CWDP: Certified Wireless Design
Official Study Guide

MW00845995

Exam PW0-250 Objectives

OBJECTIVE	CHAPTER
Network Planning	
1.1 Identify and describe best practices for pre-deployment information gathering and network planning tasks.	1
1.2 Identify the business justification and the intended goals for the WLAN.	1
1.3 Determine the budget for a WLAN project and plan a solution accordingly.	1
1.4 Discover the client device types to be used and understand their impact on design requirements.	2
1.5 Determine the desired applications to be supported and understand the requirements for specific applications.	1, 2, 3
1.6 Determine the intended end users for the WLAN and describe best practices for planning a network to accommodate different user groups.	1
1.7 Identify the physical environment(s) for the network and describe best practices for network deployments for different physical spaces.	8
1.8 Demonstrate a detailed understanding of RF propagation behaviors and relate these characteristics to WLAN design for specific environments.	6
1.9 Determine RF link requirements and demonstrate common planning techniques and deployment approaches for outdoor networks.	6, 9
1.10 Understand the role of regulatory compliance requirements in network planning and demonstrate best practices for maintaining compliance.	4
1.11 Determine network service requirements and implement Service Level Agreements (SLA) accordingly.	12
1.12 Describe best practices for updating or modifying an existing WLAN.	13
1.13 Discuss migration strategies for upgrading to 802.11n.	7, 9
1.14 Explain the importance of building-specific planning considerations.	8
1.15 Implement and understand the role of documentation in network planning and design.	13
1.16 Determine and prioritize equipment selection criteria for a WLAN deployment and recommend an appropriate solution.	5, 7, 9
1.17 Explain the functionality and purpose of network planning tools.	8, 9
Enterprise WLAN Design Strategies	
2.1 Demonstrate a detailed knowledge of WLAN architectures and solutions. Identify best practice design concepts for each architecture including the following considerations: Management solutions; Protocols for communication and discovery; Data forwarding models; Scalability and bottlenecks; Redundancy Strategies; Device location in the network; Encryption and decryption; VLANs; QoS; Roaming considerations; Architecture-specific security considerations; RF and channel planning; Capacity planning; AP-Controller associations; Licensing; Advantages and limitations	5

Sybex®
An Imprint of
WILEY

802.11 Security Design

Design Troubleshooting

NOTE

Exam objectives are subject to change at any time without prior notice and at CWNP's sole discretion. Please visit CWNP's website (www.cwnp.com) for the most current listing of exam objectives.

Sybex®
An Imprint of
WILEY

OBJECTIVE	CHAPTER
4.5 Understand the purpose of, and challenges related to, creating a balanced RF link between the AP and client devices.	6, 7
4.6 Demonstrate a detailed knowledge of the common problems related to high user densities and describe effective strategies to address them.	2, 3, 5, 9, 10
4.7 Illustrate best practices for data rate/MCS configurations to manage client connectivity.	2, 3, 6, 7
4.8 Understand the details of Dynamic Frequency Selection (DFS) and describe its impact on WLAN design.	2
4.9 Describe the role of Transmit Power Control (TPC) in WLANs and explain when and how it should be implemented.	14
4.10 Describe the purpose of, and techniques for, controlling and shaping RF to improve WLAN functionality.	7, 9
4.11 Identify and explain factors that motivate AP and WIPS sensor placement.	11, 12
4.12 Describe the role of load balancing in RF spectrum management.	5, 9, 14, 15
4.13 Understand how Distributed Antenna Systems (DAS) work with Wi-Fi and how they impact RF design for a WLAN.	5
4.14 Understand common RF accessories and other components used in WLAN communications.	6, 7

Advanced Site Surveying

5.1 Explain the steps and procedures associated with site survey preparation.	8
5.2 Explain how to conduct a proper WLAN site survey according to industry best practices.	8, 9, 14
5.3 Demonstrate a detailed and thorough understanding of surveying types and methodologies.	9
5.4 Explain the metrics, data, and other information collected and reported during a site survey.	9
5.5 Explain how surveying methodologies may differ when preparing for specific applications.	3, 9
5.6 Discuss how surveying approaches differ depending upon PHY and feature support.	9
5.7 Illustrate how a site survey facilitates hardware (APs and antennas) placement and mounting decisions.	8, 9
5.8 Describe how antenna selection, placement, and orientation is determined by an RF site survey.	7
5.9 Describe how channel planning and output power configurations are determined by an RF site.	9
5.10 Understand the differences in tools, methods, and purpose between outdoor and indoor site surveys.	8, 9
5.11 Understand how survey methodologies and requirements differ depending on network architecture.	5, 9

Sybex®
An Imprint of
 WILEY

Sybex®
An Imprint of
WILEY

CWDP™
Certified Wireless Design
Professional
Official Study Guide

CWDP™
Certified Wireless Design Professional
Official Study Guide

Shawn M. Jackman
Matt Swartz
Marcus Burton
Thomas W. Head

Wiley Publishing, Inc.

Acquisitions Editor: Jeff Kellum
Development Editor: Denise Santoro Lincoln
Technical Editors: Jennifer Huber; Jerome Henry
Production Editor: Dassi Zeidel
Copy Editor: Liz Welch
Editorial Manager: Pete Gaughan
Production Manager: Tim Tate
Vice President and Executive Group Publisher: Richard Swadley
Vice President and Publisher: Neil Edde
Media Project Manager 1: Laura Moss-Hollister
Media Associate Producer: Doug Kuhn
Media Quality Assurance: Shawn Patrick
Book Designers: Judy Fung and Bill Gibson
Proofreader: Publication Services, Inc.
Indexer: Ted Laux
Project Coordinator, Cover: Katie Crocker
Cover Designer: Ryan Sneed

ISBN: 978-0-470-76904-1

ISBN: 978-1-118-04159-8 (ebk.)

ISBN: 978-1-118-04161-1 (ebk.)

ISBN: 978-1-118-04160-4 (ebk.)

For general information on our other products and services or to obtain technical support, please contact our Customer Care Department within the U.S. at (877) 762-2974, outside the U.S. at (317) 572-3993 or fax (317) 572-4002.

Wiley also publishes its books in a variety of electronic formats. Some content that appears in print may not be available in electronic books.

Library of Congress Cataloging-in-Publication Data

CWDP : certified wireless design professional official study / Shawn M. Jackman . . . [et al.]. —1st ed.
    p. cm.
    ISBN 978-0-470-76904-1 (pbk.)
    1. Wireless LANs—Design and construction—Examinations—Study guides. 2. Telecommunications engineers—Certification. I. Jackman, Shawn M., 1974- II. Title: Certified wireless design professional official study guide.
    TK5105.78.C94 2011
    621.384076—dc22

                                                                                        2010054032

10 9 8 7 6 5 4 3 2 1

Dear Reader,

Thank you for choosing *CWDP: Certified Wireless Design Professional Official Study Guide*. This book is part of a family of premium-quality Sybex books, all of which are written by outstanding authors who combine practical experience with a gift for teaching.

Sybex was founded in 1976. More than 30 years later, we're still committed to producing consistently exceptional books. With each of our titles, we're working hard to set a new standard for the industry. From the paper we print on, to the authors we work with, our goal is to bring you the best books available.

I hope you see all that reflected in these pages. I'd be very interested to hear your comments and get your feedback on how we're doing. Feel free to let me know what you think about this or any other Sybex book by sending me an email at nedde@wiley.com. If you think you've found a technical error in this book, please visit http://sybex.custhelp.com. Customer feedback is critical to our efforts at Sybex.

Best regards,

Neil Edde
Vice President and Publisher
Sybex, an Imprint of Wiley

We dedicate this book to our families and the continued support that has helped to make this book possible.

Acknowledgments

Shawn Jackman would like to thank his wife, Joy, and his children, Summer, Pierce, and Julia, for the years of unwavering love and support.

Marcus Burton would like to thank his beautiful God, his beautiful wife, and his beautiful kids, Noah and Amalia. Lindsey, I love you today!

Marcus would also like to give an honorable mention to his significantly less beautiful brothers in arms, Devin, Josiah, and the Pudloafs.

Matt Swartz would like to thank his wife, Christie, and children, Lauren and Kyla, for their constant love and support.

Tom Head would like to thank his wife, Meridith, and his children, Laura and Ethan, for their loving support during the writing of this book.

We would all like to thank the following individuals for their support and contributions during the entire process:

We must first thank Sybex Acquisitions Editor Jeff Kellum. Jeff is an extremely patient and understanding editor who occasionally sends a nasty email message, especially when our day jobs take us away from writing for too long. We would also like to thank our development editor, Denise Lincoln. We also need to send special thanks to our editorial manager Pete Gaughan and our production editor Dassi Zeidel, and Liz Welch, our copyeditor. We also want to thank Jennifer Huber and Jerome Henry, our technical editors.

In addition, we thank Kevin Sandlin and Marcus Burton with the CWNP program (www.cwnp.com). You should be proud of the international renowned wireless certification program that you and your team have developed. It has been a pleasure working with all of you over the years.

A special thank you goes to Young Kim for his contribution to Chapter 15. Young's expertise is deep and wide in both networking and wireless, and his many years of experience with troubleshooting wireless networks is a valuable contribution for all readers.

Shawn would also like to thank the following co-workers and professional colleagues who contributed to this book and his career: Devin Akin, Nico Arcino, Marcus Burton, David Coleman, Ken Fisch, Tom Head, Jon Krabbenschmidt, Charlie Nowak, Zack Ryan, Adam Schembs, George Stefanick, and Matt Swartz.

Tom would also like to thank Elena Bogorad for assistance with proofreading.

Matt would also like to thank his manager at Cisco Systems, Jon Leary, for consistently encouraging him to meet new challenges that have fed his thirst for unsolved problems and driven his technical and personal development.

We would also like to thank the following individuals and companies for their support and contributions to the book:

Aerohive Networks (www.aerohive.com)—Devin Akin, Adam Conway

AeroScout (www.aeroscout.com)—Gabi Daniely

AirMagnet (www.airmagnet.com)—Dilip Advani, Bruce Hubbert

AirTight (www.airtightnetworks.com)—Gopinath KN

Aruba Networks (www.arubanetworks.com)—Andy Logan, Chris Leach

Cisco Systems (www.cisco.com)—Chris Allen, Brian Cox, Jim Florwick, John Helm, Young Kim, Sudheer Matta, Fred Niehaus, Sean Simmons

InfoLogix (www.infologix.com)—Katrina McSweeney

Meraki (www.meraki.com)—John Bicket

Meru Networks (www.merunetworks.com)—Joe Epstein

Phoenix Antennas (www.phoenixantennas.com)—Stephen Tilston, David Tilston

Ruckus Wireless (www.ruckuswireless.com)—GT Hill

SunWize Technologies (www.sunwize.com)—Charlie Bachman, Laurie DuBois

TerraWave (www.terrawave.com)—Carter Burke, Felicia Carreon

VeriWave (www.veriwave.com)—Eran Karoly

Vocera (www.vocera.com)—Chris O'Donnell, Brian Sturges

WildPackets (www.wildpackets.com)—Stephanie Temples

Xirrus (www.xirrus.com)—Violet Smith, Bruce Miller

About the Authors

Shawn Jackman designs and establishes new product offerings and sets Wi-Fi direction for one of the United States' largest hospital systems, Kaiser Permanente. Shawn coauthored the *CWSP Certified Wireless Security Professional Official Study Guide: Exam PW0-204* (Sybex, 2010). He has traveled the United States and internationally, designing wired and wireless networks, from concept to completion, for healthcare, warehouse, hospitality, education, metro/municipal, government, franchise, and retail environments. Shawn is a member of the CWNE Roundtable, a group of individuals who work with the CWNP Program to provide direction for the CWNE exam and certification. He lives in the San Francisco Bay Area with his wife, Joy, and their three children, Summer, Pierce, and Julia. Shawn is CWNE #54, and he can be reached via email at shawn.jackman@cwne.com.

Marcus Burton is the Director of Product Development and primary content developer at CWNP. Marcus has authored or co-authored numerous WLAN exams (CWTS, CWNA, CWSP, CWAP, and CWDP), course guides, whitepapers, and articles. In addition, he has served as technical editor for numerous whitepapers as well as the *CWTS: Certified Wireless Technology Specialist Official Study Guide* (Sybex, 2009) and the *CWSP Certified Wireless Security Professional Official Study Guide* (Sybex, 2010). At CWNP, Marcus actively participates with many WLAN vendors in product engineering, testing, and design; he also has in-depth experience with a comprehensive range of WLAN technologies and vendor products. Marcus is CWNE #78.

Matt Swartz is a Technical Leader within Cisco's Advanced Services Wireless Practice. He delivers scalable designs that enable mobility solutions across many verticals for Cisco's largest customers. Matt's most recent focus is on high-density wireless as he drives new technology to expand capacity in these environments. Prior to joining Cisco in 2003, Matt held network engineering positions with a number of service providers and enterprises. He is CCIE #13232 (Routing/Switching & Wireless) and CWNE #57. He also holds a BS degree from Old Dominion University, and is a member of the CWNE Roundtable. Matt can be reached at matt.swartz@cwne.com.

Thomas Head has been an engineer and manager in the wireless industry for over 20 years. Tom graduated from Rensselaer Polytechnic Institute with a degree in physics. He was an engineer, then manager, of radio design at Lockheed Martin's spacecraft division. He was also manager of radio programs for Lucent Technologies' third-generation cellular base station. At Flarion Technologies, Tom was responsible for RF and network testing of Flarion's innovative Flash-OFDM wireless system. He formed his own company, Aereo Networks, in 2006, which provided wireless test services and software for the US Army, Army Reserves, and major healthcare systems. He can be reached at head@aereonetworks.com.

Contents at a Glance

Contents

Foreword

So you want to design an enterprise wireless network? "I can't connect to the Wi-Fi!" is what you're going to hear if you don't get your Wi-Fi right. How do you permanently remove this wonderful end user complaint from your WLAN? It starts with proper design.

I actually considered starting and ending this foreword to the *CWDP: Certified Wireless Design Professional Official Study Guide* with just the above sentiment. That sums it up, but there is much more to it. Today's end user expects the wireless network to just work, period. When it doesn't, customers leave, employees complain, managers scream, and your network is always to blame . . . even when it isn't.

A few years ago, before Polycom bought them, SpectraLink ran into quite a few of these complaints, only the complaints were "These phones don't work!" and it really was the network. What did SpectraLink do? They created a services team to design and build their customers' WLANs properly, so that the SpectraLink phones running on those WLANs would work. It wasn't the phones. It was the network. The network was not properly designed to support Wi-Fi phones. That was five years ago. Imagine what the network has to support today, thanks to Mr. Steve Jobs!

Whether you're designing for a coffee shop hotspot or the Super Bowl, your design before the network is implemented will determine hero or goat status. The fun part is, much like security, it gets noticed only when it doesn't work. If everything works flawlessly, you've done your job. When you hear that soulful end user scream—"Mine's broken!"—then you know you've missed the mark.

So how do you design for something you can't see? RF is a strange animal indeed, often referred to as black magic, or smoke and mirrors, so you must know RF cold. That includes the RF math, behavior, and characteristics, in addition to the building(s) for which you are designing the network. That's right: you have to know building materials! RF acts differently around cement, metal, drywall, plaster, wood, trees, fences, and, yes, people. That's part of the reason we require a CWNA before you can be a CWDP. You have to know RF, and you have to know RF really well before you can claim to be a WLAN designer.

And, oh, wouldn't it be nice if every new WLAN was a sweet new greenfield implementation? Sorry, not going to happen. You will most likely be replacing an old 802.11b or 802.11g WLAN with an 802.11n system. And wouldn't it be nice if it were just rip and replace? Ha! Life should be so easy! If your manager or your customer suggests rip and replace, you'd do well to suggest that they find someone else to do this job. That should get someone's attention. Then it's your job to explain, for example, how differently an 802.11g network and an 802.11n network behave, not only in that particular environment, but in any environment.

With a/b/g, multipath and interference were the bane of your existence. Now, multipath is good for 802.11n Wi-Fi. That means a complete change in the way you design the WLAN for any environment.

Ah, but we don't design only for the environment, do we? No, no, we don't. We must design for the specific applications, and the type(s) of and number of devices that will utilize the WLAN, and the specific industry, and the number of end users . . . the list goes on and on. And then there's VoWiFi and video. How many people have you seen watching (fill in the blank) on YouTube on the wireless LAN? Your WLAN has to support that kind of bandwidth, lest you hear the cry of the end user: "Mine's broken!"

Reliable enterprise Wi-Fi starts with the design of the wireless network. So where do you start to end up with a great design? You guessed it: your old friend the RF site survey. Missed it, didn't you? What's wrong? Haven't climbed enough towers, scaled enough ceilings, pushed enough carts, dropped enough handhelds, or walked enough miles lately? It's time to go back to where you started, and improve your game not just a little but a lot. When you did your first 50 RF site surveys, were you thinking about the design of the network, or were you thinking about getting the survey done as quickly and with as little pain as possible?

Now return to the RF site survey with the—no, with *your*—network design in mind. This time, you're doing the survey for the purpose of designing a reliable, scalable, secure, mission-critical enterprise wireless LAN. It's not just Internet access anymore; it is the new access layer technology for the 21st century.

You want to design my wireless network? Start with this book, and see where it takes you.

Kevin Sandlin
Co-Founder and CEO
CWNP, Inc.

Introduction

The content of this book is focused on the *real world* of wireless design. While this book provides all of the necessary information to pass the CWDP exam, the content is primarily focused on providing tangible value to immediately expand your wireless expertise. The knowledge you will obtain from this book will not only prove valuable if you plan on performing or participating in wireless designs, but will also help you understand what makes WLANs tick, spot design mistakes, troubleshoot pesky clients and applications, understand and quantify RF issues, and more.

Writing a book on wireless design in order to certify career professionals on designing for any equipment vendor isn't a light undertaking. Vendors differ in their approach. There are even different architectures that greatly vary in the way they work, which is certainly the case between equipment vendors, but major architectural differences can even be found between product lines from a single equipment vendor.

The approach taken with the CWDP is far deeper in one area in particular than any other CWNP curriculum has ever embarked upon before—RF. Radio frequency fundamentals is an extremely tough area to teach and is probably the single least understood area of wireless networking across technical professionals. This book aims to change some of that. After all, a house can't be built on a bad foundation. A wired network can't be built using bad cabling. A supersonic jet . . . you get the point. Without the proper foundation for a wireless LAN, the performance will suffer and your network may ultimately fail.

The total focus of this book isn't just the wireless network infrastructure—we also explore the client devices that the wireless network infrastructure supports. In Wi-Fi, the communication link of a wireless client and an AP must be in parity with each other. For example, if you switch phones, even with the same mobile network carrier, your experience will vary. Where you may have once had good reception, you won't now, and vice versa. It is no different with Wi-Fi. In fact, it is worse. Mobile network carriers have incredible control over the phones they will support and perform a great deal of engineering before placing them into the hands of customers. Wi-Fi, on the other hand, has many different equipment infrastructure vendors, an even greater disparity of operating modes, and a far greater variety of client devices with comparatively very little rigor and testing between them. Industry standards have a lot of wiggle room, and as a wireless network designer, you need to take this fact into account from the onset. After all, the very reason a wireless network exists is to support client devices.

If you have purchased this book or if you are thinking about purchasing this book, you probably have some interest in taking the CWDP® (Certified Wireless Design Professional) certification exam or in learning more about what the CWDP certification exam is about. We would like to congratulate you on this first step, and we hope that our book can help you on your journey. Wireless networking is one of the hottest technologies available today and demands for mobility are great among a wide variety of industries. As with many fast-growing technologies, the demand for knowledgeable people is often greater than the supply. The CWDP certification is your opportunity to distinguish yourself from others and a way to prove that you have the knowledge and skills to support this growing industry. This Study Guide was written with that goal in mind.

This book will teach you about wireless networking so that you have the knowledge needed not only to pass the CWDP certification test, but also to be able to design, install, and support wireless networks. We have included review questions at the end of each chapter to help you test your knowledge and prepare for the test.

Before we tell you about the certification process and requirements, we must mention that this information may have changed by the time you are taking your test. We recommend that you visit www.cwnp.com as you prepare to study for your test to determine what the current objectives and requirements are.

> To adequately study for the CWDP exam, you need to do more than just study the questions and answers in this book! The practice questions we have supplied are designed to test your knowledge of a concept or objective that is likely to be on the CWDP exam, but to really learn this material, you need to read and study the chapters in the book. Please note that the practice questions will be different from the actual certification questions, but if you learn and understand the topics and objectives, you will be better prepared for the test.

About CWDP® and CWNP®

If you have ever prepared to take a certification test for a technology that you are unfamiliar with, you know that you are not only studying to learn a different technology, but probably also learning about an industry that you are unfamiliar with. It is therefore important for you to familiarize yourself with CWNP.

CWNP is an abbreviation for *Certified Wireless Network Professional*. There is no CWNP test—a common misunderstanding. The CWNP program develops courseware and certification exams for wireless LAN technologies in the computer networking industry. The CWNP certification program is a vendor-neutral program.

The objective of CWNP is to certify people on wireless networking, not on a specific vendor's product. Yes, at times the authors of this book and the creators of the certification will talk about, demonstrate, or even teach how to use a specific product; however, the goal is the overall understanding of wireless, not the product itself. If you learned to drive a car, you had to physically sit and practice in one. When you think back and reminisce, you probably do not tell someone you learned to drive a Ford; you probably say you learned to drive using a Ford.

There are seven wireless certifications offered by the CWNP program, but only five of them have exams:

CWTS™: Certified Wireless Technology Specialist   The CWTS certification is a recently introduced certification from the CWNP program. CWTS is an entry-level enterprise

WLAN certification, and a recommended starting point prior to the CWNA certification. This certification is geared specifically toward both WLAN sales and support staff for the enterprise WLAN industry. The CWTS certification verifies that sales and support staff are specialists in WLAN technology and have all the fundamental knowledge, tools, and terminology to more effectively sell and support WLAN technologies.

CWNA®: Certified Wireless Network Administrator   The CWNA certification is a foundation-level Wi-Fi certification; however, it is not considered an entry-level technology certification. Individuals taking this exam (exam PW0-104) typically have a solid grasp on network basics such as the OSI model, IP addressing, PC hardware, and network operating systems. Many candidates already hold other industry-recognized certifications, such as the CompTIA Network+ or Cisco CCNA, and are looking for the CWNA certification to enhance or complement existing skills.

CWSP®: Certified Wireless Security Professional   The CWSP certification exam (PW0-200) is focused on standards-based wireless security protocols, security policy, and secure wireless network design. This certification introduces candidates to many of the technologies and techniques that intruders use to compromise wireless networks and that administrators use to protect wireless networks. With recent advances in wireless security, WLANs can be secured beyond their wired counterparts.

CWAP®: Certified Wireless Security Professional   The CWAP certification exam (PW0-270) was reintroduced by CWNP in the fall of 2010. The CWAP certification is focused on a deep-level analysis of the components of the 802.11 protocol. This certification is possibly the most difficult CWNP certification to obtain because it requires an intimate knowledge of frame analysis, spectrum analysis, and WLAN troubleshooting. For consultants and engineers who troubleshoot the most difficult networks, CWAP is a perfect certification to hold.

CWDP®: Certified Wireless Design Professional   You may not need any background on the CWDP certification since you're holding this book in your hand, but we will include it anyway. CWDP was introduced for the first time by CWNP in early 2011. As WLAN technology proliferates, CWNP was consistently confronted with the need for network designers to be taught how to properly deploy a WLAN. This request reached our ears, and CWDP is our response to help prepare and validate the skill of design engineers across the globe.

CWNE®: Certified Wireless Network Expert   The CWNE certification is the highest-level certification in the CWNP program. By successfully completing the CWNE requirements, you will have demonstrated that you have the most advanced skills available in today's wireless LAN market. The CWNE certification was previously a rigorous and thorough exam covering advanced WLAN analysis, design, troubleshooting, quality-of-service (QoS) mechanisms, spectrum management, and extensive knowledge of the IEEE 802.11 standard. Since many engineers want to pursue their WLAN training in a piecemeal fashion, we have broken down the CWNE topics into individual professional-level exams. After earning all the professional certifications, candidates may apply for the CWNE certification. As the capstone certification, CWNE requires that candidates demonstrate their expertise by meeting several rigorous criteria that are validated via a CWNE application and review process.

CWNT®: Certified Wireless Network Trainer   Certified Wireless Network Trainers are qualified instructors certified by the CWNP program to deliver CWNP training courses to IT professionals. CWNTs are technical and instructional experts in wireless technologies, products, and solutions. To ensure a superior learning experience for our customers, CWNP Education Partners are required to use CWNTs when delivering training using official CWNP courseware.

How to Become a CWDP

To become a CWDP, you must do the following three things:

- Agree that you have read and will abide by the terms and conditions of the CWNP Confidentiality Agreement.
- Pass the CWNA certification exam.
- Pass the CWDP certification exam.

The CWNA certification is a prerequisite for the CWDP certification. If you have purchased this book, there is a good chance that you have already passed the CWNA exam and are now ready to move to the next level of certification and plan to study and pass the CWDP exam. That is the recommended path to achieving CWDP certification; however, there is no requirement to take the exams in order. You can take the CWDP exam prior to passing the CWNA exam, but you will not become a certified CWDP until you have passed both exams.

 If you have not yet taken the CWNA exam, we recommend purchasing the *CWNA Certified Wireless Network Administrator Official Study Guide* by David D. Coleman and David A. Westcott (Sybex, 2010).

When you sit to take the test, you will be required to accept a confidentiality agreement before you can continue with the test. After you have agreed, you will be able to continue with the test, and if you pass the test, you are then a CWDP.

 A copy of the CWNP Confidentiality Agreement can be found online at the CWNP website.

The information for the exam is as follows:

- Exam number: PW0-250
- Cost: $225 (in U.S. dollars; price subject to change)

- Availability: Register at Pearson VUE (www.vue.com/cwnp)
- Duration: 90 minutes
- Questions: 60
- Question types: Multiple choice/multiple answer
- Passing score: 70% (80% for instructors)
- Available languages: English

When you schedule the exam, you will receive instructions regarding appointment and cancellation procedures, ID requirements, and information about the testing center location. In addition, you will receive a registration and payment confirmation letter. Exams can be scheduled weeks in advance or, in some cases, even as late as the same day.

After you have successfully passed the CWDP exam, the CWNP program will award you a certification that is good for three years. To recertify, you will need to pass the current PW0-250 exam or earn your CWNE certification by passing the CWSP and CWAP exams and completing the CWNE application process. If the information you provided the testing center is correct, you will receive an email from CWNP recognizing your accomplishment and providing you with a CWNP certification number. After you earn any CWNP certification, you can request a certification kit. The kit includes a congratulatory letter, a certificate, and a wallet-sized personalized ID card. You will need to log in to the CWNP tracking system, verify your contact information, and request your certification kit.

Who Should Buy This Book?

If you want to acquire a solid foundation in wireless networking and your goal is to prepare for the exam, this book is for you. You will find clear explanations of the concepts you need to grasp and plenty of help to achieve the high level of professional competency you need in order to succeed.

This book is also helpful for anyone who works in wireless in any fashion. This book was not only designed to give you everything you need to pass the CWDP exam, but to go well above and beyond that by providing real-world experience, knowledge, and recommendations on how to design nothing short of world-class wireless networks.

If you want to become certified as a CWDP, this book is definitely what you need.

How to Use This Book and the CD

We have included several testing features in the book and on the CD-ROM. These tools will help you retain vital exam content as well as prepare you to sit for the actual exam.

Assessment Exam   At the beginning of the book (right after this introduction) is an assessment test that you can use to check your readiness for the exam. Take this test before you start reading the book; it will help you determine the areas that you may need to brush up on. The answers to the assessment test appear on a separate page after the last question of the test. Each answer includes an explanation and a note telling you the chapter in which the material appears.

Chapter Review Questions   To test your knowledge as you progress through the book, there are review questions at the end of each chapter. As you finish each chapter, answer the review questions and then check your answers—the correct answers appear on the page following the last review question. You can go back and reread the section that deals with each question you answered wrong to ensure that you answer correctly the next time you are tested on the material.

Electronic Flashcards   You will find flashcard questions on the CD for on-the-go review. These are short questions and answers, just like the flashcards you probably used in school. You can answer them on your PC or download them onto a Palm device for quick and convenient reviewing.

Test Engine   The CD also contains the Sybex Test Engine. With this custom test engine, you can identify weak areas up front and then develop a solid studying strategy that includes each of the robust testing features described previously. Our thorough readme file will walk you through the quick, easy installation process.

In addition to the assessment test and the chapter review questions, you will find three bonus exams. Use the test engine to take these practice exams just as if you were taking the actual exam (without any reference material). When you have finished the first exam, move on to the next one to solidify your test-taking skills. If you get more than 95 percent of the answers correct, you are ready to take the certification exam.

CWNP Authorized Materials Use Policy

CWNP does not condone the use of unauthorized training materials, aka "brain dumps." Individuals who utilize such materials to pass CWNP exams will have their certifications revoked. In an effort to more clearly communicate CWNP's policy on use of unauthorized study materials, CWNP directs all certification candidates to the CWNP Candidate Conduct Policy at

http://www.cwnp.com/exams/CWNPCandidateConductPolicy.pdf

Please review this policy before beginning the study process for any CWNP exam. Candidates will be required to state that they understand and have abided by this policy at the time of exam delivery. If a candidate has a question as to whether study materials are considered "brain dumps," they should perform a search using CertGuards engine, found here:

http://www.certguard.com/search.asp

Exam Objectives

The PW0-250 exam, covering the CWDP certification objectives, will certify that the successful candidate possesses the skills necessary to design a high-performing, reliable, and secure enterprise WLAN in a broad range of applications. As a professional-level certification, this exam requires a detailed understanding of the material and will test these concepts in depth.

The skills and knowledge measured by this examination were derived from a survey of wireless networking experts and professionals. The results of this survey were used in weighing the subject areas and ensuring that the weighting is representative of the relative importance of the content.

The following chart provides the breakdown of the exam, showing you the weight of each section:

Subject Area	% of Exam
Network Planning	10%
Enterprise WLAN Design Strategies	25%
Infrastructure Design and Network Services	10%
WLAN RF Design	20%
Advanced Site Surveying	25%
802.11 Security Design	5%
Design Troubleshooting	5%
Total	**100%**

Network Planning – 10%

1.1 Identify and describe best practices for pre-deployment information gathering and network planning tasks.

1.2 Identify the business justification and the intended goals for the WLAN.

1.3 Determine the budget for a WLAN project and plan a solution accordingly.

1.4 Discover the client device types to be used and understand their impact on design requirements:

- Applications supported
- MAC feature support

- PHY support
- Antenna type, transmit power, and other RF characteristics

1.5 Determine the desired applications to be supported and understand the requirements for specific applications:

- Coverage requirements
- Capacity requirements
- Security requirements
- High Availability (Reliability/Redundancy)
- Latency requirements
- Other application-specific considerations

1.6 Determine the intended end users for the WLAN and describe best practices for planning a network to accommodate different user groups:

- Corporate users
- Remote users
- Guests

1.7 Identify the physical environment(s) for the network and describe best practices for network deployments for different physical spaces:

- Common areas (cubicles, offices, hallways, rooms, etc.)
- Service areas (elevators, stairwells, restrooms, etc.)
- Industrial areas (manufacturing, warehousing, etc.)
- Guest areas (conference areas, lobbies, small businesses, waiting areas, etc.)
- Outdoor areas (bridging, transportation networks, outdoor stadiums, etc.)

1.8 Demonstrate a detailed understanding of RF propagation behaviors and relate these characteristics to WLAN design for specific environments:

- RF propagation characteristics
- Common construction practices
- Building materials and attenuation characteristics
- Outdoor RF characteristics

1.9 Determine RF link requirements and demonstrate common planning techniques and deployment approaches for outdoor networks, including:

- Point-to-point bridging
- Point-to-multipoint bridging
- Mesh deployments

1.10 Understand the role of regulatory compliance requirements in network planning and demonstrate best practices for maintaining compliance.

1.11 Determine network service requirements and implement Service Level Agreements (SLA) accordingly:

    1.11.1 Creation

    1.11.2 Monitoring

    1.11.3 Reporting

    1.11.4 Action

1.12 Describe best practices for updating or modifying an existing WLAN:

    1.12.1 Phased upgrades

    1.12.2 Upgrading clients

    1.12.3 Redesigning to support new applications

    1.12.4 Pre-deployment testing and verification practices

    1.12.5 Firmware or software upgrades

    1.12.6 Implementing new features with existing hardware

    1.12.7 Replacing hardware

1.13 Discuss migration strategies for upgrading to 802.11n.

1.14 Explain the importance of building-specific planning considerations:

    1.14.1 Structure characteristics

- Square footage
- Ceiling height
- Number of floors

    1.14.2 Number of buildings or other campus-specific characteristics

    1.14.3 Blueprints / floor plan (image file)

    1.14.4 Access restrictions

- Plenum
- Mounting
- Safety and health regulations and concerns

    1.14.5 Power sources

    1.14.6 MDF and IDF locations

    1.14.7 Wiring limitations

    1.14.8 Existing WLAN information

    1.14.9 Aesthetic requirements

1.15 Implement and understand the role of documentation in network planning and design:

1.15.1 Scope of work

1.15.2 NDA

1.15.3 Hold harmless

1.15.4 Network deployment acceptance criteria

1.15.5 Network design deliverable (topology map, solution explanation, design requirements, etc.)

1.15.6 Site survey deliverable

1.15.7 Bill of Materials (BOM)

- Hardware
- Software/licenses
- Support contracts

1.16 Determine and prioritize equipment selection criteria for a WLAN deployment and recommend an appropriate solution:

1.16.1 Cost

1.16.2 Appropriate use

1.16.3 Capabilities

1.16.4 Architecture

1.16.5 Accessories

1.16.6 Aesthetics

1.17 Explain the functionality and purpose of network planning tools:

1.17.1 Predictive RF modeling

1.17.2 WLAN simulators

1.17.3 RF Calculators

Enterprise WLAN Design Strategies – 25%

2.1 Demonstrate a detailed knowledge of WLAN architectures and solutions. Identify best practice design concepts for each architecture, including the following considerations:

- Management solutions
- Protocols for communication and discovery
- Data forwarding models
- Scalability and bottlenecks

- Redundancy strategies
- Device location in the network
- Encryption and decryption
- VLANs
- QoS
- Roaming considerations
- Architecture-specific security considerations
- RF and channel planning
- Capacity planning
- AP-Controller associations
- Licensing
- Advantages and limitations

2.1.1 Centralized WLAN Architectures

- Local MAC
- Split MAC
- Remote MAC

2.1.2 Autonomous WLAN Architectures

2.1.3 Distributed WLAN Architectures

2.1.4 WLAN Arrays

- Hardware arrays
- Antenna arrays

2.1.5 Mesh Networks

- Mesh as a failover mechanism
- Extension of network access with mesh as a primary backhaul technology
- Client support in a mesh

2.1.6 Remote APs (VPN)

2.1.7 Bridged Networks

- PTP
- PTMP

2.2 Describe design models and considerations for both Multiple Channel Architecture (MCA) and Single Channel Architecture (SCA) WLANs.

2.3 Discuss data forwarding models and how they impact network design:

2.3.1 Centralized forwarding

2.3.2 Distributed forwarding

2.3.3 Split-tunnel forwarding

2.4 Describe how a Distributed Antenna System works and understand its impact on WLAN design and deployment.

2.5 Explain the functions and components of the WLAN operational planes and identify their presence in a given scenario:

2.5.1 Data

2.5.2 Management

2.5.3 Control

2.6 Demonstrate a thorough understanding of design strategies and considerations specific to WLAN client devices:

2.6.1 Client application support

2.6.2 Application-specific (e.g., VoWiFi phones) vs. multi-application client devices (e.g., laptops)

2.6.3 Client management considerations

- Driver selection, configuration, and feature support
- Client utility selection, configuration, and feature support
- Endpoint network agents

2.6.4 Authentication, encryption, and security protocol support

2.6.5 MAC feature support

2.6.6 PHY support

2.6.7 Hardware components

2.6.8 Antenna type, transmit power, and other RF characteristics

2.7 Explain best practices and address common design considerations for industry-specific WLAN deployments in the following markets and scenarios:

2.7.1 Carpeted offices

2.7.2 Industrial – Warehouse and Manufacturing

2.7.3 Healthcare

2.7.4 Government

2.7.5 Hospitality

2.7.6 Education

2.7.7 Retail

2.7.8 Guest Access and Hotspots

2.7.9 Transportation

2.7.10 Mobile Office

2.7.11 Mesh/Outdoor

2.7.12 Remote Networks and Branch Offices

2.7.13 Bridging and Last-mile/ISP

2.7.14 High Density (e.g., arenas, conference halls, trade shows)

2.8 Illustrate application-specific design approaches and requirements, including the following:

- Application behavior
- Protocols
- RF requirements
- Performance requirements/metrics (i.e., throughput, jitter, delay, latency, loss)
- Security requirements
- High Availability (Reliability/Redundancy)
- Other application-specific considerations

2.8.1 Data

- File sharing
- Email
- Web Browsing
- Image sharing

2.8.2 Voice

2.8.3 Video

2.8.4 Location and Tracking

2.8.5 Barcode scanners and picker systems

2.8.6 Wireless security cameras

2.8.7 FMC – Fixed Mobile Convergence

2.8.8 Other real-time applications

2.9 Explain best practices for common WLAN feature support, configuration, and deployment strategies, including:

2.9.1 QoS

- Application-level support
- Client configuration
- AP configuration

2.9.2 Power Management

2.9.3 Protection Modes and PHY Compatibility

2.9.4 WLAN Profile parameters

- SSIDs
- Data Rate and/or MCS support

- Discovery parameters (Beaconing, probe request/response parameters, DTIMs, etc.)
- Advanced parameters (Peer-to-peer blocking, RTS thresholds, aggregation, fragmentation, client limits, proprietary optimization features, etc.)

Infrastructure Design and Network Services – 10%

3.1 Demonstrate a detailed understanding of the role that the wired network infrastructure plays in WLAN design:

3.1.1 Backhaul speeds and capacity

3.1.2 Backhaul redundancy

3.1.3 Multicast support

3.1.4 PoE support

3.2 Explain design approaches related to specific layers of the OSI model.

3.3 Discuss power supply and cabling options for WLAN devices:

- AC power in MDFs and IDFs
- AC power in distributed locations
- Endpoint PoE
- Midspan PoE
- 802.3af and 802.3at (PoE+) PoE
- Solar power
- Data cabling

3.4 Explain the significance of QoS in multi-service WLANs and illustrate a comprehensive understanding of the following:

3.4.1 WLAN arbitration

3.4.2 WMM and EDCA operations and parameters

3.4.3 Policy-based queuing

3.4.4 802.1p (802.1D/Q) CoS priority tagging

3.4.5 Differentiated Services Code Point (DSCP)

3.4.6 Admission control

3.4.7 End-to-end QoS

3.4.8 Airtime fairness mechanisms

3.5 Understand and describe VLAN use in wired and wireless network segmentation:

3.5.1 Access ports

3.5.2 Trunked ports

3.5.3 VLAN distribution

3.6 Describe load balancing, what purpose it serves for the network, and when and how it should be implemented:

   3.6.1 Client RF/Spectrum load balancing

   3.6.2 Load balancing clients among APs

   3.6.3 Load balancing APs among controllers

   3.6.4 Device licensing

3.7 Describe common design practices for high availability and redundancy:

   3.7.1 Redundancy strategies (N+1, N+N+1, etc.)

   3.7.2 Controller failover

   3.7.3 Dynamic RF adjustments – channel, power, etc.

   3.7.4 Mesh as a failover backhaul option

3.8 Illustrate best practices for roaming support in a WLAN:

   3.8.1 Planning roaming boundaries

   3.8.2 Understanding and managing client roaming behaviors

   3.8.3 Application roaming requirements

   3.8.4 L2 roaming

   3.8.5 L3 roaming

   3.8.6 Inter-controller roaming

   3.8.7 Maintaining user policies and security

3.9 Consider the following network services and protocols as they relate to wireless interaction with the wired network:

   3.9.1 RADIUS

   3.9.2 Directory Services (LDAP)

   3.9.3 DHCP and forwarding

   3.9.4 DNS

   3.9.5 NTP

   3.9.6 Certificate Authority (CA)

WLAN RF Design – 20%

4.1 Understand the basics of 802.11 arbitration processes and wireless contention domains, and describe how these factors influence network design.

4.2 Demonstrate a detailed understanding of RF behaviors and characteristics and relate these concepts to WLAN RF design.

4.3 Discuss design concepts related to frequencies and bands used for WLAN communications:

4.3.1 Bandwidth

4.3.2 Utilization and capacity

4.3.3 Regulatory licensing requirements

4.3.4 Transmit power regulations

4.4 Illustrate a comprehensive understanding of the role of channel planning and usage in network design:

4.4.1 Channel width selection

- 20 MHz
- 20/40 MHz

4.4.2 Understand the role of interference in channel selection and usage; describe and implement tactics to minimize interference:

- Co-channel interference
- Non-overlapping adjacent-channel interference
- Overlapping adjacent-channel interference
- Non-802.11 interference

4.4.3 Understand how to perform static channel plans that maximize efficiency and minimize network contention and interference

4.4.4 Understand the use of automated channel planning, calibration, and adjustments/audits.

4.4.5 Multiple Channel Architecture (MCA) considerations

- Channel utilization
- Reuse patterns
- Transmit power
- Microcell (picocell)

4.4.6 Single Channel Architecture (SCA) considerations

- Channel blankets/spans/layers
- Channel selection

4.4.7 Mesh Channel planning

4.5 Understand the purpose of, and challenges related to, creating a balanced RF link between the AP and client devices.

4.6 Demonstrate a detailed knowledge of the common problems related to high user densities and describe effective strategies to address them:

- Microcell plans
- Antenna arrays

- SCA channel blankets
- Client modifications (e.g. custom drivers)
- Band steering

4.7 Illustrate best practices for data rate/MCS configurations to manage client connectivity.

4.8 Understand the details of Dynamic Frequency Selection (DFS) and describe its impact on WLAN design:

4.8.1 Test procedures to determine if DFS channels should be used

4.8.2 Understand the impact of excluding or including DFS channels

4.8.3 Understand the impact that a BSS channel switch may have on network performance

4.9 Describe the role of Transmit Power Control (TPC) in WLANs and explain when and how it should be implemented.

4.10 Describe the purpose of, and techniques for, controlling and shaping RF to improve WLAN functionality:

- Antenna selection
- Transmit power
- AP and/or antenna mounting locations
- Enclosures and device form factor
- Antenna orientation and polarization

4.11 Identify and explain factors that motivate AP and WIPS sensor placement:

- Application performance (e.g., location services)
- Controlling RF propagation
- Coverage and capacity design
- RF environment

4.12 Describe the role of load balancing in RF spectrum management:

- Client load balancing across a spectrum
- Band Steering

4.13 Understand how Distributed Antenna Systems (DAS) work with Wi-Fi and how they impact RF design for a WLAN.

4.14 Understand common RF accessories and other components used in WLAN communications:

4.14.1 RF cabling

4.14.2 RF connectors

4.14.3 Lightning protection

4.14.4 Enclosures (e.g., environmental, safety, security)

Advanced Site Surveying – 25%

5.1 Explain the steps and procedures associated with site survey preparation:

5.1.1 Determining facility specific requirements and making appropriate arrangements:

- Arranging escorts
- Meeting access requirements, clearance, and badges
- Collecting and reviewing floor plans and/or blueprints
- Onsite training (safety and operations)
- Arranging equipment (e.g. lifts and ladders)
- Understanding industry-specific requirements (e.g. union assistance)

5.1.2 Preparing manual site survey tools for measuring RF characteristics:

- Spectrum analyzer
- Manual site survey software
- Protocol analyzer
- Throughput analysis software
- APs
- Battery packs
- Antennas
- Temporary mounts
- Other equipment

5.2 Explain how to conduct a proper WLAN site survey according to industry best practices.

5.3 Demonstrate a detailed and thorough understanding of surveying types and methodologies, including:

- Advantages, disadvantages, and purpose of each method
- Tools used to perform each type of survey
- Gathering the proper data during a site survey
- Interpreting the results of a site survey
- Applying survey data to a WLAN design
- Configuration and appropriate use of surveying tools

5.3.1 Spectrum Analysis

5.3.2 Predictive Surveys

5.3.3 Manual Surveys

- Active
- Passive

5.4 Explain the metrics, data, and other information collected and reported during a site survey:

  5.4.1 Signal metrics

  - RSSI

  - SNR

  - Noise

  - Interference

  5.4.2 Cell coverage and overlap

  5.4.3 Application and connectivity data

  - Data rates

  - Throughput

  - Latency

  - Jitter

  - Loss

  - Retries

5.5 Explain how surveying methodologies may differ when preparing for specific applications:

  5.5.1 Data

  5.5.2 Voice

  5.5.3 Video

  5.5.4 Real-time location services (RTLS)

  5.5.5 Other applications

5.6 Discuss how surveying approaches differ depending upon PHY and feature support:

  5.6.1 802.11a/g infrastructure

  5.6.2 802.11n infrastructure

  5.6.3 Mixed 802.11a/g/n infrastructure

  5.6.4 Client PHY support

  5.6.5 Beamforming support (i.e., transmit beamforming, dynamic beamforming, static beamforming)

5.7 Illustrate how a site survey facilitates hardware (APs and antennas) placement and mounting decisions:

  5.7.1 Cabling

  5.7.2 Power availability (e.g. PoE, AC power)

  5.7.3 Use of enclosures

802.11 Security Design – 5%

6.2 Recommend appropriate data encryption solutions and explain design concepts related to their use:

    6.2.1 TKIP/RC4

    6.2.2 CCMP/AES

    6.2.3 Proprietary encryption

6.3 Explain best practice security design concepts for guest and public access Wi-Fi networks:

    6.3.1 Captive portal

    6.3.2 Network segmentation

    6.3.3 Content filtering

    6.3.4 Terms of use

    6.3.5 Access control

    6.3.6 VPN

6.4 Illustrate common deployment and design strategies for AAA, especially RADIUS:

    6.4.1 AAA framework

    6.4.2 Local RADIUS servers

    6.4.3 Remote RADIUS servers

    6.4.4 Integrated RADIUS servers (in WLAN Controllers or APs)

    6.4.5 Protocol support

    6.4.6 RADIUS Proxy

6.5 Understand design strategies for integration of client authentication with directory services:

    6.5.1 Local user directories

    6.5.2 Remote directories

    6.5.3 Integrated user directories

    6.5.4 LDAP

6.6 Describe deployment and design strategies for Wireless Intrusion Prevention Systems (WIPS):

    6.6.1 Integrated

- Dedicated
- Part-time

    6.6.2 Overlay

    6.6.3 System configuration and defining policies

6.7 Demonstrate the importance of, and design considerations related to, Fast BSS Transition (Fast/Secure Roaming):

    6.7.1 No Fast Roaming Support

    6.7.2 Opportunistic Key Caching (OKC)

    6.7.3 802.11r/k (Voice-Enterprise)

    6.7.4 Preauthentication

    6.7.5 PMK Caching

    6.7.6 Proprietary mechanisms

        ▪ Virtual BSSID

        ▪ CCKM

6.8 Identify the role and limitations of client capabilities in security planning.

6.9 Describe the methods of designing a secure network with segmentation and filtering:

    6.9.1 VLAN segmentation

    6.9.2 Firewalls

    6.9.3 ACLs

    6.9.4 Role-based access control

6.10 Identify weak security solutions and protocols, and provide acceptable alternatives.

Design Troubleshooting – 5%

7.1 Identify the appropriate uses of spectrum analysis in network design and troubleshooting.

7.2 Perform and interpret an RF analysis for an existing WLAN deployment.

    7.2.1 Coverage

    7.2.2 Capacity and channel utilization

    7.2.3 Channel reuse and transmit power settings

    7.2.4 Wi-Fi and non-Wi-Fi Interference

    7.2.5 Communication link quality

7.3 Illustrate the use of a protocol analyzer and interpret the results to identify problems with the following aspects of network design:

    7.3.1 Security setup and configuration

    7.3.2 Roaming

    7.3.3 PHY rate analysis

CWDP Exam Terminology

The CWNP program uses specific terminology when phrasing the questions on any of the CWNP exams. The terminology used most often mirrors the same language that is used in the IEEE 802.11-2007 standard. While technically correct, the terminology used in the exam questions often is not the same as the marketing terminology that is used by the Wi-Fi Alliance. The most current IEEE version of the 802.11 standard is the IEEE 802.11-2007 document, which includes all the amendments that have been ratified prior to the document's publication. Standards bodies such as the IEEE often create several amendments to a standard before "rolling up" the ratified amendments (finalized or approved versions) into a new standard. The complete scope of the standards document is beyond the scope of the CWDP certification, but this book covers all of the terminology that is required for you to pass the CWDP exam.

For example, you might already be familiar with the term *802.11g*, which is a ratified amendment that has now been integrated into the IEEE 802.11-2007 standard. The technology that was originally defined by the 802.11g amendment is called Extended Rate Physical (ERP). Although the name 802.11g effectively remains the more commonly used marketing terminology, exam questions will often use the technical term ERP instead of 802.11g.

To properly prepare for the CWDP exam, test candidates should become 100 percent familiar with the terminology used by the CWNP program. This book defines and covers all terminology; however, the CWNP program maintains an updated current list of exam terms that can be downloaded from the following URL:

www.cwnp.com/exams/exam_terms.html

The CWNP Dictionary is also a useful resource for becoming familiar with all WLAN acronyms.

Tips for Taking the CWDP Exam

Here are some general tips for taking your exam successfully:

- Bring two forms of ID with you. One must be a photo ID, such as a driver's license. The other can be a major credit card or a passport. Both forms must include a signature.

- Arrive early at the exam center so you can relax and review your study materials, particularly tables and lists of exam-related information.

- Read the questions carefully. Do not be tempted to jump to an early conclusion. Make sure you know exactly what the question is asking.

- There will be questions with multiple correct responses. When there is more than one correct answer, a message at the bottom of the screen will prompt you to either "choose two" or "choose all that apply." Be sure to read the messages displayed to know how many correct answers you must choose.

- When answering multiple-choice questions you are not sure about, use a process of elimination to get rid of the obviously incorrect answers first. Doing so will improve your odds if you need to make an educated guess.

- Do not spend too much time on one question. This is a form-based test; however, you cannot move backward through the exam. You must answer the current question before you can move to the next question, and after you have moved to the next question, you cannot go back and change your answer on a previous question.

- Keep track of your time. Because this is a 90-minute test consisting of 60 questions, you have an average of 90 seconds to answer each question. You can spend as much or as little time as you like on any one question, but when 90 minutes is up, the test is over. Check your progress. After 45 minutes, you should have answered at least 30 questions. If you have not, do not panic. You will simply need to answer the remaining questions at a faster pace. If on average you can answer each of the remaining 30 questions 4 seconds quicker, you will recover 2 minutes. Again, do not panic; just pace yourself.

- For the latest pricing on the exams and updates to the registration procedures, visit CWNP's website at www.cwnp.com.

Assessment Test

1. You have been hired to come up with a network design for a new customer. What should your first step be?

   A. Present the customer with information on past designs you've done.

   B. Ask about their existing network infrastructure.

   C. Present the customer with a high-level design that can be fine-tuned once the requirements are discovered.

   D. Gather the customer's business and technical requirements and assess the possible solutions that would meet their needs.

2. When referencing a network design, the term CRD stands for which of the following:

   A. Customer requirements document

   B. Change request document

   C. Customer relations department

   D. Customer requested design

3. A project postanalysis is being performed and the analysis team is investigating why a critical technology upgrade was missed in the planning meetings. What should be considered as a root cause?

   A. Expectations were not clarified.

   B. Key participants failed to participate.

   C. Scoping was improperly performed.

   D. A technical findings document wasn't produced.

4. You are planning a new 2.4 GHz network and are determining which PHY rates and channels you will support in your design. In order to configure 9 Mbps PHY rate as a basic rate, what must you confirm as a minimum requirement with your client devices?

   A. 802.11b support

   B. 802.11n support

   C. 802.11g support

   D. 802.11a support

5. A client device spec sheet claims support of up to 200 mW of transmit power. What factors might influence the actual power output that is used? (Choose all that apply.)

   A. Client devices always transmit at maximum power.

   B. Regulatory domain requirements for the frequency in use

   C. Radio resource management protocols designed to mitigate co-channel interference

   D. DTPC requirements enforced by neighboring clients

   E. PHY rate

6. You are validating client performance on a new 802.11n network installation and a client device you've supported on your previous Wi-Fi network isn't connecting. Other devices of different types are connected. What should you first confirm?

    A. Signal levels

    B. Antenna polarity

    C. MAC feature support

    D. IP address

7. When using SSH over wireless, what should you ensure the WLAN supports?

    A. Opportunistic key caching (OKC)

    B. AES, because SSH uses it for encryption

    C. Maintained IP connectivity during roaming

    D. TLS session resumption

8. What technique is used by real-time applications to mitigate the impact of excess jitter?

    A. Lossless codecs

    B. Buffers

    C. RTP

    D. Fast secure roaming

9. Different equipment vendors who manufacture VoWiFi handsets often differ in support for which MAC features? (Choose all that apply.)

    A. WMM

    B. Power saving

    C. Codecs

    D. Frequency band

10. Warehouse environments can tend to have RF conditions that change drastically depending on which of the following?

    A. The amount and type of inventory stocked on the shelves

    B. Environmental conditions due to office doors being left open during hot days

    C. The height of AP mounting locations

    D. Power outages

11. Infusion pumps are frequently found in which of the following verticals?

    A. Enterprise

    B. Offshore drilling

    C. Healthcare

    D. Mining

12. Wireless security is a big concern for a large university campus. What important design consideration should be discussed with the university staff?

   A. Need for firewalls

   B. Disparity of client devices

   C. Dynamic VLAN assignment

   D. Propagation over large spaces

13. Which statement correctly describes the remote MAC variation of the centralized WLAN architecture?

   A. All data handling and non-real-time functions are handled directly by the AP.

   B. The AP performs distributed forwarding and control functions are split between the AP and WLAN controller.

   C. The AP has minimal data or control functionality. Real-time and non-real-time functions are offloaded to the WLAN controller.

   D. Due to the architecting of real-time functions, the remote MAC model provides the greatest flexibility for AP-to-WLAN controller interconnectivity.

   E. Almost all functions, real-time and non-real-time, are handled directly by the AP. The WLAN controller is on standby for remote failover.

14. In your network design, you are trying to minimize data switching latency and prevent bottlenecks at the WLAN controller. With those objectives in mind, what data plane model is recommended?

   A. Split tunneling

   B. Distributed forwarding

   C. Centralized forwarding

   D. Anchored forwarding

15. Which WLAN architecture is most prevalent in today's Wi-Fi market?

   A. Centralized WLAN architecture

   B. Autonomous WLAN architecture

   C. Distributed WLAN architecture

   D. Mesh WLAN architecture

   E. SCA WLAN architecture

16. What is the difference between dB and dBm?

   A. There is no difference.

   B. dB measures gain; dBm measures the difference in power.

   C. dB is a relative measure; dBm measures an absolute power.

   D. dB is used to measure noise; dBm is used to measure an amplifier.

   E. dBm is 2.14 units more than dB.

17. What is the receive sensitivity of a radio receiver?

    A. The gain of the receiver's antenna and front-end LNA

    B. The ability of the receiver to amplify a signal

    C. The ability of the receiver to detect a signal in the presence of noise

    D. The noise figure of the front-end LNA

18. What happens when someone puts an input signal that is 5 dB higher than its rated power into a simple transmitter amplifier (one without gain control)?

    A. The amplifier will draw too much current.

    B. The amplifier will distort the output signal.

    C. The amplifier will blow up.

    D. The amplifier will become unstable.

19. What is a transmission line?

    A. Twisted pair cable

    B. A medium to transfer microwave energy from one place to another using one or more conductors

    C. A medium to transfer microwave energy from one place to another using one conductor

    D. A medium to transfer microwave energy from one place to another using dielectrics

20. What are the two main properties that determine if an antenna is suitable for an application?

    A. Efficiency, gain

    B. Gain, power

    C. Gain, frequency of operation

    D. Power, polarity

21. What technology gives 802.11n its highest boost in throughput over legacy 802.11 standards?

    A. Spatial multiplexing

    B. MRC

    C. Higher coding rates

    D. Smaller guard interval

22. Kellum Kites, Inc., would like to establish a PTP link between their two factories. They will rely on this link for VoIP communications between buildings. What is the first action item that needs to be completed before a survey is performed?

    A. CAD drawing

    B. Satellite image review

    C. Walkthrough

    D. Predictive survey

    E. Fresnel zone calculation

23. What type of information may be pertinent to a network architecture decision in which the designer is deciding between a distributed forwarding architecture or a centralized forwarding architecture?

    A. Layer 3 segmentation

    B. Routing tables

    C. VLAN databases

    D. Device-to-AP ratio

24. When preparing to analyze a customer network for a new 802.11n network, what aspects of the wired network should be reviewed that will affect throughput? (Choose all that apply.)

    A. Uplink ports

    B. Access ports

    C. Routers

    D. Security protocol

25. What is the most important part of an RF site survey?

    A. Determining power levels

    B. Determining channel assignments

    C. Quantifying AP placement

    D. Analyzing the wired LAN

26. Passive surveys using survey mapping software are limited in what aspect? (Choose all that apply.)

    A. Quantifying retransmissions

    B. Predicting PHY rates

    C. Downlink RSSI measurements

    D. Uplink SNR information

27. When performing an 802.11n survey that will also support legacy 802.11 clients, you should do which of the following?

    A. Try to create multipath.

    B. Perform an active survey with the least capable client device.

    C. Use an 802.11n client that matches the AP capabilities.

    D. Always use 24 Mbps basic rates.

28. Approximately what is the typical, and generally recommended, setting for beacon intervals?

    A. 10 time units

    B. 100 time units

    C. 200 time units

    D. 1 second

    E. 100 μs

    F. 1024 μs

29. What phrase best describes the way in which WMM provides quality of service priority for different ACs in a BSS?

    A. Statistical probability

    B. Guaranteed access

    C. Round-robin selection

    D. Polled opportunities

    E. Scheduled intervals

30. Multicast video applications typically require special treatment on the Wi-Fi network due to the limitations of multicast traffic. Many vendors implement proprietary multicast-to-unicast conversion for this reason. Which of the following is not a valid reason for special treatment of multicast traffic?

    A. Multicast is assigned to the best effort (AC_BE) queue.

    B. Multicast is not acknowledged on the wireless medium.

    C. Multicast must always be transmitted with omnidirectional antennas.

    D. Multicast is always sent at a rate in the Basic Rate Set.

31. What is the term used to describe the process of assigning specific permissions and policies to users or groups?

    A. Authentication

    B. Association

    C. Authorization

    D. Allocation

    E. Accounting

32. What cipher suites are specified for use in WLANs by the 802.11 standard? (Choose all that apply.)

A. IPSec

B. TKIP

C. CCMP

D. TLS

E. SSL

F. Shared Key

33. What is a best practice security design strategy for networks in which many client devices do not support modern (WPA/2) security settings? (Choose all that apply.)

A. Plan a single SSID that supports multiple encryption types so that devices with weak security will benefit from strong security for group addressed traffic.

B. Implement MAC authentication and authorization with an up-to-date user database. Offer critical network services to important end users as needed, and deny network privileges for guests.

C. Provision separate SSIDs for weak and strong security options with segmentation and filtering as necessary.

D. Layer the security strategy for weak devices by implementing MAC filtering, SSID hiding, the best available encryption, and filtering.

34. What parameters must be configured on the RADIUS server for connectivity between the RADIUS server and the authenticator? (Choose all that apply.)

A. Shared secret

B. Authenticator IP address or subnet

C. X.509 certificate type

D. LDAP port

E. Client IP addresses

F. Communication ports

35. You are tasked with selecting an EAP type that provides robust security for university staff and students. Client usernames and passwords are required for authentication and broad client support across operating systems is also important. What EAP type best suits these requirements?

A. EAP-TLS

B. EAP-TTLS/MSCHAPv2

C. EAP-LEAP

D. PEAPv0/EAP-MSCHAPv2

E. PEAPv1/EAP-GTC

36. What are common endpoint security solutions for protecting clients on wireless networks? (Choose all that apply.)

   A. Captive portals

   B. Personal firewalls

   C. Antivirus software

   D. Endpoint agents

   E. Network access control (NAC)

37. Characterize the purpose of high-level design (HLD) documents used in WLANs.

   A. HLDs provide details about VLAN standards.

   B. HLDs provide IP addresses of critical infrastructure components.

   C. HLDs describe the hardware involved in a design.

   D. HLDs provide an architectural overview for WLAN designs.

38. Network monitoring documentation would fall under what type of document?

   A. Technical requirements document

   B. Low-level design

   C. Operational and maintenance plan

   D. High-level design

39. Bills of materials (BOMs) are a component of what document?

   A. Technical requirements document

   B. Low-level design

   C. Operational and maintenance plan

   D. High-level design

40. What is the first step to a postinstallation validation?

   A. Assessing RF

   B. Identifying interference

   C. Validating configuration

   D. Testing performance

41. When performing a wired network assessment that serves a new WLAN installation, what type of wired interface statistic output should you focus on?

   A. Speed and duplex

   B. VLAN tagging

   C. QoS marking

   D. IP services

42. When performing a QoS validation for a voice network, what value should voice media frames be marked as? (Choose all that apply.)

    A. 4

    B. 5

    C. 6

    D. 7

    E. 8

43. Which of the following are examples of non-WiFi interferers? (Choose all that apply.)

    A. Co-channel interference

    B. Microwaves

    C. Bluetooth

    D. Adjacent channel interference

44. Your company is located in a downtown high-rise building. You've configured your network so that your lowest mandatory rate is 12 Mbps. Users are complaining about poor throughput. Upon inspection, you notice that over 90 percent of the traffic is being sent at 1 Mbps. What is the most likely cause?

    A. Smart phones and/or laptops in ad hoc mode beaconing at 1 Mbps data rates

    B. An AP that has lost its connection to its controller and is flooding management frames

    C. The neighboring networks from above and/or below are very busy and have the lower data rates enabled

    D. Nothing, because this is normal

45. You are troubleshooting an autonomous AP deployment. One of the SSIDs works, but the other one is not passing any traffic. What should be suspected as a likely cause?

    A. Portal services

    B. Spanning tree

    C. 802.1p markings

    D. VLAN tagging

Answers to Assessment Test

1. D. The very first step in a network design should always be gathering the customer requirements. For more information, see Chapter 1.

2. A. The customer requirements document is a summary of requirements that have been gathered through the discovery phase and interview process. The purpose of this document is to ensure that both parties are in agreement regarding the project requirements. For more information, see Chapter 1.

3. B. When key participants are not present in planning discussions, many details can be missed. For more information, see Chapter 1.

4. C. The correct answer is 802.11g support because 9 Mbps is an OFDM rate only available in 2.4 GHz with 802.11g or 802.11n. For more information, see Chapter 2.

5. B, C, D, E. All of these options factor into whether a client will be able to transmit at an available transmit power. For more information, see Chapter 2.

6. C. Older devices may not be able to support all the MAC feature sets confirmed on newer equipment. You should confirm feature parity of encryption, PHY rates, and other factors. For more information, see Chapter 2.

7. C. Session-based protocols like SSH and Telnet will experience application disruption if the IP address of the client changes when roaming. For more information, see Chapter 3.

8. B. Applications will intentionally build in a delay mechanism (which is barely perceptible to humans) with real-time traffic in order to smooth out variability in 802.11 frame delivery, which would otherwise result in audio and video quality. For more information, see Chapter 3.

9. A, B. Codecs and frequency band are not MAC features. For more information, see Chapter 3.

10. A. Warehouse environments are very dynamic, with inventory typically always moving in and out. Depending on inventory levels and the density of the inventory itself, RF conditions within a warehouse can change substantially. For more information, see Chapter 4.

11. C. Infusion pumps are the devices that administer intravenous (IV) fluids. They are located with the patients at the bedside and are one of the most mobile and commonly used items in a hospital. For more information, see Chapter 4.

12. B. When implementing in educational environments, you have little control over the client devices and their capabilities. This makes implementing wireless security a significant challenge. For more information, see Chapter 4.

13. C. The Remote MAC architecture is one in which the MAC functions of the AP are moved to the WLAN controller. In this architecture subtype, real-time and non-real-time functions are handled by the WLAN controller, which means that the AP-to-controller connectivity must be cautiously planned. Oftentimes, the AP must be directly connected to the controller. For more information, see Chapter 5.

14. B. With centralized WLAN architectures, when all data is passed through the WLAN controller (centralized forwarding), the controller can potentially be a traffic bottleneck. This is especially true when the controller supports many 802.11n APs that are heavily utilized and when processor-intensive features like stateful packet inspection are supported. For more information, see Chapter 5.

15. A. The centralized WLAN architecture commands a strong leading percentage of today's Wi-Fi market share. With the advent of 802.11n and distributed intelligence, this may change as more vendors move data forwarding to the edge. For more information, see Chapter 5.

16. C. dB is a relative measure of power, a comparison between one power level and another. dBm is an absolute measure of power. It is power as compared to one milliwatt. For more information, see Chapter 6.

17. C. The lowest signal power level that can be given to a receiver and still communicate is the receiver sensitivity of the radio. It is largely a function of the loss between the antenna and the receiver and the noise performance of the receiver's first amplifier. It can also include a receiver's ability to lock on to a signal. It changes with the connection speed (e.g. from 1 Mbps to 54 Mbps). For more information, see Chapter 6.

18. B. The amplifier distorts the transmitted signal. The spectrum of the signal grows beyond the bounds of its assigned channel and interferes with adjacent channels. Generally an amplifier will not blow up or become unstable if it gets a high input power signal, though this may happen if the amplifier is not designed properly. The amplifier actually becomes more efficient when it approaches saturation, so current will generally decrease. Some transmit amplifiers have gain control at their input and will reduce the power of the signal going into the amplifier if it detects a high input signal. In this case, distortion would be kept to a minimum. For more information, see Chapter 6.

19. B. A medium to transfer microwave energy from one place to another using one or more conductors is the most general description. One conductor describes only some transmission lines, like waveguide. Twisted pair is only one type of transmission line. Dielectrics are used in transmission lines, and in special circumstances can form a transmission line by itself, but in general don't describe transmission lines. For more information, see Chapter 7.

20. C. The gain and frequency of operation are the starting points to knowing whether or not an antenna is suitable for an application. Important secondary considerations are efficiency, size/form factor, and polarity. For more information, see Chapter 7.

21. A. 802.11n gets its biggest boost in performance from spatial multiplexing, which is at the heart of MIMO operation. For more information, see Chapter 7.

22. C. When about to survey for a point-to-point (PTP) link, it is always wise to perform a walkthrough to investigate feasibility and properly prepare for the site survey measurements. For more information, see Chapter 8.

23. A. OSI Layer 3 segmentation information, and where it occurs, is one of the single largest determining factors that will affect whether autonomous or centralized forwarding architectures are most relevant to an existing network design. For more information, see Chapter 8.

24. A, B, C. Switching speeds and capacity at access and uplink ports in addition to routing speeds and capability are critical wired network factors for determining network throughput performance. For more information, see Chapter 8.

25. C. Beyond all else, RF site surveys need to use a thoughtful method of quantifying AP placements based on RF propagation. For more information, see Chapter 9.

26. A, B, D. Passive surveys are valuable, but not in all cases. You should consider active surveys when you need to obtain additional information about RF links between clients. For more information, see Chapter 9.

27. B. WLAN design needs to be designed to support the lowest common denominator client device that will be supported in the final design. For more information, see Chapter 9.

28. B. In the 802.11 standard, beacon intervals are measured in time units. A time unit is equal to one kilomicrosecond, which is 1,024 microseconds. Most WLAN infrastructure vendors set the beacon interval at a default value of 100 time units, which is equal to 100 kilomicroseconds (102,400 microseconds or 102.4 milliseconds). This is approximately 10 beacons every second. For more information, see Chapter 10.

29. A. In WLAN contention, no absolute guarantee is made for quality of service priority. Instead, stations and ACs contend for medium access using processes that create a statistical likelihood for priority. For more information, see Chapter 10.

30. C. Many WLAN vendors have implemented proprietary multicast-to-unicast conversion protocols to allow applications that use multicast to work properly. Despite the fact that multicast addresses are group addresses, APs with any antenna configuration are capable of transmitting multicast frames. There is no restriction for omnidirectional transmission. For more information, see Chapter 10.

31. C. There are several important layers to effective enterprise security, and one of those components is to ensure that users only have permission to access the network services that they are entitled to use. Authorization is the process of assigning the appropriate policies to users. For more information, see Chapter 11.

32. B, C. The 802.11 specification designates three encryption protocols for use in WLANs. WEP, TKIP, and CCMP are the three ciphers, though WEP has been deprecated and is no longer recommended. TKIP deprecation will also come sometime soon. For more information, see Chapter 11.

33. C, D. In some network deployments, business requirements prevent security designers from implementing the ideal security solution for all devices. In those situations, the best practices are to implement separate network policies for weak and strong security solutions, to filter and segment to ensure that few network resources are exposed, and to layer all available security solutions for maximum protection. For more information, see Chapter 11.

34. A, B, F. When configuring the RADIUS server for connectivity to the authenticator, generally only a few parameters must be configured. Specifically, the authenticator's IP address, the Layer 4 UDP port, and the shared secret are necessary configuration parameters. The X.509 certificate must be installed on the RADIUS server for client authentication, but is not necessary for communication with the authenticator. For more information, see Chapter 12.

35. D. EAP selection depends on a number of criteria that differ from one organization to the next. In the scenario described here, EAP-TTLS/MSCHAPv2 and PEAPv0/EAP-MSCHAPv2 would be the only acceptable options. EAP-TTLS comes in as a close second to PEAPv0 because client support for EAP-TTLS is not as pervasive as is PEAP. For more information, see Chapter 12.

36. B, C, D, E. All of the options are viable client endpoint security solutions except captive portals. Though clients may have to authenticate through a captive portal, this is more of an infrastructure security gatekeeper than it is a client solution. For more information, see Chapter 12.

37. D. The most correct answer is D because an HLD doesn't detail specifics of any single installation, but rather the approach and guidelines that actual implementations must be based on. For more information, see Chapter 13.

38. C. Monitoring network devices falls under the category of operating and maintaining a healthy network. For more information, see Chapter 13.

39. B. BOMs should be included in low-level designs that encompass an actual installation that includes any unique components that installation requires. For more information, see Chapter 13.

40. A. Once a network is installed and preconfigured in preparation for a postinstallation validation to occur, the assumption is that the LLD has been fully implemented in the new network. Once the network is ready to be validated, whether a manual or automatic RF configuration is used, the network should have had a sufficient settling-in period. Therefore, RF configuration components should have already been validated and you can now perform a full RF assessment. For more information, see Chapter 14.

41. A. When you are performing a wired analysis, Ethernet ports that are in the data path of the wireless LAN traffic should be analyzed for speed and duplex matches along with key indicators that indicate mismatches of these values. For more information, see Chapter 14.

42. C, D. 802.11 User Priority (UP) values should be marked as either 6 or 7 for voice media frames. For more information, see Chapter 14.

43. B, C. Co-channel and adjacent channel interference are examples of Wi-Fi interference and therefore are not non-Wi-Fi interferers. Bluetooth and microwaves are non-Wi-Fi interferers. For more information, see Chapter 15.

44. C. While it could potentially be a software issue on an AP, there's a much higher likelihood that this is coming from a neighboring network near your network. For more information, see Chapter 15.

45. D. SSIDs are VLAN tagged to different VLANs. When multiple VLANs are used across a single Ethernet link, the switch that the AP is connected to needs to be configured to allow VLAN tagging. For more information, see Chapter 15.

Chapter

1

Gathering and Analyzing Requirements

THE FOLLOWING CWDP EXAM TOPICS ARE COVERED IN THIS CHAPTER:

- ✓ Identify and describe best practices for pre-deployment information gathering and network planning tasks.

- ✓ Identify the business justification and the intended goals for the WLAN.

- ✓ Determine the budget for a WLAN project and plan a solution accordingly.

- ✓ Determine the desired applications to be supported and understand the requirements for specific applications.

- ✓ Determine the intended end users for the WLAN and describe best practices for planning a network to accommodate different user groups.

- ✓ Determine network service requirements and implement Service Level Agreements (SLA) accordingly.

In this chapter, we will discuss the importance of gathering and analyzing customer requirements. In the many stages of the network design process, understanding customer requirements should be the very first step and is likely the most critical step of a successful network design. Knowing your customer's needs is the foundation on which all other decisions and design stages are built. Unfortunately, this step is commonly overlooked, as many engineers tend to run headlong into the technical details of a design without first having a clear understanding of the customer's business needs.

Discovering the customer's needs requires that several questions be asked and answered, including:

- What are the specific goals for the network?

- What challenges (either business or technical) are being addressed?

- How will the customer measure the success of a network deployment?

It may seem overly simple to state, but it is difficult for network engineers to meet design requirements when they do not have a clear picture of the requirements to be met. So although these questions may seem basic, understanding the answer to each is essential.

This chapter will delve deep into these questions so you can understand them more fully. We will also provide a framework and best practice recommendations for approaching the requirements phase of a network design. Customer satisfaction is always the end goal, and these questions should help you understand the scope of your customer's needs so you can meet that goal.

Preparation and Planning

It is often said, "If you fail to plan, you plan to fail." While clichés like this may get tossed around too much, this phrase is surprisingly relevant to the soft-skills aspect of network design. Making a good impression on the customer is important, and is usually accomplished with a little planning and research before the project even starts. That's right: network design begins before you ever meet the customer face to face.

Prior to the first customer meeting, it is important that you learn as much as possible about the customer and their business. Think about it as an interview. Something as simple as typing the customer name into a search engine to review articles or client reviews of the business, or reading the "About Us" section on the customer's website, can get the network planning phase off to a successful start. Identifying key aspects of the customer's business is an important first step to planning a network.

You should seek to answer a few basic questions during this research phase, such as:

- In what industry does the customer operate?
- What is their primary business focus?
- Who are their customers?
- What products and/or services do they offer?
- In what type of building is the network being designed (high rise, campus, healthcare, warehouse, etc.)?

Arming yourself with critical pieces of information in advance like this can make the initial customer meeting much more productive. For instance, if your customer is in the retail industry, you can expect that certain security aspects, such as PCI (Payment Card Industry) compliance, will likely need to be considered in the design to ensure that customer credit card information is kept secure. Knowing this detail up front allows you to research the latest PCI requirements and ask the right questions when you sit down with the customer. You will likely find that not many customers are as up-to-date on industry compliance regulations as they should be. Consider this an opportunity: come prepared with specific details on the latest requirements as well as recommendations that you can offer to help drive the design discussions off to a proper start.

While everyone desires certain performance features from their network, the way you tackle priorities in the network design is always relative to the customer's business case.

Another important soft-skill recommendation is to prepare for certain topics of conversation with your customer. It is a good idea to read recent press releases and news articles published about your customer. This step can prove useful by alerting you to any major announcements that may end up becoming a topic of conversation while you are at the customer site. News such as new product launches or services could be the focus of network changes and provide insight as to why you are being brought in to help this customer with a new network design. Customer satisfaction will increase if you instantly engage in a conversation about this new product or make recommendations or ask specific questions related to how new business ventures may be integrated into their network upgrade.

Similarly, a little research can alert you to topics that should be avoided in conversation, such as recent or rumored job cuts. In general, the best practice for casual conversation is to avoid bringing up topics that may be sensitive in nature, unless they apply directly to the task at hand.

Real World Scenario

Preplanning with the Customer

We recently had a firsthand experience that demonstrates the importance of the pre–customer planning phase. I was asked by an ISP to participate in the design of a campground wireless network for one of their customers. My contact at the ISP knew very little about the customer's network goals or the facility itself, so research was helpful for me to prepare before interacting directly with the customer.

A simple web search returned information about the potential customer's business model as well as a layout of their park. Interestingly enough, the site map alone exposed several network hurdles, such as wireless distribution from the clubhouse to the campers. Of course, camper parks with numerous large metal RVs are not ideally suited to radio frequency (RF) propagation, so I knew that proper coverage planning would increase the number of access points (APs) and require specific antennas.

This is a fairly basic example, but knowing the customer's industry and some of the challenges inherent in their network environment allowed me to begin planning a low-cost solution before meeting with the customer. It also provided enough information for me to make an educated estimation of their business intentions—simple Internet-only guest access—which I later found to be correct. All of these planning steps saved both the client and me time, as it helped me to set the customer's expectations and gauge their commitment to a successful deployment early on. It also provided some handy topics of conversation to break the ice. While this story demonstrates my point about how important planning ahead can be, also note that planning for a small customer, like the camping site, is much different than the planning process for a large enterprise customer.

Meeting the Customer

After doing your homework, you're ready for the first customer meeting. Each situation is different, but generally speaking, your goals for this meeting are simple:

- Identify the key decision makers for the project and where they fit into the organizational structure.
- Identify an overall high-level scope of the project.
- Identify the key business and technical requirements.

Identify Key Decision Makers and Participants

From the onset of any project, it is imperative for the network design participants to have an accurate understanding of the individuals with whom they are working. Specifically, it is important to identify the following:

- Who is responsible for and capable of making decisions?
- Who has the information and authority to answer questions?
- Which individuals should participate in the design phase?

Over the course of a large project, network designers may interact with a diverse set of people, from maintenance technicians to network engineers and chief information officers (CIOs). So answering these questions will allow you to sort through the roles and responsibilities of a particular organization so you can streamline the process and prevent costly mistakes.

In addition to identifying the key decision maker(s), you must seek out the *project sponsor*. The project sponsor is the person who is responsible for the political momentum the project has, which usually involves the financial backing. Sometimes a project sponsor isn't involved in the design of the solution, so you may not be introduced to this person initially. But remember to seek out this person as soon as possible and at least interview them before going any further with the project. They are a key decision maker whether it is stated or it is implied. Often when a project sponsor isn't involved in the design phase of a project, the translation of the solution requirements may be misinterpreted or not properly communicated to you. Get the information from the most direct source possible. Secondhand information can add risk to the project for both you and your primary contacts.

Key decision makers can come from nearly any part of an organization. Information technology (IT) is becoming an integral part of many businesses and is no longer relegated to the interests of those directly part of the IT organization. CIOs are a perfect case in point here, as they represent both the technical strategy as well as the strategic business strategy.

You may or may not work with the key decision makers on a daily basis throughout the project, but understanding who is capable of making final decisions is critical. The design phase of a network implementation is inherently subject to change, and most changes require approval. A good design engineer will often be able to steer a customer based on their needs, but there are critical points when a decision needs to be made. That decision must come from a source of authority, such as a key decision maker or project sponsor. Once a major decision is made, it must be absolute and in writing.

🌐 **Real World Scenario**

Things Aren't Always What They May Seem

Consider a scenario in which a company is upgrading their infrastructure to support 802.11n. Unfortunately, the company still uses many legacy Wired Equivalent Privacy (WEP)-only scanning devices, which are problematic both for security and performance reasons. Per the Institute of Electrical and Electronics Engineers (IEEE) 802.11n amendment, WEP (and even Temporal Key Integrity Protocol [TKIP] for that matter) cannot be used with 802.11n modulation and coding scheme (MCS) rates. If the customer did not plan to upgrade their WEP devices, they must be informed of the incompatibility between WEP and 802.11n, or many of the benefits of the upgrade will not be realized. As the infrastructure designer, you can, and usually should, make recommendations to ensure that the network's integrity is optimized and performance maximized. Ultimately the customer needs to determine what security policies will be upheld, and at what financial and operational costs.

The decision to upgrade WEP-only devices impacts the way a network is designed. Knowing who has the overriding authority to accept or reject an important proposal is helpful to you during these times. You will usually have to educate your customer to these important facts, which they might not have thought were an issue to begin with. Your reputation is at stake, so you must ensure that the decision maker is getting accurate, timely, and complete information relating to the network's design, which will allow for a well-informed decision.

In addition to understanding the roles of decision makers, you should keep in mind that only certain individuals may be aware of the plans for network improvements. Although these plans may not be secret, some of the company representatives with whom you spend time may not have enough information to authoritatively answer questions or verify critical details. There may be times when you should simply make note of questions you would like to ask a person who maintains a role of authority rather than relying on the incomplete perspective of someone convenient. For example, some of the initial onsite design tasks may include a facility walk-through, which may be relegated to a maintenance technician who maintains a master key set. If a representative of the networking group is not present, questions or concerns may arise during the walk-through that the maintenance technician couldn't answer.

Depending on your role in the business process, you may also need to ensure that initial discussions about network implementation include input from all network stakeholders, which may include executive management, IT managers, building facility personnel, IT engineering and support staff, and even end users. In most cases, not all of these roles must be represented, but each scenario is different.

Identify a High-Level Scope

When you build a new house, you don't start with carpet or faucet fixtures. Before you get to the details, you must understand the big picture: do you want a ranch, colonial-style, Cape Cod, modular home, or something else altogether? This approach holds true for network design as well.

Knowing the high-level scope of a project comes before the selection of a security model, RF settings, or even wireless local area network (WLAN) equipment vendors. This sequence of events is necessary because the selection or configuration of the technical details is usually dependent on the big picture.

One of the first steps in a network design is to ask the customer to provide an overview of the desired goals for the network. To avoid getting lost in the weeds of technical detail, this initial conversation should be kept as high level as possible, and should serve as the framework for all subsequent plans. The idea is to establish a general scope of the project and to answer some basic questions, such as the following:

- Is this a new network installation or a modification to an existing network?

- Why is a network upgrade desired?

- What is the scale of the new network? For example, is this a small pilot to test a new video-over-wireless application, or is it a large nationwide rollout of an employee telecommuting project that extends corporate wireless into each employee's home?

- What are the primary applications?

- Will the project be implemented as a single rollout, or will it be implemented in phases?

- Is there a specific deadline that must be met?

Several other questions will be answered during this high-level discussion, but the basic function is to identify the initial framework before further investigation takes place. There will always be more details to gather, more questions that need answering, and other network recommendations to explore later.

Identifying the major objectives up front will properly frame and set boundaries for these other needs. In one sense, it provides a target to aim for. After you acquire the target itself, then you can narrow down to the bull's-eye.

Understand the Customer's Expertise

As you interview your customer, it is critically important to build your own profile of the customer's level of expertise in all the technical subject areas involved in wireless. Because WLANs are a marriage of several IT disciplines, areas of weakness need to be identified quickly. It is important to note that areas where the customer is weak might limit your solution design because of their ability (or inability) to provide continuing support and day-to-day troubleshooting.

These areas include:

- RF technologies
- Wired networking concepts primarily related to routing and switching
- Backend systems on which the wireless network is dependent
- Security solutions
- 802.11 protocols and operation
- Wireless equipment configuration and monitoring

It is highly likely that a customer's knowledge is weak in the area of RF in particular. It is the least understood subject matter for the average IT professional. While customers will typically rely on you as a Certified Wireless Design Professional (CWDP) to provide that expertise, it is important that you try to help guide the customer in the dos and don'ts of operations and configuration management once the project is complete.

A technique to understanding the customer's networking knowledge is to have them explain their current network design. Try to determine whether a vendor/integrator did this for them and to what extent they were involved in the effort. Also ask your customer to explain how they make changes to their network and, without it sounding like an interview, maybe have them provide you with some examples.

Inquire about the backend systems the customer has deployed. You will likely have to interface with some or all of these, so it is imperative to learn as much as you can. These systems can consist of (but are not limited to) RADIUS servers for authentication, Microsoft Active Directory or Lightweight Directory Access Protocol (LDAP) user databases, and Domain Name System (DNS) and Dynamic Host Configuration Protocol (DHCP) servers.

Security is a broad topic. It is also a complicated topic and likely an area in which the customer will not have a great deal of expertise. The same rule that applied for networking also goes for security: interview them. Ask them questions about the security infrastructure devices they have today. If your customer has existing wireless today, what is their current security model? Have them show or tell you their client security configuration as well.

Answers to these questions will help you understand how hard it will be to sell certain design features you might propose. It could also give you an idea how eager the person is to learn. If they aren't eager to learn and don't have a good technical understanding, you will have to keep the final solution very simple.

From an operational perspective, you should note how your customer responds to incidents and what analysis tools they currently have and *actually* use. Again, this speaks to the need for simplicity.

Gathering the Requirements

After obtaining a high-level overview of the network's objectives, the next phase is to drill down and begin the more detailed information-gathering phase. Ask lots of questions, such as:

- What applications and protocols will be in use?
- How many users will you need to support?
- What types of client devices will be in use?

After you've identified the key players in the company, this should be a snap, right? Unfortunately, it's not that easy. There are often several people involved in this process as well, along with various ways to gather this information. Again, each network is different, and the methodologies are not always cut and dried. Face-to-face meetings, conference calls, and detailed questionnaires each have their own place in this phase, with advantages and limitations for each. When possible, interactive discussion is preferable as it provides the best opportunity for clarification and further questioning if any issue remains unclear. It is also often the hardest because you must get all the decision makers into a single room at the same time.

Questionnaires can be helpful tools in the initial information-gathering phase, but they are not always the best means to the information-gathering end. With a good bit of planning and experience, you can draft a fairly comprehensive set of questions to ask a customer. Questionnaires have the benefit of convenience, as they can be filled out and returned without synchronized schedules or physical proximity; however, there are always details left for discussion or further clarification.

As we've discussed, all successful network design efforts should start with an understanding of customer requirements, which can be gathered in different ways. To facilitate the design process, design requirements are typically broken down into two primary classifications: *business requirements* and *technical requirements*. While there is not always a firm distinction between the two, in general, requirements typically fall into one of these two areas.

Business Requirements

When it comes to gathering requirements, always start with the business requirements because these drive the technical requirements. We've already established that a designer should research the customer's basic business products and services prior to the initial meeting, but at this point in the process, much more detail from the customer is needed. In this stage, the customer is providing information that clarifies the core business needs that are being addressed by the network upgrade. Some of the most common business objectives asked of a wireless network include:

- Decreasing operating expenses by migrating to a predominately wireless infrastructure, thereby reducing the cost and maintenance of access switches
- Increasing employee productivity by enabling mobile applications via the corporate Wi-Fi infrastructure
- Extending the network to previously unreachable locations to allow new applications
- Providing Internet access in a for-profit model to generate revenue

- Providing network access to guests as a complimentary service to increase the business's appeal

- Maintaining industry compliance certification with all networking infrastructure

- Offering service level–related business requirements, such as wanting 99.999 percent uptime on their network

Whatever the business drivers may be, they must be clearly articulated by the customer and understood by the designer, as the success of the project will be based on the accomplishment of these requirements.

In addition to understanding the actual objectives, it is important to comprehend the customer's method for measuring these objectives. For example, reliability, resiliency, and strong application performance may be desired, but how will these criteria be measured? To provide you with measurable evaluation criteria, the customer should explain what conditions validate a successful network deployment. Conversely, what will happen if the project fails? What business functions rely on the success of the network deployment? These questions absolutely, without question, need to be asked.

As we have mentioned previously in this chapter, it should be noted that business requirements cannot be gathered from an isolated representative. Ensure that all interested parties have an opportunity to provide input. During these interview sessions, conflicts regarding network goals may arise between different groups or individuals, leaving you to play the role of interpreter or possibly to appeal to a previously discovered authority. Diligently maintaining documentation will prove a valuable step in the process of uncovering, communicating, and resolving conflicts. This issue will be covered in more detail in the section "Politics," later in this chapter.

Technical Requirements

Finally, after all the business-related rigmarole is addressed, you'll find yourself at home talking tech. Now that you've learned what the customer needs to accomplish, and what metrics will determine the project's success, it's time to address the technical requirements.

Gathering Technical Information

Your customer will likely have a general idea about some of the common technical aspects such as high availability and scalability, as well as performance and capacity planning. However, you will want to ascertain as much information as possible about the customer's technical requirements, including:

- What client types will be used on the wireless network? You should ask questions like:
    - In what bands do they operate?
    - What features or standards do they support?
    - Are they Wi-Fi certified?
    - What drivers and firmware will be used with them?
    - How difficult will it be, if needed, to upgrade their driver and supplicant?

- What applications will be supported by the wireless network and how will the applications be used? Find out the following:
  - What are the application's requirements?
    - Throughput
    - Latency
    - Jitter
    - Loss
  - Are there any application-specific dependencies?
  - Are there any custom applications?
- What existing infrastructure is currently in place to support the wireless network? Ask about the following:
  - Security requirements, such as Authentication, Authorization, and Accounting (AAA) servers, user databases, Network Access Control (NAC), or other security-related policies
  - Routing and switching infrastructure considerations, including quality of service (QoS), throughput capacity, virtual local area network (VLAN) configurations, Power-over-Ethernet (PoE)
- Has an equipment vendor already been selected? If so, how will this vendor's architecture be deployed?
- What network-wide security policies are in place, and how will the wireless network's security posture be maintained?

Although this list is not exhaustive, the point should be clear that there are many details to collect if the planning phase is to be comprehensive.

Designing for High Availability

Let's now take a look at a single aspect of the technical requirements discussion and explore the types of information that are helpful to know. Toward the top of any enterprise network's goals is that of high availability. Given that wireless has become ubiquitous in many enterprises in recent years, there has been a fundamental shift in the perception of wireless networks from "nice to have" to "must have." That being said, any network manager who cares about their job is thinking about network uptime. This requirement spans many areas of the network design, and includes vendor selection and implementation, RF availability, AP redundancy, WLAN controller redundancy/failover (if a controller-based architecture is implemented), access switch connectivity planning, and many other areas. To plan effectively for high availability, it is important to understand how all these puzzle pieces collectively meet the need for high availability.

To reinforce the point, let's elaborate just a bit on each of these steps. Some wireless vendor architectures are inherently more resilient to a single lost device than others. Large arrays, for example, may represent a single point of failure that impacts many end users. Similarly, a WLAN controller without redundancy also represents a single point of failure that may cause problematic AP reassociations and network downtime.

To accommodate RF redundancy, AP cell planning—by means of an effective site survey—should be carefully conducted. This includes physical AP spacing, transmit power settings, as well as channel selection criteria that ensure appropriate cell overlap—without causing excessive interference in normal operating conditions. While it is not always the most effective way to control RF settings, dynamic RF management features may be helpful here, as they can automate AP configuration changes to compensate for an AP that is nonfunctional. The goal is to ensure that infrastructure device outages have a limited impact on network functions for the end user.

Of course, no high availability plan is complete without first considering the network to which wireless devices are attached. First, Ethernet cables and switch ports fail. A first line of defense may be to configure one of two AP radios (in a dual-band setup) to fail over to mesh connectivity with another AP when the Ethernet link is nonfunctional. Next, suppose there's a modular switch in the network closet with six network switching modules installed. Each module contains 48 available Fast Ethernet PoE ports. Now, let's say there are 30 APs homed to this closet. Surely a single network module could accommodate all APs with ports to spare, but if that module happens to experience a failure, a major RF coverage problem results!

When designing for high availability, you must focus on the finer details beyond the typical AP-to-controller failover features that vendors offer. Let's go back to the network closet. How about we spread those 30 APs evenly across the 6 modules? Now, if a single module is lost, we've minimized the damage from that outage to only 5 APs instead of 30. But it doesn't stop there. Each switch receives power from somewhere. Does it have redundant power supplies? If so, great! Uptime is sustained even if a power supply fails. Are the redundant power supplies plugged into different power sources? If high availability is of utmost importance to your customer, suggest having those redundant power supplies plugged into separately fed power sources.

These types of subtleties are easy to overlook but are critical to designing for high availability. This is why it is important to gather as much information as possible about the technical requirements as well as the business requirements. When you know that high availability is important, all of these factors must be addressed. Successful network design depends on it.

Using a Customer's Existing Assets to Save Time and Money

When designing a WLAN, you want to leverage your customer's existing assets that can be incorporated into some component of the design solution. Following are types of existing customer assets you may come across and examples for how you can use them:

Using an Existing Certificate Authority   If an existing certificate authority is available, it will greatly influence the type of 802.1X/EAP that you recommend. If the customer has only 2.4 GHz–capable devices and tight budget constraints, this might influence whether dual-band APs will be recommended. If the customer is already trained and familiar with products from a particular vendor, it may influence the vendor selection.

Using Existing Databases   Centralized user databases are one example of key network components. These include Active Directory, LDAP databases, or other existing databases that are typically incorporated into enterprise WLAN design. 802.1X/EAP types that use usernames and passwords all need to leverage an existing, ideally central, user database. With Active Directory you can also make use of computer (a.k.a. machine) accounts. With these machine accounts, you can either enforce an additional restriction that users must authenticate from known corporate resources or use machine authentication to allow the machine onto the WLAN before a user has logged into it. This allows remote access, software updates, and the ability for the user to authenticate to Active Directory from a live connection and not use noncached credentials.

Using Existing Servers   Existing RADIUS servers would be another asset to take advantage of. If the RADIUS server is also used for virtual private network (VPN) authentication, it is possible to leverage the authorization policies for WLAN network access as well—that is, if your WLAN vendor has an embedded firewall offering.

Understanding the Deployment Environment

For an RF technology like 802.11, understanding the target deployment environment before a *statement of work* (SOW) for a design solution is presented is paramount. Following are some items to consider:

Type of Building or Facility   *Deployment environment* can refer to an office building, hospital, university campus, warehouse, outdoor environment, or something else. Each of these environments has their own unique RF characteristics.

Indoor Requirements   Indoor WLAN deployments can also possess widely variant RF characteristics. For instance, the material used in some wall construction may only minutely affect RF propagation, while other materials might stop it dead in its tracks. But wall material shouldn't be your only consideration. Items such as fully loaded bookshelves, metal filing cabinets, storage shelving, and other large pieces of furniture or building equipment can all greatly affect RF signal penetration through them.

Buildings such as warehouses introduce unique indoor RF challenges. Think for a moment if you would recommend doing an RF site survey in a warehouse when the shelves are full or when they are empty. If you said empty, you might have a few house calls to make once those shelves are covered with supplies and inventory. Filling shelves in a warehouse is likely to alter the RF propagation and signal levels may degrade, making your customer frustrated that their devices now only work in certain areas of the facility. Also pay attention to what a customer plans to do with a room, from the supplies they stock on their shelves to the furniture or equipment they house in a facility—these may hinder reception as well.

Ceiling Height   Another important item to consider is ceiling height of the space you're working with. Where do you typically place antennas in large building? The ceiling structure is the most likely place. Now, think for a minute about antenna patterns. If you need to provide coverage to devices that are 50′ below the antenna and you need to provide strong coverage on the horizontal plane, what type of antenna might provide the best coverage on the floor where users will be walking with the devices? If you said a vertically polarized high-gain omni, that would not be the best choice. On the other hand, if you were building a mesh backhaul solution, that antenna would be an excellent choice. At 50′ in the air, APs mounted just about the shelving with no walls between them will result in virtually all the APs seeing each other at high signal levels.

Outdoor Spaces   Outdoor areas offer their own set of challenges. In outdoor open spaces, signals can potentially travel quite far. Depending on antenna choice, signals can literally travel miles—assuming open and unobstructed space. Foliage, however, is a common RF obstruction that many inexperienced designers fail to properly consider. Trees grow. They lose leaves. They get rained and snowed on.

If you do an RF site survey in late fall when all the leaves are off the trees, you'll get vastly different results than you would doing the site survey in late spring. The key takeaway here is to plan for tree growth, moisture, and heavy leaf content.

Understanding the type of environment when you are scoping out the costs and time estimated to complete an RF survey is important. Pre-survey walk-throughs are often performed before finalizing an SOW or a final price is quoted. Remember, you can never underestimate these critical factors that affect RF and no automated RF planning software can predict these factors.

Perform walk-throughs in and study your deployment environments before proceeding with the survey process. Most of all, plan for contingencies.

Constraints

Inevitably, network design efforts will meet head on with various types of constraints at some point in the process. The following are some of the most typical constraints that arise during the design process.

Budget

Wouldn't it be nice if we could design optimized networks and never bat an eye at the cost? I'm sure salespeople would be happy in that world. In the real world, however, economies are unstable, corporations are often fiscally conservative, and everyone seeks a maximum return on their network infrastructure investment. In the highly competitive global economy, companies are scrutinizing their spending more than ever. The net effect of this is that you may end up with a design that meets some requirements but does not meet others, which may include keeping the cost below a certain threshold.

Inevitably, budget constraints are a large factor in most network deployments today. In fact, it is fairly common for the list of technical demands to exceed the financial means to supply. In this case, as network designer you must either meet as many technical requirements as possible—while staying within the budget—or reset the customer's expectations regarding the cost of their technical demands.

Another approach to dealing with budget issues is to apply the menu approach. Instead of coming up with a single design, craft multiple choices from which your customer can choose. This puts the onus of responsibility back on the company to pick their poison. The options may look like this:

- Expensive, but full featured—has all the bells and whistles but with the highest cost
- Balanced cost and features—meets most requirements, but may come with some compromises
- Economical, but feature poor—meets some requirements with low cost, but is lacking severely in one or more areas

With this approach, you can come up with a couple of initial design models and explain the pros and cons of each. This strategy allows the customer to evaluate their requirements and decide how much money they will spend on the project.

When you have enough experience, you will be able to identify business and technical conflicts related to budget very quickly. You can address this obstacle early on by including evaluative criteria in the information-gathering phase. For example, one method is to break down the customer's network expectations into subcategories, such as *absolute*, *important*, and *optional*. A similar technique is to ask the customer to rate their implementation goals on a sliding scale of importance (e.g., 1–10). This type of scalar weighting provides a better frame of reference for you to meet the needs of your customer, beginning with the most important demands first. You can then compare these criteria with previously gathered business objectives and address potential conflicts.

Timeline

Another constraint that frequently affects the network design stage is the timeline, or schedule. Many network deployments are placed within a tight timeline in order to meet a specific business-related deadline. When aggressive timelines are enforced, it is possible that a multiphase deployment approach will be necessary. This would allow for a scaled-back first phase that meets the initial business and technical requirements within the constraints of the timeline. Then a second phase would be conducted at some point in the future to accomplish any outstanding goals.

Of course, your customer may have demanding priorities that require expedience from you, but there is always a risk factor to consider. If the timeline is pushed too aggressively, the network design could suffer. Also, critical details may be missed in the design phase, and they will usually come back to bite you if they're not addressed at some point. When timelines are rushed, often the information-gathering phase is compromised. This usually results in missed requirements that compromise the solution.

There is a common saying in business that is fitting here: *Low Cost, High Quality, Quick Service: Pick two!* In other words, an overreaching emphasis on one or two of these aspects will often have an adverse impact in another area. If you want your work done quickly and with high quality, you better be prepared to pay. On the other hand, if you want it quick and cheap, you're likely to get an incomplete or nonfunctional product. This truth applies as much to network design as it does to any other business.

Politics

Network designers who are brought in from outside the company are often faced with delicate interpersonal politics at the customer's site. Just because the business is supposed to cooperatively integrate with information technology doesn't mean that it will be a cooperative process. It's an unfortunate fact that interoffice politics may make an impact on network designs, but they do. When possible, the best practice is to avoid taking sides. When in doubt, come back to the soft-skill strategy of understanding the roles of individuals at the company. Assess the political tensions, identify the hot topics and where individual alliances lie, and when all else fails, fall back on the decision makers and sources of authority.

Interestingly enough, network vendors can also play a role in heightening political tension. Larger vendors with political leverage often engage executive-level management at potential customers to participate in design processes—especially vendor selection. You may find yourself in a precarious situation if the IT staff is in conflict with other management because the business-level requirements are taking precedence over technical-level features or functions.

Guiding the Customer

Customers have business objectives to meet. They are most likely meeting with a wireless design professional for two reasons: to meet their goals and to get someone who understands wireless technology involved in the project.

Discussing the Future

It's also important to help the customer clarify any upcoming changes to their environment. Ask if their space will undergo construction, have new floor-to-ceiling shelving installed, or anything else that could affect reception. If a building will be installed between a point-to-point communication link, there is a strong possibility wireless communications will be disrupted.

As a designer of a WLAN, there is little you can do about how a customer will change their environment in the future. Your job, however, is to educate the customer at the beginning of the project about these possibilities.

Setting the Right Expectations

Wireless will arguably never have the same reliability capability as wired communication lines. This is especially true when you are dealing with unlicensed radio spectrum, as a customer's WLAN isn't the only user of that RF real estate.

Be honest with your customer, whether that is a co-worker or a customer who hired you or your company for a project. Remember, you didn't design the 802.11 standard or invent RF, so don't be afraid to educate them on design challenges related to the technology and their requirements and project goals. Most importantly, tell them what you are or will be doing in your design to address their specific needs.

This type of discussion sets the right expectation for the customer's technology investment. Be careful not to phrase limitations or concerns in a way that will scare them away from the project; you should, however, strive to educate your customer in the best way you can.

It's also important to give customers your initial feedback on feasibility, timeline, and cost expectations at the beginning of a project—at least at a high level. Don't wait until later; having this conversation early on may save you time and money while waiting to discuss these matters could potentially cost you both of these things.

Creating the Customer Requirements Document

After you've met with the customer, discussed the network objectives and requirements, and addressed any initial obstacles, the next step is a move toward communicating these findings via formal documentation. The benefits of documentation are numerous, and one of the most important is to ensure that the network goals are understood and agreed upon by both parties. In fact, there is a specific document just for this purpose.

The *customer requirements document* (CRD) is a summary of requirements that have been gathered through the discovery phase and interview process. The purpose of this document is to ensure that both parties are in agreement regarding the project requirements. As one of the final steps before the formal design work takes place, the CRD should be completed and signed by both parties. This document then serves as a reference in the event that confusion or conflict arises later in the design process. It can also be updated and changed as required, assuming both parties are in agreement with the change. The CRD is also an integral document in composing the SOW, which is discussed in the next section.

Statement of Work

The statement of work (SOW) is the formal agreement that is reached between the designer and customer. It should explicitly detail the deliverables, timelines, scope of the project, and pricing. A well-written SOW will clearly define which tasks the customer should complete and which tasks the designer should complete.

The SOW is what protects the consultant from what is commonly referred to as *scope creep*. Scope creep refers to the common tendency for customers to ask consultants and designers to complete new work that was not in the original scope of work. In this way, they continually creep up the scope to get additional services from the consultant for free. This isn't always intentional. In fact, it often is not intentional behavior on behalf of the customer.

Given that competition for work is tense, consultancies typically price their services competitively to win contracts. If they end up doing significantly more work than they originally anticipated and quoted for, their margins suffer. In some cases, a consultant simply makes less money than planned, but in extreme cases, they may even lose money on the project. Having a well-written SOW is the protection they need against this. When the customer requests work that is outside of the SOW, a *change order* (CO) can be drafted and the consultant can be paid accordingly for the work that is performed outside the original SOW.

The success of a project is tied directly to the SOW. It's viewed differently, however, depending on which side of the SOW the success is being measured from.

From the consultant/integrator side of things, success is measured by their ability to deliver the tasks outlined in the SOW while staying within reasonable timelines and budgets. If scope creep becomes too prevalent, their margins will suffer. If they suffer to the extent that the project is no longer profitable, the project as a whole is a failure to them, even if they have a happy customer.

Success from the customer point of view is measured by having a network design implemented successfully while staying within time and budget constraints. Just as scope creep can affect the vendor/integrator, it can affect the customer. Suppose the customer did not realize all that they *really* needed from their network project at the time that the SOW was written? What can happen is they will make requests to have these overlooked items added to the scope, which (as previously discussed) will come in the form of a CO and ultimately drives up the cost of the project. In extreme cases, some SOWs have grown to more than double their original cost estimates, which is viewed as a project failure in the eyes of the project sponsors.

Summary

In this chapter, you learned about the importance of gathering and analyzing customer requirements. By clearly defining the requirements of a network design, a consultant vastly improves his or her chances of satisfying the customer. If not for this process, consultants would be aiming at a target blindly, hoping that their assumptions line up with the customer's expectations. There are many times when questions are more valuable than answers, and the information-gathering phase of a network design is definitely one of those times.

You also learned the importance of meeting with the customer and identifying the key stakeholders. The ability to grasp who has decision-making ability early on will help you tremendously over the course of the project. In the event you are faced with constraints that may alter the course of the project, those same decision makers will be needed to keep the project on course.

Finally, once you've completed this information gathering, you're ready to create the customer requirements document (CRD) and the statement of work (SOW). These two documents contain the details of the requirements-gathering phase and should clearly define what is required and what work will be performed.

An engineer recently summed up this process quite nicely: "I can build you any network you like, but if I don't know what you need, there's a slim chance that you're going to like it."

Exam Essentials

Prepare and plan for your project.   Research your customer's business prior to the first meeting. Identify with their needs and be ready to discuss solutions to meet those needs.

Interview your customer.   Be able to identify key decision makers and determine the high-level scope of the project. Be able to gauge the customer's experience level and knowledge of their current network.

Gather requirements.   Identify the differences between business and technical requirements as well as be aware of how outside forces such as internal politics can change the design. The outcome of this phase should map directly to the CRD.

Evaluate the Customer's Assets and Deployment Environment.   Understand what existing assets can be utilized into the design.

Manage constraints.   Understand that budgets and timelines can and will impact designs. Prepare a methodology to deal with such events.

Evaluate and Understand the Politics and Success Criteria.   Understand who the key players are and learn their success metrics.

Meet technical design challenges.   Keep in mind that the most technical design is not always the most useful or manageable for a customer.

Review Questions

1. Which of the following describes the statement of work (SOW)?

    A. A legally binding document that states the dates and times that the engineer will perform work.

    B. A document the customer presents to prospective vendors/integrators explaining what work they wish to have completed.

    C. A legally binding document that the vendor/integrator presents to the customer for approval. The document should state the definition and scope of the work to be performed. This is driven by the CRD and onsite interviews.

    D. A document that is presented to the customer upon completion of a project. This document details the work that has been completed.

2. If a customer requests work that was not included in the SOW, which of these options are true? (Choose all that apply)

    A. The vendor/integrator can choose to implement the work out of scope and incur any associated costs.

    B. The vendor/integrator can issue the customer a change order detailing the costs required to perform the work, then wait to see if the customer chooses to pay.

    C. The vendor/integrator must fulfill all customer requests, and must complete the out-of-scope work and incur any associated costs.

    D. The customer can cancel the entire project.

3. When you are designing a customer network, which of the following should be your first step?

    A. Present the customer with a detailed technical design.

    B. Gather the customer requirements and assess the possible solutions that would meet their needs.

    C. Present the customer with a high-level design that can be fine-tuned once the requirements are discovered.

    D. Ask the customer what their technical design should look like.

4. When gathering requirements for a client device, which of the following questions would not be considered a technical requirement?

    A. The client device must be certified by the Wi-Fi Alliance.

    B. The client device must support both 802.11g as well as 802.11a.

    C. The client device must cost under $500.

    D. The client device must be easy to use.

5. The project sponsor will always be able to answer what type of question about the project?

   A. The type of security model to use

   B. Which business objectives must be met

   C. The hardware vendor that will be deployed

   D. The client adapters that should be used given the environment

   E. Regulatory or legal requirements

6. Which of the following items could be considered constraints when performing a network design? (Choose all that apply.)

   A. Budget

   B. Timeline

   C. Personnel

   D. Politics

7. The customer requirements document can be changed using what tool?

   A. Technical requirements document

   B. Site survey analysis

   C. Industry regulations

   D. Change order

8. Prior to meeting with the customer for the first time, you should do which of the following?

   A. Decide which vendor they will benefit most from.

   B. Research the customer as much as possible. Try to understand what their business is, who their customers are, and any other information you can find regarding product lines and recent press announcements.

   C. Find out what vendor their competitors use.

   D. Plan an initial design to present to them.

9. Which of the following is *not* a business requirement?

   A. The new network design must improve employee productivity.

   B. The new network design must cut operating expenses.

   C. The new network design must make employees happy to come to work.

   D. The new network design must provide support for 802.11n.

10. An enterprise customer is subject to the highest standards for network uptime. When designing their wireless network, you should consider which of the following? (Choose all that apply)

   A. The failover of the wireless network only

   B. The failover of the wired network only

   C. The failover of the wireless and wired network

   D. The physical aspects such as power and cabling

11. When surveying for an outdoor network, which of the following should you consider? (Choose all that apply)

    A. Whether or not the spanning tree protocol is active

    B. Whether or not the trees have leaves

    C. The typical atmospheric conditions as they relate to relative humidity, rainfall, snowfall, and average temperature

    D. The phase of the moon.

12. You have initiated a site survey to be performed and the team has been onsite and is halfway through gathering the necessary data. The project sponsor just asked you to make sure the WLAN supports radio frequency identification (RFID) location tracking. How would you possibly characterize this situation?

    A. Scope creep has occurred.

    B. Any WLAN will support location tracking.

    C. The 802.3af RTLS standard should be incorporated into the AP configuration.

    D. The 802.11g standard incorporates location tracking.

    E. The power requirements on the UPS need to be evaluated.

13. A customer wanted an outdoor bridge installation between two buildings. They specified frequencies that need to be avoided beforehand. Once the system was installed, they asked why they didn't have coverage for their laptop outside between the buildings. What went wrong?

    A. The antennas have too much gain, thus not allowing enough vertical coverage.

    B. There was a failure to gather all the customer requirements.

    C. The technical specifications of the equipment were not properly understood.

    D. The bridge link is not serving DHCP addresses to the laptop.

    E. The bridge laser alignment flux capacitor needs bananas.

14. What are examples of technical constraints? (Choose all that apply.)

    A. Cabling length restrictions

    B. Aesthetics

    C. Not enough UPS power

    D. Existing spectrum usage

    E. Supported client types

15. A company would like to deploy a 5 GHz 802.11n WLAN. Their location is between a large shipping port, military installation, and microwave oven testing facility. What type of requirement analysis should you be concerned about?

    A. Customer politics

    B. Leveraging existing assets

    C. Understanding your deployment environment

    D. Understanding business constraints

    E. Seasonal rainfall pattern analysis

Answers to Review Questions

1. C. The SOW is a document that is generated by the vendor/integrator that details the work to be done. The details of the document are generated through the various interview sessions, as well as the CRD.

2. A, B. The SOW is a legally binding contract between the two parties, so the customer cannot cancel it based on requesting work that is out of scope. The consultant can choose to do the work for free or issue a CO, but cannot be forced to complete work that was not agreed upon and signed off on in the SOW.

3. B. The very first step in a network design should *always* be gathering the customer requirements.

4. C. Cost is a business requirement, not a technical requirement.

5. B. The project sponsor is the champion for the project but cannot be expected to have technical knowledge. Most times the project sponsor is more focused on the business and relies on the engineers to provide the technical expertise. Regulatory or legal requirements would not always be known to a project sponsor. These requirements would need to be conveyed to the project team by a regulatory or legal domain expert.

6. A, B, C, D. All of the choices can be considered constraints that you may encounter when working with a customer on a design.

7. D. The CRD can be changed providing that both parties are in agreement about the change. Furthermore, changes in the CRD can result in changes to the SOW, which *may* require a change order.

8. B. You should always do as much research as possible prior to meeting the customer. Do not form opinions too early, especially before you've had a chance to gather their requirements.

9. D. Specific support for a given technology is a technical requirement rather than a business requirement.

10. C, D. When designing a network for high availability, be sure to take all factors into consideration. Even if you are only responsible for the wireless portion, if the wired network is not fully redundant, you run a high probability that your wireless network will not be either.

11. B, C. Things such as leaves on trees and atmospheric conditions have an effect on the propagation of wireless signals and should be considered when designing an outdoor network.

12. A. A project sponsor approaching you halfway through the site survey introducing a new requirement is an example of scope creep.

13. B. The customer wanted a PTP bridge link between buildings, and once the system is installed it's too late to have this link also serve as a Wi-Fi connection for a laptop. This indicates a failure to communicate early in the project.

14. A, C, D, E. Aesthetic requirements do not fall into the technical constraint category.

15. C. The company will need to be made aware of the deployment environment for their new WLAN. They are sitting in between a harsh RF environment.

Chapter

2

Designing for Client Devices and Applications

THE FOLLOWING CWDP EXAM TOPICS ARE COVERED IN THIS CHAPTER:

- ✓ Discover the client device types to be used and understand their impact on design requirements.

- ✓ Demonstrate a thorough understanding of design strategies and considerations specific to WLAN client devices.

- ✓ Illustrate best practices for roaming support in a WLAN.

- ✓ Understand the basics of 802.11 arbitration processes and wireless contention domains, and describe how these factors influence network design.

- ✓ Demonstrate a detailed understanding of RF behaviors and characteristics and relate these concepts to WLAN RF design.

- ✓ Discuss design concepts related to frequencies and bands used for WLAN communications.

- ✓ Understand the purpose of, and challenges related to, creating a balanced RF link between the AP and client devices.

- ✓ Demonstrate a detailed knowledge of the common problems related to high user densities and describe effective strategies to address them.

- ✓ Describe the role of Transmit Power Control (TPC) in WLANs and explain when and how it should be implemented.

- ✓ Describe how channel planning and output power configurations are determined by an RF site.

- ✓ Recommend appropriate authentication solutions and explain design concepts related to their use.

- ✓ Identify the role and limitations of client capabilities in security planning.

To design a network that will ultimately support the target client devices, there is a great amount of detail to consider *besides* what will be installed as the infrastructure. Client devices and applications (which are covered in the next chapter) are the most commonly overlooked and under-engineered component in WLAN designs. At the same time, the number of client devices typically exceeds the number of infrastructure devices by a significant amount.

After all, doesn't the WLAN exist to support the users and the client devices they use? Users can't see what infrastructure product is installed; all they see are the client devices they operate. Nowadays, these include not just laptops, but smart phones, handheld computers in line-of-business (LOB) applications, wireless printers, desktop computers, and more. Users also have no tolerance when they don't have a reliable connection; they simply want it to work.

Your challenge as a WLAN designer isn't just understanding the technical and design components for infrastructure WLAN products; you must also understand the client devices that will be running on this WLAN and even the protocols they use to communicate. It may seem like a lot to learn, and, well, it is. However, doing so will pay off in higher performance and network stability.

The primary goal of this chapter is to properly arm you to accomplish this task. As you'll see, understanding and profiling your client devices is one of the single most important components in driving the infrastructure design. Documenting and analyzing this information is often the difference between the success and failure of a WLAN project.

General Client Design Factors

Clients come in an ever-growing list of different form factors, such as laptops, Voice Over Wireless Fidelity (VoWiFi) phones, Real-Time Location System (RTLS) tags, dual-mode cell phones, and even more. Yet one thing is for certain: the number of wireless devices isn't decreasing. Industry analyst group ABI Research predicts that one billion Wi-Fi chipsets will ship in 2011 alone and by 2012, some 5 billion chipsets will exist cumulatively.

Even mobile network carriers who resisted and perceived Wi-Fi as a threat to their industry are now embracing it in order to offload data traffic from their increasingly congested data infrastructure. Televisions and home theater devices are now also coming with WLAN radios. A laptop without a WLAN radio? That's crazy talk.

The point is that Wi-Fi radios are now mainstream, making their way into about every type of mobile computing product made nowadays. But what flavor of Wi-Fi do all these devices support? 802.11g? 802.11a? 802.11n? It's also important to know what type of security modes are supported, what application protocols are used, whether the applications require multicast, and how many of these devices may be running at any given time.

Answers to these questions drive the primary design considerations of the WLAN. A WLAN infrastructure design that lacks support for one single critical component required by an important client device will result in a very unhappy customer. Furthermore, how a client device is used, carried, or even worn may change the RF propagation of the device and must be factored into the infrastructure design requirements. It's also important to note that each client device that will operate on the WLAN must be documented and investigated for its support of different capabilities.

PHY Support

Just like in home building, a foundation is largely considered the most important design consideration: it limits or allows for the extent of future expansion. WLAN device PHY (physical layer) support is no different.

Client devices that only support limited speeds can severely limit the number of devices and also the configuration options for the WLAN infrastructure. Devices that support only 2.4 GHz versus ones also allowing 5 GHz will affect the WLAN survey and AP model choices.

The modes of physical layer support of client devices can be broken down into two primary categories: frequency band and speed (modulation and coding). We will also discuss considerations for each of the major different PHY types.

Frequency Band

The most predominant band for Wi-Fi has been the 2.4 GHz Industrial Scientific and Medical (ISM) band. It seemed that for far too many years the only type of WLAN radio you could buy just supported 2.4 GHz. Before 802.11n was developed, support for 802.11a was almost nonexistent for several years. In fact, there was a time that many people were concerned whether 802.11a was going to make it at all. Still today, you will be hard-pressed to find a WLAN device that only supports 5 GHz Unlicensed National Information Infrastructure (UNII) operation. They exist—it's just that they tend to be rare because there is little market for them. Conversely, support for 2.4 GHz operation with 802.11b or 802.11g is almost a given if the device has a WLAN radio at all.

Wi-Fi isn't the only device that uses the 2.4 GHz band. It has gotten an unwarranted bad reputation in some cases where many people consider it undesired real estate to build a WLAN on. Devices using Bluetooth also operate in this band, which has gained in popularity over the years. The other usual culprits for producing 2.4 GHz interference are microwave ovens, wireless video cameras, and cordless phones.

Microwave ovens aside, it is important to note that over the years manufacturers of these devices have become better at making some of these products that utilize the wireless spectrum more efficiently. Speaking of wireless phones in particular, it is largely the older devices that tend to cause the most interference to Wi-Fi devices. Often, simply replacing old devices with newer models can help a great deal.

 More details on interference and methods of interference mitigation are covered in Chapter 9, "Site Survey RF Design."

Outside of 2.4 GHz we have the 5 GHz spectrum. A 4.9 GHz band is also available for licensed public safety or municipal use, which will be discussed in Chapter 4, "Industry-Specific Design Considerations." In September 2008, the IEEE 802.11y-2008 specification was published; it allows for a lightly licensed high-power band (up to 20W Effective Isotropic Radiated Power [EIRP]) operating from 3.65 to 3.7 GHz in the United States. However, for the vast majority of WLAN designers we only have the 2.4 GHz and 5 GHz bands to work with. Table 2.1 shows a frequency map of the 5 GHz band and how Wi-Fi incorporates this band for a variety of regulatory bodies.

TABLE 2.1 5 GHz Frequency Map

Frequency Band	Channel ID	FCC (GHz)	ETSI (GHz)	MKK (GHz)	SG (GHz)	ASIA (GHz)	TW (GHz)
Lower Band (36 = default)	34	—	—	5.170₁	—	—	—
	36	5.180	5.180	—	5.180	—	—
	38	—	—	5.190	—	—	—
	40	5.200	5.200	—	5.200	—	—
	42	—	—	5.210	—	—	—
	44	5.220	5.220	—	5.220	—	—
	46	—	—	5.230	—	—	—
	48	5.240	5.240	—	5.240	—	—
Middle Band (52 = default)	52	5.260	5.260	—	—	—	5.260
	56	5.280	5.280	—	—	—	5.280
	58	5.300	5.300	—	—	—	5.300
	60	5.320	5.320	—	—	—	5.320

Frequency Band	Channel ID	FCC (GHz)	ETSI (GHz)	MKK (GHz)	SG (GHz)	ASIA (GHz)	TW (GHz)
H Band	100	—	5.500	—	—	—	—
	104	—	5.520	—	—	—	—
	108	—	5.540	—	—	—	—
	112	—	5.560	—	—	—	—
	116	—	5.580	—	—	—	—
	120	—	5.600	—	—	—	—
	124	—	5.620	—	—	—	—
	128	—	5.640	—	—	—	—
	132	—	5.660	—	—	—	—
	136	—	5.680	—	—	—	—
	140	—	5.700	—	—	—	—
Upper Band (149 = default)	149	5.745	—	—	5.745	5.745	5.745
	153	5.675	—	—	5.675	5.675	5.675
	157	5.785	—	—	5.785	5.785	5.785
	161	5.805	—	—	5.805	5.805	5.805
ISM Band	165	5.825	—	—	5.825	—	5.825

Note: Channel 34 is the default channel for Japan.

Source: http://ftp.hp.com/pub/networking/software/59906056.pdf

The 5 GHz band has some caveats. The UNII bands are divided up into UNII-1 (indoor), UNII-2 (indoor/outdoor), UNII-2 Extended (indoor/outdoor), and UNII-3 and 5 GHz ISM (outdoor bridge/indoor). Each UNII band has its own maximum power output, with the most limiting being UNII-1. For example, in the United States APs set to UNII-1 channels have a maximum power output of 50 milliwatts (mW).

In October 2004 a new Federal Communications Commission (FCC) ruling loosened up some of the requirements for the 5 GHz UNII bands, which included removing the restriction of requiring an integrated (permanently attached) antenna for use at UNII-1.

The ruling allows for external antennas as long as the regulatory restrictions of transmitter power are followed. One of the other significant components to this ruling was clarifying the allocation of additional spectrum to the 5 GHz UNII band referred to as the UNII-2 Extended (UNII-2e) band.

Furthermore, because of IEEE 802.11h, you also need to be aware of radar avoidance mechanisms in your designs that utilize 5 GHz. The UNII-2 and UNII-2 Extended bands are designated as *Dynamic Frequency Selection (DFS)* bands. DFS bands need to monitor for existence of radar and perform a disruptive procedure to monitor and look for another available channel when radar is detected. It is a disruptive and time-consuming process.

Radar has been reported to be detected near large naval shipping channels, airports, and territories outside the United States.

  To learn more about regulatory issues that make up DFS, refer to FCC Part 15.407(h)(2).

Different regulatory domains require different adherence to power emissions and allowed channels. Transmissions not only occur from infrastructure devices, but client devices as well. Client devices operating within different regulatory domains need some mechanism to understand where it is operating. For example, a user who is traveling from one regulatory domain to another and brings his mobile computing device needs to have an automated way of becoming aware of this. Therefore, the IEEE developed 802.11d, which advertises the regulatory domain in beacons and probe responses in order for client devices to conform accordingly.

Deciding what frequency bands to support is largely based on client device support. Let's explore the factors that influence your choices.

The challenge for WLAN designers is when client devices support different and potentially incompatible PHYs. Take the 802.11b PHY, for example. As a review, 802.11b operates at 2.4 GHz and only supports four data rates, also known as *PHY rates*—1, 2, 5.5, and 11 Mbps. The modulation used for these rates are Differential Binary Phase Shift Keying (DBPSK), Differential Quadrature Phase Shift Keying (DQPSK), and Complementary Code Keying (CCK) (5.5 and 11 Mbps), respectively. The 802.11g PHY operates using Orthogonal Frequency Division Multiplexing (OFDM) modulation and PHY rates of 6, 9, 12, 18, 24, 36, 48, and 54 Mbps. The 802.11g specification requires backward compatibility support for 802.11b. However, 802.11b has no support for the 802.11g PHY.

If your APs are set to 802.11g-only modes or if a single OFDM rate is set to basic or "mandatory," it will eliminate every 802.11b device from ever associating to the AP. Basic rates are data rates that *all* client devices must support in order to join the Basic Service Set (BSS).

We recommend that you design a WLAN for both 2.4 GHz and 5 GHz. This provides spectrum redundancy and resiliency in the face of interference. Operating on two spectrums using clients balanced between the two provides up to double the network capacity per AP.

When considering 802.11n APs using both spectrums, if the radio was fully utilized on both frequencies, a 100 Full Ethernet connection would be the limiting factor for bandwidth.

Speed: Modulation and Coding

Modulation is the process of modifying a carrier signal and in 802.11 transmissions, it is used to represent a data stream. There are many techniques for modulating an RF carrier to represent a single bit of data. An individual manipulation of the RF carrier is represented as a *symbol*. Each symbol can represent one or more digital bits of data. Modulation also defines the symbol rate of an RF transmission.

RF designers have also built in a method to avoid interference and transmission anomalies: chip codes. *Chipping* is a way to use several symbols to represent a single bit of data that a device is trying to send to another. For example, let's assume you want to send a binary 1 to a receiver. To represent that single binary bit of data, you could use an 11 chip Barker Code as used in the 802.11 Clause 15 PHY.

A Barker Code of 10110111000 is exclusive OR'd (a Boolean mathematical operation) with the data stream to represent a single bit of data. A Barker Code has certain mathematical properties that make it ideal to modulate radio waves. If some of the symbols were not received correctly, the receiver can recover the original transmission based on this Barker Code.

The transmitter, a 2.4 GHz radio in this case, would use a modulation technique such as Binary Phase Shift Keying (BPSK) or Quadrature Phase Shift Keying (QPSK) for 1 and 2 Mbps, respectively. For example, to transmit a 1 Mbps frame, the radio sends a 2.4 GHz carrier wave with the Barker Code–encoded data stream using BPSK modulation. Each bit of the encoded data stream would be represented by a single-phase shift for each bit. If a 2 Mbps frame was transmitted, QPSK modulation would be used, but this time using four possible phase shifts to represent 2 bits for each symbol. Therefore, the encoded bit stream arrives twice as fast. Examples of BPSK (1 Mbps PHY) and QPSK (2 Mbps PHY) coding are defined in Figure 2.1 and Figure 2.2, respectively.

FIGURE 2.1   BPSK constellation

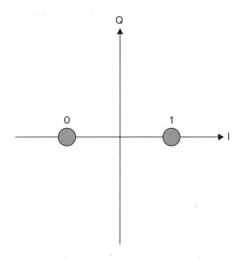

FIGURE 2.2 QPSK constellation

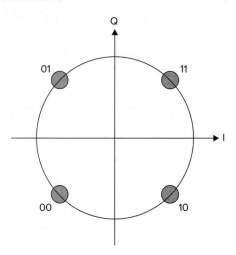

We provide these detailed examples to explain the primary components that affect RF data transmissions. So, when we talk about different PHY rates and modulation and coding scheme (MCS) rates that are used with the 802.11n PHY, modulation and coding are two primary components that change the data rate of these transmissions.

For example, Table 2.2 details the 802.11a PHY rates along with their modulation and coding rates.

TABLE 2.2 802.11a Modulation and Coding Rates

Data Rate (Mbps)	Modulation	Coding Rate (R)	Coded Bits per Subcarrier (N_{BPSC})	Coded Bits per OFDM Symbol (N_{CBPS})	Data Bits per OFDM Symbol (N_{DBPS})
6	BPSK	1/2	1	48	24
9	BPSK	3/4	1	48	36
12	QPSK	1/2	2	96	48
18	QPSK	3/4	2	96	72
24	16 QAM	1/2	4	192	96
36	16 QAM	3/4	4	192	144

Data Rate (Mbps)	Modulation	Coding Rate (R)	Coded Bits per Subcarrier (N_{BPSC})	Coded Bits per OFDM Symbol (N_{CBPS})	Data Bits per OFDM Symbol (N_{DBPS})
48	64 QAM	2/3	6	288	192
54	64 QAM	3/4	6	288	216

Source: http://cp.literature.agilent.com/litweb/pdf/ads2008/dgwlan/ads2008/80211a_Transmitter_
System_Test_Using_Instrument_Links.html

 Modulation is covered in more detail in Chapter 6, "RF Communication Principles."

The point of illustrating the differences in modulation and coding that are used for different PHY and MCS rates is to highlight the complexities involved. Different devices have different capabilities in communicating with different modulations and coding methods.

Considerations for Various PHYs

The IEEE 802.11 standard includes sections for each specified PHY and keeps amending the standards as new PHYs are developed. These are included in the standard document's sections called *clauses*. As any standard develops, new clauses are added while others are amended to support new capabilities.

 For more information on the latest 802.11 standards, please visit http://ieee802.org/11/.

In this section, we will briefly explore the clauses that pertain to each 802.11 PHY you will commonly encounter in real-world environments.

Clause 15 (Original 802.11) – DSSS PHY Specification for the 2.4 GHz ISM Band

Clause 15 covers the PHY specification we largely refer to as the *original* 802.11 specification operating at 1 and 2 Mbps. For many of you reading this, 802.11 and even 802.11b (Clause 18) are old news. However, the data rates specified with Clause 15 are also grandfathered into the 802.11b specification. In other words, the Clause 15 and even Clause 18 PHY rates will be around for a long time.

Picking up nearly any infrastructure WLAN hardware device, you will see that not only are 1 and 2 Mbps supported but they are specified as *basic rates*. Briefly, basic rates are rates that must be mandatorily supported for a client device to join the BSS. A nasty side effect of making 1 Mbps a basic rate is that the 802.11 standard specifies that certain 802.11 frames (e.g., management, broadcast, and multicast frames) will be transmitted at the lowest basic rate.

So what's the problem with that? Suppose you're trying to access the Internet from Aunt Sally's house while you're on vacation and she still has a dial-up account. After you sigh . . . loudly . . . you use her connection to download a 500 kB email attachment. From a time perspective, that same 500 kB email attachment was hardly noticed over your home or office high-speed connection. In the end, you still got the attachment. It just took a lot more time to transfer it. The same goes for the 1 Mbps data rates versus higher data rates. While this may be obvious, we need to build on this scenario.

Now, let's suppose you're now wirelessly transferring a 500 kB 802.11 frame using the 1 Mbps data rate versus 54 Mbps. Sure, it took a lot less time with 54 Mbps, but *time* has another consequence. The longer the transmission takes, the higher the likelihood that the frame will be interfered with—and the longer other devices that want to transmit need to wait to use the channel.

The more mature or rural readers of this book will remember the days of dial-up when you shared a phone line between your computer and primary telephone number and maybe even had call waiting. What happened when you got 95 percent through that file transfer and the phone rang? Your transfer got interrupted and after you picked up whatever it was you threw across the room, you started all over again.

The interrupting phone call on the dial-up connection is just like when an 802.11 frame receives interference. For example, if a 1 Mbps frame is being transmitted and another 2.4 GHz transmission is transmitted at the same time, there is a strong likelihood that the second transmission will corrupt the original and also the second transmission.

Furthermore, let's use a similar scenario, but this time with two differences: we're sharing a wireless medium with other users and different data rates are available for use (making other assumptions, of course). Next, we have a device transferring a large file at 1 Mbps PHY rate and another needing to transmit notices that someone is already using the *wireless medium (WM)*. The second device capable of using high PHY rates defers until the WM is available. The second device has to contend for the same airtime while the other device hogs it up because it is using such a slow transfer speed.

The WM is capable of higher efficiency, but because the slower rates are supported and being used by even one device, it basically takes the available airtime away for others. In other words, it is like a bad neighbor.

It is worth drawing out this analogy because it is critically important to understanding the effects of data rates with respect to interference and the number of devices that can use the WM. A good understanding about PHY rates will pay off in all your wireless designs and troubleshooting exercises.

Chances are that you'll likely never encounter pure 802.11 devices anymore. If you do encounter them, they are usually relegated boxes in storage rooms (or this author's garage). You might even find that 802.11b is still rare. Some enterprise networks have eliminated all their 802.11b devices.

The problem is that these data rates are still the default on enterprise WLAN infrastructure devices, and that's just how client device vendors test their products. Client device vendors that design for the enterprise space likely also test their gear by disabling these rates because this is a common practice for multi-AP environments. However, other client vendors do not.

To disable these rates, you must test your client devices to ensure that they still operate properly. If you find that a client device has problems when they are disabled and you still have high signal quality, likely a client driver or firmware update will resolve the issue.

Clause 18 (802.11b) – High Rate Direct Sequence Spread Spectrum (HR/DSSS) PHY Specification

HR/DSSS can be thought of as 802.11b, which is intentionally presented out of numerical order before Clause 17 (below) because it builds onto the 802.11 specification, adding 5.5 and 11 Mbps PHY rates. It uses the same 2.4 GHz ISM band as Clause 15 does.

The details of the modulation and coding are covered elsewhere in this text, so we will not review them here. From a design perspective, the same principles apply from Clause 15 802.11 PHY.

You would be hard-pressed to find a *new* 802.11b device to purchase anymore. Most of the design constraints you are likely to encounter with 802.11b are legacy devices. However, where you will find 802.11b devices still being sold today are in industry verticals such as healthcare, retail, warehousing, and certain outdoor client devices. This will not continue for long because chipset and part suppliers that manufacturers use aren't even making them anymore.

To be blunt, if someone is still making 802.11b-only capable devices nowadays, they just simply don't care or they are dealing with some strange constraint. Using an 802.11g device would provide the same or better performance but at least with the ability to use higher PHY rates.

The best recommendation we can give you as a designer or implementer of 802.11 WLANs is to push, fight, kick, or whatever else you can do to eliminate all 802.11b devices only capable of Clause 18 compliance. They will be a continuous anchor around your neck weighing down the performance of all other users and further limiting the number of devices supported per AP.

When nearly all the VoWiFi vendors supported 802.11b, designers and troubleshooters felt a lot of pain. We determined that (fairly consistent across manufacturers) only about seven simultaneous phone calls could happen per AP. VoWiFi vendors have now been supporting 802.11g for a few years, and some have even adopted 802.11a as well. Some vendors have even announced support for 802.11n. Table 2.3 shows the 2.4 GHz ISM band for a variety of regulatory domains.

TABLE 2.3 2.4 GHz ISM Frequency Plan

Channel	Frequency (MHz)	Regulatory Domain			
		FCC	ETSI	Japan	China
1	2412	X	X	X	X
2	2417	X	X	X	X
3	2422	X	X	X	X

TABLE 2.3   2.4 GHz ISM Frequency Plan *(continued)*

Channel	Frequency (MHz)	Regulatory Domain			
		FCC	ETSI	Japan	China
4	2427	X	X	X	X
5	2432	X	X	X	X
6	2437	X	X	X	X
7	2442	X	X	X	X
8	2447	X	X	X	X
9	2452	X	X	X	X
10	2457	X	X	X	X
11	2462	X	X	X	X
12	2467	—	X	X	X
13	2472	—	X	X	X
14	2484	—	—	X	—

Source: IEEE 802 11b-1999 standard

Clause 17 (802.11a) – Orthogonal Frequency Division Multiplexing (OFDM) PHY Specification for the 5 GHz UNII Bands

OFDM is the modulation scheme that nearly all modern-day wireless communications are built on. This includes 802.11a/g/n, proprietary point-to-point (PTP) links, and even 3G and 4G cellular systems. The OFDM PHY is very different from the DSSS PHY used with Clause 15 (802.11 DSSS) and 18 (802.11b). 802.11a was the first 802.11 PHY that made use of OFDM. 802.11a operates exclusively at the 5 GHz UNII bands.

OFDM is made up of many narrowband tones carrying data in an orthogonal fashion. DSSS uses a spread spectrum modulation technique that is less resilient to interference. Figure 2.3 illustrates the frequency mask of the two schemes.

FIGURE 2.3 DSSS and OFDM spectral mask

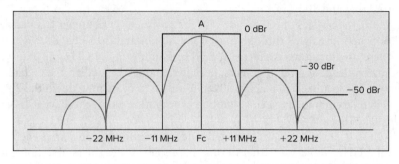

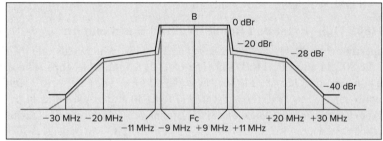

802.11a has the primary benefit of not requiring backward compatibility. Until 802.11n, 802.11a was the only IEEE 802.11 PHY operating at 5 GHz. The other main benefit is the number of channels available at 5 GHz.

The design challenge with 5 GHz involves transmit power limitations at different parts of the UNII band. For example, UNII-1 requires a maximum transmit power of no more than 50 mW, UNII-2 no more than 250 mW, and UNII-3 can go up to 1 W.

If you are deploying a WLAN, you can't count on power greater than 50 mW unless you want to eliminate the UNII-1 band from your channel plan. In other words, you've just found your upper limit in transmit power on which you should base your entire design and RF survey.

To make matters worse, some manufacturers allow you to set a transmit power up to 100 mW for 802.11a but fail to provide a way to inform the user of something important: when an AP with a 6 decibel isotropic (dBi) built-in antenna is set to UNII-1, the AP power will change to 12.5 mW without telling you in any visible way. You may have to dig quite deep to discover what the channel is configured for. Fortunately, you bought this book and now you can avoid encountering this mistake.

The other main challenge with Clause 17 is that it has been largely an option or upgrade for 802.11 clients. If you purchase a client device capable of 802.11a, chances are that it also supports 802.11b or 802.11g (Clause 15 and 18, respectively). In comparison, you are far more likely to find that devices support 802.11b or 802.11g but may not always support 802.11a. This therefore usually means that you wouldn't design just an 802.11a network.

So, in order to gain an 802.11a network you have to do a survey and AP placement design for both 802.11b/g and 802.11a.

Furthermore, the physics of RF dictate that the propagation of higher frequencies do not travel or penetrate as well through most obstructions and the signal decays faster over distance. Therefore, the range is shorter at 5 GHz than it is at 2.4 GHz.

Depending on the design requirements, designer, and/or the facility, the differences in propagation has lent itself to placing 802.11a-only APs or turning down the 2.4 GHz radios enough to accommodate a close enough propagation pattern to have a 1:1 ratio of dual-mode 802.11b/g and 802.11a APs.

With 802.11n (Clause 20) now entering the design picture, the primary benefit for 802.11n is at 5 GHz. Table 2.2 earlier in this chapter illustrates the modulation and coding schemes for OFDM, which is used by 802.11a.

Clause 19 (802.11g) – Extended Rate PHY (ERP) Specification

Clause 19 specifies the 802.11g PHY operating at 2.4 GHz, which adds OFDM rates in addition to the 802.11 and 802.11b DSSS rates of 1, 2, 5.5, and 11 Mbps. The additional OFDM rates include 6, 9, 12, 18, 24, 36, 48, and 54 Mbps. The Clause 19 specification is most commonly referred to as Extended Rate PHY (ERP) and implies 802.11g.

The biggest challenge with Clause 19 (802.11g) has been backward compatibility for DSSS-only capable devices (802.11 and 802.11b). Simply put, legacy devices simply can't understand it. To DSSS-only devices, Clause 19 is nothing more than gibberish.

For example, if a DSSS-only device wanted to transmit on the WM and an OFDM transmission was in progress, the DSSS device might not be able to detect that an OFDM transmission was in progress. Therefore, the DSSS-only device might simply transmit right over it, causing a wireless collision.

To prevent this, Clause 19 specified certain protection mechanisms for these DSSS-only devices. What these protection mechanisms do is essentially transmit a DSSS transmission that the WM will be in use for a specific time period. Since every 802.11 device must honor these types of medium reservation protocols, the DSSS devices do not transmit during the reservation period specified by the protection mechanisms. Production mechanisms include RTS/CTS and CTS-to-self.

For additional details on how virtual carrier sense, or network allocation vector (NAV), and clear channel assessment (CCA) work, please refer to Chapter 10, "MAC Layer Design."

Problem solved, right? Well, the issue is that the overhead involved with these protection mechanisms can nearly eliminate all benefits of using OFDM transmissions in many circumstances.

Nowadays, most organizations have eliminated most of the 802.11b devices from their environment and these protection mechanisms are not as relevant. However, many devices may still use protection mechanisms even when no 802.11b device is present, which causes unwarranted overhead.

We do not recommend that you bypass Clause 19 (802.11g), but it is important to understand that when a mixture of Clause 18 and 19 devices are present in the same infrastructure, protection mechanisms are required by the standard. The main point is to be mindful of your device population and the configuration of your infrastructure devices.

Clause 20 (802.11n) – High Throughput (HT) PHY Specification

Clause 20 marks the long-awaited arrival of 802.11n. In September 2009 the IEEE Task Group N (TGn) approved a final draft of the specification. The benefits of 802.11n have been advertised heavily and likely every reader of this book knows that the speeds have greatly improved.

For many of us using 802.11n at home, going really, really fast until your PC's traffic arrives at your 5 Mbps broadband connection has some limited appeal. Yes, doing file transfers between PCs and other similar activities will allow you to realize the benefits, but there is another major feature that isn't marketed nearly as well as it should be: *multiple-input, multiple-output (MIMO)*.

Likely you have already heard of some of the features of MIMO, but the significance of the technology is rarely explained well enough to hit home. In *single-input, single-output (SISO)* networks (which is every other type of network other than 802.11n at this point), the RF technology involved in these radios is fairly simple. In fact, when comparing the technology to 802.11n, it already seems archaic. Outside of the speed, the other biggest benefit of 802.11n that is made possible by MIMO is RF link *stability*.

In SISO technology, when multiple signal paths of the same signal arrive at the radio receiver, signal distortion happens. This phenomenon, known as *multipath*, is nearly impossible to avoid. In certain environments—such as warehouses, outdoor container yards/shipping ports, and multifloor, high-density indoor facilities—a great deal of multipath typically occurs. Since the beginning of 802.11, we have worked very hard in our designs to mitigate multipath as much as possible. Multipath causes the signal fading and frame corruption when too much multipath interference exists. Although the use of diversity antennas has helped to mitigate some of the effects of multipath, problems still crop up and will continue to be a performance barrier for SISO technology.

MIMO, on the other hand, employs advanced signal processing techniques to use to its advantage multiple signals arriving at different phases and minor timing differences. MIMO utilizes a signal rake processing technique that can take multiple waveforms and perform an additive signal processing technique to mathematically increase the received signal strength. This technique is called maximal ratio combining (MRC).

The different phases arriving at different phases and time of arrival can be referred to as different space-time streams. An 802.11n transmitter can create different space-time streams intentionally if the 802.11n transmitter has multiple radios. The methodology in transmitting multiple spatial streams is a bit more complex than simply creating a multipath stream, but the basic premise still applies.

We will spend a great deal more time discussing 802.11n, including the benefits and features it employs, in Chapter 7, "RF Hardware and 802.11n." We will leave the additional details for the later chapters.

As for clients, or even an AP for that matter, you need to pay close attention to the type of 802.11n radio that the device supports. You will commonly see nomenclature stating two numeric values, such as 2x2, 2x3, or 3x3. This value refers to the number of radios and antennas that are used in the 802.11 MIMO array. The first number is the number of radios; the second is the number of discrete antenna elements. Therefore, an 802.11n client like the Intel 5300 and 6300 WiFi Link is a 3x3 design, which employs three radios and three antennas.

What is critically significant about the meaning of this value is understanding the capabilities of the client. It reflects the capability of both speed and receive performance. For example, a 1x2 802.11n client has only a single radio but two antenna elements. The number of radios dictates *transmit performance* that affects uplink speed. For example, a single radio 802.11n design can transmit up to 150 Mbps. Each additional radio adds a theoretical 150 Mbps increase in speed. Therefore, a three-radio 802.11n client such as the Intel 5300 mentioned earlier can transmit up to 450 Mbps (150×3 spatial streams).

The number of antenna elements dictates the maximum possible speeds the client is capable of in the *downlink* direction. For example, the 1x2 radio mentioned earlier is capable of 300 Mbps (150×2 spatial streams) in the downlink or receive direction. Using the Intel 5300 again as an example, it can receive up to 450 Mbps in the downlink direction.

More antenna elements allow for more receive spatial streams, and if the antenna elements are separated appropriately, they can greatly increase the stability of received signal quality to nearly eliminate the negative effects of multipath distortion. The result is a much more stable RF link and therefore a more positive end user experience.

In other words, all 802.11n isn't created equally and as a designer you must understand this concept well.

Remember that when looking at 802.11n clients, both the 2.4 GHz ISM band and the 5 GHz UNII bands are available for use. This means that you will find some clients that only support one band whereas others support both. Pay particular attention to these details.

We are not including Clause 14 FHSS specification details because it is not used in modern wireless designs. Refer to the CWNA curriculum for details about IEEE 802.11 FHSS. We suggest you check out *CWNA: Certified Wireless Network Administrator Official Study Guide: Exam PW0-104*, by David D. Coleman and David A. Westcott (Sybex, 2009).

Radio Characteristics

WLAN radios are similar, in some ways, to human beings. Some people can hear better than others. Some people can even talk louder than others. Some people talk faster and slower. In this section we will explore the important characteristics of WLAN radios and how they affect your overall WLAN design.

It is important to understand that WLAN radios are not individually calibrated devices. It usually only makes sense, economically, to individually calibrate expensive and specialized RF equipment. High-priced RF equipment like handheld spectrum and vector network analyzers that are used for a variety of RF applications is calibrated to specifications as closely as possible. Typically this is +/– 0.20 to 0.25 dB of accuracy for measuring absolute power over the entire range of the spectrum analyzer. A handheld spectrum analyzer from companies such as Agilent, Anritsu, or Tektronix are usually shipped to the customer only after undergoing a manual calibration procedure by a trained technician. Typically, the device ships with a printed certification document indicating the results.

WLAN radios, on the other hand, are usually manufactured up to approximately +/– 3 dB or higher of variance. You will typically find far less variance than that in highly automated circuit board designs, but it is important to understand that not all devices will perform equally. If you remember that a difference of 3 dB is half (–3 dB) or double the power (+3 dB), this is a significant difference. This kind of variance can be found from a device from the same manufacturer of even the same model. That doesn't mean that a device from a different manufacturer falls within the same tolerances.

You should also note that WLAN device manufacturers take a WLAN radio *chipset* from a manufacturer and then develop an antenna design into their manufactured end product, which can even further change the RF characteristics.

Laptops are an excellent example of this case: several laptop vendors or even models from the same manufacturer use the same WLAN chipset, but because of their antenna design, antenna cabling, placement, and orientation, effectively the performance of some laptops is better than others. Intel WiFi Link and Atheros are common WLAN radios you will encounter in original equipment manufacturer (OEM) laptops from manufacturers such as Lenovo, HP, and Toshiba. The antennas for the WLAN radio, however, can be placed just about anywhere in the laptop designs. The placement of the antennas and the polarity are equally important.

For example, one laptop manufacturer might place the antenna in the base of the laptop and another might place it in the lid with the monitor. The types of antennas used by one manufacturer could be quite different from another. Even the placement and orientation of the antenna elements in the lid can change the performance. If the antenna element is placed near certain other electronics, it can change some of the characteristics of the antenna performance. Suffice it to say that a great deal of testing and thought is put into antenna choices, where they are placed, the types of antenna cable, and other related factors that ultimately result in the final performance.

The important takeaway in this section is to understand that all devices are unique in their own ways.

Chipsets are manufactured by Atheros, Broadcom, Intel, Marvell, Ralink, and Texas Instruments, among others. These chipsets are responsible for the radio and MAC functions. From a radio perspective, the chipset itself singularly sets the stage for the 802.11 PHY capabilities of the device.

Understanding Client RF Performance

To understand the RF performance of a client device, you must explore several key factors. We will identify and discuss the primary areas that specifically affect RF performance.

Transmit Power

How often have you been told a client device is capable of, say, 100 mW? They lied. Well, maybe whoever said this believed this information themselves, but let's just say they stretched the truth unintentionally. Let's cover a little more background information to explain why.

When a radio is about to transmit data, a background process is involved that determines the data rate of the RF transmission, otherwise known as the PHY rate. This process is performed for *each* 802.11 frame. For example, let's say you are using an 802.11g client and you have a signal level of –75 dBm of received signal strength indicator (RSSI). Furthermore, this particular client adapter determines that a PHY rate of 36 Mbps (16 quadrature amplitude modulation [QAM] at 3/4 coding rate) will be used. Don't worry about the details for now, as we're just trying to explore the larger concepts here.

This same client adapter needs to modulate and code the 802.11 frame using a great deal of fidelity. The occurrence is much like when you are watching a blockbuster action movie and a big scene occurs where an incredible diversity of sound needs to be reproduced, sent to the home stereo amplifier and eventually to the speakers. If you watch that same scene at a lower volume, the sounds will be much clearer than they would be at a loud volume.

At loud volumes when an amplifier has too much to do, *distortion* often occurs. At the same volume when there isn't much sound being reproduced, you may not hear any distortion. The issue is when a burst of high-fidelity information is sent to the amplifier where it has to reproduce the sound at loud volumes. That is when the amplifier gets saturated and distortion occurs.

In data communications, distortion is disastrous. Usually, it is so bad that the transmission isn't perceptible at the receiver. To get around this, manufacturers essentially back off on the "volume" before that high-fidelity frame is transmitted.

How big of a problem is this? Usually not much. Part of the reason is that when you are transmitting high PHY rates, you typically have high signal levels, which means the client should be close enough to the receiver for a transmission to still be heard. This does present a problem, however, when the client is located at the edge of where a particular data (PHY) rate can be heard (rate boundary) and the client cannot reproduce the sound loud enough at the required fidelity for the signal to be received by the AP.

So, the problem usually is only visible if you are running an AP at full power and the clients cannot reproduce high PHY rates at the same transmit power levels as the lower PHY rates. As you will read later in this section, the range can easily be 15 mW up to 100 mW in transmit power depending on the transmitted PHY rate.

RF amplifiers have other nasty problems when they are driven too hard. They can cause effects known as spectral regrowth, as shown in Figure 2.4.

FIGURE 2.4   Spectral regrowth

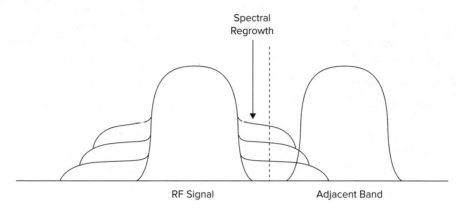

Spectral regrowth is a distortion condition that is caused by intermodulation distortion, which typically occurs when an amplifier's gain is set too high. Better amplifiers have fewer of these side effects. However, better amps also cost more—sometimes a great deal more than the market will bear.

Many consumer and business hardware purchase decisions are driven by cost. While you generally get what you pay for, if you don't understand the benefits of one system over another then you are not likely to pay more.

Imagine a customer who is about to make a large, strategic investment in 802.11n. It is easy for executive management to tout that they are offering 802.11n to employees and key stakeholders, but out of ignorance they didn't spend the extra $15 per client radio upgrade in their laptops and ended up with a 2x2 802.11n chipset versus a 3x3 one. The 3x3 chipset would result in better radio performance in both throughput and stability.

Receive Sensitivity

Earlier we said that radios are similar to humans in how well they receive and give information. Like people—some of whom have better hearing than others—radios can receive in different ways. Some radios simply have greater *receive sensitivity* than others do. Receive sensitivity is basically how faint an RF signal can be heard and understood by a receiver. For example, some radios might be able to decode an 11 Mbps Complementary Code Keying (CCK) transmission at 2.4 GHz up to –91 dBm whereas another might not be able decode the same transmission less than –89 dBm. If you remember that a difference of 3 dB is half or double the power, this can make a difference in some instances of being able to connect. It may also mean that the client with the lower receive sensitivity has a lower PHY rate that is used versus the one with better receive sensitivity operating at a higher PHY rate.

The higher the PHY rate, the higher the signal needs to be heard in order to properly demodulate the signal. Because some 802.11 modulation techniques incorporate amplitude modulation, the receiver needs to be able to distinguish small differences in received signal amplitude.

Receive sensitivity, however, has nothing to do with antenna gain as antenna gain is additive to a base receive sensitivity of the WLAN radio itself. In other words, receive sensitivity never changes. However, a signal coming in the direction of the antenna's direction of highest gain would be increased compared to a signal received in a direction that is part of the antenna's lowest gain, which would result in a reduced signal level.

Reading Spec Sheets

To quantify receive sensitivity and transmit power for WLAN hardware, you will want to refer to detailed spec sheets providing this information. Radio spec sheets should be referenced before performing an RF site survey or designing a new WLAN. Products from reputable manufacturers will provide a detailed spec sheet that outlines the performance of the radio for each PHY rate for both receive sensitivity as well as transmit power.

In the case of receive sensitivity, a detailed table like the one in Table 2.4 would be provided.

TABLE 2.4 Example Receive Sensitivity Radio Specification

802.11g	802.11a UNII-1
–94 dBm @ 1 Mbps	–87 dBm @ 6 Mbps
–93 dBm @ 2 Mbps	–87 dBm @ 9 Mbps
–92 dBm @ 5.5 Mbps	–87 dBm @ 12 Mbps
–86 dBm @ 6 Mbps	–87 dBm @ 18 Mbps
–86 dBm @ 9 Mbps	–82 dBm @ 24 Mbps
–90 dBm @ 11 Mbps	–79 dBm @ 36 Mbps
–86 dBm @ 12 Mbps	–74 dBm @ 48 Mbps
–86 dBm @ 18 Mbps	–72 dBm @ 54 Mbps
–84 dBm @ 24 Mbps	
–80 dBm @ 36 Mbps	
–75 dBm @ 48 Mbps	
–71 dBm @ 54 Mbps	

Table 2.4 tells us that, for example, when a signal is received at –84 dBm for 802.11g, the best possible PHY rate that can be understood, or received, would be 24 Mbps. If any environmental noise or interference conditions existed, the PHY rate would likely be 18 Mbps or less.

These same spec sheets should also detail transmit power specifications based on band and PHY rate. Table 2.5 provides an example of this information.

TABLE 2.5 Example Transmit Power Specifications

802.11b/g	802.11a (UNII-1)
20 dBm (100 mW) @ 1, 2, 5.5, and 11 Mbps	16 dBm (40 mW) @ 6, 9, 12, 18, and 24 Mbps
18 dBm (63 mW) @ 1, 2, 5.5, 6, 9, 11, 12, 18, and 24 Mbps	14 dBm (25 mW) @ 6, 9, 12, 18, 24, and 36 Mbps
17 dBm (50 mW) @ 1, 2, 5.5, 6, 9, 11, 12, 18, 24, and 36 Mbps	13 dBm (20 mW) @ 6, 9, 12, 18, 24, 36, 48, and 54 Mbps
15 dBm (30 mW) @ 1, 2, 5.5, 6, 9, 11, 12, 18, 24, 36, and 48 Mbps	11 dBm (13 mW) @ 6, 9, 12, 18, 24, 36, 48, and 54 Mbps
13 dBm (20 mW) @ 1, 2, 5.5, 6, 9, 11, 12, 18, 24, 36, 48, and 54 Mbps	10 dBm (10 mW) @ 6, 9, 12, 18, 24, 36, 48, and 54 Mbps
10 dBm (10 mW) @ 1, 2, 5.5, 6, 9, 11, 12, 18, 24, 36, 48, and 54 Mbps	

As you can see in Table 2.5, when sending a 54 Mbps 802.11 frame at 802.11g, a maximum transmit power of 13 dBm (20 mW) is allowed. It isn't until we hit 36 Mbps that we can get up to 17 dBm (50 mW). 100 mW transmissions are only possible with this particular radio with Clause 15 and 18 PHY rates only. For this particular radio, this tells us that we will have a variable transmit power based on the data rate.

If the AP that this client connects to is using a full 100 mW at 54 Mbps PHY rates and the client can only perform at a maximum of 20 mW using the same PHY rate, it should follow that the area that 54 Mbps can be heard by a client is larger than the area that a client can transmit and be heard at 54 Mbps. Therefore, the uplink range of the client for the same data rate is smaller.

The figures in Table 2.4 and Table 2.5 are merely an example of a radio chosen at random. Each radio incorporated in a final product solution will differ based on many factors, although the WLAN chipset itself forms most of the capabilities by itself. In other words, chipsets are a key differentiator.

Access points will typically allow up to 100 mW of power at almost any rate except OFDM rates. If an AP's power change based on the PHY rate, effectively the cell size (usable range) would change along with it. This is not necessarily the case with all APs. If it is, this may present problems of hidden node collisions and clients exhibiting unpredictable behavior at the AP's cell edges.

Access points typically use better hardware components and are more rigorously engineered than client devices are. Because the price point for access points are typically higher, better amplifiers can be used because higher power is available that also allows more equal transmit power performance across all PHY rates.

Using Client Use Cases

When devices are used in their intended function, it is possible that some performance degradation can occur. For example, a Wi-Fi–enabled smart phone worn in a pocket using a headset will perform differently versus it being held directly to the user's head. These factors must be considered in a WLAN design.

Designing for the intended use cases usually involves some testing that you can easily do with fairly little effort. For those of you not familiar with the term *use case*, it is a term often used when describing how something that you are referring to is used. In particular, if you are testing a phone, the use cases are having the phone in your pocket when not on a call, holding the phone to your ear when on a call, and so forth. Here's a list of what you need to do at a minimum:

1. Use an AP that provides real-time client uplink statistics and the intended client device configured to associate to a test AP.

2. Next, associate the client to the AP and develop a baseline of uplink RSSI information while using the client ideally at a distance (testing should rarely be done right next to an AP). For your baseline, the client should be placed more or less in free space without obstructions.

3. Once a baseline is established, use the client in the intended fashion it will normally be used.

4. Now, start taking readings to observe variance to the baseline. You may want to also rotate the client's orientation to the AP in cases where the device might be worn, such as with a Vocera communications badge, or a device that experiences a variety of antenna polarity changes. Ninety-degree increments would be fine to get a gauge.

5. If the data shows a high degree of variance in the use cases, angle, or orientation to AP, factor this into your design.

For example, let's say you are getting satisfactory signal readings near the edge of the building from the APs placed in the hallways when you surveyed with a professional surveyor utility. However, a new device you tested using the method just described shows a wide RF performance variance depending on its orientation to the AP. Let's assume you were testing a handheld computer that will be used at waist height. Let's also assume that your testing showed that when a person using the device while facing away from the AP dropped the signal by –10 dB versus when facing the AP directly.

Because the combination of that particular device facing away from the AP and a person standing between the signal propagation to the AP lowered the signal strength by approximately –10 dB, you might experience problems with these devices when used in production at the edges of the RF cells.

Some examples of device-specific use cases that should be considered include the following:

Handheld Computers   This includes ones used by warehouse staff—possibly at different elevations if forklifts or man lifts are used.

Vocera   This is a VoWiFi device that is worn in the center of a person's chest.

RFID   The signal of this usually tiny RF device might be obstructed depending on how it is mounted to assets or people.

Mobile Workstations   These are sometimes referred to as computer or workstations on wheels (COWs or WOWs).

Vehicles   Vehicle mount antennas require careful placement and are often more sensitive to polarity symmetry.

We are not suggesting that you need to scientifically analyze every use case with all your client devices. We want you to be aware of situations that can degrade performance when devices are used in the intended use cases.

At the highest level, understanding your client devices and how they will be used must be taken into account.

MAC Feature Support

Many of the advancements that have been made over the last few years with 802.11 have been at the MAC layer, which is part of the OSI Layer 2 framework. The challenge with making changes to the MAC layer is that they need to be made on both ends of the Wi-Fi link. Client device code must be upgraded just like infrastructure code in order to take advantage of newer MAC features.

Some of the most significant MAC features, those that play an important role in client design, will be discussed next.

802.11i/WPA/WPA2

The 802.11i amendment to the 802.11 standard was a critical milestone for the Wi-Fi industry. Confidence was lost with Wi-Fi security due to WEP being broken, and the industry feverishly struggled to address the weaknesses and ultimately restore confidence in the technology.

Together with Wi-Fi Protected Access (WPA and WPA2), we have an interoperability standard and a testing methodology to ultimately ensure intervendor compatibility on two primary criteria:

Enhanced Data Privacy   Both TKIP/RC4 and CCMP/AES were introduced with 802.11i. While CCMP/AES is required, TKIP/RC4 is optional and was designed to leverage existing deployed hardware that could be software upgraded. CCMP/AES— often referred to as just CCMP or even just AES—generally required a hardware upgrade, but was standard with 802.11g and more recent 802.11a hardware. All 802.11n chipsets must support AES.

The challenge you have as a designer is handling devices that do not support the encryption cipher you intend or that do not support it in a way that meets your business requirements. An example of this is a business-critical LOB application running on an 802.11b device that doesn't support AES. Another example is fast roaming support with one cipher but not the other.

Enhanced Authentication   Two methods were defined with 802.11i: IEEE 802.1X port-based authentication and preshared keys (PSKs). IEEE 802.11i did not specify which Extensible Authentication Protocol (EAP) types were to be supported with IEEE 802.1X, but not all EAP types are created equally.

A full discussion of EAP types isn't important for this particular topic, but the most important aspect from a design perspective is to understand which clients support which EAP types. Some EAP types are much more widely supported than others whereas others have much more overhead. Many vendors even vary in their implementation of certain EAP types. It is unfortunately far too common to encounter software bugs with client devices or a lack of ability to support certain EAP types.

It is absolutely critical to test your target client device population for support of your target EAP types and also ensure you are achieving the performance your application requires.

For additional details on 802.1X EAP types and WLAN security, refer to Chapter 11, "Basic WLAN Security Design."

Designing your WLAN and client devices to support efficient roaming using strong security is the holy grail of WLAN design—no compromises. Since IEEE 802.1X provides the strongest security, every WLAN design should accommodate it. However, the primary problem with 802.1X is that it adds overhead to the authentication and every roam.

We have relied on vendor-specific features (Cisco Centralized Key Management [CCKM] or *single-channel architecture [SCA]* vendor AP-based roaming) and cross-vendor early-stage prestandardized enhancements until recently (PMK caching, preauthentication, and opportunistic key caching [OKC]). Now, with the ratification of IEEE 802.11r we have a full framework that will provide big performance gains for time-sensitive applications such as video and audio while at the same time using the strongest of security mechanisms.

Target roaming times for 802.11r are less than 50 ms. This would result in no perceptible audio or video degradation.

Client devices, and infrastructure for that matter, that do not yet support 802.11r – Fast BSS Transitions, or just *FT* for short, mechanisms will unfortunately have to continue to use the same methods previously available or simply use full authentications on every roam.

Expect voice and other real-time device hardware to be the first to support any new roaming mechanisms. No support for 802.11r is available in any vendor equipment as of this writing, but the Wi-Fi Alliance is starting a big push for a Voice Enterprise specification based on 802.11r and 802.11k in 2010.

Once that specification is available, vendor support for 802.11r – FT will start to make its way into voice and video devices rather quickly. However, as of this writing, vendor participation in Wi-Fi Alliance PlugFest events has been minimal, which will likely mean further delays in seeing any fruit from the labor involved in developing the new standards.

802.11e/WMM

Client support of 802.11e and Wi-Fi Multimedia (WMM) features is particularly important for QoS support and a new form of power saving called *U-APSD*. U-APSD stands for Unscheduled Automatic Power Save Delivery, otherwise known as WMM Power Save. Most literature refers to U-APSD directly.

IEEE 802.11e is a QoS specification amendment to the 802.11 standard that is now rolled into IEEE 802.11-2007. Its features are mandatory for all 802.11n stations but optional with legacy devices such as 802.11a/b/g.

The Wi-Fi Alliance created an interoperability specification for 802.11e called WMM, which included specific features of the 802.11e specification. Without going into too many of the finer details, they are mostly the same thing and the names are often used interchangeably.

IEEE 802.11e specified certain options like *Point Coordination Function (PCF)* and *Hybrid Coordination Function(HCCA)* that were not included in the WMM specification. WMM incorporates the *Distributed Coordination Function (DCF)* and *Enhanced Distributed Channel Access (EDCA)* as the only modes of operation. These features will be explained in Chapter 10.

802.11e/WMM also specifies a *block acknowledgment (BA) policy*, which allows the option of a flexible frame acknowledgment policy. You will find BA policies particularly valuable in fragment bursting in order to utilize the WM more efficiently. BA is somewhat comparable to the TCP Sliding Window protocol for segment acknowledgments. Optionally, a BA policy of NoAck can be negotiated for all frames marked with QosNoAck in their header. A BA policy of NoAck policy is especially useful for real-time applications for time-critical data.

One of the biggest benefits that 802.11e/WMM provides is a more controlled wireless medium *contention* or *arbitration* policy. For example, applications to which we would like to provide a higher QoS prioritization (real-time applications) would be allowed the ability to transmit before lower-priority communication (Internet and email traffic).

Configurability

Client devices have incredible diversity. Some provide the ability to control a great deal of the device behavior whereas others offer hardly any at all. The ability to tune a client device to operate in a network designed for specific features, bands, and functionality can pay big performance and stability benefits.

Another consideration with client devices is that they tend to be tough to upgrade once they have been placed into production. Sure, you can manually collect each device, reconfigure it, and put it back into production, but as networks become larger and larger, that becomes far less of an option.

Consider a client device that only connects via Wi-Fi and you upgrade the firmware or WLAN driver of the device. If that process goes wrong or there isn't an automated recovery procedure for it, havoc will ensue.

Vendors are becoming increasingly familiar with the challenges enterprises are facing with managing their client device populations. Expect more attention to be focused on these challenges in the coming years. It is long overdue.

Modifying Scan Behavior (Band and Channels)

Roaming algorithms are not dictated by the standard, and they tend to be coveted intellectual property of WLAN device vendors. That is still the case even when they are poor. For instance, consider a network design where only 5 GHz is available but the client device favors 2.4 GHz, or vice versa. Using the first example, on every roam, the device scans and probes 2.4 GHz before it does 5 GHz and adds time to each roam. We have little control over the process that mobile devices use.

One of the areas we usually can control is what bands the client radio will scan. You can see from Figure 2.5 that the Intel client driver allows the administrator to select specific Wi-Fi modes of operation.

FIGURE 2.5   Client band selection

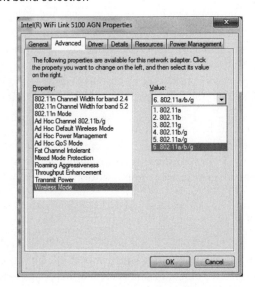

By selecting 802.11a instead of 802.11a/b/g, you would be selecting 5 GHz as the operating mode and excluding 2.4 GHz. Although this is an 802.11n adapter, Intel includes 802.11n-specific modes in a different field.

Channel scanning can be a useful tweak to make a client adapter configuration. Many client adapters will scan using passive, active, or both methods to discover access points. If your design incorporates a three-channel plan—for example, channels 1, 6, and 11—it would be quite useful for optimize your client scan behavior. This aspect is especially important if you are using a VoWiFi device that has high sensitivity to roaming delays.

Now consider the 5 GHz band. Depending on the regulatory domain where your network is operating, there could be 20 channels in the 5 GHz bands alone to contend with. If your voice device is attempting to roam without knowing what channels your infrastructure is operating, the time involved in brute-force scanning channels you don't even use can cause unnecessary delays and unhappy end users. Figure 2.6 is an example of a client capable of channel optimization.

FIGURE 2.6   Cisco 7921/7925 channel configuration

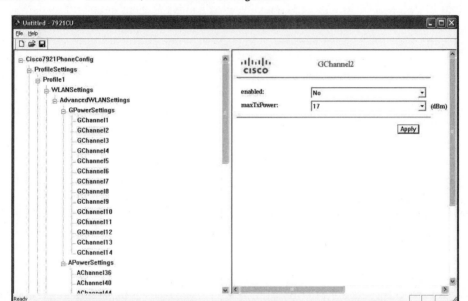

The main point to understand about adjusting scanning behavior is that if you are deploying on only a single band or only on certain channels in your design, you will get better performance when roaming and during initial association if you tune variables like these. Also, if you would simply like to force clients to a specific band, adjusting scanning behavior is a great way to do it.

Roaming Thresholds

WLAN device vendors also have their own model for determining the roaming algorithm used in their roaming procedure. Some devices allow you to control how aggressive or conservative the signal value will be that kicks off the roaming process. For example, if the signal level dropped to –70 dBm, the client would start to look for another AP to roam to.

Vendors typically give you a value to set the signal value to, such as a number from 1 to 5, as with Intel WiFi Link client adapters, as shown in Figure 2.7.

FIGURE 2.7   Roaming Aggressiveness client settings

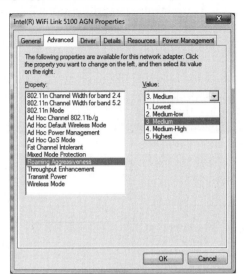

What does "3. Medium" mean? How does that differ from "1. Lowest"? While Intel does provide an explanation, it isn't a technical one. They don't tell you what RSSI value in dBm that "3. Medium" represents. We're not picking on Intel; all vendors seem to do it if they even offer the feature at all.

Remember, in an 802.11 WLAN, the client determines where and when to roam. Some WLAN client vendors determine this solely on signal strength. Others might use a more sophisticated approach of also looking at other values such as retransmissions, signal-to-noise ratio, or PHY rate fluctuations.

If you are using a SCA vendor like Meru that uses a virtual BSSID, the client device essentially never roams. Usually entire floors or large areas are deployed on a single channel, and when a device moves between these areas, the client will then need to roam. If this is the case, you would likely want to modify any variables in your WLAN device driver settings to use the most conservative roaming settings available. In other words, you would want to tell your client to never roam, which is "1. Lowest" with Intel adapters or maybe "2. Medium-Low" depending on the architecture and your design details. Although the infrastructure vendor might likely tell you that you don't need to modify the client settings, understanding the client behavior and how your network is deployed is the essential point.

In a higher-density, *multichannel architecture (MCA)* enterprise WLAN, you would likely find the default works best with most *newer* firmware releases. However, in the past, there were poor performers that essentially never roamed. You would associate to an AP and start walking down a hallway, pass another AP, and the client would drop its connection and then finally reassociate. This "sticky" type of behavior would spell disaster for your end users. The issue is quite simply a client issue.

The best recommendation that we can offer you is to upgrade your client drivers. We have learned a lot in the WLAN industry over the years and the methodologies that vendors are using have improved—sometimes drastically—in only a few years.

Fragmentation

Fragmentation involves adjusting the frame size of each WLAN frame before it is transmitted on the WM. For example, a fragmentation threshold of 512 bytes would fragment any frame larger than that into multiple frames.

Controlling fragmentation thresholds has lost favor over the years. When you were dealing with 1 Mbps PHY rates and transmitting large frames, you had a very high likelihood that another transmission in the same channel would result in a corrupted frame, causing it to retransmit again. For each retransmission you might still find that the same interference was recurring, and the vicious cycle would continue until perhaps the client disassociated from the network out of futility.

Changing the fragmentation value to a lower setting could have allowed some frames to be transmitted successfully; only certain fragments would have been affected and therefore would have had to be retransmitted. Essentially, the communication link could carry on, albeit at some reduction of throughput.

Be careful, though, because forcing fragmentation when it isn't needed will add overhead to the network connection and therefore reduce your overall throughput. Figure 2.8 illustrates a 1500-byte data transmission where one is using fragmentation (bottom) and the other is not (top). The transmission takes longer on the bottom when RF interference is not a factor. However, as the figure shows, there is a big savings when you are faced with an RF environment where interference is frequent.

FIGURE 2.8   Frame fragmentation

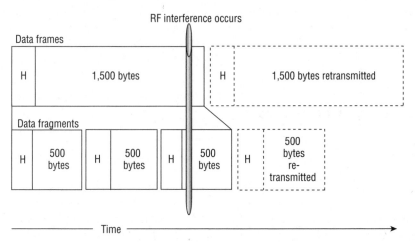

Nonetheless, fragmentation is important to consider when other options may not exist. This might be helpful in PtP links, mesh backhaul links, long-range client connections, or other scenarios, especially when low PHY rates are used.

User Lockout

Most causes of production wireless problems reside in recently induced configuration issues of some sort. Even the most well-intended users can make configuration changes to the WLAN settings and prevent them from connecting successfully or reliably to the WLAN. Infrastructure configuration decisions need to be made in concert with client configuration choices. Once the proper testing has been done and the right settings are chosen, you should lock them in.

One way to do that is to lock users out of muddling with them. Some WLAN supplicants can lock users out of many of the options. This can be as restrictive as preventing users from opening the WLAN client utility at all or perhaps just locking them out from changing certain profiles and client adapter/driver settings.

Locking users out of the WLAN client utility is usually appropriate when a certain client device will never leave the premise and unknowledgeable users will be using the system. This method might also be used when providing corporate assets to employees where security policy requires that users only connect to specific, company-provided Service Set Identifiers (SSIDs).

Also, one of the biggest vulnerabilities for hackers to gain entry to your WLAN is through improperly configured supplicant settings. For example, if you are using PEAP/MS-CHAPv2 and a WLAN supplicant was configured to not validate the server certificate, a giant security hole has been created for your network.

There are many reasons why user lockout can be a useful feature, and it is something you should look for in an enterprise supplicant.

 For more information on WLAN security vulnerabilities, we suggest you check out *CWSP: Certified Wireless Security Professional Official Study Guide: Exam PW0-204*, by David D. Coleman, David A. Westcott, Bryan E. Harkins, and Shawn M. Jackman (Sybex, 2010).

Management Features

The ability to manage a client device once it has been deployed into operation usually is limited to specific features or perhaps no options exist at all. Only in rare cases have vendors designed full management functionality of client devices.

There are several areas of interest that require management, which we will explore in this section. Proper management of client devices should start with a consistent firmware and driver for all device families. WLAN profiles are the next area, and bulk configuration is of particular interest especially once a large number of client devices are under management.

Firmware and Drivers

Probably the most disruptive change you can make to a client adapter is updating the device firmware or driver, yet this option can have the biggest payoff. Usually, making changes to client device radios require a reboot and you run the risk of the possibility the device will not reconnect at all post-upgrade. If the devices are in a local facility, perhaps that isn't as big of a problem. However, if you are an international retail chain with distribution centers, warehouses, and retail facilities across the globe, well, an upgrade gone badly might have disastrous financial ramifications.

That being said, some of the biggest gains in device performance reside with updating firmware. When WPA came out on the market and we were moving from dynamic WEP to TKIP, it required a client firmware or device driver upgrade in order to use TKIP and in order to support WPA altogether. That is just one example.

Sometimes a firmware upgrade might fix a poorly roaming client device due to a flaw in its roaming algorithm. It also might mean support for an EAP type that wasn't supported previously that your organization standardizes on. Whatever the case may be, updating the radio firmware may have big payoffs, but how can this be done?

Some VoWiFi phone vendors have built this functionality into their phone operations and can literally be updated in mass quantities simultaneously. Outside of VoWiFi device vendors, the functionality is almost nonexistent.

WLAN Profiles

WLAN profiles are simply WLAN settings for a specific infrastructure environment. It usually contains the SSID, authentication, and association settings needed to join a WLAN. Figure 2.9 and Figure 2.10 are two examples of enterprise, third-party WLAN client utilities that allow a high degree of WLAN profile management.

FIGURE 2.9   Odyssey Access Client screen shot

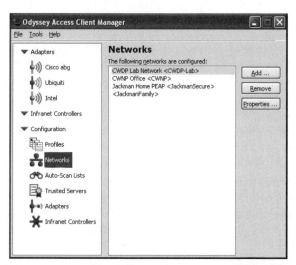

FIGURE 2.10   Cisco SSC multiple profiles

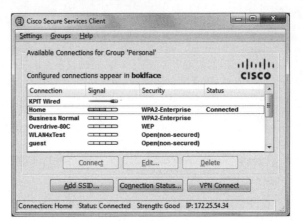

Having multiple client profiles would give users the ability to connect to multiple WLANs. If it is your laptop that you take between many different environments that have WiFi, then that is fine. If it is a device that will never leave a facility where a single WLAN is installed, this would not be a recommended practice.

Deploying third-party WLAN client utilities, sometimes referred to as client supplicants, typically comes at an added cost. Although the cost for these utilities is not that much on a per-seat basis, when you multiply that by thousands or even tens of thousands, it can become quite a large budget line item.

Keep in mind that some client utilities will cycle through available WLANs on a regular basis. Other client utilities may have other WLAN profiles installed, but one can be selected and will include the ability to look for and connect to only a *single* WLAN profile. The ability to configure a client to connect to a single profile is a very nice feature and one that is available in many enterprise-grade supplicants.

In terms of manageability, using a highly featured and manageable WLAN client utility/supplicant is one of the most beneficial items to update. If any infrastructure WLAN setting was changed or the security policy was changed, being able to roll out a new WLAN profile to every supplicant in your client population is a dream that hopefully comes true one day.

We are unfortunately very far from that right now, but many manufacturers are beginning to realize this and hopefully we will see some solutions in the near future.

Bulk Configuration

The concept of bulk configuration in this section refers to the ability to perform one administrative action that affects an entire population of devices.

Think for a second about the value that WLAN controllers or wireless network management systems (WNMS) products have offered administrators when it comes to managing a large population of APs. Using these products, a single mouse click can initiate a systemwide configuration change nearly instantly.

Let's also say that your network design incorporates a few hundred APs. Now, consider the fact that you might have 10 times that many client devices. What's more, they are mobile and even if you wanted to make changes, you may not be able to find them—they might be powered off or they might be off premises.

Most of the time, client devices require their settings to be modified manually. Some clients allow packaged updates to be rolled out via an enterprise software deployment/ management platform, but all clients do not fall into this category.

There is no standard for bulk client device management—but there needs to be. Some vendors have incorporated bulk configuration capabilities into their products. For example, configuring several hundred or perhaps even several thousand VoWiFi phones is not a simple task. Some of these vendors have a built-in default profile to join a configuration SSID and look for their management device to pull down a device configuration.

If you are using a Windows Active Directory network and computers are both part of a Domain and using Microsoft's built-in client utility, you can roll out Group Policy updates to your client population. The problem is that the Windows client utility has had performance and security vulnerabilities for Windows XP and Vista and many enterprises do not use it. Perhaps more supplicant vendors should leverage Active Directory using a specialized Active Directory Organizational Unit (OU).

Overall, vendors who have developed these bulk configuration capabilities should be applauded. These features should be touted as selling points to administrators of large organizations or administrators of large client populations.

A great deal of work still needs to be done in this area.

Common Client Device Form Factors

In this section, we will explore the various types of client devices and the considerations that will affect your WLAN design. Different client device form factors require different equipment manufacturer design decisions that ultimately affect antenna placement, options, and even WLAN radio choices. These differences, in turn, affect your WLAN design.

Laptop Computers

It's a safe assumption that everyone who is reading this book owns or regularly uses a laptop computer. In this section, we are loosely referring to laptops as a category of mobile computers, including notebooks and netbooks. Nowadays, taking Wi-Fi away from a laptop is like taking all the tires off a car.

Students, corporate users, and others traversing conference rooms, moving between airports, hotels, cafes, around their residence, and many other places have become dependent on Wi-Fi. Just think that Wi-Fi used to be an optional accessory with laptops. Today, the thought of not including wireless seems ridiculous.

Laptops vary in their WLAN radio performance—unfortunately by a very wide range. For example, have you ever upgraded your mobile phone to a newer, fancier model only to find that you then had more dead spots and dropped calls than you did before (assuming you didn't change spectrum or RF technology such as moving from CDMA, GSM, etc.)? What happened? You stayed with the same carrier. The towers didn't move!

Newer devices don't always mean better RF performance. Although the new device may have a newer operating system with better applications and other features, sometimes the antenna design may be worse. What this illustrates is that some phones have better RF performance than others. Laptops are no different.

Wi-Fi Adapters

Whereas Wi-Fi adapters used to be plug-in adapters in the form of PCMCIA/Cardbus (a.k.a. PC Card), USB, and now PC Card Express (or ExpressCard), they are now integrated into the design of the laptop.

In days past, we were required to insert a PC Card adapter into our laptop in order to have wireless access because WLAN radios were not built in. Nowadays, just about every mobile electronic device has a WLAN radio installed. That means we are typically only using a radio that isn't built-in when we want to use a different WLAN radio technology like 802.11n or when performing specific activities like WLAN analysis (which many of you reading this book are likely familiar with). For most users, the built-in radio is more than sufficient.

As a Wi-Fi professional, you may have noticed that some of the embedded adapters are not always supported by WLAN analysis software systems. Because of this, we tend to still use the PC Card radios. The industry is making it harder on us because finding a laptop with a PC Card slot is nearly impossible. The industry is shifting toward the newer PC Card Express slot. The problem is that not many PC Card Express WLAN radios have been adopted in the enterprise.

Embedded Radios

Embedded antenna design is an entirely different subject. The antennas can be built into the laptop monitor lid or even into the base of the laptop. Older SISO radios usually have *antenna diversity*. Antenna diversity is when two antenna elements are separated by a certain distance, often at least a quarter wavelength apart. With antenna diversity, the radio then switches the antenna element that is uses based on the best signal it receives. MIMO uses an entirely different method, which we will explore in Chapter 7.

 The wavelength of 2.437 GHz (the center of the 2.4 GHz ISM band in many regulatory domains) is 4.8465 inches, or 12.31 cm; 5 GHz has a much wider variance in frequency width. Using an approximated center of the 5 GHz range of 5.475 GHz, the distance is 2.1573 inches, or 5.48 cm.

When using an embedded radio like the Intel WiFi Link (formerly known as Centrino), you are relying on the OEM laptop manufacturer's embedded antenna design. Even the placement of the WLAN radio makes a difference in the laptop circuitry itself. Some of the electronics used in a laptop can emit forms of RF that are interpreted as noise to the WLAN radio. The more experienced laptop manufacturers are now properly shielding and grounding the electronics causing these forms of interference, but with some older laptop models this has been an issue.

To help paint the picture of how antenna diversity is used, have you ever been driving a car and listening to the radio and as soon as you stop at a red light the sound quality drops significantly? You then creep the car forward slowly and the signal comes in clearer? The antenna on your car is likely in a multipath null.

Newer 802.11n radios use an entirely different radio concept called MIMO, as previously discussed in this chapter. MIMO requires the use of several antenna elements and even multiple radios in a single chipset. While 802.11n can come in a variety of antenna elements and radios, laptop manufacturers need to design these antenna elements into their laptop designs.

As of this writing, laptops were being built with two to three different antenna elements. The smaller laptops (notebooks and netbooks) are typically based on two antenna element designs. Higher-end and physically larger laptops would typically have three. If 4x3 or 4x4 client adapters become available, four antenna elements will need to be included into the laptop design.

The point is that laptop designs can change WLAN performance simply based on how their antennas are placed.

Without getting into the details that are covered elsewhere in this text, the more antenna elements and the greater the length of their extension cables, placement, separation, and polarization, the more the differences in performance become apparent. Therefore, in your design you will need to consider your current and future client device population and the relative performance of each device.

Chipsets and Drivers

There are a handful of types of WLAN chipset vendors on the market. The main vendors for *laptop computers* are Atheros, Broadcom, and Intel. There are other chipset vendors, such as Marvell, Ralink, and TI, that develop radios for smart phones, USB adapters, and infrastructure radios.

Drivers and firmware, on the other hand, control the behavior of the radio. Manufacturers often rush a new chipset to market but have not quite perfected the driver to perform well against all infrastructure products with all the different 802.11 modes. Although this is understandable, it must be something you consider when you are deploying the latest and greatest chipset in your design. This is why many enterprises wait until products mature before putting them into mass deployment.

Some chipsets have gotten a bad name over the years largely based on poor roaming performance. However, some of them have changed that reputation by developing new drivers that alter the behavior. A driver can take a poor-performing chipset to a good one by modifying the roaming algorithms, rate shifting algorithms, power saving modes, and other factors.

The important message of this section is that if you find yourself experiencing poor performance with particular clients, it is important to understand the effect that drivers have on WLAN chipsets. If you find yourself in this situation, you should consider performing tests using different driver versions and then selecting a specific one that you will deploy across your entire device population.

Client Utilities and Operating System Considerations

The next area you should consider after the WLAN driver is the *WLAN client utility*. The client utility will also play the role of an *802.1X supplicant* when using WLAN security.

Client utilities control what SSID the client radio will connect to using a specific mode. For example, if you are using Wi-Fi at a cafe or hotel, you are likely using an open, unencrypted communication mode. When you are connecting to a corporate network, you are likely using 802.1X/EAP with WPA or WPA2.

Some client utilities work with a single WLAN radio, whereas others are designed to work with multiple adapters. Enterprise client utilities (often referred to simply as *supplicants*) can be packaged and deployed en masse to entire populations of laptop computers that run a variety of client adapters. These client utilities can also have default WLAN profiles, which are usually the enterprise SSID along with the pertinent security policy that is used at all facilities. You can even lock users out of changing this profile, but still allow them to add more for their home network as well as anywhere else they travel. You can also restrict users from ever using certain EAP types if that is important to your organization's security policy.

In some cases where devices do not leave a particular facility, you may even want to lock out users from even opening the WLAN client utility software completely. This way, you are ensuring users do not make changes that can affect the stability or compromise the security of that computer. Here's some information for the most used systems:

Windows Operating Systems that Run on a Domain   These can make use of Group Policies that can deploy client profiles down to groups of computers. Group Policies can deploy WLAN profiles for computers running Microsoft's built-in, free client utility. Group Policies can even lock down the utility in various ways.

For information on Active Directory Wireless Group Policies, refer to the Microsoft TechNet Library article at: http://technet.microsoft.com/en-us/library/cc758512(WS.10).aspx.

Microsoft Windows' Built-in Client Utility with Windows XP (Wireless Zero Config) These have limitations of EAP type support, which is why many corporations have adopted using third-party supplicants such as the Juniper Odyssey Client, Cisco Secure Services Client, or others. Windows 7 has used a more open approach to allow third-party vendors to write add-ons for the built-in utility for different EAP types that Windows does not ship with.

Macintosh Computers   Macs have a single option for a wireless client utility; you get what you get.

You can see that there are many options for deploying laptop computers. Depending on your design, this can change clients' behavior significantly.

Tablets

Tablet computers have their place in many mobile LOB applications. Over the years they have come in and out of fashion usually because applications weren't being written for pen or touch screen input. The use of tablet computers has exploded recently with the availability of tablet devices from Apple and Blackberry, and ones based on the Google Android operating system. Tablet computers nearly always incorporate internal-only WLAN adapters.

From a design perspective, tablet computers are not that different from laptops. Here are a few key differences:

- Performing user authentication can be more challenging than with laptops because of the lack of a keyboard.
- Long usernames and complex passwords can be a big annoyance for users, which can affect your security design methodology.
- Smart cards or biometrics may be an option for performing device-level authentication where perhaps machine authentication may be used afterward.

A new breed of tablet devices has recently come to market. In the medical field, devices have been designed with handles that can more easily survive drops, can survive certain contact with fluid exposure, and have embedded barcode and RFID scanners and even cameras. Since the iPhone has hit the market, there has been renewed interest in touch screen devices for a variety of applications. The Apple iPad was just being introduced as of this writing.

You can expect to encounter tablet-based computing devices more and more in your WLAN designs, especially as applications are now aggressively being written for them.

Thin Clients

Thin clients have traditionally not been candidates for WLAN use. Thin clients are a category of computing devices that generally do not have an operating system installed on them. Traditional thin clients usually use a special boot procedure (BOOTP) to load their entire lightweight operating system at boot time in order to establish a glorified terminal session to a server cluster. The benefit of this type of computing device is that a central operating system image can be updated and all the thin clients can be updated simply by rebooting them.

In order for a thin client to boot from a WLAN network, they would essentially have to build a fully featured WLAN supplicant into their BIOS and establish a WLAN connection before they can do anything useful. That is why these devices have been traditionally Ethernet-only devices.

Some thin client computers are using an embedded Windows operating system on a read-only hard drive, but this is arguably not a traditional thin client device.

Without mentioning specific makes and models of thin client vendors, it is important to know the details of their network traffic. There are some that will require a sustained, constant network traffic flow. While the bit rate might be measured in hundreds of kilobits per second, the more devices you have per AP problems might surface due to more data transmissions and discrepancies in PHY rates based for different clients. Roaming events and variable network conditions might cause an undesirable user experience for thin client computers.

What about a wireless network bridge device that plugs into the thin client computer's Ethernet port? It is possible to do this. It certainly adds to the cost and deployment complexity of the system. It is usually not economically feasible to use a thin client computer in this fashion to use a WLAN bridge device.

Handheld Computers

Handhelds are used mainly in retail and warehousing applications. If you look at workers in supermarkets and large retail chains, you will likely see these devices in action. They are typically equipped with barcode scanners to assist with inventory operations. Handheld computers typically run a version of Windows CE or Windows Mobile operating system. These systems have limited options for WLAN client utilities and supplicants.

WLAN radios on handheld computers are nearly—if not always—embedded radios. The wireless performance of these devices has improved greatly over the years. Because they are typically used by highly mobile users, their roaming algorithms are designed for heavy roaming activity.

The biggest challenge with handheld computers usually has to do with EAP type support. Usually this is easily solved with a WLAN driver and supplicant upgrade.

Application-Specific Devices

Application-specific devices (ASDs) are devices with proprietary operating systems and, as the definition implies, are designed for specific applications only. These include devices such as wireless printers, mobile medical devices, VoWiFi phones, home theater devices, and a variety of others.

ASDs are often some of the hardest devices to manage. You are usually limited to only the options that the single vendor provides, such as firmware, supplicant, MAC features, and EAP type support.

Smart Phones

Smart phones are devices like the Blackberry, iPhone, Palm, and Android. The smart phone category alone is probably the largest set of incoming devices into the WLAN space. With few exceptions, these devices have been carrier-only devices and have viewed 802.11 WLANs as a competitive and disruptive technology to the wireless carrier's bottom line.

Now, virtually all of these devices are coming equipped with 802.11 radios built into them, and users are already starting to connect them to WLANs. Wi-Fi networks are faster than the carrier networks, and users are interested in gaining whatever speed advantage they can. In some areas a usable wireless carrier data connection may not even be possible, which is another advantage to users. Furthermore, wireless carriers are being inundated with exponential data usage growth on their existing networks. They are simply running out of available data network bandwidth.

Network designers need to be planning for a great deal of growth in the number of devices that they should expect to support. This affects IP addressing schemes, wireless data security, compatibility testing, and many other factors.

Already applications are making their way onto mobile phones that allow users to use the data connection from their smart phones to make VoIP calls. If a user already has a VoIP telephone service at home, this will potentially save the user a great deal of minutes on their wireless carrier bill.

In-Building Voice Devices

Especially in large facilities with a large number of people, wireless voice communication is a must. No longer are users willing to tolerate the walkie-talkie type of communication using Family Radio Service (FRS) or General Mobile Radio Service (GMRS) frequencies because the channels are too heavily used by others within range.

In places like large warehouses, hospitals, and large office complexes, in-building wireless voice devices have become a staple requirement for productivity. In-building voice device networks largely began as 900 MHz systems. They have largely transitioned into VoWiFi networks, but there are at least two companies, Ascom and SpectraLink, that also make an enterprise Digital Enhanced Cordless Telecommunications (DECT) 6.0 system. In fact, 900 MHz voice systems are barely being manufactured anymore, if at all. Most of the market has transitioned to either 802.11g or 802.11a. 802.11n handsets are just starting to appear.

Each manufacturer is listed in alphabetical order in the following sections.

Ascom

Ascom is credited as introducing the first 802.11g phone, i75, to arrive on the market. Its handsets are typically made for tough environments like healthcare, industrial, and warehouse environments where users are usually brutally tough on their electronics.

Ascom announced support for an 802.11n handset in March 2010. As stated earlier, they also have a DECT 6.0 offering. DECT 6.0 operates at a noninterfering frequency range to all 802.11 WiFi (1920–1930 MHz). DECT 6.0 is a protocol designed from the ground up to service voice communications, and the protocol is highly efficient at roaming and other areas that WiFi can struggle with. Data speed, on the other hand, is something that DECT 6.0 does not have. If your customer is looking for mainly a voice communication system that is easy to deploy and isn't concerned about a selection of handset options, then this solution can be attractive.

Ascom also offers a native application integration platform built into their product platform that allows customized messages to be sent to and from handsets from a variety of application platforms and protocols.

Ascom handsets are H.323 and Session Initiation Protocol (SIP) capable.

Blackberry

Although it is not very well known, Blackberry is starting to make their way into the in-building only market. Their existing phones that are already shipping with 802.11 radios are starting to hit the market without requiring a cellular contract or service plan.

Blackberry has a host of large enterprise users already using their devices and an equally large development community. The operating system used by Blackberry is very feature rich, and all the devices can also be managed via the Blackberry Enterprise Server (BES).

Their devices boast large, high-resolution color displays that can be used to access enterprise applications; serve as a phone; and quite simply could be the only device some users may need.

While Blackberry handsets shouldn't be considered ruggedized, they take a beating from the user base already. Blackberry handsets can work with the Mobile Voice System (MVS) server and also integrate to the Cisco Unified Communications Manager.

Cisco

Cisco initially came to the WiFi market with an 802.11b phone. Their first phone offering was predominantly designed for carpeted office space and less harsh environments.

Cisco later developed the 7921, which was not only an 802.11g-capable phone but also operated at 802.11a. Again, the 7921 was largely a carpeted office space–only phone, but Cisco later introduced a rugged version called the 7925 with nearly all the features and performance benefits of the 7921.

Cisco's latest WiFi handset offering is 802.11 feature rich and has good 802.11 industry-standard support. Both of Cisco's recent handsets support a color screen and allow for application integration features into the handset from various application integration gateway products.

A great deal of application integration development is being made on Cisco's wired and wireless products within healthcare, call center, and industrial environments where access to time-sensitive information is critical. As of this writing, Cisco's handsets are only Skinny Client Control Protocol (SCCP) (Cisco proprietary) capable.

Polycom (SpectraLink)

Polycom, who purchased SpectraLink, has been around a long time in the in-building voice communications space. SpectraLink 900 MHz products have been widely deployed throughout hospitals, warehouses, and enterprises. SpectraLink was one of the first vendors to offer an 802.11 VoWiFi product.

Prior to the implementation of standards-based QoS mechanisms, SpectraLink developed their own method of QoS called SpectraLink Voice Priority (SVP). The SpectraLink proprietary solution requires an SVP server that is used for three main purposes:

Call Admission Control (CAC)   Proprietary mechanisms are used to limit the amount of active voice calls per access point.

SRP Encapsulation   All audio packets are encapsulated using a proprietary protocol called SpectraLink Radio Protocol (SRP). When a voice packet arrives from the PBX, the SVP server encapsulates each voice packet with an SRP protocol 119 header.

Timed Delivery   All SRP packets are sent from the SVP server to a WLAN controller or autonomous AP in 30 ms intervals.

When an SVP solution is deployed, the WLAN controller or autonomous AP is used to prioritize SRP protocol 119 packets for transmission on the 802.11 medium by always using a zero random backoff timer. SpectraLink's method of using a zero random backoff timer effectively guarantees that voice transmissions will always take priority over all other types of data transmissions. Unfortunately, this is at the expense of every other VoWiFi or QoS-sensitive device.

WARNING   It is very important to not mix other VoWiFi products with Polycom products that are still using the SVP server and SRP protocol. Because the SRP protocol is not standards compliant, it will not play fairly with other VoWiFi products.

Although many of Polycom's customers still use the proprietary SVP solution, it should be noted that Polycom's SpectraLink phones now fully support WMM standards-based QoS mechanisms and can mixed with other VoWiFi products in a WMM environment. Polycom VoWiFi phones also support OKC and Cisco Compatible Extensions (CCXv4).

Vocera

Vocera is largely known for their voice device that is worn around a user's neck that completely operates off speech recognition. Vocera has an amazing software application that allows users to push a large button on the front of the device and issue voice commands.

Clicking the button on the device announces, "Vocera." That prompt is your key that the device is awaiting a voice command. If Matt Swartz said, "Call Shawn Jackman," the badge that Shawn is wearing would hear a brief jingle and say, "Would you like to talk to Matt Swartz?" A simple response of "Yes" or "No" is all that is needed.

When a user picks up a fresh badge at the beginning of their work shift, they click the button and a voice prompt asks them to say their name. When they do, the user is logged in, and that is how users are located by the system. In order to find them, all the server needs to know is which badge a user is logged into.

Vocera has a unique solution in that no phone numbers are ever needed. The devices are shared among other users, and users log in using voice commands. Once a user logs in, the system automatically associates that specific device with that specific user. Users communicate with each other by actual names or groups. This allows one-to-one and group-based communication.

Healthcare is the primary market for Vocera and is quite useful for clinical and nursing staff who have to handle patients and infectious items. If their hands are involved with a patient, they don't even have to touch anything in order to communicate with other staff members.

Vocera has taken some significant leadership in helping to evolve the world of telephony in a positive way.

From an RF perspective, these pesky little badges have been the disdain of many RF engineers. Because they are worn in the center of the chest region, the RF characteristics (as shown in Figure 2.11) tend to make it somewhat directional. When facing away from the AP at the edge of a patient room, the wearer might experience a lower RF link quality than when using a device held to their head with more or less equal RF propagation in all directions.

FIGURE 2.11   Vocera B2000 radiation pattern

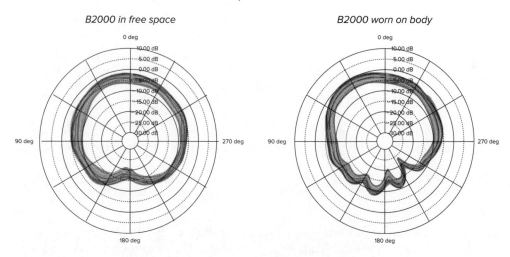

Vocera also incorporates the use of multicast. Multicast has dependency on the wired LAN as well as the WLAN. Professional services are generally recommended when Vocera is a target device to run on the WLAN.

That being said, a good voice-grade design usually yields a positive outcome.

Video Devices

Video devices come in several forms. Each form they come in will result in different capabilities. The most common types of video devices are PC based and ASDs, sometimes referred to as appliances.

PC Based

PC-based video technology should incorporate some of the best video codec and compression technology available on the market. This is due to the fact that PCs have very fast CPUs. When you are dealing with slower hardware, you may need to use a variety of compression methods and codecs because many of the higher-end codecs require additional computing power.

PCs generally have other limitations, though. Generally speaking, PCs are not configurable in terms of 802.11-based QoS. Although the PC can mark the traffic using IP Differentiated Services Code Point (DSCP) values, that fact will provide advantages only when the traffic hits the AP and sends it upstream within the network.

One of the most important aspects of 802.11e/WMM is making use of the backoff timers. IEEE 802.11e specified the capability for *access categories (ACs)* that devices can take advantage of. Within each of these ACs are specified timing windows when a device making use of a specific AC may start to transmit with (*CWmin*), as shown in Figure 2.12. In fact, as part of the *CSMA/CA* procedures in order to avoid transmit collisions, there is also an upper limit (*CWmax*) that a transmitting device will randomly select a value between.

FIGURE 2.12   Example Enhanced Distributed Channel Access (EDCA) access categories

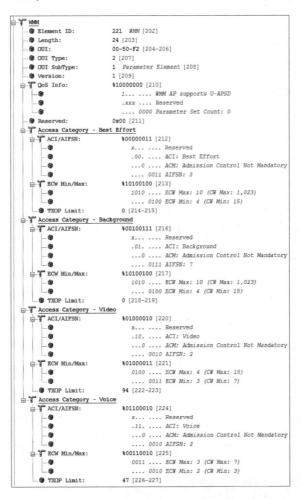

From a wireless medium perspective, one of the main mechanisms used to provide QoS traffic prioritization is related to transmit timing. If you cannot configure a PC-based device to participate using EDCA categories and specify how the transmitter should mark traffic, do not assume that the device supports 802.11-based QoS timing mechanisms.

Another mechanism to provide QoS prioritization is by using a traffic specification, or *TSPEC*. An 802.11 station, or STA, may use a TSPEC to reserve airtime with the WLAN infrastructure. Again, a laptop that is simply transmitting traffic from its applications would not send a TSPEC to the WLAN infrastructure in order to reserve airtime. Video is the type of traffic that should be allowed to have transmit favoritism over web-based and other general-use network traffic.

The WLAN radio on the PC has to perform this task. Drivers for client WLAN radios do not inspect the traffic coming into the transmit queue and determine how to prioritize that traffic in an 802.11 WLAN today. If the driver did not automatically detect these values, the application itself would have to instruct the client WLAN radio accordingly.

At this point, this feature is not possible, which makes using PC-based video applications more challenging from a QoS prioritization point of view than purpose-built ASDs designed from the ground up for video.

Video Appliances

Video appliances would be considered ASDs. They are typically a rack mount or a device that sits near a video screen that runs a proprietary OS exclusively built for performing videoconferencing.

You will typically find highly configurable QoS settings that allow the marking and tagging of traffic at finite levels of detail. For example, this might mean that data traffic from these devices that wasn't part of a real-time media stream can be sent at a normal traffic classification. Call setup and teardown (a.k.a. signaling) can be set at a middle level QoS level (802.11 User Priority [UP] of 4) whereas video and audio are given two different markings (802.11 UP of 5 and 6, respectively).

The downside of video appliances is that they haven't yet been designed to operate over WLANs. If a WLAN or PC Card slot is available, it is nearly guaranteed that there is only the very basic support for 802.11. QoS features and fast, secure roaming would not be available. In other words, WLAN support on these devices is almost nonexistent or not highly recommended at this point.

Summary

WLAN infrastructure exists to support the devices and applications that run on them. As a design professional, you cannot lose sight of this. Truly understanding the way your devices will perform on the WLAN is critical to a proper wireless design.

Designing and supporting client devices starts with understanding and analyzing the type of PHY support available. You learned that it is important to know what PHYs are supported and which one performs best in a given situation.

You also learned that clients have different radio characteristics and that certain factors affect their performance. Knowing these factors is critical to planning and designing for a robust WLAN that will support *all* your target client devices.

MAC feature support was another topic that we explored. You learned that some devices may not support all the features in your WLAN design. Client and infrastructure feature support is the most important area to focus on.

Of course, no network design would be complete without a proper support model. We discussed a variety of options devices use. We showed you techniques that can be used to configure clients to support certain features and to apply WLAN profiles.

We also explored a variety of client device form factors and important design considerations.

We cannot stress enough how important it is to pay close attention to your client devices. One of the most common mistakes that WLAN administrators make is paying too much attention to the infrastructure and too little attention to the client devices. Most of the time WLAN performance problems can be traced back to client devices, but infrastructure equipment certainly is often at fault as well. Now you have learned about WLAN client devices and have the opportunity to improve your designs.

Exam Essentials

Understand client device characteristics.   Be able to explain how the various types of PHY support client devices are used and how to incorporate them into an infrastructure design. Know the design differences in client device radio characteristics and how MAC feature support will affect WLAN design.

Understand device spec sheets.   Know how to interpret client device specification documentation and how to relate that to WLAN infrastructure design.

Be able to configure client devices.   Understand the impact on performance when client devices are configured based on frequency bands, channels, transmit power, and other criteria.

Understand client use cases.   Understand how each client device will be used in the WLAN and how it affects WLAN infrastructure design.

Review Questions

1. If radar has reportedly been detected on your WLAN deployment, what bands would you consider avoiding?

   A. 5 GHz UNII-1 and 2

   B. 5 GHz UNII-2 and 3

   C. 5 GHz UNII-2, 2e, and 3

   D. 5 GHz UNII-2 and 2e

   E. 5 GHz UNII-1, 2, and 3

2. In October 2004, the FCC ruled to allow for which of the following? (Choose all that apply)

   A. 100 mW EIRP for UNII-1

   B. External antenna option for UNII-2e

   C. Required permanently attached antenna for UNII-1

   D. External antenna option for UNII-1

   E. Allocating extended spectrum to 5 GHz UNII–UNII-2e

3. Modulation can be defined as:

   A. The process of incorporating a chipping code to build resilience

   B. The process of encoding data symbols using a carrier frequency

   C. The process of modifying a carrier signal to represent data

   D. The process of representing data using RF coding techniques

4. HR/DSSS specifies the following PHY rates:

   A. 1, 2

   B. 1, 2, 5.5, 11

   C. 6, 9, 12, 18, 24, 36, 48, 54

   D. MCS 1–15

5. What power level in the United States might you not want to exceed if you survey for a 5 GHz deployment with a 3 dBi antenna that will use auto-channelization features?

   A. 25 mW

   B. 50 mW

   C. 100 mW

   D. 250 mW

6. Receivers using MIMO benefit from which RF phenomena? (Choose all that apply)

   A. Multipath

   B. Constructive interference

   C. Destructive interference

   D. Beam shaping

   E. STBC

7. What frequency and power did 802.11y provide?

   A. 5.65–5.7 GHz, 5W EIRP

   B. 5.25–5.35 GHz, 10W EIRP

   C. 3.7–3.75 GHz, 15W EIRP

   D. 3.65–3.7 GHz, 20W EIRP

8. What are the two primary categories for understanding what type of PHYs a client supports? (Choose two)

   A. Antenna tuning

   B. Frequency band

   C. MCS rates

   D. PHY rates

   E. WPA/WPA2 support

9. Which of the following statements are true regarding SISO? (Choose two)

   A. SISO is the technology used for 802.11b/g/n only at 2.4 GHz.

   B. SISO is used with 802.11a/b/g when no antenna diversity is used.

   C. SISO is used with 802.11a/b/g when antenna diversity is used.

   D. SISO is capable of handling only one real-time application stream where MIMO can support multiple.

   E. SISO can leverage several spatial streams using advanced DSP processing from multiple antennas.

10. With 802.11n, if a radio has three receive chains and two transmit chains, which of the following must be true? (Choose all that apply)

    A. Receive throughput is capable up to 300 Mbps.

    B. Receive throughput is capable up to 450 Mbps.

    C. Receive throughput is capable up to 600 Mbps.

    D. Transmit throughput is capable up to 300 Mbps

    E. Transmit throughput is capable up to 450 Mbps

11. In 802.11, clients are required to be calibrated for RSSI and SNR reporting to:

   A. Within +/−5 dB

   B. Within +/−3 dB

   C. Within +/−1 dB

   D. Within +/−0.5 dB

   E. Within +/−0.25 dB

   F. No specific value

12. Which of the following is false regarding transmit power?

   A. Power should be balanced between client and AP.

   B. DTPC must be enabled at 2.4 GHz.

   C. At high signal strength, client power may be reduced to provide high PHY rates.

   D. Per most regulatory restrictions, transmit power is not equal across 5 GHz.

13. What contributing factor might cause two different types of clients to perform differently at the same location and at the edge of coverage?

   A. AP transmit power

   B. AP receive sensitivity

   C. Client receive sensitivity

   D. Fragmentation threshold

   E. Noise floor

14. What might be considered a valuable feature in a client supplicant for enterprise customers? (Choose all that apply)

   A. User lockout

   B. Remotely updating profiles

   C. Controlling fragmentation

   D. Updating chipset firmware

15. A client device with high angular or orientation variance of antenna performance would result in which of the following? (Choose all that apply)

   A. The client attempting to roam at inconsistent locations at the edge of coverage

   B. Higher degree of variance of PHY rates within similar geographical locations

   C. Sporadic reports of limited/degraded connectivity at the edges of coverage

   D. Higher degree of retransmissions for highly mobile client devices compared to other clients

16. What is the target roam time using 802.11r with 802.1X/EAP authentication?

    A. 25 ms

    B. 50 ms

    C. 100 ms

    D. 150 ms

    E. 250 ms

17. What two 802.11 amendments deal with regulatory and transmission requirements?

    A. 802.11f

    B. 802.11h

    C. 802.11i

    D. 802.11d

    E. 802.11k

18. When performing an analysis of device roam times, which of the following would be sufficient?

    A. Doing standard ping tests

    B. Configuring your analyzer to scan the channels of nearby APs

    C. Locking your analyzer into the specific channel your client is currently on

    D. Using a multichannel capture utility

    E. Looking at RADIUS server logs for reauthentications on roams

19. From an 802.11 QoS perspective, how are many laptop devices constrained?

    A. Laptops do not support 802.11 QoS.

    B. WLAN client drivers usually do not provide facilities for applications to control radio behavior.

    C. Laptops fully support 802.11-based QoS mechanisms because many are now 802.11e compliant.

    D. If the client is "Wi-Fi Certified," it should support QoS facilities for applications to take advantage of.

20. Video applications running over a laptop computer will likely not support which of the following? (Choose all that apply):

    A. TSPECs

    B. WMM Power Save

    C. A-MPDU

    D. Transmit timing control

    E. Fragmentation

    F. 802.1X/EAP

Answers to Review Questions

1. D. IEEE 802.11h specified the UNII-2 and 2e bands as DFS bands, which require mechanisms for avoiding radar.

2. D, E. The October 2004 FCC ruling removed restrictions for an integrated antenna for UNII-1 devices and allocated more spectrum for unlicensed use. Many other updates were also included in this update, such as encouraging the use of smart antennas and the use of MIMO.

3. C. Modulation is the process of taking a carrier frequency and modifying it in a way that the receiver can decode data from the modifications to the carrier frequency.

4. B. HR/DSSS is the other name for the 802.11b specification and what the 802.11 standard refers to the technology in its documentation.

5. A. UNII-1 is limited by the FCC to 50 mW EIRP (25 mW of transmit power with a 3 dBi antenna equals 50 mW EIRP). Even though UNII-2–3 allows for higher EIRP, auto-channelization features of infrastructure devices would require cells using UNII-1 channels to not exceed 50 mW EIRP. If a survey was done at a higher transmit power, it might result in poor coverage at cell edges of APs configured for UNII-1 channels.

6. A, B, C. The same RF transmission that is reflected off multiple objects that are received at the receiver's antenna can cause corruption of the RF signal in SISO technology. MIMO leverages this phenomenon by being able to hear these multiple signal paths received on different antenna elements to reconstruct a better received signal. Constructive and destructive interference are effects of multipath. Beam shaping and STBC are transmission techniques.

7. D. 802.11y specifies a lightly licensed spectrum for high-powered data networks operating up to 20W EIRP.

8. B, D. Supported frequencies are the first major factor and speed (or PHY rates) is the other. Modulation is part of the method used in determining PHY and MCS rates. WPA/WPA2 support is out of context.

9. B, C. SISO stands for single input, single output and has nothing to do with diversity of lack of diversity. However, it is used with 802.11a/b/g. SISO is not just a 2.4 GHz technology, and it has nothing to do with real-time applications and cannot use spatial streams.

10. B, D. Each receiver or transmitter element is capable of handling a PHY rate of 150 Mbps. If three receive chains are used, then $3 \times 150 = 450$ Mbps of receive PHY throughput. For transmit, since only two transmitters are used, $2 \times 150 = 300$ Mbps is the maximum PHY throughput capable.

11. F. 802.11 clients are not calibrated.

12. B. Dynamic transmit power control (DTPC) is not a requirement for any 802.11 operation, assuming devices adhere to regulatory restrictions.

13. C. AP transmit power and receive sensitivity would affect both of the clients located at the same position. Fragmentation threshold is related to keeping frame sizes lower, usually to avoid interference or constrain to the lowest MTU of the DS medium. Noise floor will also affect both clients equally. Client receive sensitivity will cause a variety of responses.

14. A, B. The ability to lock out users from changing profiles and remotely update profiles to mass client populations is a highly desired enterprise feature with clients.

15. A, B, C, D. Devices with a high degree of orientation variance (the angle how the client is oriented to the AP) will suffer from bigger swings in RF signal strength, depending on how the device is oriented to the AP. Such swings will cause all these conditions to be more prevalent compared to other devices.

16. B. IEEE 802.11r is targeting sub-50 ms roam times for roaming from AP to AP within an ESS.

17. B, D. IEEE 802.11h and 802.11d cover, among other elements, regulatory and transmission requirements for IEEE devices operating in the 2.4 GHz ISM and 5 GHz UNII frequency bands.

18. D. Only a simultaneous multichannel capture utility will provide accurate roam times. Standard ping tests are not granular enough because a WLAN operates on submillisecond-level timing. Scanning or locking your analyzer to specific channels with a single WLAN adapter will provide only a partial picture. RADIUS server logs would not be sufficient for many reasons, but most importantly because the server may never know a client roams in some WLAN architectures if the client is still operating within a valid authentication time frame.

19. B. WLAN client drivers do not provide QoS configuration options to control 802.11-based QoS markings or EDCA Access Category (AC) timing mechanisms. Therefore, even though applications might mark IP (Layer 3) QoS values, a laptop usually does not do anything special with it within the wireless medium.

20. A, D. Because laptops are designed to support many applications (unlike ASDs), they do not provide granular levels of control over WLAN radio behavior that can be used to gain 802.11-based QoS benefits.

Chapter 3

Designing for Applications

THE FOLLOWING CWDP EXAM TOPICS ARE COVERED IN THIS CHAPTER:

- ✓ Determine the desired applications to be supported and understand the requirements for specific applications.

- ✓ Illustrate application-specific design approaches and requirements.

- ✓ Understand the purpose of, and challenges related to, creating a balanced RF link between the AP and client devices.

- ✓ Demonstrate a detailed knowledge of the common problems related to high user densities and describe effective strategies to address them.

- ✓ Illustrate best practices for data rate/MCS configurations to manage client connectivity.

- ✓ Understand the details of Dynamic Frequency Selection (DFS) and describe its impact on WLAN design.

- ✓ Explain how surveying methodologies may differ when preparing for specific applications.

- ✓ Discuss how surveying approaches differ depending upon PHY and feature support.

- ✓ Explain best practice security design concepts for guest and public access Wi-Fi networks.

A wireless network must support an increasing number of applications these days. Whereas wireless infrastructure was once seen as a convenience, it is now often a requirement in many environments. So, as applications that are being run over the WLAN have increased in complexity, the design criterion for the infrastructure has had to change along with it. Complexity can come in many forms, particularly when dealing with difficult applications and protocols that weren't designed to operate over wireless networks.

Applications vary a great deal based on several factors, such as the amount of traffic they send, the protocols they use, the frequency of transmissions, and a variety of other factors that will influence your overall WLAN design. Real-time applications like audio and video are especially important when it comes to traffic latency and other overall time factors. This chapter will examine vendor-neutral design guidelines for voice and video applications. Designing for video is an entirely new industry application that is gaining a great deal of attention for WLAN usage.

It is likely that you have already heard of different grades of WLANs, such as data, voice, and location-grade networks. Yet what may not be widely understood is that along with each of these grades, the price tag to design and deploy them also increases. In this chapter, we'll explain how these overall design grades affect your design and, therefore, your overall budget.

One of the fastest-growing killer applications for WLANs is guest access. Providing guest access to visitors, contractors, vendors, and customers is often the biggest driver to deploy a WLAN in many industry verticals. We'll cover this topic in detail and discuss the design objectives and deployment considerations for various types.

Understanding WLAN Applications

In this chapter, we'll explore a variety of issues relating to applications, along with common applications that run on WLANs. As you'll see, several considerations regarding these applications will affect your WLAN designs. Knowing some of the details related to how these applications operate will pay off.

These details include understanding the protocols used in the applications and how to handle difficult ones. Some applications are not as friendly to WLAN behavior as others. Latency-sensitive applications like voice have their own unique requirements, and a variety of factors need to be considered in any WLAN that is to employ audio or any real-time application.

Real-time location tracking doesn't fall into the real-time application as voice and video, but generally refers to being able to locate devices based on relatively real-time information. Those of you who have had some exposure to Real-Time Location Systems (RTLSs) in WLAN designs can probably agree that a great deal of confusion exists regarding how to design for real-time location tracking. We'll cover this topic in depth.

Applications that require multicast have traditionally been difficult to deploy on WLANs. We'll discuss several vendor-neutral design factors that will help you when faced with those applications.

Familiarizing Yourself with Application Protocols and Behavior

Simply put, there are some applications that simply weren't designed for momentary lapses of connectivity loss. Some applications may survive roaming between different IP subnets whereas others will not. Understanding the details related to the applications you are supporting is yet another important aspect of WLAN design.

The first part of analyzing a particular application is to look at the protocols that are being used.

A protocol is a method of communication that a software designer uses to communicate over a computer network. A protocol can be a well-defined, standards-based protocol, or applications can, and often do, design their own. This includes decisions at several layers of the OSI model in addition to the contents carried by these protocols that cause the application to behave a certain way.

Well-known protocols are usually much easier to handle because a great deal of knowledge already exists about them. Terminal protocols are so heavily used in some industry verticals that we are including a specific discussion on that one alone. An introduction on voice and video protocols will also be presented.

Using Well-Known Protocols

If the applications you are required to support are well-known protocols, most of your research is done already. For example, web-based applications operating over TCP ports 80 and 443 have predictable behavior. Generally speaking, you can assume that the application layer is stateless and each communication exchange is a simple request/response transaction. Also, you can generally assume that even if the client device changed IP addresses between transactions, usually this will not pose a problem.

TCP in general is a well-known protocol that will likely account for most of the traffic that occurs over typical WLANs. Operating at OSI Layer 4, it is one of the protocols that is used to establish a session-based communication session and focuses on increasing the reliability of traffic delivery. TCP has built-in mechanisms for handling difficult network conditions that can result in lost transmissions, duplication, and segments delivered out of order. When establishing a session between two hosts, TCP accomplishes this, in part, by using a numbering scheme for every segment. The focus of TCP is on trying to obtain greater reliability of transmissions.

Frames, Packets, and Segments

When referring to individual network transmissions, most people simply refer to them as "packets." This is not entirely accurate, and the distinction can be misleading when referring to the details of network communications. At OSI Layer 2, which is what IEEE 802.11 focuses on as well as Ethernet (802.3), we are to refer to these transmissions as "frames." At the IP layer, OSI Layer 3, we are to refer to these transmissions as "packets," whereas transmissions at OSI Layer 4 (TCP and UDP, for example) we refer to as "segments."

UDP, on the other hand, is focused on timeliness of delivery. UDP uses less overhead in the protocol and is best used when the reliability of the network medium is good. Applications that use UDP are often designed to handle lost segments at the application layer. UDP is often the protocol used for real-time applications like voice and video.

Understanding Terminal Protocols

Contrast HTTP to a session-based protocol like Telnet or SSH(2), which requires a consistent, stateful connection with the peer device at high-layer protocols. From a historical perspective, Telnet was largely based on a method of providing a mechanism for remotely running applications from a lightweight computing device. With terminal protocols, each network transmission (a.k.a. packet) builds on the last communication, all the way down to the keystroke.

Many handheld computers used in retail and warehousing applications as well as some medical systems will use a Telnet type of protocol. The challenge from a wireless perspective is that when a short loss of connectivity occurs or when the device changes IP addresses the connection is severed. This requires the end user to set up the session all over again, and likely all of the data the user was working on is lost. Protocols like Telnet are some of the most challenging protocols for WLAN designers because momentary lapses of connectivity can greatly impact productivity.

VLAN segmentation design is critical in environments where IP mobility isn't managed. In other words, if one AP was connected to one VLAN and another AP was connected to another VLAN, depending on the infrastructure capabilities, the client device might require an IP change. Therefore, if a session-based protocol like Telnet is used, the connection will be lost.

Campus-based LANs can be performed using a variety of methods. One of the more recent and promoted methods is to run Layer 3 all the way down to the access layer of the network. That means that every Ethernet switch would have its own IP segment. If it were not for the advent of WLAN controllers tunneling traffic back to a central VLAN, regardless of what VLAN the actual AP is on, we would have been in serious trouble with

WLANs for quite some time now. However, not every environment has moved to a WLAN controller or similarly capable model.

Handling Voice and Video Protocols

Not all voice and video protocols are created equally. In fact, incredibly remarkable differences exist between them. Some of the earliest audio codecs, for example, have little to no compression, and slight variations in jitter or frame ordering can result in a noticeable audio impact. Video codecs are the same way. Some of them are very raw and frankly weren't originally designed to operate on any type of packetized network, whereas others are designed to operate over WAN links and can even have highly variable bit rates.

We're going to spend more time on the topic of voice and video protocols later in this chapter, but for now, this short introduction to application protocols should be enough to detail how some applications are more sensitive than others to WLAN performance issues.

Proprietary Protocols

Application programmers often develop their own protocols. Those same developers may also write their software in such a way that an application cannot tolerate any type of dropped packet or disruption of network connectivity. These types of applications can be the hardest to address not only because their behavior is less known, but because there is little that you can do about it.

When you find that your target WLAN will support a propriety application that hasn't been tested to operate over a WLAN where connectivity might be unavailable periodically, you should immediately escalate this issue to your management and request that testing be performed.

Handling Difficult Protocols

In early stages of wireless implementations of large or metropolitan area networks, many of the protocols that were needed to be accessed fell into the category of difficult protocols, as described earlier. Metropolitan network users were often public safety, ambulatory, and city personnel who frequently required access to Telnet-based applications. But this all changed when a new breed of applications that helped to proxy these types of stateful applications emerged on the scene. It was learned that one of the best ways to handle difficult applications and protocols over wireless networks, or just about any unreliable network for that matter, was to change the way the device connects to the application host.

New proxy applications began to fill a niche where WLANs didn't share a common IP subnet, and stateful application connections would simply reset due to lapses in connectivity or IP subnet changes.

Consider a design where you have every WLAN client perform a remote desktop type of session to a traditional server that resides on a wired network that has a consistent, reliable connection. Conceptually, if the WLAN device establishes a terminal session to this server and the application is launched from there, you could use this application in a reliable way. In this case, the application is essentially being accessed only from the server and not the WLAN client. Screen updates are sent down to the WLAN device, but the application itself is never opened from the WLAN client.

So, what happens when the WLAN client loses its connection to the server? The terminal server application residing on the server in this case never closes down the session when it loses connectivity to the WLAN client. This is much like you walking away from your computer, running to the kitchen for a drink of water, and then sitting back down again; your computer is still running your applications, but you just stepped away momentarily. The trick to configuring the terminal server application on the server is to make sure that, when the WLAN client reestablishes network connectivity and logs back in, the server presents the same session as it had previously.

Because each WLAN client can be assigned its own login credentials, this is not too difficult a task.

Another design option is using a product that proxies the application from the WLAN client through a home agent. The home agent would be just like the server in the first example that is running a terminal server software package. In this case, the client would launch its own application, but the traffic that application sends would traverse through the home agent device.

The WLAN client would have an application running on it that facilitates this process and also performs authentication and encryption to the home agent. In some respects, it operates like a dynamic VPN tunnel to the home agent. The application running on the WLAN client can have an embedded unique identity that allows that home agent to discern which session to establish for which WLAN client.

Techniques like this are commonly used in metropolitan WLAN designs. They can also be used in situations where the connection medium might change from WLAN to a cellular connection depending on where they are physically. This is sometimes called a form of *mobile IP*. Mobile IP is used to refer to other technologies, but this is a form of it.

Real-Time Applications: Voice and Video

Some of the fastest-growing application types to be run on WLANs are the real-time applications of voice and video. Voice applications in the enterprise have traditionally been used over *application-specific devices (ASDs)* like the ones mentioned in Chapter 2, "Designing for Client Devices and Applications." As a reminder, ASDs are devices specifically built for a particular application. Now, smart phones and personal computing devices are starting to run software agents that can place calls using a compatible device with a built-in Wi-Fi radio. Even laptops are being used to run a soft-phone application that traveling users in particular can use anywhere they go. International travelers are making heavy use of this technology because even a single business trip abroad can result in many hundreds of dollars in phone calls and data connection fees using traditional mobile phones, such as with the application shown in Figure 3.1. The software application will allow a user to use a Wi-Fi network to place calls, thereby eliminating telephone toll charges.

FIGURE 3.1   Cisco Mobile Communicator

Voice is a subset of video from a technical point of view. While we think of video as just moving images, the human mind intrinsically expects audio to accompany video. After all, you don't watch TV with the sound off. Or, better yet, you wouldn't have a videoconferencing session with somebody else without an audio stream. If anything, it would be the opposite. So, technically speaking, there are at least two media streams for any given real-time video session: one for audio and one for video. Humans are intrinsically auditory, and sound is an essential part of video communication.

For clarity's sake, when we are referring to real-time video over Wi-Fi, we are implying that it is a videoconferencing session. There are significant differences between this and a one-way, real-time video and audio stream for security surveillance or broadcasting purposes. In one-way transmissions, we do not suffer from the same scrutiny of round-trip delays. If a one-way broadcast stream is received, even a multisecond delay would not be an issue in the vast majority of cases. However, if you are having a videoconferencing session and you have to wait several seconds before you hear the other side respond to you, that delay is not generally considered to be acceptable.

In prerecorded broadcast voice and video transmissions, the application handling the communication can buffer the traffic. In other words, the transmission isn't a communication session and doesn't require a real-time reaction from a participant on the other end. This is much like watching videos over a network. You are not communicating in real time with a party at the other end; you are simply viewing the audio and/or video stream. Buffering creates an initial time delay in the arrival of the start of the media stream. In return, it takes away the irregular breaks in speech or dropped video frames when network traffic conditions can't keep pace with regular traffic delivery. Essentially, what the application is doing is like building a little savings account. When the media stream doesn't arrive when expected, it can still deliver an uninterrupted audio and video stream as long as the application can keep the buffer from becoming empty. If traffic conditions become bad enough so the deposit rate into the buffer can't keep pace with the withdrawal rate from the buffer, then a disruption would certainly occur at some point. Therefore, this is much like a real-life savings account, comparing continual withdrawals to regular paycheck deposits. If the withdrawal rate keeps steady, but the deposits stop arriving, there will be no more funds to consume.

So, from a design perspective, let's exclude non-live, one-way, and non-interactive streaming of voice and video traffic from our design discussion. What we really need to be concerned with are the real-time, bidirectional voice and video streams.

Vendor-Neutral Voice Design Guidelines

Every vendor has unique guidelines for designing voice applications. This is true not only for vendors of voice handsets or software applications, but also for infrastructure vendors. You can reference a number of vendor documents on this topic for implementing a specific voice technology on a specific infrastructure product. However, what do you do if the customer you are designing a WLAN for hasn't chosen a vendor yet? This is a tricky subject, particularly since this might even mean that they haven't chosen an infrastructure vendor as well as a voice vendor. Worse yet, perhaps there may be multiple voice vendors that the wireless infrastructure will be required to support.

As this situation of not knowing exactly what manufacturer's product will be deployed is becoming increasingly common, creating neutral voice design guidelines is growing in importance. It frankly doesn't matter what voice technology you will deploy when initially designing a WLAN infrastructure, assuming you follow a series of rules that will be discussed in this chapter. Arguably, designing for voice vendor neutrality is more important than designing for a particular one because the voice product choices may evolve over time.

That said, you should note that all the major vendors generally agree on certain design criteria. Because there aren't too many WLAN chipset vendors, you typically find that competitors may often use the same WLAN chipset. When that happens, differences primarily lie in antenna design, use-case restrictions, and application protocol differences.

Where voice vendors may differ is with respect to the nerd knobs on various infrastructure products. For example, some may prefer WMM to be disabled, whereas others may want it supported or even required. QoS and multicast handling behavior are other issues that may differ with various equipment manufacturers' products. Regardless, these have nothing to do with Layer 1 and how your RF survey and design practices change. Sure, some may differ by +/−2 dB, but we aren't completely convinced that this difference is based on empirical data or just serves as an additional fudge factor for designers to shoot for based on how the product is used.

After all, having slightly more coverage is less of a problem than having slightly or drastically less. WLAN design is indeed like Goldilocks: my WLAN is too hot, my WLAN is too cold. Too much same-channel overlap in coverage will create too much contention. Too little RF coverage will result in RF dead spots and an inability to connect. But if RF coverage has just enough coverage for devices to have a smooth transition, Goldilocks would say it is "just right."

For those of you who might already be familiar with some manufacturer design guidelines, let's forget for a minute about what you might have been told or what you've read regarding WLAN design practices. Sure, some of you are already thinking you know exactly what RSSI metric or SNR value your design target at cell edges should be, but we're asking you to forget about all that for a moment so you can explore how many vendors have generally come to the same value. What's more, let's also explore how this value can be misleading and you wouldn't want to use it in all cases.

Remember, vendors have to provide general design guidelines that apply in as many situations as possible. When those break down in specific cases, vendors will generally provide additional guidance on the topic. These topics should at a minimum include:

- PHY rate link budget
- Rate shift boundaries
- Roaming characteristics and target RF metrics
- Cell edges and transition zones

Understanding the PHY Rate Link Budget

In Chapter 2, we explored the reasons why WLAN radios perform rate shifting as they are further away from their RF peer. Knowing the factors involved with rate shifting is critical to understanding the primary factors governing enterprise WLAN designs. Essentially, as the signal strength gets weaker, the less fidelity can be deciphered from the received signal. Therefore, the radios shift their PHY rate to a less intense modulation or maybe the coding rate decreases. This usually does the trick for the other end to decode the transmitted message at the other end of the RF link.

That section in Chapter 2 also explored the time factor differences involved in WLAN transmissions at different PHY rates. While VoWiFi traffic isn't very bandwidth intensive, it requires reliable transmission and reception of each end of the voice communication. Even a small amount of data can result in a lot of airtime usage as PHY rates degrade to lower levels. As other conversations and traffic might be present, the longer transmissions involved in the lower PHY rates create RF contention. Furthermore, RF *contention* means that devices need to wait until the WM becomes available before they can transmit. When waiting is incurred, *jitter* starts to enter into the communication link, resulting in unfavorable voice quality or voice delays.

It doesn't always mean that contention is playing a role. What is important to know is that when devices perform rate shifting, it is usually because some of their transmissions aren't being properly heard. For example, when the AP can't decode 802.11 received frames without error from a VoWiFi device, the 802.11 protocol states that the receiver should not send an ACK frame even if it could tell if the traffic was destined for itself. Also per the standard, when the transmitter didn't get an ACK frame, it implies that the transmission wasn't heard by the receiver of the message (unless a block ACK policy is negotiated, but we will defer that discussion for now). What's more, when a WLAN device is required to send a retransmission, it must perform a random backoff before it tries to gain access to the medium again. The methodology for that policy is out of scope of this topic, but as more retransmissions start to occur, the backoff timer keeps doubling. As more consecutive retransmissions occur, the longer the backoff timer value becomes, which can result in substantial delays from a voice quality perspective.

 For more information on RF contention and backoff operations, please refer to Chapter 10, "MAC Layer Design."

We're sure you can see that as this process continues, more jitter occurs in the communication link. Keep in mind that this may only occur in one direction of traffic. In other words, if you had an imbalance in the RF link budget or one end was experiencing more interference, it might only affect the received traffic or it might affect the *clear channel assessment (CCA)* method for the transmitted traffic.

Now let's walk through this process a bit more slowly to grasp what is happening at the 802.11 frame level with respect to time:

1. Assume the connection begins at the highest level of quality using 802.11g and the PHY rate is operating at 54 Mbps.

2. The mobile device starts to walk away from the AP, and as it is sending all of its traffic, the signal gets weaker and weaker.

3. As the signal reaches a certain point, eventually the 54 Mbps PHY transmissions will not be decipherable by one or both ends of the communication link. When that occurs, no ACK is sent, and perhaps the device simply tries again at 54 Mbps. The client will perform this for a device-specific number of retries.

4. While all rate shifting algorithms are different and are considered the "secret sauce" of each vendor, let's assume that the device tries up to two additional times at 54 Mbps, which can be regularly observed by several devices. Remember, time is still ticking and nothing has come through to the other end of the link.

5. Now, the device sends a 48 Mbps frame and still doesn't get an ACK.

6. The device then changes to 36 Mbps, and then it finally gets an ACK. Likely both sides then rapidly flush their buffered frames that have been continually recorded as you have been talking.

At 54 Mbps going down to 36 Mbps in this fashion, depending on the voice products, the delay may not even have been perceptible. The timing of these events is measured in hundreds of microseconds. In fact, the application layer of the transmitter device may not even know that the device had to retransmit one or more times until communication finally recommenced.

Once the RF conditions stabilize even at a lower PHY rate, voice quality will start to improve again. As long as the WM isn't overloaded, there should be plenty of available transmit opportunities, even at middle- and lower-level PHY rates, to sustain a normal conversation where users may not notice any degradation of quality.

The WLAN driver and 802.11 state machine do a lot at Layer 2 without being asked to or needing to tell anyone what has happened. It is like a super diligent employee, exhausting all of its available resources before coming to management to indicate that a problem has occurred and assistance may be required.

However, when too much of this happens, usually voice-quality degradation will occur. As PHY rates continue to drop, the time to transmit the 802.11 frame becomes longer. And, as the 802.11 frame is retransmitted multiple times, it has a combined result of greater jitter delay and even packet loss.

Determining Rate Shift Boundaries

Now that you understand link budgets, let's consider how RF signals affect the actual PHY rates that clients use. Fluctuations in PHY rates in a downward (slower) direction is nearly always the result of frame retransmissions. In the case of highly mobile devices, signal-to-noise ratio (SNR) values are constantly in flux due to these changing RF conditions.

Voice devices do share some things in common. Generally speaking, with modern voice devices, transmit power can be assumed to be 25mW. Yes, some voice devices are advertised to do more, but from a vendor-neutral design perspective, it gives you an adequate value to use for your design without requiring peak transmit power from some voice devices. Remember, we are looking for battery savings as well, and the lower we keep transmit power, the better the battery performance.

With that assumption, let's take into account the knowledge you gained from Chapter 2 regarding radio characteristics. Since we assume that voice clients transmit at a maximum of 25mW, the AP transmit power should be reciprocal. We've just determined the maximum AP transmit power for the survey. If you will be using an automated RF management mechanism, you can even back off this transmit power by an additional 3 dB (and, therefore, use 12.5 mW of AP transmit power) to give yourself a little headroom and still stay within your link budget if it is ever warranted.

If you refer to a spec sheet for an AP, you should see specific receive RSSI values in dBm indicating where the radio will need to change to a different PHY rate. You will learn techniques in Chapter 9, "Site Survey RF Design," to perform this task, but if you were to mark a map where these dBm values are by taking actual measurements, this would indicate the locations where rate shift boundaries should occur. Perform this for the 54 to 48 Mbps threshold all the way down to the 36 to 24 Mbps threshold.

At this point, we've determined an optimal AP transmit power based on general characteristics of VoWiFi client devices. Using that transmit power, we marked on a map using a client device the RSSI values where 54 Mbps will transition to 48 Mbps and where 48 Mbps will transition into 36 Mbps, and so on.

Now, let's consider a client adapter to perform these measurements. One adapter that many WLAN RF site survey professionals have used over the years is the Cisco

AIR-CB21AG adapter. This is largely due to its popularity as well as its support for many of the RF survey software and analysis tools. It is an Atheros-based Cardbus (PC Card) adapter, and Cisco also provides a great spec sheet, as shown in Figure 3.2.

FIGURE 3.2   Cisco CB21AG receive sensitivity

Receive Sensitivity 802.11b/g (typical)	• −94 dBm @ 1 Mbps • −93 dBm @ 2 Mbps • −92 dBm @ 5.5 Mbps • −86 dBm @ 6 Mbps • −86 dBm @ 9 Mbps • −90 dBm @ 11 Mbps • −86 dBm @ 12 Mbps • −86 dBm @ 18 Mbps • −84 dBm @ 24 Mbps • −80 dBm @ 36 Mbps • −75 dBm @ 48 Mbps • −71 dBm @ 54 Mbps

What is nice about this adapter is the ability to control the transmit power. If you configure this adapter for 25 mW, just as a general voice device is assumed to be, you can start to perform some measurements. It is important to note that other client adapters could suffice here as well, but you do not want to use one that is markedly better than any of the voice devices that might be under consideration. For example, an 802.11n adapter usually is not the best choice in this type of measurement.

Referring to the section of the table for receive sensitivity, as shown in Figure 3.2 for 802.11g, we see that −71 dBm and better will support an 802.11g PHY rate of 54 Mbps and that −75 dBm and better will support a PHY rate of 48 Mbps. Therefore, around these signal levels you would expect to see PHY rates fluctuate. However, keep in mind that these values were determined in an RF interference–free area such as in an anechoic chamber. That means that the noise floor and other interference conditions at the time would likely be at an ideal value and not necessarily reflective of real-world conditions that you might have in your target WLAN environment.

What that essentially means is that at −71 dBm you might not be able to communicate at the 54 Mbps PHY rate. Ambient RF transmissions at a distance will collectively assemble to look like an elevated noise floor to a WLAN radio, and, therefore, the SNR of −71 dBm in the anechoic chamber will be higher than it would be at −71 dBm in your operating environment.

More details related to this topic are covered in Chapter 7, "RF Hardware and 802.11n."

Another important consideration must be made: directionality. The adapter used in this example doesn't have a perfect isotropic sphere. In fact, this adapter is somewhat directional, especially when it is placed into the side of a laptop. So, −71 dBm at the optimal beamwidth of its antenna will read differently when standing in the same physical location, but just facing the adapter in a different direction. In other words, when the adapter (in the laptop) is oriented at one angle to the AP, it will perform differently than it will at another angle, say, when you face the other way.

You may think that there's a lot to consider here. You're right. This is why equipment manufacturers don't explain the process to this level, because you don't want to perform science experiments every time you do an RF site survey design.

Knowing When Devices Roam

We have just learned why client devices shift PHY rates in different RF conditions. Knowing when client devices will roam is important to understanding how you should design your areas of signal overlap, or areas referred to as AP transition zones.

Vendors design their roaming algorithms around chipset characteristics and antenna performance. Some use an SNR value while others use a raw RSSI value irrespective of noise floor.

When a device vendor provides a design recommendation as to what the infrastructure RF cell edges need to be based on, this is certainly a clue where their roaming algorithm is likely to kick off. Assume it is below that value because a device doesn't want to start looking where to roam once it is at a place where retransmissions are expected to occur. The roaming process can take some time to complete, and the device even needs to probe off its currently associated channel (active scanning).

Some of you reading this book might already have seen a value of −67 dBm promoted by several VoWiFi vendors. Assuming an elevated noise floor from the perspective of the client adapter, a design target of −67 dBm ups the ante of our low −70-ish dBm number (depending on the chipset) to a higher value where rate shifting is likely to occur at 54 Mbps in the 802.11g PHY. That likely brings the value more aggressively higher than the −67 dBm number, to perhaps even something in the mid −60s.

Keep in mind that your goal shouldn't be to sustain 54 Mbps everywhere. That's just not feasible, and if you were to design for data rates that high, co-channel interference would kill your performance anyway in a large WLAN deployment. Remember, you want to design your RF porridge to the Goldilocks metaphor—not too hot, not too cold.

A good general design goal in your final deployment is to have your 802.11g VoWiFi phones operating at or better than 24 Mbps on a consistent basis, which includes at the RF cell edges during their roam. A simple RF frame capture utility can validate this for you.

Keeping PHY rates above 24 Mbps will limit the extent of the rate shifting and, therefore, the backoff timer events. At the same time, it will hold up high PHY rates where the WM airtime is still being used most effectively. An efficiently used WM means that devices are operating at high PHY rates, getting on and off the WM in the shortest amount of time possible, which in turn yields support for a higher quantity of VoWiFi clients.

Real World Scenario

Observing Roam Times and Behavior

When using a single WLAN radio with a WLAN analyzer to perform analysis, you cannot properly test client roaming behaviors. When associated clients look to roam to another AP, they will change channels temporarily and send probe requests looking for more APs servicing the same SSID the client is currently on.

Monitoring a single channel will not pick up any off-channel activity that the client is doing. Furthermore, there is no clear indication on the client's associated channel that the client is about to go off channel for any particular reason. There are clues but nothing definitive. Therefore, using a single WLAN radio to capture a roaming client can't be done in a way where you would still catch all the frames.

As of this writing, only a few options are available to simultaneously capture multiple channels while also using the same laptop. Here's the list:

- AirPcap adapters from CACE Technologies using Wireshark

- Linksys USB 802.11n adapters with WildPackets OmniPeek

- Several adapter options from AirMagnet Wi-Fi Analyzer from Fluke Networks

By the time this book is published, more options may exist.

Using a multichannel capture utility is highly recommended to perform analysis of voice and video clients in particular.

−67 dBm Isn't Always −67 dBm

When taking measurements during this design exercise, consider for a moment that you are using an embedded WLAN client adapter using a particular make and model of a laptop that reports an RSSI of −67 dBm. You then place another laptop in that same location, with a different client adapter, and you receive a different value. You then insert a PC Card into the laptop, and it reports yet another value. Which is right?

Measurements in dBm are absolute values and not relative, unlike measurements in dB. However, why did one client adapter see the RF environment differently? Antenna gain, orientation, multipath distortion, receive sensitivity, receive gain using MRC (Maximal Ratio Combining) if the adapter is 802.11n, and other issues are likely the factors to blame.

The reported value you should use for surveys should be the one that is equal or as close to the *worst* WLAN RF performer that the network will support. Therefore, if that adapter is chosen to perform the RF site surveys, then your bases should be covered.

We intentionally did not discuss QoS features in this section on voice design. Please refer to Chapter 10 to learn QoS design considerations for voice and video applications.

Vendor-Neutral Video Design Guidelines

We are still quite early in video's adoption of WLANs. There aren't any vendor guidelines that we know of at this time to reference and very little work has been done in this area for enterprise WLANs. We will, however, tackle this subject and provide some early guidance for designing for this technology. Although as of this writing there aren't any popular, vendor-neutral guidelines for WLAN video design best practices, video is still rather new to be used on 802.11 WLANs. What is important for you to consider is what is different about video than, say, voice designs.

As we discussed earlier in this chapter, real-time video also includes voice. So, video includes both a media stream for audio and a media stream for video. In fact, there are up to two other streams for call setup and teardown (call signaling) as well as a data exchange stream for sending documents and screen sharing between users or any other type of data that needs to be exchanged during the communication session. Our focus will be on the audio and video streams for the sake of this discussion.

For a moment, recall your experiences watching online video streams. Have you ever seen an online video in which the video was choppy but the audio was still intact? Have you ever seen the reverse, where the video is intact but the audio is choppy and you can't quite make out what was being said?

Video, unless you are performing a real-time, remote medical surgery, likely takes a back seat to audio. In other words, video has a higher loss tolerance than audio in the vast majority of cases. This is due to the fact that more information is conveyed during a typical communication by audio than by video. Choppy audio during a videoconference would likely be highly disruptive, causing participants to ask the speaker to repeat him- or herself. If a few video frames are dropped but the audio is clear, that would likely result in no loss of meaning.

Because video and audio are separate streams, we have the opportunity to handle them differently. This includes how they are queued, transmitted, and marked. Remembering this is important because you need to understand the differences in the network traffic characteristics and how they affect your design.

The first unique characteristic related to video traffic is the data length of each network frame. Video frames are very large—about as large as can be allowed without violating maximum transmission unit (MTU) sizes. In contrast, audio frames are usually only a few hundred bytes, including all overhead. Also keep in mind that even though 802.11 frames prior to 802.11 can be upward of 2,436 bytes, we are 99 times out of 100 traversing a wired Ethernet network when communicating between endpoints. 802.11n frames can even be larger. Therefore, the MTU size for 802.11 transmissions decreases to usually around 1,600 bytes or slightly less in most Ethernet networks.

This is why you will see frame sizes around 1,600 bytes when looking at video traffic on an 802.11 network. If you are configuring your own video endpoint device to operate over a WLAN, you will likely need to trim down the frame size to the MTU size your organization has already adopted.

You are then relying on the application to fragment payloads higher than this value (inclusive of overhead) before placing onto the WM. It is possible you may experience 802.11 fragment bursting. No video clients that we are aware of currently make use of these more recent and advanced 802.11 mechanisms. 802.11n A-MPDU or A-MSDU frame aggregation features are not likely to be as beneficial as you might think. Network transmissions occur in regularly spaced intervals, and we want each single network transmission to arrive at its destination well before the next transmission is ready to be sent. This is what provides a seamless video experience. Frame aggregation in this case will only affect very large frame sizes where individually fragmented frames can be packaged up into very short fragment bursts. However, as higher definition video transmissions become increasingly common, each network frame transmission will be greater, which will result in higher payloads where frame aggregation can provide some benefit.

We will now explore what affects video quality and identify some important information to take with you on your next WLAN that requires video.

Understanding the Effects of Video Quality

To understand how to design for video, you need to be familiar with the areas that affect the quality of video and areas that are uniquely specific to WLANs. Regardless of the equipment vendor, video endpoint devices implement a variety of controls, such as the following:

Video Window Size (Width and Height)   This refers to the number of pixels that a video window uses, typically represented in width and height values.

Frames per Second (fps)   This value is not to be confused with 802.11 frames; we're talking about video frames in terms of how many pictures per second make up the end user viewing experience.

Bit Rate   This value typically tries to cap bit rate to a certain value that can affect compression and fps.

Codec   We will be discussing codecs later; for now, know that a codec is the coding and decoding algorithm used to transmit video (and audio) traffic over a network medium.

These values will allow you to fine-tune the video session in order to conform to your bandwidth and perhaps even CPU constraints.

Changing to higher values can exponentially increase the amount of workload the 802.11 network will experience. If you are running 802.11n without protection mechanisms (because you are supporting legacy clients), you may be able to realize near broadcast quality video assuming everything else is designed appropriately.

When more workload is required in order to transmit the data, the more 802.11 frames you will see per second. This usually includes more fragmentation and might even occupy the medium in longer durations.

Fragmented 802.11 frames are allowed a much higher priority on the 802.11 medium before other data traffic can commence. When this is the case, other clients need to hold off their transmissions.

In turn, if the current PHY rate of those transmitted frames is low, you can expect some potentially serious impact to other clients. Therefore, it is critical when implementing video that you have highly optimized 802.11 clients and infrastructure.

Simply put, the video industry isn't there yet. Video companies specialize in video and not WLAN technology and likely only have the bare minimum expertise in 802.11 as necessary. Use cases for video of Wi-Fi are just starting to take hold, and many of the largest companies are probably just beginning to ramp up their expertise in WLANs.

Video appliances from companies like Polycom and Tandberg (recently acquired by Cisco) are purposely built hardware appliances that simply aren't designed to be mobile. Making them mobile at this point requires a bit of an engineering exercise in order to optimize them for 802.11. Based on what is on the market as of this writing, the fix isn't as easy as placing a $100-ish 802.11 client bridge device. Client bridges have tended to be a very small majority of overall device sales and something that customers do not want to spend much money on. Those two facts combine to minimize the focus a client bridge product is going to garner within a manufacturer's committed roadmap.

One option is to take a higher-end AP device that has the ability to operate in client bridge mode (while also supporting advanced 802.11 features such as QoS) and also exhibit good roaming performance. This should allow you to provide an interim solution in the short term while video manufacturers ramp up their 802.11 expertise and product offerings in the years to come.

Video Design Takeaways

From a vendor-neutral perspective, designing for video over Wi-Fi isn't that much different than designing for voice. That said, it does place additional requirements onto the same set of design logic that voice uses. Although this process is harder than designing for voice, the same principles apply; you need optimized RF cell edges, good-quality roaming algorithms, and the ability to keep PHY rates high.

Assuming that the video clients will operate in a voice-optimized network, the next best payoff when designing for video is to focus on the WLAN radio the video endpoints will use. That means focusing on the antenna types and placement, radio technology, MAC feature support, QoS, and other similar factors.

We will cover this topic in the "Codecs and Protocols" section in a bit, but for now a great deal of attention needs to be placed on the codec being used, such as the ones designed to be used over packetized networks.

Retransmissions are a performance killer. If you are experiencing retransmissions of 802.11 frames, you need to determine the root cause and seek to eliminate it.

Using 802.11n will certainly help. The best recommendation is to use 802.11n at least on the client side of your video endpoint even if your infrastructure currently doesn't support it. That way, when you are ready to roll out 802.11n, you only have to optimize your client settings—the MIMO radio benefits of the 802.11n client will already be there.

Real-Time Applications: Most Stringent Design Criteria

As you have read, designing for real-time applications over 802.11 isn't child's play. At the very least, it should make you appreciate the value and importance of a well-done RF site survey if you don't already have that appreciation.

If there are any deficiencies in the RF infrastructure (AP) design such as poor RF signal strength, these applications all suffer the consequences. In our previous discussions, we have assumed that clients have the ability to roam to an AP when they need to do so. That is a really big assumption.

Knowing *why* you need to support this design criterion is the first step. The next step is for you to make this happen.

Not all designs require this functionality today. As you learned in Chapter 2, you must analyze your customer and assess not only their needs today but what you think they'll need within the next three or more years. If you see there is business value based on your experiences, you can guide the customer appropriately. In two years they will not remember saying "no" when you asked them, "Do you want to support voice?" When the time comes, the customer will try to deploy voice anyway, and when they have performance problems, you will likely receive some or all of the blame. Yes, producing documented deliverables stating design objectives and exclusions will protect you financially and legally, but customers often have convenient memories.

The best recommendation we can give you is to design for real-time applications today. Some customers do not want to and that's fine, but the best recommendation we can give you is to educate the customer and guide them accordingly. It is your responsibility to explain the pros and cons of data only wireless networks and how this may affect future business needs.

Redundancy and High Availability

As we rely on WLANs for critical functions such as voice and video communications, we must pay careful attention to redundancy and high availability.

In Chapter 13, "Documentation and Finalizing the Design Solution," we will discuss these factors in greater detail, so for now we'll simply touch on a few areas that highlight the importance for real-time applications.

RF high availability is hard (and expensive) to achieve. Some vendors offer failover type of support, which requires deploying a secondary AP at each location. This secondary AP is always performing a heartbeat check with the primary AP, much like the Hot Standby Router Protocol (HSRP) or Virtual Router Redundancy Protocol (VRRP) does in IP routing networks. This obviously substantially adds to the cost and complexity of a deployment.

All in all, APs fail infrequently for indoor environments. Outdoor locations are another animal. Outdoor conditions, especially in some parts of the world, can be rather harsh. Even some indoor industrial environments can be hard on equipment. Highly intensive indoor environments like stock trading floors and hospital operating rooms might be candidates for a more complex and expensive approach as life and high dollars are at stake.

Another consideration is how these devices are powered. If a Power-Over-Ethernet (PoE) switch were to fail, it can mean an outage for quite a large area. One design method that can be used is to stagger adjacent APs onto two different PoE switches so if one switch fails, at least half of the APs will still be online and cover the same physical area. The coverage will be spotty, but it is far better than a complete service outage.

Codecs and Protocols

The more complex the compression and *codec* that is used on a real-time media stream, the higher the computation requirements. Whenever computation is involved, you are increasing the time to process the information. From a design perspective, you must be sensitive to processing delays incurred from more complex codecs used with real-time applications. This will be less and less of a concern as technology progresses where faster and faster CPUs are common. Nonetheless, the number of workload devices needed to perform is constant because audio and video streams are constant. In most use cases, each device is not only decoding the information it is receiving, but also encoding its audio and/or video sources.

Bigger CPUs have traditionally been accompanied by greater energy requirements—something that is undesirable for battery-driven mobile devices. Faster CPUs also bring with them more costs that are added to the final end product.

Understanding Common Audio Protocols

Many real-time applications have opted to use less computationally complex and, therefore, higher bandwidth codecs. One example of this is G.711, which is an International Telecommunication Union-Telecommunication Standardization Sector (ITU-T) standards-based Pulse Code Modulation (PCM) audio codec. G.711 more or less transmits data in a raw, uncompressed fashion, carrying with it very low latency and optimal voice quality. Each direction of a G.711 audio stream takes up 64 kbps of payload (160 bytes per segment), which when you add segment, packet, frame headers, and other overhead (802.11 ACKs and encryption), it increases the workload to approximately 215 kbps for each wireless phone attached to the AP. This includes a two-way voice stream in each direction. If you were having a conversation from one VoWiFi phone to another on the same RF cell or channel, you would double that number to 430 kbps.

When making field measurements from wireless packet captures and analysis tools, you may notice greater bandwidth is consumed. Actual wireless bandwidth consumed will vary. It is dependent on several factors such as RF conditions, roaming protocols, 802.11 retransmissions, and other application protocol overhead.

G.711 is the most common protocol you will encounter in VoWiFi implementations and even video systems. Because different types of VoIP handsets, desksets, and voice gateways have to support each codec for each type of make, model, and firmware you intend to use in your design, the lowest common denominator tends to be chosen. However, more modern VoIP systems will negotiate the codec at the time of call setup, depending on the capabilities of the peer. Keep in mind that if you transfer a call in progress, that may mean a new codec has to be negotiated or the call may be dropped.

Another protocol that has gained a lot of attention but usually only exists in single or limited vendor implementations is G.729. G.729 drops the bit rate requirement from 64 kbps with G.711 to 8 kbps. Some voice quality is lost in the process, but not as much as other protocols with similar bandwidth benefits. The problem with G.729 is that the encoding device requires high CPU speeds to perform the calculations to gain the bandwidth benefits.

Because wireless bandwidth is large enough to support multiple G.711 streams, especially at high PHY rates, the payoff for using G.729 is not as great as it would be if you were trying to send this data over a T1 Internet connection between offices. Table 3.1 shows several of the more popular audio codecs and how each translates to the 802.11 workload.

TABLE 3.1   Audio Codecs and Properties

Format	Description	MOS	Payload (B)	PPS	Payload b/w (kbps)	Wireless b/w (kbps) *	Two Phones (kbps) **
G.711	Pulse Code Modulation (PCM)	4.1	160	50	64	214.4	428.8
G.722	7 kHz coding at 64 kbps	4.13	160	50	64	214.4	428.8
G.726	Adaptive Differential PCM	3.85	80	50	32	150.4	300.8
G.729	Speech coding @ 8 kbps	3.92	20	50	8	102.4	204.8

* Assumes TKIP encryption (20 Bytes)
** Wireless medium bandwidth consumed from a voice conversation between two wireless voice devices (eg., VoWiFi phones)

Understanding Voice and Video Codecs

You can expect more and more codecs to be used for different applications. For voice communications, a narrowband codec is sufficient because human speech operates in only a small section of the sound spectrum. Wider band codecs are starting to be incorporated into telepresence types of video and audio conferencing, especially where a wider sound spectrum will need to be encoded. Telepresence is a term used when attempting to create as real of an in-person experience as possible. Using a wider sound codec (and higher definition video) ultimately means higher wireless workload. For example, protocols like G.719 scale up to 128 kbps.

As for video codecs, the industry has mostly adopted the MPEG standard of compression codecs: MPEG-2 and MPEG-4. MPEG-2 has been the most popular codec to be implemented among these systems and is the current standard for DVDs and digital television as of this writing. MPEG-4 is gaining popularity for several factors.

First, MPEG-2 has no inherent capabilities to synchronize the audio with the video stream, which is why you often see audio getting out of sync with video especially over a longer viewing period. MPEG-2 quality is technically capable of impeccable quality, but is not designed for network or streaming applications. Therefore, what we see when we're watching MPEG-2 delivered over a network connection is often quite poor. On the other hand, MPEG-4 was designed for network-based delivery, and you will often see that the quality is much higher and is the first MPEG protocol that truly enables videoconferencing capabilities.

Second, MPEG-2 requires much higher network bandwidth than MPEG-4. Less network bandwidth also translates to smaller file sizes, thus reducing disk space requirements for storage. MPEG-4 achieves this by eliminating redundant information from the data by comparing more video frames at one time than does MPEG-2.

Using Multicast

One of the least viable means of communicating over 802.11 is with multicast because of reliability problems. When using multicast with 802.11, it is never known if the frames have been received by the destination device.

To give an example, let's consider an AP that received a multicast frame that had to send it to several of its current associated devices. Upon receiving this frame, it simply broadcasts it out to all of its associated stations in a single event. Comparing that to normal unicast communication we typically encounter, each transmitted frame requires an acknowledgment by the receiving device that it received the frame. If no ACK is received, then the frame is transmitted.

The benefit of multicast is to be able to reach a large audience of devices with the highest network efficiency possible. However, the way the 802.11 multicast standard is written today, we can't have both. From an 802.11 perspective, multicast isn't any different from broadcast frames.

There are potential drawbacks with multicast when multicast traffic needs to be received by clients using some form of power save. Power saving–enabled clients will have to wait until the next Delivery Traffic Indication Message (DTIM) in order to receive the frames. When multicast is enabled, DTIM values are usually set to the lowest possible value of 1.

Video is starting to seriously take hold in the WLAN industry. Multicast has huge benefits to a half-duplex medium, which all 802.11 operates within the bounds of today. However, if we have poor reliability with multicast message reception, the end user experience will be poor, resulting in unhappy users.

Given this fact, some vendors are starting to do some creative things with multicast. Here are some examples:

IGMP Snooping Multicast Let's assume an AP has three associated stations currently operating at PHYs of 54 Mbps, 24 Mbps, and 11 Mbps, respectively. Remember, PHY rates are dynamic based on signal strength, capabilities, and other factors. So, let's assume the PHY rates of these stations are not based on client capabilities; instead, RF conditions have dictated these PHY rates.

Before proceeding, we are assuming that each of the three associated clients need to receive the multicast stream. The AP can determine the clients who need to receive the multicast stream if the AP were to watch Internet Group Management Protocol (IGMP) join requests from its associated stations. An IGMP join request is used by stations wishing to join a specific multicast group. Furthermore, if the AP has no associated stations that are joined to that multicast group, it would be optimal to not transmit any portion of the multicast stream.

Now, consider a multicast frame that has to be received by each of these stations. In a normal 802.11 standards-based fashion, the AP would usually just send out a single multicast frame at the lowest basic rate, which is typically a default of 1 Mbps. Some operators have tuned this value based on their RF design, but it is rarely more than 11 Mbps.

This is generally the first method that equipment vendors employ to limit the amount of multicast traffic from being transmitted by every AP. This way, only the APs that have associated clients who want to receive the stream transmit the traffic.

Converting Multicast to Unicast   Another option being implemented by some enterprise vendors is to convert the multicast to unicast frames at the AP. Turning the traffic stream into unicast would dictate that, in this example, three unicast frames would need to be delivered: one to each associated station.

Having now converted the multicast frame to unicast, we now have two primary benefits. The first is reliability. Each frame can then follow normal unicast transmission conventions, which would include retransmissions if the client didn't hear it properly the first time. The implication of this feature would mean that the end user experience should be much better because far less frame loss occurs.

The second benefit could be transmission speeds. Using the word *could* is an operative word in this case. Changing from a single frame transmission to three certainly isn't more efficient, and it also requires frame acknowledgments after it is sent. Well, if you transmitted a 54, 24, and 11 Mbps frame to each associated station instead of a single 1 Mbps multicast frame, it should be more efficient on the wireless medium.

Suppose the 11 Mbps client moved closer to the AP and signal strength improved. The PHY rate of that client would change from 11 Mbps to upward of 54 Mbps, thereby allowing the multicast frame to be transmitted to that station with greater spectral efficiency.

Multicast to PHY Optimized Multicast   If the number of associated stations reaches a certain quantity, the multicast to unicast conversion might result in more overhead. At some threshold, the traffic stream would revert back to multicast. However, another option that equipment vendors are employing is to send the multicast traffic at the lowest common denominator PHY rate. For example, if we use our initial three-client example with 54, 24, and 11 Mbps PHY rates, that would mean the multicast stream would be transmitted at 11 Mbps.

Another consideration regarding multicast is related to QoS. By definition in the 802.11 standard, multicast transmissions are assigned to the lowest QoS traffic category of Best Effort (BE). If a vendor were to employ these types of nonstandard multicast to unicast enhancements, even QoS prioritization could be incorporated into the transmissions.

Location and Context Awareness

Location-based technology has garnered a lot of attention in WLAN designs in the past few years. Most manufacturers tout some sort of location capability with their products. Some have features that are built-in, while some offer integration hooks to third-party vendors who specialize in location technology and have sophisticated software applications related to specific industry verticals.

We have only begun to touch on the incredible offerings that location ability can offer us. Knowing where something or someone is at a given point of time has the opportunity to shape workflow processes and even improve our social interactions. Removing time searching for items or knowing where someone is eliminates waste and inefficiencies in so many ways. We are already seeing applications becoming available to our smart phones that help us return to our parked car, find out where our social network is, track employees to help dispatch the closest person to a specific location, and more.

When you search the Internet, many web browsers use the context of where you are searching from. For example, if the IP address you are connecting from (say, a home broadband connection) is in Walnut Creek, California, and you searched for "movie times," web browsers are using the context of your location to enable better search results. At the same time, the advertisers listing with the search engine you are using might want to target you as an advertisement recipient. The advertiser can enable certain ads based on your geographic location. For example, if a local restaurant wants to advertise to their community, they can place ads with an advertiser that incorporates the use these geo-location features. The point is that many, many location-based applications are beginning to make their way into our lives.

For enterprises with large and multiple facilities, location technology helps staff be much more efficient, while at the same time improving safety in some cases. Let's look at a few examples.

Healthcare is one of the biggest users of location-based technology today. Because there are 24/7 shifts of employees and shared assets, it lends itself to items being moved without knowing where they went. Even in a single-family home without many people, items are constantly being misplaced or stashed away. Multiply that by hundreds or even thousands of assets in larger and larger places with hundreds of staff members and you can see how big this problem is.

Consider a safety example. Infusion pumps that are used in healthcare environments get a lot of attention with location technology. They are some of the highest mobile and sought-after devices in a hospital and also require a certain workflow to follow after they are used. This makes them move from storage, to the patient room, to a dirty room for cleaning staff to pick up, over to one or more sterilization facilities, and back out for use. On top of that, drug libraries need to be updated on these devices from time to time. This requires a specific group of hospital workers to find these devices, take them out of service, and then perform the library update.

Just finding all of the infusion pumps is a daunting task. Even mid-sized healthcare facilities can have hundreds of these pumps. Location technology makes performing preventive maintenance and other tasks like updating the drug libraries a far more simple task. From a safety perspective, a drug library being out of date might mean lost lives. This is a serious consequence.

Location in technology can be called many things. Here's a list of a few:

RFID   RFID is a very general term used for identification using radio frequency technology. RFID is commonly employed in retail environments using passive tags such as clothing labels and stickers on books. Some metropolitan railways are using RFID for tickets in lieu of the ubiquitous magnetic strip technology.

RTLS   RTLS stands for Real-Time Location System, which implies the ability to locate items in real time wherever they may be. This is the most common term in use today when referring to Wi-Fi-based location tracking where 802.11-based active RFID tags are used.

RTAS   RTAS stands for Real-Time Awareness System, which implies more than just location. Awareness implies that contextual information might be learned as well. RTAS is another marketing term for RTLS, implying active RFID tags are being used with a sensor-based feature set.

Context Awareness   Context awareness is a term much like RTAS where additional contextual information might also be learned and leveraged. Our infusion pump analogy from earlier is a great example for how context awareness provides additional information regarding the location of the device, such as whether the device is in use, dirty, available, or broken. How this information might translate into a workflow application could be similar to when nurses need an infusion pump and do a search. When the nurses search, they are likely looking for one they can use immediately. They don't care about the four other ones nearby behind closed doors that are in use. The person involved in collecting and returning the pumps to a central storage facility, however, would want the exact opposite information.

If the mobile device the nurse was carrying was associated with the group "nurse" and the staff member collecting the used pumps was associated with the group "cleaning staff," this could automatically enable their device searches to be even more efficient.

This is simply a high-level introduction. Once location technology and our mobile devices evolve, we will undoubtedly experience a paradigm shift in more ways than we can imagine today.

In the rest of this section, we will discuss the common use cases, how the technology works, what types of approaches different vendors are taking, and different design considerations for Wi-Fi-based location tracking.

Common Use Cases

When trying to learn about a new technology, it is always helpful to understand what business objectives people are trying to solve with it. In this section, we will discuss some of the most popular uses of location tracking technology with respect to WLANs.

In our introduction to location and context awareness technology earlier, outside of a healthcare scenario, we haven't fully discussed all the types of things that can be tracked. Quite simply, this could be anything with an 802.11 radio. Or it may be a specialized RFID tag that is affixed to an asset that perhaps doesn't have one today. People may also wear an RFID tag, or perhaps they are associated with VoWiFi phones instead.

The most common set of use cases for location tracking falls into three areas of benefit: assets, people, and workflow.

Assets

For most enterprises, asset tracking is the first step to realizing a return on their investment in the technology. Asset tracking allows people to find commonly used objects more efficiently, which will maximize staff productivity and reduce costs.

Placing tags on assets can help deter theft and discarded assets that might make their way into storage boxes, such as bunched-up bedding and clothing. Tags can be placed on containers in warehouses where individual items are known to be included.

Not losing assets means that a company maximizes the usage of the ones they *already* have. Businesses end up purchasing more assets or perhaps even leasing them when they can't find what they need, a practice that costs them both time and money.

People

Tags may be worn by staff members, children at amusement parts, hospital patients, prison inmates, and more. Each has its own value proposition, which can reduce costs, improve efficiency, and enhance safety.

 The type of tag that is used in real-time location tracking is not the type of tag used with applications such as paper RFID tags (for inventory management and theft prevention applications) or microchipping, like what is done with dogs and other pets. Those types of tags must be scanned using a specialized reader from close proximity—usually well under 2 meters. In some cases, this may be only several inches. Location tracking in the context of our discussion will center on real-time tracking using a variety of means that utilize a ubiquitous infrastructure technology.

Workflow

Workflow is the process involved in performing a certain set of activities. Workflow processes are based on currently available information and what systems already exist. Newer technologies like location and context awareness are offering new information that can be incorporated into existing workflow processes to optimize steps involved.

Even simply using an 802.11-based computer without a tag can yield some of the same benefits. Here are some examples:

- Using a Wi-Fi handheld device to display information about the museum exhibit you are currently viewing using an available wireless infrastructure to triangulate your location.

- Using an 802.11-based device such as a VoWiFi phone that has a specialized button programmed for certain alerts. An example of this could be a prison staff member who is under duress, and they simply double-click that button. Because it is a VoWiFi phone, the wireless network could know where that staff member was and immediately send an emergency alert to other staff members along with the location, allowing the person being assaulted to have minimal interaction.

- Having employees in a large manufacturing facility use mobile devices to pinpoint their locations for quick on-site availability. This example involves location and contextual information.

- Using RFID tags on vehicles at a rental car facility to automate the tracking of where cars are parked, when they arrive, if they have been cleaned and prepared for service again, and when they leave the premises.

 Real World Scenario

Healthcare Workflow Optimization

In a hospital, if a patient is admitted to the emergency room, a certain series of steps need to be performed by specific staff members. Here's a list of what may occur:

1. The patient might first need to go to Triage and be assessed.

2. Based on that assessment, say the patient is then admitted to a room.

3. A nurse must visit the patient to perform a set of tasks to get information such as patient vital data.

4. Say the patient has to then go to radiology for an X-ray.

5. Once the X-ray is taken and the results are available, a doctor will then need to visit with the patient.

6. Then, at some point the patient will be discharged or admitted.

Each of these milestones can incorporate location tracking technology that can generate timestamps when each event occurred. If a hospital is trying to find ways to improve the patient experience, these timestamps and existing workflow processes can be monitored. If a workflow process is monitored and a part of the process took too long, the application can signal hospital staff to take remediation measures. Management may be interested in this type of data, such as:

- How long did the patient wait to be triaged?

- How much time passed until the patient was seen once admitted to the ER?

- How long did it take for the doctor to see the patient?

- What was the total time the patient spent in the ER?

Answers to these questions can be valuable in helping management make decisions on staffing levels, ensure patient satisfaction, reduce costs, and more.

Hopefully, you see just how important a wireless network can be in many environments. Your job as a designer of wireless networks plays one of the most significant roles in allowing for location-based services.

We will review the technology and different vendor offerings in the Design Approaches by Major Vendors section later in this chapter. We will then describe various design options that you can use to include location-based services in your designs.

How 802.11-Based Location Tracking Works

In simple terms, tracking an 802.11 device, or just about any RF or ultrasound device for that matter, is based on signal strength. As you may have learned from the CWNA curriculum, RF (and sound) follow a propagation model commonly referred to as *free space path loss (FSPL)*. As an RF signal propagates through free space, the signal strength over that distance traveled is highly predictable. The signal degrades using an inverse log curve, otherwise known as the *inverse square law*, as shown in Figure 3.3.

FIGURE 3.3   Inverse log curve

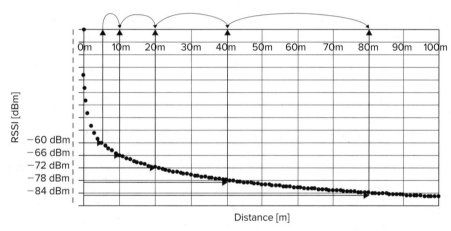

Distance [m]

Courtesy of AeroScout

The closer you are to the transmitter, the higher the change in signal strength. For example, looking at Figure 3.3, when a transmitter is 5 meters from a receiver, it reads a signal strength of −60 dBm. Moving only 5 more meters away, the signal drops to −66 dBm. That is a change of 6 dB within only 5 meters, which would provide incredible location accuracy if that model held up for every 5 meters. Unfortunately, that isn't the case. While still referring to Figure 3.3 and extending this model out to the difference in signal strength between 40 meters and 80 meters away, there is a change of only 6 dB. This example of the inverse square law illustrates the need to have the receivers as close to the transmitters as possible in order to obtain good location accuracy.

Unfortunately, it's not that simple for most environments. In buildings we have walls, shelving, multiple floors, and a variety of other obstructions that affect signal strength. Therefore, a new model began to develop that more closely resembles the real world, which is called *RF fingerprinting.*

RF fingerprinting is a way of mapping x,y locations on a map based on recorded RSSI values. In concept, if you were to record relatively closely spaced measurements throughout an entire map using a single device, the calculations would factor in all the environmental characteristics of a location coverage area. This RSSI fingerprint information is fed into the location calculations, thereby improving the accuracy.

At some point, around −67 dBm, you reach a point where the signal starts to normalize with distance. Visually speaking, in reference to Figure 3.3, this is the signal level where the line starts to flatten out. At that point, this is where you reach diminishing returns, and another receiver should also be able to pick up the transmission in order to keep location accuracy optimized.

Design Approaches by Major Vendors

Different vendors have approached accomplishing real-time location in a variety of ways. Each major vendor in this space has intellectual property and offers a unique value proposition. Some vendors' technologies apply better to certain environments and use cases.

For simple business requirements, all of the vendors covered here will likely work very well. As you start to look at more complicated business cases, some have a clearer advantage in certain environments and for specific use cases.

Not all location technology uses 802.11 or even RF. As a Certified Wireless Design Professional, you should know all the options to present to your customer or stakeholders.

At this point there is no clear, single technology that looks like the Holy Grail of location technology. Some of the best implementations incorporate 802.11-based RF and others use different RF or sound-based technologies.

The following are examples of how some major vendors have accomplished real-time location.

AeroScout

AeroScout was one of the first vendors to offer an 802.11-based location technology. They found a creative way to use the 802.11 protocol in their tag technology to minimize overhead and configuration. Their software application can track regular 802.11 radios as well as their RFID tags into a software interface, MobileView, which may be customized for specific workflow applications. Even passive RFID tags from Reva Systems can be integrated into MobileView.

Because tracking an 802.11 device is dependent on the layout of your APs and isn't inherently accurate down to granular levels of detail, you will find location purely based on the 802.11 radio accurate from a few feet to 10 meters in most designs. One of AeroScout's initial offerings was to include a device called an *exciter.*

Exciters are designed to cover areas like entrances, exits, and shelving locations. They send a 125 kHz signal in a defined area that is configurable in range. When an

AeroScout RFID tag is in range of the exciter, it will then send an 802.11-based tag transmission along with the exciter information, and perhaps other data such as current tag battery level, thereby alerting the location system to the fact it is in immediate range of the specific exciter.

An exciter will not trigger any activity on an 802.11 client. The signal from the exciter uses the 125 kHz wavelength to cause the AeroScout tag to generate an 802.11-based tag transmission.

AeroScout also offers an ultrasound exciter option. Ultrasound is capable of locating devices within a matter of inches. In this case, an 802.11 tag is being located by the Wi-Fi network in a normal fashion in various parts of the coverage area. Then, should that tag enter the range of the ultrasound exciter, the tag will then be tracked anywhere in range of that ultrasound signal down a series of inches.

The use cases of being able to track items down to a series of inches are few and far between. Most of the time, people want to know at least what wing an item is in and as far down as to what room. Where inside the room the item is located is usually a lot less valuable but is still important in some, albeit rare, use cases.

Cisco Location Appliance/MSE   There are two ways of deploying AeroScout's technology. Because Cisco has a large part of the enterprise WLAN market share, AeroScout offers a specific solution designed just for their infrastructure.

Cisco's split-MAC, or controller-based architecture (formerly Airespace), was one of the first technologies to offer a location device. This device was called the 2700 Series Location Appliance. This device collected all of the tag and 802.11 radio information from a series of controllers and performed the detailed location calculations, ultimately providing an x,y location on a specific map or building floor.

The Cisco 2700 Series Location Appliance has been replaced by the 3300 series Mobility Services Engine (MSE). The MSE is capable of tracking a great deal more tags and is also a server platform to place code from partner companies like AeroScout and others. Part of AeroScout's code is placed on the MSE, allowing a better integration with the MobileView platform.

Everyone Else   Because AeroScout tags do not actually associate to the WLAN, AeroScout tags use a specially formatted 802.11 transmission that can be uniquely identified by infrastructure APs. Tags are typically programmed to talk on all of the deployed 802.11 channels in the 2.4 GHz band in a given environment. For example, if the tag needs to transmit, it will do so on channels 1, 6, and 11 if that is how the infrastructure is currently configured.

This allows the maximum amount of APs to hear that tag wherever it may be located. The APs in turn send along this tag transmission to a centralized location server along with the RSSI signal strength of the tag transmission.

In other words, AeroScout has worked with all of the major enterprise manufacturers to detect the AeroScout 802.11 tag transmission and then perform the necessary steps of forwarding that information to an AeroScout location engine or perhaps only the WLAN infrastructure vendor's own location platform.

Awarepoint

Awarepoint is not an 802.11-based location technology. Instead, it uses ZigBee, which incorporates IEEE 802.15.4. IEEE 802.15.4 is a PHY and MAC specification that operates at 2.4 GHz using configurable channels. Awarepoint commonly operates at IEEE 802.15.4 channel 26, which is outside the frequency mask of IEEE 802.11 channel 11 so the two technologies do not interfere, as depicted in Figure 3.4.

FIGURE 3.4   802.11 and 802.15.4 PHY comparison

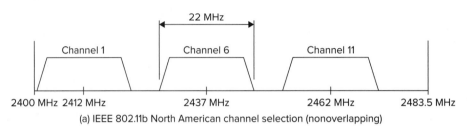

(a) IEEE 802.11b North American channel selection (nonoverlapping)

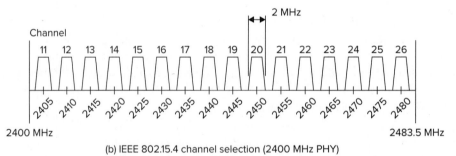

(b) IEEE 802.15.4 channel selection (2400 MHz PHY)

Awarepoint offers a simple plug-in sensor device that can be placed into any common wall outlet to form a mesh network back to a bridge. The bridge device is wired and aggregates all the information from its meshed sensors and forwards it back to the location server.

What is nice about Awarepoint's solution is that you can quickly deploy it in areas were WLAN coverage isn't available or doesn't make sense.

Awarepoint's location algorithm also uses 3D RF information that many of the other location vendors do not. This information ultimately allows for Awarepoint's solution to be more accurate.

While the use of this technology might seem outside the scope of your current interpretation of wireless design, you nonetheless need to consider all the options available to you. Because you may not be able to deploy an 802.11-based network in a ubiquitous fashion, that restriction might lend itself to needing non-802.11-based solutions. When this is the case, you must plan your spectrum accordingly, which means coordinating what channels an 802.15.4 solution is configured for along with your 802.11 and even other networks.

Ekahau

Ekahau has also been in the location market for quite some time. They have taken the approach of using 802.11 tags that associate to the WLAN. While that means that each tag needs an IP address and that each tag must be configured to operate over your WLAN security policy, Ekahau tags have a bidirectional communication link that can be exploited. So, essentially, they are capable of being two-way communication devices.

Ekahau tags have the ability to determine their location based on how they hear the WLAN infrastructure. In contrast to Ekahau's model, AeroScout is based on how the infrastructure hears the tag.

Because you do not always need a bidirectional tag for all applications, Ekahau has also released a tag that will operate in a similar fashion to AeroScout's model discussed earlier.

Ekahau tags also feature the ability to operate over any WLAN infrastructure because they associate to the WLAN.

Earlier we mentioned that exciters are used with AeroScout's technology. Ekahau offers a similar solution called location beacons, but instead of using RF or ultrasound, they have employed infrared (IR) light. IR has the benefit of providing highly accurate location resolution. The disadvantage is that IR light can be obstructed far more easily than RF technologies. We are all likely accustomed to this same phenomenon: television remote controls have to be pointed in the relative direction of the receiver or the IR light is not seen. Ekahau's location beacons, however, have the option of using few narrow beams of IR, so the effect we are accustomed to with our television remote controls is not the same.

Radianse

Radianse is another overlay, non-802.11 technology operating at 433 MHz (UHF). It utilizes tags and transmits to receivers that are typically located in rooms.

The accuracy of the system is reported to be within a meter, which is quite good.

Sonitor

Sonitor has taken a different approach: their overlay technology requires in-room ultrasound devices. Sonitor is known for their high accuracy, attributed to the physics of ultrasound.

Location Design Considerations

A lot of confusion exists regarding how to design for Wi-Fi location-based tracking. Some people say you have to stack the APs, others say put APs at the building edges, and some people say you have to double the number of APs.

Although an entire chapter could be dedicated to designing for location, we'll discuss the design only at a high level. The best recommendation is to augment the information you will learn in this book with vendor-specific training by the manufacturer to learn their particular system and best practices. However, if you are designing a WLAN and want to simply find your 802.11 clients and perhaps some 802.11-based tags with better accuracy, then keep reading.

What we recommend, based on experience, is to start with a sound voice-grade design as a baseline. A solid voice-grade design is one that meets some of the most stringent performance requirements possible.

Next, *only* where the added location resolution is necessary, you can implement listen-only APs that are optimized for location-configured channels. In listen-only mode, you gain all the benefits of hearing the 802.11 devices and RFID tags, but you do not interfere with the integrity of the WLAN performance.

This concept is critical. Too often customers purchase too many APs, and the result is that the performance of the network is horrible. These customers were typically doing what the sales engineer or vendor told them. Unfortunately, not enough authoritative information has been readily available to prevent disasters like this. Furthermore, location tracking using Wi-Fi is still in its infancy, and the industry is still learning. Although mistakes like this are understandable, using the basic rules in this section should be well worth the price of this book.

Another factor worth considering is AP placement. Because 802.11-based location tracking requires some level of triangulation to work, you next need to look at AP placement adjustments.

For example, in the case of long rectangular building structures, APs placed down the center of the hallway will only locate you between APs and not in rooms on each side of the hallway, as is shown in Figure 3.5.

FIGURE 3.5   AP placement limiting location tracking

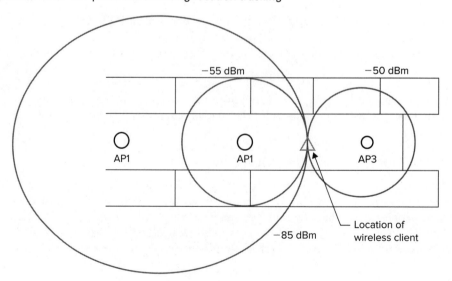

Moving a few of the APs into the rooms or simply adding a few listen-only APs should pull the devices off of the hallway center line.

Generally speaking, it is easier for a location algorithm to triangulate from the outside in. For example, at edges of a building, you will not have an accurate location resolution if your APs are placed toward the inside of the structure. Fewer APs are going to hear the 802.11 devices or RFID tags, which means less reliable location resolution.

In summary, a sound voice-grade design is the starting point for a location-grade Wi-Fi network. See what you get with that as a starting point. If business requirements dictate that you need greater location resolution in some areas, then add listen-only APs.

Incorporating Other Location Technology Components

If business needs require reliable in-room accuracy or specific features that cannot be accomplished with built-in 802.11 features, you need to look to incorporating an RTLS vendor solution.

Furthermore, if your business needs require an application designed for end users to manage assets, create alerts to enhance workflow, deter theft or any of the other benefits that a standard 802.11 WLAN provides, then you also need to look to a third-party location vendor.

There is certainly the option to augment the WLAN only where the added requirements exist. Depending on your WLAN infrastructure vendor, they may have stronger integration with some platforms than others.

If you are looking to leverage a mixture of 802.11 devices with tags, then you have only two major vendors available today: AeroScout and Ekahau. These are the companies who have been around the longest, and even other vendors are structuring OEM relationships with them.

For AeroScout, you have the option of installing exciters or ultrasound along with their 802.11-based RFID tags. Ekahau uses infrared location beacons that work in the same way.

Other No-Location-Based Benefits

Many of the RTLS vendors are also offering other features of particular interest, such as temperature and humidity monitoring. Other benefits might include tamper-resistant tags and even motion sensors. A device can sit idle and transmit only a few times to provide the location server its current location. It can then sit idle and not have to transmit again until the device starts moving again.

This approach will further extend the battery life of the RFID tag.

Guest Access

Guest access, or public Wi-Fi, has proven to be a big enough business driver to justify a ubiquitous deployment of 802.11 WLANs in many areas. In places like educational campuses, businesses, hotels, coffee shops, restaurants, airports, hospitals, and even large metropolitan areas, guest access is often a critical business driver.

Airports, restaurants, and hotels were the first to embrace Wi-Fi for public guest access. Entire businesses were and are still being formed to deploy and manage Wi-Fi infrastructure at thousands of locations. Starting in the early 2000s, companies like Wayport and Cometa Networks started to aggressively blanket as many public places around the United States and even around the world.

Understanding Business Drivers for Guest Access

When we think about public Wi-Fi, many of us may think about Starbucks, Panera Bread, and other retail chains that have taken an aggressive stance on adopting a public wireless. The benefits are clear to them. Many a weary business traveler has plugged in business names into their GPS in order to gain Wi-Fi access to send out a critical email or document.

Customers sitting for longer lengths of time lead to more revenue. Knowing that public wireless is available at certain locations will draw users to walk in the door. For retail applications, the value proposition is clear.

Hotels and airports are another clear-cut example of how valuable public Wi-Fi can be to travelers. Anybody with a laptop with idle time on their hands or needing to be productive for business purposes yearns for wireless connectivity. Often that means that they are willing to pay. Airports and hotel chains generate substantial revenue from public Wi-Fi. Of course, smaller hotel chains and smaller airports tend to give it away as an incentive.

Healthcare also has a strong value proposition for inpatient stays. Recovering patients cherish the ability to have a stronger connection to the outside and another form of passing the time, while family members have the ability to work remotely while still caring for their loved ones.

Education is one of the largest fields using Wi-Fi with campuses full of both students and teachers carrying laptops these days. Educational environments often ask users to perform a login to a simple web page once they connect with their campus credentials, and they are then granted Internet access.

Business offices also have a strong use case for guest wireless when they have vendors and visitors to accommodate. One of the biggest values of placing vendors and visitors on a guest wireless segment is to protect the business from computer viruses and other security vulnerabilities that may exist on foreign, unmanaged laptops. Guest access usually provides a completely segmented network to prevent these types of vulnerabilities from manifesting.

Models for Guest Access

Guest access can come in many forms. Typically, a guest access model incorporates an unsecured and broadcasted Wi-Fi network advertising the ability to join. Once a user joins, they are typically restricted from passing all traffic until some sort of authentication has been performed. Authentication is typically performed with a web browser using a variety of methods. Some of these methods require a username and password whereas others might be a simple acknowledgment of an *acceptable use policy (AUP)*.

The main types of guest access are:

- Sponsored access
- Public access
- Fee-based access

We will now discuss each of these in detail.

Sponsored Guest Access

Think of sponsored guest access as a means of providing guest access to known users. Known users can be vendors, contractors, and escorted guests. Sponsored guest access is typically used in business office environments, but is also sometimes available in other venues where the owner is trying to control access to a greater extent. This includes some conferences and even hotel venues.

Sponsored guest is a great solution when a vendor is visiting a location to present a slideshow, for example. The vendor may also need to use a web-based presentation platform to present the slides to users who are attending the meeting remotely. If the presentation resides on the vendor's PC, then transferring that file could be problematic as the vendor would need to either go through a variety of traditional file transfer methods to transfer the slides or plug into the corporate network. Plugging into the corporate network is the worst solution because it could potentially expose the business to a host of security threats. If a wired network jack is not available, the vendor would also need to get their computer configured for the businesses' wireless security policy. In this instance, sponsored guest access provides the most effective solution.

In this case, sponsored guest access can be made available via an office administrative assistant or any authorized employee using a web-based form to create a temporary username and/or password for the visiting vendor (or any guest at the facility). The lifetime of that temporary account would typically be 8 hours or could even be extended for several days if needed. Now, without any further administrative action, that account will expire automatically, and the user will be able to do exactly what they need to do while not presenting any security threat to the place of business.

Several WLAN vendors offer guest access features as part of their base platforms; they may also have add-on devices and infrastructure that extend the features of the WLAN infrastructure. There are companies like Nomadix, Bluesocket, and Colubris (now HP) who have helped shape the guest access industry with inexpensive *access control gateways*. Access control gateways are devices that restrict all network traffic until some form of authentication or acceptance occurs. The access control gateway redirects the user to a web portal once they open their web browser and try to access a web page. Many of you have likely encountered this web-based redirection while using just a public Wi-Fi network.

Many of the WLAN controller vendors and a few others have fairly robust guest access functionality built into their base product offerings. This has made sponsored guest access much more feasible for many office environments because the platform is built into the base platform.

Public Guest Access

Public guest access is typically self-service, and the entity providing the guest access services does not know who the intended user is. Public guest access is common in a long list of venues nowadays, including hotels, airports, and coffee shops. When public guest access is used, typically a richer user experience is provided to the end users. A web page with detailed instructions for obtaining access is provided, and usually several websites can be browsed, such as the company web page or other basic websites that may be of value to visitors, such as weather and travel websites. Frankly, whatever the provider thought was important to their guest users or the organization can be presented.

Public access websites are manually configured into a *whitelist*, which allows users to view certain web pages without authenticating through the network. Before a user is granted authorization to have access to the general Internet, two items are of particular interest. The first is that users acknowledge an acceptable use policy (AUP) that essentially says they aren't going to launch any Internet attacks or view explicit material. The second item of interest to the organization is some sort of identifying information about that user, such as an email address or member ID.

If a user was found to be causing malicious activity or an audit needed to be performed by an outside agency, this information proves valuable to investigators, and the provider would have to show due diligence by collecting this type of guest access information. This information can be in many forms, but should be something that allows the provider to identify a specific user.

Fee-Based Guest Access

Guest access started off as a paid service. Entire companies were founded on the premise that guest Wi-Fi access would take off in a big way. Hotspots were being treated like cell towers and were being thought as multi-tenant devices. For example, the thinking was that you might pay an extra $10 per month on your mobile phone bill for hotspot access available at thousands of locations. A wholesale hotspot provider would then provide the managed service offering. When a user accessed that location's guest access environment, a small portion of that money would be exchanged between the mobile phone carrier and the individual location operator.

At least two things happened that got in the way of this business model. First, as a competitive measure, companies would give away Wi-Fi if their competitor was charging to win consumer appeal. The second has to do with mobile carrier data access getting cheaper. If you have to pay $10 for each venue to get Internet access for a short period of time or even by day, it would be far cheaper to simply subscribe to a mobile carrier data plan if you had to do this more than a handful of times over the course of a month. There are certain venues that still charge for Internet access, and they will likely continue to do so as long as it is profitable and they do not have competitive pressure.

After a successful sign-on or guest purchase, an immediate notification needs to be made to the access control device that the user is authorized to use the Internet. This requires the provider to have a full e-commerce engine and merchant account. E-commerce infrastructure, however, costs money to maintain, and there are monthly charges incurred even to maintain a credit card merchant account whether or not there are billing transactions.

If the venue desires a highly customized web page that includes up-to-date information such as weekly news, events, sales, and other information, maintaining the content is also an operational consideration and an added cost. This could perhaps be assumed as a marketing cost regardless of whether the guest access is a paid service.

All of this adds complexity and overhead to a guest access implementation. If a reasonable volume and financial return is expected, it might be worth the effort. Otherwise, the added development, maintenance, operational costs, and support may not be worth it. One consideration is that customers visiting your venue where a guest access solution is provided may perceive the free guest Wi-Fi as a major attractor, and it may pay off in other, indirect transactions.

Network Design Approaches

There are many ways to accomplish a guest network design. Depending on your design requirements and constraints, you may have to exercise different options in different scenarios. These options include segmenting VLANs, tunneling traffic to different network locations, and limiting the amount of network usage any single user or perhaps the entire group of users may generate.

VLAN Segmentation

The simplest way to implement a guest access solution is to dedicate a nonroutable VLAN to guest traffic. This approach assumes that the wired network isn't segmented with Layer 3 boundaries within the LAN. In other words, it would mean that all VLANs are trunked or 802.1Q tagged to each switch where APs are plugged into.

If the network is using a split-MAC architecture, it would only mean that a guest segmented VLAN would need to reside where the WLAN controller resides. Therefore, even if you have Layer 3 segmentation down to the access layer switches, this design is still viable and is quite simple.

By creating a new VLAN that has no gateway on the existing wired LAN with the addition of simple ACLs to block all traffic to and from the guest VLAN, you now have a fully segmented network. Next, you drop a DSL or cable modem circuit onto this VLAN and whammo, it works!

If you add a third-party access control device or your vendor's WLAN controller has the necessary features built in, you can even implement a wired guest access solution. This will allow all wired traffic to traverse the same access control system that wireless users do.

Tunneling and Anchoring Traffic

Many WLAN controller vendors tout using WLAN controllers in other ways than just serving APs. They have proposed an alternative to the VLAN approach by allowing APs to tunnel traffic to a secondary controller located outside the internal enterprise LAN. This is typically in a DMZ partition or somewhere in the transit network on the way out to the Internet.

In this scenario, a WLAN client would establish a connection to a guest SSID from the lightweight APs. The APs then perform their normal process of sending all of their traffic back to the WLAN controller in whatever type of protocol the vendor supports, like Control and Provisioning of Wireless Access Points (CAPWAP) or Lightweight Access Point Protocol (LWAPP). Once the guest traffic hits the WLAN controller, it forwards all traffic to a different WLAN controller (we'll call it the guest controller) located on the outside of the internal network.

The guest controller then serves up a DHCP address from a new scope you would define for all guest users. That scope can either be logically pertinent to the DMZ zone the controller resides in or perhaps a completely virtual scope that is only locally significant to the WLAN controller. If the latter is chosen, the traffic is sent to the wired network using *Port Address Translation (PAT)*, otherwise known as *NAT Overload*.

Therefore, when this approach is taken, no changes need to be performed on the wired LAN. Added cost is incurred for the guest controller, but that might be a preferred approach for some organizations.

Rate Limiting

One desired feature that most organizations like to implement is some form of traffic rate limiting. The guest network should take a backseat priority in most networks such as in healthcare, business offices, and several other environments. You do not want guest users hogging up all of the local RF channel bandwidth and/or the Internet circuit for noncritical business use.

Rate limiting features are typically supported by just about any guest access solution available today. It also gives fair and balanced access to all users that are on the guest wireless network. The recommendation in most cases is to use a separate Internet circuit for the guest users. This eliminates the contention on the Internet circuit that is used for business purposes.

Let's say, for example, that you are running a 2.4 GHz 802.11g/n network. Let's also say that you only have 802.11g/n-capable devices. The WLAN will be running in at least an 802.11g fashion without the use of protection mechanisms. Then, when you introduce guest access, users then come in with 802.11b devices. What has just happened is that your native 802.11g network performance just lost a lot of efficiency.

Some vendors allow you to advertise only Orthogonal Frequency Division Multiplexing (OFDM) rates in order to prevent these 802.11b devices from associating altogether. Yes, those users will not be able to connect. However, if they cannot connect, they are also not bringing down the performance of all the corporate devices.

Summary

Some of the most popular, primary applications that you will encounter in discussions when designing or augmenting a new WLAN will be VoWiFi, location tracking, and guest access. Video is quickly making its way into the set of primary applications, and you should start to think about it in your designs today.

You will be expected to understand each of these primary applications very well. You will be tested on the fundamental aspects of these design approaches, and your customers will expect you to know them as well.

Exam Essentials

Understand applications and protocols.   Be familiar with difficult network protocols and applications and know how to address them in WLAN design.

Real-time applications.   Be able to describe design differences needed to support real-time applications like voice and video. Understand how these differences will affect the infrastructure RF survey and design.

Location tracking.   Be able to understand how real-time location tracking works with a variety of technologies and how they can be incorporated into WLAN design.

Guest access.   Be able to explain guest access design fundamentals and how this can be incorporated into different network topologies.

Review Questions

1. What types of applications would be heavily disrupted if the client device were to change IPs? (Choose all that apply.)

   A. Telnet

   B. SIP

   C. SSH

   D. HTTP

   E. FTP

2. As a general design practice, what minimum PHY rate is recommended to ensure VOWLAN quality?

   A. 11 Mbps

   B. 18 Mbps

   C. 24 Mbps

   D. 36 Mbps

   E. 54 Mbps

3. What of the following solutions ensure that client devices do not change IP addresses as a device roams? (Choose all that apply.)

   A. Use a WLAN controller or an infrastructure AP that incorporates IP mobility features.

   B. Use larger IP subnets for your device pool and ideally disable broadcast suppression.

   C. Use a mobile IP software product that can be used to traverse different operators' networks.

   D. Do not turn the device off after it has powered up.

   E. Keep each floor of a building to a single subnet and hopefully devices will not move between floors.

4. When the timing of voice traffic arrives with a high degree of variable timing, what is this considered?

   A. Latency

   B. IFS

   C. TDOA

   D. Jitter

5.   As a device starts to shift to lower PHY rates, what factors usually influence a device decision to shift to lower PHY rates? (Choose all that apply.)

   A.   Signal degradation

   B.   Retransmissions

   C.   Interference

   D.   Packet loss

6.   Videoconferencing over Wi-Fi may contain what kinds of network traffic? (Choose all that apply.)

   A.   Session initiation and teardown

   B.   Data

   C.   Real-time video

   D.   Real-time audio

   E.   MOH

7.   What type of codec should be avoided using video over Wi-Fi?

   A.   AVI

   B.   QuickTime

   C.   MPEG-2

   D.   MPEG-3

   E.   MPEG-4

8.   What are methods of providing RF high availability?

   A.   Use the HSRP/VRRP protocol.

   B.   Use dual spectrums.

   C.   Deploy 802.3af.

   D.   Power APs to maximum power.

   E.   Deploy using 100 percent overlap.

9.   What design considerations should you be concerned about when using 802.11-based multicast frames for real-time applications? (Choose all that apply.)

   A.   Multicast frames are not acknowledged.

   B.   802.11 multicast frames are sent using the lowest basic rate in the BSS.

   C.   802.11 multicast frames are sent using the highest basic rate in the BSS.

   D.   Delivery assurances for clients with power saving enabled

   E.   Wired network co-dependency to enable multicast applications

10. Left to its simplest form, what method does a location algorithm use to determine location within a WLAN coverage area?

    A. Inverse cube law

    B. FSPL

    C. RF fingerprinting

    D. 802.11 clause 16

11. How does an exciter using 125 kHz communicate information over a Wi-Fi network?

    A. Exciters incorporate 802.11 radios or use Ethernet backhaul.

    B. Exciters relay information through a WLAN client MMPDU.

    C. Exciters use simplex transmission and merely inform WLAN radios they are in range.

    D. Exciters can only be heard by tags with a 125 kHz receive circuit.

    E. Exciters can detect when tags are present, like passive RFID, and inform the location server.

12. Regarding AP placement, what placement method would result in the least location accuracy?

    A. Straight lines

    B. Floor-to-floor staggering

    C. Listen-only APs

    D. Use of an SCA

13. What might limit the ability to locate 802.11 clients using a WLAN infrastructure without an 802.11 tag? (Choose all that apply.)

    A. RF channel selection

    B. Lack of 802.11k support

    C. When its radio is disabled

    D. When it is off

14. Looking at a client radio specification sheet that states Receive Sensitivity of −82 dBm @ 18 Mbps would mean:

    A. It is only capable of transmitting at 18 Mbps PHY rates at −82 dBm.

    B. It must hear a signal >−82 dBm in order to demodulate the 18 Mbps PHY rate.

    C. It must hear a signal <−82 dBm in order to demodulate the 18 Mbps PHY rate.

    D. It would need to hear a signal <−82 dBm in order to use the 24 Mbps PHY rate.

15. How is a whitelist used in guest access design?

    A. Provides a list of URLs that are restricted

    B. Provides a list of application protocols that are allowed over the guest network

    C. Provides a report of known and valid guest users

    D. Provides a list of authorized URLs that are allowed before authentication

16. What are important guest access network design considerations? (Choose all that apply.)

   A. Circuit reliability

   B. Traffic tunneling and anchoring

   C. Network traffic segmentation

   D. Rate limiting

   E. 802.11 supported rates

17. When charging for guest access, what additional costs need to be factored in? (Choose all that apply.)

   A. Credit card merchant account

   B. Customer support

   C. Web page development

   D. Uptime

   E. Quality

18. What factors are key features when designing a guest network for a large enterprise? (Choose all that apply.)

   A. 802.11n

   B. Rate limiting

   C. 802.1X security

   D. Traffic tunneling or anchoring

   E. SSID segmentation

19. An acceptable use policy will result in what benefit for the provider? (Choose all that apply.)

   A. Attempts to protect the organization from users performing illegal actions

   B. Attempts to protect the organization from data loss to the guest user device while using the guest network

   C. Requires users to adhere to the laws dictated by the provider while using the network

   D. Provides a contract that users must accept that governs their use of the network

20. Location technology (RTLS) can use which of the following methods? (Choose all that apply.)

   A. Passive RFID

   B. Active RFID

   C. 802.11-capable laptops

   D. UWB

   E. UHV

   F. Sound

   G. Infrared

Answers to Review Questions

1. A, B, C, E. Session-based protocols like Telnet, SIP, SSH, and FTP will cause the session to be terminated if a client device were to be assigned a new IP address.

2. C. It is unrealistic to maintain 54 Mbps PHY rates—client devices will never decide to roam. However, dropping too low will cause more rate shifting than desired and impact the performance of other wireless devices. 24 Mbps is a good metric to design for the lowest PHY rate during device roams in MCA environments.

3. A, B, C. Options A, B, and C are all valid options. Option D will not provide any value unless one or more of A, B, or C is used. Option E is not a valid solution because RF propagates and reflects between floors of a building.

4. D. Jitter is caused by variability in the time traffic is sent and received.

5. A, B, C, D. All of these factors can result in rate shifting of wireless stations.

6. A, B, C, D. Two-way, real-time videoconferencing over Wi-Fi will at least contain video, audio, and some type of call/session setup and teardown protocol. Many videoconferencing systems allow data to be transmitted to the other parties as well, such as presentation slides and other data.

7. C. MPEG-2 was not originally designed to be transported over a data network and has many negative attributes that result in poor quality relative to other codecs.

8. E. HSRP/VRRP is an IP networking failover feature. Dual spectrums will not provide RF redundancy if an entire AP would fail or clients only support one spectrum. 802.3af is only an alternative powering mechanism for APs. Increasing transmit power to fill in RF holes can fill in holes only if you are downlink-limited to begin with; unless client devices support the same maximum power (which is usually unlikely), it will not help. Deploying using 100 percent overlap would result in poor performance but would at least provide some level of RF redundancy. It is worth noting that some vendors provide proprietary mechanisms to failover standby APs if the active one were to fail.

9. A, B, D, E. Using multicast over Wi-Fi networks for real-time applications requires a lot of attention to detail. Several infrastructure equipment manufacturers are currently developing enhancements to multicast traffic delivery.

10. B. The free space path loss (FSPL) propagation model is used to determine device location between APs within a coverage area. The question was based on the premise of using the simplest form.

11. D. Exciters are only transmitters that need to be powered using a variety of means and can only be detected by RFID tags with 125 kHz receive circuits. Tags then relay the exciter information over to the Wi-Fi network.

12. A. APs located in a straight line would only be able to locate devices in a straight line between its neighboring APs.

13. C, D. 802.11 devices cannot be located when they are powered off or if their WLAN radio is disabled or not transmitting.

14. B. This client's receive sensitivity specifications state that a signal level of −82 dBm or greater must be heard in order demodulate a 18 Mbps PHY rate.

15. D. A whitelist is a list of URLs that may be accessed before a guest user is authenticated.

16. A, B, C, D, E. All of these are important considerations for guest network designs.

17. A, B, C, D, E. When giving away guest access to users, it is very different from the expectations users will have when they pay for it. Unless the number of paying guest users is expected to be high, charging for guest access may not financially be a good idea.

18. B, D. Guest clients need to be limited in their ability to monopolize the available 802.11 bandwidth. Traffic tunneling and anchoring are important features that can help segment and direct guest network traffic from the organization's network traffic.

19. A, B, C, D. All of these areas should be addressed with an appropriate AUP.

20. B, C, D, F, G. Passive RFID cannot be used for real-time tracking purposes. Active RFID and 802.11-capable devices transmit 802.11 frames, and many enterprise APs and infrastructure can track these devices. UWB (ultra-wideband), sound (ultrasound), and infrared are technologies used by some manufacturers or RTLS solutions.

Chapter

4

Industry-Specific Design Considerations

THE FOLLOWING CWDP EXAM TOPICS ARE COVERED IN THIS CHAPTER:

- ✓ Identify the physical environment(s) for the network and describe best practices for network deployments for different physical spaces.

- ✓ Demonstrate a detailed understanding of RF propagation behaviors and relate these characteristics to WLAN design for specific environments.

- ✓ Determine RF link requirements and demonstrate common planning techniques and deployment approaches for outdoor networks.

- ✓ Explain the importance of building-specific planning considerations.

- ✓ Explain best practices and address common design considerations for industry-specific WLAN deployments.

- ✓ Understand the differences in tools, methods, and purpose between outdoor and indoor site surveys.

What design book would be complete without useful insights to design challenges for various types of installation environments? This chapter explores the most common industry verticals as well as some interesting WLAN design scenarios. This is valuable information that you can put to use right away in your own projects.

Healthcare, retail, and education are the three verticals that comprise most WLAN equipment sales. Depending on the equipment manufacturer, one of these industry segments might make up over 50 percent of their equipment sales. Each of these will be discussed with enough detail that you'll gain enough knowledge to begin your first installation. In the same vein, for those of you who have worked in these verticals before, we provide new information that you'll be able to incorporate into your next designs.

This chapter will also discuss outdoor environments because they present some unique challenges that you will not likely encounter in indoor deployments.

Healthcare

Deploying wireless in healthcare environments, multifloor hospitals in particular, is one of the more challenging tasks for Wi-Fi designers. Users and their devices are often highly mobile and their needs are great. Caregivers need timely access to a vast amount of electronic information, and they need to be able to efficiently communicate with their fellow caregivers and other co-workers. Their co-workers, in turn, need timely and efficient access to them.

Healthcare facilities tend to be rather large. Covering an entire facility usually requires a high number of access points (APs), with coverage possibly overlapping on several floors.

Application support for voice, location services, and guest access is typically considered to be a "standard" feature request in the majority of today's healthcare WLANs. By default, it's fair to assume that these applications will be required in new WLAN deployments.

In healthcare, the number of devices utilizing wireless networks has been rapidly increasing each year with no real end in sight; if an electronic medical device is mobile and is used for patient care, there is likely either WLAN support today or near-term plans for WLAN support on the device manufacturer's product roadmap. On top of mobility demands, running physical cables for network devices is expensive; even if cost wasn't a concern, it is highly disruptive to busy facilities that don't have office hours. Healthcare facilities are often running around the clock.

Hospitals have been using WLANs for many years now. These networks were likely working well for their initial purposes, but as the number of devices has grown and their applications have become more demanding, legacy WLANs are starting to show signs of stress. The growing channel utilization metric is a perfect illustration of this reality.

The need to design better, higher capacity networks in the healthcare vertical has never been more critical.

Supporting Data, Voice, Guest, and Location Services

When it comes to supporting data, voice, guest, and location tracking services on a single RF network, deciding on a design specification may seem overwhelming. Each of these applications may call for different design specifications based on client and vendor requirements. For instance, a typical data network in a healthcare environment is normally designed to approximately −73 dBm, but most voice designs have RSSI targets of −65 to −67 dBm, depending on the voice device vendor. To complicate things further, when you add in location, you now have to devote much more thought to *where* you place the access points, as we discussed in Chapter 3, "Designing for Applications." This may mean you need more APs in some areas of the hospital in order to facilitate higher location resolution for 802.11 devices (in listen-only mode).

As a WLAN designer in a healthcare environment, you need to be aware of a couple of critical factors as well:

- You are dealing with patient lives. Make no mistake about it. As hospitals become more and more electronic (and all of them are), they will increasingly rely on the hospital WLAN.

- Hospital IT and business decision makers tend to be risk adverse. So even though a hospital may not plan to initially deploy VoWiFi or location-based services, they almost always have future plans to do so.

So what do you recommend to your customer or management? We strongly recommend that you explain the demands of common applications and how the WLAN must be designed to support the organization's current and potential future needs. Furthermore, you want to impress on them that it is not an option to design for anything less than voice, location, and even video capabilities. The additional cost and effort put into the initial design represents a small amount of money and time compared to the costs of augmenting the network at a later date. After all, when designing for voice and video, you are designing for a high-performance WLAN, which should support every other application that they will likely ever deploy.

Now that we are assuming that a new hospital WLAN design will support real-time applications like voice and video as well as location services, we can move forward with design specifications. Those sets of applications are the most demanding that you can deploy today.

Build for Growth

One thing is for sure with hospital WLANs: the network needs to be built to support a growing number of mobile devices. Building for a large number of client devices is not unlike designing for the stringent demands of real-time applications. In other words, installing more APs (while still being careful to avoid overdeploying) is often required to accomplish this task. This is additional fuel to sway your customer to design to the metrics recommended for use with voice and video.

To help you understand the types of devices that are or will be using the WLAN, let's explore a few examples.

Infusion Pumps

Infusion pumps are the devices that administer intravenous (IV) fluids. They are located with the patients at the bedside and are one of the most mobile and commonly used items in a hospital. A medium-sized hospital typically has many hundreds of infusion pumps. Biomedical engineers want these devices on the WLAN to help them manage their fleet of devices by ensuring that they are in proper working condition. These devices also have electronic drug libraries that require updates from time to time, and unless staff has some way of communicating with the devices, they must manually gather them to perform the update.

Along with any other type of electronic device, infusion pumps require regular maintenance. Devices that are highly mobile and highly sought after can be difficult to perform maintenance on because they are hard to find and in short supply. Finding them is also a challenge; because they are so heavily used, nursing staff have tended to create a stash. After they are used, the pumps are sent to be sterilized, but as new ones return, it is not uncommon for them to be stashed away. This is where a Real-Time Location System (RTLS) can solve the location, and potentially the device status, problem. Even without an RFID tag, assuming the infusion pump is on the WLAN, the pumps can be located.

Now that the use case for infusion pumps using the WLAN is clear, we can assume several hundred infusion pumps will be using the WLAN. It is not uncommon to see over a thousand infusion pumps in larger hospitals.

VoWiFi

Voice over Wi-Fi (VoWiFi) has become commonplace in the healthcare vertical. Many hospital systems have had Voice over IP (VoIP) systems installed, at least in a limited fashion, for many years and are now extending the capability to their wireless network. The advantages of VoWiFi are simple. It costs less than cellular and it allows two-way voice communication to critical hospital members as they move freely throughout a facility.

These benefits are not without a wide array of technical challenges. Deploying a wireless network in a hospital that meets vendor requirements is demanding. Suppose, for example, the vendor requires −67 dBm signal coverage and less than 1 percent *packet error rate (PER)*. Now let's say they also recommend the phone sees at least two access points meeting those criteria for seamless roaming at cell edges.

Sound easy? Sure, you simply put in a lot of access points and you can ensure coverage that meets this requirement. Heck, say you even add your own special contribution to their requirement and have four APs at −67 dBm or better. Will it work well? Likely not. Why not? Well, because you will have created too much *co-channel interference*, which in turn will wreak havoc on both your APs and your clients trying to use the network.

The problem arises when heavier usage occurs and too many devices and APs on the same channel are trying to contend for transmit time.

As you will read throughout this book, the key concept when designing voice- or even video-grade WLANs is getting the coverage you need without also getting excessive co-channel interference. Expect this point to be driven home very thoroughly. In the 2.4 GHz spectrum, being limited to three channels (see Figure 4.1) makes this very challenging. Many times, networks are deployed poorly in the 2.4 GHz spectrum but no one notices because the channel utilization is very low. Over time, as more and more phones and other devices are added to the network, the channel utilization rises and co-channel interference rears its ugly head.

FIGURE 4.1   2.4 GHz ISM band channel plan

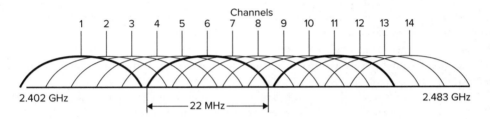

In the 5 GHz spectrum there's a bit more flexibility due to the increased channel support (see Figure 4.2). It's important to see which channels your APs support and compare them to the channels that your clients support to make sure you aren't using channels on the APs that the clients have no way of using.

FIGURE 4.2   5 GHz UNII band channel plan

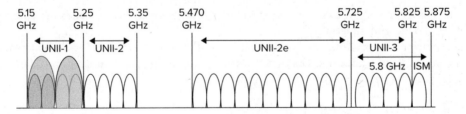

An important note on the use of the 5 GHz channels is that they don't all have the same maximum transmit power. That being said, it's in your best interest to review your channel plan to ensure you will be able to produce the power you need, where you need it. This maps directly to the power selected on the AP during the original survey. Taking this one step further, many vendors have features that dynamically select channels and power settings for the APs based on what the surrounding RF environment "hears." These features will be capped by the regulatory restrictions for that channel. As a network designer, you must take this under careful consideration.

Smart Phones

Hospital workers are highly mobile. Nurses are constantly moving from room to room and are not sitting at a computer desk. Doctors have an even greater footprint to cover because their patients may be in many different parts of the hospital. In fact, doctors and specialists often cover many buildings where only cellular devices may be sufficient. Doctors and nurses need to respond to their patients in real time. Quite literally, lives hang in the balance when communication is not sufficient.

In times past, hospital staff carried pagers because they operated at low frequencies and could usually be successfully communicated to just about anywhere the staff would go. However, pagers are limited in that they don't offer the same two-way real-time interaction that phones do. Today, almost everybody carries a cellular or mobile phone. Increasingly so, these devices are becoming smart phones and not simply devices that support just telephony services. Texting, email, web browsing, and custom applications are now the focus.

As mobile carrier networks are more and more oversubscribed with the rapid growth of data usage, the carriers have now equipped their devices with 802.11 radios in an attempt to offload some of the network load. Users do not mind this shift because the speed of 802.11 is far greater than that of carrier networks—especially if the servers these devices are communicating with are local to the WLAN.

In healthcare environments, smart phones are being used as advanced notification devices. Not only can they be used to notify clinical staff of critical lab values of their patients, but also graphical information can be sent to these devices for remote diagnostic events. While not all information that can be transmitted to a smart phone is appropriate for a clinical decision to be made, it is amazing just how much actually is.

Communicating with nursing staff can also be greatly improved by advancing past a simple telephony device. Nurses are responsible for interacting with the electronic patient record, and having access to that information wherever they may be also lends incredible efficiency to their job functions.

Equipping doctors, nurses, and other hospital staff who interact with the clinical process usually amounts to many hundreds of devices at any given time, 24 hours a day. In larger hospitals this can reach well over a thousand devices.

Mobile Carts or Computing Devices

For nursing and clinical staff to interact with the electronic medical record, they must have access to full-featured computing devices in order to enter data using a normal keyboard and monitor. It is common to see COWs (computers on wheels) or WOWs (workstations on wheels) deployed throughout hospital environments, as shown in Figure 4.3. These devices can be shared between patient rooms and can even be assigned to a single nurse for the duration of the shift, depending on the workflow. Charting all of the patient data is not always proper to do directly at the patient's bedside or in the patient room, so having access to a mobile device that can be wheeled into and out of rooms is often desired.

This means that several hundreds of mobile carts and other computing devices involved in the patient's electronic medical record must also be added to the hospital WLAN. For larger hospitals, this can amount to more than 500 mobile carts alone.

FIGURE 4.3   Example Mobile Cart (a.k.a. COW or WOW)

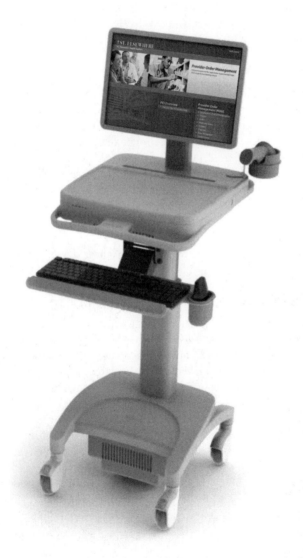

Image courtesy of InfoLogix, Inc.

Beds and Nurse Call

Even hospital beds are becoming electronic devices. Some hospital bed manufacturers are building in sensors and other features to alarm hospital staff of particular interest to caregivers. This may include a "bed rail down" or "out of bed" alert for patients that may be at risk of falling or other clinical conditions.

Beds are also mobile in hospital environments. They are often wheeled in and out of hospital rooms between departments where services are rendered. A medium-sized hospital is usually considered to be characterized by several hundred "beds." Interestingly enough, the term "bed" is often used to speak to the size of a hospital in lieu of square footage. As a WLAN designer, square footage is your benchmark on the size of the WLAN that will need to be designed. In other words, you can likely count another several hundred beds into the future load of the WLAN.

EKG and Sonogram Devices

Electrocardiography (EKGs or ECGs) devices interpret the electrical activity of the heart over time captured by electrodes placed on the skin. Sonogram devices create images or animations of internal organ activity and are also used on pregnant mothers to view the womb (ultrasounds). These are commonly mobile devices that are wheeled into patient rooms when they need to be used. As electronic medical records are becoming increasingly sophisticated, saving these images for further analysis, a second opinion, or even for legal purposes is becoming more and more important.

Next to voice and video communication, these devices can send a great deal of data. For a single hospital to generate a gigabyte of video and image data over a 24-hour period is not unheard of.

It would not be uncommon to see 50 or more of these devices located at a medium-sized or larger hospital.

Mobile X-ray Devices

A growing trend in healthcare X-ray machines is to avoid the use of film. Several manufacturers are replacing the detector plate that is usually where the film resides with an electronic imager. The X-ray machine projects X-rays from a source pointed at a patient by passing them through an area of focus, which is finally picked up by the detector plate. Detector plates are being redesigned as Wi-Fi devices that communicate the X-ray image back to the system over a Wi-Fi network. Images taken during this process are usually quite large and will consume a great deal of bandwidth in short bursts. While most of the time nothing is being sent by the detector plate, data transfers will spike after each X-ray operation.

Most of the vendors at this time are designing their own proprietary Wi-Fi networks, but this is often seen as a liability to IT personnel. Time will tell if they will continue to reside on their own network, but likely they will start to integrate. If these devices are separate, you are still faced with the issue of channel contention for all nearby co-channel APs.

The number of these devices at a single facility will be small (likely fewer than 10), but the data that they send is large.

RFID Tags

As you have already learned in Chapter 3, the use of RFID tags in healthcare is becoming quite popular. Specialized software applications designed for use by hospital, nursing, and support staff are available to locate any hospital asset, patient, or staff member.

For assets, this can be anything with or without an 802.11 radio. Why would you put an RFID tag on a device that already has an 802.11 radio? The internal 802.11 radio might be off or there may be the need to use chokepoint technologies such as RF, ultrasound, IR, or ultra-wide bandwidth (UWB) to provide near-exact location granularity for some applications or workflow purposes.

The number of assets alone in a hospital is usually in the tens of thousands. This includes wheelchairs, beds, mobile computers, and a host of other specialized equipment that has to be located quickly when it is needed for patient care. Another reason is that equipment and supplies used in healthcare environments tend to be very expensive. In an effort to deter theft or accidental loss, these types of assets are being *tagged* by hospital staff for cost-saving purposes.

Outside of assets, many hospitals are starting to employ patient tracking. Dashboard displays can be automatically updated on nursing and clinical staff displays wherever the patient (or staff) may go. Patients waiting too long in an area can automatically trigger an alarm that something is out of the norm and the patient likely requires some kind of attention.

Timestamps based on location are also generated that can help hospital management determine where improvements in their processes may be made in order to save time and efficiency. These reports can also be used to supply more granular data to help hospital administrators provide the appropriate staffing levels to support historical averages. All of the potential uses of location data are still being discovered as these systems are being deployed.

As the designer of a hospital WLAN, you might have already guessed that the number of RFID tags can eventually reach into the tens of thousands for larger hospitals. In fact, many hospitals have deployed that many tags today.

 Real World Scenario

RFID Tagging to Improve Patient Flow

A hospital in a large metropolitan area has been getting negative feedback from the patients who come to the hospital for care. The feedback is mostly directed at the emergency room wait times, and the CEO of the hospital demands an answer as to why the wait times are so long. The IT director suggests that patients be tagged with RFID tags upon entering the hospital in an effort to better understand the patient flow from admittance to discharge.

After several months, the CEO learned quite a bit from these tags. He found out that although his emergency room staffing was adequate, his X-ray room staffing was not. The results of the RFID study concluded that many patients entering the emergency room got through their admittance paperwork and initial exams within a satisfactory period of time. The study showed that the bottleneck turned out to be an understaffed X-ray room during peak hours. With so many patients entering the emergency room in need of X-rays, this created a logjam that caused several-hour waits in the emergency room. The CEO was able to address this issue by increasing the staffing in that area and allowing the use of an additional X-ray room during peak times.

Telemetry

Telemetry, from a medical perspective, is a term used for the systems involved in remotely monitoring patient vitals. It is also referred to as *biotelemetry*. Traditionally these systems have used a different dedicated wireless spectrum other than what Wi-Fi uses. The frequency ranges for older telemetry systems have traditionally been able to operate on an unlicensed basis using vacant television channels (174–216 MHz and 470–668 MHz) and on a licensed basis using land mobile radio operations. Many hospitals have used the 608–614 MHz range, which is close to where digital and HDTV transmissions occur. This has resulted in the Federal Communications Commission (FCC) setting aside a new frequency spectrum called *Wireless Medical Telemetry Service (WMTS)*. Some states have newer compliance standards that are requiring the use of the 1.4 GHz allocated space.

Frankly, the WMTS spectrum usage is a little messy and not all countries are in agreement with the FCC. This has resulted in medical telemetry manufacturers starting to adopt the ISM bands for telemetry use. While there is a dedicated wireless spectrum available for just this use, some of these manufacturers have begun to use Wi-Fi. You really can't get better provisioning than to have your own dedicated wireless spectrum for a communication system. Having to share the same spectrum between different types of communication devices is a compromise. From many people's perspective, this falls into the "you can, but should you?" category.

Some hospitals unknowingly have purchased a telemetry system that uses the 2.4 GHz ISM band and later went to install a Wi-Fi system, only to then understand that they aren't friendly neighbors.

The data originating from these systems is critical to patient lives. Arguably, it is more important than just about any data sent in a hospital environment. The data from these systems are sent back to a head-end monitoring system usually installed at a nurse station where several people can monitor it for critical alarms. Once an alarm occurs, the data generated from telemetry systems is usually sent as a secondary notification to VoWiFi and smart phone handsets.

Hopefully the point has been driven home in terms of building for growth in hospital WLANs. These device categories are only the big ones, but there are even more devices that are also beginning to utilize the WLAN in healthcare environments.

High Availability

When designing a WLAN for use in hospital environments, you must fully consider redundancy. Redundancy involves not just having something as simple as spare devices ready to deploy, but also involves power distribution. Remember, most APs connect to Ethernet switches both for data connectivity and for power. In the event of a switch failure, several issues occur, including lost power to those APs, switch uplink failure, and possibly traffic congestion on offload switches, requirements for router redundancy, WLAN controller redundancy, and potentially more, depending on several factors.

It is difficult to provide RF redundancy. Although you can perform spectrum redundancy using dual-mode APs (using 2.4 GHz and 5 GHz simultaneously), if you lose an AP, there will be some impact on performance. Many manufacturers tout the benefits of automatic RF configuration and its ability to compensate for coverage holes. If you lose an AP and other APs decide to power up to fill in that cell, client devices don't necessarily increase power along with the APs. Don't be surprised if these algorithms don't always make the best decisions. Testing with these features on and off has often shown that it's best to disable the feature that allows an AP to power up to fill in a coverage hole. Sometimes the result of the AP powering up for one hole will negatively impact other areas surrounding the hole itself.

Without going into intricate details about automatic RF configuration features, suffice it to say that there will be an effect on coverage if an AP fails. Too much overlapping RF negatively impacts performance just as when not enough coverage exists. While too much RF isn't usually as bad of an impact in a light to moderately used WLAN, too little RF would be bad regardless of current usage. The point to be made here is that automatic RF configuration does not replace a site survey and, in fact, only works well when a proper site survey and AP placement were performed with the automatic RF feature in mind.

In WLANs, providing high availability down to the AP level usually requires onsite spares. This doesn't equate to high availability by most IT professionals' definition. In response, some vendors have built in features for dual deployment of APs using a hot-standby feature should an AP fail. It is almost unheard of to see these features in existing deployments, and recent vendor offerings usually have deprecated the feature set. The good news is that failure of enterprise-class APs is quite rare.

Some vendors have also allowed for the use of monitor mode (listen-only) APs that can be deployed in a WLAN environment around active ones. If an active AP fails, the system will turn on an adjacent monitor mode AP and the WLAN should exhibit minimal impact on the quality of service users will experience.

It is important to keep in mind that there are limitations to providing redundancy within the RF medium itself.

Real World Scenario

Converting from Static Channel and Power to an Automatic RF Feature

A hospital has decided to convert their wireless network from a static channel and power configuration to one that utilizes the new automatic RF feature that their vendor has implemented. The time comes to convert the APs, and the maintenance window goes as planned.

The engineers know they that the new feature takes time to calibrate, so they wait until the next morning to begin their verification tests. Before testing can begin, however, they are flooded with complaints of poor and spotty coverage inside the patient rooms combined with unusable phones, dropped calls, and so forth. In a panic they decide to revert back to their old static channel and power plan.

What happened? The automatic RF feature is reliant on how the APs "hear" each other. With all APs mounted in the hallways, they "hear" each other very loudly, which causes them to lower their power levels. This action results in poor coverage in the rooms—hence the complaints. The reality is the static power and channel plan was working, but it shouldn't be considered optimal as it also came with an abundance of co-channel interference. When the automatic RF feature was turned on, it tried to overcome that interference and turned down the power on the radios, which in turn caused the coverage problems in the patient rooms.

Can it be fixed? Sure it can! There are two options when confronted with this scenario. The first is to tune the algorithm to allow it to have very hot (high powered) neighbors. This will essentially let the APs run with hot neighbors and have quite a bit of co-channel interference, but as stated earlier, that is no different than when things were statically configured. The second option is to re-survey the facility and relocate the APs with the algorithm in mind. This involves moving APs into patient rooms, which give you the benefit of better AP isolation as well as improved patient room coverage. There will undoubtedly still be a need for some number of hallway APs, but that number will be far less than in the previous configuration. Graphic 4.1 shows this latter process in action. Previously, the APs were mounted in the hallways, but to migrate to an automated RF system, the APs were moved into hospital rooms, accommodating the automated RF management system.

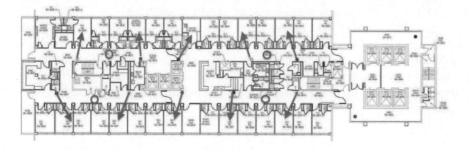

Aesthetics

As in many business settings, healthcare environments are sensitive to the aesthetics pertaining to equipment being installed in the environment. This aspect doesn't always have to do with keeping the environment pretty.

For example, psychiatric units or locations with mentally ill patients may be alarmed by the blinking of the AP's LED lights generated by normal usage of the WLAN. Physical tampering of the device may also be a concern. Fortunately, there are options to overcome most of these challenges. Most vendors provide a configuration option for disabling the blinking lights, for example. Also, many third-party companies offer a wide range of covers, in-ceiling mounting options, enclosures, and other products that allow for flexibility in terms of aesthetics and physical security of the access points. Many products are now manufactured with internal antennas so that the APs blend with the surroundings and antennas are hidden from view.

Other considerations in terms of aesthetics include the following:

Operating Rooms (ORs) Operating rooms usually have limitations as to what can be installed in them. Many times these rooms need the ability to be fully wiped down with a cleansing solution and thus a third-party enclosure is desirable.

Stairwells and Elevators Stairwells and elevators are always challenging, both from an RF perspective as well as from a building code and aesthetics perspective. Depending on the locality and its building codes, you may or may not be able to mount access points inside an elevator shaft or stairwell.

Patient Rooms Hospital policies typically encourage IT staff to avoid patient rooms when possible, but by avoiding installation of APs in patient rooms, RF propagation may be not ideal. There are many complications with mounting an AP within a patient room. The biggest issue is that the room has to be taken out of service for the installation of the AP and subsequently needs to be taken out of service in the event the AP has to be replaced. While the latter is a rare occurrence, over the longer term this situation can present challenges. That being said, from an RF perspective, it's highly desirable to mount the APs in the patient rooms as doing so affords the ability to have better isolation of APs, thereby reducing the co-channel interference that is so detrimental to a design where all APs are mounted in the hallways.

Access Restrictions

When doing any type of work in a hospital, it is important to keep in mind that you are often at the mercy of hospital operations. Getting into ORs at all usually requires scheduling the activity after hours (or during slow hours) and well in advance. Even then, it is possible that unforeseen patient needs will require that you reschedule the activity.

You also need to note that sterile environments are usually physically marked by red lines painted onto the floors, as shown in Figure 4.4. These lines usually exist before doors and you must not cross these lines unless you are wearing the proper attire. Failure to do so might cause you a great deal of political damage with your customer.

FIGURE 4.4 Hospital floor marking sterile area

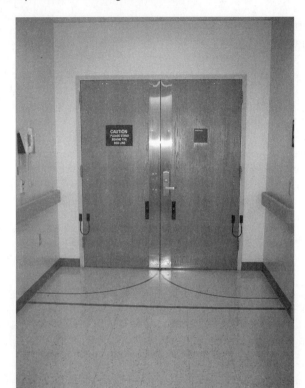

Multifloor RF Propagation

When it comes to designing a wireless network for healthcare, one of the often overlooked details is the RF propagation between floors. It is imperative that you pay careful attention to RF propagation if you expect the design to scale and fully support the range of devices and applications being used in healthcare today.

The specifics of survey best practices will be covered in detail in Chapter 9, "Site Survey RF Design," but it's worth noting here that floor-to-floor propagation can cause serious issues with high-density wireless networks due to co-channel interference. A common mistake surveyors make is to find an AP layout that works on a floor and then assume they can replicate that same layout on the rest of the floors. That should work since the rest of the floors have identical layouts, right? Wrong!

Depending on the construction of the building (and this varies from facility to facility), the vertical attenuation may be substantially less than the horizontal. This is often common with older building construction where thick, load-bearing walls are used but the floors have less structural support. What this means is that you might have an AP on the third floor, whose hottest RF neighbors are the APs on the second and fourth floors.

For situations like this, careful testing and planning needs to be done to prevent any issues with floor-to-floor co-channel interference. It should also be noted that improper "stacking" of APs floor over floor (see Figure 4.5) has been known to have detrimental effects for the before-mentioned automatic RF feature that some vendors deploy.

FIGURE 4.5   Avoid stacked APs between floors.

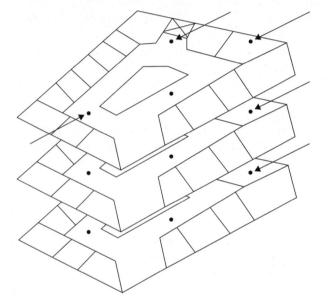

Regulatory

Working in a healthcare environment, you need to be made aware of certain regulatory agencies that you may encounter. The most well known is *JCAHO*, otherwise known as the *Joint Commission*. JCAHO is a nonprofit organization in the United States responsible for the accreditation of hospitals in the United States. They periodically perform surprise audits at hospitals, which often puts the hospital staff in a minor state of emergency. Hospital staff are trained to immediately make it known that JCAHO is onsite and a series of trained responses will likely need to be followed. If you are planning on working in a hospital and JCAHO shows up when you are there, you might as well plan on coming back once the audit has been performed, which can take several days.

Some states have their own regulatory agencies that control other aspects of hospital infrastructure. One example of this is the Office of Statewide Health and Planning Development (OSHPD), a California agency that regulates, in part, what is allowed to be installed in a hospital. The approval process to run cable and install APs needs to be documented and submitted to OSHPD for all California hospitals. The approval process has been known to take six months or more. This can add significant time to WLAN projects when regulatory agencies like this one must be catered to.

Lead Walls

Hospitals have some areas where lead has been incorporated into the wall material in order to shield unwanted X-ray radiation from escaping from radiology areas in order to provide a safe environment for X-ray technicians and hospital staff.

Lead walls tend to present their biggest challenge during the site survey if not properly anticipated. While this chapter is not focused on the survey process itself (see Chapters 8, "Site Survey Preparation," and 9, "Site Survey RF Design"), it is appropriate to briefly discuss this topic to avoid pitfalls when surveying healthcare facilities.

The main issue that tends to arise with lead walls is specific to site survey software's prediction of RF coverage. Different survey vendors have different default settings for RF coverage prediction, and it's crucial to know how far away from the surveyor the software is predicting the RF coverage. Why is this important, you may ask? Suppose you are surveying an area of a hospital and have measured the RF data on three sides of a room by surveying the hallways and rooms surrounding that area. The survey software will take those known, collected data points surrounding that room and predict the coverage inside the room using default prediction algorithms. Unaware that the wall is lead lined, the software may show that the RF coverage is within your designed minimum up to 20 feet away from where you walked and took data points. This can make the room appear to have ample coverage when in fact, it does not. You can avoid this problem in a couple of ways:

- First, it's highly recommended in VoWiFi surveys that you lower the number of feet the survey software is predicting coverage away from the surveyor. A common range to be used is generally around 10 to 15 feet.

- Second, you can avoid this type of misleading survey data if you mandate that the surveyor *must* enter every room that is considered a part of the intended coverage area. You can verify this via the path file to ensure your directions were followed.

Never trust what people tell you. Measure it! Data doesn't lie.

Constant Construction

Whenever construction occurs, it will more than likely change RF propagation patterns. Therefore, construction changes invalidate the existing RF survey for the new area.

Furthermore, when performing a site survey, you should look carefully for old and new parts of the building. Different survey and deployment techniques might be necessary depending on the construction techniques and materials used.

It is not uncommon to survey a hospital and then return 12 months later to find that an entire wing has been remodeled. Walls now exist where there were no walls before. While you can't tell your customer not to change their building's composition to meet their own needs, you should make them aware that these changes directly impact the way RF propagates through the facility. Such changes can cause serious issues for the operation of the devices that rely on the wireless network. Be upfront with your customer and let them know that these physical changes have to be planned for well in advance to allow time for proper surveying and resulting AP additions and adjustments to accommodate the change.

Outdoor Access

Areas between buildings where users walk need voice coverage. Break areas and outdoor eating areas should have coverage for critical alarm notification devices such as smart phones and VoWiFi handsets. It's best to cover these areas with APs dedicated to these areas as opposed to trying to cover them with APs that are covering the indoor areas. To attempt to cover them using indoor APs may work in some situations, but more often than not, you will have to turn up the AP power to a level that is more than that used for indoor coverage areas.

Later in this chapter we will discuss outdoor environments in greater detail.

Guest and Patient Internet Access

Guest and patient Internet access is now commonplace in most large healthcare facilities. Although providing this service is not an absolute requirement, in today's connected world it's getting close to becoming a must-have.

When it comes to designing for guest access, keep the following in mind:

- Guest networks should be given a lower QoS priority than any of the healthcare facilities networks that are being used for day-to-day operations. Typically, guest users are given "best effort" markings.

- It's impossible to predict what devices guests will bring into a facility. For that reason, we recommend that you configure the guest network as bare bones as possible. Avoid any advanced configuration features as they may or may not play well with all chipsets and drivers.

- Per-user rate limiting and/or website/protocol restrictions should be deployed on web gateways. Application protocol restriction usually includes denying real-time streaming protocols and peer-to-peer file sharing applications. URL filtering is also important to restrict access to known websites of inappropriate nature.

Refer to Chapter 3 for further information on designing for guest access.

Retail

There are several types of industry categories that we are including in the retail design category. Categories include warehouses and industrial environments, retail branches, and food franchise locations. All of these environments usually are remote to a centralized IT facility. Each typically requires some form of centralized authentication infrastructure and, depending on the number of client devices and availability requirements, may even need certain infrastructure located at some locations.

Warehouses and Industrial

Warehouses and industrial environments are a unique environment in which some WLAN designers have specialized. These environments come with a unique set of challenges from an RF perspective in that they typically have the most difficult and constantly changing physical environments.

Several factors make warehouse and industrial environments unique. These include the devices and applications that are most commonly used as well as the unique challenges that enter into RF propagation design from varying inventory levels. We will now discuss several unique factors and design methods for dealing with them.

Incorporating Computing Devices and Applications

Warehouses are most commonly known for using handheld computing devices. Laptops are rarely used. There are even wearable computers complete with a microphone headset for voice recognition picking systems. What makes this environment different from others usually starts with the devices used. Many of them are designed primarily for this industry vertical and tend to be very rugged.

In Chapter 2, "Designing for Client Devices and Applications," we discussed handheld computers and some common design practices to be aware of when they will be used. It will be helpful to recall those application-specific needs and challenges as you consider deploying Wi-Fi in warehouse and industrial environments. In simplest terms, many handheld systems used in industrial and warehouse environments require very minimal throughput. The important requirement for these applications is pervasive and consistent connectivity and mobility.

In addition to these factors, VoWiFi is a type of device and application that is starting to gain more momentum in this vertical. Warehouses have constantly changing inventory levels, which can vary the RF performance considerably. Multipath interference has also been one of the primary challenges that have affected some warehouse VoWiFi deployments that used 802.11abg technologies. However, 802.11n should provide a big benefit over the previous *single input, single output (SISO)* technologies. However, don't forget that if you deploy 802.11n APs, but your client devices are still 802.11abg, the multipath problem still exists in full.

If you asked anybody who has worked in warehouse environments what application is the most common, there would be a clear and consistent answer among everyone polled: Telnet. Most of the applications that run on the handheld devices over the network use Telnet as the application protocol. Some client applications convert Telnet information into a graphical user interface in order to allow for some tasks to be performed by simply clicking a button. In the end, from a WLAN designer's perspective, the application is still Telnet.

One thing in particular can greatly impact an end user's experience with Telnet: roaming. Roaming is especially problematic if reassociations experience excessive delay or if the user is forced onto a new subnet during a roam. If you deploy your WLAN to operate using different IP subnets or VLANs and the client device roamed between two segments while in an active Telnet session, the session would be lost—unless some type of L3 mobility tunneling protocol is used. The user would have to reconnect and would likely lose whatever data they were handling at the time.

If the network architecture uses a model where Layer 3 segmentation is done at the access layer, autonomous APs would not be a good design choice unless some form of a mobile IP system was used. In these environments, using a centralized forwarding data model would be a good choice if the switching design will not accommodate tunneling between APs at the edge.

Centralized data forwarding will be discussed in detail in Chapter 5, "Deciding on an Equipment Vendor."

Design Challenges

There are many design challenges you must consider when working with warehouses and industrial buildings. Imagine a warehouse with 50-foot-high metal storage shelves that form rows from one end of the building to the other. That in and of itself is challenging due to the multipath caused by all the metal, but let's zoom in a bit and focus on some of the less noticeable items:

Dealing with Inventory Changes   Most warehouses are in a constant state of change with inventory always on the move. Some days the aisles will be full; other days they may be close to empty. The amount of inventory and the composition of that inventory can have a drastic effect on the RF propagation within the building. From a survey and design perspective, you will want to plan for a worst-case scenario of having a full inventory of very dense product to ensure you will have adequate coverage when shelves fill up!

Using this technique, you will ensure that minimal levels of RF coverage are available regardless of the inventory levels at any given time. The trade-off is too much coverage when the shelves are emptier. It is an acceptable compromise because too little coverage will render wireless communication unreliable or completely unusable. Too much coverage will affect overall performance, but likely a fully usable data connection will persist. In this scenario, it is important to also remember that automated RF management may require more precise tuning with higher thresholds (changes are made less frequently) to prevent the WLAN from a constant process of changing channels and transmit power levels in accordance with fluctuating stock.

Finding the Best Location for Mounting APs   Let's assume you've done your survey and, from an RF perspective, know where you need your APs to be located. Questions you should ask yourself to find the best AP mounting locations are:

- Is it even feasible to mount an AP in those locations?

- Can you get Ethernet to those locations and stay within the specified Ethernet limitation of 100 meters?

- Is there a surface on which to mount the AP?

- Is a wireless backhaul (mesh or bridge link) required?

- What equipment may be necessary for mounting in those locations?

Designing with High Ceilings in Mind   Warehouses usually have very high ceilings with few obstructions other than the metal rafters holding up the roof. This makes for a unique challenge when designing a wireless network. Having the APs mounted up high leaves concerns about getting adequate coverage down to the floor—where your clients are. There's also the issue with containing co-channel interference, as the ceiling-mounted APs are typically all within clear RF line-of-sight view of one another. This can lead to the same RF problems discussed earlier in this chapter where APs are mounted in the hallways. While all of this sounds bad, it's still common practice to mount the APs either in the ceilings or high up on the walls of a warehouse because there's often not a better option.

Incorporating Office Space into Your Design   These environments typically have some small amounts of office space inside them that need coverage. The coverage model for the office environments will differ greatly from the warehouse itself, so you should approach the design by essentially breaking it into two separate methodologies. Achieving balance between the two separate environments is not an easy task. Careful consideration is needed on the AP placement, antenna selection and orientation, and channel and power plans. This is discussed further in the next sections where we cover some antenna selection criteria for industrial and warehouse environments as well as later in this chapter as we look at designing for carpeted office use.

Accommodating Normal Disruptions   Warehouses typically house a great deal of staff. The eating areas usually have a large bank of microwave ovens available for the workers to heat up their food. Interference from the microwaves may pose a minor disruption if users all take their breaks at the same time and they do not rely on a 2.4 GHz–based VoWiFi system for their communication system during the breaks. If the break times are staggered, it is likely that the combined effect of multiple microwave ovens in use at once will substantially degrade the wireless performance of the 2.4 GHz band in the area surrounding the microwaves.

Building-to-Building Communication Links   If there are several warehouse building structures as stand-alone buildings, it is not uncommon to need to enhance the building-to-building communication links for the new WLAN. Installing a Point-to-Point (PtP) or Point-to-Multi-Point (PtMP) network backbone system may be a great option to provide higher-speed links between buildings, and may also be used to augment existing communication lines in an additive, failover strategy.

Methodologies for Warehouse and Industrial Building Design

So how do you handle a challenging environment like this? For the warehouse portions, directional antennas can be a useful component to your RF propagation strategy. Start at the outermost part of your required coverage area and find a spot on a wall that is clear of adjacent obstructions and ideally has a clear line of sight down inventory aisles. Try placing a directional antenna at this location, using an appropriate amount of *down-tilt* on the antenna. Antenna gain from 6 to 12 dBi may be suitable depending on the circumstances.

A common, yet fallacious, initial design approach is to place APs high in the ceilings, upward of 50 feet high, and also use higher-gain omnidirectional antennas—usually 5.5 dBi or so. The result of this design style is shown in Figure 4.6.

FIGURE 4.6 Example of poor antenna choice for warehouses

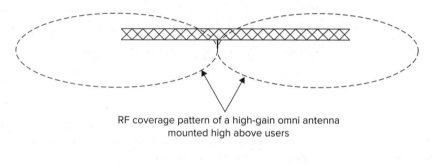

RF coverage pattern of a high-gain omni antenna
mounted high above users

Consider a ceiling full of APs mirroring the one shown in Figure 4.6. This would result in incredible range high above users' heads because the antennas are usually above the highest inventory shelving and there is usually nothing obstructing the RF signals directly horizontal to the antenna placement. In other words, APs would hear each other at very high signal levels, but the vertical directional focus (making your doughnut flatter) leaves users on the floor without coverage. This happens when three-dimensional coverage is not factored in.

In Figure 4.7, an elevation propagation pattern (looking straight on at the antenna to understand horizontal propagation) is shown for a 5.2 dBi omnidirectional antenna. Notice the direction of gain is horizontal, which is the direction perpendicular to the length of the antenna when it is held in a vertical orientation.

FIGURE 4.7   5.2 dBi omnidirectional antenna

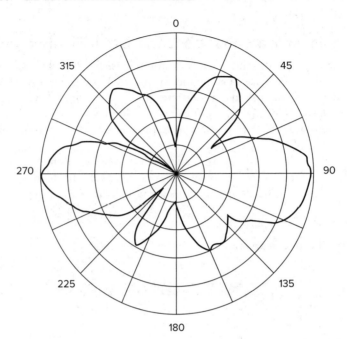

It can be possible to get too much distance, so you might find that a large amount of down-tilt needs to be placed on the antenna. As with a light bulb reflector, you are looking to maximize the amount of signal intensity within an acceptable range. Down-tilt would be used if the antenna is mounted on a wall instead of the ceiling because even with an omnidirectional antenna, down-tilt would create an effective directional propagation pattern. The advantage here is that by focusing energy directionally, you can minimize excessive multipath, manage contention with other APs, and also provide appropriate coverage overlap for mobile devices as they roam between APs.

Once you have taken this approach around all the edges of the building, you can then start to fill in the coverage holes (if any exist) using low-gain omnidirectional antennas. If ceiling heights are approximately upward of 50 feet high, you might consider a low-gain patch antenna. For example, a 6 dBi patch antenna has a wide field of view and provides two important other benefits to the overall design. First, it has some RF rejection to the other APs installed in the ceiling and the APs mounted high on the surrounding walls. In other words, you will have substantially reduced co-channel interference. Second, you are not wasting energy in any direction where you do not have WLAN clients located. Signal isn't going into the ceiling and to other APs in the ceiling. An example of a low-gain patch antenna used with high ceilings is shown in Figure 4.8.

FIGURE 4.8   Example showing a low-gain patch antenna

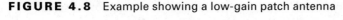
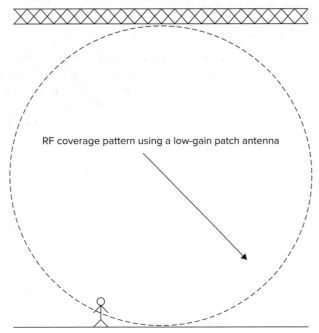

RF coverage pattern using a low-gain patch antenna

Pay particular attention to receiving and shipping areas. These areas tend to have more concentrated usage of WLAN devices and are usually considered higher-priority locations for signal quality.

Another important area (or in some cases, areas) is where merchandise selection, otherwise known as "picking and packing," occurs. Some warehouses have areas where workers receive a packing slip and have to walk between many different shelves with inventory usually broken into individually sellable items. A handheld scan gun is typically used to scan the packing slip and the holding shelf for each quantity of item that was removed. This helps to maintain a master inventory record and provide a level of quality assurance that the right item was picked and packed for the final customer.

These picking and packing areas have a lot of WLAN activity. A slow-performing network in this area can result in directly attributable monetary loss.

Retail Branches

The retail branch category is defined as any brick and mortar store, from small to very large retail facilities, that can number in the hundreds or even thousands of locations. This can include grocery chains, electronic retailers, and other large retail chains with a large number of branch locations. Retail branches by our definition have at least one centralized datacenter where services are provided. In other words, not all of the applications and services are provided by onsite computing devices.

Retail environments usually do not have a large quantity of client devices, comparative to other enterprises. There are two main categories:

Handheld Devices   These are typically incorporated for use in inventory or labeling tasks. As inventory is placed on the shelves, it is scanned where the *point-of-sale (PoS)* equipment debits from the inventory levels as goods are sold. The pricing that the PoS system uses for each item that is scanned at the register is kept in a centralized database. PoS devices are typically wired devices. Some credit card processing equipment may also use the wireless network. Some handheld devices have a card reader built into them and will utilize the wireless network to authorize each purchase.

Price Check Stations   These are common in many stores where consumers are interested in taking an item and scanning it to check the item's price. Some of these systems use Wi-Fi as a backhaul and query the same database as the PoS registers do.

We present both of these categories in order to understand the potential security risks they present. One or both of these systems may use the WLAN, but even if a WLAN is present, chances are that the systems that house this information may be accessible from the WLAN network. In other words, pricing information and credit card accounts might be transmitted wirelessly and proper security precautions need to be made.

More than one retailer has been exposed by international media from being susceptible to security vulnerabilities where credit card data has been captured. The Payment Card Industry Security Standards Council has developed a set of data security standards called *PCI DSS*, also simply referred to as *PCI*. It was designed to help merchants who process credit card transactions prevent fraud. The PCI DSS standard applies to all organizations that hold, process, or exchange cardholder information. The PCI standard is responsible for a great deal of the security practices implemented in the retail industry today.

   More information about PCI can be found at
https://www.pcisecuritystandards.org/security_standards/pci_dss.shtml.

VoWiFi is a driver for retail environments as well. It is more common to see VoWiFi at larger retail facilities than smaller ones.

Larger retail branches also typically have multiple APs per location. This means that roaming performance will need to be considered if VoWiFi is to be used. Some retail branches can exhibit similar characteristics to warehouse facilities in that inventory levels can fluctuate and therefore so will the RF propagation.

From a management perspective, each retail branch facility will likely have the exact same WLAN infrastructure configuration as well as a common WLAN device image. This lends itself very well to a centralized management system. Centralized WLAN controllers might not necessarily be the best choice for these environments if too much WAN latency or too many link reliability issues are present. If a large number of APs are at each facility, an onsite WLAN controller might be justifiable, but with many facilities with just a few

APs or less, the cost of controllers can add up. Otherwise, a centralized WNMS might be the best choice. This is especially true if the types of APs installed in each retail branch can vary between two or more vendors or even between divergent architectural types from the same vendor.

Consistency of configuration, firmware and application versions are key for geographically dispersed organizations. This makes for easier troubleshooting and usually a well designed and tested solution is the result of this type of design. Equipment and software purchases can be combined that will also result in higher discount levels.

Range is usually a key design component to retail environments. The concept of "range versus rates" is used in these types of environments because data rate is less important to minimizing the IT footprint at each facility where WLAN infrastructure is installed. If a large amount of data doesn't need to be transmitted and there aren't a lot of client devices contending for wireless access simultaneously, lower data rates are certainly acceptable. This may allow you to sometimes double the square footage of coverage for each AP in some environments. Just be careful to leave yourself plenty of link budget for fluctuations in RF signal quality where a solid, stable RF link can still be maintained.

Guest access is not a major concern for retail branches, but in certain retail environments it is looked upon quite favorably in order to keep customers at the store for longer lengths of time.

One of the interesting developments in retail stores is the use of a WLAN for guest services that facilitate targeted advertising on mobile devices. For example, if a customer enters a retail big box store and accesses the guest network via their smart phone, they may be offered specific coupons or discounts. This use will continue to emerge in the coming years.

Food Franchises and Shopping Destinations

Food franchises are defined as major brand-name coffee merchants, chain restaurants, and fast-food purveyors. Shopping destinations such as large shopping malls are also grouped into this category because of their similarities to guest access requirements.

The design challenges for smaller food franchises or shopping destinations doesn't differ that much from the retail branch model. The primary differences for food franchise locations primarily center on the following:

- They might need only a single AP.
- They are more likely to have neighboring APs (friendly rogues).
- There is a greater emphasis on guest access.

In terms of all applications in these environments, guest access reigns king. Actually, the web portal that is presented at these locations is considered prime real estate for marketing and promotion. Even customer satisfaction surveys can be performed using the web portal. Especially in restaurants and coffee shops, the presence of guest access will encourage customers to stay for longer periods of time. Charging for guest access in these environments is also commonly done. As different franchise operations are often competitive with each other, some have opted to give it away for free.

Each franchise location likely needs its own Internet access at least to form a VPN connection to the corporate franchise office. Therefore, the guest traffic might also be shared with the franchise operational activity. When this is the case, you do not want the guest access activity to impact the franchise operations. Two simple options exist. First, a separate circuit can be used for just the guest access system. The other option is to perform traffic policing using the quality of service (QoS) queues that may be present on the border router. Guest traffic in these environments is sometimes tunneled to a centralized location, usually a datacenter, where the web portal is presented and the URL filtering occurs. This tunneled traffic can be placed in the low-priority QoS queue or even rate limited and marked before it enters the WAN circuit.

Providing RF coverage at these locations is not usually much of a design challenge. However, the same management issues apply as with the retail branch model. It is important to have an absolutely consistent, standardized and centralized WLAN design and configuration model throughout every location.

Education

The education vertical, for the sake of our discussion, is defined by campus environments encompassing several buildings and open spaces where students dwell between classes. Smaller campuses and single buildings are simpler versions of the educational campus design scenario that we will focus on.

Nearly all students are carrying laptop computers. The "when I was a kid" cliché simply won't work for parents anymore who are trying to fight the ever-increasing gadget appetite of their children; it is a part of their education. Some high schools and nearly all higher education institutions require their students to have laptops.

But laptops are not the only devices students are carrying. Smart phones and other secondary computing devices like tablets and e-readers are also carried by many students. Students tend to be heavy users of rich media applications and also use their computers more than other user demographics. That equates to more and more network utilization per user.

Educational institutions have at least two classes of users: faculty and students. Faculty members are likely provided an enterprise asset that conforms to a platform standardization policy. At least these devices can be engineered and tested for WLAN compliance. Students, on the other hand, will carry just about whatever the hot device of the month is, which as we stated earlier, might even be more than one device. In contrast to faculty, virtually no standardization can be had across the student computing devices, which puts the institution in a bind when it comes to enterprise security and certain WLAN feature support. Of course, user-based security is important so that each student has their own access credentials and privileges as well as privacy.

Students also want to work just about anywhere they can sit or lay down. This means open spaces, outdoor areas, and public space is fair game for WLAN coverage. Similarly, they want to be mobile. If they're using their smart phone or tablet on their way to class, they want continuous connectivity the whole time.

One of the big challenges with classrooms is the device density. The number of devices that can be present in small areas can be quite large. Classrooms might even need more than one AP in some cases. Using a single AP with both 2.4 GHz and 5 GHz radios can be an enormous advantage because each radio can handle a portion of the client load. That does assume that a fair number of the client devices are dual-band capable. The other benefit of dual-band APs is that their costs are not that much higher than single-spectrum APs. In fact, it almost takes a concerted effort to purchase an enterprise, single-radio AP anymore.

Let's combine what we have already discussed and put it into perspective. In educational environments we find the following attributes:

- High device quantities
- High device density per AP
- Outdoor and public space coverage demands
- Heavy users of network bandwidth
- Lack of device standardization
- Some level of user-based security
- Application mobility

This is certainly one of the most demanding sets of design challenges. We will focus our discussion on user densities, lack of device continuity, and security, the three areas that are the biggest hurdles and have the most unique challenge in this segment.

Handling User Density

In both K-12 and higher education deployments, user densities are very high. Many classrooms, with one device per student, require at least 30 connections to an AP. Depending upon the building characteristics of the classrooms, APs are often deployed in every other classroom. In other words, each AP usually must handle 60 student connections, sometimes more. Enterprise APs are perfectly capable of handling that many client associations, but the applications used by the students will dictate how well the 802.11 protocols and WLAN products hold up to the load.

You will often find that education deployments for the classroom are not overly taxed because the applications are not high bandwidth, but with that many users on an AP, it doesn't take a very demanding application to cause noticeable performance issues for each student. Supporting low-latency, streaming applications in this environment is usually out of the question.

Because of this challenge, we must rest on our design laurels and ensure, via thorough testing, that our AP density is sufficient to handle user numbers and applications, while maintaining adequate co-channel separation so as to avoid contention problems with adjacent cells. With such density, this is tough.

In extra-high density areas, such as conference rooms and some libraries, you will find that AP placement and antenna choice is very important. One vendor, Xirrus, builds an array that handles high densities very well by providing multiple radios in each unit connected to directional antennas that covers a limited horizontal section of the environment. Each piece of the pie, as an analogy, is served by a different radio and directional antenna, creating multiple different contention domains. Other vendors are capable of providing a similar version of a directional antenna array as well, though it takes a little more strategic planning and hardware selection. We will discuss this technique in greater detail in Chapter 5.

Lack of Standardization

There are a few primary issues where lack of standardization rears its ugly head in education—primarily higher education. Just about every student brings a different device to campus, and each device will have its own software bugs, feature incompatibilities, implementation variances, unique configuration strategies, and other problems. You must design with this in mind.

You'll certainly find that some client devices don't play well in your network. This is usually a result of a driver bug or some type of implementation error from the client manufacturer. It helps to keep spreadsheets of known issues and to provide recommended drivers or software upgrades for client devices. In most cases, the primary design take-away from this tendency is to avoid any advanced feature sets that require client support. These features will only lead to support problems. Even in those features that, in theory, should work for all clients, problems will show up. It is the designer's responsibility to keep the network as simple as possible while still securely providing all desired services.

In addition to a wide array of support problems, the other main issue with lack of standardization is security. We will discuss the security challenges next.

Security Challenges

Because of the complexity of different computing devices and operating system platforms, implementing an 802.11-based security policy is usually one of the greatest challenges in higher education. However, for the sake of user security, it must be done. Most higher education institutions prefer 802.1X for primary student connectivity. Since students usually have a username and password for other campus services, the Wi-Fi network can draw from this credential (stored in a database) for an 802.11 access credential.

One of the design criteria to consider here is whether 802.1X is necessary, and if so, what EAP type to implement. We discuss EAP in Chapter 12, "Advanced Enterprise WLAN Security Design," but for now, there are a few key points. First, the EAP method will have to be a ubiquitously supported method across all devices and operating systems. Second, the access credential used by EAP will generally have to be a username and password pair to tie in with existing student credentials. PEAPv0/EAP-MSCHAPv2 is the most common choice in this implementation, but many universities also use EAP-TTLS.

Finally, students generally cannot configure their own devices for an 802.1X connection profile. So, the IT staff must provide a web-based method or a software executable file that performs this setup for the student. Many institutions use a third-party software program that is compatible with a wide range of OSs for this purpose. This process usually includes the creation of a WLAN profile on the supplicant as well as installation of a server certificate into the trusted certificate store of the client device. The key point here is that the chosen configuration method be compatible with the broadest possible range of computing devices. Alternatively, the IT staff can provide detailed instructions for the student to follow, though this is not a preferred method because it is very difficult for IT staff to provide comprehensive instructions for setup of all devices and OSs.

If 802.1X is not the chosen security method for primary access, a good alternative is to use a per-user PSK (PPSK), which is a proprietary option offered by some vendors. We will discuss this security type in more detail in Chapter 11, "Basic WLAN Security Design." For now, you should know that a per-user PSK allows each device or set of devices to have a unique access credential that provides relatively strong, individualized data privacy for the user. This solution will be easier to manage than 802.1X but may be slightly more difficult than a simple PSK. All device types will support it, too.

As we've discussed already, many students will have a primary computer as well as other peripheral devices, such as mobile phones, tablets, and other Wi-Fi capable devices like gaming consoles and printers. The trick with these devices is to include them in the primary access method (like 802.1X) where possible, but to provide an alternative SSID for devices with weak security. Gaming consoles are a perfect example of this. Since the school may not offer an SSID with a PSK, devices that don't support 802.1X will often be moved to a tightly filtered and restricted open network that implements some type of MAC address filter. Students register their devices and MAC addresses with the IT staff and provisions are made. This is not ideal security, but for devices like gaming consoles, it is better than providing a wide open network.

There are many other considerations to make as well.

Staff and Guests   Educational staff will often use a separate SSID than the students, though they are often secured with 802.1X. Some type of guest services are usually provided on a separate network as well, though the access method on these networks will vary by institution. Some will be open with a captive portal, while others will require that visitors and guests obtain a temporary password from the IT staff.

Rogue Devices   Another security challenge is rogue devices in student dorm rooms or lab facilities. Without realizing the potential problem, a student might plug in their consumer Wi-Fi router and unknowingly provide DHCP services to other users of the LAN. This would cause serious problems for the other users because they would not have a valid IP address for the school network and would be unable to use the network until the rogue Wi-Fi router was removed. These rogue devices might also offer another entry point to the campus LAN in areas where it may be undesirable to do so. Some type of wireless intrusion detection system (WIDS) is usually recommended to prevent this, and making the usage policy known to students may help too.

Virus Containment   One method of limiting the exposure of viruses and similar threats is to block peer-to-peer traffic. It is more challenging to do this with wired networks, but many WLAN equipment vendors have features that can restrict all peer-to-peer user traffic. Obviously this feature would be bad for a voice network where phones need to call each other, but for normal laptop and general computing devices, this feature can provide a lot of value.

Network Access Control   One way to handle the lack of device standardization is to use *network access control (NAC)*. Because students manage their own devices and no antivirus or malware protection may be present, NAC provides a technology framework to interrogate devices before they can gain normal access to the network. For example, a device that doesn't meet the minimum criteria can be dynamically placed on a quarantine VLAN that is segmented from the rest of the network. The VLAN will usually provide a web portal with instructions for the user to take action to meet the minimum requirements to use the network.

Roaming   Roaming requirements tend to be less demanding in education than in some other verticals, such as healthcare, but they are still important in most higher education deployments as students and faculty want to remain connected as they are on the go. Many mobile devices are taking advantage of the Wi-Fi network for real-time interactive applications, which will require roaming. We will discuss roaming and security in greater detail in Chapters 10, "MAC Layer Design," and 12, "Advanced Enterprise WLAN Security Design," and we will help designers make the best choices for each environment.

 Real World Scenario

Eduroam

Eduroam is an international initiative that allows members of educational establishments to gain Internet access at other member sites easily, using credentials from their home site in a secure manner. Authentication details (username/password) are configured on the user's computer and tested at the home site before departure. These details are used automatically at the destination site when the computer discovers the Eduroam network is available.

Eduroam uses realm-based RADIUS authentication for user authentication. A user from one university would perform an 802.1X authentication and present their username along with a realm identifier that specifies which user database to query for the specified user. In other words, there is a network of RADIUS servers that are part of Eduroam, each providing authentication services for their home users wherever they may travel to.

Other Verticals

Although healthcare, retail, and education are some of the largest WLAN verticals, others exist that you should be familiar with as well. They include typical carpeted office environments, hospitality segments such as hotels and conference venues, SOHO venues, and a variety of outdoor environments.

Office Use

Office environments are heavy adopters of Wi-Fi. Offices are becoming more and more mobile as time goes on. Workers telecommute and many employees travel a great deal, spending less time in front of a traditional desk. Most office workers with laptop computers are likely to have Wi-Fi at home. Naturally, when they go to the office, their expectations are that the user experience is at least as good as it is at home.

Companies also have a financial incentive to unwire the office. That means that they run and support less cabling to each worker desk. Away from the desk, conference rooms are highly critical areas where Wi-Fi is required; this is because when workers are in the conference room, they need to have access to the same resources that they have when they are at their desk.

One big shift in office space network design has been to nearly forego Ethernet switches and *unshielded twisted pair (UTP)*—Cat5, 5e, 6, etc.—cabling to employee workspaces and to leverage Wi-Fi as the primary means of connectivity. Many new office spaces are taking this step, though existing facilities that already have UTP do not have the financial incentive to cut the wire. To be clear, you usually can't forego the cabling and Ethernet connectivity altogether, but instead of using multiple runs per cubicle, perhaps one line would be run. It is quite common to find office environments that have run up to four cable pulls to each cubicle or small office.

Frankly, in terms of raw performance, wired is better than wireless for the type of connectivity that doesn't require mobility and that demands highly reliable connections. (And you thought this was a wireless book!) That is, wired performance will likely always have an edge over wireless performance in terms of speed, latency, loss, reliability, and availability. However, cost is always a consideration as well, and not everyone needs the performance enhancements offered by wired connectivity.

We all know that with earlier Wi-Fi offerings, speeds were insufficient to handle even the simplest tasks for a handful of users. This fact has discouraged migrations to fully Wi-Fi-based environments, but 802.11n has changed the game with speeds and reliability sufficient to support mission critical business applications. There are several factors involved in this migration, but the most important of them is what applications are in use by the office workers. If it is primarily engineering and the staff needs large amounts of bandwidth, wiring may be best. But, for most environments with some file sharing, web access, email, and the like, wireless provides the perfect blend of performance and cost along with mobility.

Let's look at a few attributes of Wi-Fi used in office environments:

- Mobility requirements are somewhat limited. As VoWiFi adoption increases in this space, mobility needs will increase.
- Heavy usage of Wi-Fi in conference and training rooms
- Guest access for vendors and visitors

Office users do not usually require the type of seamless mobility that highly mobile workers do because office users are typically stationary for longer lengths of time. Even if they are mobile, aside from VoWiFi, most office applications can tolerate a moderate amount of latency during a roam. Because of this, they have less stringent design requirements for roaming. When meetings are held, office workers often take their computing device to a conference room where Wi-Fi would be expected in order for them to be productive during the meeting.

Guest access for customers and visitors is another important WLAN feature that companies are quick to embrace.

The physical environment for office space tends to be fairly open with some drywall offices. Cubicle farms are perfect examples of this. The cubicles usually only extend 5 to 6 feet in height, allowing ceiling-mounted APs to have a fairly large coverage area. Open space with few obstructions allows for pretty straightforward RF design. The primary issue is finding balance between application demands with user densities and preventing interference with neighboring cells.

Each office environment will have its own unique characteristics and needs, but the design process is pretty straightforward and follows the best practices explained throughout the rest of this book.

Hospitality

Travelers have come to *expect* that Wi-Fi will be available at their hotel or airport. This, believe it or not, has grown to include cruise ships and some other transportation services, like airplanes. While the operations crew might have a need for Wi-Fi, chances are that the primary driver for Wi-Fi is guest access. There are a number of common factors to consider in network deployments for hospitality.

Cost   Giving away Wi-Fi for free usually limits the cost an organization is willing to pay to provide that service. This may translate to budget-conscious deployment techniques using the lowest number of APs and the lowest-cost model of a manufacturer's APs. This often requires a single-band (2.4 GHz) deployment using internal antennas. Even eliminating cable drops is sometimes desirable if mesh features are available and can be used. Not every organization is like this, but many are.

Some hospitality venues still rely on a fee-based Wi-Fi solution. In many public areas, such as airports, this is more common. Service providers will generally have a network service here, so you can subscribe to and access these networks wherever you travel.

Hotels are moving away from this trend for their guests, though one area where a hotel might be able to charge for Internet access is a conference area. These areas often even use a different SSID than the guest room, providing some guaranteed level of service, such as 1 Mbps downlink connectivity. Having revenue-generating areas like this may help justify purchasing higher quality APs and better Internet bandwidth to use for the entire WLAN deployment.

Services   One of the interesting facets of designing for hospitality networks is that Internet access is the primary—or sole—service, and the Internet connection is usually the network bottleneck. For that reason, designers can often focus less on high bandwidth WLAN design (ensuring high data rates and throughput), and alternately spend their time ensuring that all areas are well covered with reliable client connectivity and even modest data rates. The WLAN should at least provide adequate service to stay ahead of future improvements in Internet speeds.

Backhaul   In many hotels, AP backhaul can be a challenge. Ethernet cable drops may not be available in the most desirable locations for APs. For this reason, some vendors have manufactured a walljack AP device that uses the existing (in hotel rooms) Ethernet cabling for connectivity. The AP is built into the walljack unit, and the device also provides Ethernet ports out to the room for VoIP connectivity, wired network access for guests, and other possible Ethernet needs.

In some cases where Ethernet drops are not available, mesh backhaul may be used. The problem with using mesh features and eliminating the need for an Ethernet cable drop is that APs still require power. Running a new AC electrical line tends to be more expensive than running a UTP cable drop. However, if AC is available in the mesh location, then it is certainly an option.

Aesthetics   Since most hospitality venues are highly aesthetically conscious, most APs will be hidden from sight. For those that are not, internal antennas are usually recommended. From an RF perspective, it may make the most sense to put an AP in a room, but this may cause objections in aesthetic concerns as well as for potential theft issues.

Security   Hospitality networks nearly always use open networks with captive portal authentication for "security." After associating to the network, traffic from each user is intercepted by the guest appliance (or the Wi-Fi infrastructure itself) that will present an authentication page and an acceptable use policy (AUP) agreement before users can gain Internet access.

The authentication process usually relies on an authentication PIN or passphrase that is provided to the guest during check-in. For design purposes, there are several different types of systems that can accommodate this need, but one of the important aspects to consider is that hotel (or staff members from other hospitality industries) staff will be responsible for on-site administration of the platform. Therefore, either an automated process should be used, or the guest credential platform should be very user friendly to administer.

From a business perspective, captive portals with an AUP satisfy the liability concerns, but users' Wi-Fi traffic remains susceptible to attack. The WLAN designer should enable peer-to-peer blocking, and if more advanced features—like broadcast traffic filtering, DHCP snooping, ARP inspection, ARP proxy—are available, to implement them as well.

There are many attacks that can be performed when users are using Wi-Fi open security. For business travelers, one way around this is to use VPN, but not all consumers and even small companies will be able to make use of it. For this reason, some Wi-Fi equipment vendors allow for VPN termination to their devices, but that becomes an IT headache for hospitality staff to support.

SOHO Remote Offices

In this category we will focus on single-AP deployment locations that are not directly connected to a corporate network. These environments are essentially for employees who work remotely at home or at small, satellite corporate offices. In this design section we are also assuming these locations have one or two people using the network from an inexpensive broadband Internet connection.

For telecommuters, there are benefits to supplying a corporate AP to certain types of employees. If the SSID is the same that is used in the office environment, the SSID is likely already configured for the user. If we assume that the office extension AP is reliable and doesn't add much to the IT support model, that decision may actually minimize support costs. Some of the most IT-challenged corporate users who work remotely insist that IT support staff help them set up their home environments in order to be productive. Companies that employ these types of remote employees who need remote access might justify the expense of having their IT support personnel not only help configure the environment initially, but also continue to support user needs for troubleshooting and upgrades.

There are security benefits to this model as well. Hackers seeking to compromise certain corporate users, like company executives or product management, might find that the best place to do it would be at their residences. Home users typically configure their equipment with minimal security features, if security is enabled at all. This makes their devices and the traffic they send open to attacks that could be prevented if they were using a strong corporate security policy at home. The only logical way to accomplish this would be to supply them with an AP that enforces a strong corporate security policy.

The following are features for the small office, home office (SOHO) and remote office vertical.

Encrypted Tunnel

Newer capabilities of WLAN equipment include the ability to install APs at remote locations with an Internet connection and have the AP form an encrypted tunnel back to the corporate offices. Control and Provisioning of Wireless Access Points (CAPWAP), a protocol used for AP communications, supports an encryption protocol called *Dynamic Transport Layer Security (DTLS)*. CAPWAP allows the AP to "phone home" to a WLAN infrastructure device, usually a WLAN controller, and then negotiate an encrypted tunnel to pass WLAN traffic from the remote AP back into the corporate network via this secure tunnel.

The traditional method for accomplishing this type of security required a WAN router with IPSec VPN capabilities. The configuration for these features was complex, and it took a substantial amount of engineering effort to bring these locations online. Even once these locations were brought online, physical security for these devices was a major concern. For example, if a device was placed at an employee's home office, a family member with an infected PC might connect to the encrypted tunnel, where this traffic could then make its way back into the corporate office. When the VPN router is exchanged for a remote AP, the corporate network access is tied to a specific access profile, one that only corporate users can access.

802.1X and Wired Ports

Some APs from enterprise WLAN equipment vendors have the option of using multiple Ethernet ports on the remote AP to provide flexible connectivity options for remote users. These ports may be used by a wired VoIP phone for the home user or perhaps a desktop PC. The ports are more of a concern than the Wi-Fi network because usually no security features are configured for wired Ethernet ports. In response, equipment vendors are offering wired 802.1X features or web-based portal authentication pages, although adoption of 802.1X on the wire has been somewhat slow. Portal authentication pages are an attractive option and could even be tied into a two-factor authentication mechanism that may already be used for traditional VPN access.

Configuring a Personal SSID

Another possible option for office extension APs is the ability to configure multiple SSIDs, specifically a corporate SSID and a personal SSID, as shown in Figure 4.9. In this scenario, you could tie each SSID to a tunneling profile. For example, the corporate SSID would send traffic down the encrypted tunnel to the enterprise network, and the personal SSID would drop the traffic off locally just like a normal AP would do.

FIGURE 4.9   Office extension APs using personal SSIDs

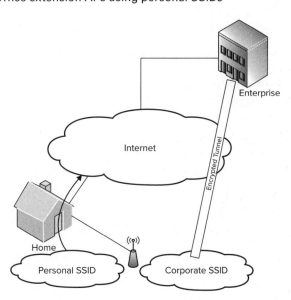

Installing Secondary Ethernet Ports

Secondary Ethernet ports can also be configured for personal communications just like the personal SSID. This means that a single AP can be placed at an employee's home, and it would allow the employee and their personal machines to work off the same equipment.

Other devices like VoIP phones can also be plugged into the secondary Ethernet port, enabling an even more office-like experience for heavy telecommuters.

Providing Wi-Fi Outside

Outdoor Wi-Fi deployments are some of the most challenging networks to design because of these factors:

- Mounting locations are limited.
- RF interference is harder to control
- Backhaul connectivity may be difficult to achieve
- Heating, cooling, and other environmental considerations need to be factored in.
- Power may not be readily available for access devices.
- Environmental variables may be out of the network owner's control

Not every outdoor environment has all these challenges, but many do. Let's examine some common outdoor environments and discuss the design considerations for each.

Metro

Metropolitan Wi-Fi networks were once considered one of the fastest-growing market segments of Wi-Fi. Nearly every city was embracing a ubiquitous Wi-Fi strategy for a variety of uses, including:

Public Safety   Use cases for public safety include police, fire, and ambulatory.

Video Backhaul   If you have ever looked around busy intersections and various roadway locations, you will see video cameras. These cameras need to transmit a signal to a remote location via some backhaul connection. While this can be done via landlines provided by the local telephone company, it may be more cost effective in the long run to handle this transmission with a wireless connection.

Parking Meters   New parking meters have the ability to utilize a network connection to efficiently operate and monitor parking areas. Sensors are embedded in these meters and give updates to a central location. Alerts can be sent to a local parking enforcement officer to issue a ticket.

Economic Stimulus and Tourism   Local government is always looking to make their town more attractive to tourists. The logic is that consumers might be more likely to patronize businesses that have wireless access compared to those that do not. This also means that outdoor parks, cafes, and gathering areas will also attract consumers to nearby businesses.

When designing for outdoor coverage, you have to take into account a few design factors. The first is the amount of traffic users will need to transmit and receive versus the amount of distance you must cover with each AP. Next, you need to research whether the environment is subject to harsh weather conditions as such conditions would limit the mounting options and add design requirements. Available mounting locations and techniques in general need to be understood along with power and data backhaul options, if any exist. Your design may require a wireless backhaul and/or renewable energy options like solar power.

Ranges vs. Rates

When designing for outdoor locations, you will typically be faced with having to provide the maximum amount of coverage per AP. In other words, you are designing for maximum range as opposed to maximum data rate. As you will learn in Chapter 6, "RF Communication Principles," when you maximize the amount of range an AP will cover, you have to give up something: data rates—or density.

One way you add range is with directional antennas. Using directional antennas means that you are taking signal amplitude and focusing it in one direction, which generally reduces signal amplitude in other directions.

Harsh Environments

Equipment placed outdoors should be designed to handle harsh outdoor conditions. Typically, WLAN equipment designed for outdoor environments is intended to work in extreme weather conditions. This includes desert conditions with the hottest of temperatures and sandstorms to the extreme opposite—climates with sustained subzero temperatures. Regardless of the conditions, it is important to check the equipment's temperature ratings during the selection process.

If you are placing an AP outside, the heat from the sun is enough of a challenge. If you've ever stepped into a car that has been parked in the sun for a few hours on a warm summer day, you know how interior spaces can heat up when exposed to the sun. Placing equipment into a metal enclosure without proper planning can be a bad move. *Solar loading* is the term used to denote the amount of sunlight an object endures that will be converted to heat. Direct sunlight on an enclosure will heat up the interior. Simply shading a device can decrease the solar load substantially and should always be considered. This strategy may be difficult as the object shading the enclosure might also limit the RF propagation if the antennas are next to the enclosure.

Freezing temperatures are also troublesome. While some APs are designed to operate at very low temperatures, others are not. Be careful when choosing APs; many that can be operated at very low temperatures might need protection from overheating. For APs that do not provide low-temperature options, you might need to include a heating element with a thermostat for colder periods.

When using heating and cooling elements, you can assume that Power over Ethernet (PoE) is not possible. When you are placing National Electrical Manufacturers Association (NEMA) enclosures outside, it is usually best to provide standard A/C power to them for expansion and to power the accessory elements that might also be housed in the enclosure.

Using a *NEMA enclosure* to place equipment inside is great for the electronics but not for the RF propagation. You will generally use an external antenna when using a NEMA enclosure. That means you must penetrate the enclosure to run an antenna extension cable. This task needs to be done in two parts.

First, you run a cable from the antenna connector on an AP equipped with external antenna connectors to a bulkhead connector on the NEMA enclosure. This cable is also referred to as a *pigtail cable*. Usually you want to place the bulkhead connector on the bottom of the NEMA enclosure, as shown in Figure 4.10.

FIGURE 4.10   RF extension cable and bulkhead connector

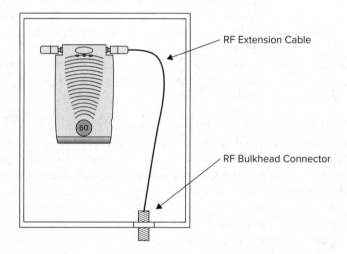

Never go short with the length of the RF extension cable that extends from the AP antenna connector to the bulkhead connector. Leave at least an extra 6 inches. Also, you need to confirm, and then double confirm, the connector choice because there are so many options when ordering cables with specific connectors for different antennas and AP makes and models.

Placing the bulkhead connector on top of the NEMA enclosure might result in water penetrating the NEMA enclosure. It is almost always best to place the bulkhead connector on the bottom of the enclosure. Water will find its way into even the smallest of openings. As the years progress with the expansion and contraction of the enclosure materials due to heating and cooling, seals that used to be airtight often develop very small leaks. Antenna connectors located at the bottom of the NEMA enclosure also provide the greatest protection from the elements.

Once you place the bulkhead connector on the bottom of the unit, you can connect an antenna. Depending on the RF coverage pattern you need, a variety of antenna types can be used. A notable exclusion in this process is surge suppression, which we will cover later in this section.

After the antenna has been connected to the outside portion of the bulkhead connector, you should seal it. There are two types of sealant you can choose from. One is a tape, and the other comes in a form similar to a block of clay. After the antenna connector has been placed on the bulkhead connector and tightly fastened, you want to completely wrap the connector and every possible opening to protect the metal from corrosion and from Mother Nature's elements.

Mounting Location Restrictions

When designing an outdoor network, you have to consider several factors regarding where you plan to mount the equipment. First, you have to take into account cable length and power restrictions. For instance, if you need to mount an AP more than 100 meters away from an Ethernet switch, you might need to consider using fiber or using an RF link as a backhaul.

Second, electrical power is a concern. If you plan on placing an AP in a particular location, never assume that you can tap into any available lighting fixture or conduit carrying electricity. Three primary factors weigh into this consideration:

Voltage   Electrical lines, especially those used in commercial construction, carry a variety of voltages. It is possible that a transformer might be required to step down the voltage from a nearby line to what the AP can use for input power.

Amperage   Every electrical line has a finite capacity it can carry. You need to factor in the maximum load your outdoor AP solution will consume (assuming heating elements, media converters, etc.) and consult a licensed electrician.

Always-on vs. Switched Power   A mistake people often make is assuming that the power available in an electrical line is always on. When these lines are used for outdoor lighting, the power source may be switched from a photovoltaic sensor, timer, or manual switch.

If you do find a continuous power source that also has available capacity for the electrical load that you require and at the voltage you need, *and* you are given permission, consider yourself lucky. Again, while there might be electrical power nearby, you need to confirm these primary factors before you can plan on tapping into the power source.

Electrical power is a functional mounting restriction. Other factors come into play in the form of aesthetics. Not everybody likes to look at metal boxes and large antennas sticking up on the sides of their buildings. Quite often you will find yourself having to camouflage your outdoor solution into the façade where you are mounting. This may even include painting the antenna and enclosure. Double check with the product manufacturer, as painting may void your warranty. Also, darker-colored paints will absorb more sunlight than lighter-colored paints, thus creating a higher solar load. However, if you have to paint your antennas, pay careful attention to the type of paint being used; some paint contains metal flakes or other materials that can change the RF characteristics of your antenna. Note that painting the NEMA enclosure for your AP can additionally heat the inside of the enclosure.

Another important consideration when mounting anything outside is *how* you are going to install it. The optimum location to mount an antenna isn't always the most accessible. Man lifts and other heavy construction equipment may be required to perform the labor. Rental fees for this equipment should be factored into the installation budget. Don't just consider the initial installation; you also need to factor in maintenance and troubleshooting activities that might have to occur well after the initial installation.

Next, think about how maintenance will be performed. If an AP is placed on a pole 100 feet in the air, it may be possible to put a junction box at the bottom of the pole that has a serial line connected to the device's console ports. This approach can save a lot of money in the long run if problems occur that require equipment rental or specialized labor to gain access to the equipment.

Everything considered, safety should always be the highest of priorities. Always think of safety first before performing any installation and maintenance activity that involves heights, opportunity for electrical shock, and other situations that you may not be specifically trained to handle.

RF Propagation

RF propagation in outdoor environments can vary over time. As discussed previously, temperature will not affect Wi-Fi propagation to any significant degree.

Differences in vegetation will affect RF propagation. While reviewing a propagation path, you will need to take all the various trees and plants into account. But what you may not realize is that you also have to plan for each plant's growing cycle. Deciduous plants and trees lose their leaves after their growing season, so consider a loss or a gain of leaves in these areas, depending on the time of year. Some plants and trees do not lose their leaves, but if they are in a cold climate, they may become laden with a large amount of snow. You always need to figure the worst-case scenario when planning the area of RF propagation. In other words, a RF site survey performed in late fall or winter will often yield far different results in late spring or summer.

Tree growth is another big factor, particularly in PTP links. Some trees experience significant growth from year to year whereas others do not. Research is in order if trees are planted between the areas where ends of a PTP link will be located requiring a signal from a particular mounting location. Document the type of tree, its maximum future height, and when it is expected to grow to that height. You can usually gauge height by other trees of the same variety in the surrounding area. Height calculations need to be factored into your long-term plan.

Directional Antennas

When planning an outdoor setting, using directional antennas is usually more favorable than using omnidirectional antennas. Directional antennas offer connections at a greater distance and can also provide greater rejection to sources of RF interference.

We've already discussed the relevant factors that need to be taken into account for electricity and backhaul. When using directional antennas outdoors, it's a common practice to use multiple APs at mounting locations and to install directional antennas. The primary concern with this approach involves the channel planning and adjacent channel power from the other radios. One way to mitigate this concern is to separate the antennas for each AP by a minimum distance. Usually a distance of at least 2 meters is preferred. The more distance you have, the better off you are.

Some directional antennas have different characteristics that help when co-locating them. *Sector antennas* are essentially high-gain omnidirectional antennas that have a material used on the back that directs all of the RF energy in a primary direction. Antennas always have some energy in secondary areas, usually called *sidelobes* or *backlobes*. *Yagi antennas* are notorious for having backlobes.

Figure 4.11 shows an antenna pattern for a sector antenna. Notice there is fairly little RF energy that is radiated behind the antenna.

FIGURE 4.11   Sector antenna propagation pattern

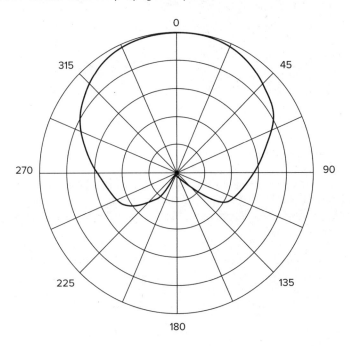

Figure 4.12 illustrates a sample radiation pattern for a yagi antenna. Notice the backlobes in various directions.

FIGURE 4.12 Yagi antenna propagation pattern

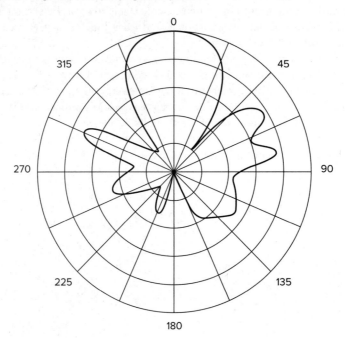

When using a single mounting location for different radios, be sure to take into account the energy the radios will pick up from one another.

You also can't assume that using different channels will resolve the problem of adjacent or co-channel interference. The IEEE 802.11 standard specifies the frequency mask that must be adhered to for 802.11 transmissions, as shown in Figure 4.13.

FIGURE 4.13 Sample frequency mask for DSSS transmissions

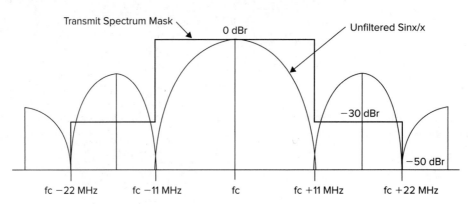

Figure 4.11 was taken from the IEEE 802.11-2007 standard. It illustrates that there is nonprimary RF energy that accompanies most 802.11 radio transmissions. The standard requires that the first signal set, adjacent to the primary transmission signal, must transmit a signal amplitude of 30 dB lower than the peak of the primary transmission signal. That may seem like a lot, but another antenna placed on an adjacent channel can pick up enough energy that will cause interference and channel contention.

A good way to test how it will perform in your installation is to set up the antennas in your lab the same way you intend to deploy them (while cabling one antenna up to an AP and the other to a WLAN analyzer using a client adapter with an external antenna connector). To do this, follow these steps:

1. Place the AP on one channel and lock your client adapter on an adjacent channel.

2. From the WLAN analysis software, look at the signal levels you are receiving from the AP beacons and play with different distances to determine where the least signal is heard.

3. If the AP you are planning to use has a receive sensitivity adjustment, you will want to set it above the signal level you are receiving from the adjacent channel.

Just keep in mind that mobile device transmissions heard below that threshold will be ignored. Also remember that in this test scenario, client adapters typically have poorer receive sensitivity than AP radios, so you will want to factor that into your data assessment.

Solar and Wind Power

Sometimes you need to install an AP where no electrical power exists. That usually means you have to use a wireless backhaul connection as well; therefore, two APs might need to be powered at that same location. One solution to this problem is to use solar or wind power.

These power sources come with some major drawbacks. Solar- and wind-powered units are expensive. They also require maintenance because they store their power in batteries. Batteries have a finite life, and depending on the climate in which they are used, battery life can be shortened by extreme temperatures. Figure 4.14 shows a solar-powered energy source and enclosure.

Wind-powered units are less common than solar because the amount of available wind is more variable than the amount of sunlight. It always depends on your installation scenario.

When determining the size of the solar panel, consider the load that will be drawn from the batteries along with the available sunlight in the area where you will be installing the panel. Some climates are much more efficient with solar power than others. The amount of shade in the area you plan to install the panel also plays a role. The type and quantity of batteries also needs to be considered. Consult manufacturer guidelines before specifying a solar solution.

FIGURE 4.14 Sample solar enclosure

Image courtesy of SunWize Technologies, Inc.

Surge Suppression

There are two types of surge suppression that should be included in your outdoor designs. The first is related to any physical, wired connection you use to supply power or wired backhaul connection. The second is related to electrical surges from lightning or airborne electromagnetic activity.

Most of us are already well aware that electrical surges can occur through power lines. However, not all of us are accustomed to electrical surges that can occur over copper-based Ethernet connections. Any equipment placed in outdoor locations should employ surge protection for both power and copper-based data connections.

When you are placing surge suppression in your system and it is wired to an Ethernet switch, both ends of the line should be protected. For example, the AP needs protection as well as the Ethernet switch.

Surges due to lightning or electrical storms will cause an electrical surge through the antenna and make its way to the AP's radio(s). In some parts of the world, lightning and electrical storms are more common than others. Yet remember that lightning doesn't need to be present for an electrical storm to occur.

Some types of surge suppression reportedly can survive moderate surges without you having to replace the surge suppressor. One form of surge suppressor that can be used for antenna transmission lines is based on *gas tubes*.

Security

Outdoor equipment should have physical security precautions in place. Access to these network devices involved in your design might reveal sensitive information that can be used to gain network access or decrypt traffic traveling over the wireless network. Equipment connections need to be secured from anyone attempting to access them. Most of the time a simple lock on the enclosure will do.

Backhaul

Outdoor wireless devices might be able to leverage options other than an Ethernet connection to bridge it into the network. Separate, dedicated radios can be used for backhaul connections. Some wireless devices have secondary radios that can be used for these purposes, or an entirely different wireless device might be required that connects the two via Ethernet.

If a second radio is used for backhaul, it is usually recommended that this be done using a different radio spectrum. For example, if the wireless network is designed to service 2.4 GHz for 802.11b/g/n clients, the backhaul connection could use 5 GHz. There are other wireless spectrums that may be leveraged for these connections, including 900 MHz. While the speed of a 900 MHz connection might be less than what 2.4 GHz or 5 GHz may provide, 900 MHz might be the only way a backhaul connection can be provided. 900 MHz can travel further and even provide a reliable connection in *non-LOS* situations. WiMAX and LTE are also candidates worth consideration for backhaul connections, but it will come with a monthly recurring cost to a wireless carrier.

Mesh is another way of providing wireless backhaul. Mesh connections usually provide more than one connection to the network infrastructure. For example, in Figure 4.15 mesh AP number 1 has formed a backhaul connection to mesh APs number 2 and 3.

FIGURE 4.15   Single-radio backhaul mesh example

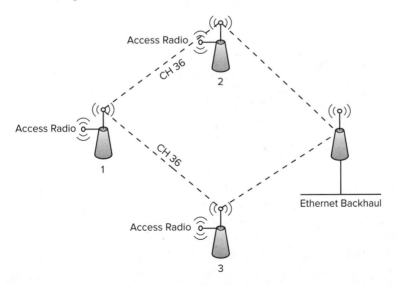

A typical mesh AP will use a single radio for backhaul. That means that in order to communicate with more than one other mesh AP, the mesh channel needs to be shared. For example, the entire mesh backhaul system shared among all mesh APs should be configured using the same RF channel.

Some mesh vendors have more than one secondary radio that can be used for a mesh backhaul. This means that if you use the same network as shown in Figure 4.15 and add a second radio, you form two different mesh backhaul connections using two different channels, as shown in Figure 4.16. This strategy usually costs more and requires more diligent channel and link planning.

FIGURE 4.16   Multiradio mesh backhaul example

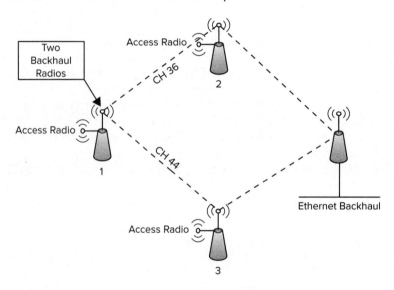

The multiradio mesh backhaul option will provide the highest throughput of both options.

Another way of providing backhaul, especially for APs in remote outdoor environments, is via traditional data circuits from a local service provider. While cable modem, DSL, or T1 type of service can be used, wired data circuits are usually the more expensive option.

Shipping Ports and Terminals

Shipping ports and terminals are another common and difficult environment that leverages Wi-Fi to provide communication for the field operations staff. Sophisticated software systems manage the container locations and workflow management for the vehicles that pick the right container for the right tractor trailer that will take the container to its final destination by ground. Figure 4.17 shows intermodal containers stacked on top of each other, a scene that is common in shipping ports and terminals.

FIGURE 4.17 Intermodal container stacking

The difficult design component of these locations is the fact that the shipping containers used to transport goods are constantly in a state of flux. In some shipping areas, the containers can be stacked four or five high with only narrow aisles between them. That makes for an incredible challenge to provide consistently reliable wireless coverage down these aisles to where the workers are using their computing devices. Typically the client computing devices are mounted to the vehicles that move the containers throughout the facility. Or the client device may even be handheld computers.

Environments such as these are also highly ridden with RF signal multipath due to the metal materials and shapes used in the shipping container construction. RF signals reflect and scatter off the shipping containers and affect the performance of the Wi-Fi network. Before the availability of 802.11n, these environments typically suffered from multipath performance degradation.

Typically the only places to mount radios in these environments are the light poles. They are often the only tall, permanent structure in shipping yards. These tend to be difficult installation locations because they are very high and sometimes have motorized lighting fixtures that allow the actual lighting fixture to be lowered for maintenance and lightbulb replacement. Just as the lights are designed to provide light from an elevated position in order to provide light in the aisles between containers, mounting directional antennas with down-tilt is also a common practice. Height is your friend in these locations. High mounting locations are often the only way to get coverage down into the aisles between containers.

Some people have experimented with straddling devices on carriers or cranes. These are motorized vehicles, sometimes on rails, that are used for stacking and moving containers where containers are received and loaded on ships. While these cranes don't often change orientation, they do move back and forth along a straight line and sometimes over some distance. In this case coverage will move right along with this crane as it moves. Larger terminals can be several square miles. The backhaul network for these locations can be a difficult design task.

Sometimes a design calls for erecting new towers or poles to service the wireless network. This is often an expensive proposition. The company commissioning the network often hasn't factored in large construction costs for the wireless network implementation. The best analogy for instances like this is a light pole. Light poles are large, expensive structures that require a great deal of engineering and construction. Each light pole must be cabled back to where the electrical service originates, requiring trenches to be dug in the ground. In the end, it is just a lightbulb on the top of this expensive structure that is providing the value. If you find yourself designing for environments like this and you need to construct a tower, it is best to bring up the possibility early in the project.

Transportation

Communication systems used for transportation—such as airliners, cruise ships, and trains—have their own set of issues. Each type of transportation requires quite different design approaches and has its own unique elements that warrant specific techniques.

The use case for this design scenario is generally for guest access. Also, while placing APs in vehicles will provide coverage based on whatever technique makes sense, the backhaul is an entirely different consideration altogether. In the following list, we look at some common solutions for transportation sources.

Airliners   Airliners can either use satellites or a new network of terrestrial-based communication towers with antennas facing toward the sky. The airplane backhaul communication system will roam between towers just as a Wi-Fi client will between APs. Satellite-based communications will likely have greater latency but may be the only option when traveling over large ocean waters.

Cruise Ships   Cruise ships also typically fall into the category of needing satellite-based communications. The only viable option that currently exists is satellite-based backhaul systems. We all know that satellites are expensive. That means that providing Internet service for an entire ship full of people costs a great deal of money. The cruise ship operators typically charge for this service for the passengers who want to take advantage of the service.

Trains   Rail-based transportation is a different animal altogether. Although more options exist for backhaul, it can still be a difficult challenge to incorporate that backhaul into each train car. For example, if a head-end unit used for backhaul is placed in the engine car, making that connection usable to each train segment is a design challenge.

Train cars are like building blocks; they can be removed and added in an ad hoc fashion. Physical connections between the cars exist to carry electrical power between cars but perhaps not for communication. Mesh radios could be used to carry this signal, but as you get further away from a *root mesh node* (the one with a direct backhaul connection), higher latency occurs and reliability decreases.

Backhaul is one thing. To get signal coverage for client devices in these environments, APs should be placed where the client devices will reside. Airlines are pretty straightforward. Trains aren't that difficult either, except for providing a backhaul connection. Cruise ships, on the other hand, have developed a reputation of difficulty. Cruise ships are constructed of thick metal, and metal and RF aren't exactly best friends. The problem is that the long metal hallways on cruise ships tend to act as waveguides carrying the RF signal from an AP quite a large distance. With no APs in the passenger rooms, the APs placed in the hallways experience a great deal of interference and contention from other same-channel APs' traffic.

For these design scenarios, there are likely several options used with varying levels of success. We have mentioned a few scenarios in order to give you some perspective of different design approaches for each of these environments.

 We would be remiss if we didn't mention regulatory domain restrictions. Every country has different rules for transmit power and channel usage. As a cruise ship crosses into different regulatory domains, certain rules need to be followed.

Summary

This chapter has provided insight into various industry verticals and the most common design challenges that accompany them. No two environments are completely alike, and customer decisions can change the design requirements drastically.

You should familiarize yourself with the design issues that are involved in the big three Wi-Fi industry verticals of healthcare, education, and retail. Even if you haven't worked with one of these industries, you might find yourself faced with a design opportunity in the future. Being aware of the challenges that a wireless design professional commonly faces will go a long toward earning you credibility with customers.

Each of these industry verticals has security and performance requirements. Some even have their own regulatory compliance requirements in addition to the technical design challenges. It is important to know the primary characteristics of each industry vertical and to educate your customer accordingly.

In the next chapter, we will discuss several factors that should help you make equipment vendor decisions. We will also explore the various WLAN architectures on the marketplace today.

Exam Essentials

Identify physical environment and best practices.   Be able to identify different deployment environments and the best design practices that accompany each environment.

Understand design considerations for healthcare environments.   Be able to explain the design factors pertaining to healthcare environments, including the various applications and devices.

Understand design considerations for retail environments.   Be familiar with design practices for warehouse WLAN deployments and RF propagation considerations. Also be able to explain design considerations for retail branch offices, including management considerations and guest access deployments.

Understand design considerations for education.   Know the design factors that pertain to educational WLAN network designs and the design constraints and workarounds for WLAN security.

Understand deployment approaches for outdoor environments.   Be able to understand the unique design considerations for outdoor WLAN deployments and the additional design elements that pertain to installation of equipment outdoors.

Review Questions

1. What are the three biggest WLAN enterprise verticals? (Choose all that apply.)

    A. Education

    B. Warehouses

    C. Retail

    D. Healthcare

    E. Office environments

2. What U.S. regulatory agency governs hospital accreditation and can cause a disruption to project schedules if they show up unexpectedly?

    A. PCI

    B. FCC

    C. JCAHO

    D. OSHPD

    E. IETF

3. What WLAN applications are typically considered standard features for new designs? (Choose all that apply.)

    A. Data

    B. Video

    C. Voice

    D. Location

    E. Guest Access

4. What particular WLAN concern are healthcare organizations faced with in terms of client devices?

    A. 802.11r support

    B. Voice support

    C. Band steering support

    D. Growth of devices

5. Your customer is asking you to place a WLAN into a psychiatric unit in a hospital. What design considerations should immediately come to mind for consideration? (Choose all that apply.)

    A. LED lights

    B. RTLS support

    C. Physical tampering

    D. Ability to blend in

6. When considering high availability in a WLAN design, what design considerations should be made? (Choose all that apply.)

   A. Switch redundancy

   B. Onsite AP spares

   C. Listen-only APs

   D. UPS power

7. When performing a site survey in a hospital, what area(s) might have schedule restrictions for access? (Choose all that apply.)

   A. ORs

   B. Patient rooms

   C. EDs

   D. Morgue

   E. Stairwells

8. In healthcare environments, what is one important consideration justifying the need to perform RF propagation measurements to determine AP placement?

   A. Floor-to-floor propagation

   B. Construction changes

   C. Client density

   D. Lead walls

9. What type of application protocol would you commonly find in warehouse environments?

   A. SSH

   B. Telnet

   C. SCCP

   D. HTTP

10. One of your warehouse customers called you reporting problems with their WLAN in some locations that you designed and installed over a year ago. What should be one of your first considerations for your line of questioning?

    A. Changes in receive gain

    B. Rogue APs from neighbors

    C. Inventory changes

    D. DHCP lease exhaustion

11. You are designing a WLAN for a large warehouse and IDFs containing network switches are spaced quite far apart. What design options do you have to keep cable lengths under 100 meters?

   A. Install directional antennas.

   B. Use mesh APs.

   C. Use fiber media converters.

   D. Use CAT6 UTP.

12. What is a common design consideration for placing APs high above inventory shelves in warehouse deployments?

   A. Number of mesh root nodes

   B. Co-channel interference

   C. Antenna diversity

   D. Mounting locations

13. A warehouse customer always complains that the WLAN experiences problems during employee break times. What should immediately be investigated as a potential concern?

   A. Microwave ovens

   B. Client devices are updating

   C. Timed Auto-RF events

   D. Black body radiation

14. What regulatory standard should be considered in retail WLAN networks?

   A. JHACO

   B. ESS

   C. PCI DSS

   D. FCC Part 15

15. What type of security might be recommended as a possibility to be used for student computing devices?

   A. WEP

   B. WPA-PSK

   C. Open

   D. Shared

   E. 802.1X

16. What RF design challenges are education institutions faced with? (Choose all that apply.)

    A. High device density

    B. Encryption overhead

    C. High network utilization

    D. Roaming

17. What type of standards-based encryption is used by office extension APs for the traffic tunnel? (Choose all that apply.)

    A. LWAPP

    B. AES

    C. CAPWAP

    D. DTLS

    E. TKIP

18. What type of protection should be provided to outdoor antenna installations?

    A. A/C spikes

    B. Lightning surge suppression

    C. Static electricity

    D. Brownouts

19. When designing for a PTP outdoor link, what important consideration should be made about local vegetation? (Choose all that apply.)

    A. Leaves

    B. Water density

    C. Tree height growth

    D. Reflection factor

20. When mounting more than one antenna and AP in a single mounting location, what design factors should be considered? (Choose all that apply)

    A. Antenna backlobes

    B. RF channel and band selection

    C. Backhaul connectivity

    D. Antenna adjacency

Answers to Review Questions

1. **A, C, D.** The three biggest WLAN verticals as of this writing are education, retail, and healthcare.

2. **C.** JCAHO, also known as the Joint Commission, is responsible for hospital accreditation and regularly performs audits and can disrupt project activities such as site surveys and other implementation activities.

3. **A, C, D, E.** While video is gaining momentum as a WLAN application, the four most common WLAN applications in healthcare environments are data (which is usually implied), voice, location, and guest access.

4. **D.** While different technical features are always of interest, the biggest concern that healthcare organizations are dealing with today is an explosive growth in the number of devices utilizing the WLAN.

5. **A, C, D.** Psychiatric units need special consideration for abnormal LED blinking activity and how and where the equipment is installed. Physical tampering with equipment is quite possible and the ability for the equipment to blend into the environment is highly desirable.

6. **A, B, C, D.** All of these features are important when designing for high availability. Switches often provide power to APs, and should the switch fail, it is best to not place every AP in an area on a single switch. Onsite AP spares are important because if an AP fails, automatic RF features are usually not enough to compensate for a loss of an active radio. Listen-only APs might be able to be converted to active APs should a nearby AP fail, or they might be moved to replace the active ones that failed. UPS power is equally important when designing for high availability.

7. **A, B.** Operating rooms (ORs) are one of the most difficult areas to survey because emergency surgeries can happen at any time in many healthcare facilities. Patient rooms must also be reserved for service ahead of time.

8. **D.** Areas of construction where lead walls might be used in radiology areas might not be evident when walking a facility. X-ray areas might have moved over the years, and the older location might still have lead walls. Always perform RF measurements to base AP placement on. No predictive site survey is going to help in these situations.

9. **B.** Telnet is the most common protocol used in warehouse deployments today.

10. **C.** The most common problem in warehouse WLANs is inventory changes in the environment. This includes the movement of shelving and client device activity.

11. **A.** Options B and C might be potential solutions for placing APs beyond the 100 meter cable length restriction, but both require A/C electrical power where APs are to be placed. In the case of the mesh AP, it must also have ample RF signal from a mesh neighbor.

12. **B.** A series of APs placed in warehouse ceilings above inventory shelving will all hear each other quite strongly. This will result in a great deal of co-channel interference if your RF signal propagation isn't factored into your designs.

13. A. Microwave ovens are a common source of RF interference for WLANs operating in the 2.4 GHz ISM band (802.11b/g/n) particularly around staff break times.

14. C. PCI DSS is a data security standard for the payment card industry. The WLAN network must abide by PCI requirements, which include compliance and auditing activities.

15. B, C. Don't ever recommend WEP—ever. WPA-PSK should be commonly supported by nearly every WLAN client device. Open security is likely the only other option where a web-based portal authentication can be used at least for authentication purposes. Shared is a long-time deprecated security method and should be removed from your 802.11vocabulary for any new WLAN design discussion. Using 802.1X is nearly impossible to support among a wide range of consumer-based client computing devices.

16. A, C. High device density and heavy network usage are two concerns that translate to RF design challenges for educational institutions. The combination of these two elements lends itself to high channel utilization.

17. D. DTLS is the encryption's mechanism that is adopted into the CAPWAP protocol standard.

18. B. Antennas placed outdoors, and especially in environments prone to electrical storms, should incorporate lightning surge suppression.

19. A, C. Outdoor PTP links should first factor in vegetation growth over the coming years. Additionally, if an RF survey is performed on a remote link with trees close to the RF communication path, the survey should be performed when all the trees still have their leaves, if possible.

20. A, B, D. When installing multiple APs in a single location, pay careful attention to adjacent channel interference for each antenna and AP placement.

Chapter

5

Vendor and WLAN Architecture Selection

THE FOLLOWING CWDP EXAM TOPICS ARE COVERED IN THIS CHAPTER:

✓ Describe best practices for updating or modifying an existing WLAN.

✓ Determine and prioritize equipment selection criteria for a WLAN deployment and recommend an appropriate solution.

✓ Demonstrate a detailed knowledge of WLAN architectures and solutions. Identify best practice design concepts for each architecture including the following considerations:

- Management solutions
- Protocols for communication and discovery
- Data forwarding models
- Scalability and bottlenecks
- Redundancy Strategies
- Device location in the network
- Encryption and decryption
- VLANs
- QoS
- Roaming considerations
- Architecture-specific security considerations
- RF and channel planning
- Capacity planning

- AP-Controller associations
- Licensing
- Advantages and limitations

✓ **Describe design models and considerations for both Multiple Channel Architecture (MCA) and Single Channel Architecture (SCA) WLANs.**

✓ **Discuss data forwarding models and how they impact network design.**

✓ **Explain the functions and components of the WLAN operational planes and identify their presence in a given scenario.**

✓ **Explain design approaches related to specific layers of the OSI model.**

✓ **Describe common design practices for high availability and redundancy.**

✓ **Illustrate best practices for roaming support in a WLAN.**

✓ **Illustrate a comprehensive understanding of the role of channel planning and usage in network design.**

✓ **Demonstrate a detailed knowledge of the common problems related to high user densities and describe effective strategies to address them.**

✓ **Understand how Distributed Antenna Systems (DAS) work with Wi-Fi and how they impact RF design for a WLAN.**

If you're familiar with the vendor-neutral stance of CWNP, you may be surprised to see the title of this chapter. A chapter relating to the selection of an equipment vendor? Yes, that's right. The intention of this book is to address all topics relating to WLAN design from start to finish, so it seemed fitting to include a discussion about vendor-specific architectures and best practices, as well as how to select a solution based on customer requirements and the advantages and disadvantages of specific architectures based on design scenarios. While we won't recommend purchasing from any particular vendor, we will provide the education necessary to help decision makers understand the options and make solid decisions based on the factors important to design requirements. Because these decisions are important, an industry-wide knowledge of architectures and vendor solutions is expected for passing the CWDP exam.

The process of selecting a solution from the list of vendor offerings can be a bit intimidating. Vendor marketing is more compelling and competitive than ever, and it seems that WLAN architectures are becoming more differentiated by the month. Of course, each solution makes its way to market with promises of best-in-class performance, future readiness, and unmatched value. All in all, each vendor usually excels in one or more particular areas and often fulfills a unique role in the market. Depending on the deployment environment, budget, industry vertical, client devices, operational staff, and many more factors, some vendor solutions gain or lose appeal.

Customers ultimately shoulder the burden of analyzing their deployment scenario, understanding the types of available architectures, and determining which one fits their needs best.

Yet this topic is not only important in the vendor evaluation process, it also has significant implications for the actual wireless design after a vendor has been selected. Each vendor's solution is unique in some fashion, and to take advantage of its benefits, you must design and configure the network according to its strengths. For example, if you purchase a *single-channel architecture (SCA)* system and then deploy it as a *multiple channel architecture (MCA)* system, the network will not operate as intended and the user experience will be poor. Network design is not a one-size-fits-all approach for all WLAN architectures. What works well with one solution may not be optimal for another vendor's solution. Network designers must understand the equipment vendor's design and deployment of best practices.

This chapter will address the topic of WLAN vendor solutions and network architectures with a focus on solutions in the market today. In addition to exploring architectural differences, we will briefly discuss the role of competitive testing and technical comparisons in an equipment selection process.

Consumer vs. Enterprise Equipment

Before we explore the ins and outs of modern WLAN architectures, it is important to note that there are two major subgroups of WLAN products: consumer grade and enterprise grade.

Understanding Consumer Wi-Fi Devices

In most cases, you will find consumer-grade Wi-Fi devices—usually WLAN routers—from major electronic retail stores. Several consumer brands compete for the business of homes and small offices, but these devices may also be found in larger networks. Consumer APs are one example that reflects the "autonomous WLAN architecture," which is described later in this chapter. Autonomous APs are designed to operate in a stand-alone fashion without centralized network control or management functions. An example is shown in Figure 5.1.

FIGURE 5.1   Example of an autonomous AP

Courtesy of Belkin International, Inc.

Since most consumer APs are deployed in homes or offices small enough for a single AP, simplicity is important. You will usually find a minimal set of wireless features in these devices. Due to this and other reasons, consumer-grade APs should be relegated to homes and small businesses with just a few APs. Usually businesses that have deployed multiple APs find that consumer gear is not as reliable, scalable, or capable of supporting the enterprise-level features that businesses ultimately require.

Understanding Enterprise Wi-Fi Devices

Enterprise-grade WLAN devices are designed for large network installations and provide vastly more features than consumer-grade products. Because enterprise networks are large and often complex, enterprise products typically offer a high level of configuration flexibility and feature support. Of course, any time there is a wealth of features, complexity tends to be fairly high. Similarly, enterprise-grade equipment comes with a higher price tag than the consumer-grade counterpart. Enterprise wireless customers tend to invest significant amounts of money into their network infrastructure, so enterprise wireless vendors typically use different distribution models for the sale of their equipment. This often includes direct sales from the equipment vendor itself as well as distribution channels and value-added resellers. In any case, you will not find enterprise WLAN equipment in retail electronic stores. Figure 5.2 shows a sample portfolio of enterprise products.

FIGURE 5.2   Some examples of enterprise products

Courtesy of Cisco, Copyright 2010

It is not uncommon for an enterprise WLAN vendor to develop distinct products to fit each market opportunity. While the distinction between consumer and enterprise— and possibly a third category, mid-market—grade is not always clear-cut, this book is focused on equipment that is designed for the enterprise. Small networks can be installed with minimal competence and often zero planning, but an enterprise network requires forethought, intentional configuration, and a carefully chosen design solution.

The Difference Between Consumer and Enterprise Products

While many WLAN products have a variety of features, the core components of these solutions are basically the same. A small office, home office (SOHO) Wi-Fi device needs to have a WLAN radio chipset just as an enterprise one does. All Wi-Fi manufacturers purchase chipsets from the same few WLAN chipset manufacturers. However, the difference in volume between purchases of consumer and enterprise chipsets is staggering.

Interestingly enough, the consumer demand for Wi-Fi products is what financially motivates most chipset vendors. In fact, for the major vendors who produce both consumer and enterprise chipsets, the difference in sales volumes is so great that if all enterprise chipset purchases were to disappear, the impact would be minor.

Enterprise products are the ones that usually need the latest industry standard features, such as the ones introduced with 802.11i (enhanced security), 802.11e (QoS and performance), and more recently, 802.11r (improved roaming performance using enterprise security). Although some of the features in these amendments will benefit consumer products, others will not.

Enterprise product support for these new features always starts with the WLAN chipsets. Until a chipset supports these features, the vendors using the chipsets are limited in the capabilities they can support. Due to the overwhelming sales demand in the consumer market, the economic motivation for chipset vendors to develop enterprise-only features is minimal. This is important to keep in mind when you, as a WLAN designer, are researching feature support with equipment vendor products.

While Wi-Fi will continue to grow in the consumer market, it will also continue to grow in the enterprise market. To draw a parallel to another industry, automobile manufacturers do not participate in the Formula One racing events because they will be offering products with the same features. Rather, they use this experience at the high end to learn from the engineering exercises and innovation. The fact is that enterprise equipment vendors are the ones who push the envelope of performance and features, and chipset manufacturers participate at the enterprise level because it ultimately makes their consumer products better.

Management, Control, and Data Planes

Because WLANs can be terribly complex, comparing vendor solutions can come with a significant amount of confusion. One way to help organize and frame the differences between network architectures is by dividing the network functions into three major categories or planes. These three planes are shown in Figure 5.3 and include the following:

- Management plane
- Control plane
- Data plane

FIGURE 5.3 Management, control, and data plane responsibilities

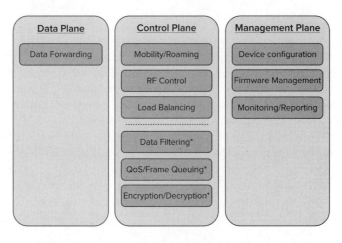

As you review Figure 5.3, you may notice that some of the functions in the control plane column (as indicated by asterisks) look more like data plane functions. If we were to be perfectly precise, these fit somewhere between Data and Control, in a column that may be called "services," but for the sake of simplicity, they are more closely related to the control plane than the data plane.

As vendor solutions become increasingly divergent, it is important to understand how a specific architecture functions; specifically, it is important to know *if, how, and by which devices* the most common network functions are being performed.

In modern WLAN equipment, network functions are often divided between different devices, such as a WLAN controller and access point. As you read vendor documentation or compare vendor architectures, you may begin to realize that each vendor puts a unique twist on the structure of the three operational planes. Consider this framework as you explore the technologies.

 Do not confuse the management, control, and data planes with the three 802.11 frame categories: management, control, and data. The terms in this section relate to architectural functions of vendor implementations and not to 802.11 frame types.

Management Plane

The functions of the *management plane* include:

- Network configuration
- Status reporting and monitoring
- Firmware management
- Other common management-related tasks

Functions at this level are not a part of the moment-by-moment network operations, but they are critical to a network's scalability and overall usability in the enterprise. Manageability of enterprise WLAN equipment is critical because performing independent, management-level configurations on thousands of devices individually is simply impractical and infeasible.

In the early days of autonomous APs, management was performed directly on an AP-by-AP basis, and this was a *major* scalability drawback. Initially, WLANs did not have shared management, which meant that administrators had to deliberately access and manage each device independently, often doing so using methods prone to human error. *Wireless network management systems (WNMSs)* came into play to address this need for management and monitoring of autonomous APs. While this addressed some of the concerns related to early autonomous systems, other limitations related to performance and inter-AP communication remained.

After the centralized WLAN architecture was introduced in 2002, WLAN controllers became a primary and effective way to centrally manage access points. However, in larger enterprise networks multiple WLAN controllers are required, which also necessitates central management of WLAN controllers. In essence, the management functions became abstracted one more level because you still had to manage a large quantity of WLAN controllers in larger networks. The WNMS usually comes back into play for that purpose.

Management of WLAN devices is an important consideration for all networks with multiple APs, which is why many vendors have developed dedicated management platforms. For enterprises, it is also recommended that you consider the management of the wired network, as some vendors distribute NMS platforms for both wired and wireless devices. In addition, companies with multiple vendors' wireless devices may consider a unified management solution that can manage devices across multiple vendors. This type of solution may not have full management functionality of all vendors, so it is important to understand the management limitations of such an approach.

In fact, many enterprises still have a mix of autonomous and controller-based environments. Despite the fact that controllers added some important network functions, controllers aren't a silver bullet in all circumstances; many still feel there is a need for specific features commonly found in autonomous APs. The reasons include cost, deployment size and complexity, and some of the specialized modes that autonomous APs allow. Given these trends, a unified approach to the management plane can save a considerable amount of time for network administrators and is important for network continuity.

Control Plane

The *control plane* includes the "control" functions related to cooperation and interaction *between* wireless equipment in a network. Example functions include:

RRM Coordination   Specifying channel and power settings for automated RF management

Mobility Management   Using fast secure roaming, IP mobility, and uninterrupted policy management during BSS transitions

Load Balancing   Collecting and sharing AP load and performance metrics to improve ESS-wide functionality

Infrastructure Controlled Roaming   Coordinating client associations to specific APs (e.g., in single-channel networks)

In today's networks, these operations are usually performed within a WLAN controller, though some solutions use protocols between distributed wireless nodes to perform the same function, abstracting the WLAN controller to a virtual level.

Similar to management plane functions, early networks with autonomous APs did not have a shared control plane and did not perform many—if any—control-related functions at all. Multi-AP deployments may have shared a common distribution system (an

Ethernet network) for network connectivity, but the APs did not communicate with one another to facilitate a coordinated network operation. For the early wireless networks that embraced wireless as a secondary network access method, control functions were mostly inconsequential. Wi-Fi was deployed only in conference rooms, for guests, or in places that could not be wired, so little control functionality was necessary. However, the shift from wireless as a convenience to pervasive and mission-critical required many control enhancements not provided by basic autonomous APs.

As the size of wireless deployments grew and the demands placed on the wireless network increased, control functions became critical for scalability and performance if application demands were to be met. WLAN controllers were introduced and have been embraced as the de facto solution to address the requirements of the control plane, where many of these operations are centralized into one device or a smaller group of devices that communicate with all the APs.

Similar to the management plane, when multiple controllers are present in large enterprises, control protocols are required between controllers as well. So, again, controllers abstracted some of the control plane, but that only works until multiple controllers are deployed. Every WLAN controller vendor recommends a redundant controller in case the primary one fails or in some cases to distribute the load. Therefore, the control plane effectively only moved.

Scalable modern networks require sophisticated network control, which is why this aspect of the network architecture is very important. Each solution addresses control functions in a proprietary way, which should lead network architects to carefully consider these mechanisms in the design phase.

The *Control and Provisioning of Wireless Access Points (CAPWAP)* protocol is gaining momentum as a WLAN control protocol, as it is now used by multiple vendors and is replacing the *Lightweight Access Point Protocol (LWAPP)*.

Data Plane

The *data plane* includes the handling of data within a network. The two devices that usually participate in the data plane are the AP and the WLAN controller. Autonomous APs handle all data forwarding operations locally, but controller-based APs may have some variation of data handling. There are two types of data forwarding:

Centralized Data Forwarding   Where all data is forwarded from the AP to the WLAN controller for processing, it may be used in many cases, especially when the WLAN controller manages encryption and decryption or applies security and QoS policies.

Distributed Data Forwarding   Where the AP performs data forwarding locally, it may be used in situations where it is advantageous to perform forwarding at the edge and to avoid a central location in the network for all data, which may require significant processor and memory capacity at the controller.

As 802.11n is now becoming increasingly prevalent in large, enterprise networks, *centralized data forwarding* is becoming more difficult due to the traffic loads that can now be generated on the WLAN. WLAN controller manufacturers are now beginning to embrace *distributed data forwarding* in different ways.

As with the management and control planes, each vendor has a unique method and recommendations for handling data forwarding. Data forwarding models will be discussed in greater detail later in this chapter when we discuss the centralized architecture, but for now, you should remain aware of the role that data forwarding will play in different architectures.

Understanding How the Management, Control, and Data Planes Work Together

We've just introduced the management, control, and data networking planes. The combination of these three operational groups generally comprises a modern WLAN's functionality. To make the most sense of a new or old WLAN architecture, it may help to consider organizing features according to these three planes. Proper system planning and architecting demand that you understand how, and by which devices, these processes are performed.

Differentiation in these functions and where in the network they are performed is often the reason that one vendor may be a better choice than another in a specific design scenario.

Architecture

At a fundamental level, Wi-Fi is a marriage between wired networking and radio communications. Early WLANs reflected the basics of this approach with the autonomous AP. With Wi-Fi as a convenient method of network extension, the functionality provided by these devices was simple and sufficient for the time. APs were placed strategically where wireless access was needed, devices were managed independently, and basic connectivity was provided for file sharing, email, web browsing, and other basic network functions.

The initial problem with this design was that autonomous WLAN architectures were independent. They were not managed collectively—or centrally—and they did not cooperate with one another to form seamless and robust extended service sets (ESSs). This led to scalability and performance restrictions.

Centralized management was introduced in the form of a WNMS, and some of the management-level problems were solved. As users became accustomed to wireless access—largely driven by ubiquitous wireless Internet connectivity at home—demand for greater network coverage grew, and applications that were previously restricted to the wire found their way onto the wireless network. With new performance demands, new network control issues became clear.

To address many of these problems, the centralized WLAN architecture was introduced. Absorbing the management, control, and some data functions, the WLAN controller introduced a new era of WLAN architecture dominance. Many variations of this architecture came to market. WLAN controller-based networks currently reign as market share king. APs in this system come with many designations, including lightweight, thin, controller-based, and access ports.

Each vendor that offers a centralized WLAN architecture solution has a name for their access points. Some call them lightweight APs, some call them access ports, and others prefer to call them wireless termination points. In the past, "lightweight APs" was the preferred term for CWNP exams, but to maintain vendor neutrality in the changing market landscape, CWNP has chosen to use the neutral term "controller-based APs."

Despite the strong market presence of the centralized WLAN architecture, many vendors have introduced variant architectures, including some that are pioneering distributed network design models without a WLAN controller. In these networks, the controller is replaced with a management appliance or simply a server. Recent innovations have looked to bring "autonomous" APs back into view with improvements on management and control functionality. The future of wireless architecture remains to be seen, and there is certainly no lack of competition and innovation.

After analyzing the top 10–15 WLAN vendors in the market today, three primary WLAN architectures begin to emerge and can be broken down as follows:

- Autonomous WLAN architectures
- Centralized WLAN architectures
- Distributed WLAN architectures

While most WLAN infrastructure products can fit into one of these three architectural categories, some solutions bear traits of multiple architectures. We will discuss these variations in the next section as well. Further, there are other significant architectural variations to account for, such as channel use methods and RF distribution techniques. We will discuss a few of the most significant ones in this section.

Autonomous WLAN Architectures

The original 802.11 access point in its simplest form is what may be referred to as an autonomous AP. This type of AP bears many names, including fat, thick, stand-alone, or autonomous, and may be a SOHO or enterprise-class model. This solution has the longest history in WLANs and is the second most common enterprise architecture still being deployed today.

Due to the many variant naming conventions for "autonomous" APs, CWNP's exams attempt to avoid potential confusion and use the generic term "autonomous APs."

Wireless networking has largely been driven by home users, who can usually provide wireless access to an entire house with a single wireless device. For this reason, some of the earliest access points were often home routers, which provided all-in-one functionality to home users. Although enterprises have always been served with more sophisticated routing and switching infrastructure, autonomous APs in the enterprise were originally only slightly more sophisticated than SOHO APs. In some cases, early enterprise deployments simply used SOHO wireless APs without the routing functions.

In today's WLAN, it is not uncommon to see customers replacing this type of autonomous AP system with a new architecture that can handle the end-user application demands of modern networks. These APs still hold many uses for home networks, small companies, as well as for some limited uses in the enterprise.

As we have touched on already, the autonomous WLAN architecture consists of APs that perform all 802.11 functions locally and independently, requiring no assistance from other devices. Autonomous APs are characterized by local management, distributed data forwarding, and little or no network-wide control functionality. A sample network following the autonomous WLAN architecture is shown in Figure 5.4. Both *distribution services* and *integration services* are included within the AP. The stand-alone nature of this architecture reflects limited cooperation—and thus, limited feature support—between APs of a shared ESS.

FIGURE 5.4 Simple wireless network using an autonomous architecture

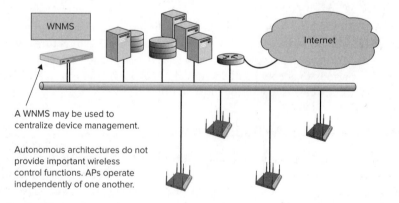

A WNMS may be used to centralize device management.

Autonomous architectures do not provide important wireless control functions. APs operate independently of one another.

Drawbacks to an Autonomous Architecture

In previous sections of this chapter, we have already highlighted some of the drawbacks of this type of independent system, but it bears stating explicitly that independent autonomous APs are not generally recommended for robust wire-replacement enterprise-class networks.

802.11 Services

The 802.11-2007 specification defines 802.11 architectural *services* that are a mandatory part of the 802.11 architecture. Understanding these services is an important part of understanding the many different WLAN architectures in the industry today. The defined services include:

- Authentication

- Association

- Deauthentication

- Disassociation

- Distribution

- Integration

- Data confidentiality

- Reassociation

- *MAC service data unit (MSDU)* delivery

- DFS

- TPC

- Higher layer timer synchronization (QoS facility only)

- QoS traffic scheduling (QoS facility only)

We've mentioned the integration and distribution services, which are two of the 802.11 services that are most difficult to understand. Interestingly enough, the IEEE did not want to limit the vendor architecture for 802.11 networks, so they use a high-level explanation for these services, which can be somewhat nebulous. This topic is beyond the scope of the CWDP exam, but for more information, see IEEE 802.11-2007, Section 5.3. You can download the full IEEE 802.11-2007 specification from http://standards.ieee.org/getieee802/802.11.html.

Here are a few of the main drawbacks to using an autonomous architecture. We will list all the strengths and weaknesses later in this section.

Limited Manageability   When discussing the autonomous WLAN architecture, the first drawback that must be addressed is that of limited manageability. Since autonomous systems are not designed for centralized network management or control, the result is significantly limited scalability. For enterprises with hundreds or thousands of APs, managing APs one at a time is impractical. Network management systems are often used as the answer to this issue. A WNMS is a purpose-built management platform for managing wireless devices and typically has a graphical interface to allow monitoring and configuration control of multiple APs. New configurations and firmware can be pushed to APs via the Simple Network Management Protocol (SNMP) instrumentation or other command-based management methods native to the autonomous AP. The dashboard of a WNMS that may be used for managing autonomous APs is shown in Figure 5.5.

FIGURE 5.5   Example of a WNMS for autonomous APs

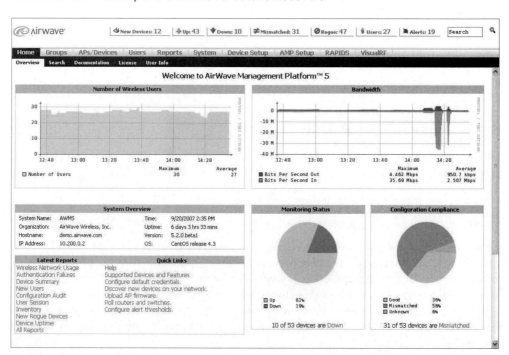

However, when autonomous APs are not purpose-built to be managed by a WNMS like this, there are often limitations to their use, including some features or commands that cannot be performed centrally. The integration of such a WNMS is commonly via a third-party vendor and will not be the tight integration of a system built by a single design team.

Furthermore, configuration changes can also be performed on APs manually without the use of the WNMS, which can cause incongruence between the WNMS configuration and the AP configuration. Or worse yet, this may prevent the WNMS from communicating with the autonomous AP at all. Figure 5.6 shows a configuration audit that reveals an "Out of Sync" configuration. The very concept of a configuration mismatch between an AP and a centralized configuration should immediately alert you that the management plane lacks cohesiveness in this architecture.

FIGURE 5.6 A WNMS configuration audit reveals a mismatched configuration.

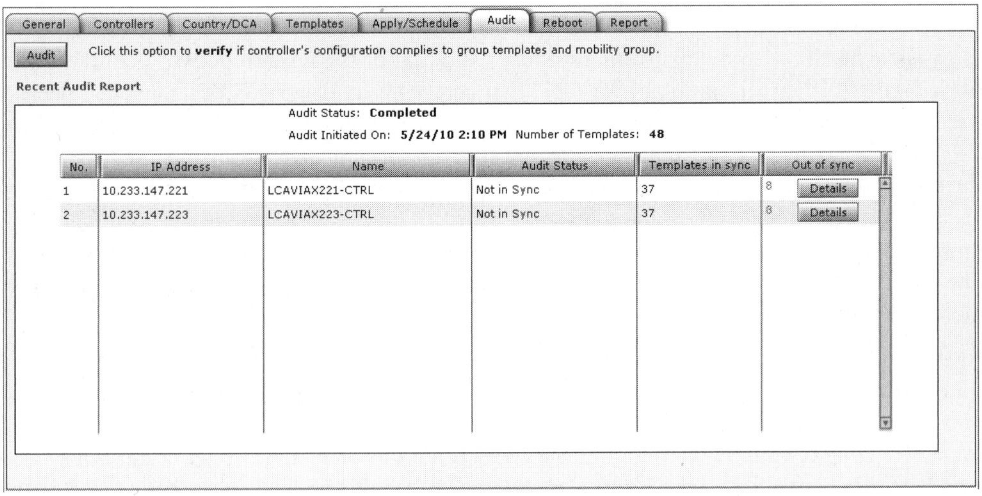

	General	Controllers	Country/DCA	Templates	Apply/Schedule	Audit	Reboot	Report

Audit   Click this option to **verify** if controller's configuration complies to group templates and mobility group.

Recent Audit Report

Audit Status: **Completed**

Audit Initiated On: **5/24/10 2:10 PM** Number of Templates: **48**

No.	IP Address	Name	Audit Status	Templates in sync	Out of sync	
1	10.233.147.221	LCAVIAX221-CTRL	Not in Sync	37	8	Details
2	10.233.147.223	LCAVIAX223-CTRL	Not in Sync	37	8	Details

Also, newer features available in stand-alone products may not be initially available with the WNMS, and it may take WNMSs a software revision or two in order to keep up with these features. This means that upgrading the WNMS is a maintenance requirement.

Configuration Mismatches

Configuration mismatches are not relegated to the autonomous WLAN architecture. In fact, anytime there are two separate methods for managing a device, configuration mismatches may be possible. This is true for autonomous, centralized, and distributed WLAN networks, and this is an important point to address in a network policy that specifies a method for device management.

Configuration Continuity within a Network   This management limitation also leads to the problem of configuration continuity within a network. While APs in a modestly sized system typically share many of the same configuration parameters, some configuration parameters are unique for each AP. Attempting to maintain configuration and firmware unity across a large company with limited centralized management or strong change control procedures is quite difficult and may also pose security vulnerabilities if change management authorization is not tightly guarded. The value of time should also be considered here, as independent management of each device exponentially increases the amount of management workload for network administrators.

Network Control Functionality   Despite the obstacle of centralized management, the impassable hurdle with independent autonomous APs is at the level of network control functionality. When autonomous WLAN architectures were originally designed, engineers weren't concerned with fast secure roaming with 802.1X, automated RF tuning, *load balancing* between APs and spectrum, or similar control-intensive features. In reality, the 802.11 specification originally intended for the access points to provide all necessary network functionality, and roaming features were not highly factored into the original 802.11 specification design. Other wireless protocols designed for mobile phone standards, like DECT 6.0 for example, have rich feature sets for inter-base station communication for mobile roaming events.

At that time, the processing and memory requirements of robust distributed intelligence for control functions was cost prohibitive. For that reason, when these features became important for enterprises, WLAN controllers were introduced as the sensible solution for centralizing control functions, and the "AP" functions were split between multiple devices. Since controller-based solutions were the only viable answer to the problem at that time, all vendors with competitive enterprise-class products embraced it, and enterprise-class vendor development efforts largely halted in expanding the autonomous WLAN architecture. Stated again for emphasis, limited control functionality is the primary hurdle for deployment of autonomous WLAN architectures in the enterprise.

Dealing with Potential Security Risks   In addition to the security vulnerability of network continuity mentioned previously, autonomous APs may also pose security risks if local secrets or passphrases are not appropriately protected within the AP. Stolen or otherwise compromised APs may pose a risk to breached security information that compromises the wireless and/or wired network. This includes SNMP strings, RADIUS shared secrets, and management usernames and passwords that might be centrally shared among other network devices or network operating systems.

The primary takeaway here is that the intended use of a wireless device is always the determinant of its features. Independent autonomous APs were designed with feature sets to meet the needs of early enterprise networks, and today's autonomous WLAN architectures often still reflect these limitations.

When Autonomous APs Fit in the Enterprise

From the perspective of an enterprise network, independent stand-alone APs are usually only useful in select roles, such as bridging, single-AP deployments where there are cost constraints, or network extension with mesh. This type of AP may also be useful for those enterprises that only desire network access in specific locations of a facility not requiring more sophisticated control functions. In a highly geographically distributed WLAN network, such as with international retail or franchise locations, a good WNMS might be sufficient to overcome the management-related drawbacks. Figure 5.7 shows an autonomous AP that may be configured in different roles.

FIGURE 5.7   Autonomous APs may often serve different roles.

While highlighting the limitations of autonomous systems for the enterprise, it is not our intention to cast a pall over these APs, as they are useful in several environments. For example, many small businesses save a notable amount of money by using autonomous wireless systems as the primary network access method. Autonomous APs with a moderate feature set can serve small businesses adequately and often provide features that are too advanced for these deployments. After all, some smaller organizations set their configurations and have no need to go back to change them unless something goes wrong.

Advanced Features of Autonomous APs

Despite the aforementioned limitations inherent in autonomous WLAN systems, some standardized features have been developed that may minimize the limitations of autonomous WLAN architectures. For example, although sophisticated policy retention is not possible during a roam between autonomous APs—because this type of control-related information is not shared between APs—both preauthentication and PMK caching are available to reduce roaming times in an 802.1X environment. Better fast secure roaming mechanisms are available in centralized and distributed WLAN solutions, but these autonomous-friendly roaming options will still be beneficial as long as they are supported by the client devices.

Similarly, 802.11k provides radio resource management enhancements that may facilitate some RF-related network controls. As a note of caution, 802.11k was ratified in 2008, and though it is standardized by the IEEE, has not been widely implemented in any autonomous WLAN architectures thus far. With these considerations in mind, it is easy to see why it is important to understand what features are required for a given network and what limitations are present in a given solution.

Some AP vendors have also built impressive lists of advanced features into their autonomous APs, including:

- DHCP server
- Built-In RADIUS and user databases
- QoS support
- Fast switching due to locally bridged data plane
- Mesh, Repeater, and Bridge modes
- VPN client or server functions
- Client-mode operation to operate as a wireless to Ethernet bridge
- Automated channel selection and power settings

Despite the impressiveness of these features, for the enterprise the weaknesses of autonomous WLANs still outweigh the strengths.

Comparing the Weaknesses and Strengths of Autonomous WLANs

As you can see, an autonomous architecture is quite useful for some deployments, especially smaller networks. However, in most enterprises, autonomous WLANs simply don't offer the feature sets, system capabilities, or scalability that are required for large, high-performance networks. A comparison of the autonomous architecture's weaknesses and strengths follows.

Weaknesses

In comparison with robust enterprise-class architectures, independent autonomous APs have several drawbacks, including:

May Require Independent Management   Although a WNMS can be used to overcome this drawback, limitations remain. Firmware and configuration continuity can be difficult to sustain across the enterprise.

Lacks Centralized Oversight   Modern networks often require a method of sharing and collecting network-wide data and using this holistic perspective to make decisions that improve performance across the network. The autonomous WLAN architecture does not have a method of centralizing data collection and making adjustments according to network-wide needs.

Lacks Sophisticated Radio Resource Management Functionality   While APs can automate channel selection based on their perspective of the RF environment, this approach is limited and lacks sophisticated systemwide control mechanisms. Coordinating these parameters in unison across the network in accordance with changes to the dynamic RF environment is important to sustain resiliency in the face of environmental variables.

Provides Minimal Scalability   Scalability is minimal due to control, management, and other limitations.

Lacks Advanced Contention Management and Transmission Control Features   Many modern features are designed to enhance performance on the wireless network by providing intelligent coordination, control, and adjustments to channel access procedures. This type of feature is not possible with independent autonomous systems.

Has Significant Weaknesses in Mobility Management   Fast secure roaming support is limited to preauthentication and PMK caching, which both have significant limitations. Also, user policy continuity (such as security filtering, QoS policies, and VLAN assignment) is not gracefully maintained during client mobility.

Cannot Perform Load Balancing   When neighboring APs are not aware of one another's client load, effective client load balancing is not possible. This feature is often considered dangerous to deploy in many environments, and it is a minor point.

Has a Security Risk   Due to the local storage of passwords on autonomous APs, compromised APs may provide a security risk if an intruder can recover network secrets.

Strengths

Although enterprises will have a difficult time overcoming the list of drawbacks inherent in autonomous systems, there are several strengths to note:

Role Flexibility   Many autonomous APs are designed to serve several different roles, depending on the network application. Examples include mesh AP, repeater AP, wireless router, or bridge.

Low Cost   Because they are often used for small businesses and homes, independent autonomous APs—as a system—typically have a lower price tag.

Simplicity   With a single self-contained device for all network functions, traffic flows and feature configuration are often fairly simple.

Network Performance   Because network traffic is bridged locally, autonomous APs avoid performance drawbacks of centralized data forwarding networks. Specifically, centralized forwarding models with WLAN controllers require that WLAN traffic be forwarded to the controller and then to its destination. This traffic U-turn adds some delay and may become a traffic bottleneck. That being said, the delay may be short enough where it is not noticed by the user.

Real World Scenario

Independent or Cooperative Autonomous APs

CWNP has decided to use two terms (*independent* and *cooperative*) to differentiate between the implementations of the generic "autonomous" AP device. In the traditional reference, an "autonomous" AP is a stand-alone AP that is deployed in an autonomous WLAN architecture, such as in a home, without intentions of providing control functions along with other APs. This type of AP, as discussed in the autonomous WLAN architecture section, has many limitations that prevent it from scaling well in the enterprise.

The term *autonomous AP* is usually recognized as a sort of legacy AP with limited use in the enterprise, but some vendors have introduced enterprise-ready architectures that use "autonomous" access points with the intention of providing shared control between APs across the network. In this implementation, the AP still does all data processing and forwarding locally, but the control plane exists *between* autonomous APs. Protocols are used between APs to share important real-time network information and are often vendor proprietary to some level. This type of autonomous AP is significantly different from the legacy (or completely stand-alone) type of autonomous AP in which no greater wireless network awareness is provided.

The term *independent autonomous AP* may be used to refer to the AP that does everything independently and does not participate in control functions with other APs (autonomous WLAN architecture). The term *cooperative autonomous AP* may be used to refer to solutions that use autonomous APs as a sort of cooperative—or virtual—WLAN controller and cooperate with one another to form a robust system of autonomous APs (distributed WLAN architecture).

The distributed WLAN architecture, which may be composed of cooperative autonomous APs, is discussed later in this chapter.

Centralized WLAN Architectures

The fundamental characterization of a centralized WLAN architecture is that the 802.11 functions are executed across a hierarchy of devices instead of within a single device, as in the autonomous and distributed WLAN architectures. Centralized WLAN architectures are often referred to as split-MAC architectures because parts of the 802.11 MAC layer features are split between two separate network devices.

The 802.11 specification defines PHY and MAC services in great detail but does not dictate how these services are to be implemented. This allows for a significant amount of flexibility in vendor implementations, which leads to diverse architectures. As an example, the 802.11-2007 definition for an "access point (AP)" is as follows: "Any entity that has station (STA) functionality and provides access to the distribution services, via the wireless medium (WM) for associated STAs" (IEEE 802.11-2007, Clause 3.3).

This is a generic definition that does not limit an "AP" to a single physical device. It is an "entity," which is nonrestrictive and provides freedom for its functions to be divided among multiple network entities. As you can deduce from the need for this chapter in a WLAN design book, vendors have embraced this freedom and have implemented the services required by the 802.11 standard with many variant architectures. Even within the centralized WLAN architecture subtype, the amount of centralization varies from very minute centralization to almost absolute centralization.

As you might expect, when vendors begin implementing highly divergent technologies, terminology also becomes confusing and widely variant. Each vendor—or network organization—often introduces a new set of terms to describe their implementation. In fact, WLAN controllers were first introduced as *wireless switches*. However, before we discuss the most common terminology, let's look at the basic 802.11 functionality and how it is divided among different devices.

Basic 802.11 Functionality

At a high level, 802.11 functions can be categorized as PHY and MAC functions. Here's an overview of each:

PHY Functions These are those mechanisms performed at Layer 1 of the OSI model (the physical, or PHY, layer) and includes transmission and reception of RF traffic. Obviously, these functions are always performed by the device in which the RF transmitter is housed and to which the antennas are connected.

MAC Functions There are many of these, and they are divided up as *station services (SS)* and *distribution system services (DSS)*. These include association, authentication, confidentiality, QoS facilities, distribution, integration, and several other services defined within the 802.11 specification.

Although they are not defined by the 802.11 specification, there are also control-related functions. According to the IEEE 802.11 standard, the required services within an 802.11 network are to be provided by "access points" and may be divided among multiple network entities. Control-related functions are only necessary when the MAC functions are split between multiple entities, as in the centralized WLAN architecture. Now that we've had a look at the services to be performed, let's look at the terminology.

In most circles, including the CWNP community and most vendor marketing materials, the terms *access point and WLAN controller* have been overwhelmingly embraced to identify the two primary entities that compose the centralized WLAN architecture. In other circles, IETF terms used in *RFC 4118* are recommended. In RFC 4118, the authors seek to delineate between the generic *access point* definition from the 802.11 specification—a network entity—by using the terms *wireless termination point (WTP)* and *access controller (AC)*.

Access Points (AP) or Wireless Termination Points (WTP) A wireless termination point (WTP) is the same as the common industry term for an access point: that is, the physical entity that contains the RF transceiver and antenna, performs RF transmit and receive functions, and may or may not perform MAC or some control-related functions, depending on how the centralized architecture divides these roles.

WLAN Controllers or Access Controllers (AC)   The term *access controller* (AC) is used to describe the centralized controller whose function is related to the management and control planes and may also include MAC functions, again depending on the specific implementation.

A conceptual illustration of the centralized architecture as presented in RFC 4118 is shown in Figure 5.8, and a sample network following the centralized WLAN architecture is shown in Figure 5.9.

FIGURE 5.8   RFC 4118 illustration of the centralized WLAN architecture

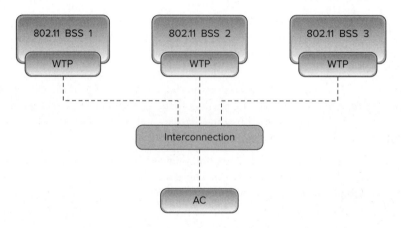

FIGURE 5.9   Centralized architecture example

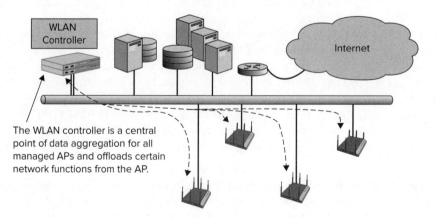

Centralizing WLAN Control

We've seen that vendors have taken advantage of the freedom inherent in the 802.11 specification and have designed proprietary architectures that divide 802.11 functions between access points and WLAN controllers. This architecture is known as *centralized* and may also be called a controller-based, split-MAC, lightweight, or other WLAN architecture terms. Don't be surprised if even in this single book all of them are used.

The centralized WLAN architecture, and thus, the WLAN controller, was largely borne out of the necessity for better management and control functionality on larger, multi-AP wireless networks. In the first few years of the 21st century, hardware limitations for processing and memory prevented distributed architectures; thus WLAN controllers emerged as the centralized point in the network where services could be aggregated. The centralization of network services also provides a unified perspective on the network's operations, which optimizes—and enables—features like centralized RF configuration, access point management, network-wide state monitoring, *mobility management*, and more.

Variations of the WLAN Architecture

Each vendor using a centralized architecture sees the customer market differently and seeks to optimize their solution according to perceived customer needs or desires. Given the overwhelming market share of centralized architecture vendors and the desire for solution individualization, the centralized WLAN architecture has many variations. This architecture can be roughly subdivided into three categories:

- Local MAC
- Split MAC
- Remote MAC

It is fairly common to hear the term *split MAC* as a synonym for the centralized architecture, as the split MAC subtype is the most widely used. The correlation is not exact.

As we think about the division of services between two separate devices, it is important to consider the benefits and drawbacks of dividing functions between multiple devices. Further, the dynamic and often latency-sensitive nature of WLANs dictates that the types of services offloaded away from the network edge and onto WLAN controllers (usually located in the network core) be carefully planned. Issues like bandwidth, encryption, latency, processing and memory requirements, utilization, and others impact network performance, so they must be considered. As one example, if there is a significant amount of latency between the AP and the WLAN controller, the processing of simple control frames may be delayed to such an extent that the wireless network cannot complete a simple authentication. Keeping these issues in mind, we will explore the differences between the subtypes of centralized WLAN architectures next.

Figure 5.10 provides a graphical representation of the three subtypes of the centralized architecture: local MAC, split MAC, and remote MAC.

FIGURE 5.10   Centralized architecture subtypes

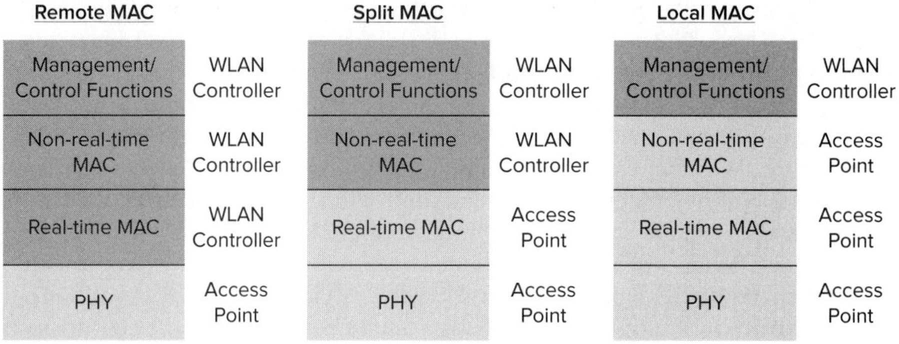

Remote MAC		Split MAC		Local MAC	
Management/ Control Functions	WLAN Controller	Management/ Control Functions	WLAN Controller	Management/ Control Functions	WLAN Controller
Non-real-time MAC	WLAN Controller	Non-real-time MAC	WLAN Controller	Non-real-time MAC	Access Point
Real-time MAC	WLAN Controller	Real-time MAC	Access Point	Real-time MAC	Access Point
PHY	Access Point	PHY	Access Point	PHY	Access Point

Local MAC

The *local MAC* subcategory refers to implementations in which most, if not all, MAC functions remain local to the AP. Control and management planes are offloaded to the WLAN controller, but the AP retains most of the network processing functions. The basic logic in effect here is that most services are kept at the AP, which provides the broadest flexibility for connectivity options between the AP and WLAN controller, and also lessens the processing burden on each WLAN controller, allowing the WLAN controller to scale to a greater number of APs.

In other words, multihop wired connectivity is not problematic in this case because the WLAN controller is *not* participating in any real-time functions like handling most management and control frame types, encryption and decryption of MSDUs, as well as QoS functions like classifying, scheduling, and queuing.

Non-real-time services like integration services (translation between 802.11 and 802.3 frame types), distribution (forwarding MSDUs based on association tables), authentication, deauthentication, association, and disassociation are also handled by the AP. A minimal amount of services requiring centralization are moved to the WLAN controller, not the least of which may be the 802.1X authenticator function.

Local MAC might also be used in geographically dispersed locations traversing a WAN link. These locations might be at retail or franchise locations or even in employee homes with one or only a few APs. In many cases, equipment vendors provide remote AP modes that are used for remote applications like this.

Due to the increased traffic loads of 802.11n networks as well as the increased use of latency-sensitive applications with wireless, local MAC architectures are becoming more popular. In fact, many vendors that previously relied on the WLAN controller for most functions are beginning to move these functions back to the AP. This move prevents the controller from becoming a bottleneck and allows for the distribution of intelligence to the AP, providing better scalability.

Remote MAC

In contrast with the local MAC model, the *remote MAC* subtype seeks to offload all possible services to the WLAN controller. In theory, this method allows for the most "lightweight" AP, which is marketed as providing lower cost for each AP. This method keeps the PHY functions local to the AP, but all MAC, management, and control functions are provided by the WLAN controller, including real-time services. For this reason, implementations using the remote MAC model are limited in the way in which they can be designed, as real-time functions may cause performance problems if the network is not sufficiently capable. A direct connection between the AP and controller is recommended in this case—no Ethernet switches or routers should be in between. For robust enterprise networks, this model is becoming less practical and less common.

Split MAC

As the most popular of centralized architecture subtypes, the split MAC implementation is the most diverse in implementation. Of all the MAC functions to be split, vendors each have their own view of the best method. RFC 4118 puts it this way: "Split MAC Architectures are not consistent regarding the exact way the MAC is split" (IETF RFC 4118).

The most common trend is to split the functionality among real-time and non-real-time processes. However, vendors are not always in agreement as to what is real-time and what is not. Generally speaking, the following are considered real-time and kept at the AP:

- Control frame processing
- Some management frame functions, like beacon generation and probe responses
- Retransmissions
- Rate adaptation
- Reassociation (this is considered real-time in environments with high mobility, due to latency-sensitive roaming)
- Frame buffering
- RF data collection

The following are generally considered non-real-time and moved to the WLAN controller:

- Some QoS functions like classifying and scheduling (queuing is up for grabs)
- Distribution and integration
- Association, disassociation, authentication, and deauthentication
- Most management frame processing
- Fragmentation and defragmentation
- 802.1X functions and security key management (encryption and decryption are up for grabs)

Most notably in the split MAC subtype, network management, monitoring, and control functions are also handled by the WLAN controller. This includes mobility management,

RF management and tuning, AP configuration and firmware oversight, and processing of network-wide state information.

Data Forwarding Models

You may have noticed that no mention of data frame handling was made in the previous sections. This is because there is no consistent trend in this regard. All three subtypes (local, split, and remote) of the centralized WLAN architecture may use centralized or distributed data forwarding models, which are shown in Figure 5.11 and Figure 5.12, respectively. As you can see from the figures, centralized data forwarding relies on the WLAN controller to forward data. The AP and WLAN controller form a tunnel, and all traffic is passed to the controller for forwarding (or comes from the controller). In essence, the AP plays a passive role in data handling here. It simply does what the controller tells it to do. In distributed forwarding scenarios, the AP is solely responsible for determining how and where to forward data traffic. The controller is not an active participant in these processes. This includes the application of QoS or security policies to data.

Generally speaking, the device that handles the majority of MAC functions is also likely to handle data forwarding. The decision to use distributed or centralized forwarding is based on a number of factors.

FIGURE 5.11   Centralized data forwarding

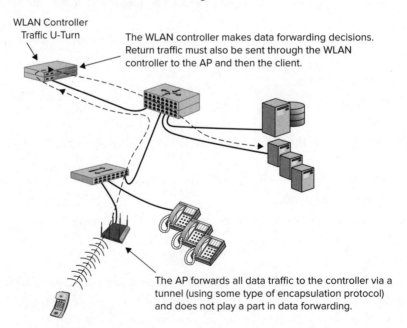

WLAN Controller
Traffic U-Turn

The WLAN controller makes data forwarding decisions. Return traffic must also be sent through the WLAN controller to the AP and then the client.

The AP forwards all data traffic to the controller via a tunnel (using some type of encapsulation protocol) and does not play a part in data forwarding.

FIGURE 5.12   Distributed data forwarding

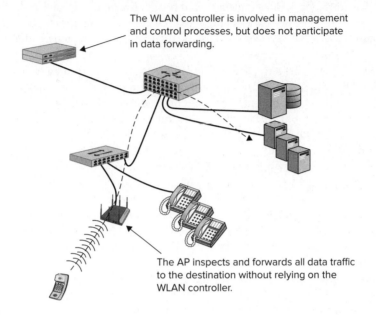

The WLAN controller is involved in management and control processes, but does not participate in data forwarding.

The AP inspects and forwards all data traffic to the destination without relying on the WLAN controller.

Security considerations are often at the forefront of this decision. Addressing one of the initial drawbacks in autonomous systems, centralized architectures allow for the transition of security keys from autonomous APs to centralized WLAN controllers. Since APs are mounted in areas that may be subject to theft, moving this security component to a WLAN controller that is locked in a wiring closet is a notable advantage when legacy APs are in use—newer APs tend to provide sufficient security of keys. Of course, if this is a concern, encryption and decryption must also take place on the WLAN controller.

Data forwarding occurs somewhere after the point encryption or decryption takes place. Of course, this is more of a forced decision if key storage is desired on the WLAN controller. Authentication and key management (AKM) is typically performed on the WLAN controller, but to support distributed forwarding, the keys are pushed out to the APs as well.

In a similar vein, many institutions, especially governments, desire for network traffic to be encrypted from the access layer infrastructure all the way to the core infrastructure. When data traffic is encrypted from the client all the way to the WLAN controller in the network core, eavesdropping from the access layer of the wired network is better prevented. The alternative is to decrypt data at the edge and forward it through the wired network to its destination as unencrypted traffic. Ultimately, this benefit is fairly minor and depends on the use case. For example, if you are forwarding data into the network core as encrypted traffic, it is protected on the way in. But if the WLAN controller will then be forwarding that traffic back out as unencrypted traffic, the benefit is negligible, because it must still pass through the network unencrypted. Of course, some protection may be better than none, and the access layer switching infrastructure may be the most vulnerable to intrusion.

Interestingly enough, there are also security advantages to distributed forwarding at the access point instead of the WLAN controller. Stateful firewall inspection is a popular feature among security-conscious network vendors and is an important feature in many network environments. From a basic security design perspective, it is usually desired to provide filtering at the edge or entry point of a network so as to keep unwanted traffic off the network. When firewall features are moved to the edge of the network (in the AP) instead of the core of the network (in the WLAN controller), the security policy may be applied to filter unwanted traffic at its points of entry so that it never enters the network in the first place and does not have a chance to get to the core of the network. This point is demonstrated well when you compare it to wired firewalling from the Internet. Where is the firewall placed in the network? It is placed at its outermost point of connectivity to the unsecured network. Just as countries secure their geographic borders from foreign insurgents, network defense is treated much the same.

In addition to security considerations, edge switching design practices are also important. Specifically, in a centralized forwarding model, traffic is tunneled to the WLAN controller on the native VLAN of an access port, and the data's VLAN assignment is provided on egress from the WLAN controller, which is connected via trunked ports. With distributed forwarding, VLAN assignments must be carried all the way to the edge switches, which may require configuration changes on all access layer switches.

The primary traffic type on the network should also be considered as a part of data forwarding. When latency sensitive data plays a major role in the network's traffic, it may be advisable to avoid the WLAN controller U-turn for data processing. In this case, it is much faster to process data at the edge where no additional network latency is added. Of course, the impact of the WLAN controller U-turn is dependent on your wired network design and the amount of traffic volume on the WLAN that is being sent to the WLAN controller. In some cases, this may be a nominal amount of latency, whereas other deployments may have several hops between an AP and WLAN controller, adding significant latency. On the other hand, if latency-sensitive traffic is not a large part of the network, some of the security advantages of centralized data forwarding may be more important.

Another consideration of the centralized data forwarding model is when using 802.11n. With the adoption of 802.11n, it is possible even with lower-end enterprise APs to generate in excess of 200 Mbps of network workload from wireless users. If your network design requires those kinds of speeds, the centralized data forwarding model will likely result in a bottleneck where the WLAN controller attaches to the network. In Figure 5.13, a WLAN controller is shown using a 10 Gbps Ethernet link to the network. In a centralized data forwarding model, this means that traffic from the APs must be directly sent to the WLAN controller. The network traffic must then exit the same Ethernet link when it is placed onto the network. Therefore, the 10 Gbps link is reduced to nearly half of its perceived 10 Gbps capacity because the link must be double taxed.

FIGURE 5.13 Centralized data forwarding congestion

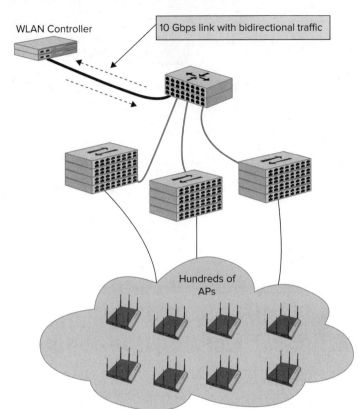

In some deployments, split-tunneling may be employed to apply different data forwarding policies within an AP. If robust filtering is desired (or perhaps unnecessary) for a certain type of traffic—such as a specific user group, SSID, data type, or destination address—a data forwarding policy may be applied to dynamically decide how to forward data. This is common in remote networking situations in which some traffic is simple web traffic not requiring additional security, whereas other traffic goes to the corporate network via a VPN. Instead of using a static policy that applies to all data, more dynamic models may be applied based on the advantages or drawbacks therein.

Despite the seeming advantage of a dynamic split-tunnel forwarding policy, many network security designers look unfavorably at split-tunnels. This is largely because the unsecured side of a split-tunnel policy (usually traffic to the Internet) may serve as an entry point for security vulnerabilities that are filtered to the secure side of a split-tunnel policy (usually traffic that goes through a corporate VPN). This is a common scenario for remote users that connect to the corporate network through a tunneled VPN. Figure 5.14 shows a conceptual example of split-tunnel forwarding.

FIGURE 5.14 Conceptual view of split tunneling

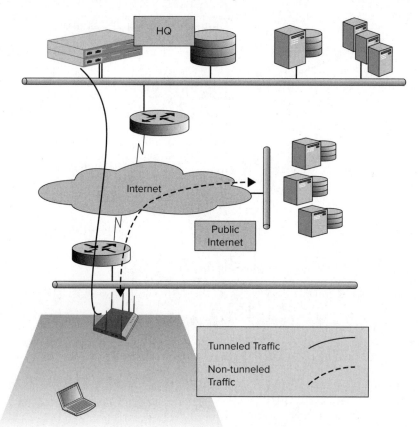

These are just a few of the important motivating factors for data forwarding policies.
Most vendors today recognize that a one-size-fits-all architecture is not broad enough
to maximize market penetration in different verticals and deployment scenarios. For that
reason, many vendors are making data forwarding models a configurable option. With
the same equipment, you can deploy in a distributed or centralized fashion, depending on
your need. Of course, the device that performs data forwarding must be outfitted with
the hardware capacity to support the amount of traffic passing through it. In many cases,
centralized WLAN vendors optimize their solution for a specific type of forwarding model,
so it is important to understand how a vendor has designed their solution. For example,
you may find that the APs have minimal processor and memory hardware because the
WLAN controller was designed to bear the data forwarding load. In other situations, the
APs may have more robust hardware, but the controller may not be suited to handle the
data forwarding load.

Can Autonomous or Distributed Architectures Do Centralized Forwarding?

While composing this study guide, we intentionally chose to discuss data forwarding models as a part of the Centralized WLAN Architecture section. As a WLAN designer, you may be looking at this topic in different ways. If you've already purchased a centralized system, you may be wondering whether to choose distributed or centralized forwarding. However, if you're comparing WLAN systems prior to choosing a WLAN architecture, you will find that the autonomous and distributed WLAN architectures must use distributed data forwarding because there is no central node to perform data handling. However, we should elaborate.

Most data in a WLAN can be handled either centrally or at the network edge. However, even in distributed data forwarding models, some data traffic will still be handled centrally, so to speak. This caveat refers to those networks in which data is tunneled from one AP or controller to another (such as with tunneling for L3 roaming or guest tunneling to a DMZ). In these cases, the immediate AP to which the client station is associated is only handling a limited amount of data forwarding. That is, it is only doing what is necessary to get the traffic to the node that will perform the real data handling. This process looks more akin to centralized forwarding.

Also, it is important to mention that our comparison of centralized and distributed forwarding models in this section generally applies the same to autonomous, centralized, and distributed WLAN architectures. So, it may aid in comparing a centralized WLAN architecture vendor (especially one that is built on centralized data forwarding) to a distributed WLAN architecture vendor.

Primary Advantages of the Centralized WLAN Architecture

As a whole, the centralized WLAN architecture solves a number of problems. The primary advantages of the architecture include:

Centralized Management   WLAN controllers provide exceptional control of multiple network devices from a centralized network location. Firmware and configuration continuity are more easily managed and sustained across the enterprise.

Centralized Data Aggregation   WLAN controllers are a sensible solution for aggregation of network-wide state information, which enables effective and automated decision making based on a holistic perspective of the network.

Sophisticated Radio Resource Management Functionality   A centralized controller allows you to collect data from the RF monitoring function of APs to inform and then control systemwide channel selection and transmit power settings.

Scalability   Centralized networks can handle the needs of large-scale deployments with centralized management, control, and monitoring functions. While centralized WLAN scalability is better than autonomous WLANs, there are still drawbacks to the way in which this scalability is achieved (see the weaknesses section).

Sophisticated Contention Management and Transmission Control Features   Some wireless networks provide automated adjustments and real-time control of network arbitration and AP transmission parameters. Centralized control is required for this functionality.

Mobility Management Capabilities   Fast secure roaming support is maximized by easily sharing security keys, state information, and policies within and between WLAN controllers.

Load Balancing   Controllers can use association state information and a network-wide perspective to effectively manage client load between frequency bands and between neighboring APs.

Secure Key Management and Centralized Encryption/Decryption   Network keys are centrally stored in devices that are not likely to be physically compromised. Also, it allows centralized encryption/decryption into the core of the network.

Flexibility in Data Forwarding Models   With WLAN controllers, the centralized architecture enables flexibility in data forwarding practices. This may be advantageous if end users want different forwarding policies for each SSID or traffic type or if they want to minimize feature configuration on access layer switches.

Primary Drawbacks of the Centralized WLAN Architecture

Some of the potential drawbacks with centralized WLAN architectures include:

Cost   Due to the need for robust controller and AP hardware, high-speed Ethernet switch ports, redundant controllers, and licensing of controllers, costs are typically higher (sometimes much higher) than autonomous or distributed architectures.

Complexity   By splitting the network functions between multiple devices, additional complexity may be added to the network to split these functions, especially for protocols like multicast and IP mobility.

Latency   Adding an additional redirection in the data path will add latency to the flow of wireless network traffic.

Bottlenecks   Though most wireless network designers are careful not to oversubscribe their WLAN controllers, it is quite possible for a WLAN controller to become a network bottleneck. Ethernet links and WLAN controller capacity must be carefully planned to avoid this. Often, the amount of capacity planning comes down to cost considerations.

Scalability   While centralized WLAN architectures are capable of great scalability, WLAN controllers also have scalability limitations. Each WLAN controller can handle only a limited number of APs, which may mean multiple WLAN controllers and additional devices to centrally manage the multiple WLAN controllers. Similarly, controller upgrades and licenses come in intervals (often called stair steps), so you may pay for capacity or licenses that you don't need.

Subject to Single Point of Failure   The WLAN controller represents a single point of failure in the network in which the outage of one device could cause a network outage to a wide group of users or locations. While WLAN controllers are commonly deployed in a redundant fashion, failover processes may still cause noticeable service outages. Some solutions provide better redundancy and failover strategies than others, though all redundancy comes at a cost.

Distributed WLAN Architectures

Now that we've looked at the autonomous WLAN architecture as well as the centralized architecture, it should be easy to define the distributed WLAN architecture. It combines aspects of both the autonomous as well as the centralized solution. Distributed WLAN architectures are modeled after traditional routing and switching design models, in that the network nodes provide independent distributed intelligence but work together as a system to cooperatively provide control mechanisms. Full MAC functionality is provided in each device in this type of system. As peer entities, each device can stand alone, but by sharing network information with one another, they form a distributed network infrastructure. This is shown in Figure 5.15.

FIGURE 5.15   Basic distributed architecture

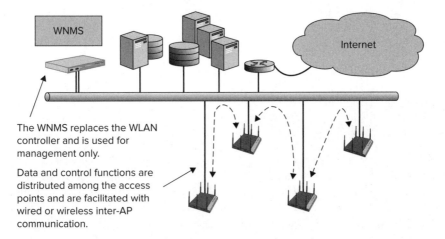

The WNMS replaces the WLAN controller and is used for management only.

Data and control functions are distributed among the access points and are facilitated with wired or wireless inter-AP communication.

Mesh Networks as a Distributed WLAN

The most popular example of distributed WLAN architectures is found in mesh networking. Mesh access points are often self-contained—meaning they perform all MAC functions locally—and interoperate with other mesh devices using some type of proprietary inter-mesh protocol to provide control mechanisms and share state information with one another. In this way, they can manage some of the features that are not possible with autonomous WLAN architectures. Figure 5.16 shows a sample illustration of a mesh network.

FIGURE 5.16 Wireless mesh node coordination

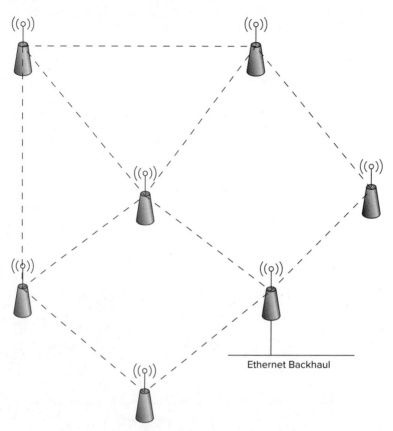

Ethernet Backhaul

In today's networks, mesh networking protocols are proprietary. However, the 802.11s amendment, which is in draft format as of this writing, will attempt to standardize the way in which mesh APs operate. However, support for 802.11s is waning, and some believe it will not reach ratification.

Generally speaking, mesh networks form a mesh using distributed networking protocols. Similar to the OSPF routing protocol, neighboring nodes share link state information with one another and maintain a catalogue of the network topology. These regular state messages serve to update mesh APs of changes in the network topology, including new devices or a change to a forwarding path.

Fully Distributed Enterprise WLANs

Some vendors have also designed their entire WLAN system around the distributed architecture. In these systems, cooperative autonomous access points are used, and control functions are enabled in the system with inter-AP communication via protocols such as

CAPWAP. In this way, they form a sort of virtual WLAN controller by providing control functions via protocols instead of dedicated hardware platforms. Since management cannot be virtualized, the management plane functions are typically offloaded to a separate device, such as a WNMS, which is not critical to minute-by-minute network functionality.

One of the reasons that the distributed WLAN architecture has come to market is 802.11n. As we've discussed earlier in this chapter, the centralized WLAN architecture can use distributed data forwarding or centralized data forwarding, depending on the customer's need. Interestingly enough, with the traffic loads that are possible with 802.11n, most vendors are beginning to enhance their offering for distributed forwarding. As distributed forwarding becomes more important and necessary, it seems like an evolution of the WLAN architecture to minimize the capabilities of a WLAN controller in terms of the data plane. Some vendors that sell a distributed WLAN architecture have decided to remove the WLAN controller altogether or to integrate the WLAN controller with the AP.

New Architectures May Create New Challenges

With this shift in control functionality, distributed architectures must find a new way to address control-related mechanisms. Aerohive Networks was the first company to adopt a fully distributed architecture, and they have chosen to use a proprietary implementation of CAPWAP to perform control-related functions via protocols. However, instead of sharing all control data throughout an ESS, APs use a neighbor concept to determine how to share information. For instance, let's look at how this works with fast secure roaming by comparing it with the centralized architecture.

For more information about specific implementations of distributed network architectures, you should read Aerohive's and Bluesocket's whitepapers. Aerohive's paper is titled Cooperative Control Architecture Whitepaper and may be downloaded at http://www.aerohive.com/resources/whitepapers.html#3. Bluesocket's paper is titled vWLAN Whitepaper and may be downloaded at http://bluesocket.com/media/download/2010-07-05_vWLAN_Whitepaper.pdf.

SECURE MOBILITY

WLAN controllers have provided incredible performance advantages with 802.1X/EAP because they are centrally performing the authenticator role for a number of APs. Thus, the keys and state information are all stored right within the WLAN controller. When a mobile device authenticates and forms a *robust security network association (RSNA)*, as the mobile device roams to another AP within the same ESS, it may be able to bypass the EAP authentication phase of the 802.1X process. This is because the WLAN controller already knows about that client device and whether it still has a valid authentication lifetime and security association. It also knows the valid pairwise master key (PMK) for the client.

In a centralized model, the WLAN controller manages AKM processes and can share keys within mobility groups, allowing seamless client roaming across APs. Since distributed architectures don't have a centralized controller, they must share keys and state information directly with one another. However, since clients are only going to roam to neighboring APs, it does not make sense to share client keys across an entire network with hundreds or thousands of APs. Instead, APs share mobility information with neighboring APs for which this information is relevant. At regular intervals (and when state information changes), APs share information with one another to maintain important control functionality.

IP MOBILITY

IP mobility is one of those unique challenges that has been solved by WLAN controllers and is fairly well understood by wireless network engineers. As you deploy a WLAN across an enterprise that spans several network closets, you will surely cross several Layer 3 segments on the network infrastructure. This is even more prevalent when networks are designed with Layer 3 down to the access layer switches. Of course, as clients roam throughout the network, they will cross VLAN boundaries and require IP mobility to maintain connectivity to the proper VLAN that supports proper functionality of the application. In order to achieve this, the distributed APs form traffic tunnels to each other when the mobile device associates to APs that will normally drop users on different VLANs and, therefore, different IP subnets. This is essentially the same function that WLAN controllers have performed.

RADIO RESOURCE MANAGEMENT

A similar approach can be taken with automated channel and transmit power settings. APs share information with neighboring groups of APs (up to a specified number of hops), and automated modifications can be made in accordance with the insight gathered from other neighbor APs. In this way, the control-related functionality inherent in WLAN controllers can be performed with regular inter-AP communications in which APs share state information with one another.

EDUCATION AND END-USER TRAINING

However, just as WLAN controllers established a new way to do wireless networking when they were introduced, distributed networking vendors have an uphill battle to inform the industry about their new solution. Most wireless network engineers that have studied WLANs in the past understand how centralized architectures work, but few have really gotten a handle on the distributed architecture. The WLAN industry has become accustomed to certain types of deployments, which means that distributed networks will introduce new obstacles.

REMOTE CONNECTIVITY

A fully distributed model has a potential drawback when using APs for remote access connectivity from small branch offices or telecommuter environments. The WLAN controller plays the role of the termination point for the remote APs to connect to, often over a public, untrusted network. Without a WLAN controller, some device needs to play the role of this function and also have the ability to scale.

RADIUS AUTHENTICATOR GROUPS

Another potential challenge is with 802.1X. In a centralized model, the WLAN controller plays the role of the authenticator for many APs, and the convenient side effect of this role is that this minimizes RADIUS server configurations. Replacing the WLAN controller with distributed APs may require a number of additional configuration steps, which may be a task for a completely separate IT group who owns the security configuration of the RADIUS authentication infrastructure. This is arguably a minor point, but depending on the customer's security policy, it may be possible to minimize this issue. Specifically, the authenticator must be added to the RADIUS server, which is typically done by a single IP address. However, in a distributed WLAN model, it would be beneficial to configure the authenticator in the RADIUS configuration by opening up an entire subnet that contains the APs used as authenticators such as 10.1.54.0/24. This syntax would allow any authenticator from a source address of 10.1.54.X that is using the proper RADIUS shared secret. Assuming precautions are made around the sharing of the RADIUS shared secret, this should be a sufficient approach.

As we've discussed, a fully distributed model will require that the distributed APs perform a great deal of inter-AP communication in order to share network state information across sister APs that are part of the same ESS. The few vendors that currently implement distributed networks have kept the control traffic fairly lean, so this should not pose a problem for wireless or wired link utilization.

As of this writing, the distributed WLAN architecture is still fairly new to the industry, but it seems to address many of the weaknesses of centralized WLAN architectures.

Advantages to Distributed WLANs

As you can see from mesh networks as well as enterprise-wide distributed architectures, one of the significant advantages is that they can be resilient to change. By closely maintaining and monitoring state information, they can quickly fail over or alter communication paths to avoid a network failure. They are commonly referred to as "self-forming and self-healing" because they build resilient communication pathways and may be able to navigate around a network failure. Of course, with distributed networks, there is no single point of failure in the network, so individual device failures only affect a limited area and set of users.

Other advantages of the distributed WLAN architecture include:

Scalability   Since distributed architectures use autonomous WLAN devices and are not dependent on a controller, scalability is linear and potentially unlimited.

Cost   By removing the manifold costs of WLAN controllers from the network, distributed architectures are typically able to offer lower solution costs than their centralized counterparts.

Resiliency and High Availability   As we demonstrated with mesh networks, distributed architectures are well suited to construction of a web of interconnectivity that is resilient to network changes.

No Single Point of Failure   Given the autonomy of network nodes, no device represents a single point of network failure. Single device failures can be overcome with forwarding path changes and automated radio responses (radio resource management [RRM] changes, mesh failover, etc.).

Filtering and Forwarding at the Edge   Since all system intelligence is at the edge of the network, distributed architectures are ideally suited to filter and control network traffic from the edge. Similarly, appropriate forwarding policies are applied to data traffic immediately.

Disadvantages to Distributed WLANs

There are a few disadvantages with distributed WLAN architecture:

Relatively New   Entirely distributed WLAN architectures are fairly new, and there are only a few players in the current market. This may indicate a limited amount of training and documentation resources.

Encrypted Tunnel Termination   As mentioned previously in this chapter, controllers are typically used as encrypted tunnel terminators for remote APs, but distributed architectures may have a centralized high capacity appliance for aggregation of services like encrypted tunnel (VPN) termination.

802.1X Configuration   In some situations, AAA server configurations may be more time consuming and intensive for authenticator provisioning.

Inter-AP Communication Overhead   Distributed network nodes must communicate with one another in regular intervals to maintain current state information. In most networks today, this is a minor amount of traffic, but it could be considered a potential drawback.

As of this writing, Aerohive Networks, Bluesocket, and Xirrus Networks are the three primary enterprise vendors competing with distributed WLAN architectures. The distributed approach is relatively new to market for all of these vendors, though they have demonstrated pretty strong value claims for this architecture. It is fairly clear that distributed intelligence is becoming more popular in the marketplace, and the advantages offered by distributed solutions are significant.

Other WLAN Architectures

So far we've taken the time to define three fairly concrete architectures:

- Autonomous
- Centralized
- Distributed

However, not all solutions fit entirely into one of these architectures. For that reason, it is important to understand this fourth, slightly less distinct architectural category that is a sort of catchall for variant offerings. Most vendor offerings can be categorized into one of these three groups, but some fit into two of those groups.

Hybrid WLAN Architectures

Although the hybrid architecture is not a traditional subtype of network architecture, it is important to note that distinct architectural lines are starting to fade. As variant architectures proliferate in the market, the best aspects of multiple architectures are being adopted into "hybrid" models. For example, controller-based mesh networks may be implemented by vendors whose traditional architecture reflects the centralized model. Similarly, purpose-built hardware arrays, which we will discuss in the next section, combine the WLAN controller and multiple APs into a single hardware device. This technology is offered by Xirrus and reflects a distributed architecture but also includes a hardware WLAN controller. Other vendors implement autonomous APs that mimic behaviors of both distributed and autonomous architectures. The APs are stand-alone and are managed by a centralized WNMS but perform minimal systemwide control operations. It is difficult to distinguish whether this implementation fits as a distributed or an autonomous model.

Similarly, some centralized models allow for distributed or remote data forwarding and even allow the AP to continue to function if the controller goes offline. Controller-based remote APs represent a hybrid operational model. The remote APs in some modes may not rely on the WLAN controller for forwarding or all control functions, but they do rely on the WLAN controller for management and some control functions. In some scenarios, controller failure would restrict the capabilities of the AP, but in other scenarios few functions are impacted. We highlight this section simply to illustrate that the three primary WLAN architectures are not hard and fast distinctions. It is important to understand how your vendor's (potential or current) equipment functions and to evaluate its values accordingly.

Arrays

Xirrus is the only vendor in the market today that manufactures a true multi-AP WLAN array. Other vendors, such as Ruckus Wireless, have designed APs that use integrated antenna arrays, but these are a different RF animal altogether. A point worth considering is that few companies focus much attention by innovating at the RF layer with antenna techniques, which our industry should highly encourage. Innovative RF techniques and smart antenna technology can drive critical gains in technology advancements as we have seen with 802.11n and MIMO. That being said, in this section we want to focus on the architectural concept of multi-AP arrays, such as with Xirrus.

In this type of array technology, the RF fabric is composed of a series of high-gain directional antennas designed to add range and also to operate independently from other antenna element transmissions. In this architecture, a WLAN controller and multiple APs are integrated into a single hardware unit. Each AP is connected to a single (or a set, for MIMO) directional antenna that is designed to provide RF coverage in a directional pattern. A single array is designed and configured such that the sum of radios and directional antennas provides 360 degrees of omnidirectional coverage in the desired band (i.e., 2.4 GHz, 5 GHz, or both). Figure 5.17 shows a hardware array top from Xirrus and an expanded view of the internal components, including multiple-directional antenna elements.

FIGURE 5.17   Xirrus array

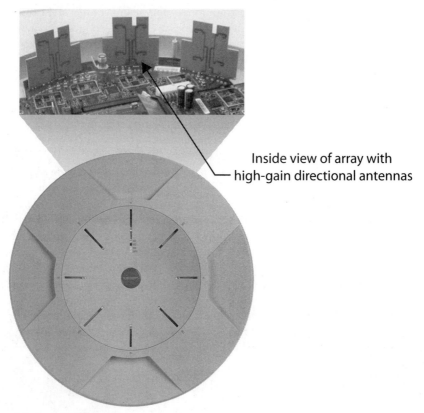

Inside view of array with
high-gain directional antennas

Courtesy of Xirrus, Copyright 2010

The value claim for this setup is typically based on increased range and better client capacity per single wireless network infrastructure device. By using high-gain directional antennas, the array is able to provide increased range for network access regardless of the client capabilities. We know from our RF background studies (CWNA) that by focusing RF energy directionally, we will have more gain than if we were to transmit a signal with the same energy omnidirectionally. Xirrus applies this logic to their array, combining multiple Wi-Fi radios and antennas together into an array to form a multi-AP node. The challenge that WLAN arrays have is keeping transmissions from other radios/antennas within the array itself from interfering with uplink reception on other radios within the array. Under the hood of the array, you'll see that RF shields are installed to minimize backlobes and sidelobes within the array. Arguably, small amounts of backlobe interference may not cause a problem or may be restricted to the same channel communications. However, if the backlobes and sidelobes are not properly controlled, high-powered transmissions could interfere across "nonoverlapping" channels within the array as well. For these reasons, channels should not be reused within an array.

In the case of a WLAN array, the antenna elements are housed in the same physical device and are located close to each other. This may cause some impact to performance unless advanced RF design techniques are employed. Because this level of technology is highly proprietary and difficult for a third party to test, we will not explore much further down this road. One of the deployment strategies in which arrays have been highly effective is in high-user-density environments such as convention centers, conference areas, arenas, and high-traffic libraries. They also have unique appeal for disaster relief situations in which large areas need Wi-Fi coverage with minimal hardware and minimal preparation. While arrays have the benefit of using fewer devices to support a larger geographical footprint—this also saves considerably on the cost of Ethernet switch ports, cable runs, and the overhead required to install them—they also have the advantage of restricting the wireless contention domain by using directional antennas. Further, by integrating a number of APs (up to 16) within the array, high user densities can be served quite well.

 Real World Scenario

Providing High Density with a WLAN Array

Xirrus is well known as a (possibly "the") premiere vendor for supplying high-density Wi-Fi connectivity for conference areas and other dense user environments. It is common practice for all vendors to deploy multiple APs with directional antennas in a panoramic method so as to eventually provide omnidirectional coverage. This is perfectly acceptable, and where one vendor is chosen exclusively, there's nothing wrong with it. However, when you consider the extra workload that goes into this type of deployment, the virtues of a hardware array begin to become apparent. Consider some of the additional steps, including:

- Selecting and installing RF connectors and RF cabling to attach external antennas to AP radios.

- Selecting and installing the appropriate antennas to provide the coverage necessary for the deployment. This issue is made worse by dual-band MIMO, which often requires specialized antennas and up to six RF cable runs.

- Determining the number of APs and antennas necessary to accomplish the task.

- Mounting the APs and antennas in a way that minimizes or prevents co- or adjacent-channel interference.

- Supplying Ethernet to each and every AP.

This is not an exhaustive list by any means, but it highlights several of the manual tasks that may be on the shoulders of the WLAN designer or end user instead of the WLAN vendor. With hardware arrays, all of this work is absorbed by the WLAN manufacturer in a proven form factor, and it eases the design, installation, and deployment tasks for the designer and end users.

If you are looking to service a large geographic area (compared to the footprint of a traditional AP) with a minimal amount of hardware devices, a WLAN array might be a good design choice. It's amazing what antenna gain can do to effective range. However, in the same light, as you aggregate multiple services into a single device, you come back to the issue of a single point of failure. As you try to expand a single device's reach, you also open up opportunities for a large area to suffer a service outage. This is a trade-off worth considering.

In the end, the best advice we can offer regarding WLAN arrays is to conduct competitive testing to see how this product fares in your environment. Also compare the theoretical advantages of such a solution with your deployment needs.

Important Architectural Distinctions

Thus far in this chapter, we've looked at the primary WLAN architectures at a high level—what 802.11 services are provided by a given architecture and how are they provided. In that discussion, we just finished looking at hardware arrays, which are a unique solution for RF distribution. In this section, we will look at two other architectural distinctions that are important for RF distribution and control. Specifically, we will look at the two architectures related to channel use: multiple-channel architectures and single-channel architectures. After that discussion, we will look at distributed antenna systems (DASs), which is a way of distributing RF throughout a building. DAS is becoming more common in other wireless disciplines, and it is important that we speak to its merits and drawbacks for Wi-Fi here.

Channel Use

It is well known that the wireless medium is half-duplex and shared among users operating on overlapping channels. 802.11 contention processes are, therefore, designed to arbitrate and avoid collisions to maximize channel efficiency in light of this limitation. As with most aspects of 802.11 network operation, vendors build proprietary mechanisms in addition to the required 802.11 mechanisms to maximize performance in the face of this channel utilization challenge. Of course, each implementation is a bit different, but two primary trends have emerged, with one as the thought leader in the market:

Multiple-Channel Architecture (MCA)   The dominant architecture, MCA attempts to spread radio communications across all the available nonoverlapping channels within a frequency band.

Single-Channel Architecture (SCA)   The less common implementation, SCA seeks to isolate all communications on a single channel (within a particular band) in an attempt to manage the RF medium with sophisticated proprietary algorithms and control mechanisms.

These architectures are identified by the way in which they spread or concentrate communications within a frequency band and what design approach they rely on to maximize performance. While the overwhelming majority of wireless professionals are more familiar with the multiple-channel approach—it commands approximately 95 percent of the enterprise market share—there are also some potential advantages to the single-channel system.

Multiple-Channel Architecture (MCA)

To facilitate the standardized arbitration processes, ESS networks using the MCA are typically designed in such a way that physically co-located APs (neighbors) are not also operating on the same channel. This is done by carefully controlling the transmit power and channel selection of each AP using a design technique called a *channel reuse plan*. Of course, the radio spectrum is limited, so channel reuse and same-channel cell overlap are inevitable in enterprise systems. A sample channel reuse plan is shown in Figure 5.18.

FIGURE 5.18   Example channel reuse plan for 2.4 and 5 GHz networks

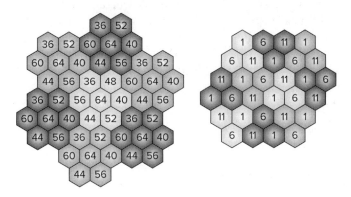

This architecture is very popular because the logic on which it is based is easy to understand and is convincing. Each channel has a finite capacity. There are multiple channels. Therefore, to maximize capacity, each available channel should be used. This line of reasoning is ultimately true and even single-channel vendors wouldn't argue that the use of multiple channels is one way to increase and maximize system capacity. Thus, the strength of the multiple-channel approach is that each neighboring AP operates in a different spectrum or a different *contention domain*. This is also one of the stated drawbacks of the MCA; that is, especially in the 2.4 GHz band, it is impossible to completely isolate all APs from one another. This ultimately leads to co-channel interference with neighboring cells.

Due to the channel spreading of MCA networks, they tend to be more resilient to interference—both from Wi-Fi as well as non-Wi-Fi sources—than their single-channel counterparts. For example, an MCA system operating in the 2.4 GHz ISM band may be configured to operate on channels 1, 6, and 11, and an automated channel planning and transmit power solution may be in place to manage AP channel and power assignments.

If approximately one-third of the APs are operating on channel 11, then interference on channel 11 will only affect one-third of the network. If the system recognizes a need for these APs to switch channels, only one-third of the network experiences a temporary outage during the channel switch. Conversely, the entirety of a single-channel system could be impacted if an interference source is detected on its operating channel.

The most notable advantage to MCA networks is capacity. While this section serves as a fairly brief introduction to the multiple-channel approach, some of the operational strengths and weaknesses of a multiple-channel system are best understood by looking at single-channel systems.

Single-Channel Architecture (SCA)

So, given the inarguable truth of multiple channels and system capacity, what is the deal with the single-channel architecture? Why do SCA vendors operate on a single channel and leave this capacity unused? The primary reason is that the single-channel approach provides a high amount of system control to the infrastructure. In other words, it shifts some of the control from the client to the infrastructure. This is important because client devices and drivers are notoriously unpredictable, nonstandard, unreliable, or worse. Providing control to the infrastructure relieves some of this instability offered by clients. Even with high-quality client devices, most enterprise networks have many different clients in their environment.

Single-Channel Architecture Caveats

SCAs are vendor proprietary and used by only one of the top competing enterprise vendors, Meru Networks.

Before we go into the details, we should note that in a typical MCA network, each AP has a BSSID (radio MAC address) for each SSID. Traditionally, the BSSID represents a BSS (the network provided by a single AP radio), which is usually part of a larger ESS. Client devices see many BSSIDs throughout an MCA ESS and thus associate each BSSID with an individual AP.

In contrast, in an SCA network the use of a BSSID changes. The most popular SCA vendor, Meru Networks, has two distinct technologies that are used. They originally introduced the concept of *virtual cell*, which used an ESS-wide BSSID for all APs. In other words, the same MAC address is used by all APs in an ESS. In this way, clients do not see any differentiation between APs—that is, for a single SSID. The other option is known as *virtual port* and reflects a per-client BSSID across the ESS. This has a similar net effect but also provides some other, more granular functionality. Figure 5.19 illustrates the differences between BSSID usage for MCA and SCA networks. In Figure 5.19, you will notice that only the virtual cell (an ESS-wide BSSID) is shown for SCA networks.

FIGURE 5.19 Comparing BSSID usage between MCA and SCA networks

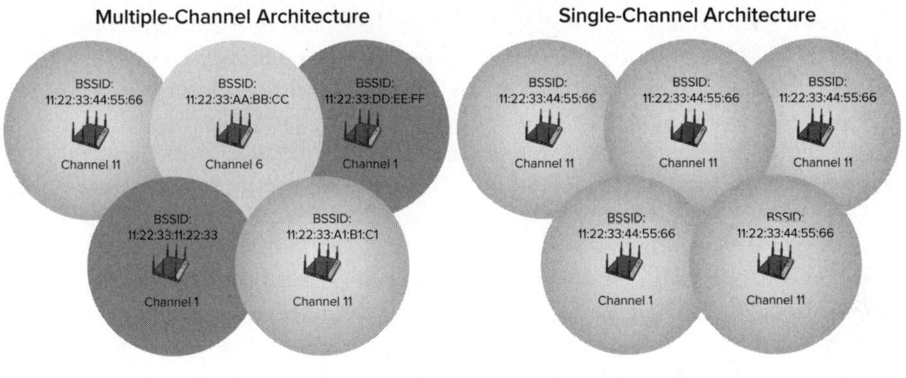

Multiple-Channel Architecture

Single-Channel Architecture

By operating entirely on a single channel and using this proprietary BSSID setup, the network infrastructure—specifically the WLAN controller—can coordinate system performance and functions since all APs are operating on the same channel. This is largely because client devices only see a single BSSID. Because they're on the same channel, APs can hear neighboring APs and clients in the same physical area all the time, which provides the ability to adjust network behaviors (such as uplink contention parameters and downlink transmission control) in accordance with network or environmental changes. Based on a network-wide perspective of all STAs, uplink and downlink transmissions can be effectively coordinated such that a single channel's capacity is maximized. By using proprietary algorithms to do this, they are able to surpass the capacity and predictability—which is important for many sensitive applications—offered by relying only on the 802.11 protocols.

ADVANTAGES TO OPERATING ON A SINGLE CHANNEL

Admittedly, the 802.11 protocol may prevent the SCA system from reaching the same systemwide performance levels as a well-designed MCA system (this is a hotly debated topic), but the performance of a well-tuned SCA system can exceed many critics' expectations of what can be done using only a single channel. In one sense, it is important to qualify what is meant by "performance." If we're talking strict throughput, an MCA network often has more capacity than an SCA network. However, in an SCA network, communication reliability can be greatly improved in ways that are not possible in an MCA network.

One advantage of operating on a single channel is that clients can be *tricked* into thinking that all APs collectively form a single large AP. In this way, the fact that the infrastructure is composed of multiple APs is transparent to the client. As we've already mentioned, this is done via a systemwide virtual BSSID or a per-client BSSID. Because of this transparency to the client device, the client never perceives a need to roam from one AP to another—assuming the single-channel network is properly designed to provide sufficient coverage and signal quality across the enterprise so that client roaming algorithms are never kicked in. This allows the infrastructure to intelligently coordinate which AP receives and transmits to any given client, providing seamless roaming throughout the network. This mechanism provides for imperceptible roaming events and is a considerable advantage for SCA networks, especially given the somewhat tenuous and sparse fast secure roaming support in the client market today.

This type of infrastructure-controlled roaming is beneficial in a few ways. First, reassociations in MCA networks usually take 50 ms or more and may take as long as several seconds. This may be a major problem for application performance. The answers proffered by the industry to solve the fast secure roaming problem all come with drawbacks. With an SCA, this issue is removed completely because, from the client's perspective, security associations do not move from one AP to another. Roaming events can occur in as little as a few milliseconds' time, which is typically sufficient to adjust a client's association on a frame-by-frame basis, if necessary.

Second, by creating a blanket of coverage on a single channel and controlling client associations in the infrastructure, SCA networks can create AP-to-client links with consistently high SNR. This is important because high SNR (among other RF and channel-related factors) often leads to high communication rates, high throughput, and better reliability. When the AP and client can maintain an optimum communication rate (e.g., 36, 48, or 54 Mbps), channel efficiency is much higher than it would otherwise be if client stations were in control of associations and were operating at low data rates because they are not associated to the optimum AP.

DISADVANTAGES TO OPERATING ON A SINGLE CHANNEL

Despite these improvements, the capacity limitation of a single channel is still an obstacle. To overcome that criticism when high capacity is a concern, single-channel vendors recommend the use of channel blankets (spans or stacks) to scale the single-channel design so that capacity from multiple channels can be used. A channel blanket is essentially the process of designing a comprehensive single-channel network on more than one channel. In network environments where high user densities are an issue, multiple-channel blankets can be co-located to provide high system capacity across multiple channels, while maintaining the benefits of a single-channel system. This could scale well beyond the capacity of a well-planned MCA network. However, the major drawback in this approach to high density is that co-locating multiple APs across an enterprise like this can become cost prohibitive very quickly.

One of the major weaknesses of the single-channel architecture is that it is supported by only a few vendors, and only one of those vendors (Meru Networks) is a competitor in the enterprise market. There has been a lot of debate and discussion about the use of the SCA, largely because it comes with a heavy dose of proprietary technology.

The other common concern about SCA deployments is that the contention domain is very large. While AP transmissions are coordinated to minimize collisions with other APs, the RF medium is highly dynamic and, even with proprietary technologies, client behaviors cannot be controlled with absolute precision. Minimally, the number of retransmissions of a heavily used SCA would likely be higher and with less peak throughput than an MCA.

Although proprietary features can be great for product differentiation, they can also draw fire from competing vendors. This is especially true when "proprietary" begins to look like "nonstandard," which is another problem altogether. Many competing vendors have criticized SCA vendors for violating the standards, but this is where the discussion becomes very gray. We won't presume to say what should and shouldn't be done by vendors, but the real litmus test for potential customers should be whether an infrastructure system works with the customer's client devices, applications, and use cases. We strongly encourage interoperability testing of equipment from both MCA and SCA vendors. To that end, unfortunately, deploying few APs in an IT-specific area doesn't constitute a proper test. To properly test SCA versus MCA, designers need a larger network of APs and distributed client devices operating in real-world traffic conditions. Unfortunately, almost no customer has the opportunity to perform such a thorough test and publish it without perhaps some backing from one side of the channel use camp.

In addition to the technical strengths and weaknesses of each solution, it is important to weigh the role that education plays in the vendor selection and deployment process. Due to its proliferation, the MCA is understood far better than the SCA. Because of this, network engineers, administrators, and consultants are more likely to understand the operation of an MCA network. Of course, this does not mean that SCA should not be deployed. But the knowledge level of the network staff should be a factor in vendor selection. Similarly, educational resources and documentation should be considered as well.

Distributed Antenna Systems

It's no secret that modern technology is increasingly mobile, a fact that means wireless systems of all kinds are on the rise. Many businesses now employ multiple services that rely on a wireless infrastructure of some type. These may include Wi-Fi, 3G/4G and cellular, RTLS, medical telemetry, wireless door locks, paging systems, fire and safety systems, and more.

Some vendors have recognized the potential challenge (and opportunity) this affords and offer a solution to capitalize on it. *Distributed antenna systems (DASs)* come in many sizes, shapes, and flavors. Here, we are focused on *neutral-host DAS*, which is also known as multiband DAS. These systems are end-to-end converged wireless infrastructure systems designed to meet the needs of many wireless systems by means of a single RF infrastructure. This is accomplished by distributing multiple-service RF cabling infrastructure and antennas throughout a facility for use by multiple radio systems.

The infrastructure hardware (APs, in the case of WLANs) of each wireless system is then connected to the shared RF infrastructure for distribution throughout the building. This is typically done in a network closet where an AP antenna lead is cabled into an input of the DAS. As with any architecture, many vendor variations of distributed antenna systems exist, and this architecture is entirely proprietary.

DAS wasn't originally designed for Wi-Fi systems. The cellular and two-way radio industries needed a way to get a footprint into large indoor locations, especially where high device density can be present. Because of the way construction materials attenuate RF, the signal can only penetrate the building so much from outdoor sites, regardless of the power levels used. Using a DAS allows for the ability to use low-powered transmissions both on the infrastructure and mobile devices, which also increases mobile device battery life. Due to the fact that customers don't want to install a different infrastructure for each different RF system, there is some logical basis that can support the argument of a single antenna system for multiple RF infrastructure systems.

Because DAS has not been widely implemented as a Wi-Fi technology, we don't want to fixate on this topic; however, it is worth highlighting the value proposition of DAS as well as some notable drawbacks that come along with it. InnerWireless (www.innerwireless.com) and MobileAccess (www.mobileaccess.com) are two of the leading DAS vendors that can also provide Wi-Fi services.

The Value Proposition for DAS

The primary industry for which DAS is targeted is healthcare, while hospitality, convention, industrial, and manufacturing facilities are also a notable target. As an industry where the workforce is highly mobile and communication requirements are high, healthcare tends to deploy many different types of wireless systems. Also, many healthcare facilities have areas where antennas or cabling may not be desirable, such as in sterilized surgical rooms. In these areas, minimal intrusion with a single antenna system may be preferable to multiple different types of antennas mounted in the ceiling.

One of the primary touted advantages of DAS is that a single-antenna infrastructure system will have cost advantages when compared with deploying antenna systems for multiple divergent technologies. The logic here seems simple. If you have four wireless technologies requiring their own infrastructure, you pay for four instances of RF infrastructure. If, on the other hand, you implement a single type of wireless infrastructure for all four services, you save money. This is the basic value proposition for DAS.

Drawbacks for Using DAS

However, while this argument holds some surface validity and may hold up with some RF systems, this position should be carefully scrutinized, especially if the WLAN is being designed for 802.11n or even if 802.11a/b/g with antenna diversity is considered a value.

Many WLAN infrastructure and client vendors have far differing opinions regarding DAS and for good reason. One important factor for customers to consider when evaluating a DAS solution is whether the WLAN vendor (manufacturer of APs) either recommends or will provide support for this type of system. Although many vendors attempt to keep a positive relationship with DAS providers, in private their perspective is much different. Many vendors have opted to refuse technical and implementation support for customers who choose DAS. Instead, they defer to the DAS vendor to ensure that the system will meet performance expectations and communicate this caution clearly to the customer. There are many technical reasons for this.

First, design techniques for DAS are generalized for all services. Stated in reverse, DAS designs are not Wi-Fi specific. If you're reading this book, you must already know that WLAN requirements are stringent and often demand strict and thoughtful design techniques for high-performance and highly reliable systems (or you wouldn't be reading this book). Sensitive WLAN deployments will often find that DAS does not adequately address the RF challenges of modern WLANs. They are, by definition, not purposely built for WLANs.

Further, not all DAS vendors are created equal. Some implementations pose significant challenges to the fundamental channel access algorithms specified by 802.11. Others are limited in the types of features and applications they can support. In fact, the choice to implement a DAS should be weighed against the sensitivity of RF applications desired.

For example, traditional WLAN-based RTLS services absolutely should not be deployed on modern DAS. Other sensitive applications like VoWiFi should use DAS with extreme caution or not at all.

To support VoWiFi on a DAS, the density of DAS antenna elements, transmission lines, and headend equipment increases the cost of the DAS, sometimes many times over. After all is said and done, customers may end up overengineering and overpaying for a DAS that might give you some level of acceptable performance with Wi-Fi. Furthermore, at the end of the day, calling for support to your WLAN manufacturer might result in the vendor's refusal to help you if the problem even smells like an RF issue.

Of specific relevance in today's WLAN deployments is the fact that most DAS vendors have limited or no support of MIMO or even antenna diversity. This means you're spending money today to deploy a SISO system (802.11a/g) without diversity, and who wants to do that? For those DAS vendors that do support MIMO, there are other problems. Specifically, MIMO requires multiple separate RF chains and antennas, which requires more RF cabling infrastructure and different antennas. Want to guess what impact this has on cost? Needless to say, the value claims of DAS begin to crumble when MIMO comes into the picture. New patent applications have been submitted that may address this complication, but nothing in the market today shows much promise for MIMO.

In addition to MIMO RF complications, several DAS—and WLAN infrastructure vendors—have reported problems with *radio resource management (RRM)* when a DAS infrastructure is in use. The reason for this is that RRM algorithms are often designed to work with directly connected antennas and not with antennas that are connected via additional hardware, including extended lengths of RF cable as well as inline amplifiers. In other words, most DAS implementations use long RF cable runs to extend the antenna to its mounting location. For this reason, some type of amplifier is often required to maintain signal amplitude to the antenna. This creates an imbalance both in RF reporting from the antenna as well as precise RF control to the antenna from the AP. Some DAS vendors claim to have solved this problem by coordinating the amplifier's output with the AP's radio, but many vendors remain skeptical.

Another major hurdle for DAS is that of RF expertise. In today's WLAN education landscape, it is fairly common for network administrators to be well versed in the networking technology but weak in the RF technology. This is understandable because RF has only begun to be folded into the network landscape within the past decade or so. DAS introduces even more sophisticated RF technologies into a WLAN system, which make for a steep RF learning curve for administrators. A high degree of RF expertise is highly recommended if DAS is to be implemented in your organization or customer's environment.

It is the strong opinion of the authors of this book to absolutely, without question, not attempt to install a DAS yourself. Furthermore, if you intend to use it for Wi-Fi, you should seek the smartest and most capable RF engineering firm you can get to design and install it for you. We have seen mistakes on DAS installations that would never be noticed by most installers but that have created a significant negative performance impact.

Finally, evaluation of a DAS is largely a theoretical exercise. In some larger campus implementations, it may be possible to do trial runs in single buildings, single floors, or in isolated wings. However, in many cases, it is difficult to install a full DAS solution that supports multiple services on a trial basis. It is not uncommon for a customer to implement DAS for Wi-Fi, experience a significant number of problems, and then remove the WLAN from the DAS infrastructure. This obviously poses a problem for cost, time, and lost service periods. For this reason, most companies deploy DAS for other wireless services but refrain from supporting the WLAN on it.

As you can see, it is our opinion that distributed antenna systems have a significant number of challenges that must be addressed. As a disclaimer, this section addresses DAS as seen in the market at the time of publishing. It is quite possible that methods and WLAN-specific design approaches will improve, but as of this writing, we maintain a position of caution when it comes to supporting Wi-Fi services over DAS.

Additional Vendor Selection Considerations

When deciding on a wireless network vendor, it is important to evaluate each vendor against the competition in the market. Several criteria must be evaluated before a choice is made, and the method used to perform this evaluation is significant. A simple list should help demonstrate the point:

Reliability   Many polls have shown that this is the most important aspect of a wireless network.

Performance   Throughput, capacity, dependability, stability, coverage, latency, delay, and jitter are all important performance-related considerations.

Industry Standard Compliance and Certification   At a minimum, Wi-Fi equipment should be Wi-Fi Certified. More stringent standards-compliance evaluation and testing could be conducted as necessary.

Solution Scalability   Systems should be evaluated by their ability to handle high traffic loads and many clients and to not require excessive cost or management at large scale.

Ease of Use   The learning curve for management, configuration simplicity, documentation quality, and other factors should be considered as part of "ease of use."

Future Readiness and Application Support   Customers should evaluate their normal buying cycles and compare this against a solution's ability to meet their needs now and into the future.

Customer Support Scale and Quality   Large enterprise customers should evaluate their vendor based on its capacity to provide the necessary support and customer care required for large organizations.

Vendor Maturity and Stability   No customer wants their vendor to go out of business, so it is important to evaluate a vendor's stability and market maturity as well.

Cost   It should go without saying that cost varies from one vendor to the next.

Security   Security features often vary from one solution to another.

Remote Networking Capabilities   Distributed office locations and mobile employees often demand specific mobile networking features. Some vendors excel in this area.

Feature Support   This is a broad aspect that may include many different things, such as regulatory compliance (DFS, for example), mesh support, failover options, QoS and airtime fairness, integrated WIPS, and more.

Holistic Network Design and Management Needs   This includes aspects such as how the wireless network fits into wired network continuity goals.

Depending on your design situation, some of the items in this list might have higher priority and weight than others.

There is a common saying in the industry: all vendors lie. This is pretty pessimistic. The point, though, is that it is important to validate all claims made by vendors by performing your own testing. It is always recommended to invite your top selection of vendors to do competitive testing and to demonstrate the qualities of their equipment in your network environment. When possible, you should prepare evaluation criteria and design a pilot phase for your network design to select a vendor.

Furthermore, performing a test using only a few APs over a small coverage area or with a small number of client devices is not a useful gauge of performance. Consider that RF is three-dimensional, and heavy client traffic at one part of the network might impact performance of other device transmissions in adjacent areas. For example, if a client on a given channel is taxing the network heavily, what is the impact for similar types of client traffic on immediately adjacent APs on the same channel? What about one more AP distance away? Is heavy client traffic in one area significantly impacting performance on the same channel at a greater distance than you would expect?

Also, as you evaluate vendor equipment yourself, you should consider the value of published tests conducted by vendors and third-party organizations. It is important to note that many tests are biased in some way or another—again, this may sound pessimistic, but it is true. Some published tests are paid for by third-party marketing arms of the vendor themselves, so they may not be reliable (both in procedure and in scope). Read these types of vendor evaluations with astute attention to detail and pay careful attention to wording. Always evaluate competitive tests with rigorous criteria, and use your own pilot testing as a heavily weighed factor in your selection criteria.

As you analyze published tests, be critical. We've outlined a few important criteria that may be helpful in this process:

- Verify that each vendor represented in the test had input as to how their solution (and even the client devices) were configured and which hardware and software was used. It is important that publicly available hardware and software was used.

- Verify that the test methodology was published. Usually the details are hidden. Preferably, this would include full details about all hardware/software for the infrastructure and client devices, as well as test methodologies including scripts and test software.

- Verify that the test is valid. This includes the repeatability (reliability), validity (measures what it purports to measure), and relevancy (applicable to your situation) of the test.

- Verify that the test was audited. Ideally, a neutral group participated in the test in one way or another.

- Verify the test network design scenario. Ensure it is an acceptable, real-world test from your perspective. Testing a few APs in a lab environment is not likely to satisfy anyone's appetite. Is the test environment skewed to one vendor versus the other, making it an unfair comparison?

Although most customers are capable of testing and assessing wireless vendors quite adequately, it always helps to get third-party opinions from analyst firms and technology reviews. While CWNP doesn't necessarily agree with all the conclusions in these reports, yearly articles like Gartner's Magic Quadrant may be helpful for comparing the relative strengths of weaknesses of each vendor. This type of analysis may be helpful in selecting a vendor for your network environment, a task that can be stressful and overwhelming.

Summary

As you can see, making an equipment vendor decision is tough. Hopefully, the knowledge in this book and perhaps other CWNP curriculum will arm you to make the most informed decision possible. While CWNP takes a vendor-neutral stance, what we never want is unfairness and imbalanced rhetoric in the marketplace. That breeds confusion and is an injustice to the professionals who strive to make sound, educated, and informed decisions based on the best information possible.

Network design is one of those topics that there is rarely ever a single, clear correct choice. Your job as a Certified Wireless Design Professional is to inform and educate your fellow decision makers while being as fair and balanced as you can be. That may also mean that your first and perhaps second choice may not be the one that is chosen. Sometimes those experiences are some of the best you will ever have and provide an incredible perspective to the path that perhaps you might usually take.

The good news is that there are so many great vendors in the marketplace today that should technically perform for most deployment scenarios.

Exam Essentials

Understand and explain the differences in WLAN architectures. Be able to explain detailed differences among autonomous, centralized, and distributed WLAN architectures.

Understand the various modes of centralized WLAN architectures (local MAC, split MAC, and remote MAC). Be able to explain local MAC, split MAC, and remote MAC within the centralized WLAN architecture approach.

Understand the operational planes of WLAN designs. Be able to explain the roles and responsibilities of control, management, and data planes within all WLAN architectures.

Describe design models and considerations for different RF models and identify their use in deployment scenarios. Explain the fundamentals and strengths of Multiple Channel Architecture (MCA) and Single Channel Architecture (SCA) WLANs.

Discuss data forwarding models. Understand centralized forwarding, distributed forwarding, and split-tunnel forwarding models. Know how they impact network design and which design scenarios and use cases best apply to each model.

Describe distributed antenna systems. Know how a DAS works and understand its impact on WLAN design and deployment.

Review Questions

1. Which operational plane would be responsible for performing automated RF management?

   A. Control

   B. Distribution

   C. Data

   D. Management

   E. Integration

2. What operational plane would a WNMS primarily interact with?

   A. Integration

   B. Management

   C. Control

   D. Data

   E. Distribution

3. What types of WLAN architectures employ distributed data forwarding models? (Choose all that apply.)

   A. Autonomous

   B. Controller

   C. Distributed

   D. Centralized

4. A distributed WLAN architecture contains everything *except* which of the following?

   A. Coordinated security key caching for roaming enhancements

   B. A WLAN controller for management and control functions

   C. A stand-alone management application or server to centralize device configurations

   D. IP mobility across Layer 3 boundaries

5. What architecture suffers the biggest limitation for sharing control information across APs?

   A. Independent autonomous

   B. Controller

   C. Distributed

   D. Centralized

   E. Cooperative autonomous

6. RFC 4118 attempts to deal with what modern wireless challenge?

   A. CAPWAP interoperability with LWAPP

   B. Enterprise mesh control protocols

   C. RRM functions within a centralized architecture

   D. Taxonomy of CAPWAP

7. What subcategories comprise the centralized WLAN architecture? (Choose all that apply.)

   A. Bridged MAC

   B. Remote MAC

   C. Big MAC

   D. Local MAC

   E. Split MAC

8. What centralized WLAN architecture subtype is the most prevalent?

   A. Split

   B. Local

   C. Remote

   D. Split and remote, which are roughly the same.

   E. Split and local, which are roughly the same.

9. With the new MCS rates of 802.11n, what should you consider as a potential throughput bottleneck in a very large WLAN design?

   A. Local MAC operation

   B. Distributed data forwarding

   C. Centralized data forwarding

   D. Remote AP operation with local forwarding

10. What are potential drawbacks of centralized WLAN architectures? (Choose all that apply.)

   A. Scalability

   B. Single point of failure

   C. Cost

   D. Latency

   E. Complexity

11. What are potential drawbacks of distributed WLAN architectures? (Choose all that apply.)

   A. Encrypted tunnel termination

   B. Does not support legacy devices

   C. Inter-AP communication overhead

   D. Centralized data forwarding

   E. Poor failover operation

12. A WLAN array incorporates what two major design differences from other architectures?

  A. Added RF cabling

  B. High antenna gain

  C. DTLS encryption

  D. Greater number of radios

13. What type of DAS incorporates Wi-Fi services? (Choose two.)

  A. Autonomous

  B. Neutral-host

  C. Distributed

  D. Multiband

  E. Dedicated-host

14. DAS design is largely based on, and most effective for, what antenna technology?

  A. SISO

  B. SIMO

  C. MISO

  D. MIMO

15. By operating on a single-channel design and using a single BSSID, what does an SCA eliminate?

  A. Spectrum load balancing

  B. Contention domain

  C. Client roaming decisions

  D. Management frame poisoning

16. In a normal enterprise deployment scenario, what channel architecture will provide the greatest aggregate throughput capacity?

  A. MCA

  B. HCA

  C. SCA

  D. DCA

17. What parallel term in RF terminology can be used to compare to a broadcast domain with Ethernet networks?

  A. Channel reuse

  B. Spectrum load balancing

  C. Contention domain

  D. RRM arbitration

18. What functions do the control plane of centralized and distributed WLAN architectures help solve? (Choose all that apply.)

   A. Channel reuse plans

   B. Transmit power

   C. Mobility management

   D. Load balancing

19. Of the WLAN architecture, channel use, and antenna technologies listed, which ones represent the main market share in each category? (Choose all that apply.)

   A. Distributed architecture

   B. Centralized architecture

   C. MCA

   D. SCA

   E. Static antenna array

   F. DAS

   G. Fixed dipole antennas

20. When analyzing published competitive tests by equipment vendors, what items are the tests usually lacking? (Choose all that apply.)

   A. Detailed configurations of each vendor's equipment

   B. Detailed test methodology

   C. Client devices and configurations

   D. Audit by a third party

Answers to Review Questions

1. A. The control plane is responsible for coordinating channel and power settings for automated RF management among network devices.

2. B. A wireless network management system (WNMS) would primarily interact with the management operational plane.

3. A, C, D. Autonomous and centralized WLAN architectures both use a distributed data forwarding model.

4. B. Distributed WLAN architectures support all of these options without the use of a WLAN controller as is used with a centralized architecture.

5. A. Independent autonomous APs do not have robust control planes to share with APs of the same ESS. Cooperative autonomous APs may be able to share control information.

6. D. RFC 4118 is titled Architecture Taxonomy for Control and Provisioning of Wireless Access Points (CAPWAP).

7. B, D, E. The three subcategories of a centralized WLAN architecture are local, split, and remote MAC.

8. A. Split MAC architectures are the most popular method of centralized WLAN architecture models. Local MAC is gaining more momentum as 802.11n and remote or office extension APs are gaining in popularity.

9. C. If a large number of APs are used for a single WLAN controller using a centralized data forwarding model, it is possible that the WLAN controller Ethernet connectivity links might become a traffic bottleneck.

10. A, B, C, D, E. Although scalability is both a benefit and a drawback, each of the other options are all notable concerns for centralized WLAN architectures.

11. A, C. In addition to encrypted tunnel termination and increased inter-AP communication, two other items were noted in the chapter: distributed architectures are relatively new and there is added 802.1X configuration overhead.

12. B, D. The primary differentiator of WLAN arrays is their use of high antenna gain and the number of WLAN radios.

13. B, D. Neutral-host, otherwise known as multiband distributed antenna systems (DAS), incorporate Wi-Fi services.

14. A. DAS designs as of this writing incorporate single-input, single-output (SISO) antenna technology without the use of diversity.

15. C. An SCA using a single BSSID eliminates client roaming, assuming proper RF propagation.

16. A. When an SCA system is deployed using a single channel, multichannel architectures (MCA) can usually provide more aggregate throughput capacity because they take advantage of more frequency real estate. When SCA channel stacks are used, an SCA system can exceed the capacity of even the best designed MCA systems.

17. C. A contention domain is the geographic area an RF transmission can be heard and, therefore, contend with other transmissions using the same channel.

18. A, B, C, D. All of these functions are provided by the control plane of both the centralized and distributed WLAN architectures.

19. B, C, G. Of the three technology categories included in these answer options (WLAN architecture, channel use, and antenna type), the centralized architecture using multiple channels with fixed dipole antennas is the most popular. While some of these other options are gaining popularity, the correct answers still hold strong market share leadership.

20. A, B, C. Often published competitive tests are audited by third parties, but they are not always objective third parties.

Chapter

6

RF Communication Principles

THE FOLLOWING CWDP EXAM TOPICS ARE COVERED IN THIS CHAPTER:

- ✓ Demonstrate a detailed understanding of RF propagation behaviors and relate these characteristics to WLAN design for specific environments.

- ✓ Demonstrate a detailed understanding of RF behaviors and characteristics and relate these concepts to WLAN RF design.

- ✓ Understand the purpose of, and challenges related to, creating a balanced RF link between the AP and client devices.

- ✓ Illustrate best practices for data rate/MCS configurations to manage client connectivity.

- ✓ Understand common RF accessories and other components used in WLAN communications.

- ✓ Describe common causes and symptoms of high channel utilization, detect this problem in an existing network, and explain design best practices for remediation.

Modern radio communications are quite complex. What started in the nineteenth century as a relatively simple yet novel method for telegraph communications has become a sophisticated technology for over-the-air data transfer. Radio technology today is a dizzying array of equipment, configurations, environments, threat vulnerabilities, and networking complexities.

Yet as complex as the technology now is, its principles date back many decades—some even before the turn of the twentieth century. This chapter explores these age-old RF concepts. You might ask why a modern wireless expert needs to know these old-fashioned ideas. How could radio principles developed in the 1960s possibly have any relevance today? Contemporary radio equipment is governed by the same principles as radios designed and built in the last century. Therefore, a practical understanding of these principles will ensure that your wireless designs are sound. Wireless engineers who ignore these foundations will do so at their own peril. Simply put, you are not a wireless expert until you understand basic RF principles.

Understanding Basics of RF

Equipment suppliers have tried to make the radio component of a wireless LAN as simple as possible. A modern enterprise system of APs has centralized control, automatic power, and frequency adjustments, and some even have coordinated station handoff. You might be fooled into thinking that you need to place APs only every 100 feet and let the automated system do the rest. In some fairly undemanding scenarios, this might be all that is required. However, networks that service mission-critical and diverse applications are where things will start to break down unless the radio parts of the network are examined carefully. To help you better understand all this, we will explore the physical layer of a wireless network in some detail. This discussion should give you a solid background in the more subtle aspects of RF networks.

> **The Growth of Radio in the 1960s**
>
> It was during the 1960s that microwave radio communications really took off. Space exploration had a lot to do with this. The astronauts who landed on the moon communicated to the earth at a frequency around 2.2 GHz, close to the band used for 802.11 b/g Wi-Fi radios today. Communication satellites were launched with microwave radios on board during that period. Advances in instrumentation made accurate measurements of radio performance possible; instruments like the spectrum analyzer and network analyzer became widely available in the 1960s.

Importance of RF Design to a Successful Network

Designing a successful wireless network requires careful consideration of over-the-air propagation. Bad RF design can kill network performance. It is very common to see situations where way too many or too few access points are deployed, their power levels not set properly, frequencies not planned properly, and no thought given to the type of traffic in the network. A basic understanding of what affects transmitter and receiver performance is a good starting point to avoid these kinds of disasters. Let's now explore some basic radio engineering so you can create your own robust wireless network designs.

RF Is Like Bad Cabling

We've repeated in this book that bad RF is like bad cabling, but we should take this metaphor a step further. Using RF in any fashion is like using bad cabling.

It is truly amazing that radio communications is even possible over the air. The link is full of noise, contention, bandwidth constraints, and latency—all phenomena that degrade data transfer. At one time, cable connections were similarly handicapped. The 802.11 MAC layer avoids contention using Carrier Sense Multiple Access with Collision Avoidance (CSMA/CA), a technique first developed for Ethernet collision avoidance. Modern switches and routers have all but eliminated the need for this protocol as part of Ethernet, but it is unavoidable in over-the-air communications. Communicating over the air is like making connections through a noisy, malfunctioning Ethernet hub. The best you can do is minimize the degradation.

The points raised thus far haven't even taken into account multiple devices and device types using completely different and interfering transmission techniques. Especially when dealing with unlicensed bands such as 2.4 and 5 GHz, we not only contend with our own devices, but we also do so with other, foreign devices.

Radio Propagation

A lot can happen to a radio wave as it travels from a transmitter to a receiver. Its power level decreases as it travels, even if there are no obstructions between the two radios. If there is something between, such as buildings and trees, the power level will decrease even more rapidly. Understanding the way in which a radio signal attenuates and how much the signal attenuates as it travels is critical to a sound wireless system design.

It all starts with frequency. Just as with AM/FM radio and television, WLANs operate in different channels, and similar to the older radio technologies, each channel is used as a separate communication path. Each channel exists at a different frequency, which affects the ability for radio waves to propagate. We will now focus on radio propagation at different frequencies and its impact on WLAN performance.

802.11 Operating Frequencies

Governments regulate radio transmissions. There are good reasons for this. It helps standardize the equipment and also reduces chances for interference. The two basic types of regulatory frameworks for radio operations are as follows:

Licensed Operators that have purchased or leased bands from the government are using licensed frequencies. Licensed bands are used for cellular phone, government, and satellite service, among many others. It might be surprising to know that 802.11 exists in a licensed band at frequencies between 3.65 and 3.7 GHz. This is called 802.11y and it shares spectrum with another licensed OFDM technology called IEEE 802.16, widely known as WiMAX. Because the licensed band is highly controlled and has limited ownership, the source of interference is limited and well understood. The operating RF power levels are considerably higher than those used in the unlicensed band.

Unlicensed Unlicensed bands can be used by anyone with a radio. No license is required from the government. The government controls interference by limiting power levels. 802.11 uses unlicensed bands at 2.4 GHz and 5 GHz.

The unlicensed frequency at 2.4 GHz is called the Industrial, Scientific, and Medical (ISM) band. This band was initially designated for industrial equipment like RF welders and microwave ovens so that they could radiate without causing interference to radio communications. When radio networks became more capable of handling interference, manufacturers lobbied governments to allow radio communications in these bands. Currently the 2.4 GHz ISM band allows several kinds of radio networks, including 802.11, Bluetooth devices, baby monitors, and cordless phones.

All the devices that are not related to 802.11 interfere with WLAN communications. The frequency range used by 802.11b/g devices is broken up into 11 channels in North America (1–11), 13 channels in Europe and most of the world (1–13), and 14 channels in Japan (1–14). (Channel 14 is only allowed for 802.11b.) Table 6.1 shows the channel numbers and center frequencies of each channel in the 2.4 GHz band. It is clear from the table how only three channels are noninterfering (Japan can have four). In the United States, channels 1, 6, and 11 can be used on a noninterfering basis. To avoid interference, no other channels should be used. The maximum allowable power radiated is 1 W with a 6 dBi antenna.

Table 6.1 shows the channels, frequencies, and allowed power.

TABLE 6.1   Frequencies, channels, and allowed power level for 802.11b/g

Channel number	Frequency (MHz)	Maximum output power (up to 6 dBi antenna gain) FCC limits
1	2412	
2	2417	
3	2422	
4	2427	
5	2432	
6	2437	
7	2442	1 W
8	2447	
9	2452	
10	2457	
11	2462	
12	2467	
13	2472	
14	2484	

In North America the 5 GHz 802.11a primarily occupies what is called the Unlicensed National Information Infrastructure (UNII) band and is divided into these parts:

- 5.15 to 5.25 GHz in the UNII-1 band
- 5.25 to 5.35 GHz UNII-2 band
- 5.47–5.725 GHz in the UNII-2 extended band
- 5.725–5.825 GHz in the UNII-3 band
- 5.725–5.875 GHz in the 5.8 GHz ISM band

Table 6.2 shows the 23 possible channels in the UNII bands. In countries outside of North America a similar number of channels in this band is used. Unlike the 2.4 GHz band, the 5 GHz band only allows channels numbers that do not interfere with each other. The third column in both Table 6.1 and 6.2 show power level limits that are allowed for each band by the FCC in the United States. Other countries have similar limits on power. A detailed discussion of these limits is found in the Regulation section below.

TABLE 6.2   Frequencies, channels, and allowed power levels for 802.11a

Band	Channel numbers	Center Frequency (MHz)	Maximum output power (up to 6 dBi antenna gain)
UNII band 1 5.15 to 5.25 GHz	36	5180	50mW
	40	5200	
	44	5220	
	48	5240	
UNII band 2 5.25 to 5.35 GHz	52	5260	250mW
	56	5280	
	60	5300	
	64	5320	
UNII band 2e 5.47-5.725 GHz	100	5500	250mW
	104	5520	
	108	5540	
	112	5560	
	116	5580	
	120	5600	
	124	5620	
	128	5640	
	132	5660	
	136	5680	
	140	5700	
UNII band 3 5.725 to 5.825 GHz	149	5745	1000mW
	153	5765	
	157	5785	
	161	5805	
ISM 5.8 GHz 5.725 to 5.875 GHz	165	5825	1000mW

Path Loss and Range

Most people have had some experience with radio path loss. For example, you might have a problem with your cell phone indoors, determine the signal level (indicated by bars) on the phone to be too low, and move outside for a better signal. People intuitively know that buildings can dramatically affect radio signal levels. When one walks into a building, the difference in power can be as much as 20 dB, meaning that the signal level outside can be 100 times higher than just inside the doors of the building. The exterior walls and tinted glass of the building absorb the microwaves from the cell tower so that there is less power available inside the building than outside.

There are several ways a signal can be attenuated as it travels from a radio transmitter to a receiver. The primary source of loss is strictly a geometric one. As an ideal radio signal propagates outward, its total power stays constant and the area over which it spreads gets larger.

Consider an analogy of a water sprinkler. There is a finite amount of water being expelled from the sprinkler head that is projected in a specific pattern. For our analogy, let's assume it is a 360° sprinkler. If you stood at the edge of the sprinkler pattern versus being very close to the sprinkler head, you would not get as wet, as illustrated in Figure 6.1.

FIGURE 6.1   Power per area example

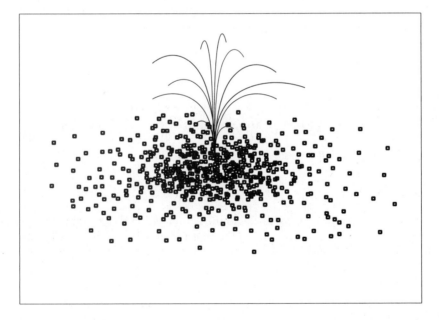

As you can see, as you get farther from the radio, the power per area gets smaller. As the antenna of the receiver collects power over a constant area, the energy it can receive diminishes when the receiver moves farther away from the transmitter. It receives a smaller and smaller percentage of the total available power as the signal spreads over a larger and larger area.

To understand loss, you first need to calculate what happens to the transmitted signal. The following equation demonstrates how the surface area of a sphere, S, is related to its radius, R.

$$S = 4\pi R^2$$

The loss of a radio signal over distance is related directly to this equation. For a special kind of antenna, called an *isotropic antenna*, power radiates equally in all directions. We calculate W_t, the power transmitted from an isotropic antenna per square area, on the expanding sphere:

$$W_t = P_t/(4\pi d^2)$$

d replaces R as the distance between the transmitter and receiver, and P_t is the RF power out of the transmitter. With a transmitting antenna that has gain G_t the value of W_t becomes larger by the factor G:

$$W_t = P_t G_t/(4\pi d^2)$$

This only tells half the story. The receiving antenna has a certain effective area, A_e, that is related to the receive antenna gain and the wavelength of the radio signal, λ (lambda). This area can be thought as the amount of area on the sphere over which the receive antenna gathers energy:

$$A_e = G_r\lambda^2/(4\pi)$$

The received power, P_r, is then found by multiplying the transmitted power per square area over the sphere by the amount of area presented by the receive antenna:

$$P_r = W_t A_e = [P_t G_t/(4\pi d^2)][G_r\lambda^2/(4\pi)] = P_t G_t G_r[\lambda/(4\pi d)]^2$$

$$P_r = P_t G_t G_r/[(4\pi d)/\lambda]^2$$

This is called the Friis transmission equation. This equation states that the receive power is related to the transmitted power, gain of the transmit and receive antennas, and a factor $[(4\pi d)/\lambda]^2$. This is the free space path loss, L.

$$L = [(4\pi d)/\lambda]^2$$

Expressed in dB:

$$L(dB) = 10 \log ([(4\pi d)/\lambda]^2) = 20 \log ((4\pi d)/\lambda)$$

Finally, this last equation is the same as the one previous but in a form that is easier to work with:

$$L(dB) = 20 \log(d) + 20 \log(f) - 27.55,$$

where *d* is the distance in meters and *f* is the frequency in MHz.

The thing to note here is that loss measured in dB increases by the logarithm of both distance and frequency. Doubling the frequency from 2.4 GHz to 5 GHz results in a 6 dB difference in path loss. As the receiving station moves farther away from the transmitting radio, changes in loss become less. Most of the dramatic differences in path loss occur near the transmitter. When the distance from the transmitter changes from 1 meter to 2 meters, the loss goes up by a factor of 6 dB. This same change in loss occurs when the distance changes from 1 km to 2 km. A graph of free space loss is shown in Figure 6.2.

FIGURE 6.2   A graph showing free space loss over distance for 2.4 GHz and 5 GHz signals

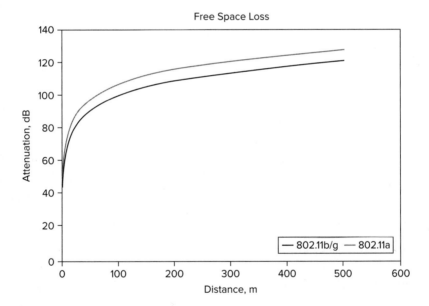

Engineers who are familiar with 802.11 will note how far a 1 Mbps will propagate as compared to a 54 Mbps rate. The primary reason for this is the difference in receiver sensitivity for the two rates. A 1 Mbps signal can be received at a power level of –94 dBm whereas a 54 Mbps signal requires a –71 dBm power level (these numbers were taken from a typical enterprise access point). This 23 dB difference in power in a free space loss model corresponds to a distance that is 14 times farther. In free space, 1 Mbps signals can be received 14 times farther than 54 Mbps. This distance ratio is likely smaller in a real-life scenario, but the calculation demonstrates the idea that lower data rates propagate further than higher ones.

The free space loss equation is not extremely useful in practice for accurate loss measurements, as radios typically do not float in space (at least WLAN radios don't). They are usually surrounded by objects either indoors or outside, including the ground, walls, people, trees, and furniture. These objects will reflect and absorb radio signals, greatly increasing the loss over distance. Many loss models have been developed that take into account these effects. A simple model that is commonly used is shown here:

$$L(dB) = 10\,n\log(d) + 20\log(f) - 27.55$$

Here the free space loss model has been modified to include a value n. When $n = 2$, loss follows the free space model. Indoor deployments will use an increased number, typically something around $n = 3$. A very crowded office with a lot of obstructions might use an n value of 4. Outdoor deployments will use an n value between 2 and 3. This model too has limited accuracy, but is generally more accurate than the free space model.

Building materials will absorb microwaves in different ways. Table 6.3 shows some typical absorption characteristics of common building materials. It is likely that nothing on this table will be on the test, but we include the table as a useful reference.

TABLE 6.3 Attenuation values for common building materials at 2.4 GHz and 5 GHz

Material	5 GHz Attenuation (dB)	2.4 GHz Attenuation (dB)
Solid Wood Door 1.75″	10	6
Hollow Wood Door 1.75″	7	4
Interior Office Door w/Window 1.75″/0.5″	6	4
Steel Fire/Exit Door 1.75″	25	13
Steel Fire/Exit Door 2.5″	32	19
Steel Rollup Door 1.5″	19	11
Brick 3.5″	10	6
Concrete Wall 8″	13	10

Material	5 GHz Attenuation (dB)	2.4 GHz Attenuation (dB)
Concrete Wall 18"	30	18
Glass Divider 0.5"	8	12
Cubical Wall (Fabric) 2.25"	2	1
Interior Hollow Wall 4"	3	5
Interior Hollow Wall 6"	4	6
Interior Solid Wall 5"	16	14
Marble 2"	10	6
Bullet-Proof Glass 1"	20	10
Exterior Double Pane Coated Glass 1"	20	13
Exterior Single Pane Window 0.5"	6	7
Interior Office Window 1"	6	3
Safety Glass-Wire 0.25"	2	3
Safety Glass-Wire 1.0"	18	13

Please note that this table was a result of a test done by 3Com, and should not be considered absolute or typical values.

There is often a great variation in wall and ceiling attenuation in buildings. In Chapter 9, "Site Survey RF Design," we discuss making signal level measurements before WLAN deployments. This is necessary because it is difficult to predict how far signals will penetrate in a building without measurement. It is common that older buildings will have more densely packed walls that attenuate more than newer buildings. Exterior walls will generally attenuate more than interior ones. The layout of a building can change in such a way that a wall that once was an exterior wall has been made to be an interior one, causing an unexpected increase in attenuation. Some ceilings and floors will hardly attenuate signals at all and some will greatly attenuate signals. For example, hospitals might move their Radiology department to a new location but leave in place its lead-lined walls. Having measured wall attenuation personally, the authors of this book have found values greater than 50 dB in some areas that are currently or used to be Radiology departments.

As Table 6.3 shows, 5 GHz signals will not penetrate as well through many materials as 2.4 GHz signals. Not only is free space loss higher for the higher frequency, the increased attenuation will further limit its coverage. Sometimes if 802.11b/g is collocated with 802.11a, it is necessary to power down the b/g radios to produce the same coverage area as the radios.

Given the large variations in attenuation, it is very important to measure signal propagation in every building where a WLAN is deployed and for every frequency band (2.4 GHz and/or 5 GHz), especially in mission-critical areas.

Multipath and Diversity

802.11 WLANs are used in many different environments. Whether indoors or outdoors, the radio signal does not necessarily reach the receiver in a direct path from the transmitter. Radio signals will reflect off objects and may take many paths to reach the receiver. Occasionally the direct line-of-sight (LOS) path is not the strongest signal path. It may not even exist. The multiple versions of the same radio signal picked up at the receiver can be a source of interference. In this section we will explore the impact of multipath on radio performance.

A simple multipath situation is shown in Figure 6.3. The main LOS modulated signal leaves the transmitter and is picked up by the receiver some time later. The distance between the two radios and the speed of light ($3x10^8$ meters/sec) determine this time of flight. A reflected signal has to travel a greater distance and will arrive some time later. This difference in time between the various received multipath signals is called the *delay spread*. Typically delay spread varies from 30 to 270 nanoseconds (ns) for indoor systems depending on distance between radios and how much clutter (people, furniture, walls, etc.) there is in the environment. Outdoor deployments can have much higher delay spread.

FIGURE 6.3   Multipath diagram

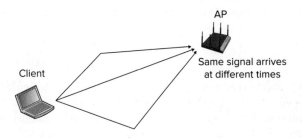

The concern with delay spread is that the digital data that is sent over the air on different paths will interfere with each other. The signals from the different paths will enter the receiver and join, causing different symbols from the same data stream to interfere with each other. This is called *intersymbol interference (ISI)*. For a delay spread of 270 ns, the data symbol rate would have to approach 3.7 Msymbol per second (Msps) for the symbols to be close enough to each other in time to totally interfere ($1/(270 \times 10^{-9}) = 3.7 \times 10^6$). Smaller delay spreads would impact even higher symbol rate communications. As you will discover in the sections that follow, the symbol rates for 802.11 are lower than 3.7 Msps, so the impact of 270 ns and below delay spread on WLANs is minimal. The 802.11 standard is designed so that delay spread does not cause much ISI, at least for indoor applications.

The other effect that multipath has on data communications is related to the frequency of the radio carrier. If one adds two radio signals that are at the same frequency, they can add to each other (constructive interference) or subtract from each other (destructive interference). The relative phase and amplitude of the two signals determines the amplitude of the combined signal. Signals that are in-phase will add constructively and the amplitudes of the two will add together. Those out of phase (180° phase difference) will add destructively, resulting in a lower amplitude that is the difference of the two amplitudes. This change in amplitude is called *fast fading* because the signal can fluctuate dramatically and quickly as a client radio moves short distances.

The wavelength of a radio carrier in air is calculated as a function of frequency and the speed of light. In the following equation λ is the wavelength, c is the speed of light $(3.0 \times 10^8$ m/s), and F is the frequency in Hz:

$$\lambda = c/F$$

At 2.4 GHz, the wavelength is 12.5 cm $(3.0 \times 10^8$ m/s $/ 2.4 \times 10^9$ Hz $= 12.5$ cm). At 5 GHz that wavelength is 6 cm. Movements on the order of that distance can bring the receiver from a deep fade to a strong signal. Access points will typically have two antennas used for what is called *receive diversity*. The purpose is to minimize the impact of multipath fading. If one antenna is experiencing a fade and the error rate increases, the receiver would typically check the other antenna to see if it has a better signal. If the signal is better, it would use that one to receive. The receiver will constantly compare the two signals and use the best one. By separating the antennas by a wavelength, the access point designer or installation engineer maximizes the likelihood that a fade in one antenna means a strong signal in the other. Setting the distance to be a multiple of a wavelength works well too, as long as the two antennas are not more than around four wavelengths apart. Diversity antennas that are too far apart will start to cover different areas.

 Real World Scenario

Using Diversity Antennas

One of the authors remembers a particularly bad antenna configuration found in a hotel where he was staying. There was an 802.11b/g access point in a hallway corner with the two ports connected to high -gain antennas. The antennas were pointing in two different directions down each hallway. It seemed that the hotel owner thought that he could save access points if he could use the two antennas to cover different areas. The problem with this configuration is that beacon messages are transmitted on only a single antenna. Radios on one hallway could never associate with the access point. What the hotel owner didn't know was that the two antenna ports are designed for receive diversity and depend on the fact that both antennas cover the same area.

Regulations

The Federal Communications Commission (FCC) in the United States and other world regulatory agencies will limit the amount of power that can be emitted from an 802.11 AP and client. This is done in an effort to limit interference levels in the unlicensed band. The rules quoted here are FCC rules. The Institute of Electrical and Electronics Engineers (IEEE) has similar but slightly lower power rules that are accepted worldwide. Where they differ is indicated in parentheses. It is important to follow the local rules governing transmit power whenever deploying a wireless system. Typical indoor installations will not run into problems unless very high-gain antennas are used. The only exception to this is the lower 5 GHz frequency band 5.15 GHz to 5.25 GHz, which has strict limits to transmit power. Deploying high-power outdoor systems is where you can run into problems, and you should carefully consider the limits.

Point to Multipoint

An access point communicating to client devices is described as a point-to-multipoint (PtMP) system. 802.11b and g regulations allow up to 30 dBm or 1 watt (W) of transmitter power with a 6 dBi antenna. Indoor access points do not transmit energy at levels as high as that limit; 15 to 20 dBm is more typical. Outdoor access points are likely to transmit at the regulatory limits. The regulations further stipulate that the radio's transmit power be reduced by 1 dB for every dB of antenna gain over 6 dBi. *Effective isotropic radiated power (EIRP)* is a measure of the power that would be radiated out of an isotropic antenna and is typically measured in dBm or watts. It can be calculated by adding transmit power measured in dBm to the antenna gain measured in dBi. That would put the EIRP limit for 802.11b and g at 36 dBm or 4 W.

802.11a operates in four 5 GHz bands and has different PtMP rules. The low frequency band runs from 5.15 GHz to 5.25 GHz and has a maximum transmit power of 50 milliwatts (mW) (40 mW IEEE) with a 6 dBi antenna. It is limited to indoor use. The middle frequency bands run from 5.25 GHz to 5.35 GHz and 5.47 GHz to 5.725 GHz, with a maximum power limit of 250 mW (200 mW IEEE) with a 6 dBi antenna. They are designated for indoor and outdoor use. The high-frequency band runs from 5.725 GHz to 5.825 GHz and has a maximum transmitter power of 1 W (800 mW IEEE) with an antenna gain of 6 dBi. It is used both indoors and outdoors. Typical indoor APs will only radiate 17 dBm (50 mW) transmit power over all the bands.

Point to Point

The FCC defines point-to-point (PtP) systems as having a single fixed radio on both sides of the link. Typically a PtP system would be used to relay IP traffic from one fixed point to another and would use high gain antennas to achieve links over long distances and limit interference to radios outside of the link. The FCC generally allows higher EIRP for a PtP system than a point-to-multipoint system. With 802.11b and g, for every 3 dB of antenna gain over a 6 dBi antenna, you need to reduce the transmit power 1 dB below 30 dBm. An 18 dBi antenna, for example, has a gain that is 12 dB over a 6 dBi antenna. The transmit power would have to be reduced by 4 dB from 30 dBm or 26 dBm. The total EIRP in this case would be 44 dBm (18 dBi + 26 dBm = 44 dBm) or 25 W.

The PtP rules for the lower and middle 5 GHz bands (5.15 GHz to 5.725 GHz) are the same as with PtMP. The upper band (5.725 GHz to 5.825) allows for 1 W or 30 dBm transmit power with a 23 dBi antenna for outdoor PtP links. The power reduces 1 dB for every 1 dB of gain increase above 23 dBi. This caps the upper band EIRP to 53 dBm or 200 W.

Modulation

A single frequency microwave tone carries no information. A single tone is also called a *carrier wave (CW)*, or just carrier for short. Just as a tone of sound contains no information unless it changes pitch or amplitude, the CW must be modulated or changed in order to convey information. There are three basic ways that a radio tone can be modulated: changing phase, frequency, and amplitude (frequency changes can be considered a form of phase change, just continuously changing). In addition, a single carrier tone can be broken up into multiple subcarriers, each subcarrier having its own modulation. WLAN systems combine these modulation techniques in complex ways. In this section, we will explore how modern digital communications has transformed your grandmother's simple AM radio into a sophisticated data transfer system.

Digital Modulation

There are three ways that a radio carrier tone can be modulated to convey information. We are all familiar with frequency modulation (FM) and amplitude modulation (AM) radio signals where a radio transmitter uses sound to change the frequency and amplitude of a carrier, respectively. An FM or AM receiver will then convert the modulated carrier back to sound. Similarly, a digital radio transmitter will modulate a carrier with digital data. A digital receiver then converts the modulated carrier back to the original digital data stream. A digital radio modulates a carrier just like an FM or AM radio does. Instead of sound, the information sent is digital data. The basic principle is the same. In fact, the earliest data radios used the same circuits as FM radios. Over time, radio design has been optimized around data communications. Our focus here is on these modern digital modulation techniques.

Constellation

A *constellation* is a convenient way to visualize a digitally modulated signal. Modulation causes the amplitude and phase of a carrier to change. A constellation is a map of these changes on an X-Y coordinate system. Mapping every point of amplitude and phase is not important. The focus is on the points in time where the receiver detects amplitude and phase. This is the point where an analog signal is converted to digits. The transitions between the detection points in time are less important and are generally not shown as part of the constellation.

In this section ideal constellations with no distortion or noise are explored. The "Communications Link" section later in the chapter will investigate the effects of noise on the constellation.

Figure 6.4 shows a graph of a sinusoid wave at four different phases: 45°, 135°, 225°, and 315° and with constant amplitude.

FIGURE 6.4   Sinusoidal waveform showing four phases, 00 = 45°, 01 = 135°, 11 = 225°, and 10 = 315°. The constellation sample point in the figure is where the phase and amplitude sample is taken for the constellation.

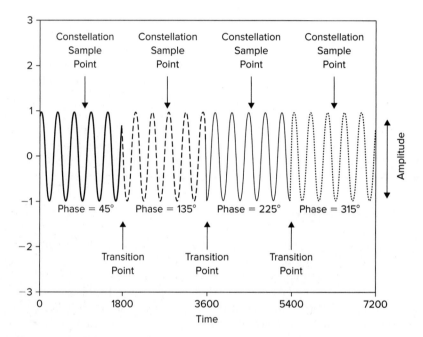

A digital transmitter with a phase modulator is designed to change the phase of a carrier according to its digital input. With the four phases in Figure 6.4, two bits of information can be represented: 00 = 45°, 01 = 135°, 11 = 225°, and 10 = 315°. A phase demodulator in a receiver would detect the phase and amplitude and recover the digital signal in the middle of the signal, far away as possible to the transitions from one phase to the next. The arrows in Figure 6.4 show the detection point used by the receiver.

The detected four-phase signal can be shown on an X-Y grid, as shown in Figure 6.5. This dot pattern is called a constellation. It shows in one graph both amplitude and phase of an RF signal.

FIGURE 6.5   Constellation dot pattern of a QPSK modulated signal

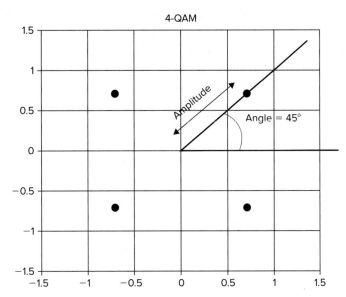

The amplitude of the signal is represented by the distance from the origin, point 0, 0 and one of the four points in the figure. The phase is represented by the angle, as shown in the figure. It illustrates how the transmitter's modulator varies the amplitude and phase. Each dot in the constellation is a snapshot of the phase and amplitude at the detection arrow point of the modulated carrier shown in Figure 6.4. Over time the dot position changes from one state to the other as the modulated signal changes from 00 to 01 to 10 to 11 in the data stream order. The four-dot pattern constellation shows a modulation type called *quadrature phase shift key (QPSK)*. The horizontal axis is known as the I or *in-phase axis*. The vertical axis is known as the Q or *quadrature phase axis*.

Binary phase shift key (BPSK), QPSK, and the more general *quadrature amplitude modulation (QAM)* are the basis for much of modern digital radio communications. They are at the heart of the 802.11 physical layer. Earlier, we discussed QPSK, which has four phase states, 45°, 135°, 225°, and 315°. BPSK involves only two states with phase 0° and 180°, where 0° represents 0 and 180° represents 1. QAM is an extension of the idea for QPSK. Instead of four states, 16-QAM and 64-QAM has 16 states and 64 states, respectively, arranged in a square. QPSK is also a type of QAM modulation called 4-QAM. In 16-QAM, 64-QAM and higher orders, both the amplitude and phase of the carrier is modulated. The constellation patterns for each of these modulation methods are shown in Figure 6.6.

FIGURE 6.6 Constellation pattern of QPSK, 16-QAM, and 64-QAM

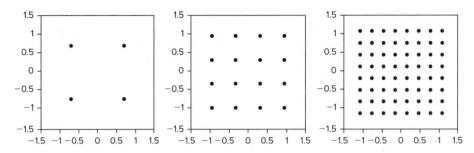

Each point on the constellation represents a digital symbol. The order of the QAM modulation determines the number of bits represented by the symbol. For 16-QAM, the symbol represents 4 bits ($2^4 = 16$), for 64-QAM the number of bits is six ($2^6=64$). Figure 6.7 shows the 4 bits represented by each of the points in the 16-QAM constellation.

FIGURE 6.7 Four-bit pattern for a 16-QAM constellation

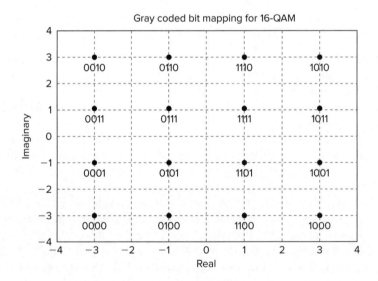

Gray coding is discussed later in this chapter.

A digitally modulated carrier will spend some time hanging at a point in the constellation. It will quickly transition to another point in the constellation and then hang there for some time. Any point in the constellation can transition to any other point. Figure 6.8 shows all the possible transitions for a 16-QAM and 64-QAM signal. In digital radio communications, symbol rates are important since a modulated carrier is sending symbols, not individual bits. It acts like a parallel digital bus, sending multiple bits at a time. A 64-QAM signal has a 6-bit symbol. Its bit rate is six times higher than its symbol rate. A BPSK and 64-QAM signal running at the same symbol rate will have bit rates that differ by a factor of 6.

FIGURE 6.8 Constellation pattern of 16-QAM and 64-QAM signal showing transitions

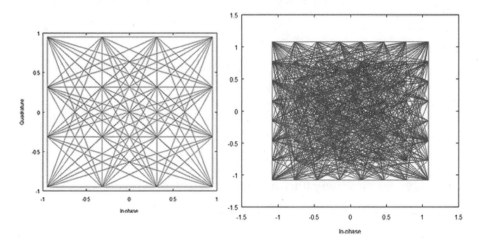

What is the reason for adding points to a modulated carrier? As points are added to the modulation, the bit rate increases. Stuffing more and more points on to the modulated carrier results in a constant symbol rate and a higher data rate. Remarkably, this higher data rate does not require more spectrum. All the different digital modulation methods discussed have the same spectrum for a given symbol rate. There are trade-offs, however. The increased data rate does not come without drawbacks: a higher-quality signal is necessary to transmit at these higher rates and a more linear (more expensive, less efficient) amplifier is needed to transmit the modulated carrier without affecting signal quality.

Receiver performance in the presence of noise and signal quality as it relates to modulation order will be explored later in the section "Communications Link."Amplifier saturation and the effect of high order modulation on spectrum quality will be discussed as well.

DBPSK and DQPSK

802.11 at 1 and 2 Mbps and 802.11b at 5.5 and 11 Mbps uses two different modulation techniques:

- *Differential binary phase shift keying (DBPSK)*
- *Differential quadrature phase shift keying (DQPSK)*

They are very similar to the modulation schemes discussed earlier and have the same number of bits per symbol. Instead of the bit stream determining directly the phase of the carrier, in differential keying, the bit stream sets the change in phase. The differential scheme has some advantages over the direct phase method. If a receiver loses signal momentarily, it can recover quickly. The receiver does not need to detect an absolute phase of the carrier but need only figure out the change in phase from one symbol to the next.

DBPSK has two changes possible: 0° and 180°. A zero bit corresponds to a 0° change (no change) and a one bit corresponds to a 180° change. DQPSK is similar. The phase change for DQPSK is 0°, 90°, 180° and 270° for symbols 00, 01, 11, and 10, respectively.

Spectrum of a Modulated Carrier

The spectra of a BPSK, QPSK, 16-QAM, and 64-QAM modulated carrier are all identical if the modulator is running at the same symbol rate for each. Figure 6.9 shows the spectrum of a BPSK, QPSK, 16-QAM, and 64-QAM signal that has not been filtered The carrier frequency is at 500 Hz and the symbol rate is 62.5 symbols/sec. The primary nulls next to the main lobe at 500 Hz are at 437.5 Hz (500 – 62.5 Hz) and 562.5 Hz.

FIGURE 6.9 Frequency spectrum of a BPSK, QPSK, 16-QAM, and 64-QAM signal

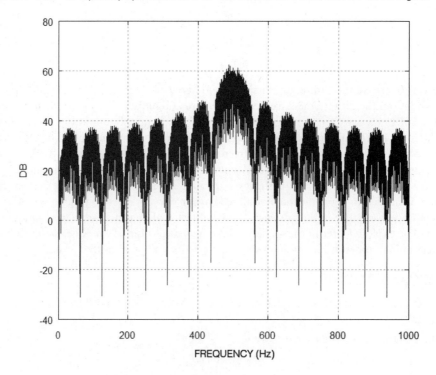

The spectrum has a classic shape to it. It follows a mathematical curve called SinX/X. The shape of that curve is shown as amplitude and as a dB value in Figure 6.10.

FIGURE 6.10 SinX/X function shape shown as amplitude (left graph) and in dB (right graph)

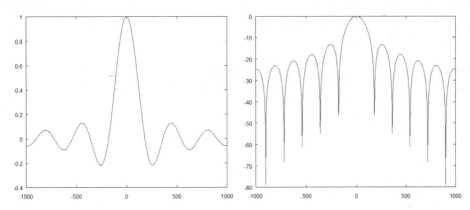

The first side lobe of the spectrum comes up to 13 dB below the main lobe. This shape will become important later when we discuss OFDM. The higher frequency lobes of the spectrum outside of the main lobe are due to the rapid transitions in phase and amplitude between the steady state constellation points. They can be filtered without much change in the quality of the modulated signal. Figure 6.11 shows a filtered 16-QAM spectrum. With filtering, the side lobes are over 30 dB lower than the main lobe. This reduction in side lobe from 13 dB results in lower interference to neighboring channels.

FIGURE 6.11 Filtered 16-QAM spectrum

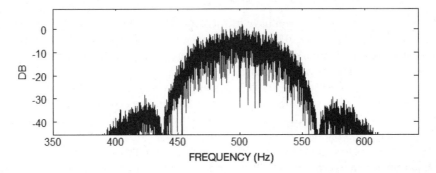

The effect of the filtering on the 16-QAM constellation is shown in Figure 6.12. Note the "+" located at the constellation sampling points. The filtering does not significantly affect the location of the points.

FIGURE 6.12   Filtered 16-QAM constellation

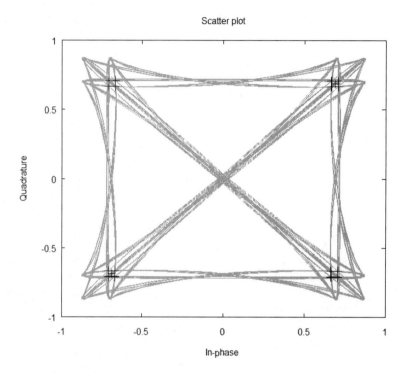

802.11 Modulation and Coding

In this section you'll take what you have learned about basic digital modulation and apply it to the 802.11 standard. The 802.11 physical layer has evolved from a strictly 1 to 2 Mbps data rate standard to the 802.11g and rates that go to 54 Mbps. 802.11n introduced PHY rates up to 600 Mbps, using more bandwidth and advanced spatial processing techniques. The carrier frequency for the original 802.11 standard was 2.4 GHz, a frequency that was set aside for unlicensed communications. The first step in this evolution achieved the 1 to 2 Mbps data rate by a coding technique called *direct-sequence spread spectrum (DSSS)*. This was the original 802.11 standard released in June 1997.

Spread spectrum was a technique developed for the military to protect communications against jamming and interfering signals. In 1999, the standard was expanded to include 5.5 Mbps and 11 Mbps data rates, which also used DSSS but in a slightly more complex fashion called *Complementary Code Keying (CCK)*. That part of the standard was designated with the letter b. That year also saw a standard called 802.11a that used a very different kind of modulation called *Orthogonal Frequency Division Multiplexing (OFDM)*. The data rates for that standard include 6, 9, 12, 18, 24, 36, 48, and 54 Mbps and use a carrier frequency in the 5 GHz band, also in an unlicensed band. The 2.4 GHz band was upgraded in 2003 with the 802.11g standard. It was designed to be backward compatible with the 802.11b standard and included the data rates used in both the b and a standards. 802.11g was specified by using a mixture of DSSS and OFDM depending on the data rate. Though the standard allows for frequency-hopping spread spectrum (FHSS), it is not commonly used and will not be covered in this book.

DSSS

DSSS is a spread spectrum method that takes a narrow band data signal and transmits it with more bandwidth than is necessary. The receiver of this signal converts the wide bandwidth signal into a narrow band one by a process called *despreading*. There are two basic of advantages to doing this:

- The signal is robust against narrowband jammers or interferers. When the receiver takes in a narrowband signal along with the wideband one, the despreading process will narrow in frequency the wanted signal and spread out the unwanted one. The receiver can then use a narrowband filter to remove most of the energy of the interfering signal.

- There is a gain related to the increase in bandwidth. Called *processing gain*, it affects the required signal to noise in a DSSS signal. In 802.11, the 1 Mbps and 2 Mbps data rates have a processing gain of 10.4 dB. Processing gain will be addressed in the "Noise" section later in this chapter.

Original 802.11

The 1 Mbps and 2 Mbps data rates achieved by the original 802.11 used a method of spreading using a *Barker code*. Barker codes have special properties that make them ideal for a spread spectrum system. The spread signal results when you combine a relatively low-bandwidth data stream with a high-bandwidth Barker code. For each bit of data, a series of 11 pulses called chips are sent over the air, which spreads out the signal in frequency. The low data rate 1 Mbps stream is combined with a Barker code running at a high rate, called a *chip rate*, of 11 Mchips per second. The resultant bandwidth of the signal is 22 MHz.

Figure 6.13 shows what happens when an 11 chip Barker is combined with a two-bit data sequence of 1 and then 0. The 0 and 1 are represented by –1 and 1, respectively so that the data and Barker code are shown combining using a multiplication operation. This is equivalent to a binary operation called XOR. There are some important things to note. For every data bit, there are 11 Barker code chips. The chip rate is 11 times the data bit rate. The resulting data stream is 11 times faster than the original data and requires 11 times the bandwidth to transmit.

FIGURE 6.13 Barker code combined with 2-bit data

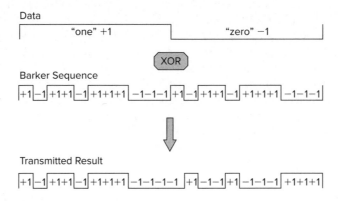

The 1 Mbps 802.11 data rate uses the DBPSK modulation that you learned about in an earlier section. If you were to modulate the 1 Mbps data signal directly on to the carrier, the resulting bandwidth would be 2 MHz. The modulator is running at 1 Msymbol per second (1 Msps) so the nulls of the SinX/X spectrum is at 1 MHz on each side of the carrier. Of course, this isn't how 802.11 is transmitted. The 1 Mbps data rate signal is spread before modulation. The data stream is combined with the Barker code. After the Barker code is applied, the data signal is now 11 times faster at 11 Mchips per second and the modulator now runs at 11 Msps. The spectrum nulls are at 11 MHz on each side of the carrier, for a total of 22 MHz bandwidth.

The 2 Mbps 802.11 data rate is transmitted in much the same way. The only difference is that it uses DQPSK. The symbol rate is the same for both, but since DQPSK, just like QPSK, has 2 bits per symbol, the data rate is double. Both data rates, 1 and 2 Mbps, use the same 22 MHz bandwidth.

When the chip rate sequence is received, it must be despread. Figure 6.14 shows what happens in a DSSS receiver that uses Barker codes. The demodulated chip sequence is XORed with a Barker code and the result is the original data stream. This in itself is not remarkable. Any 11-digit data sequence will do this. What is special about the Barker code is that it has strong autocorrelation properties. The next set of figures will demonstrate what that means.

Figure 6.15 shows a data stream that has been despread using a Barker code. The bit streams are the result of XORing the received chip sequence with the 11-chip barker code. The smaller-amplitude data streams are the result of the Barker sequence shifting by various chip amounts before the XOR operation. Unless the Barker sequence is lined up exactly—that is, zero offset—the amplitude of the XORed result is much smaller. The Barker code was chosen for this property. It allows the receiver to easily detect the original data stream that was spread by the same code.

FIGURE 6.14   Received spread signal combined with Barker code

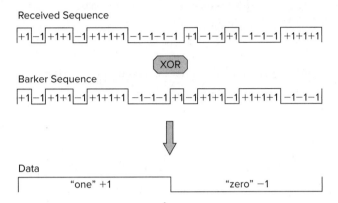

FIGURE 6.15   Received data stream after despread from Barker code, shown with various chip offsets

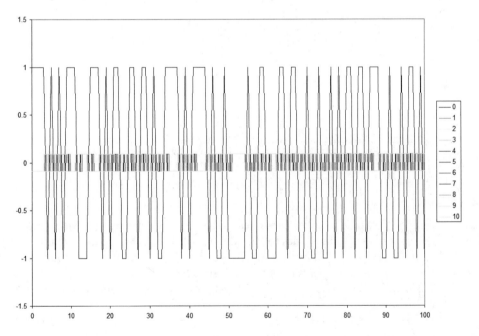

Figure 6.16 shows what happens when two of the chips are changed in the Barker code sequence, which means that it is no longer a Barker code and has a reduced autocorrelation property. The amplitude in many of the offset sequences are not very different from the 0 chip offset case. Some 11-chip sequences result in no amplitude difference between the various offsets. The strong autocorrelation property of the 11 chips in the Barker code

allows it to reject or lower the amplitude of any sequence that does not contain the correct Barker code sequence at zero offset. Noise or jammers will have a reduced effect on the data output of the receiver.

FIGURE 6.16   Received data stream after despread from non-Barker code, shown with various chip offsets

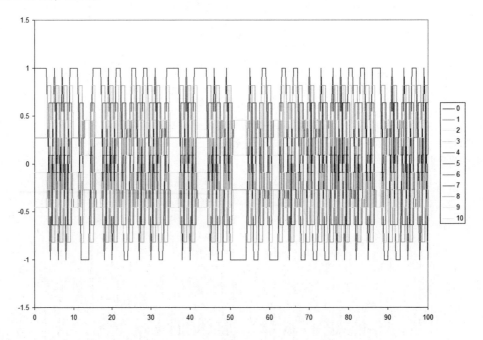

802.11b

802.11b introduced two new higher data rates to the original standard, 5.5 Mbps and 11 Mbps. These data rates also use codes to spread the spectrum, but the codes are not a single code as it is with the 1 and 2 Mbps data rate Barker code. The 5.5 Mbps uses four different 8-chip codes; the one used depends on the data itself. The 11 Mbps uses 64 different 8-chip codes, also depending on the data stream. The codes used for these data rates are part of the CCK methodology.

The basic idea is this. The 5.5 Mbps data rate works with 4 bits at a time. The 11 Mbps data rate works with 8 bits. The first 2 bits are used as data input to a DQPSK modulator. The rest of the bits—2 in the case of 5.5 Mbps and 6 in the case of 11 Mbps—are used to choose an 8-chip code. Two bits can choose one of four different codes; 6 bits can choose one of 64. The chosen 8-chip code then spreads the data stream formed from the first

2 bits. The 8-chip code keeps changing as data passes through the transmitter. The input symbol rate is no longer 1 Msps as it was with the earlier 802.11 standard; it is now 1.375 Msps. This is the symbol rate of the first 2 data bits that are modulating the DQPSK modulator. The CCK scheme sneaks more data into the spread spectrum by using the remaining 2 or 6 bits to choose the spreading code. The resulting data stream in both the 5.5 Mbps and 11 Mbps is an 11 Mchip/s (1.375 Msps $\times$ 8 chips = 11 Mchips/s) spread spectrum signal.

When the CCK signal is received, the first 2 bits are demodulated. The next step is to figure out which 8-chip code was used to transmit the signal. Just as with the Barker codes, the 8-chip CCK codes have good autocorrelation properties. So each possible 8-chip code is tried until a strong correlation is found. That strong correlation indicates that the proper chip code has been found. In the case of 5.5 Mbps communications, four different 8-chip codes are tried. In the case of 11 Mbps communications, 64 different 8-chip codes are tried. Once a chip code is found, the rest of the 4- or 8-bit group sent by the transmitter can be determined. The first 2 bits are found by the XOR operation on the received signal. The rest—2 bits in the case of 5.5 Mbps and 6 bits in the case of 11 Mbps—is determined by which 8-chip code worked. When calculating total throughput needs, you need to include the bits that were sneaked into the spreading code. Instead of 1.375 Msps sending only the first 2 bits, it sends 4 and 8 bits for a true throughput of 5.5 Mbps (4 $\times$ 1.375) and 11 Mbps (8 $\times$ 1.375). It's like having parallel data streams of 1.375 Mbps. Two of them are sent using DQPSK. The other 1.375 Mbps streams are sent by choosing the 8-chip spreading code.

DSSS systems are fairly robust to multipath and delay spread. If two signals are received at different times, a DSSS receiver will be able to isolate the two signals. The autocorrelation property of the Barker code and CCK codes makes it possible to detect one multipath signal and suppress others. One of the multipath signals would have a 0 chip offset whereas the others would be offset by some chip interval. The paths with a non-zero offset would be reduced in signal level as compared to the path detected at 0-chip offset. A special type of receivers is available that takes advantage of this isolation and will find the separate multipath data streams and add them coherently. This type of receiver is called a *rake receiver.*

The spectrum of the 802.11 DSSS signal is that of a filtered DBPSK or DQPSK modulated carrier. Figure 6.17 shows the FCC requirement for filtering of the signal. The first side lobe of the SinX/X spectrum would reach –13 dB from the peak of the center lobe if there were no filtering requirement. The FCC puts a limit on the levels of the first and subsequent side lobes of –30 dB and –50 dB from the peak of the main lobe. The purpose of this is to limit the amount of energy that is allowed to interfere on adjacent channels. Generally the side lobes are not required for communications, so limiting their levels improves the overall performance of the system. Figure 6.17 is called a *spectral mask* and is a common way to show spectrum regulatory requirements. Figure 6.18 shows the 802.11b spectrum measured at the output of an access point.

FIGURE 6.17   FCC spectral mask for 802.11b

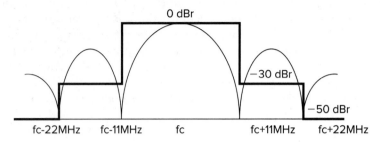

FIGURE 6.18   Measured spectrum output of an 802.11b access point

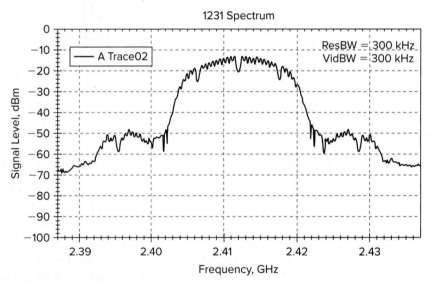

OFDM

In a multipath environment, delay spread can cause ISI. A single carrier modulated with a high symbol rate data stream is particularly susceptible to ISI. As the symbol rate increases, the delay spread needed to cause ISI becomes smaller and the likelihood that interference will occur rises. OFDM sends a single data stream on many closely spaced carriers. The symbol rate on any single carrier is relatively low. OFDM's low symbol rate reduces the effects of ISI while maintaining a high overall data rate.

Figure 6.19 shows the subcarrier spacing of an OFDM signal. The term subcarrier is used to differentiate it from the main carrier. The subcarriers are spaced quite close together. The spacing is designed so that the typical SinX/X nulls of one carrier fall into the center of the other. The symbol rates for each subcarrier are designed to equal the spacing of the subcarriers. It is by this means that the frequencies are considered orthogonal. It means that they are spaced in such a way as to not interfere with one another.

FIGURE 6.19   OFDM subcarriers

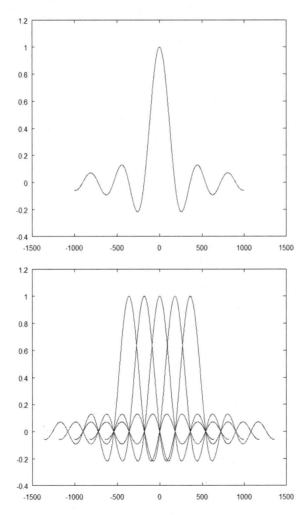

The 802.11 g and OFDM signals are made up of 52 subcarriers, 48 of which carry data. The other four are called *pilots* and help the receiver demodulate the OFDM signal. Each carrier is sending data symbols at a rate of 250 kilo samples per second (ksps). Some overhead is associated with each subcarrier related to framing, amplitude, and timing information. The largest overhead is due to something called the *guard interval (GI)*. GI is one feature of OFDM signals that helps prevent ISI in a high-delay spread environment. You will learn more about GI in Chapter 7, "RF Hardware and 802.11n," when we discuss 802.11n. The true symbol rate for the modulated subcarrier including overhead is 312.5 ksps, which is directly related to the subcarrier spacing. The 802.11 OFDM standard starts with 64 subcarriers. It divides 20 MHz into 64 parts, which produces the 312.5 kHz spacing (20 MHz / 64 = 312.5 kHz). Keeping the subcarrier spacing the same as the 312.5 ksps SinX/X frequency spectrum ensures the orthogonality of the modulated subcarriers. The peak of one subcarrier lines up with the null of the others.

Twelve of the 64 subcarriers are turned off, including the center subcarrier. It is always a good idea in radio design to suppress the center carrier of any modulated signal. The reason has to do with the real-world problems associated with the modulation process. The six lowest frequency subcarriers and five highest frequency subcarriers are also turned off. It is interesting to note that the 802.11 OFDM signal is slightly wider on the higher frequency side than the lower. These 11 subcarriers are turned off so that the OFDM signal can meet its spectral mask requirements. Those spectral mask requirements are shown in Figure 6.20. The spectrum of an 802.11g OFDM signal is shown in Figure 6.21.

FIGURE 6.20 FCC spectral mask for 802.11g and a OFDM signals

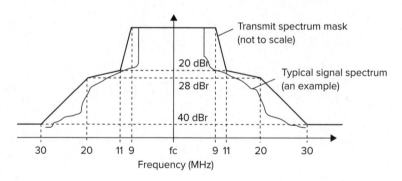

Federal Communications Commission

FIGURE 6.21   Spectrum of an 802.11g OFDM signal

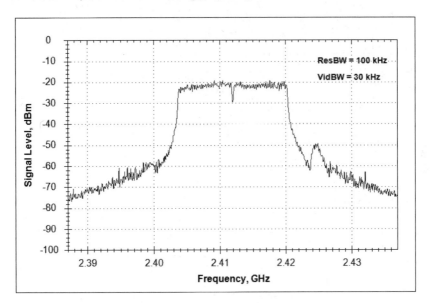

Coding

It should be clear by the discussion so far that a radio channel is not very friendly to communications. Coding adds bits to the transmitted data stream to add redundancy. The extra bits are used in the receiver to overcome the effects of noise, interference, and fading encountered in the channel. The main idea behind coding is to reduce the required signal-to-noise ratio (SNR) for a given bit error rate (BER). As code bits are added, the radio signal can tolerate more noise. 802.11g and 802.11a uses convolution coding, interleaving, and Viterbi decoding. Some of the data rates—9, 18, 36, 48, and 54 Mbps—use a coding technique called *puncturing* that limits the redundant bits and allows higher data rates.

Figure 6.22 shows a basic block diagram of the coding and decoding process. The data signal is first stuffed with extra bits with a convolution coder. A ½ convolution encoder will add 1 bit for every existing bit. The data stream then goes through an interleaver. The interleaving scrambles the bits around so that if there is a burst of bit errors, the reassembled bit stream does not contain sequential errors. Burst errors are common in a fading environment. The signal is then modulated and transmitted across a radio channel. At the receiver, the process is reversed. The received bit stream is demodulated, and then goes through a deinterleaver and then into a Viterbi decoder. The deinterleaver will reassemble the bits that were scrambled into the correct order. The decoder is quite complex and will make a decision on the greatest likelihood a received bit is a 1 or a 0.

FIGURE 6.22 A block diagram of the coding/decoding process

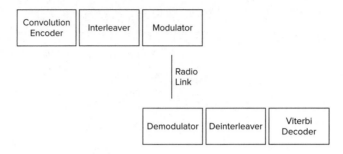

A similar block diagram showing the puncturing and depuncturing that occurs with the ⅔ and ¾ coding rates is shown in Figure 6.23. The puncturing process starts with a bit stream that has been ½ convolution encoded. The ⅔ coding results when, for every 4 bits after the encoder, 1 bit is punctured or stolen.

FIGURE 6.23 A block diagram of the coding/decoding process, including puncturing and depuncturing for code ⅔ and ¾

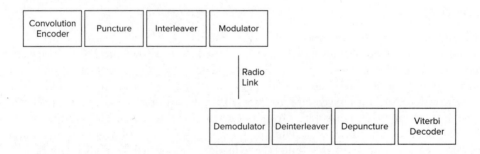

The coding changes from ²⁄₄ (same as ½) to ⅔ (2/(4 − 1)). This is shown in Figure 6.24. On the receive side, the receiver adds back the stolen bits but tells the Viterbi decoder that there is no confidence in the added bits. Then, ¾ coding results when, for every 6 bits after the encoder, 2 bits are punctured. The coding changes from ³⁄₆ (same as ½) to ¾ (3 / (6 − 2)). This is shown in Figure 6.25.

FIGURE 6.24 ⅔ code puncturing and depuncturing

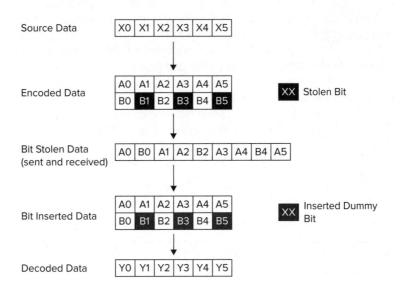

FIGURE 6.25 ¾ code puncturing and depuncturing

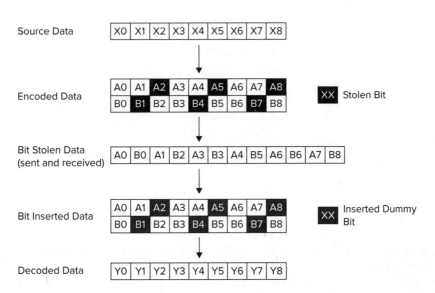

Coding increases the number of bits that are required to be sent for a given amount of true data sent. It requires a certain amount of overhead. Using a ½ code sends 2 bits for every 1 data bit. Using a ¾ code sends 4 bits for every 3 data bits. The trade-off in radio design is noise immunity versus data throughput. Later in this chapter, in the section "Communications Link," we will show how error rate and SNR are related. Receiving data at a given data error rate requires a higher SNR if no coding is used compared to whether coding is used.

The 24 Mbps and 36 Mbps 802.11 data rates both use 16 QAM as their modulation format. The only difference between the two is the coding that is used: 24 Mbps uses a ½ code, and 36 Mbps uses a ¾ code. The ratio of the two codes is 1.5/1. This is the same ratio of the data rates (36/24). It is also the same ratio of the SNR required to receive the data rates.

The 802.11g and 802.11a OFDM is available in eight different data rates. Table 6.4 shows the data rates, modulation, and coding rates used on the data subcarriers. Knowing the modulation type and coding rate, the data throughput can be easily calculated. The highest data rate has 48 tones × 250 ksps × 6 bits per symbol (64 QAM) × ¾ coding rate = 54 Mbps.

TABLE 6.4 Modulation and coding rates used for each of the 802.11 OFDM data rates

Data rate (Mbps)	Modulation	Coding rate
6	BPSK	½
9	BPSK	¾
12	QPSK	½
18	QPSK	¾
24	16-QAM	½
36	16-QAM	¾
48	64-QAM	⅔
54	64-QAM	¾

Noise

Thermal noise can dominate radio receiver performance. Engineers need to understand the impact that noise has on their radios in order to get the most out of their system. In the following section, we will discuss the sources of noise, such as background temperature and amplifiers. You will learn how noise can be measured with common radio instrumentation. We will also describe the specs you should look at when comparing the noise performance of radio equipment.

Temperature

When a piece of metal is heated, it will start to glow and change color. It starts off as a red color; as it gets hotter it glows yellow, then white. As the metal cools off, it will again radiate at red frequencies, then infrared (invisible light below red in the spectrum), then microwave frequencies. At room temperature (25 °C or 77 °F), the piece of metal, just like all objects, radiates at microwave frequencies. This is something physicists call *black body radiation*. Everything around us in the world gives off microwave thermal noise. No microwave radio, such as a Wi-Fi access point or client, can receive and detect a signal that lies below this level of noise.

At room temperature, the amount of radiation is –174 dBm in every Hz of bandwidth. In the 22 MHz bandwidth of a Wi-Fi channel, the amount of noise is that contained in 1 Hz, multiplied by a factor of 22 million. The 22 million factor can be expressed as 73.4 dB, which would bring the total noise in the Wi-Fi band to –100.6 dBm. This number, although it varies slightly with temperature, is a practical one to use over a broad range. Any Wi-Fi signal that is below this power level would be impossible to detect by a Wi-Fi receiver. Signals have to be above this value by some amount in order to be detected. The amount above the thermal noise before signals can be detected is a function of the quality of the Wi-Fi receiver and the data rate of the transmitted signal. The two critical performance measurements related to the noise performance of a Wi-Fi receiver are receive sensitivity and noise figure.

The noise floor value of –174 dBm/Hz comes from the formula $P = kTB$, where k is Boltzmann's constant $1.3806503 \times 10^{-23}$ m^2 kg s^{-2} K^{-1} (a very small number), T is the temperature in °K (add 273.15 to the temperature in °C), and B is the bandwidth in Hz. At a temperature of 0 °C or 32 °F, the noise power is –174.2 dBm/Hz. At 100 °F (38 °C), the noise power is –173.6 dBm/Hz. As you can see, for a normal temperature range, microwave noise power does not vary much. 290 °K (17 °C or 63 °F) is considered standard noise temperature and has a corresponding noise power of –174.0 dBm/Hz.

Amplifier Noise

Other than data throughput, a receiver will report two values to a user on the health of the radio link receive signal strength indicator (RSSI) and SNR. The former tells the user how much signal there is at the receiver input, and the other expresses the quality of that signal. The receiver uses the RSSI value to calculate SNR. The other component of SNR, noise, is also measured and is the topic of this section.

Characterizing noise is critical in receiver radio design. A receiver's function is to amplify a signal at a very tiny power level and detect information from it. At such low signal levels, the effect of thermal noise dominates. Much of radio receiver performance is centered on SNR. The part of the receiver design that involves SNR is the front end, the part that gathers the signal, filters it, transports it to the first amplifier, and amplifies it. After the antenna, the SNR of the signal can only get worse as it goes through the receiver. The measure of how much the SNR degrades is called *noise figure*.

Noise figure (NF) is defined as the ratio of the SNR of the input to the SNR of the output of a device, assuming that thermal noise is the noise level at the input. Noise figure is typically expressed in dB and would be the difference in SNR at the input and the SNR at the output expressed in dB. Something with a noise figure of 5 dB has a 5 dB worse SNR at its output than input. A simple way to calculate noise figure for a receiver is to add the loss between the antenna and its *low-noise amplifier (LNA)* with the noise figure of the amplifier. Although this is not strictly the full noise figure of the receiver, it will get you to within a few tenths of a decibel of the value. A receiver with 3 dB of loss due to cables and filtering before the LNA and an LNA with 2 dB noise figure will have a total noise figure of 5 dB.

Figure 6.26 shows a diagram of a receiver front end.

FIGURE 6.26 Receiver front end showing changes in SNR as the signal travels down the chain

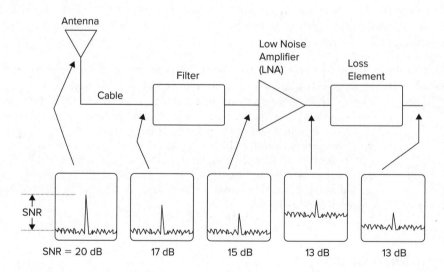

First a signal will enter into the receiver's antenna. In Figure 6.26, the SNR of the signal right after the antenna is shown to be 20 dB. After the antenna there are some lossy elements, a cable, and a filter. The filter is there to let only signals in the Wi-Fi band pass

through. Signals outside of the band will be rejected and not allowed to enter into the receiver's electronics. The loss of the cable and filter causes the signal level going into the LNA to be lower than what is coming out of the antenna—for example, 3 dB lower. The noise level at the antenna and at the input of the LNA, however, is the same. The cable and filter do not attenuate the noise like they do the signal. The noise level depends on the temperature of the object the antenna is pointed at and is a constant –174 dBm/Hz at all points along the path to the LNA. The SNR is therefore reduced as it travels from the antenna to the input of the LNA. In this case, the SNR is reduced from 20 dB to 17 dB just before the LNA. This reduction in SNR is the NF of the cable and filter. Noise figure is the ratio of SNR at the input to the SNR at the output of the cable and filter. The NF of any loss element before an amplifier is equal to the loss of the element. In this case, the NF is 3 dB.

The LNA also has an NF value. The SNR at the output of an LNA is always less than that at the input. This is because an LNA will always add noise to its output. All amplifiers do this. What is special about an LNA is that it is designed to add very little noise. A well-designed Wi-Fi LNA can have an NF of around 2 dB, meaning that the SNR at its input is 2 dB higher than at the output when the input noise level is thermal noise.

In Figure 6.26, the input noise level to the LNA was thermal noise. Therefore, the NF of the cable/filter and the LNA can be added (when expressed in decibels) to produce the total noise figure of the cable, filter, and LNA. The example in Figure 6.26 has a total NF of 7 dB (cable loss + filter loss + LNA NF = 3 dB + 2 dB + 2 dB = 7 dB). What happens to the calculated NF after the LNA? An amplifier NF is a measure of the amount of noise that the device adds to thermal noise at its output. An amplifier stage after the LNA has an input noise level that is well above thermal noise. Therefore, the SNR at the output is almost the same as the SNR at its input. In other words, adding noise after the LNA has virtually no effect on noise figure. The same could be said for loss after the LNA. Assuming the gain of the LNA is high enough, the SNR at the input of a lossy cable is the same as the SNR at the output. If the loss is several decibels less than the gain of the amplifier, the noise at the output and input of the cable are above thermal noise and the SNR is the same. This equal reduction in signal and noise is shown for a lossy element in Figure 6.26. In this example, the SNR stays at 13 dB before and after the element and therefore has no effect on the overall NF of the receiver. The total NF or total difference in SNR from the point after the antenna (20 dB SNR) and the point after the last loss element (13 dB SNR) is 7 dB.

This discussion about NF brings up some important ideas for people who deploy wireless systems to consider. If there is a long, lossy cable between the antenna and a Wi-Fi access point, there will be a direct impact on the performance of the receiver (it also affects the transmitter, but that is another discussion). Let's say the cable was quite thin (thin cables are lossy) and had an attenuation characteristic at 2400 MHz of 80 dB per 100 feet. If there is 20 feet of cable between the antenna and the Wi-Fi receiver, the total loss is 16 dB. That cable contributes 16 dB to the NF of the system. The SNR is reduced by 16 dB before it even enters the radio. Assume that the access point has an NF of 5 dB; the total NF and therefore SNR degradation of the system is 21 dB. Only clients that are sitting right under the antenna would be heard on the uplink of such a system. A better design approach would be to either bring the access point closer to the antenna with a shorter cable, or put an LNA close to the antenna. The cable loss after the LNA would have no impact on noise performance, assuming the gain of the amplifier was well above the 16 dB loss of the cable.

For 802.11, a bidirectional amplifier would have to be used instead of an LNA by itself because both the transmitted and received signal travel on the same cable. Bidirectional amplifier contains both a receive LNA and a transmit amplifier. A fast RF switch routes the signal to the appropriate amplifier path.

Measuring Noise

The spectrum of thermal noise is spread out over a broad range of frequencies. It is sometimes called white noise as an analog to visible light where the color white is a broad mixture of colors. When measuring noise, you have to consider carefully the instrument being used and what is being measured. On a spectrum analyzer, when the input is terminated with a load (50 ohms in most cases), you will see what is called the *noise floor*. This is the line across the bottom of the screen that is bouncing around. Figure 6.27 shows a single trace of a noise floor measured on an older spectrum analyzer, HP 8562A (HP microwave instruments are now made by Agilent Technologies).

FIGURE 6.27   Noise floor measured on an HP8562A

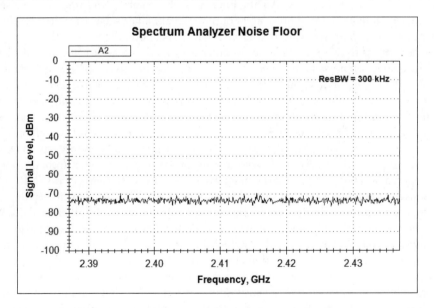

The noise is measuring –74 dBm. What does this mean? To understand this value, you need to know what the spectrum analyzer is doing. The analyzer measures power a little at a time. It has a filter that sweeps across the frequency span of 50 MHz, from 2.387 GHz to 2.437 GHz. As the filter sweeps across, it measures power over its bandwidth that is a fraction of the 50 MHz total span. The bandwidth of this filter is shown in the upper right corner of the plot. This bandwidth is called *resolution bandwidth* and is 300 kHz for this measurement. The –74 dBm signal that is measured is the amount of power that passes through the narrowband 300 kHz filter as it sweeps across the span of the analyzer. The noise floor is bouncing around because the nature of noise is such that the value changes slightly on each sweep of the filter. Knowing the bandwidth of the power measurement allows you to compare what you are measuring with the thermal noise coming from the termination on the analyzer. In a 300 kHz bandwidth, the thermal noise power coming from the 50 ohm termination would be –119.2 dBm in 300 kHz ($10 \times \log(300000) = 54.8$ dB-Hz; –174 dBm/Hz + 54.8 dB-Hz = –119 dBm in 300 kHz). The noise shown in Figure 6.27 is –74 dBm in 300 kHz. The difference is 45.7 dB. The calibration manual for the unit indicates that the instrument has a 34 dB NF at 2.4 GHz (modern instruments have a much better NF, especially if they come with a built-in LNA). That would result in a noise floor at –85 dBm, which is 11 dB below the value that was measured.

Where is the extra 11 dB coming from? One crucial piece of information was left out in the previous description. The instrument has an internal attenuator that was set to 10 dB. Because the attenuator is in front of the instrument's amplifier, it does not change the power of the noise; it only changes signals by 10 dB. The instrument adds 10 dB to the power level it is measuring so that signals appear on the screen at the correct value. It is designed to display signal levels that would have been reduced by 10 dB since the input attenuator was set to that value. To compensate for that, the instrument adds 10 dB to the measured value and displays that. This works fine for signal levels well above the noise floor. It is a different story for thermal noise. As you learned earlier, the spectrum analyzer's input noise level (at the thermal noise floor) and that coming out of the instrument's attenuator is the same value. So the spectrum analyzer reports on its screen thermal noise at a higher level than what it measures by the value of its input attenuator. The measurement of –74 dBm in 300 kHz is really –84 dBm in 300 kHz given the 10 dB attenuator offset. This would indicate that the instrument has an NF of 35 dB.

By recording the noise floor of the spectrum analyzer, we were able to determine the instrument's NF to within 1 dB. All that was required was a noise floor measurement and knowledge of the instrument's resolution bandwidth and input attenuator setting. This same methodology can be used to measure the noise figure of an amplifier. To make the measurement, you would have to first measure the gain of the amplifier accurately. This is not difficult with a spectrum analyzer and a generator. For you to make an NF measurement, the gain of the amplifier would need to be a bit higher than the NF of the spectrum analyzer. You would terminate the amplifier input with a 50-ohm load and measure the noise floor of the amplifier's output. Knowing the gain of the amplifier and that thermal noise is at –174 dBm/Hz, you can calculate the thermal dBm/Hz level at the analyzer's input (input thermal dBm/Hz = –174 dBm/Hz + amplifier gain). It is then a simple matter to determine the expected noise floor level if the amplifier had a 0 dB noise figure (input thermal dBm/Hz + ResBW dB-Hz). The difference between the measured value and the value calculated for the 0 dB noise figure is the noise figure for the amplifier.

Older spectrum analyzers used an analog resolution bandwidth filter that would measure noise bandwidth slightly inaccurately. The resolution bandwidth filter would measure about 0.5 dB higher power than would be indicated by the bandwidth of the filter. To make very accurate power measurement using these older instruments (within a tenth of a dB), you would need to calibrate each setting of resolution bandwidth to determine its noise bandwidth. This inaccuracy went away with the advent of digital filtering to measure spectral power. These days, spectrum analyzers can measure power very accurately and painlessly.

Interference comes from man-made radiating sources and is generally at higher levels than thermal noise. For licensed band operation, thermal noise is a main factor in receiver performance. There are tight controls on who radiates in these bands and therefore interference is well defined. Unlicensed bands have many systems that coexist without coordination. Interference is a constant source of degradation in the radio link. Bluetooth radios, cordless phones, and microwave ovens all contribute to the interference found in WLAN systems. It can be true that interference is so high that thermal noise is relatively unimportant. Understanding and dealing with these sources of interference is vital if communications are to be reliable.

Units of Measure

One of the most common mistakes made by engineers who have some experience with wireless technology is giving the wrong units of measure when quoting power values. Making this mistake is a quick way to be labeled as an RF newbie. The first question I ask when interviewing job candidates who represent themselves as wireless professionals is, "What is the difference between dB and dBm?" The wrong answer will lead to a very short interview. In the following sections, dB, ratio, dBm, and gain and loss are discussed in a way that assumes the reader has some experience with the concepts. A CWDP engineer would be expected to be able to read through it without having to think too much about it. Wireless experts should be able to work with decibels as though it comes to them naturally.

Decibels

Before we discuss the answer to the question about the difference between dB and dBm, we have to define our terms. As with many terms used in communications today, the decibel is a unit of measure devised by Bell Telephone Laboratories. The unit has a long history related to the attenuation of an audio frequency signal along a mile of telephone cable. What was once convenient for telephone engineers in the 1920s has turned out to be very useful for modern radio engineers. The *decibel (dB)* is a way to express the ratio of two power levels. A power ratio expressed in decibels is defined as 10 times the 10-based logarithm of the ratio. Sometimes dB is expressed as *dB relative (dBr)*.

In the following equation, the power levels need to be expressed in the same units, such as milliwatts or watts:

$$G_{dB} = 10 \times \text{Log}_{10}(P2/P1)$$

The G term can typically describe the gain of an amplifier, loss in a cable, the NF of an amplifier, or the SNR. If G is positive, the ratio is greater than 1. If G equals 0, the ratio is 1. If G is negative, the ratio is less than 1. Two decibel values an RF engineer should always know are 3 dB and 10 dB. 3 dB is a ratio of 2 (it is actually 3.01 but is close enough to 3 for any radio design work) and –3 dB is a ratio of ½. 10 dB is a ratio of 10 and –10 dB is a ratio of 1/10. You can impress your friends and neighbors if you know that 5 dB is a ratio of 3 and –5 dB is a ratio of ⅓ (it's actually 4.8 dB but 5 dB is usually close enough).

Although it looks like using such a formula complicates an RF engineer's life, it actually makes it simpler. Knowing 3 dB and 10 dB ratios allows engineers to figure out power ratios in their head. If a signal is four times higher at the output of an amplifier than the input, you can calculate the logarithm and come up with a 6 dB gain value. Alternatively, an engineer can exploit a property of logarithms. If you multiply two numbers and then take the logarithm, it is the same as adding the logarithms of the two numbers. Dividing one number by another is equivalent to subtracting one logarithm by another. If the engineer knows the decibel values, a multiplication calculation becomes an addition one and a division calculation becomes a subtraction one. We know that 3 dB is the same as a ratio of 2. A ratio of 4 is 2 × 2. In decibels, this is expressed as 3 dB + 3 dB, or 6 dB. Likewise, if the amplifier has a gain ratio of 20 (10 × 2), the gain value in dB is 10 + 3 = 13 dB. If you want to calculate a power ratio given the dB value, use the following equation:

$$P2/P1 = 10^{(G_{dB}/10)}$$

A positive gain of something being measured indicates that the output is larger than the input. If the gain is negative, this would mean that the output is smaller than the input. This is equivalent to saying that there is loss. An amplifier with 30 dB of gain has 1,000 times as much power at its output than at its input (a ratio of 1000/1). A cable with 20 dB of loss has 100 times smaller an amount of power at its output than at its input (a ratio of 1/100). You could also say that the cable has –20 dB of gain. If the amplifier feeds the cable, the two devices in series would give a total of 10 dB of gain (1000/100) = 10 or 30 – 20 = 10 dB). The output of the amplifier is 1,000 times greater than the input. The cable then divides the signal level by 100 to bring the total ratio of output to input to a value of 10, or 10 dB.

Large numbers like 200,000 that have a single digit followed by zeros can be calculated in dB without a calculator. The trick is to count the number of zeros, multiply by 10 and add the single digit value in dB. 200,000 becomes 50 dB + 3 dB = 53 dB, and 8,000,000 becomes 60 dB + 9 dB = 69 dB. When expressing bandwidth like 200 kHz and 8 MHz in dB, this technique is useful.

Typically a wireless engineer spends a good amount of time figuring out gains and losses in a cascading fashion. It could be equipment such as a cable, which is connected to an amplifier, the output of which is connected to another cable. It could be a link budget that includes antenna gain, path losses, and SNRs. The decibel formula turns many multiplication and division steps into addition and subtraction. The total gain in decibels is calculated by adding all the gains and subtracting the losses.

A good illustration of calculating loss for a series of cascading elements is a simple long cable. The cable can be thought of as a cascading series of cables. If you know that the loss in a cable is 3 dB per meter, the loss in an 8 meter cable will be 24 dB ($3 \times 8 = 24$ dB). Though it might seem obvious to perform this calculation this way, let's examine closely what is going on so that it is very clear. Each meter of cable has 3 dB of loss and so has half the power level at its output than it had at its input. The 8-meter cable is equivalent to eight 1-meter cables cascaded in series. Each 1-meter cable is halving the power, so the gain can be calculated as $(((((((1/2)/2)/2)/2)/2)/2)/2)$, or 1/256. You could have just as easily calculated the loss as $2 \times 2 \times 2 \times 2 \times 2 \times 2 \times 2 \times 2 = 256$. Calculating the gain or loss in dB results in –24 dB of gain or 24 dB of loss ($10 \times \log(1/256) = -24$ dB or $10 \times \log(256) = 24$ dB). You could also calculate the loss as $3 + 3 + 3 + 3 + 3 + 3 + 3 + 3 = 3 \times 8 = 24$ dB. The magic of logarithms has turned an exponent problem, $2^8 = 256$, into a multiplication problem, $3 \times 8 = 24$ dB.

dBm

Now we get to that question asked at the beginning of this section: "What is the difference between dB and dBm?" The lowercase m after the dB is an important clue about the meaning of *dBm*. dBm is a ratio like dB, but it is the ratio of a power level relative to one milliwatt (1 mW) or one thousandth of a watt (0.001 W). Since you know what power a milliwatt represents in absolute terms, you can express RF power in dBm. This is very different from a ratio expressed in dB. For example, an amplifier's gain and maximum power level are expressed differently as a decibel value. Amplifier gain is expressed in dB. The maximum output power of the amplifier is expressed in dBm. An amplifier gain can be expressed as 10 dB. It is not 10 dBm. This is because amplifier gain is the ratio of its output power to its input. Ten dBm is 10 mW, which is a measure of power. Its maximum output power can be expressed as 20 dBm, not 20 dB. Twenty dBm is 100 mW. Twenty dB is the ratio of 100. Expressing that a power level is 100 times larger at its output than its input does not indicate a power level at the output of the amplifier. Only when it is said that the power is 100 times larger than 1 mW is it known that the power is 100 mW. You can now answer the question properly. dB is a way to express a power ratio. dBm is a way to express an absolute power.

Calculating the Difference of Two Power Levels Expressed in dBm

When calculating the difference of two power levels expressed in dBm, you should be careful to express the result in decibels. A common mistake made by new wireless engineers is to express this result in dBm. If one radio is transmitting at 10 dBm and another is transmitting at 5 dBm, you would say that the first is transmitting at a level that is 5 dB higher than the second, not 5 dBm higher.

15 dBm − 10 dBm = 5 dB

A difference in values expressed in dBm is actually the ratio of two power quantities. Expressed as amplitude, the previous equation looks like this:

31.6 mW / 10 mW = 3.16

In this same way, a measure of accuracy and variability is expressed in dB. You would say that the 18 dBm output power of a transmitter is accurate to within 2 dB, not dBm. Likewise, you would say that that you are measuring a 10 dB variation in received power if it varied between −50 dBm and −60 dBm.

Other dB Measures

There are a number of dB measures that are relative to some known value. We will discuss these in the following sections. The letter or letters after dB indicate the type of quantity being measured.

dBW

A power level expressed in milliwatts will be 1,000 times larger than that expressed in watts. That means that a signal level expressed in milliwatts is 30 dB higher than that expressed in watts (10 + 10 + 10 in dB is the same as 10 × 10 × 10 = 1000). Similar to dBm, *dBW* expresses a power level in watts. For example, a large power level of 43 dBm is equal to 13 dBW (43 −30 = 13 dBW). This is a power level of 20 W (10 × 2 W) or 20,000 mW (10^4 × 2 mW). These high power levels are common for cellular base station amplifiers that are used to radiate signals over large areas in a licensed radio band.

Wi-Fi access points do not radiate at power levels higher than a watt. Wi-Fi client devices radiate at even lower powers. Point-to-point systems don't radiate at levels higher than a few watts. The limit is imposed by regulatory agencies worldwide because the bands of operation for Wi-Fi are unlicensed. These agencies impose the limits to curb interference between radios. For that reason, dBm is more typically used as a measure of RF power in these systems than dBW. dBW is used to characterize satellite and cellular system power levels because of the higher levels. They operate in licensed bands and are allowed to radiate at levels up to 100 watts.

dBc

dBc is a decibel measurement of a signal relative to an unmodulated radio carrier. It is typically used to characterize interference, noise, distortion or allowed spurious emissions. Because it is often difficult or impossible to turn off the modulation on a carrier, using the measure of modulated carrier power as an approximation of unmodulated carrier power is sufficient. Usually they are very close to each other. dBc measurements are primarily used by equipment manufacturers to meet performance criteria set by government regulations. The concern usually is related to the amount of power radiating into licensed bands.

dB-Hz

dB-Hz is used as a measure of bandwidth. A 22 MHz bandwidth can be express as being 73.4 dB-Hz (10 log (22000000Hz/1Hz) = 73.4 dB-Hz). When you are calculating noise power, it is sometimes useful to express bandwidth in this way. Temperature noise power is –174 dBm/Hz. In a 22 MHz bandwidth, the total noise power is –100.6 dBm (–174 dBm/Hz + 73.4 dB-Hz = –100.6 dBm). dB-Hz is often used when making link budget calculations.

dBi and dBd

The other commonly used decibel expressions used in wireless are *dBi* and *dBd*. They are used to characterize antenna gain performance. When connected to a transmitter, antennas will radiate RF energy out in many directions. Some antennas will radiate in almost all directions, whereas others will radiate in a more focused way, like a searchlight. There is an ideal antenna that is called an isotropic antenna, which will radiate power in all directions equally. The antenna pattern for such an antenna is a perfect sphere. No such antenna can exist in practice but it can be approximated. A half-wave dipole antenna does a pretty good job of approximating an isotropic antenna. It's a toroidal shaped (doughnut-shaped) antenna pattern that typically provides gain of 2.15 dB over what an isotropic antenna would provide. This means that in the direction where the highest amount of power per square area is being radiated from a dipole is 2.15 dB higher than the power per square area radiated from an isotropic antenna. The gain of the antenna is 2.15 dBi, where the "i" stands for isotropic. The measure of dBi is a gain ratio and not an absolute power since no power is associated with the isotropic antenna pattern. By definition, an isotropic antenna would have 0 dBi of gain.

Since a dipole antenna is so common, it is sometimes used as a reference for an antenna gain measure. An antenna with 5 dBi of gain has a gain that is 2.85 dB higher than that of a dipole (5 dB = 2.15 dB + 2.85 dB). This 5 dBi gain value can be expressed as 2.85 dBd—that is, a gain that is 2.85 higher that of a dipole.

Commonly Used Ratios

In the previous section we discussed dB values that referenced some absolute quantity such as watts or dipole gain. In this section we will discuss ratios that are commonly used in wireless engineering.

SNR   *Signal-to-noise ratio (SNR)* is a common ratio that is measured in radio communications. The noise power is generally considered to be thermal noise. SNR is the ratio between signal and noise power. The tricky part comes in defining the bandwidth over which the signal and noise power is measured. For Wi-Fi signals, the bandwidth is 22 MHz. Any signal outside of this bandwidth is too low to contribute to the overall signal power. Noise outside of this bandwidth will be filtered by the receiver and will not add to the noise of the demodulated carrier. An SNR of 10 dB is the limit for the 1 Mbps 802.11b/g data rate. Below that SNR level the bit error rate rapidly degrades. The 54 Mbps data rate requires an SNR of over 22 dB in order to achieve a reasonable bit error rate. The actual SNR required at these data rates will vary from vendor to vendor. The receive sensitivity specification for a specific vendor can be found in the equipment datasheet.

SIR   *Signal-to-interference ratio (SIR)* is commonly used to quantify the level of interference caused by nearby transmitters. A low SIR indicates a problem between adjacent APs that is degrading receiver performance.

PAR   *Peak-to-average ratio (PAR)* is important for transmitter performance. A signal with a high PAR like 54 Mbps Wi-Fi needs a more linear amplifier than a signal with a low PAR like 1 Mbps WiFi.

Communications Link

Radio performance is defined by two extremes: high power and very low power. On the high RF power side, there is a desire to create a large amount of RF power with the least amount of electrical power from an AC or DC power source. The radio transmitter is often the part of the radio that draws the most energy from the power source, which is of great concern to manufacturers of client devices that run on battery power. The transmitter is also often the most expensive part of the radio: the power amplifiers are the most expensive devices in the unit. In addition, the radio transmitter is potentially the greatest source of interference to itself and to other radios in the vicinity.

On the low RF power side, the radio receiver has to detect very low power signals in a noisy and high interference environment. The communication system does this by adding coding bits and changing modulation to suit the quality of the radio channel. The transmitter, receiver, antennas, and radio channel all play together to allow communications to happen. In this section we examine how each part influences link quality. It all comes together in the last section when we discuss link budgets. There the performance of each element is listed and the robustness of the link is determined.

Transmitter Performance

Transmitter performance is primarily focused on delivering signals at high power efficiently with minimal distortion. In this section we will explore amplifier distortion called saturation and its impact on the transmitted spectrum.

Amplifier Saturation

Amplifiers have a limited range over which they can amplify signal. Go beyond that limit, and the amplifier will reach saturation. *Amplifier saturation* is reached when the amplifier does not increase in output power when the input increases. Figure 6.28 shows a typical Pin vs. Pout characteristic of a microwave amplifier.

FIGURE 6.28 Pin vs. Pout curve for a 30 dB gain amplifier with a 30.8 dBm 1 dB compression point

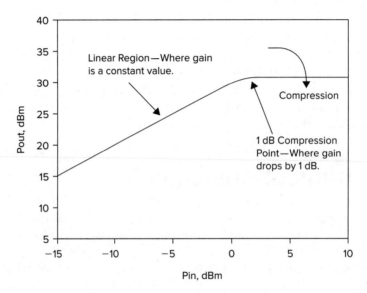

The linear region shows how for a given input power increase, there is an equal output power increase. In Figure 6.28, the amplifier has a gain of 30 dB. For an input of –10 dBm, the output is 20 dBm. Increase the input by another 5 dB and the output changes to 25 dBm. As the input power approaches 0 dBm, the amplifier starts to compress. The gain decreases rapidly and the output power stays flat with changes in input power. The 1 dB compression point of the amplifier is defined as its output power when the amplifier's gain reduces by 1 dB. It is usually expressed in datasheets as P_{1dB}. In the example in Figure 6.28, the 1 dB compression point is at 30.8 dBm. At that point, the input power is 1.8 dB, the output power is 30.8 dBm, and the gain of the amplifier is 29 dB. The amplifier is considered fully saturated when the output power ceases to increase with increasing input power. The saturated output power of this amplifier is 30.9 dBm, which is very close to the 1 dB compression point output. Compression is the main source of distortion in a microwave amplifier and has a direct effect on the quality of a radio's transmitter output.

Amplifier Backoff and Peak to Average

The importance of an amplifier's saturation becomes apparent when a modulated signal is passed through it. If a single unmodulated tone at the amplifier's center frequency was sent into the amplifier at +10 dBm, the output of the amplifier would be a tone at the same frequency and 30.9 dBm. The distortion of the amplifier would have no effect on it. A single tone has constant amplitude. If a modulated signal is sent into the amplifier with amplitude that varies, distortion on the output would be seen, but only if the amplitude peaks near the point of saturation.

With a −6.2 dBm average power input signal, the amplifier has an output of 23.8 dBm, which is 7 dB lower than the 1 dB compression point of the amplifier. The amplifier is said to be backed off by 7 dB. If the signal varies so that it peaks up at a level 9 dB higher than its average, the peak input will reach beyond the saturation point of the amplifier. Figure 6.29 shows what happens in this circumstance. The PAR of the signal is 9 dB.

FIGURE 6.29   Signal with 9 dB PAR shown as input into Pin vs. Pout for a saturated amplifier at 7 dB backoff

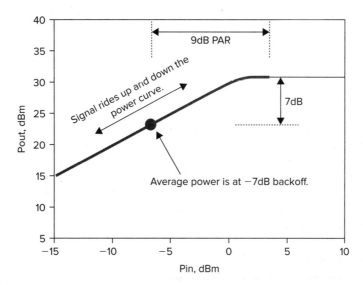

The signal rides up and down the Pin vs. Pout curve as the input signal varies. Clearly the input and output signal will differ significantly. The average power level at the output of the amplifier is 23.8 dBm. The peak however is limited to a PAR of 7 dB. The top 2 dB of the signal was clipped off the output. In order to avoid this distortion on the output of the signal, the input level would have to be reduced so that the amplifier is operating below 9 dB backoff, as shown in Figure 6.30.

FIGURE 6.30   Signal with 9 dB PAR shown as input into Pin vs. Pout for a saturated amplifier at 9 dB backoff

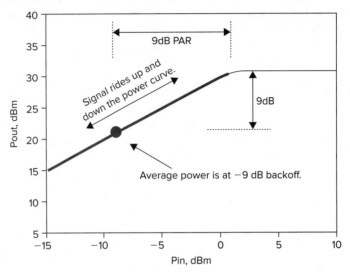

It turns out the OFDM signals can have quite large peaks. Theoretically, if all the signals in each of the tones line up perfectly, the peak of a Wi-Fi OFDM signal can be 17 dB higher than the average power of the signal. As it turns out, that doesn't happen very often and the electronics can be designed in such a way to avoid this. The PAR is a critical measure of a signal that passes through an amplifier. The PAR of Wi-Fi OFDM is around 9 dB. Equipment manufacturers need a bit more precision in the definition of PAR, such as how often the signal exceeds the peak level, but for purposes of this book, 9 dB is a good rule of thumb to use. DSSS has a PAR value of around 4 dB. Generally you can operate an amplifier closer to saturation—that is, at a higher power level—with a DSSS signal than an OFDM signal. In the next section we will explore what happens if a signal goes too close to saturation.

Spectral Regrowth

The spectrum shape of an OFDM signal with a PAR of 9 dB will pass unchanged through a saturated amplifier if it is backed off farther than 10 dB. As the input increases, however, the output spectrum will change. Figure 6.31 shows how the spectrum of an 802.11 OFDM signal changes as the input signal's average power increases from 20 dB to 3 dB backoff. The signal level increases, as you would expect. The interesting thing to note is how the spectrum outside the OFDM signal increases in amplitude faster than the signal itself. This is called *spectral regrowth*. It is caused by the distortion of the amplifier as the input signal peaks drive the amplifier into saturation.

FIGURE 6.31 Output spectrum of an OFDM signal as the average input power increases from 20 to 3 dB backoff

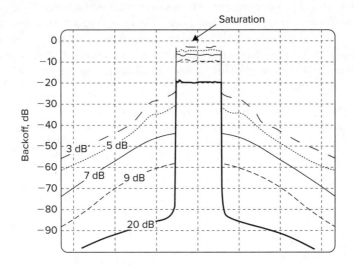

Real World Scenario

Why Not Use a Linear Amplifier?

Let's say Company B, a mobile client radio manufacturer, wants to produce a very clean output signal with no spectral regrowth. They decide to do this by using a higher-power amplifier in their designs, capable of linear operation in the whole range of input power levels. Though they have a perfect spectrum at their amplifier's output, Company B has very poor sales.

There are two good reasons for why they should have manufactured a lower-power amplifier that had a lower saturation point instead. Their amplifier is too expensive and draws too much power.

Amplifiers get more expensive as they go up in power. In an AP, manufacturers have a bit more money to spend on a higher-power amplifier than mobile device manufacturers. The AP, therefore, can transmit at higher powers and has a higher-quality spectrum. Company B, however, manufactures mobile devices, which are very price competitive. Their higher-power amplifier puts them at a price disadvantage. Amplifiers operate more efficiently as the average power approaches saturation. DC power consumption is less of a concern in APs, but can be an issue for Power over Ethernet (PoE) operation where power may be limited.

Mobile clients on the other hand have great incentive to use the lowest power amplifier possible. Both cost and power consumption, because of limited battery life, are high on a manufacturers list of concerns for client devices. Clients will typically transmit at a lower power level than APs and will run close to the spectral limits allowed by the standard. Frequency also plays a role with power amplifier efficiency and cost. Higher-frequency devices cost more and are less efficient, so all of these issues have a greater importance for 802.11a than 802.11b/g.

Company B would have had much better sales had they known that a perfect spectrum meant that their product was too costly and drained their customers' laptop batteries. The company would have been better off making their output spectrum just barely meet the spectral mask requirements.

As you can see in Figure 6.31, driving an amplifier with a signal that has a peak power beyond the 1 dB compression point will cause energy to spill out into adjacent channels. If two radios are physically close to each other, even if they are at different operating frequencies, they can interfere with each other. One radio might be trying to listen to a faint signal close to the noise floor threshold. If its neighbor is transmitting on a nearby channel at a high power level, its adjacent channel power might be high enough to swamp out the faint signal and cut off communications. It is often a good idea to limit the transmit power of an AP to a value below its maximum for this reason. This will greatly reduce the power that the radio radiates outside its operating channel.

Receiver Performance

A receiver designer spends a lot of time considering the effect of noise on radio performance. It is the function of a digital receiver to demodulate a carrier and turn the extracted symbols into a data stream. Noise degrades the constellation of the modulated carrier, which can make the received data stream prone to error. For people who study the effect of noise on receivers, the problem is largely one of geometry. As the modulation order is increased, constellation points are crowded closer together and the signal becomes more susceptible to noise. Knowing how close together the points are for a given modulation scheme, you can determine the amount of noise that results in a given bit error rate.

Receiver Sensitivity

Receiver sensitivity measures the ability of a receiver to detect a signal. The signal to noise of the received signal has a strong effect on this ability. A receiver has difficulty receiving data that is very noisy. The complexity of the modulation also has an effect on receiver sensitivity. High order modulated signals require a higher SNR in order to be properly detected. Figure 6.32 shows QPSK, 16-QAM, and 64-QAM signals at the same average power level with an SNR level of 10, 15, and 20 dB. The difference between these constellation figures and the ones shown earlier is that we have added noise to the carrier. It is clear from Figure 6.32 that it is much easier to detect QPSK than 64-QAM symbols in the presence of noise. A receiver detecting QPSK will have many fewer errors than 64-QAM. Another way of expressing this is to say that 64-QAM requires a higher SNR to achieve the same bit error rate as QPSK.

FIGURE 6.32   QPSK, 16-QAM, and 64-QAM signals at the same average power level with an SNR level of 10, 15, and 20 dB

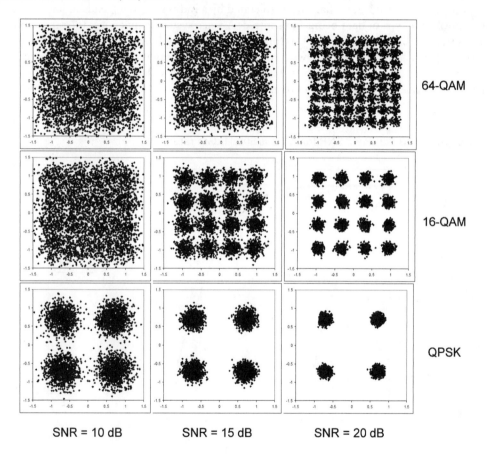

SNR = 10 dB   SNR = 15 dB   SNR = 20 dB

Gray Code

By a large margin, errors in detection happen between symbols that are adjacent to one another. A bit of noise can move the constellation point from close to its intended spot to an adjacent symbol and cause an error in detection. It is important, therefore, that radio designers make adjacent symbols vary only by 1 bit. In Figure 6.7 earlier in the chapter, the

4 bits for each symbol in a 16-QAM signal are shown. Each adjacent symbol in the diagram varies by 1 bit. This pattern of symbol bits is called Gray coding, named after a physicist at Bell Labs named Frank Gray. If this pattern were not followed, a detection error where one symbol is mistaken for an adjacent one would result in more than one bit error.

In Wi-Fi, the OFDM data rates depend on modulation order (BPSK, QPSK, 16-QAM, and 64-QAM) and coding (½, ⅔, and ¾). Because Wi-Fi uses Gray codes for its modulation, it is relatively straightforward to calculate error rates knowing the modulation, coding, and number of data tones in an OFDM signal. Figure 6.33 shows the results of such a calculation. The graph is called a waterfall plot and is well known by communications engineers. The bit error rate that can be tolerated by a radio system depends in large measure on the type of data being transmitted. A voice system is much less tolerant of bit errors than a TCP data transfer. Therefore, a voice system will need a higher SNR than normal data. The vertical axis shows error rate in scientific notation. A bit error rate of 1×10^{-3} means that 1 bit out of 1,000 is incorrect. In this plot, the effect of coding rate has been considered, so there is no further gain from that.

FIGURE 6.33   BER vs. SNR for various 802.11 data rates

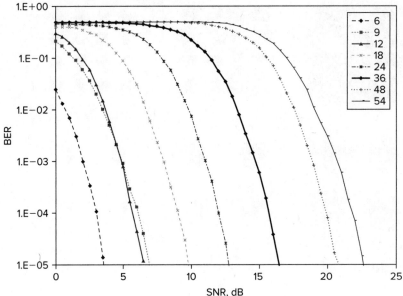

DSSS Processing Gain

A DSSS system has a noise immunity quality called *processing gain*. Normally an increase in bandwidth would require a higher signal power in order to maintain a constant SNR.

The larger bandwidth would let in more thermal noise, and a higher signal power would be needed to maintain a constant ratio. This is not true of a signal that has been spread. A spread spectrum system is designed in such a way that if the spreading code increases the bandwidth by a factor of X, the SNR required to receive at a given error rate is reduced by the same factor. Because of this, there is no need to increase signal power because the system has let in more noise with the increased bandwidth. The same signal power can be used to communicate in both the nonspreading and spreading scenarios. As mentioned earlier. the processing gain for the 1 and 2 Mbps 802.11 data rates is 10.4 dB (10 × log(11) = 10.4 dB).

Antenna Gain

The main property of antennas that relates to the communications link is gain. In the next chapter we will explore antennas in much more detail, but the focus here is gain. On the transmitter side, the antenna directs power toward the receiver. The gain of the antenna and its pointing direction will dictate how much of the power that comes out of the power amplifier is directed toward the receiver. On the receiver side, the antenna collects the power coming from the transmitter. The antenna gain and pointing direction will dictate the signal power that ends up at the receiver. The temperature of the objects that the antenna is pointing at determines the thermal noise floor at the antenna connector. Since for WLAN communications this is a constant –174 dBm/Hz, antenna gain has the same influence on SNR as it does on signal level. The signal level and SNR increase equally with higher gain.

A WLAN radio communication channel is made up of two links between the AP and client. There is the uplink (UL) from the client to the AP and the downlink (DL) from the AP to the client. When you are trying to figure out which is which, it helps to think of the AP mounted high in the ceiling. The downlink goes down from the AP; the uplink comes up from the client. In the case of 802.11 these are half-duplex links. It turns out that the UL and DL both use the AP and client antennas equally. A high-gain antenna on an AP and a low-gain antenna on a client will have the same effect on both the UL and DL. The transmit signal from the AP will be high on the DL; the received signal to the AP will be high by the same proportion because of the high-gain AP antenna.

Radio Channel Properties

The radio channel has several properties that influence the performance of a WLAN system:

- Attenuation that varies over time and space
- Noise
- Interference

Because these properties often vary in a way that is not predictable, the only way to ensure that communications occur reliably is to provide margin in the link. You can add this margin, expressed in dB, by doing the following:

- Bringing the AP and client closer (provide more APs per square area)
- Increasing AP and/or client power level

- Increasing the gain of the AP and/or client antenna
- Forcing the client and AP to use a lower-level modulation data rate than the radio channel can support

The transmit power and antenna gain may or may not be practical. For example, increasing the AP transmit power will increase the coverage and improve the margin on the DL. It won't have any effect on the UL. This can cause a situation where a DL exists but an UL is not possible. It also will add to the interference between APs and interference between clients and unassociated APs. Adding gain to an AP's antenna will limit the direction in which communications can occur. The result is coverage holes, or places where there is no signal.

Forcing the AP and client to use a lower-level data rate than is required is usually not necessary. Under most conditions, the radios can adjust rapidly enough to a changing radio channel. There are applications like voice that are very sensitive to packet loss and latency problems that might benefit if the AP and client are not allowed to achieve the highest data rates. In a high-multipath environment with large fades, this might improve performance. Often the best way to provide margin against a degraded radio channel is to bring the APs a little closer together than is strictly necessary, reduce the AP power level to balance the UL and DL, and measure a high SNR level (around 25 dB) at the points equidistant between APs. This approach eliminates the common situation where coverage is UL limited due to the client's lower transmit power. It also reduces spectral regrowth at the AP output, which in turn reduces interference levels.

As users move in a WLAN, they will hand off between APs. This requires the client to disassociate with one AP as it associates with another on the fly. There has been a lot of study in this area and great improvement in recent years in the way that enterprise WLAN systems deal with handoff. With the prevalence of WLAN voice systems, handoff performance has become very important. At the beginning of this section, we talked about the automated frequency planning and power adjustments that were possible with enterprise WLAN systems. Although these capabilities do make the job of an administrator easier, if the systems change frequency or power too often, handoff performance can suffer.

Link Budget

A link budget is an accounting method for showing how much margin a radio system has against radio channel degradation. Typically you would do this for a point-to-point system, but it would be instructive to show a link budget for a WLAN deployment.

Earlier in the chapter, we discussed path loss and the Friis transmission equation:

$$P_r = P_t G_t G_r / [(4\pi d)/\lambda]^2$$

In the equation you see that the received power is a function of the transmit power, transmitter and receiver antenna gain, distance, and wavelength (or frequency). The free space loss $[(4\pi d)/\lambda]^2$ can be replaced with different loss models, depending on the environment: outdoor, indoor, office, open space. A link budget takes these elements along with other losses in the system and lists them with the goal of determining the amount of power available at the receiver. Comparing that with the receive sensitivity determines the margin in the system.

In the link budget shown in Table 6.5, the output power, transmit cable loss, transmit antenna gain, free space loss, receive antenna gain, and receive cable loss are added together. That value is the power level in dBm presented to the receiver. The difference between this number and the receiver sensitivity is the margin for the link. In the example given in the table, the power at the receiver is –70 dBm. The receiver sensitivity for a 24 Mbps data rate is –85 dBm for this model receiver. The margin is 15 dB because the signal level received is 15 dB higher than is necessary to receive a 24 Mbps data rate signal. The radio channel could go into a 15 dB fade and still maintain that data rate.

TABLE 6.5   A typical link budget for a WLAN deployment used for either a downlink or an uplink

Radio element	Performance criteria	Value
	Output power (dBm)	15 dBm
Transmitter	Cable loss (dB)	–2 dB
	Antenna gain (dBi)	6 dBi
Radio channel	Free space loss or other loss model (dB)	–90 dB
Receiver	Antenna gain (dBi)	2 dBi
	Cable loss (dB)	–1 dB
	Receiver sensitivity (dBm)	–85 dBm
	Margin (dB)	15 dB

The link budgets can get more complex than what is shown in Table 6.5. For example, the receiver sensitivity can be derived from required SNR for a particular modulation, noise figure, and noise power within the operating bandwidth. Practically speaking, this isn't necessary because all 802.11 equipment manufacturers will publish receiver sensitivity values for the various modulation types. The simplified link budget shown is a good method for calculating link margin.

When an LNA is added to the receive chain before the 802.11 receiver, the link budget calculation becomes more complex. The receiver sensitivity value given by the radio manufacturer assumes that the noise level is due to thermal noise. Adding an LNA elevates the noise floor by the gain of the amplifier and its noise figure. Even though the signal level is increased going into the receiver, the noise is also increased.

The SNR from the LNA is different than what the receiver expects at its receiver sensitivity threshold. The noise figure of the LNA dominates the noise performance of the whole receiver chain. Receiver manufacturers generally do not publish receiver noise figures. The easiest way to deal with this is to assume that the noise figure of the LNA is the same as the noise figure of the receiver. Then you can use the same receiver sensitivity number that the manufacturer published, but the input of the whole receiver chain becomes the input of the LNA. To assume otherwise would complicate the link budget beyond the scope of this book.

Summary

Wireless technology has grown considerably from its humble beginnings. Today it is hard to imagine life without wireless technology. We use cell phones and WLANs without thinking much about the underlying principles that make radio communications possible. In this chapter you learned basic principles like receiver noise performance and transmitter distortion that have been known since World War II. We also reviewed the more modern methods of spread spectrum, coding, and OFDM. There is a basic physics principle with radio such as path loss, noise, and interference that no amount of technology can overcome. The way to have reliable radio communications is to understand its limitations and design with margin. With the information in this chapter, we have given you some of the tools you will need to design a reliable wireless LAN.

You have learned about frequency of operation and how it affects propagation. Multipath causes the signal arriving to an amplifier to have delay spread, which in turn causes ISI. You learned how receive diversity combats multipath. We explored various modulation techniques like QPSK and QAM. You learned how to view modulation in a constellation diagram and what the spectrum of a modulated carrier looks like. We also examined DSSS and CCK used in the original 802.11 and 802.11b. 802.11g and a communicate at a higher data rate and use OFDM. You also learned about how coding affects data rates and SNR. We examined noise and how it relates to temperature and receiver performance. We defined noise figure and showed you how it is measured. Other topics we covered include amplifier saturation, spectral regrowth, and receiver sensitivity. Finally, we organized system performance into a link budget so that you could calculate link margin.

Exam Essentials

Understand components of RF links.   Be able to explain noise figure, RSSI, and SNR as well as units of measure used in RF. Also be able to explain receiver sensitivity and the effect on modulation order and SNR.

Explain RF amplification concepts.   Be able to explain saturation, spectral regrowth, and PAR.

Understand transmission line effects.   Be able to calculate cascading gains and losses to arrive at a total gain or loss value.

Understand radio design concepts.   Know the various parameters that define the performance of a transmitter and receiver such as peak-to-average ratio, amplifier saturation, noise figure and receiver sensitivity

Explain modulation and coding types.   Know the different modulation types and coding rates for each of the 802.11 data rates. Also be able to explain details behind OFDM modulation.

Be familiar with radio propagation theory.   Know how frequency and environment affect propagation. Also be able to explain free space path loss.

Review Questions

1. A receiver includes a cable connected to the antenna, a filter, an LNA, and a cable, in that order. The cable connected to the antenna has a loss of 3 dB, the filter loss is 1 dB, the noise figure of an LNA is 4 dB, and the cable connected to the rest of the receiver has a 5 dB loss. The gain of the LNA is 20 dB. What is the overall noise figure of the receiver?

    A. 4 dB

    B. 24 dB

    C. 8 dB

    D. 13 dB

2. The thermal noise is at –174 dBm/Hz. A spectrum analyzer has a resolution bandwidth of 1 kHz and a 5 dB noise figure. What is the level of the noise floor?

    A. –174 dBm

    B. –139 dBm

    C. –204 dBm

    D. –144 dBm

3. An amplifier has a 1 dB compression point of 32 dBm and a gain of 20 dB. Which is the highest average input power shown here that would be safe to operate a 24 Mbps 802.11g signal so that spectral regrowth is not a problem?

    A. 10 dBm

    B. 0 dBm

    C. 5 dBm

    D. –5 dBm

4. A signal passes through a 10-meter cable, an amplifier, and then a filter. The amplifier has an output that is eight times higher in power than its input. Each meter of cable reduces the signal level by a factor of 4. The filter has a loss of 5 dB. What is the total loss/gain of the three elements in series?

    A. 37 dB loss

    B. 16 dB gain

    C. 56 dB loss

    D. 65 dB loss

5. If the amplifier in Question 4 has a noise figure of 10 dB but a gain of 0 dB, what is the total noise figure of the cable, amplifier, and filter in series?

   A. 16 dB

   B. 10 dB

   C. 75 dB

   D. 70 dB

6. The 802.11a 54 Mbps data rate uses 64-QAM. What is the symbol bit length for this modulation?

   A. 64 bits

   B. 6 bits

   C. 8 bits

   D. 1 bit

7. A high power radio system transmits at 40,000 Watts. What is this power in dBm? Solve this without a calculator.

   A. 46 dBm

   B. 66 dBm

   C. 76 dBm

   D. 56 dBm

8. Which of the following are elements that make up a basic link budget?

   A. Receiver antenna gain, thermal noise temperature, transmitter output power, and path loss

   B. Receiver antenna gain, transmitter output power, transmitter compression point, transmitter antenna gain, and path loss

   C. Receiver antenna gain, receiver noise figure, modulation loss, transmitter antenna gain, and path loss

   D. Receiver antenna gain, receiver sensitivity, transmitter output power, transmitter antenna gain, and path loss

9. Receiver sensitivity is related to what other radio performance measurements?

   A. Noise figure

   B. Antenna gain

   C. Amplifier compression

   D. Spectral regrowth

10. How much more power can a 1 Mbps 802.11b signal have than a 54 Mbps 802.11g signal if it is sent through a saturated amplifier?

   A.   2 dB

   B.   5 dB

   C.   2 dBm

   D.   5 dBm

11. The 802.11a 36 Mbps data rate signal has which of the following characteristics?

   A.   OFDM signal using QPSK and ½ rate coding

   B.   OFDM signal using QPSK and ½ rate coding

   C.   DSSS signal using BPSK and no coding

   D.   OFDM signal using 16-QAM and ¾ rate coding

12. If the client and AP are transmitting at their maximum power, area coverage is generally determined by which of the following?

   A.   Client transmit power

   B.   Client noise figure

   C.   AP transmit power

   D.   Client receive sensitivity

13. A common path loss formula is the following: $L(dB) = 10\,n\,\log(d) + 20\,\log(f) - 27.55$. What value of n would represent free space loss?

   A.   1

   B.   0 dB

   C.   2

   D.   3

14. What is the chip rate of 1 Mbps 802.11b?

   A.   11 Mchips/s

   B.   22 Mchips/s

   C.   1 Mchip/s

   D.   2 Mchips/s

15. Which of the following affect receiver sensitivity?

   A.   Noise figure of the receiver

   B.   Loss in a receiver before its LNA

   C.   Received modulation format

   D.   All of the above

16. A 16-QAM signal is sent at 1 Msps. What is the bit rate of the signal at the receiver output?

    A. 1 Mbps

    B. 6 Mbps

    C. 2 Mbps

    D. 4 Mbps

17. Using a free space model, if the frequency is doubled, the loss is increased by how much?

    A. 3 dB

    B. 6 dB

    C. 27.55 dB

    D. Unchanged

18. Antenna gain is measured in what units?

    A. dB

    B. dBm

    C. dBa

    D. dBi

19. An amplifier has a 1 dB compression point of 20 dBm. It is operated at 10 dB backoff. It has a gain of 20 dB. What is the average input power?

    A. −10 dBm

    B. 10 dBm

    C. 0 dBm

    D. 20 dBm

20. 802.11g and 802.11a have how many nonoverlapping channels in North America?

    A. 14 for g and 20 for a

    B. 11 for g and 12 for a

    C. 3 for g and 23 for a

    D. 3 for g and 4 for a

Answers to Review Questions

1. C. The noise figure of this receiver is the sum of the loss between the antenna and the LNA, plus the noise figure of the LNA. Since the gain of the LNA is higher than the loss after it, the loss after the LNA does not contribute to the overall noise figure.

2. B. Noise floor is calculated by taking the value of thermal noise, adding 30 dB (10 × log(1000)), and then adding the noise figure of its LNA front end.

3. B. A 0 dBm average input signal would be amplified to 20 dBm output. A 24 Mbps OFDM signal has around 9 dB PAR. The output of the amplifier would peak at 29 dBm, which is 3 dB below the 1 dB compression point of the amplifier. A 5 dBm input signal would result in a peak power of 34 dBm, which would cause clipping.

4. C. The loss of the cable is 60 dB (10 × 6 dB). The gain of the amplifier is 9 dB (10 × log(2 × 2 × 2) = 3 dB + 3 dB + 3 dB = 9 dB). The filter has a loss of 5 dB. The total loss is 60 − 9 + 5 = 56 dB.

5. C. This cable and amplifier combination would not be recommended for a receiver. There is 60 dB of loss before the LNA, which adds directly to the noise figure. The LNA contributes an additional 10 dB. Since there is no gain in the LNA (not exactly useful), the 5 dB loss of the filter after the LNA contributes directly to the overall noise figure.

6. B. A 64-QAM symbol has 64 possible states. These 64 states can be expressed using 6 bits.

7. C. 40,000 Watts is 40,000,000 milliwatts, which is a four followed by seven zeros. The seven zeros gives the factor 70 dB, the 4 is 3 dB + 3 dB = 6 dB. The combination is 76 dBm.

8. D. Option D contains elements of a basic link budget. Option A includes thermal noise temperature; although this could theoretically be used as an element of link budget calculation, it is not commonly used and was not discussed in the book. Option B includes amplifier compression point, which does not figure into a link budget calculation. Option C includes modulation loss, which doesn't exist.

9. A. The noise figure of a receiver is directly related to its sensitivity. A receiver with a high noise figure LNA will require a higher input signal than one with a low noise figure. Option B affects the signal level at the input of the receiver but does not change the receiver sensitivity. The other options are related to transmitter performance.

10. B. A 1 Mbps 802.11b signal has a PAR of around 4 dB. A 54 Mbps 802.11g signal has a PAR of around 9 dB. The ratio of the two is 5 dB. 2 dB is too small a difference, and Options C and D use the wrong units to express a ratio.

11. D. 802.11a only uses OFDM; 16-QAM and ¾ rate coding is required to transmit 36 Mbps data rates.

12. A. For a system where an AP is transmitting at full power, the uplink limits coverage. A is the only option that involves the uplink. Client power is usually limited and less than the full power capability of an AP.

13. C. The formula is a free space loss formula if $n = 2$. Higher values of n should be used to model the effects of multipath and material attenuation.

14. A. The 1 Mbps 802.11b uses an 11 chip Barker code. It spreads a 1 Msps signal to produce an 11 Mchip/s spread spectrum waveform.

15. D. Options A, B, and C all have an effect on receiver sensitivity. Noise figure determines how much noise is added to the input signal. Loss directly impacts noise figure. Different modulation formats are more or less susceptible to noise.

16. D. A 16-QAM signal has 4 bits per symbol. The bit rate is four times the symbol rate.

17. B. The frequency part of the free space loss model is $20 \times \log(F)$. Doubling F will add 6 dB to the loss.

18. D. Antenna gain is measured against an ideal isotropic antenna. The i in dBi is isotropic.

19. A. The output of the amplifier is 10 dBm (20 dBm − 10 dB backoff = 10 dBm). Since the amplifier has a 20 dB gain, its input power must be −10 dBm.

20. C. There are 11 possible channel assignments for 802.11g, but only 3 are nonoverlapping. There are 23 possible channels for 802.11a and they are not overlapping.

Chapter

7

RF Hardware and 802.11n

THE FOLLOWING CWDP EXAM TOPICS ARE COVERED IN THIS CHAPTER:

- ✓ Demonstrate a detailed understanding of RF behaviors and characteristics and relate these concepts to WLAN RF design.

- ✓ Understand the purpose of, and challenges related to, creating a balanced RF link between the AP and client devices.

- ✓ Illustrate best practices for data rate/MCS configurations to manage client connectivity.

- ✓ Describe the purpose of, and techniques for, controlling and shaping RF to improve WLAN functionality.

- ✓ Understand common RF accessories and other components used in WLAN communications.

- ✓ Describe how antenna selection, placement, and orientation is determined by an RF site survey.

In the previous chapter we examined the details of radio performance. This chapter focuses on the components that make up a WLAN radio system. RF cables, antennas, and filters are similar devices. RF cables are generally wide-band devices that transfer radio energy from one place to another. Antennas transfer radio energy from a transmission line to the air. These then filter the energy over frequency and space. Filters will transfer energy and filter over frequency. We will also examine the details of 802.11n radios.

RF Cables and Connectors

The most common type of RF cable is called coax, or coaxial, cable. A coaxial cable consists of a center metal conductor, surrounded by an insulating material, which is further surrounded by a tubular metal conductor. Coaxial refers to the fact that the two conductors—the wire in the center and the tube surrounding it—share the same center axis.

Coaxial cables come by different names, such as RG-6, RG-58, RG-213, LMR-195, LMR-200, LMR-400, and semi-rigid. RG stands for Radio Guide and was developed as a standard during World War II. Although RG is no longer a standard, the name designation is still used. LMR is a registered trademark of the Times Microwave Corporation and is part of their line of low-loss cables.

Cables differ in diameter, flexibility, and loss. Lower-loss cables typically have a larger diameter and are less flexible and more expensive than higher-loss cables. The size of the connectors used on either end of the cable may also dictate the type of cable used. Choosing the right cable is usually a trade-off between these criteria.

RF connectors are used to connect cables and equipment without disrupting the flow of RF energy. The quality of that connection is vital for maintaining performance of a radio system. RF connectors come in many varieties. A wireless engineer should be familiar with the names of connectors, including SMA, RP-SMA, N, MMCX, TNC, RP-TNC, BNC, and U.FL (developed by Hirose Electric Group in Japan).

Transmission Lines

What is a *transmission line*? In microwave electronics, it is a medium to transfer microwave energy from one place to another using one or more conductors. The most common transmission lines use two conductors stretched over a distance. Coax cable is a two-conductor transmission line where one conductor is a wire in the center; the other is a tube, called the *shield*, encompassing the center conductor, as shown in Figure 7.1.

FIGURE 7.1   A diagram of a coax cable

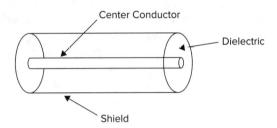

A twisted-pair cable is used for lower-frequency RF signals and medium data rate digital signals such as Ethernet. The coax cable usually has a material between the center and outer conductors called a *dielectric*. The geometry of the two conductors and the dielectric material between them determines what is called the *characteristic impedance* of the transmission line, usually denoted as Z_o. Don't worry too much about impedance for now because we'll discuss impedance in more depth in the next section.

A Cable's Nature Changes at High Frequencies

Most people have experienced a short circuit on a live voltage source. Generally things spark and heat up as a good amount of current is drawn through the short. This scenario involves three elements: voltage, current, and resistance. Put a voltage source across a low resistance and you will get high current. Make that a large resistance and the current flow is small. The resistor regulates or resists the flow of current. Two other devices affect current and voltage: capacitors and inductors. Capacitors store charge; inductors store current. Together, resistors, capacitors, and inductors determine the impedance of a circuit.

A cable that is a type of transmission line has fairly simple properties when the signals are low frequency or at zero (DC voltage). The signal at one end of the cable is the same as at the other. A cable is not a very interesting part of a low-frequency circuit.

The situation changes at radio frequencies. When the wavelength of the signal is comparable to the length of the cable, the radio properties of the cable become important. At higher frequencies (short wavelength), the signal at one end of the circuit is no longer the same as what is at the other end. The wave properties of the cable, such as impedance and loss and the effect on signals—namely reflections and attenuation—become important. The RF loss and impedance of a cable have to be factored into overall system performance. We will explore the details of factoring RF loss and impedance into your designs later in this chapter.

Coax generally comes in two different impedances: 50 ohms and 75 ohms. Fifty ohms is used for radio design, and 75 ohms is mostly used for CATV and video. Twisted pair has an impedance of around 100 ohms. A transmission line common for over-the-air television is two untwisted wires spaced apart in such a way that they create a 300 ohm impedance.

A *waveguide* is a single conductor transmission line, usually a rectangular or circular tube whose size is related to its frequency of operation. Waveguides are not commonly used at 2.4 GHz. The dimensions of standard waveguide at that frequency have a rectangular cross section of 6.5×3.2 inches, which make it a bit unwieldy. At 5 GHz, the waveguide gets a bit smaller and more manageable: $1.6 \times .8$ inches. Many of you have likely heard that a metal canister, such as ones that hold a well-known potato chip, can be used as a waveguide antenna at 2.4 GHz. While it may have a cool factor associated to it, we recommend using an actual engineered antenna.

The complexity of microwave electronics comes from its wave nature. *Wavelength* is a measure of the size of the microwave wave. At 2.4 GHz, a signals wavelength in air can be calculated as

$$\lambda = c/F$$

where λ (lambda) is the wavelength in meters, c is the speed of light (3×10^8 m/s), and F is the frequency in Hz (1 GHz $= 10^9$ Hz).

At 2.4 GHz and 5 GHz, the wavelength of a microwave signal in air is 12.5 cm and 6 cm, respectively. In a cable, the wavelength reduces by the square root of the dielectric constant of the cable's dielectric. Most coax cable uses solid polyethylene or a polyethylene foam as its dielectric. Polyethylene and polyethylene foam have a dielectric constant of 2.25 and 1.55, respectively. A cable with a polyethylene dielectric would have a wavelength of 8.3 cm at 2.4 GHz as compared to 12.5 cm in air, or

$$8.3 \text{ cm} = 12.5 \text{ cm} / \sqrt{2.25}$$

This will become important when we discuss voltage standing wave ratio (VSWR) later in the chapter.

Impedance

Impedance is a central concept in RF/microwave electronics. It is a measure of a transmission line's distributed capacitance and inductance. To grasp this concept, you have to understand a little about capacitance and inductance and how it relates to a transmission line.

Figure 7.2 shows a diagram of a capacitor. It is made up of two conductors separated by a material that has special capacitive properties called a dielectric. If opposite charges build up on each of the capacitors plates, a voltage potential builds up between them. The amount of charge stored for a given voltage is a quantity called *capacitance* measured in *farads*. Since a farad is a large quantity, capacitance is usually expressed as a value in microfarads ($1\mu F = 10^{-6}$ farads) or picofarads ($1pF = 10^{-9}$ farads). If a dielectric is present, the capacitance is higher than if no dielectric is present. If the plates are closer, the capacitance is higher than if the plates are farther. If the plates have more area, the capacitance is higher than if the plates have less area. A coax cable can be viewed as a capacitor. It has two plates, the inner and outer conductor, and a dielectric in between. There is a certain amount of capacitance per length. A typical 50 ohm cable has a capacitance of 100pF /meter.

FIGURE 7.2 A diagram of a capacitor

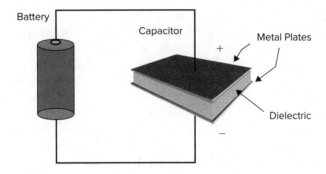

An *inductor* is a conductor that carries current. A transmission line is two conductors carrying current in opposite directions. The inductance is related to the distance between those conductors as it is with a capacitor, but in the opposite way. Inductance gets smaller as the two conductors get closer.

The impedance of a coax cable is related by the following formula:

$$Z_o = \sqrt{\frac{L}{C}}$$

where Z_o is the characteristic impedance of the cable, L is the distributed inductance, and C is the distributed capacitance.

An assumption made with this formula is that the resistance in the cable is negligible, which is generally a good assumption. It turns out that for a transmission line, Z_o depends only on the shape and separation of the two conductors, and the dielectric constant of the material between them. For a coaxial cable, Z_o is determined by the following formula:

$$Z_o = \frac{138 ohms}{\sqrt{\varepsilon_r}} * \log\left[\frac{D}{d}\right]$$

where D is the inner diameter of the shield (outer conductor), d is the diameter of the wire in the center (inner conductor), and ε_r is the relative dielectric constant of the material between the two conductors. The impedance is related to the geometry of the cable, namely the ratio of the conductor diameters, and the material dielectric constant.

In a traditional electronic circuit, the voltage increases and the current decreases as resistance or impedance increases. This also happens in a transmission line, as you will learn in the next section.

VSWR, Reflection Coefficient, and Return Loss

Why is impedance important? At low frequencies, the voltage and current of a signal at one end of a transmission line is pretty much the same as what it is at the other end. This is not true of high-frequency signals. At high frequencies the wave nature of the signal starts to take over. Microwave signals (high frequencies) are best thought of as traveling down one direction of the transmission line, reflecting off the end and traveling back the opposite direction that it began. The relationship between how much power is sent and how much is reflected back has everything to do with the impedance of the transmission line and the impedance at the ends. If the impedance at the ends does not match the transmission line, a reflection will occur at the ends. The amount of power reflected is related to how much the impedance of the line differs from the impedance of the load at the end.

There are a few important concepts in this section that you will need to focus on. You will need to understand what is a good and what is a bad VSWR, reflection coefficient, and return loss. You should know how impedance changes along a transmission line when there is a mismatch at one end, especially at ¼ a wavelength and ½ a wavelength. The formulas that are given here are for reference. It is not necessary to memorize them all for the exam, but being able to calculate VSWR from load and line impedance is important.

Normally a radio engineer will match the impedance of a load on the end of a transmission line to the line's characteristic impedance, Z_o. If there is a mismatch between them, the measured impedance of the transmission line changes from Z_o to different values all along the line. Figure 7.3 shows what happens to the impedance of a 50 ohm cable with a 50 ohm resistive termination (essentially a small 50 ohm resistor at the end). Not surprisingly, nothing that interesting happens when the impedance of the line is 50 ohms throughout its length. To makes things simple, we assume that the generator of the signal is matched to the characteristic impedance of the line.

FIGURE 7.3 Impedance along a 50 ohm cable with a 50 ohm load

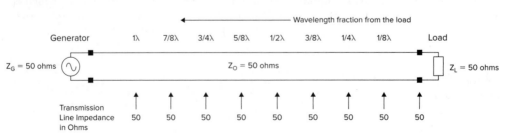

What happens when the termination does not match Z_o? It may sound weird that the impedance of the line changes from Z_o. It is important to distinguish between the characteristic impedance Z_o and the actual measured impedance in the line. They are two different things. Let's look at what happens in the extreme case when there is a short or open circuit at the end of the transmission line. The load impedance is 0 ohms for a short circuit and infinity ohms for an open circuit. Figure 7.4 shows how the impedance along the transmission line changes.

FIGURE 7.4 Impedance along a 50 ohm cable with a 0 ohm load (short circuit)

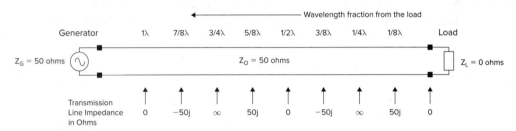

Notice that some of the impedances show a letter j after the number (some books use the letter i; it's the same thing). This shows that the impedance is complex and not strictly resistive. The j value is what is called the imaginary part of the impedance. A positive j value indicates an inductive impedance, and a negative j value indicates a capacitive impedance. A number that has both a real and an imaginary part to it has a mix of resistance (real) and capacitive or inductive (imaginary) impedance. Figure 7.5 shows the last example, which is a 20 ohm termination.

FIGURE 7.5 Impedance along a 50 ohm cable with a 20 ohm load

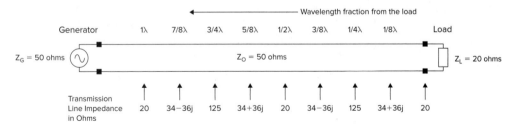

If there is a mismatch between the characteristic impedance of the transmission line and the load, the impedance fluctuates along the line. When there is a short circuit (zero impedance) load, a quarter wavelength away from the load there is the equivalent of an open circuit. Another quarter wave away, the impedance is zero again. Every half wavelength, the load impedance is repeated. This property of changing impedance along a transmission line is often used as a design tool by radio designers to tune circuits. A transmission line can be used to transform one impedance to another. But the mismatches shown in Figure 7.5 are not part of a radio design and result in lower performance.

Reflection Coefficient

The *reflection coefficient* is related to the amount of reflection coming from a load. Here is the formula for calculating the reflection coefficient, Γ (gamma) at a load impedance:

$$\Gamma = \frac{Z_L - Z_0}{Z_L + Z_0}$$

where Z_L is the load impedance and Z_o is the line characteristic impedance.

The reflection coefficient is a measure of the amount of signal reflected compared to the amount transmitted. $\Gamma = 0$ means no reflection, and $\Gamma = 1$ (Z_L is open circuit or infinite impedance) or -1 ($Z_L =$ is short or 0 ohms impedance) means total reflection. If $Z_L = 20$ and $Z_o = 50$ ohms, as in the earlier example, the reflection coefficient Γ equals -0.43. The sign of the reflection coefficient indicates something of the phase of the standing wave signal. Note that a load impedance of 125 ohms will result in the same reflection coefficient except that it is positive. The only difference is that a 20 ohm reflection has a different phase than a 125 ohm impedance. They differ on a transmission line by a quarter wavelength, which for a reflection coefficient changes the sign from $-$ to $+$.

As one measures along a transmission line away from a mismatched load, the impedance is constantly changing. The reflection coefficient will also change. If the transmission line does not have loss, the reflection coefficient will change in phase but not in amplitude. When there is a 20 ohm load on a 50 ohm transmission line, the impedance changes continuously from 20 ohms to $34 + 36j$ ohms to 125 ohms to $34 - 36j$ ohms back to 20 ohms, and so on. The phase of the reflection coefficient changes continuously but remains at a constant 0.43 amplitude. The amount of power reflecting back is the same along the lossless transmission line; the phase, however, changes.

Return Loss

Return loss (RL) is the amplitude of the reflection coefficient expressed in dB power. It is the ratio of the power reflected to the power sent by the transmitter. The following is the formula that is used to calculate return loss: $RL = -20 \log |\Gamma|$, where $|\Gamma|$ is the amplitude of the reflection coefficient. Because $|\Gamma|$ is always less than 1, the logarithm is negative and *RL* is always positive.

A return loss of 0 dB indicates that all the power sent is reflected back. There is no loss between the transmitted signal and the one reflected back. A return greater than 15 dB is quite good and indicates almost no reflected power. Alternatively, a 20 ohm or 125 ohm load on a 50 ohm transmission line would result in a 7.3 dB return loss ($-20 \log(0.43) = 7.3$ dB), meaning that the reflected power is 7.3 dB less than what it would be if the load fully reflected the power. All along a lossless 50 ohm transmission line terminated with 20 ohms, the return loss is a constant 7.3 dB.

VSWR

The *voltage standing wave ratio (VSWR)* is another way to measure the degree of mismatch existing between a load and transmission line. The variation of impedance goes hand in hand with the variation in voltage along the transmission line. Although both the current and voltage vary down the line, it turns out the voltage is easier to measure, so traditionally the standing wave ratio refers to a voltage ratio. The maximum voltage on a transmission line occurs where the impedance is real and at a maximum. This is when the line is at 125 ohms in the previous example. When the line's impedance is real and is at a minimum, voltage is at a minimum. This is when the line is at 20 ohms in the previous example. VSWR is the ratio of maximum voltage to minimum. There are a couple ways that VSWR can be calculated. One way is to take the larger of Z_o/Z_L and Z_L/Z_o. The other way is to calculate the following:

$$VSWR = \frac{V_{MAX}}{V_{MIN}} = \frac{1+|\Gamma|}{1-|\Gamma|}$$

For a load resistance of 20 ohms and transmission line with a $Z_o = 50$ ohms, VSWR is 2.5 (50 ohms/20 ohms = 2.5 or $(1 + .43)/(1 - .43) = 2.5$). It is sometimes expressed as 2.5:1. VSWR can range from 1 to infinity. When VSWR equals 1, there is no reflection. When it is infinite, there is a full reflection. Rearranging the math on the previous equation shows the reverse expression. which can be used to calculate the reflection coefficient and return loss from VSWR:

$$|\Gamma| = \frac{VSWR-1}{VSWR+1}$$

and as shown before, RL $= -20 \log |\Gamma|$

We mentioned earlier that 15 dB return loss shows a good match between the transmission line and the load at the end of the line. This corresponds to a reflection coefficient of 0.178 or -0.178. The VSWR is 1.4:1 and the load resistor for a 50 ohm transmission line is 72 ohms or 35 ohms.

Up to now we have discussed a mismatch between a transmission line and a load and how that causes a reflection. If the transmission line itself changes its characteristic impedance—for example, by a change in geometry—the result will also be a reflection at the discontinuity. A bad ground on a connector, or a sharp bend or a crimp on a cable, changes its geometry. The resulting change in impedance will cause a reflection of microwave signals. No connector is perfect and will cause some discontinuity in impedance at the connection point. In general it is a good idea to limit the number of connectors in a system and take care not to damage cables by bending them with too tight a radius.

Generally a high VSWR should be avoided. It is important to match the transmission line with a load that is as close as possible to its characteristic impedance. Any power reflected back is power that is not available to the load. Generally a VSWR below 1.5 or a return loss above 15 dB is considered to be good. A VSWR above 2.0 or a return loss below 10 dB will likely cause problems. If there are multiple places where reflections occur, the ability of the signal to pass can become severely degraded. Worse yet, the transmitted power level becomes dependent on frequency. Large ripples in transmitted power can occur across a wide-band signal.

It is possible that a lossy cable can mask a VSWR problem. It can make a large mismatch seem much smaller than it really is. Take an example of a cable with 5 dB of loss. Even if there is the worst VSWR, a short circuit at one end, measurements at the other end will show a return loss of 10 dB. This happens even though there is a full reflection at the short. This is because the transmitted signal is reduced by 5 dB on the path toward the short and is reduced a further 5 dB on the return trip. The return loss of the short isn't being measured; the lossy cable and the short in combination are being measured. It's important when measuring return loss that you know the attenuation of the cable used to make the measurement. Two times this cable attenuation value should then be subtracted from the return loss value of the cable and the load combination. This will give you the return loss of the load by itself.

Measuring cable loss can be done a number of ways with various instruments. One method uses the property of return loss discussed in the previous paragraph. An RF network analyzer (sometimes called a vector network analyzer) measures return loss directly. If you have this instrument, an easy way to determine the attenuation of a cable is to short out the end and measure the return loss. Half of the dB value will be the cable loss. This method is useful if you are measuring the loss of a cable and you have access to only one end. The other end may be on the top of a building and you are in the basement. As you learned earlier, an open circuit and a short circuit give the same full reflection. So measuring with one end open is almost as good as a short. We say *almost* as good because the open, if it is not designed as a pure open circuit, can radiate and add more loss to the measurement than is in the cable.

Usually the open circuit is a lousy antenna and does not radiate much, so the method produces a pretty accurate result. It is also possible to measure cable loss using the method if there is an antenna at the other end of the cable. You would just need to measure the reflection well off the center frequency of the antenna where it is fully reflecting the signal.

A filter and antenna can have a very good VSWR match in its band of operation. It acts like a 50 ohm load in this frequency band. Outside of the band it usually looks like a high VSWR load like a short or open. This kind of VSWR frequency dependency is expected and will normally not cause problems as long as the frequency of operation stays within the low VSWR region of the filter or antenna. In other words, as long as the radio is using frequencies within the frequency region that the filter isn't affecting, there should be no negative impact.

Connectors

There are many different types of RF connectors. Since we are mostly interested in connectors used in radio communications, we will concentrate on 50 ohm connectors. We will also focus on those commonly used for WLAN radios.

If you deal with a variety of manufacturers' products, we highly recommend that you own an assortment of connector adapters to convert from one type to another. While connectors can become bad, especially when frequently connected and disconnected, they usually provide little RF signal loss.

The connectors you will need to be familiar with are as follows:

RP (Reverse Polarity) Connectors   In an attempt to discourage nonprofessionals from installing RF equipment to high-gain antennas, the FCC forced manufacturers of WLAN radios to use nonstandard connectors. The nonstandard connector chosen for these radios were like the standard ones, but modified to be incompatible. To comply with this requirement, manufacturers came up with reverse polarity versions of standard connectors. Since these connectors became so widespread, they became de facto standards along with the usual types. The FCC requirement for nonstandard connectors ended up doubling the types of connectors in the marketplace.

SMA/RP-SMA   An *SMA connector* is relatively small. Figure 7.6 shows both a male SMA connector and a female RP (reverse polarity) version.

FIGURE 7.6   A male SMA connector and a female RP-SMA connector

Male
Source: Meggar via Wikipedia.

Female
Source: Lzur via Wikipedia

SMB   The SMB connector is a bit smaller than the SMA and is a snap-on type connector. Figure 7.7 shows a male SMB.

FIGURE 7.7   Male SMB connector

Source: Petteri Aimonen via Wikipedia

N   The *N connector*, shown in Figure 7.8, is one of the largest connectors used for WLANs and has higher power handling capabilities than the SMA. It is often found on outdoor WLAN systems.

FIGURE 7.8   N connector

Source: Peter Schwindt via Wikipedia

RP-TNC The *TNC connector* is midway between the N and SMA in size. The RP-TNC is very common on indoor access points. It is shown in Figure 7.9.

FIGURE 7.9 RP-TNC connector

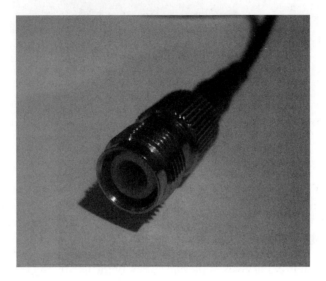

MMCX The micro-miniature coaxial *MMCX* is a small connector that is sometimes used on client device radios such as PC Card and some USB.

MC Card MC Card is nearly identical to MMCX and is used by some manufacturer client devices and even radios within AP products.

U.FL *U.FL* connectors are very small connectors often used on the WLAN radio circuit boards within the WLAN electronic housing.

Filters

Microwave filters are passive devices that pass signals at some frequencies and block others. The most common type of filter is a *bandpass filter*, which will pass signals within a band and stop signals with frequencies above and below the *passband*. A common bandpass filter that has low loss is a *cavity filter*. A cavity filter is shown in Figure 7.10.

FIGURE 7.10   Cavity filter

You see in the figure a metal box with a lot of screws in it. The larger screws are used by the manufacturer to tune the filter. A filter is similar to a musical instrument. For example, a flute produces a note by creating a standing sound wave within the flutes tube. A flute player shortens and lengthens the tube by opening and closing holes in the side of the tube. The standing sound wave of the flute is directly analogous to a standing microwave signal inside a cavity filter. The manufacturer changes the dimensions of the filter cavity by turning the screws in and out, thus changing the tone of the cavity. At certain frequencies the cavity resonates and sets up a standing wave. At those frequencies, the cavity will pass the signal through. By putting several cavities in series, each with a slightly different resonance, the manufacturer can create a wide-band filter with a high rejection of signals outside the passband.

Figure 7.11 shows the dB magnitude of the signal that passes through the filter and the signal that is reflected for a typical cavity filter. A vector network analyzer would be the type of instrument that could make these measurements. The figure shows that there is low loss inside the passband and high loss outside it. Inside the band, signals are attenuated by a little over 1 dB. Outside the passband they are attenuated or rejected by at least 31 dB. Most signals are rejected by even more than this. It is interesting to note what happens to signals outside the passband.

Where did the signals go if they did not pass through the filter? The plot of reflected signal level is greatest outside the passband. It is clear from the plots that signals that have frequencies inside the band are passed through; those outside are reflected back and little gets through. The filter shown in Figure 7.12 would be used on channel 11 for an 802.11g radio, for example. A radio equipped with this filter could tolerate very high RF signal on channel 6. It would also not interfere with any radios on that channel. If the radio connected to this filter were tuned to another channel—say, channel 6—almost all the power coming out of the radio would be reflected back into the transmitter. The radio is usually designed to handle this, but it would not work very well. Similarly, the signals received from the antenna would be heavily attenuated by the time they passed through the filter and onward to the radio receiver.

FIGURE 7.11   Frequency plot of a cavity filter

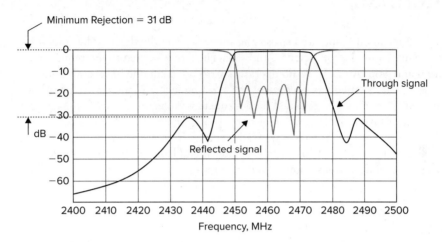

Figure 7.12 is the same as Figure 7.11, but the amplitude scale has changed from 10 dB per division to 0.5 dB per division. At this scale you can see more detail. The passband shows a maximum insertion loss of 1.2 dB. The bandwidth is 25 MHz. Bandwidth is typically expressed as a 3 dB bandwidth. It is measured at the points in which the passband signal drops by 3 dB. The insertion loss of 1.2 dB for this filter is pretty good, given this bandwidth. The variation in insertion loss in the passband is called *ripple*. The ripple for this filter is 0.3 dB, which is typical for this kind of filter.

FIGURE 7.12   Higher-resolution frequency plot of a cavity filter

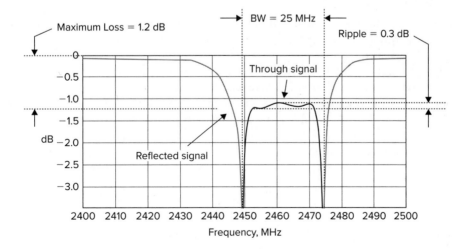

Antennas

Antennas come in all shapes and sizes. The shape is generally dictated by trade-offs between gain, bandwidth, efficiency, and size. The size is related to its frequency of operation and gain. Amateur radio operators working from one to several hundred MHz use very large antennas because of the low frequency. A microwave phone antenna is quite small due to its low gain and high frequency. Antennas for use in spacecraft communications from the ground are generally large due to their high gain.

The job of the antenna is to transfer radio energy from an electronic circuit/cable to the air (or vacuum in the case of spacecraft antennas) and from the air to a cable/circuit.

Let's now explore various antenna types and properties.

Antenna Types

Antennas are a critical part of any communication system. Choosing an antenna usually results from answering the following questions:

- What is the frequency range needed?
- How much gain is needed?
- What antenna pattern is required?
- Are the radios moving or stationary?
- How will the antenna be mounted?
- What front-to-back ratio is required? (We'll explain this concept later in this chapter.)
- Are wind and weather a factor?
- Are aesthetics a factor?

The most important factors that will influence antenna selection are gain and antenna pattern: where you want the signal to go and with how much amplification. Generally the two factors are related.

If it is important to confine an antenna pattern to a single direction—say down a long hallway or stairwell—a patch or panel antenna might do well. It doesn't protrude very far from the wall and can have a nice amount of gain. For instance, yagi antennas do well outside; they have very little wind loading and generally high gain. If very high gain is required, as with a point-to-point link, a parabolic dish may be required. Table 7.1 shows the gain range of several common antenna types.

TABLE 7.1 Gain range of several common antenna types

Type	Typical gain range (dBi)
Omni	2 to 12
Dipole	2
Patch	5 to 17
Parabolic Dish	12 to 36
Horn	7 to 18
Panel (Patch array)	7 to 22
Yagi	5 to 20
Sector	14 to 20

Omni

Omni antennas will radiate equally in the horizontal direction (H-plane) but may be confined to a relatively narrow range of angles in the vertical direction (E-plane). The higher the gain of the antenna, the narrower the range of angles it will radiate vertically. This kind of antenna is ideal for mounting on a ceiling inside a building. Ceiling mount omni antennas are designed to point downward slightly so that it will radiate into the rooms below and not waste energy radiating up. Depending on the mounting height and area of coverage, 3–6 dBi is a good gain value to use. A high gain omni antenna is not the best choice for a ship at sea as the wave motion would cause the radio link to vary in signal strength too much. A low 2 dBi gain omni is more appropriate for that application.

If an extra antenna is available, it is a good idea to take it apart and look at the parts inside. Often the plastic covering, called a *radome*, comes off easily. Antennas vary widely in quality and it is very easy to hide poor workmanship under a nice-looking plastic radome. Even the radome itself can be examined. One of the authors was evaluating a 2.4 GHz antenna and found very poor workmanship inside. What was most interesting, however, was what happened when the author put the radome in a microwave oven and baked it for 40 seconds. It came out very warm. The radome that covered the antenna actually absorbed microwave radiation at 2.4 GHz. The material used to manufacture this radome was obviously a poor design choice used by the antenna manufacturer.

Dipole

A dipole antenna is a very common low-gain antenna. It is sometimes called a stick, rubber duck, or whip antenna. This section will explore the basic constructions of a few types of dipole antennas.

Figure 7.13 shows a simple dipole. One element of the dipole is connected to the center wire of a coax cable. The other is connected to the shield. Each element is a ¼ λ (lambda or wavelength), which makes the total length ½ λ. The impedance of a ½ λ dipole is 73 ohms, which makes it ideal for 75 ohm cable systems. To match 50 ohms, a small device called a transformer needs to be part of the antenna to transform the 50 ohm cable to the 73 ohm antenna. The transformer is also called a *balun*. The gain of a ½ λ dipole is 2.13 dBi. Increasing the dipole's length will increase its gain and change its impedance. A 2 λ, 4 λ, and 8 λ dipole has a gain of 3.6 dBi, 5.4 dBi, and 8.5 dBi, respectively. Each different length requires a different balun design for impedance matching. Sometimes a dipole is shorter than ½ λ due to size constraints. These antennas are low gain and not very efficient.

FIGURE 7.13   A diagram of a ½ λ dipole

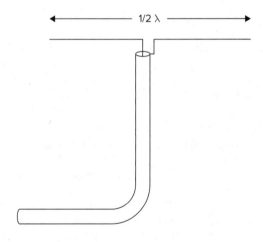

Figure 7.14 shows a folded dipole. Note that the radiating element is made of two parallel wires connected at the ends. Its input impedance is around 300 ohms and has a higher bandwidth than the ½ λ dipole. This kind of antenna can be fed with a 300 ohm twin wire used for TV antennas.

FIGURE 7.14   A diagram of a ½ λ folded dipole

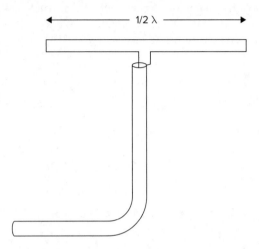

Figure 7.15 shows a common ½ λ dipole design used for so-called "rubber duck" antennas that are used on retail access points. The cable's shield (outer conductor) is extended and folded back on the cable. The folded shield and the center conductor form the dipole.

FIGURE 7.15   A diagram of a ½ λ "rubber duck" dipole

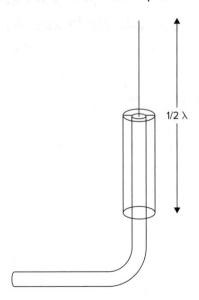

Figure 7.16 shows a picture of this type of antenna with the plastic removed. Note that the center conductor is only 2.6 cm long instead of 3.1 cm, which is ¼ the wavelength of 802.11g in air. The reason for this is that the pin is surrounded with a dielectric material that has an effective dielectric constant of 1.42. The wavelength shrinks by the following factor:

$$\sqrt{1.42} = .19$$

which occurs in the presence of the dielectric.

FIGURE 7.16   A ½ λ "rubber duck" dipole without plastic covering

Figure 7.17 and Figure 7.18 are similar types of dipole antenna. Figure 7.17 shows a cable with a ¼ λ antenna connected to the center pin. The shield is connected to a ground plane. The ground acts as a mirror, so the other part of the ½ λ antenna is a reflection of the center pin ¼ λ element of the antenna. The antenna is called a ¼ λ whip antenna but it is really a ½ λ dipole. The second half of the dipole is a virtual ¼ λ element. This is a common design for automobiles and trucks. The ground plane is the vehicle itself. Sometimes if the ground plane is impractical because of size, the type of antenna in Figure 7.18 is used. The ¼ λ radials are wires that extend out, usually at a 45° angle from the horizontal plane. The radials act just like the ground in the previous figure. The ¼ λ radials are a high impedance (open circuit) at one end. As you learned earlier when we discussed transmission lines, if one end of a radial is open, the end connected to the coax shield is a short or ground. Just like the ground plane in the previous figure, the radials will act as a mirror and reflect the ¼ λ element on the center conductor providing a second virtual ¼ λ element.

FIGURE 7.17   A diagram of a ¼ λ whip antenna

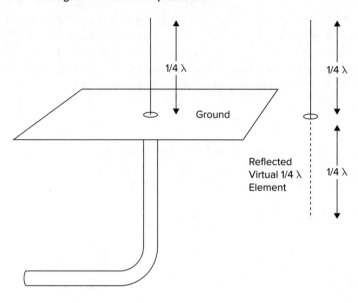

FIGURE 7.18   A diagram of a ¼ λ whip antenna with grounding radials

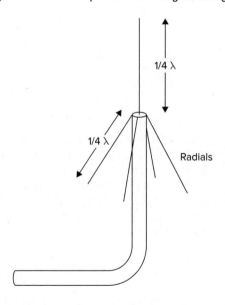

Patch

Most ceiling mount omni antennas are patch antennas with a gain from 3 to 6 dBi. Their low profile make them ideal for that application. A patch antenna is essentially two metal plates connected to a cable. It has a ground plate that is connected to the shield of the cable. The center conductor is connected to the other plate, which acts as the antenna. There is a dielectric between the antenna and the ground plate. Figure 7.19 shows a diagram of a rectangular patch antenna.

FIGURE 7.19   A diagram of a rectangular patch antenna

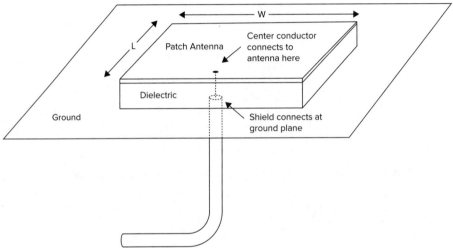

Where the center conductor connects to the antenna plate is the main factor that determines the input impedance of the antenna. The dimension L (length) determines the resonance frequency of the antenna. The dimension W (width) affects bandwidth and gain and has little effect on the frequency of operation. Generally a wider patch has a wider bandwidth and higher gain. If the width gets too large, however, the antenna pattern will degrade with high side lobe levels. A rectangular patch closely mimics two ½ λ dipole antennas that are separated by the width W. The dimension L is a ½ λ in length.

A patch antenna can also take on shapes other than a rectangle; a circle is one of the popular ones.

Parabolic Dish

A dish or parabolic antenna is commonly used for point-to-point links given its high gain. Figure 7.20 shows a typical parabolic antenna.

FIGURE 7.20   A parabolic dish antenna

Source: Bidgee via Wikipedia

The dish of the antenna concentrates the signal to a focal point where there is a small directional antenna. The gain of a dish is directly related to its aperture. The aperture of a dish is simply the area of the circle made by its outer rim.

$$G = \frac{4\pi\eta A}{\lambda^2}$$

where η (eta) equals the efficiency of the dish, A is the aperture, λ (lambda) is the wavelength, and G is the power gain over an isotropic antenna. Calculating gain in dBi is 10 * log(G). A dish typically has a 60 percent efficiency though it can vary from 40 to 80 percent with different feed configurations. The difficulty illuminating the dish uniformly with the feed antenna at the focal point leads to the relatively poor efficiency of the dish. There is a desire to spread out the power evenly over the whole dish without allowing power to spill out past the edges. Other inefficiencies are due to surface roughness of the dish and feed blockage (the feed partially blocks the signals coming to and from the dish). Surface roughness becomes a larger issue at high gain levels—that is, greater than 35 dBi. You will find lower gain parabolic antennas in noncritical applications constructed with a mesh dish. Surface roughness is measured as a function of wavelength. As long as the sides of the squares that make up the mesh are less than ⅛ λ, the surface roughness will be low enough for most applications. For high-performance, high-gain applications, such as satellite dish antennas or terrestrial microwave links, the dish should be solid or a fine mesh and smooth.

Horn

A horn is a medium- to high-gain waveguide antenna. Figure 7.21 shows a diagram of a rectangular horn. It is fed with a small dipole antenna or probe in a cylindrical or rectangular box. The box has a closed end and an open end. The open end of the box is attached to a cone or pyramid that has a continually increasing aperture. The cone/pyramid part of the horn is used to transform the impedance of the waveguide box at one end to a value that can efficiently transfer power to the air. Horns generally have wide bandwidths and are very efficient (low loss). They are commonly used as feed antennas for dishes.

FIGURE 7.21   A diagram of a horn antenna

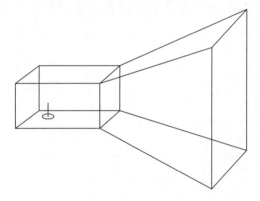

Phased Array

A phased array is an antenna that is composed of several antennas joined together by a feed network. The array can be made up of any type of antenna. Typically the antennas are arranged in a line or over an area. Each element in the array gets a copy of the signal with its own phase and amplitude. The phase change can be used to steer the antenna, as shown in Figure 7.22. In this figure, the phase of antenna element 1 is adjusted to constructively interfere with 2, 3, and 4 in the direction toward the right. Elements 2, 3, and 4 are similarly adjusted. In other directions, the phases destructively interfere and the amplitude is reduced.

FIGURE 7.22 A diagram of a phased array antenna

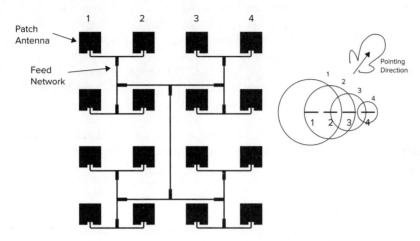

Phased arrays for 802.11 are generally high-gain antennas designed for a fixed angle. High-gain panel antennas are often phase array patch antennas. Keeping the loss of the phased array feed network low is the most challenging part of an array's design. Air dielectric feeds tend to be the lowest loss. A feed network made from a cheap printed circuit board or thin cable can be lossy and cause inefficiencies. If you are unsure, take the antenna apart and examine it.

Yagi

The yagi antenna was invented by H. Yagi and S. Uda in 1926. The yagi is a type of array antenna that is relatively easy to design and is tolerant of manufacturing variations. Figure 7.23 shows the basic elements of a yagi antenna. There is one driven element that is connected to the transmission line and one reflection element that sits behind. The front of the antenna has a number of director elements that determine the gain of the antenna. Typically the elements are a thin rod, but other kinds of yagi antennas are possible, including ones that have circular disks or rings.

FIGURE 7.23 A diagram of a yagi antenna

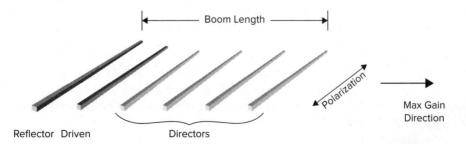

If the elements are thin (small diameter), each of the elements of a yagi antenna will have a length close to ½ wavelength. At 2.4 and 5.2 GHz, ½ wavelength is 6.2 and 2.9 cm, respectively. The reflection element is slightly longer than ½ wavelength and the director elements are slightly shorter. The driven element length is somewhere between the two. A yagi antenna with thick elements (large diameter) will have shorter elements. Typically the spacing of elements in a yagi are spaced from ¼ to ⅓ wavelength apart. The boom length, which is the distance from the reflection element to the last director element, determines the gain.

Figure 7.24 shows how gain varies with boom length with a typical yagi design. Note how a doubling of the yagi length from 2.14 wavelengths to 4.39 wavelengths increases the gain by only 2.6 dB. At gains above 20 dBi, the yagi becomes a less attractive option, given the size of the antenna.

FIGURE 7.24   A typical yagi antenna design shown as a plot of the data in Table 7.2

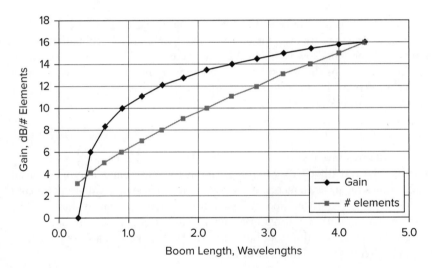

The most difficult part of yagi design is maintaining an adequate *front-to-back ratio (F/B)*. Yagi datasheets will often quote very high F/B, sometimes over 30 dB. These kinds of F/B are achievable but only over a very narrow bandwidth and for low- to medium-gain antennas. Also, even if the F/B ratio was quoted properly, the highest gain at the rear of the antenna may not be directly pointing to the back, but may be pointing at an angle off from 180°. Practical F/B for yagi antennas are values closer to 10 to 15dB. The antenna pattern of a yagi antenna is shown in Figure 7.25. This antenna is quoted to have an F/B that is greater than 20 dB. However, there are lobes at 120° and 240° that are only 15 dB below the boresight gain.

NOTE   Boresight refers to the optical axis of a directional antenna.

FIGURE 7.25   Yagi F/B and side lobes showing higher lobes to the side than back

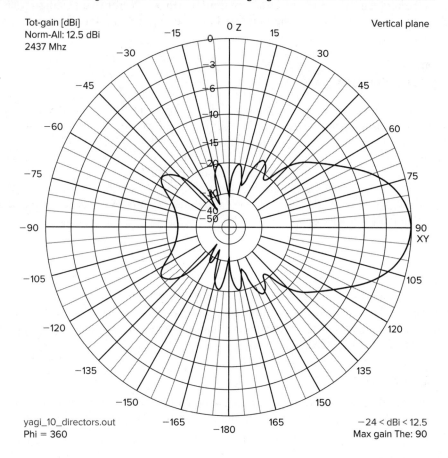

Sector Antennas

Sector antennas are used in outdoor systems to provide high gain, good front-to-back ratio, and wide coverage area. You might think that high gain and wide coverage are mutually exclusive. The sector antenna achieves broad coverage in the horizontal direction. Typically the horizontal beamwidth is 65° to 90°. The vertical beamwidth is generally 10° to 15° with a gain from 14 to 20 dBi. The pattern looks like a flat pancake. At the top of a tall tower, only a small vertical beamwidth is needed. Typically the area around the tower is split up into three equal pie slices, or sectors. The broad horizontal beamwidth of the sector antenna is used to cover one third of the area around the tower. Although sector antenna designs vary widely, they typically have a reflector behind the radiating element or elements. This increases gain and improves the front-to-back ratio (described later). The antenna reflector acts similarly to a reflector in a flashlight that directs light radiation forward. The elements in the sector antenna are often part of a phased array.

Antenna Properties

Using the proper antenna is one of the most critical components to WLAN designs. While APs that use built-in antennas work fine in most indoor office environments, external antennas can greatly improve the coverage and performance of APs. In fact, using an external antenna, you can gain coverage quality and improve distance while even shielding yourself from interference and RF transmissions from other APs.

There are more aspects to antennas than just the shape of its radiation pattern. In this section, we will discuss various factors relating to antennas and how they will affect the details of your WLAN RF design.

Gain

An antenna's gain is one of the most important properties of an antenna. It is a measure of an antenna's ability to concentrate a radio signal. It is usually measured against the performance of an ideal isotropic antenna that radiates in all directions equally. It can also be measured against the performance of an ideal quarter-wave dipole. The former is measured in dBi, the latter in dBd.

Frequency Band

Like gain, the frequency band of operation is a very important antenna characteristic. It is the range of frequencies that the antenna can maintain its pattern, gain, and return loss.

Pattern

The 3D antenna pattern of a dipole antenna is shown in Figure 7.26, and the vertical and horizontal polar plots are shown in Figure 7.27. The dipole length is along the Z-axis. Two angles determine direction: theta (θ) and phi (φ).

Figure 7.28 shows how the direction angle is referenced. The angle from the Z-axis is theta and the angle from the X-axis to the dotted line shown in the diagram is phi.

FIGURE 7.26   3D dipole antenna pattern

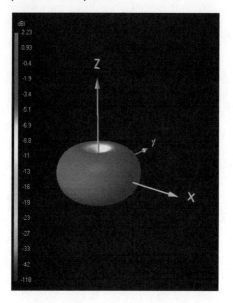

FIGURE 7.27   Vertical and Horizontal polar antenna plots

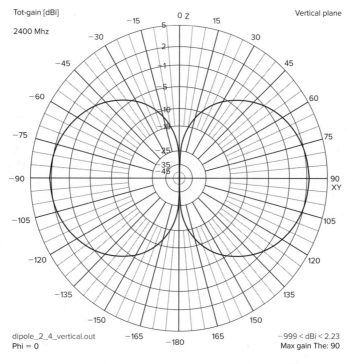

Vertical

(Continues)

FIGURE 7.27 (Continued)

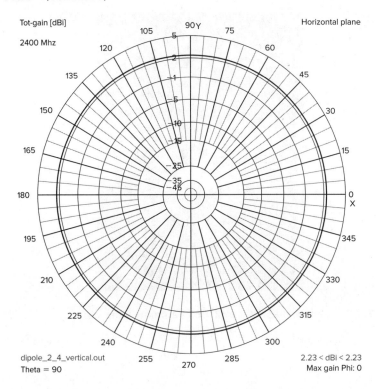

Horizontal

Along the Z-axis (theta = 0°) there is no gain. On the X/Y plane (theta = 90°), the gain is maximum and is constant over all phi directions. The 3D plots show by color the gain of the antenna in various directions. The polar plots show the same thing by the distance from the origin where the axes meet. The vertical polar plot shows a slice of the 3D plot at phi = 0°. The Z and X axes are shown. The horizontal polar plot shows a slice of the 3D plot at theta = 90°. The X and Y axes are shown. Generally the two polar plots, vertical and horizontal, will intersect the highest gain point of the antenna. That direction is usually along theta = 0° or theta = 90° and phi = 0°. In the polar plots, the true gain is often not shown. What is shown is relative gain. The highest relative gain shown in that kind of plot is 0 dB. In that case, the maximum gain in dBi or dBd should be printed somewhere on the plot.

FIGURE 7.28   A diagram showing theta (θ) and phi (φ) direction reference

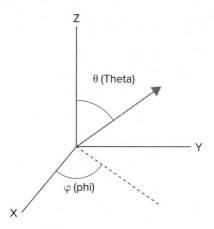

Impedance

Earlier we discussed impedance and transmission lines. An antenna is a common load at the end of a transmission line. They are designed to give an impedance close to 50 ohms at its operating frequency to match the transmission line impedance. Generally a good antenna will have a VSWR spec of 1.5:1 or better over the band of interest. This is equivalent to a 14 dB return loss. It is important that the antenna be mounted away from metal or dielectrics so that this VSWR can be maintained. Outside the band of interest for the antenna, the VSWR is generally very large, so it is important to get an antenna that is designed for the band of interest. Sometimes it is difficult for certain types of antennas to be tuned over the whole 5 GHz 802.11a/n(5) spectrum and some are designed for the upper or lower band only. Check whether this is the case before deploying.

Bandwidth

Antennas act like a bandpass filter. They will pass energy at some frequencies and reflect back power at others. Figure 7.29 shows a plot of return loss over frequency for a 2.4 GHz antenna (strictly speaking, it is the negative of the RL since RL is positive). This kind of plot is typical for an antenna. The plot shows that the antenna has a better than 15 dB return loss over the 2.4 band.

FIGURE 7.29   Antenna return loss over frequency

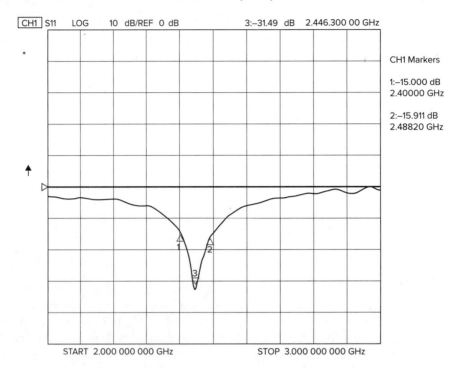

Note also that the return loss goes to 0 dB at the right of the figure. This is a good thing. It shows that the cable loss and loss inside the antenna is very small. If there was significant loss in the cable or antenna, the RL would show it outside of the tuned band. If sizable loss is showing up in the plot, the antenna may be causing problems with the radio link. Antenna power loss is power that cannot be recovered on both the transmit and the receive side. It can mean less transmitted power or higher receive noise figure. If there is loss in the cable used to make the measurement and that loss was not calibrated out, a bad VSWR in the antenna would be masked by the lossy cable. This may mean that a measured RL of 15 dB is actually 10 dB and 5 dB was added by a 2.5 dB loss in the cable.

Beamwidth

Beamwidth is related to antenna gain. A high-gain antenna sends radio power over a narrow angle. A low-gain antenna sends it over a wide angle. Figure 7.30 shows what is called the 3 dB beamwidth of the dipole discussed earlier. The 3 dB beamwidth is the angle where the gain has fallen by ½ or a decrease of 3 dB. For the dipole shown, the 3 dB beamwidth is 76°. The polar plot used to measure the 3 dB beamwidth was the vertical one, so it is actually the vertical beamwidth that is 76°. The horizontal beamwidth for the dipole is 360°, meaning that power radiates in all directions equally horizontally. A relative gain plot was used to make the beamwidth measurement. It is easy to see from the plot where the gain has fallen by 3 dB.

FIGURE 7.30   The 3 dB beamwidth of a dipole antenna is 76°.

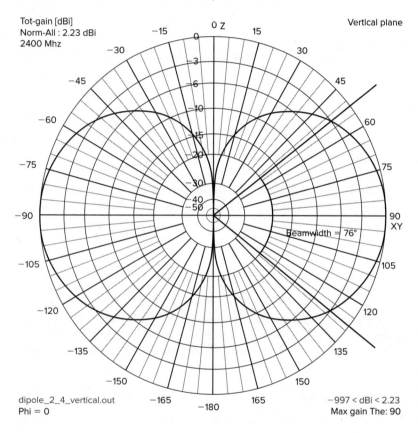

Efficiency

Efficiency of an antenna is a measure of its loss characteristics. Losses can be due to the following:

- VSWR mismatches
- Conductor losses
- Dielectric losses
- Misdirected energy

The efficiency of an antenna is the ratio of the power radiated to the input power. It is usually expressed as a percentage. The number is less than 100 percent (no antenna is completely lossless). The radiated power is less than the input of the antenna because of loss:

$$\varepsilon = \frac{P_{radiated}}{P_{input}}$$

Array antennas sometimes suffer from lower efficiency because of the signal distribution network. Parabolic dishes also generally have poor efficiency, which lowers its gain. Dipoles, patch, and horn antennas all have high efficiency and almost no loss.

Polarization

Radio waves generally come out of an antenna with what is called linear *polarization*, which is a vertical or horizontal direction or polarity. A dipole antenna that is oriented vertically sends out its radio signal with a vertical polarization. If a vertically polarized transmitted signal is received by a vertical dipole antenna, the signal at the receiver will be at a maximum. If the dipole antenna at the receiver is horizontally polarized, the received signal can be reduced by several tens of decibels. It is always critical to match the polarization of the transmit and the receive antennas. In practice, however, the signal is often reflected many times between the two antennas, which can randomize the polarization, causing less severe effects. Regardless, there is usually degradation in performance due topolarity mismatches, which should always be avoided if possible.

Circular polarization is a combination of vertical and horizontal polarization. There are also two types of circular polarization, called right hand and left hand. As with linear polarization, the transmit and the receive antennas should be matched with the same type to have maximum transfer of power. A circularly polarized signal received by a linearly polarized antenna will get half the power (−3 dB) than a correctly circularly polarized antenna.

Back and Side Lobes

High-gain antennas will radiate in directions other than that of the main lobe. The amplitude of the side lobes and the lobe in the back are important to characterize for certain applications. It is sometimes a good idea to limit power in a particular direction, such as when two APs are close together and connected to high-gain antennas pointed away from each other. Figure 7.31 shows a horizontal polar plot of a 15.7 dBi gain antenna. The side lobes shown are 17.3 dB down from the main lobe, which gives it a gain ±60° from the boresight of −1.6 dBi. The side lobe in the back is 24.6 dB down from the main lobe and has a gain of −8.9 dBi. The front-to-back ratio (F/B) of the antenna is the ratio of the gain of the front lobe to the gain of the lobe in the rear, which is 24.6 dB for this antenna. An F/B of 20 dB or better is considered to be a good value.

FIGURE 7.31   Horizontal polar antenna plot showing back and side lobes

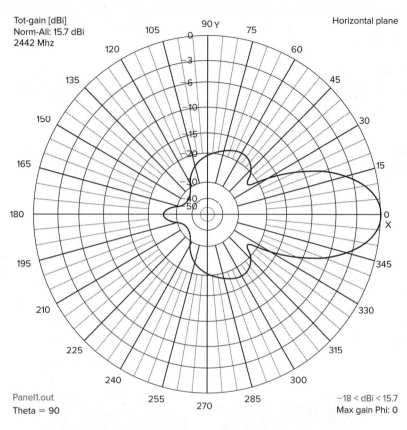

Tot-gain [dBi]
Norm-All: 15.7 dBi
2442 Mhz

Horizontal plane

Panel1.out
Theta = 90

−18 < dBi < 15.7
Max gain Phi: 0

It is feasible in some scenarios to make use of these back and side lobes in order to provide coverage to where client devices will need service.

Environmental Effects

Examine an antenna, and you will find that it is made of metal parts and dielectrics. The metal parts of the antenna do not even have to be touching each other. It should be clear that bringing metal or dielectrics close to an antenna can have a dramatic effect on performance.

Figure 7.32 shows antenna patterns of a dipole antenna near a metal plate. It shows that as the dipole gets closer to the plate, the antenna pattern changes radically. The metal plate acts as a kind of mirror to the dipole. From a far-away observer, the dipole looks like two dipoles, one actual and one reflection, each radiating with the same signal. This causes the interference pattern that you see in many of the pictures in Figure 7.32. Notice how when the antenna is brought very close to the plate, the pattern becomes well behaved. This is a common antenna design, where a dipole sits in front of a reflector.

FIGURE 7.32   3D antenna pattern of a dipole near a metal plate

In addition to the pattern, metal and dielectrics near an antenna can change its tuning. An antenna that is tuned to operate at one frequency band changes to another band. Instead of a nice transfer of power from the transmitter to the air, the antenna reflects a large amount of the power back into the radio. Placing the antenna near these materials can turn an expensive, well-tuned antenna into a device that performs no better than a coat hanger.

Metal in close proximity will have a more dramatic effect on an antenna than a dielectric. Most building materials are poor dielectrics and are not a big concern. Dry wood, wallboard, concrete blocks, and ceiling tiles are not a big concern. Water, glass, and certain plastics and ceramics can cause problems. Some building materials have metal embedded in them, such as tinted or UV coated glass and reinforced concrete. Antenna placement near these materials should be avoided. In critical deployment applications, it is important to check signal performance over the whole area covered by an antenna regardless of what is near the antenna.

802.11n

802.11n provides a substantial throughput increase over the "legacy" 802.11a/b/g standards. The standard introduced 40 MHz and MIMO (Multiple In, Multiple Out) operations, which can increase the raw data rate from a maximum of 54 Mbps to upward of 600 Mbps. The increase in frequency bandwidth from 20 MHz to 40 MHz brings about a more than doubling of the channel capacity. MIMO is a spatial multiplexing technique that allows multiple data paths to be transmitted at once. The earlier standards used SISO (Single In, Single Out) with only one data path. When all we used to have was SISO technology, we didn't become accustomed to the term, but you should start to become familiar with using SISO as a new term in Wi-Fi communications.

Yet these channel data rate increases come with a cost. The 40 MHz operation reduces the number of different frequency channels available. At 5 GHz there are enough frequencies available that this might make sense. At 2.4 GHz, although technically allowed, 40 MHz operations would effectively reduce the number of channels available from three to two: one 40 MHz channel and one legacy 20 MHz channel. This is why the Wi-Fi alliance (which certifies interoperability among manufacturers) has not certified 40 MHz operation at 2.4 GHz. Frankly put, 40 MHz channels used in the 2.4 GHz band should be strictly relegated to home use.

MIMO requires radios to have duplicate transmit and receive circuits, which draw more power and are more costly than a SISO radio. MIMO also requires multiple antennas separated ideally by at least half a wavelength, which can pose a problem for client devices.

802.11n radios use a complex system of spatial multiplexing (SM) and receive diversity to achieve high data rates in a multipath and varying SNR environment. Radio systems differ in the *algorithms* they use and how they perform under these conditions. In other words, not all manufacturers' products will perform MIMO operations equally. When comparing the performance between WLAN equipment suppliers or characterizing a selected supplier, measure actual performance in the environment in which the equipment will be used. You should vary the SNR levels (vary the distance between AP and client) and the number of clients. Be sure to perform testing in the variety of multipath conditions that will be present in the deployed location, such as crowded offices and open spaces. If the system requires mobility, such as WLAN voice, handoff testing between APs is a vital part of performance characterization.

802.11n has much higher performance than the earlier standards b, g, and a. In the following sections, we will explore where this performance comes from. You will learn about MIMO, channel bonding, guard interval (GI), and frame aggregation, all of which are changes from the earlier standard and increase data rates. We will show how each change adds up to a significant performance improvement.

MIMO

Multiple In, Multiple Out (MIMO) can have a dramatic effect on data rate. The standard allows for up to four MIMO data streams. Each data stream is capable of sending up to 72.2 Mbps of raw data, for a maximum of 288.9 Mbps in a 20 MHz channel. Figure 7.33 shows the basic operation. The radio transmitter transmits different information on each transmit antenna. Each receive antenna will receive all the signals from each of the transmitting antennas. It is the job of the receiver to tease out the original transmitted signal from the multiple copies it received. A high degree of multipath, which is typical of indoor deployments, actually helps the MIMO receiver clearly differentiate between the various data paths. There is also information imbedded in each data stream that helps the receiver estimate each data channel's properties.

FIGURE 7.33 A basic MIMO operation

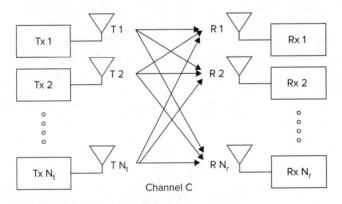

Channel C

It is important in MIMO to count the number of transmitting antennas, receiving antennas, and the number of data channels in a radio. As we have mentioned earlier in this book, 802.11n devices are not created equally. These numbers can be expressed as A × B: C, where A is the number of transmit antennas, B is the number of receive antennas, and C is the number of spatial channels.

This nomenclature is not universally accepted, but it's useful because it is compact and for that reason we will use it here. The Cisco 1250 series datasheet describes the AP as having "2 × 3 MIMO with two spatial streams" which would read compactly as 2 × 3:2. The number of spatial data channels has a direct impact on data rate. For example, three data paths can transfer three times the data rate as one. The extra antennas beyond the channel number improves the SNR of the receive signal and guards against fading by providing spatially separated duplicate versions of the same signal. Commonly available configurations in access points are 2 × 2:2, 2 × 3:2, and 3 × 3:2. Some 3 × 3:3 devices are available. Access points are required to transmit and receive on at least two spatial streams. Smaller client devices tend to have fewer antennas than access points due to limited space for antennas. This is not necessarily the case with laptop computers. Also, some clients will transmit only one stream to conserve power. Client devices are required to transmit only one stream but must receive at least two. The standard allows for 4 × 4:4 for the highest data rates.

Very high raw data rates are theoretically possible with MIMO. In practice, however, these data rates may be difficult to achieve. The technique relies on a certain amount of multipath, which is not always present. Also, spatial multiplexing (SM), which will be described in more detail in the next section, works best in a high SNR environment. Adding more paths adds more capacity. At lower SNR levels, the multiple transmit antennas do not improve transmission performance, but the multiple receive antennas do. When SNR is low, receive diversity usually provides a better capacity gain than SM. Adding more spatial paths does not always improve performance.

802.11n uses multiple transmit and receive paths within the radio as part of MIMO. The multiple paths are used for spatial multiplexing, as described earlier. They are also used for various transmit and receive diversity techniques. Space-time block coding (STBC) and cyclic shift diversity (CSD) are transmit diversity techniques where the same transmit data is sent out of multiple antennas. STBC communication is possible only between 802.11n devices. CSD diversity signals can be received by either 802.11n or legacy devices. Transmit beamforming (TxBF) is a technique where the same signal is transmitted over multiple antennas and they act like a phased array. Maximal ratio combining (MRC) is a type of receive diversity technique where multiple received signals are combined, thus improving sensitivity.

Spatial Multiplexing

Spatial multiplexing (SM) is central to the workings of MIMO. Signals from a number of transmitters (N_t) are sent out and received by a number of receivers (N_r). Each receiver detects signals from each of the transmitters. For three transmit antennas and one receiver, the combination mathematically looks like this:

$$R_1 = C_{11}T_1 + C_{12}T_2 + C_{13}T_3$$

where C_{11}, C_{12}, and C_{13} are the channels between receiver 1 and transmitters 1, 2, and 3, respectively. All of the distortions imposed on the transmitted signal by the channel, including multipath fading and loss, are included in the C number. R_1 is the combined signal received by receive antenna 1 by all of the transmitted signals through the various channels. T_1, T_2, and T_3 are the data signals transmitted by transmitter 1, 2, and 3, respectively. The formula shows that the signal received by receiver 1 is a combination of the transmitted signals from transmitters 1, 2, and 3 that traveled through the air and bounced all around.

For four receive antennas, the formula becomes a little more complex:

$$R_1 = C_{11}T_1 + C_{12}T_2 + C_{13}T_3$$
$$R_2 = C_{21}T_1 + C_{22}T_2 + C_{23}T_3$$
$$R_3 = C_{31}T_1 + C_{32}T_2 + C_{33}T_3$$
$$R_4 = C_{41}T_1 + C_{42}T_2 + C_{43}T_3$$

The trick is for the receiver to figure out what the different C components are and then, using some matrix mathematics, figure out what was transmitted as T_1, T_2, and T_3—that is, the original transmitted data.

Along with the data sent by the transmitters, training signals give the receiver clues about the various channel C values. These training signals allow the receiver to compare what it is receiving from each transmitter to what it knows was transmitted. This way, the receiver keeps track of how the channels changed each T and can continually calculate the T values as the channels change over time. More details are discussed on training signals in the section "Protection Modes."

Those familiar with matrix math may have noticed that there are more equations than unknowns. It turns out that having more receive antennas than is strictly necessary can help the receiver come up with a better estimate of the channel's C values and a better estimate of the transmitted data (T) sent.

Space Time Block Coding

Space time block coding (STBC) is a method where the same information is transmitted on two or more antennas. It is a type of transmit diversity. By sending copies of the same signal on multiple antennas, the actual rate of the data transmitted does not increase as transmit antennas are added. The rate does, however, increase the receiver's ability to detect signals at a lower SNR than would be otherwise possible. The receive sensitivity of the radio system improves.

In a two–transmit antenna STBC system, OFDM symbols are grouped in pairs. The two symbols, which we will call s1 and s2, are transmitted out of the two antennas at different times. Antenna 1 will transmit s1 and antenna 2 will transmit −s2* (the minus sign and the * will be explained momentarily). Next, antenna 1 will transmit s2 and antenna 2 will transmit s1*. Before transmitting its symbols, antenna 2 performs a mathematical operation called conjugation (denoted by the *), which flips the top of the symbol's constellation to the bottom and the bottom to the top. The negative sign flips the right side of the constellation to the left and the left to the right. By transmitting pairs of symbols in this fashion, a relatively simple receiver can be devised that combines the energy from both transmitted signals, thus improving the SNR. Larger numbers of transmit antennas require a larger number of symbols to be grouped together and transmitted at different times.

Cyclic Shift Diversity

Cyclic shift diversity (CSD) is another transmit diversity technique specified in the 802.11n standard. Unlike STBC, a signal from a transmitter that uses CSD can be received by legacy 802.11g and 802.11a devices. For Mixed mode deployments where 802.11n coexists with 802.11g and 802.11a devices, there is a need to have a way of transmitting the symbols in the legacy OFDM preamble over multiple transmit antennas. If the same signal was transmitted, the multiple antennas would act as a beamforming antenna. To avoid this, CSD is used and a cyclic delay is applied to each of the transmitted signals. The delays are calculated to minimize the correlation between the multiple signals. A conventional legacy system would treat the multiple received signals as multipath versions of the same signal. The cyclic delay is chosen to be within the limits of the guard interval (GI) so that it doesn't cause excessive intersymbol interference (ISI). An 802.11n system has no problem using the multiple signals to improve the overall SNR of the preamble.

The details of how CSD works will not be part of the CWDP exam. CSD is one of the finer and least discussed features of 802.11n but nonetheless still important to equipment vendor radio designers.

Transmit Beamforming

If there are more transmit antennas than data streams, it is possible to use the antennas as a phased array. The transmitted signals can be phased in a way that allows for pointing of the transmitted signal to improve the signal levels at the receiver. This technique works if the transmitter is told details about the channel by the receiving station. Currently, this technique is not widely used.

When transmit beamforming (TxBF) is used in a MIMO system with, for example, two transmit radios as with a 2×2 or 2×3 array, the total amount of signal power improvement that can be achieved is only *up to* 3 dB. If the number of transmitters is four, as with a 4×4 array, the total amount of signal boost is *up to* 6 dB. As you will recall, the reason for this is that with every +3 dB change in signal, the power is doubled. Adding another +3 dB doubles the signal again.

The reason why we state *up to* is that it is assumed that the transmitter has calculated and performed the phase transmission perfectly and nothing else has changed in the environment where the maximum signal level is achieved at the location of the receiver.

Maximal Ratio Combining

Maximal ratio combining (MRC) is a receive diversity technique that is more sophisticated and better performing than the legacy technique. 802.11 radios generally have more than one receive radio. In 802.11a/b/g radios, there is typically one transmitter antenna sending a signal to a set of two diversity receiver antennas with two separate receiver circuits. The number of receivers can be more than two, but the principle is the same. The two receive antennas are positioned so that if one receiver is in a deep fade, the other sees a strong signal. An 802.11a/b/g radio will reject the signal from the receiver with the worst SNR and use only the one with better SNR. Reliability of received signal is improved because the better of the two signals was selected. It is not optimum, however, if the signal that is thrown away is usable.

802.11n improves the performance of the receiver by mathematically combining both signals. It would not help to combine them directly; that would likely cause more multipath fading. The 802.11n radio detects the nature of the two channels that the signals passed through and modifies the signals according to the channel characteristics it computed before combining. Each received signal is shifted in phase so they combine coherently. Their amplitudes are modified to favor the signal with the best SNR so that noise figure is not affected. The receive-combining function occurs on a tone-by-tone basis in the OFDM signal. Each tone's SNR and relative phase is assessed before combining. This is important because fading often varies across the frequency band. This effect is even more drastic as channel widths have increased to 40 MHz.

The channel characteristics are determined using known training signals that are sent along with the OFDM signal. Each receiver branch uses the training signal to determine how much the phase has changed and the channel quality. That information is used to properly align the different received signals in phase and amplitude before combining.

Protection Modes

A typically deployed 802.11n network will have legacy 802.11a/b/g stations that coexist with 802.11n stations. This is due to minimal penetration of 802.11n-capable radios. This mixture of radio types requires three modes of operation for 802.11n systems:

- Legacy mode
- Mixed mode
- Greenfield mode

A system of APs and client stations can be operating in any or all of the three modes. The AP will sense the modes that the client devices can operate in and adjust its operating mode to accommodate them.

Legacy Mode

In *Legacy mode*, legacy 802.11a/b/g systems coexist with 802.11n systems. The transmission and reception of signals between legacy radios are unchanged from the usual method used with non-802.11n systems. Transmission between a legacy radio and a MIMO-capable system allows for the use of receive diversity in the MIMO radio, therefore improving the quality of received transmissions from legacy devices. A transmitting 802.11n radio in Legacy mode only transmits on a single antenna, mimicking an SISO radio.

The frame structure of 802.11n is the same as 802.11a and g and is shown in Figure 7.34. The first part of the preamble is called the Legacy Short Training Field (L-STF) and is made up of 10 identical short BPSK symbols transmitted at 6 Mbps without coding or GI. Not every OFDM tone contains the training field; it's on only 12 of the total number spread across the whole bandwidth. The receiver uses the short symbols of the L-STF to roughly determine the frequency and phase of the signal that allows it to lock on.

FIGURE 7.34 The Legacy mode frame structure

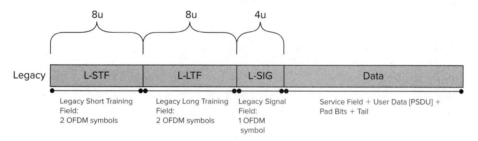

The second part of the preamble is the Legacy Long Training Field (L-LTF). It is carried on all the OFDM tones. The long training symbols are 6 Mbps BPSK signals with no coding and have a GI to protect against ISI. The L-LTF is followed by the Legacy Signal (L-SIG), which is transmitted as 6 Mbps BPSK, 1/2 rate code and uses all the OFDM tones. L-SIG contains information about the rate and length of the data field. The data field follows L-SIG and contains the data payload of the 802.11 frame.

Once the receiver locks using the L-STF, it can use the long training symbols to fine-tune timing. In order for OFDM to work properly, the receiver needs to know the exact frequency and phasing of each tone. The training symbols are known by the receiver and are used to determine the exact tone timing so that the receiver can demodulate them.

When 802.11 (1 and 2 Mbps) and 802.11b (5.5 and 11 Mbps) transmissions are sent in Legacy mode, the same protections mechanisms exist as mentioned earlier, but the protection mechanisms employed with 802.11g when 802.11 and 802.11b clients are present also apply.

Mixed Mode

Mixed mode also allows 802.11n radios to coexist with legacy equipment but allows transmissions at the higher rates. 802.11n radios signal each other with high throughput (HT) frames but can signal legacy stations at lower speeds. The preamble is identical to Legacy mode. This allows legacy systems to co-habitat in the presence of 802.11n systems and interact properly.

The difference between the Legacy and Mixed modes happens in the data payload part of the frame. Figure 7.35 shows the structure of the Mixed mode frame. The L-STF, L-LTF, and L-SIG part of the frame are identical to the Legacy frame modes of operation. To work properly, 802.11n needs specialized training sequences that are specific to spatial diversity and MRC. The HT Signal (HT-SIG) contains information about the Modulation and Coding Scheme (MCS) index, frame length, the bandwidth (20 MHz or 40 MHz), STBC, short GI (Guard Interval), and frame aggregation. The HT Short Training Field (HT-STF) contains information for the receiver to improve its understanding of signal levels in a multiple transmit/receive system. The HT Long Training Field (HT-LTF) allows the receiver to accurately estimate the channel over which the signal traveled. It compares the received signal to the known signal structure to make the estimate of each data stream channel. The number of HT-LTFs in the HT preamble is determined by the number of special data streams and number of transmit antennas.

FIGURE 7.35 The Mixed mode frame structure

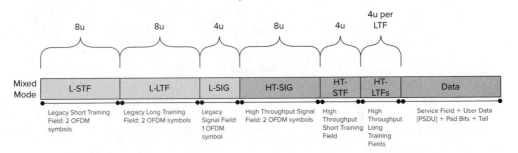

In both the Mixed and Legacy modes, HT protection requires 802.11n radios to use RTS/CTS (Request To Send/Clear To Send) or CTS-to-self messages to signal to legacy devices that the channel is in use. These mechanisms, along with the larger preamble header, lead to significant throughput reduction when compared to Greenfield mode, which we discuss next.

Greenfield Mode

An 802.11n system in *Greenfield mode* does not transmit the full legacy preamble. It does, however, transmit the L-STF that allows the radio to lock on to the signal. It then goes straight into the HT preamble.

No transmissions to legacy systems are possible when a radio is in Greenfield mode. Legacy systems will interpret Greenfield radio transmissions as noise and may transmit on top of them. This mode should only be used if there are no legacy devices, which is presently difficult to achieve at 2.4 GHz but may be possible at 5 GHz.

Figure 7.36 shows the frame structure of a Greenfield mode signal. The structure is similar to that of Mixed mode but is missing the legacy preamble and L-SIG that exist in the Legacy and Mixed modes. An 802.11n system in Greenfield mode can *receive* frames from legacy systems because its receiver features contain all the logic to support legacy transmissions.

FIGURE 7.36 The Greenfield mode frame structure

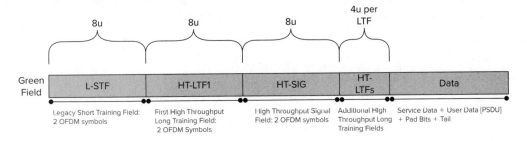

Operating Mode

The operating mode of an AP can adjust to the modes it sees operating in client stations. Using the beacon and probe response frames, HT stations can indicate to APs the types of client devices present in the environment. The HT Information Element contains the following fields:

- Operating Mode
- Non-Greenfield Stations Present
- OBSS Non-HT Stations Present

The Operating Mode field can have one of four values:

0 All stations in BSS are 20/40 MHz HT. All stations in a 20 MHz HT BSS are 20 MHz HT.

1 Some members on the primary or secondary channel (maybe in the presence of outside BSS stations) are non-HT.

2 All stations are HT but at least one is a 20 MHz–only station.

3 At least one legacy station is present in the BSS.

The Non-Greenfield Stations Present field indicates whether all the associated HT stations are Greenfield capable. The OBSS Non-HT Stations Present field indicates whether an overlapping BSS has non-HT stations associated with it. The AP sets its operating mode based on what it is able to observe from the HT Information Element advertisements from client stations.

Channel Bonding

802.11n has two bandwidth operations: 20 MHz and 40 MHz. In 40 MHz mode, two adjacent 20 MHz channels are chosen; one channel is classified as a primary channel and the other is designated as a secondary channel. In older literature they were called control and extension channels, respectively. The primary channel can be either higher or lower in frequency than the secondary. The primary channel is used to communicate to HT and non-HT 20 MHz–only stations within a BSS.

The frequency mask of a 40 MHz wide channel is shown in Figure 7.37. Note that the levels outside the 40 MHz signal are higher than those outside a 20 MHz signal. This added interference to adjacent channels can be seen in Figure 7.38.

FIGURE 7.37   40 MHz 802.11n frequency mask

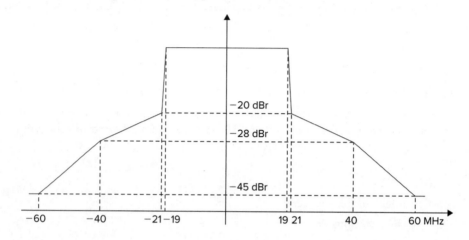

FIGURE 7.38   How a 40 MHz and a 20 MHz channel interferes with an adjacent channel

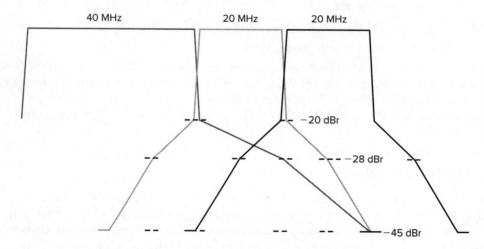

Doubling the bandwidth from 20 to 40 MHz will more than double the throughput capacity of an AP. The cost is fewer channels available for frequency reuse. A typical 2.4 GHz 802.11g deployment would use channels 1, 6, and 11, alternating the channels so that APs using the same frequency are not adjacent. This would be impossible if a 40 MHz wide channel was used. That would allow for a single 20 MHz channel at either 1 or 11 and a single 40 MHz channel. There would be no way to place APs such that adjacent APs would have different channels. For this reason, we don't recommend that you use a 40 MHz channel at 2.4 GHz. At 5 GHz there are twelve 20 MHz channels (not counting the UNII 2e range) that can be used to create six nonoverlapping 40 MHz channels.

Guard Interval

802.11g and 802.11a at the PHY rate of 54 Mbps each consists of 48 tones carrying data, which is minus the other OFDM pilot tones. Each of the 48 tones produces 250,000 symbols per second, where each symbol is 6 bits in size (64-QAM) at a ¾ coding rate. This is how we arrive at 54 Mbps. It can also be represented by the following formula:

48 tones × 250 ksps × 6 bits/symbol × ¾ coding rate = 54 Mbps

When we last discussed this topic, we mentioned that the tone spacing for 802.11 OFDM is 312.5 ksps and therefore the raw symbol rate must be 312.5 ksps to keep the tones orthogonal. The extra data is overhead that is called the *guard interval (GI)*. The data and guard interval symbol have a 4 μs (1/250 ksps = $4 \times 10 - 6$ seconds per symbol) duration. This can be broken up into the 0.8 μs (the same as 800 ns or 800×10^{-9} second) GI and the 3.2 μs data portion. The GI allows the receiver time to receive multiple versions of a signal without confusing it. It can allow up to 800 ns of delay from multipath without causing ISI.

In 800 ns, radio waves can travel a quarter of a km (800 ns * c = 0.24 km where c = speed of light). Therefore, 802.11g and 802.11a are designed to work with path differences of up to 0.24 km because they use an 800 ns GI.

Generally speaking, indoor applications have a maximum delay spread of 250 ns, which would make the 800 ns GI used in 802.11g and 802.11a overkill. 802.11n has a feature that allows the choice of GI. It can be changed from 800 ns to 400 ns, which results in an 11.1 percent throughput improvement. Except for specialized applications, a 400 ns GI is more than enough for use indoors to ensure that there is no ISI.

Modulation and Coding Scheme Rates

802.11 a/b/g physical layer data rates are pretty easy to remember; there are only a handful. 802.11n changed that situation with its MCS rates. There are 128 different possible rates; some are actually duplicated—for example, MCS index 1 and 8 have the same data rates as 5 and 11. Table 7.2 shows the breakdown of the various rates and how they relate to coding rate, modulation type, GI times, channel bonding, and spatial data channels. The 20 MHz rates are called HT20 rates (High throughput, 20 MHz) and the 40 MHz rates are called HT40 rates.

TABLE 7.2: 802.11n PHY layer data rates at varying coding rates, modulation types, GI times, channel bonding, and spatial data channels

MCS index	Spatial streams	Modulation type	Coding rate	Data rate Mbps			
				20 MHz channel		40 MHz channel	
				800ns GI	400ns GI	800ns GI	400ns GI
0	1	BPSK	½	6.5	7.2	13.5	15
1	1	QPSK	½	13	14.4	27	30
2	1	QPSK	¾	19.5	21.7	40.5	45
3	1	16-QAM	½	26	28.9	54	60
4	1	16-QAM	¾	39	43.3	81	90
5	1	64-QAM	⅔	52	57.8	108	120
6	1	64-QAM	¾	58.5	65	121.5	135
7	1	64-QAM	⅚	65	72.2	135	150
8	2	BPSK	½	13	14.4	27	30
9	2	QPSK	½	26	28.9	54	60
10	2	QPSK	¾	39	43.3	81	90
11	2	16-QAM	½	52	57.8	108	120
12	2	16-QAM	¾	78	86.7	162	180
13	2	64-QAM	⅔	104	115.6	216	240
14	2	64-QAM	¾	117	130	243	270
15	2	64-QAM	⅚	130	144.4	270	300
. . .	3	. . .	. . .	. . .	. . .	. . .	. . .
23	3	64-QAM	⅚	195	216.6	405	450
. . .	4	. . .	. . .	. . .	. . .	. . .	. . .
31	4	64-QAM	⅚	260	288.9	540	600

Frame Aggregation

802.11n has further improved overall efficiency by increasing frame size and reducing interframe gaps. Packet data received at an access point is broken up into frames for sending over the air. The maximum frame transmission size for the earlier standards was 2,304 bytes. Just as with any network protocol, each 802.11 frame comes with a certain amount of overhead. 802.11n has increased throughput by combining frames into one larger frame, thus reducing the overall overhead. There are two different methods for frame aggregation:

Aggregated MAC Service Data Unit (A-MSDU)   This can reach a length of 7,935 bytes. The *Aggregated MAC Service Data Unit (A-MSDU)* accumulates smaller frames that are heading for the same destination and are at the same quality of service (QOS) into a single larger frame. This can dramatically cut down on overhead but also makes each frame transmission more susceptible to receive errors due to RF issues like noise and interference. The benefits given by the larger frame size can only be realized in a high SNR environment.

Aggregated MAC Protocol Data Unit (A-MPDU)   This can reach a length of 65.535 bytes as compared to the standard 802.11 frame size limit of 2,304 bytes. The *Aggregated MAC Protocol Data Unit (A-MPDU)* frame aggregation is a little different. It allows a series of individual 802.11 frames to be sent one after the other with one access to the medium. Because each MPDU is sent with its headers, the overhead efficiencies are not quite as good as with A-MSDU. However, errors can be detected in individual PDU frames so that errors do not require a retransmission of the entire set of frames—just the one that was in error. This makes the A-MPDU less susceptible to noise than the A-MSDU.

802.11n also leverages the Block ACK policy introduced with 802.11e. From the perspective of frame aggregation, Block ACK is also available in 802.11n where a single acknowledgment frame is sent to confirm the receipt of multiple frames. This greatly improves efficiency by removing the need to transmit an ACK for every frame received.

Effects on Performance

The 802.11n standard has made many incremental and additive improvements to the original 802.11a/b/g standards. Changing the highest coding rate from 3/4 to 5/6 increased the MCS data rate by 11.1 percent. Increasing the number of tones in a 20 MHz frequency channel from 48 to 52 increased the data rate by another 8.3 percent. Changing the GI from 800 ns to 400 ns increased the data rate by 11.1 percent. Channel bonding two 20 MHz channels into one 40 MHz channel increased the data rate by 107.8 percent, more than doubling the data rate. The final improvement came with MIMO spatial multiplexing, which increased the top data rate by 300 percent by increasing the number of spatial streams by a factor of 4. Each of the increases adds up to a total factor of 11.11 times (1.111 * 1.083 * 1.111 * 2.078 * 4.00 = 11.11) increase in data rate. The maximum rate goes from 54 Mbps to 600 Mbps.

What about other techniques such as frame aggregation, MRC, and transmit beamforming? Frame aggregation does not affect the raw data rate capability of 802.11n. The amount of overhead and none of the CSMA/CA delays are factored into raw data rates. Frame aggregation does, however, have a dramatic effect on actual data throughput by eliminating a large amount of overhead that was in the earlier standard. Techniques such as MRC and transmit beamforming can improve on the received signal's SNR, which would make it possible to send data at higher data rates and a higher MCS index than would be possible otherwise.

Summary

Transmission lines, filters, and antennas are passive devices critical to the operation of any wireless system. In this chapter we discussed, in detail, concepts such as impedance and return loss. We also discussed the various types of connectors, cables, and antennas and their different uses. When you now look at spec sheets for antennas, you will understand the meaning of front-to-back ratio, horizontal and vertical patterns, polarization, gain, and return loss.

802.11n is gaining ground as a standard high-speed WLAN technology. Understanding its subtlety is critical to designing high-performance installations. This chapter has given you insight into the performance gains made from this technology and how to use it effectively.

Exam Essentials

Understand transmission line impedance and matching.   Understand what a good and bad VSWR is and how to calculate it.

Know the different connector types, both normal and RP.   Know what N-connector and RP-TNC connectors is are used for.

Know the various antenna types and in what applications they would be best used.

Know all the antenna properties.

Be able to read a polar antenna plot.

Understand the basic concepts of 802.11n radios.

Review Questions

1. Which connector is the largest?

   A. SMA

   B. RP-TNC

   C. N

   D. MMCX

2. Coax commonly comes in what two impedances?

   A. 50 and 300 ohms

   B. 50 and 100 ohms

   C. 50 and 75 ohms

   D. 100 and 300 ohms

3. The wavelength of a 5 GHz signal is 6 cm in air. What would the wavelength be in a cable with a relative dielectric value of 4?

   A. 6 cm

   B. 12 cm

   C. 3 cm

   D. 1.5 cm

4. There is a short circuit load on a lossless transmission line with a relative dielectric constant of 4. Where along the line would you expect an open circuit at 5 GHz?

   A. 6 cm from the load

   B. 0.75 cm from the load

   C. 1.5 cm from the load

   D. Nowhere on the line

5. A 50 ohm line is terminated with a 25 ohm resistor. What VSWR would that cause on the line?

   A. 1.0

   B. 5.0

   C. 3.0

   D. 2.0

6. A cable with 2.5 dB of loss is used to measure the return loss of an antenna. The measured value in-band is shown to be larger than 20 dB. What is the actual return loss of the antenna, and is it considered to be a reasonable value?

   A. Larger than 15 dB and yes

   B. Larger than 15 dB and maybe

   C. Larger than 17.5 dB and yes

   D. Larger than 17.5 dB and no

7. For an antenna 35 dBi of gain is needed. What antenna type should be used to achieve this gain?

   A. 4λ dipole

   B. Yagi

   C. Dish

   D. Horn

8. A conventional 2.13 dBi gain dipole antenna needs to be designed. If the application was CATV, would a balun be required in the design? What would the length of that antenna be at 5 GHz?

   A. No; 3 cm

   B. Yes; 1.5 cm

   C. Yes; 3 cm

   D. No; 1.5 cm

9. A dish has a 15 dBi gain at 5 GHz. A dish with twice the area has what gain at 5 GHz?

   A. 17 dBi gain

   B. 20 dBi gain

   C. 30 dBi gain

   D. 18 dBi gain

10. According to the 802.11n standard, what is the highest achievable raw data rate?

   A. 54 Mbps

   B. 750 Mbps

   C. 300 Mbps

   D. 600 Mbps

11. What are two different transmit diversity techniques used in 802.11n radios?

   A. MCS and SM

   B. MIMO and MRC

   C. MRC and STBC

   D. CSD and STBC

12. A MIMO radio with two receive, three transmit, and two spatial channels is designated in what way?

   A. 2×3×2

   B. 2×3:2

   C. 3×2:2

   D. 2×2:3

13. How much theoretical throughput improvement over a single channel is gained by using the total number of spatial channels available in 802.11n?

   A. Factor of 3

   B. Factor of 2

   C. Factor of 4

   D. Factor of 8

14. What part of the 802.11n preamble is common to all three modes of operation (Legacy, Mixed, and Greenfield modes)?

   A. L-LTF

   B. L-SIG

   C. L-STF

   D. HT-LTF

15. A bandpass filter has a maximum in-band loss of 1.5 dB, ripple of 0.4 dB, and a return loss of 15 dB. What is the minimum in-band loss?

   A. 1.5 dB

   B. 13.5 dB

   C. 1.9 dB

   D. 1.1 dB

16. In an outdoor 802.11n deployment, a receiver is getting strong signals that are a direct line and signals that are have bounced off buildings that are a couple blocks away. What parameter in the radio should be adjusted to ensure proper communications?

   A. Modulation

   B. GI

   C. Channel bandwidth

   D. MRC

17. What of the following directly impact the MCS rates?
    A. SM
    B. STBC
    C. MRC
    D. CSD

18. What part of the 802.11n preamble is used by the receiver to estimate the spatially multiplexed signal channel? What mode is this used in?
    A. HT-LTF in Greenfield mode only
    B. HT-LTF in Mixed and Greenfield modes
    C. HT-STF in Greenfield mode only
    D. HT-STF in Mixed and Greenfield modes

19. Two channels are bonded together to make a 40 MHz channel. Which two channels could you use in this way?
    A. Channels 7 and 11 in the 2.4 GHz band
    B. Channels 36 and 40 in the 5 GHz band
    C. Channels 48 and 56 in the 5 GHz band
    D. Channels 148 and 157 in the 5 GHz band

20. What method improves throughput in a low SNR environment?
    A. A-MSDU frame aggregation
    B. SM
    C. 64-QAM
    D. Receive diversity

Answers to Review Questions

1. C. The N connector is largest of the four connectors. It is the largest connector that is likely to be encountered in a WLAN deployment.

2. C. The common coax impedances are 50 and 75 ohms.

3. C. The wavelength in a cable is reduced from that in air by the square root of the relative dielectric constant.

4. B. Option B, 0.75 cm, is ¼ wavelength from the load with a dielectric constant of 4.

5. D. The VSWR would be 50 / 25 = 2.0.

6. A. The loss of the cable increases the return loss of the measurement by 5 dB. The return loss of the antenna is better than 15 dB, which is reasonable.

7. C. A solid dish antenna would be appropriate to use at that high gain level. None of the other antenna types could achieve 35 dBi of gain.

8. A. CATV uses 75 ohm cable and the ½ wavelength dipole has a 75 ohm impedance so no balun would be necessary. The length is ½ wavelength, which is 3 cm at 5 GHz.

9. D. Twice the area corresponds to twice, or 3 dB, higher gain.

10. D. The highest rate possible is 600 Mbps.

11. D. CSD and STBC are both transmit diversity techniques.

12. C. The designation goes Nt × Nr : number of channels.

13. C. There are four spatial channels available in total for 802.11n. Four channels result in a fourfold improvement in throughput.

14. C. L-STF is used in all the modes by the receiver to lock into the signal.

15. D. The ripple of 0.4 dB means that the in-band loss varies from 1.5 dB to 1.1 dB.

16. B. If GI is set to 400 ns, the signal a couple blocks away may interfere with the direct line signal. Setting the GI to 800ns to avoid ISI would be appropriate.

17. A. Spatial multiplexing directly impacts the MCS rates. The other techniques generally improve SNR at the receiver but do not affect the MCS rate.

18. B. The HT-LTF is used in both Mixed and Greenfield modes by the receiver to estimate the radio channel for spatial multiplexing.

19. B. Channels 36 and 40 are next to each other and could be bonded. Channels 7 and 11, along with the channels in C, are not at the right spacing. 148 is not a valid channel number.

20. D. Receive diversity improves throughput at low SNR environments. A-MSDU frame aggregation, SM, and 64-QAM are all techniques that require relatively higher SNR.

Chapter

8

Site Survey Preparation

THE FOLLOWING CWDP EXAM TOPICS ARE COVERED IN THIS CHAPTER:

- ✓ Understand the role of regulatory compliance requirements in network planning and demonstrate best practices for maintaining compliance.

- ✓ Describe best practices for updating or modifying an existing WLAN.

- ✓ Demonstrate a detailed understanding of the role that the wired network infrastructure plays in WLAN design.

- ✓ Discuss power supply and cabling options for WLAN devices.

- ✓ Explain the steps and procedures associated with site survey preparation.

- ✓ Explain how to conduct a proper WLAN site survey according to industry best practices.

When performing a site survey, you must do a great deal of preparation in order for the effort to go smoothly. Depending on the type of network you are designing, you may need to arrange equipment rentals and specialized facility access. The type of facility being surveyed may also require security escorts. These types of dependencies necessitate advanced planning and coordination.

When you are preparing for a survey, it is important to understand the *statement of work (SOW)* thoroughly and use it as your primary guide to properly prepare. You must review the business and technical requirements to understand the details outlined in the SOW, including the types of the applications, devices, performance requirements, and other factors that the customer needs the wireless network to support.

During the preparation process, you have to understand, refine, or sometimes define the criteria that spell out what the customer needs to accept your work and consider the project complete. You must plan deliverables for the entire project during this stage. You must also determine what information or data to collect during the survey process because that dictates the type of tools and methods that you will use. Finally, no project is without constraints and this also affects the site survey planning and execution.

Site survey preparation includes two primary events that will set the stage for all of the rest of the site survey preparation activities: the kick-off meeting and the walkthrough. This chapter shows you how to perform both of these activities and properly prepare for a successful site survey and therefore a well-designed wireless network.

Primary Events

It is often said that the more you prepare for something, the better it goes. This couldn't be truer when it comes to performing wireless site surveys. This chapter is dedicated to addressing important site survey preparation steps that the authors of this book have learned from many years of performing site surveys. As we mentioned, two primary events will occur during this planning phase: the kick-off meeting and the walkthrough. Let's explore these events next.

Kick-off Meeting

A *kick-off meeting* is usually the first opportunity that the survey team has to fully engage with the customer. This is an important time to not only make the proper introductions, but also explain the process involved during the site survey. You should use this time effectively in order to obtain all the information you need from your customer. Here are some helpful tips for planning for and running the meeting:

Agenda   Provide an agenda before this meeting that details the type of topics you will be discussing and what information your customer needs to bring. Usually an agenda you create for one project translates quite well to your next project. An agenda will require tweaking from project to project, but the basic structure and details should be roughly the same.

Invitations   You should invite any representative from the customer who will have a stake in the wireless network. This usually includes, at a minimum, the project sponsor, the project manager, a representative from your customer's IT department, and perhaps people from facilities, building security, end users of the network, and certain department leads. Your primary customer contact needs to determine who should be present from this list, but in order for them to properly determine whether certain parties will be needed, your primary contact should have the agenda information.

Other Preparatory Meetings   Even after the initial kick-off meeting, you may have to schedule another meeting before going onsite to start the survey process. Depending on the amount and complexity of information that your customer provides, you may need an additional information review meeting.

Kick-off Meeting Agenda Items   Kick-off meetings should minimally cover:

- Making introductions
- Reviewing the SOW
- Reviewing customer requirements
- Educating the customer about the process involved in a site survey
- Emphasizing the importance of a proper site survey
- Introducing the customer to the equipment that will be used for the survey and what it might look like in the final installation
- Explaining installation requirements for wireless network infrastructure and how installed infrastructure devices relate to aesthetics
- Detailing the reasons why you are requesting certain information
- Providing examples of site survey deliverables, such as a heat map
- Answering customer questions

Time and Expenses   When site surveys are performed, there are expenses involved, including travel and shipping costs that are incurred for each facility. To help keep costs in check, prepare your team to work efficiently and also prepare your customer for the time and materials required; otherwise, your project can get off on the wrong foot. If applicable, make sure your customer knows about the travel and expense involved and how preparation is critical in order to minimize expense.

When it come to preparing for the actual survey, if properly planning involves more than one meeting with your customer to prepare, discuss with your customer and explain how these additional meetings are the right decision in order to utilize everybody's time and money appropriately.

The Walkthrough

All site surveys should begin with a physical *walkthrough* of the entire coverage area. The walkthrough provides you with good information for an efficient and effective site survey. Perform walkthroughs in advance of the actual survey and after the initial kick-off meeting. This allows you to obtain the information you need from your customer beforehand and then use and review it during the process. If you don't have certain items, such as maps and required coverage areas before the walkthrough, the process will be less effective.

Being onsite for a walkthrough is an added expense and your customer may have an issue with that. Smaller jobs may not need a walkthrough, but larger jobs usually do unless they are not complex (which is rare). You should expect that with a higher level of complexity, a walkthrough is warranted.

The following is a set of minimum requirements that need to be met during a walkthrough:

- Confirm in-scope and out-of-scope areas.
- Mark main distribution frame/intermediate distribution frame (MDF/IDF) locations or where other potential cable termination locations may be required.
- Get a gauge of the type of building construction you are dealing with.
- Confirm the accuracy of maps and other customer-provided information.
- Get to know the customer, key stakeholders, and sponsor(s).
- Get a gauge of area(s) where a high density of devices may be present.
- Gain a good understanding of your target end users and applications.
- Explore areas where you anticipate installation of APs will be difficult.
- Identify areas that need to be scheduled separately.
- Note areas that are more complex and might require additional time.
- Keep an eye out for other existing wireless communication infrastructure.
- Identify devices such as microwaves, cordless phones, and wireless headsets that can interfere with signal quality.

A walkthrough is an excellent opportunity to continue interviewing the customer and get a feel for the deployment environment. You may also have an opportunity to meet other project stakeholders.

You should have drawings of all coverage areas before the walkthrough begins because you'll need them to reference and take notes on. If nothing else, walkthroughs help identify areas that you missed in the overall planning effort that you need to factor into the site survey. You should also confirm that maps are accurate. Often maps are out of date and may require some level of augmentation for the survey team to be able to perform their survey measurements.

Administrative Items

When you visit another company's facility, they have a set of rules and regulations for visitors. In fact, you are not just visiting their facility; you are working in their facility and will be gathering information that may even be considered sensitive to the customer. You need to be granted a certain level of access to perform your work, and you should have several assets prepared before going onsite. Let's explore these now.

Key Contacts

Every site survey should have designated points of contact. This includes contacts from both the customer and the survey team. This contact may be the project manager or a member of the technical leadership teams. Each of these parties will then coordinate all communication within their teams, providing a seamless interface to outside parties. It is important at the beginning of a project to designate a point of contact.

When dealing with your customer, this central point of contact is critical. All secondary contacts should be coordinated through this contact, which may include people from facilities, a network, network security, building security, end users, project sponsor(s), and others. All of these people have their own work schedules and meetings that you must accommodate well in advance.

Remember that some of your contacts may be hourly or part of a union. There may be additional, unplanned costs to your customer if you need to have hourly staff available to you after normal business hours. Union labor may also have certain limitations concerning which activities union workers are able to participate in, depending on their contract. For example, a union worker may be needed to operate certain equipment or run aerial equipment such as a forklift or scissor lift.

Facility Information

One of the most important assets needed when performing any type of wireless survey is a blueprint or CAD drawing of the coverage area in electronic format. The quality of this drawing is important; when converted to electronic form, such drawings are usually imported into survey mapping software packages. The integrity of scale and proportion of these drawings is critical. If a drawing was squished in only one dimension but not the other, it will not be a proper representation of the coverage area. Pay careful attention to these drawings before any work begins.

Sometimes you will find that electronic maps are not readily available or are very poor. You should try to place the responsibility for providing adequate drawings back on the customer before work begins as these maps are a critical asset to performing a wireless site survey. Hand-drawn sketches of a coverage area should be avoided because they tend to be inaccurate.

Drawings are also used to facilitate a visual set of documentation of in-scope and out-of-scope areas. Even if you determine these areas in advance, be sure to validate and reference them during your walkthrough. It is common to augment these in-scope and out-of-scope areas during the walkthrough process. Free online tools and applications can provide you with a great deal of information—sites like Google Earth and MapQuest let you access satellite imagery of a customer site, for instance. We recommend that you obtain this kind of information and print out a copy before arriving at the customer site.

Security

Some environments take security more seriously than others. Security provisions come in two forms:

- Building security
- Network security

A site survey involves both types, so it's important to have full access to the facility where the wireless network is to be designed. You should also assess any wired or wireless network with which the new network will integrate. In the case of an existing network, you will need proper security credentials in order to access the existing network and perform your assessment.

Some customers simply let you roam around without any escort whereas others require supervision, such as security guards or even a police officer. In most situations, you should wear a security badge at all times as it properly identifies you as an authorized vendor or visitor of that facility. Sometimes you will simply receive a badge without a picture; other companies may require you to have your photograph taken and a specialized badge printed for the duration of the project. Some companies even charge for this, and you may need to schedule your time accordingly to obtain your badge. You may even have to go to another facility to obtain it. Find out the customer's requirements related to security during the kick-off meeting and before showing up to begin work.

If needed, the security badge will include access to get you behind locked doors and other restricted areas for the site survey. The badge could include a passive RFID tag or magnetic strip that you can use on specialized access control devices located next to doors.

During the kick-off meeting, determine if there will be certain restricted areas, and if there are, ask whether they are always restricted or if you can access them at certain periods of the day. Factor these restrictions into your schedule.

Request security access related to computer or network assets during the kick-off meeting as well. A proper site survey includes performing an analysis of the wired network or inspecting another wireless network that the new network will integrate with. Performing this work requires a certain amount of access to any existing equipment that is already installed. We highly recommend that you request a user account with *read-only* privileges only. This does two things: First, it prevents any possibility of human error during the analysis. Second, it immediately sends a statement to the customer that you are only here to obtain information and do not want to compromise or disrupt any production activity on this equipment.

Your site survey preparation needs to include requesting both building access authorization and network security credentials, and you have to provide enough time for your customer to obtain them.

Legal and Compliance

Many large companies have training requirements for all contractors or vendors performing work for their organization. Sometimes this training may be tied to specific facilities or environments within the scope of the wireless network. You must include additional time in the project timeline to accomplish this training before work begins.

In addition to training, some companies require that you have certain vaccinations that are up to date and kept current during the scope of a project. A common requirement for healthcare environments is a test for tuberculosis, known as a TB or a PPD (Purified Protein Derivative) test. Especially if you will be working internationally, ask your customer what requirements they have well in advance of your scheduled arrival.

Governments and public safety organizations also are heavy users of wireless networks. Working for these types of customers requires that you obtain a high level of security clearance before you begin work. Airports also fall into this category as many areas of the airport demand a thorough and expensive background check.

Whether or not the customer requires it, it is always smart to initiate a nondisclosure agreement (NDA) between you and your customer. The NDA doesn't necessarily have to cost anything, especially if you use a standard document. Using an NDA shows the customer that you are sensitive to their intellectual property, and that information shared with you or anything that transpires during the course of your professional engagement will be confidential. There may be other documents, such as a *hold harmless,* that you or your organization may require. Such documents can be included in a *master services agreement (MSA)* that authoritative parties from both companies will need to sign.

It is also important to understand municipal or other governing regulatory compliance mandates that must be followed. This includes more than just wireless emission regulatory compliance and could include restrictions that affect the site survey process itself, most likely where equipment may be installed. Regulations may be dictated by insurance companies, governments, local building codes, or just about any other authoritative entity.

Certain types of clothing may also be required for specific customer locations. If the environment is under construction, you can usually assume at least a hard hat will be required. Safety vests, glasses, and certain types of shoes may also be needed. Environments like hospital operating rooms and manufacturing facilities with clean rooms may require that you wear a specific type of suit when accessing certain areas within the facility.

Ask your customer to define all regulatory and legal requirements that they require you to follow.

Environment

To design a wireless network properly, you need to know your deployment environment very well. This involves meticulous attention to detail in several areas, as you'll see in this section.

Existing Wireless

If you are designing a wireless network for a location that already has some form of wireless network installed, you need to find out more about it. Nowadays, it is quite common to find other 802.11 networks in some capacity. However, there may be other wireless network systems for telephone communications using 900 MHz or 1.9 GHz. In healthcare environments, you commonly have telemetry systems, temperature monitoring systems, paging networks, and more. In these cases it is less of a wireless networking system, but it is important to document what other wireless systems exist and what frequencies they are using.

Unfortunately, most retail networking equipment labels do not list frequencies on the packages. In some cases, you can't find this information in the spec sheet or on the product packaging. A new wireless system may therefore impact other systems that are already installed. For instance, consider what could happen if somebody installed a networking system in an entertainment room at a children's hospital that used the same frequency as medical equipment used for patient care. This may be anything from popular gaming consoles that have little impact to video-monitoring systems that could wreak maximum havoc. For your purposes, this means that you should not assume your customer has all the facts concerning equipment that uses WLAN frequencies, and so you may have to work to find this information yourself. Although many people aren't accustomed to thinking about frequency planning in their environment, you as a wireless design professional need to help your customers with this issue and educate them on the need to maintain a central list of this information. One way to do this is to get started by providing a spreadsheet of what you find on site. This spreadsheet will prove valuable to both of you.

It is also good practice to ask the customer if they are planning any upgrades to their existing wireless systems. If they are, you will want to ask them for information on the products that will be used for the upgrade. It is possible that they might be moving from one frequency that doesn't interfere with 802.11 networks to one that does, and this is the type of information you need to proceed.

Finally, consider asking the customer if a RF survey of the existing wireless networks was performed and documented. These documents may contain information that will be helpful in your planning even if existing networks are not using the same frequency.

Construction Details

On the topic of construction, there are many environmental details to pay attention to. If RF propagation was equal in all environments regardless of construction type, materials, and what is added to the environment, we wouldn't have to write much about RF survey design. The fact is that these areas have a major impact on RF propagation, and when preparing for an RF site survey, you should collect this information and understand how it affects the RF survey process. Here are some general guidelines:

Outdoor Locations   If the environment is an outdoor location, pay attention to the types of weather and frequency of electrical storms. This will determine the types of enclosures and grounding and surge suppression you need. Locations where snow or ice buildup commonly occur should also be avoided such as with certain rooftop mounts where antennas might be easily buried under snow when a large amount of snowfall occurs.

Indoor Locations   If the environment is an indoor location, ceiling types can play a major role. Since most APs seem to be designed for ceiling mounting nowadays, plan to address locations where ceiling mounting may not be possible. These places include where high ceilings exist, where there may not be ceilings at all (such as with atriums), or perhaps where ceilings will not easily accommodate installing a new AP (such as with hard or decorative ceilings).

Square Footage and Floors Covered   Knowing the total amount of square footage that the wireless network will be required to cover is also helpful. For certain types of environments, it is possible to run approximations on the number of APs that may be required given certain information about the environment. The number of floors and separate buildings is also important. If there are separate buildings, find out what type of connectivity exists between them.

Construction Material   When you're trying to plan the amount of time or number of APs an environment will need, it is helpful to gauge the type of construction that was used. Some buildings, usually older varieties, have thick concrete walls even internally to the building. Modern construction tends to not use this technique, but when you run into these types of environments, you need to factor in additional time. This type of construction can also be difficult to cable and may even limit the locations of where you will be able to place APs. Stucco or lath and plaster are another construction technique for interior walls that also limit RF propagation. While traditional lath and plaster does not, both have been known to be used with a metal screen to help hold the plaster or stucco material. You should ask someone knowledgeable with the environment what type of material the walls are made of.

Insulation   Even the type of insulation can affect your project. Asbestos was a common type of insulation used in older construction projects and has since been deemed hazardous. When asbestos is used, surface-mount cable raceways may be used to avoid exposing asbestos to the environment. While the effect of RF propagation has never been reported as a concern, the problem arises when it comes to running cable. Some insulation types come with a metal foil backing. This foil may cause more RF to reflect off the foil and affect the amount of propagation from each AP.

Plenum Area Requirements   Plenum area requirements are also important to note. These requirements limit the choices of APs and antennas that can be deployed. Usually, if a facility has plenum requirements in one part of the facility, they will likely have it in all parts, but you should ask the survey team to consider these requirements when they are designing the placement and type of APs and antennas during the RF survey.

Conduit   When cabling in outdoor and some indoor environments (including some plenum spaces), conduit may be required. Conduit is a form of metal tubing commonly used for electrical cabling. Low voltage or optical wiring used for Ethernet may need to be placed into conduit, which can substantially increase the costs of a project. In some instances the costs can far exceed the budget allowance.

Future Construction Projects   You should also ask the customer if any construction is planned within the planned WLAN coverage area. If there is, obtain some details and ideally CAD drawings of the construction plans to determine how this construction will affect the WLAN design.

Aesthetics

Some people are focused on aesthetics. In some environments it is perfectly natural to want to obscure the equipment, but in others aesthetics are simply less important.

Outdoor environments are common where the equipment being installed needs to be hidden or even painted. The larger the antennas used, the higher the likelihood you will need to face aesthetics issues. If you are ever in a passenger seat while driving around a populated area, take a look at building rooftops to reinforce this point. Radio towers are becoming common that are shaped like evergreen trees. The faux branches are made of materials that are effectively transparent to the RF frequencies that are being used on the tower.

As will also be noted in Chapter 9, "Site Survey RF Design," which will also cover aesthetics, if you are forced to paint your antennas or equipment, there are many negative outcomes from this exercise. The first part is extra labor and cost to your customer. The second is that doing so voids all equipment warranties. If equipment needs to be painted, the equipment housing usually has to be removed from the electronics and painted separately. Failure to do so might cause paint to get into the electronics, seize exhaust fans or filters, coat antenna connectors, and other problems. Even the paint used for these purposes has to be carefully selected so that it doesn't interfere with the RF propagation. The paint for the antennas might have to be different than the one used for the equipment because they are two different materials. The list goes on.

From an indoor perspective, it seems that nearly every environment the authors of this book have encountered has included some level of aesthetic concerns. Sometimes it may be just one person on the customer project team who is sensitive to changes to the current environment. The comical part of this is when the customer is overly concerned about putting a small AP on the ceiling when it is already filled with HVAC vents, fire sprinklers, smoke detectors, lighting sensors, security systems, and other required facility components either by code or for a customer business purpose.

Obscuring antennas can be a problem. The same problem would exist if you wanted to obscure lighting fixtures. If you had to put lights out of sight, it would limit the performance of the lighting fixture. The same goes for RF. Some people have installed

APs and antennas above ceiling tiles. This is similar to installing a speaker system in the same location. The sound waves would become muffled because the sound is reflecting and passing through obstructions before it is received by the human ear below the ceiling. Also, when antennas are placed above the ceiling, they cause a smaller propagation pattern than they would if they were installed below the ceiling grid.

In dark places like movie theaters and some places within hospitals, it might be important to turn off the LEDs of the AP. LEDs can be quite bright and the blinking pattern can draw attention to them. In hospitals, it is quite common to need to disable the LED lights on APs in psychiatric wards and patient rooms where patients will be sleeping.

In cases like this, it is usually best to physically label the AP with a sticker or some small, unobtrusive label that indicates the AP's LEDs have been manually disabled.

Understanding the Wired Network

Not every environment will have an existing wired network, but many already do. Perhaps part of the scope of your wireless network includes creating a new wired network or augmenting an existing one. Most WLANs integrate with wired LANs, and you therefore need to perform a thorough analysis of the network and even recommend changes that are required in order to support features of the WLAN design.

When performing a site survey, analyze the wired network, which may affect the type of WLAN architecture that you will use. Where OSI Layers 2 and 3 are segmented plays an important role in this decision. VLAN architecture, QoS capabilities, and uplink speeds are also factors in WLAN design decisions. Limited available capacity and redundancy, or lack thereof, may require that your WLAN project incorporate augmenting the wired LAN. The results of your analysis ultimately affect the final performance of your WLAN design.

Layer 3 Segmentation

Depending on the type of network architecture used, you may find LAN equipment configured in a variety of ways. Larger LANs will segment the network into logical and physical components usually called *core, distribution, and access layers*. In one or more of these layers you will find that OSI Layer 3 segmentation occurs. Simple enterprise LANs have a centralized (core) switch, usually Layer 3 capable, where access switches are uplinked to. This model combines the core and distribution layers. This is also where multiple VLANs would be created, and the switch would perform IP routing between the VLANs. This is also where the Layer 3 features of the switch are leveraged.

In larger networks, a middle layer is added usually due to quantities of access switches. These middle layers may also be used as a pseudo network core for a larger building in a multibuilding campus network design. In other words, each building may have its own set of aggregation (distribution) switches that all access switches connect back to. In turn, these distribution switches then connect back to a single building where the network core resides. Each building with a network distribution layer is commonly configured with Layer 3 features as well. These distribution switches would be an IP router for all traffic for all of its VLANs.

To take this concept even further, some enterprise networks have incorporated Layer 3 segmentation all the way down to the access layer. Therefore, each switch that PCs, printers, and even APs connect to also performs IP routing. This concept may sound fairly simple, but the problem is that it impacts mobility in certain WLAN architectures. You may have to choose a particular WLAN architecture in order to provide seamless IP mobility wherever users may roam. For example, if a user is connected to an AP and obtains an IP address originating from one VLAN and roams to another AP with a different VLAN, the wireless client would have to obtain a new IP address. A situation like this would cause a disruption of service with some applications in simpler WLAN architectures, such as independent autonomous models.

WLAN architectures that incorporate centralized data forwarding usually resolve this issue. As a review from Chapter 5, "Vendor and WLAN Architecture Selection," this architecture can place APs on any IP segment and wireless clients can roam anywhere in the WLAN deployment and still maintain a single IP address regardless of the default VLAN the AP is placed on. Other distributed architectures may also employ some IP mobility features that also provide the same benefits. The point is that with more Layer 3 segmentation, you need to concern yourself with WLAN features that perform IP mobility throughout the WLAN deployment.

While the wired architecture might not seem like a factor that you should concern yourself with in the site survey preparation process, it is important to validate all important areas of WLAN design that will either constrain or facilitate different aspects of your WLAN design.

 Wired network knowledge and fluency with configuration and analysis are part of other vendor-specific *wireless* certifications such as the CCIE Wireless certification, Aruba Certified Design Expert (ACDX), and Aruba Certified Mobility Expert (ACMX) certifications.

VLAN Configuration

Usually several wired VLANs have to be leveraged in the WLAN design. Therefore, you must find out what VLANs and IP addressing are used for each VLAN in the wired network design. VLAN design can tell you a lot about a wired network design. This design provides information about different security and access privileges that are associated with different VLANs, if any exists. VLAN design can help you quantify if any network design deficiencies exist in the wired LAN that need to be addressed prior to WLAN deployment. You should also note if any VLANs are not routed or what physical device is performing the routing functions.

People capture this information in a lot of ways At the very least, gather the information shown in Table 8.1.

TABLE 8.1 VLAN configuration example

VLAN ID	Description	Network	IP node	Device name
10	Cubicles Area 1	10.200.10.0/24	.1	Distribution-1
11	Cubicles Area 2	10.200.11.0/24	.1	Distribution-2
20	Server Farm	10.200.20.0/24	.1	Distribution-Server
30	WLAN Users	10.200.30.0/22	.1	Distribution-Service-1
34	WLAN Voice	10.200.34.0/23	.1	Distribution-Service-1
40	Guest	192.168.0.0/24	.254	Hotspot-Controller

Table 8.1 is merely an example of the high-level VLAN configuration and does not provide information such as ACLs or firewall rules dictating how traffic traverses these VLANs. Document this information based on these VLAN IDs or host-specific ranges based on the existing configuration of the wired LAN.

One possible way to amend this information would be to document a list of ACLs using a numbering scheme. If you then add two more columns to Table 8.1 titled Ingress and Egress, you can place ACL numbers into each of these columns as they apply to each VLAN.

QoS Capabilities

As you will read in Chapter 10, "MAC Layer Design," QoS is a highly complex topic. In this section, we will only concern ourselves with documenting wired device information and leave wireless QoS discussions to other chapters. As with the other wired features that require analysis, knowing what capabilities exist or do not exist in the wired LAN infrastructure will add to the wired remediation scope. Each of these devices needs to be analyzed to understand what QoS features apply to them, if any features exist at all.

An example of a device that we would be concerned about is a Layer 2 only–capable switch that did not have any ability to recognize or prioritize QoS traffic. In contrast, Layer 3 switches are typically capable of QoS features, but gaining the behavior you are looking for may require additional software licensing and most certainly detailed configuration.

In most WLAN QoS designs, what we are most commonly looking for is the ability to read and prioritize traffic on uplink or trunk ports. Features that provide marking and classifying traffic are typically not used in LAN devices. WAN devices are another matter altogether. WAN QoS configuration and design components are out of scope for WLAN design, but you will still need to understand that traffic flows and if traffic will be traversing WANs, you will need to also include WAN devices and WAN circuit link QoS capabilities into the QoS documentation exercise.

Uplink Speeds and Distribution/Core Capacity

As WLANs are both getting faster and gaining more and more usage, we need to pay much more attention to Ethernet link saturation. You must document each Ethernet switch that APs will be plugging into, and also document how they uplink to the rest of the infrastructure through the network distribution and/or core. As multiple switches that APs will reside on uplink into a distribution or core switch, the uplink ports, including redundant connections, all need to be documented.

Capacity of ports is an entirely separate topic that you must consider especially when adding new Ethernet switches as part of your WLAN design. If a network is moving from legacy 802.11 technology and upgrading to 802.11, the access switches that APs will plug into will most likely require upgrading (or you can add new ones). There is a trickle-down effect when you do this. As the access switches that APs plug into get faster and more traffic is uplinked from these switches, the distribution and core layers must also be able to absorb this additional workload. Where gigabit ports might be used today, the speed of the uplinks might be best moved to 10 Gigabit Ethernet. That means 10 Gb ports will need to be available in these other layers.

Many of the switch types that are used in distribution and core layers are modular varieties. In other words, they have a management engine with the option to install line cards with different interface types and features. It is important to note that the backplanes in these chassis-based switches as well as the management engine that runs the chassis also have performance limitations. For example, the backplane of older chassis-based switches might only be capable of 100 Gb of simultaneous traffic. If this is in the core switch with 10 distribution segments that each have 25 Ethernet switches with an average of 200 802.11n APs on them, it is quite possible that bandwidth will be constrained at the network core. In this design, it is highly likely that the distribution will be routing traffic into the core layer and the core will require less processing of each Ethernet frame. However, it is important to understand overall distribution and core capacity when it comes to aggregation of uplinks from the access and/or distribution layers.

Capacity Planning

You have several other areas that you need to document during a wired network analysis. Completing a capacity planning analysis may or may not involve performing a study as part of WLAN design SOW, but you at least need to quantify the additional load that will be placed on the existing or planned network(s). This includes both wired segments and wireless segments such as PTP or mesh links. One of the ways to facilitate this is to understand what *oversubscription ratio* is already used in the existing LAN design.

An oversubscription ratio is the factor that is used for network segment design. There may even be a different oversubscription ratio between the access and distribution layers versus the distribution to core layers. WAN links also have oversubscription ratios. Even if these values are not known to the customer, as an overall benefit to the WLAN design project, you can quite easily figure this out at least for the network device segments that you are addressing in your WLAN design. When this data is presented, it is usually an eye-opening event with customers when they find out that some of their network segments have oversubscription ratios that are too high compared to others.

Technically speaking, it is important to understand all network segments and the usage on those segments even if it is not part of the network path for wireless devices. If a distribution layer has 10 Ethernet switches that you will need to plug into to service your APs, you also need to understand the other network load that will be placed on that same distribution layer. That includes other Ethernet switches as well as end-user devices or servers that may be plugged into the distribution switch.

A lack of Ethernet capacity prior to a WLAN deployment will only add to the problem. WLANs will add more workload on the network.

Redundancy

Redundancy should always be looked at from time to time. Most customers and network designers strive to perform regular inspections of redundancy but often get bogged down with other tasks and projects that consume their time. As the WLAN designer, you also have a vested interest in the amount and type of redundancy that exists in the design. In fact, there may already be known lacking areas in the current network that staff has been unable to obtain the funding to resolve. New projects like WLAN designs are usually great opportunities to augment complementary systems that strengthen both the wireless design as well as the wired design.

In Chapter 1, "Gathering and Analyzing Requirements," we discussed how high availability and redundancy fit together. As you place devices into the network that are redundant, there may still be single points of failure that mitigate the value of this additional redundancy. For example, if a single router is used in the LAN and that fails, no matter how many redundant links, backup power systems, or even network protocols you have, the entire network is brought to its knees.

Again, you may not be commissioned to perform a full redundancy analysis for the network, but you also have a vested interest in redundancy especially when certain applications are or will be used on your WLAN design. This includes applications like voice, video, and even Real-Time Location Systems (RTLSs).

At a minimum, you need to gather information on the following:

- Port redundancy
- The redundancy protocol used

- High-level configuration of redundancy protocol
- Device redundancy
- UPS power—battery, UPS, and systems that incorporate generator-based power
- Network service redundancy such as routing, voice server, and RADIUS

Placement of Devices

Where devices are placed in a network can greatly affect performance and availability. For example, a voice server that IP phones will register to and traverse traffic through that is placed over a WAN link can affect call performance. Even if the speeds of these links are high, latency between these devices can still be a concern. For example, if a RADIUS server is local, the user database that it needs to communicate with may not be local and may reside over a WAN link with a round-trip latency delay high enough that users will notice the effect.

Devices of particular interest to WLAN designs are, at a minimum:

- Existing WLAN components
- Voice server
- RADIUS server
- User database
- NMS/WNMS

 Real World Scenario

WLAN Controller Network Placement

An enterprise IT team is evaluating a WLAN controller-based solution that incorporates centralized forwarding features. The IT team has been performing their analysis in a network lab that also has connectivity to the enterprise LAN. As a precautionary measure, the entire network lab uses a highly throttled-down Ethernet link to minimize impact to the production network in case of an unfortunate network event.

Once the team finishes their analysis, they decide to perform a proof-of-concept installation into the same facility. They install several APs configured to use the WLAN controller. Over time, the team has overlooked the fact that WLAN controllers use a centralized data forwarding model; thus, all traffic will not only have to traverse into the lab network from the production network where the WLAN controller was installed, but also traverse back out of it when using the Internet or any other enterprise resource on the network. This centralized forwarding architecture over a slow Ethernet link slows down performance so drastically that the wireless network performance is not meeting user expectations.

This scenario may seem far-fetched, but not everyone understands the finer details of various architectures. Also, employees are often involved in many projects and sometimes forget important details that can affect performance.

If this wired network design flaw had been caught during the site survey and network design process, a great deal of grief could have been avoided. In this particular case there were a lot of user complaints about the performance of the solution. The IT team involved in the WLAN infrastructure configuration blamed the end-user devices. The situation escalated to the point where a consultant was brought in to solve the problem. The consultant discovered on the first day of analysis that a single 10 Mb half-duplex Ethernet link was used between the entire network lab and all of the APs residing on the building network.

MDF/IDF Locations

When determining and qualifying placement of APs in your WLAN design, *MDF/IDF* locations can involve some limitations, so it's best to consider them when preparing the site survey. Cable lengths should be within 100 meters, which means all cable length plus patch cables between the Ethernet switch and the AP. Fortunately, when PoE was designed, it also matched the cable length limitations of Ethernet. This prevents you from using two different cable length standards depending on whether the devices will be using PoE. Remember, cable paths may not be direct and if cable needs to be run around certain obstacles, it will limit the distance APs can be placed away from these locations.

Available power capacity is another concern that should be addressed early on. All equipment closets are designed with a finite amount of maximum available power capacity. The more equipment that gets placed into a closet, the more available capacity that gets used. Many equipment closets were designed for devices that only consume the amount of power needed to power themselves. Switches that provide PoE are now changing the game. It is very likely that electrical power capacity needs to be upgraded in order to support a lot of PoE devices. Now that IEEE 802.3at-2009 (a.k.a. enhanced PoE or PoE+) has been ratified, providing up to 51 W of power using all four cabling pairs, more and more devices will start to be developed without a power cord altogether and designed to power exclusively off PoE. This list may include desktop computers, printers, and other common computing devices we are accustomed to today. The point is that you need to factor in the additional electrical load that APs will add to the MDF/IDF locations.

During your initial walkthrough, it is a good idea to inspect equipment rooms. You should look for available rack space for additional patch panels and PoE switches, including whether proper cooling or ventilation is available.

Survey Equipment

RF site surveys require a lot of equipment in order to be prepared for a variety of circumstances. As a parallel, if you have ever seen a plumber or an electrician truck pull up to a job site, you may have witnessed for yourself the number of tools and parts that they carry. Even then, they often still do not have everything and will have to go to supply store.

Equipment required for RF site surveys, fortunately, is not as demanding. However, the concept is the same. If a customer is hiring a professional to perform a job, there is an inherent expectation that the professional will be prepared to deal with a variety of common situations. It is your responsibility to develop an equipment kit to be prepared for any situation.

The following is a list of equipment that should get you started. Everybody has different techniques, and the items in this list may be tweaked. We recommend that you include the following items in your survey kit.

Tripod   Not just any normal tripod will do. A lighting tripod or the functional equivalent is the centerpiece of your survey kit. To temporarily place APs to measure RF propagation, you need a simple, lightweight device to mount an AP with the potential to go to as close to ceiling height as possible. In fact, some units can go close to 20 feet high.

Camera tripods are usually not recommended. Telescoping tripods used for lighting, or otherwise known as light stands, make excellent site survey rigs. They are designed to go higher and are often built to hold more weight.

Whatever you use for an AP mounting apparatus, you will need plenty of mounting space in order to place one or more APs and several types of antennas. It is usually best to create your own crossbar at the top of the tripod. You can then mount an AP to the crossbar to place an AP in a ceiling mount position or use it to mount antennas to. Depending on your pre-deployment survey methodology, you may want to test cell coverage of multiple APs at one time, so you may want multiple tripods.

Access Points   This may seem obvious, but yes, you will need an access point (or multiple access points) to perform a site survey. We highly recommend that you have one AP that uses internal antennas and another with external antenna capabilities.

Most customers generally prefer to purchase APs with internal antennas because they cost less and are less complicated to install. You should generally strive to use an AP that has built-in omnidirectional antennas for all locations where omni antennas are preferred. When you need to shape the RF propagation of your signal, you will need the AP that is capable of external antennas. Ideally, the survey AP should match the AP that will be used for the actual deployment.

APs that are designed to work with WLAN controllers can be more complicated to survey with. Unless you lug around a WLAN controller with your site survey rig, you will need to find another option. Consult with your equipment manufacturer for their recommendation on how to best perform an RF site survey using the same AP in these situations.

Portable Power Source   To truly be mobile, you will also need a portable power source to power the AP. There are several options that can be used for this purpose that are available for purchase from retailers. At least one manufacturer has created a specialized battery pack with a handle and PoE port for just this purpose.

This battery-powered portable PoE unit can usually last an entire workday and allow for overnight charging. You should carry two just in case you exhaust the battery supply or a malfunction occurs. The least favorable aspect of just about any battery solution is that they are heavy. Plan for extra shipping costs, or if you are building a kit, you might want to try to figure out ways to keep the combined weight of your kit below the airline weight limit before incurring additional charges.

Another option for using an all-in-one battery power PoE unit is to build a unit yourself. This option can be helpful if you have devices that require A/C power. You will want to use larger 12 volt batteries that can be found in specialty electronic stores. Look for batteries with the highest amount of capacity, which is often denoted in units of ah, or amp hours. You can then hook up a power inverter that takes a DC power input and provides a 110/220 volt AC outlet where you can hook up an AP or other devices that do not draw too much power. However, if all you need is PoE, it is more convenient to simply purchase an all-in-one battery-powered PoE unit.

Aerial Man-Lifts   In many environments, you will need to be able to access high locations by using specialized equipment. For example, if you want to place an AP on a pole at 35 feet in the air, you can rent a bucket truck or various types of aerial man-lifts, also known as boom, scissor, telescopic, or reach lifts. They are sometimes even referred to by their brand names. On the man-lift safety rails, you can mount an AP or antenna in the pointing direction you are looking for and move the man-lift into position. Even if you will be performing this task by yourself, many man-lifts allow lift operation from the ground.

Although renting this type of equipment can be fairly expensive, doing so will save more money in the long run because it allows you to test out the design and options. If you will be working in a warehouse environment and need to access high places—which is nearly all the time—check with the facility because they may have their own.

Antennas   Omnidirectional antennas aren't silver bullets. Many WLAN designers don't consider using anything else. However, many designs can benefit from shaping the RF signals from APs. The problem is that the costs are great. Not only do the APs typically have a higher cost, but you then have to buy the additional antenna that your design calls for. For this reason, we recommend that you install APs that use built-in antennas for most of the common indoor types of installations. In environments like warehouses, outdoor deployments, or any facility with large open spaces, such as stadiums, you must seriously consider using external antennas where you have better control over your RF signals. Therefore, your survey kit should contain several types of antennas of different gains.

Directional antennas can also be used to help locate sources of interference. Therefore, when you are performing a spectrum analysis and attempting to locate a source of interference, the directional antennas in your kit can serve a double purpose.

Along with a variety of antenna types, we also recommend that you keep a pack of antenna connector adapters. You can find many sources of antenna connector adapters available online and at retail electronics chains.

PC-Based Spectrum Analyzer   No survey kit would be complete without a PC-based spectrum analyzer. We recommend that you keep even the less expensive varieties in your kit along with a set of device drivers.

Measurement Device   You may often have to take distance measurements during RF site surveys. It is also common for distances to exceed the length of a common tape measure. While measuring wheels can come in handy if you take a great deal of measurements, it is yet another item that needs to be packed and will take up space in your survey kit. Handheld electronic measuring devices are also available.

Chargers   When running on battery power all day, you will need a full set of chargers in order to bring your equipment back into full running state before the next day begins. This includes chargers for portable power sources, two-way communication devices like walkie-talkies or cell phones and, of course, laptops.

Cables   Any type of equipment that you are using for your survey that requires a communication cable needs to be added to your kit. This usually includes CAT 5—both straight-through and cross-over, serial, NULL modem, and USB. Consider having different lengths of CAT 5 cables for a variety of situations. In lieu of packing straight-through and cross-over patch cables, you can include crossover adapters that are quite small and that you can add to the end of any CAT 5 RJ-45 connector.

Multi-outlet surge suppressors and power extension cables may also be needed for some surveys.

Digital Camera   This is a pretty straightforward item you should include in your survey kit. What may not be straightforward is the need for optical zoom. If you will be taking pictures of mounting locations from a distance (in the case of high ceilings or outdoor locations), you may need a digital camera with a high degree of optical zoom. Cell phone digital cameras almost never meet your needs in these situations.

USB Memory Storage   Again, this is another straightforward item, but we cannot emphasize enough that without some way to transfer files, using USB memory storage can cost you a great deal of time on a survey when time is of the essence.

Tape and Ties   There is a phrase that duct tape will fix anything. The statement couldn't be truer in some of the RF surveys that the authors of this book have performed. We also recommend that you include electrical tape, double-sided duct tape and, of course, standard duct tape.

Velcro and nylon ties can also be extremely helpful in temporarily securing antennas, cables, and APs to your survey rig as well as in other situations where you have to temporarily mount antennas in order to perform a site survey. Be careful with using Velcro for mounting devices because the adhesive doesn't always hold well. Industrial-strength adhesive is the only type we recommend for attempting to mount even lightweight items.

Velcro straps are also helpful for cable tie-downs. They can be used not only to neatly store the cables in survey kits, but also to secure loose cables to survey rigs. They even add an element of safety.

Safety Markers   We recommend using some form of safety marking, and in some environments, doing so is a requirement. Especially when the equipment will be used in environments that have heavy traffic, you should mark your equipment with fluorescent tape or other form of easily identifiable safety marker to prevent injuries or equipment damage. This can include using safety cones, painting your rig in fluorescent colors, or using marking tape that is small enough to easily fit into a survey kit and costs very little money.

Notepad   A writing pad of some sort comes in handy for many purposes and should be included in your survey kit. Graphing paper can be handy as well.

Rolling Cart   Some survey professionals prefer to have a rolling cart to carry all their survey equipment around with them. This is not something that's easy to pack, of course. Consider purchasing a cart when you arrive onsite. You may also want to check with local IT staff to see if it is possible to borrow one for the duration of the RF survey.

Laptop with RF Survey Software   All of this fancy equipment is useless if you do not have a laptop computer equipped with RF survey software. Our best recommendation is to use survey mapping software packages such as AirMagnet Surveyor, Ekahau Site Survey, or the functional equivalent.

Keep spare copies of the RF site survey software tools on a flash or portable storage device in your survey kit. Storage devices must also include the necessary licenses and even WLAN adapters if the license is tied to a specific WLAN adapter.

Extra laptop batteries are a must as well. Surveys often take all day and even if batteries last four hours at a time, they can rarely be returned to a full charge during the course of even an extended lunch break.

Onsite Temporary Storage   It often takes a bit of time to set up for a survey the first day. It is best to be able to store the equipment onsite at the customer location behind a locked door safe to protect against theft. You should also ask if this location has electrical power available in order to charge your batteries at night.

Outdoor Survey Items   In Chapter 9, we will discuss the process involved with performing PTP links and outdoor surveys in general. Depending on the type of outdoor survey you will be performing, you may want to include one or more items from the ones mentioned in the section "Survey Methods."

Basic Tools   When you are away from your office or home, you need to be prepared for a variety of circumstances, and a set of basic tools can come in extremely handy. Items we recommend include screwdrivers (small and medium), cable strippers, a battery-powered drill (hammer drills are better), assorted bits, standard pliers, needle-nose pliers, side cutters, industrial scissors, a utility knife, spare blades, and a few different types of self-tapping screws.

Point-to-Point Links

Point-to-Point (PTP) links can be some of the toughest types of RF surveys, especially when they are required to be made over long distances. The preparation that goes into a PTP survey is usually one of the most important aspects of performing the RF survey.

One of the most critical items you should perform before beginning a survey is a full walkthrough. Many PTP links require aerial man-lifts, and you may not be able to access the intended installation location during the initial walkthrough. Regardless, your job in this walkthrough is to scope out any and all locations that may be possible locations to install the antenna. How these locations will be accessed and thinking through the process involved in performing the site survey is critical to the survey team's success.

Be on the lookout for obstructions in the RF signal path and also factor in the Fresnel zone. Before the survey team goes onsite, use something like Google Earth to determine the total signal path. That way, you can calculate the size of the Fresnel zone based on the frequency that will be used for the PTP link. You can use terrain software packages, but they are not always accurate. Construction constantly changes in areas and trees constantly grow. Software is only as accurate as the data that is included with it, and it is not wise to rely on these software programs totally. If you are working with tight elevation tolerances with PTP links, you should perform measurements during a site survey.

You must also keep in mind that trees grow. If the signal path looks clear today, will the trees continue to grow? What about if trees are in the way, but they do not have leaves? Keep in mind that if the trees in the RF path are deciduous and it is wintertime, you will need to factor in the almost certain possibility that once the leaves grow back another path needs to be found. If one or more trees can be removed and new ones planted somewhere else, this is sometimes the best option when considering other alternatives.

Summary

Like many things in life, proper preparation for an activity usually pays off many times over. The more complicated the system is, the greater the emphasis should be on planning. This chapter outlined some of the most critical steps to properly plan for an RF site survey.

Always start a WLAN project with a kick-off meeting so that you can get buy-in on the SOW with all the stakeholders present and review the details of the work that will soon take place The kick-off meeting is the ideal time to explore any issues with key decision makers. This is also a great time to educate your customer on the process involved in a RF site survey.

Walkthroughs are also important because they help ensure that important details that might affect the RF survey process aren't missed. The person performing the walkthrough needs to have experience with the RF survey process in order to ask the right questions and look for the type of information that will prepare the RF survey team.

Site survey preparation helps you gauge the type of tools or construction equipment that will you'll need to perform the site survey process. A thorough kick-off meeting and walkthrough with the customer will help you determine what items are required.

Finally, analyzing the wired network and gaining an understanding of the assets and limitations that exist in the environment will go a long way to improve the overall design. This analysis might also expose other problems with the network.

Remember, preparation is the key to success. Think about it as an investment of time. Proper site survey preparation will allow for a more successful final solution—always.

Exam Essentials

Explain the importance of site survey planning events.   Understand the methods and importance involved in the kick-off meeting and walkthrough.

Explain the various aspects of survey preparation.   Know the administrative items involved in planning for an RF site survey.

Quantify the coverage environment.   Understand the environment factors that influence site survey preparation.

Describe the components of documenting the wired network.   Understand the processes and tasks involved with wired network analysis and documentation.

Describe important survey kit items.   Define the items that need to be included in an RF site survey kit and how they relate to the RF survey process.

Explain PTP link preparation components.   Understand the process involved in preparing PTP link surveys.

Review Questions

1. What preexisting document should be reviewed during the kick-off meeting with the customer?

   A. SOW

   B. Interference report

   C. MSA

   D. Acceptance criteria

2. When a walkthrough is scheduled with the customer, what parties should be invited to the meeting?

   A. IT team

   B. End users

   C. Project sponsor

   D. Facility

   E. Project stakeholders

3. During the walkthrough process, you need to be looking for which of the following? (Choose all that apply.)

   A. Areas that will require specialized tools

   B. Potential sources of interference

   C. Areas that require advanced scheduling

   D. Areas of high user density

4. An MSA commonly addresses at least which two legal categories?

   A. Nondisclosure agreement

   B. Hold harmless

   C. Indemnity clause

   D. Intellectual property protection

5. What important document should be obtained prior to the walkthrough and confirmed for accuracy?

   A. SOW

   B. LAN design

   C. NDA

   D. CAD drawing

6. What agenda items should you cover during the kick-off meeting? (Choose all that apply.)

   A. Building construction

   B. Explanation of survey process

   C. Areas of difficult AP installation

   D. Review of customer requirements

7. Which item does not belong apply to the walkthrough?

   A. Looking for areas of high user density

   B. Accessing all areas to confirm line of sight

   C. Exploring areas of challenging construction

   D. Identifying IDF/MDF locations

8. During a customer walkthrough you notice an area of the CAD drawing where it is not accurate. What next step should you take?

   A. Redraw the portions of the map that have changed.

   B. Request the survey team to do their best to walk where necessary and use the references on the map.

   C. Do not survey that area.

   D. Request a new version.

9. For what types of systems should you request read-only access to in order to perform an analysis of the customer's existing infrastructure? (Choose all that apply.)

   A. Routers

   B. Switches

   C. Clients

   D. RADIUS

   E. Active Directory

10. When working with a military organization, what type of compliance requirement might you expect?

   A. Strong security policy

   B. FIPS 140-2 encryption

   C. Security clearance

   D. Background check

11. If you are starting a new relationship with a customer that will comprise of multiple engagements, what should you consider establishing at the beginning of the project?

   A. Hold harmless

   B. VPN accounts

   C. Network security accounts

   D. MSA

12. During the course of a pre-survey walkthrough, you learn that a customer has an existing wireless phone system installed. What would be a good question to ask them? (Choose all that apply.)

    A. Is the system IEEE 802.11e compliant for QoS?

    B. Are any upgrades to the phone system planned?

    C. Can you provide a datasheet on the system?

    D. Ask if you can move that phone system to the new WLAN.

13. You run across an area in your walkthrough where decorative ceilings are installed. The customer has asked to use ceiling mounted APs with omnidirectional antennas only. What should you recommend?

    A. Install the AP on the wall.

    B. Install the AP above the ceiling.

    C. Recommend a different AP designed for wall mounting.

    D. Install a bracket on a wall to mount the AP.

14. A customer wants to deploy a WLAN that employs centralized forwarding. What LAN requirements should you look for?

    A. Routing redundancy protocol

    B. High-speed Ethernet links

    C. Layer 2 at the distribution layer

    D. Layer 3 at the access layer

15. You are installing APs in hospital patient rooms. What feature should you explore on the APs themselves?

    A. Guest access

    B. DTPC support

    C. LED suppression

    D. DFS avoidance

16. A customer has asked you to design a WLAN based on an autonomous AP architecture. During the LAN analysis you notice that the LAN uses Layer 3 segmentation down to the distribution layer. What issue should you raise?

    A. DHCP option conflicts

    B. Redundancy support

    C. That 802.3af lacks support for Layer 3

    D. Inter-subnet roaming

17. You are determining whether QoS is supported on a wired LAN. The customer has new, high-end enterprise networking gear at the core of their network. They plan to plug the APs into new access switches that support Layer 2 QoS. What insight can you offer?

    A. They may not have end-to-end QoS.

    B. IP DSCP values map to COS.

    C. Layer 2 COS is sufficient.

    D. QoS will achieve better MOS.

18. When performing a capacity planning analysis on a LAN with a large number of access switches and distribution blocks, what can you check to see if existing links have too much congestion? (Choose all that apply.)

    A. VLAN stats

    B. Uplinks from distribution to core layer

    C. Interface stats

    D. Access switch VLAN uplinks

19. You are performing a redundancy analysis for a new WLAN in a healthcare facility. They will be running VoWiFi and are concerned about availability. They appear to have redundancy in the switching architecture using STP and EtherChannel and are running routing protocol redundancy. Their current security policy requires WPA2 Enterprise, and they have a redundant voice server. UPS power seems to be sufficient. What might be missing? (Choose all that apply.)

    A. Spare APs

    B. Authentication server redundancy

    C. DHCP services

    D. Redundant power supplies

    E. Voice codec redundancy

20. You are performing a walkthrough for a PTP wireless survey. You will need to use a small communication tower to install the link. How should you plan to perform the survey?

    A. Use a lighting tripod.

    B. Temporarily install the equipment to the radio tower.

    C. Use a man-lift.

    D. Install the radio and equipment and tune later.

Answers to Review Questions

1. **A.** Kick-off meetings happen after the contract signing, and the statement of work (SOW) is an outcome of the contractual process. This document should be reviewed during the kick-off meeting with the customer to resolve any discrepancies.

2. **E.** Any project stakeholder is the most correct answer. Anybody who will have a role in the project should be invited to the kick-off meeting for at least the portion that pertains to them.

3. **A, B, C, D.** Pay careful attention to all these areas during the walkthrough.

4. **A, B.** A master services agreement (MSA) commonly addresses a hold harmless agreement and an NDA.

5. **D.** One of the most important documents is the CAD drawing. This document needs to be reviewed to ensure it is accurate during the walkthrough.

6. **B, D.** Key project stakeholders need to be made familiar with the process involved in site surveys, including the typical challenges that commonly occur that can compromise the integrity of the final design. Customer requirements should also be reviewed with the customer.

7. **B.** It is usually not possible to access all areas where radios will need to be installed to confirm line of sight. The walkthrough should document the equipment and tools that will be necessary to perform this work, along with planning for alternative locations.

8. **D.** It is best to not attempt to augment a version of the customer's map as the details may not be accurate. You should request from the customer an updated map and require that it be accurate in order to obtain higher-quality results. If one does not exist, the customer needs to understand the potential impact on results.

9. **A, B.** Routers and switches are the primary devices of focus when performing an analysis of the customer environment. For other systems, it may be important to obtain proof of how they are configured.

10. **C.** Many military organizations require a heightened level of security clearance.

11. **D.** At the beginning of a project, before any work is performed, you should establish a master services agreement (MSA).

12. **B, C.** The existing wireless phone system may not be based on 802.11 at all. Asking the customer detailed wireless or spectrum questions about their phone system will likely not yield the results you are looking for. It is best to simply ask simple questions, look up additional information if needed, and determine if upgrades are being planned that might affect the WLAN project.

13. C. The most appropriate answer is C because many ceiling-mounted APs with omnidirectional antennas are designed to provide coverage down to clients from where it is typically mounted on a ceiling and in a 360° orientation around it. Effectively placing the AP on its side will rotate this pattern three-dimensionally and you may not get the results you want. Mounting antennas above a ceiling is never recommended because building material attenuates RF signals.

14. B. The most appropriate answer is high-speed links ideally in the network core or a distribution service block. Routing protocol redundancy has more to do with redundancy factors and IP segmentation plays little to no role in a centralized forwarding infrastructure.

15. C. Guest access is a system and not specifically an AP feature. LEDs that are used on APs can be annoying and even alarming to guests, especially if they use the color red. It is best to disable them when they are used in such environments.

16. D. In a standard autonomous architecture, an AP acts as a bridge device to a local VLAN. When a client roams between APs connected to different distribution blocks, the VLAN will change, requiring the client to obtain a new IP address. This might greatly affect certain applications depending on where the segmentation occurs.

17. A. Some WLAN infrastructure as well as user applications only mark Layer 3 IP DSCP values. If the LAN does not support Layer 3 QoS, those devices will not honor prioritized traffic.

18. B, C. Generally assume the customer doesn't have sophisticated monitoring systems or they are not configured appropriately for the information you are looking for. What will always work is reviewing switch port traffic statistics. Other possible answers include links between core switches and potentially stats on backplane ports if a chassis-based switch is used.

19. A, B, C, D. All of these options except voice codec redundancy should also be investigated for redundancy.

20. C. Always use an aerial man-lift in lieu of climbing a customer's tower or installing anything prematurely. Develop a plan for a proper survey and plan your equipment purchases based on the survey results.

Chapter

9

Site Survey RF Design

THE FOLLOWING CWDP EXAM TOPICS ARE COVERED IN THIS CHAPTER:

- ✓ Determine RF link requirements and demonstrate common planning techniques and deployment approaches for outdoor networks.

- ✓ Describe best practices for updating or modifying an existing WLAN.

- ✓ Discuss migration strategies for upgrading to 802.11n.

- ✓ Explain the importance of building-specific planning considerations.

- ✓ Explain the functionality and purpose of network planning tools.

- ✓ Describe design models and considerations for both Multiple Channel Architecture (MCA) and Single Channel Architecture (SCA) WLANs.

- ✓ Illustrate best practices for roaming support in a WLAN.

- ✓ Demonstrate a detailed understanding of RF behaviors and characteristics and relate these concepts to WLAN RF design.

- ✓ Discuss design concepts related to frequencies and bands used for WLAN communications.

- ✓ Illustrate a comprehensive understanding of the role of channel planning and usage in network design.

- ✓ Understand the purpose of, and challenges related to, creating a balanced RF link between the AP and client devices.

- ✓ Demonstrate a detailed knowledge of the common problems related to high user densities and describe effective strategies to address them.

✓ Describe the purpose of, and techniques for, controlling and shaping RF to improve WLAN functionality.

✓ Describe the role of load balancing in RF spectrum management.

✓ Explain how to conduct a proper WLAN site survey according to industry best practices.

✓ Demonstrate a detailed and thorough understanding of surveying types and methodologies.

✓ Explain the metrics, data, and other information collected and reported during a site survey.

✓ Explain how surveying methodologies may differ when preparing for specific applications.

✓ Discuss how surveying approaches differ depending upon PHY and feature support.

✓ Illustrate how a site survey facilitates hardware (APs and antennas) placement and mounting decisions.

✓ Describe how antenna selection, placement, and orientation is determined by an RF site survey.

✓ Describe how channel planning and output power configurations are determined by an RF site.

✓ Understand the differences in tools, methods, and purpose between outdoor and indoor site surveys.

✓ Understand how survey methodologies and requirements differ depending on network architecture.

✓ Understand site survey tools and planners that are built into network infrastructure systems.

If you are designing a new WLAN, this will be one the most important chapters of the book to help you determine AP locations. It is as simple as this: you can never recover from bad AP placement regardless of what features may be available in an equipment vendor's system. Quite frankly, bad RF propagation is synonymous with bad or faulty cabling in a wired infrastructure. In other words, recovering from bad RF design can only be done by changing the design.

Automated RF features that are built into some infrastructure WLAN products will only help in rare circumstances. If you have already read other chapters of this book, you have consistently heard the theme that automated RF features are overmarketed and oversold.

This chapter will address all areas a proper site survey should include based on a variety of design criteria. As you'll see, site surveys are not all created equal. To complicate matters further, different design approaches and their caveats are not very well understood in the Wi-Fi industry and this chapter will attempt to quantify the areas you need to be concerned with.

RF Survey Overview

Beyond all other things, a site survey must include a method to quantify and measure RF propagation. Because RF propagates differently in different environments, your methods will vary depending on the physical environment you are attempting to cover. This includes construction and mounting options. At the beginning of this book you read that becoming a CWDP involves attention to *construction*. This chapter will quantify that statement.

If you are performing a survey yourself or you are selecting and hiring a vendor to perform this work for you, the information in this section is equally valuable. If you are outsourcing this effort, you need to pay close attention to the methodologies and criteria explained in this chapter before you make a final vendor selection. Outsourcing is a double-edged sword; you cannot outsource something that you know nothing about. It is synonymous with selecting the right employee to staff a position without knowing how to select that person. You have to know what to ask and understand the subject matter enough to ensure you have the right candidate. Outsourcing a site survey to a vendor is no different.

Furthermore, if you are striving to be a CWDP and will be performing the RF surveys yourself, this chapter will lead you well on your way.

The site survey method you should use in your designs will vary based on several factors. While the authors of this book always highly emphasize that survey methods involving actual RF measurement techniques are superior, sometimes the design may be for a building that hasn't been constructed or populated yet. In other cases you might be designing a network upgrade from one technology, doing an AP technology upgrade, or even adding a frequency band. Each requires a different set of attention and design techniques. That is why there are a variety of industry-standard survey methods.

Each method also requires different attention to detail in terms of the client device used for measurements as well as the AP configuration. Wrong settings lead to bad designs. In Chapter 2, "Designing for Client Devices and Applications," we discussed several design factors that must be considered based on devices that will run over the new network. While this chapter discusses the method to perform the RF design, the RF characteristics of your target client devices must be factored into each of these methodologies discussed. We'll provide an explanation of each.

Spectrum Analysis

The first stage of every site survey should involve an onsite *spectrum analysis*. Because Wi-Fi operates in the unlicensed bands that many other devices use, you must ensure that interference is minimal. *Minimal* is probably the best word choice because there are so many devices that use the same spectrum and it is nearly futile to think all forms of interference can be mitigated.

When a site survey is performed, nowadays it is more or less expected that an OSI Layer 1 analysis be performed. Cables need to be tested, too. Because spectrum analysis was so far out of reach for so long to WLAN designers, spectrum analyzers were not used. The complexity and knowledge required to use PC-based spectrum analyzers is far less than using traditional spectrum analyzers. What's more, costs have drastically decreased, putting spectrum analyzers well into reach for even moderately sized jobs and companies.

In the past, only some WLAN designers incorporated spectrum analysis into the cost of site surveys. Spectrum analysis is now considered a requirement.

Tools cost money, and they also need to be maintained. Therefore, the cost of performing this work must be factored into the total cost of the WLAN deployment.

The following sections will explore this topic fully.

Different Types of Spectrum Analyzers

Spectrum analysis involves the use of a specialized RF instrument and antenna(s) to listen to and analyze specific wireless frequencies. The readings the instrument provides vary a great deal depending on the capabilities of that instrument. There are various types of spectrum analyzers:

Large Bench Top Units   Traditionally, spectrum analyzers are large bench top units whose typical starting costs are over $20,000. They can cost much more than that, depending on their accuracy, frequency range, speed, and the type of measurement modes. Bench top units are great for laboratory use cases and for performing accurate (calibrated) measurements. Wireless equipment manufacturers are the primary market for these units.

Portable Spectrum Analyzers   The type of spectrum analyzer that is most useful to a WLAN designer is portable, like the one shown in Figure 9.1. In response to this, manufacturers have produced portable versions of these units that can be taken to any environment. Sometimes they are also called *field units*.

FIGURE 9.1   Portable spectrum analyzer

The type of portable spectrum analyzer shown in Figure 9.1 can be equipped with a variety of antennas depending on the frequency being analyzed. The challenge with these types of spectrum analyzers is that you need a great deal of academic background in RF along with experience in order to obtain useful measurements from them. That is why these units have traditionally been tools for equipment vendors or RF engineers who have had significant training.

PC-Based Spectrum Analyzers   In 2007, Cisco acquired a company called Cognio. Cognio made the first popular and affordable PC-based spectrum analyzer. Several companies rebranded it prior to the Cisco acquisition. The analyzer comes in a CardBus form factor that fits into a compatible laptop. For many, the most amazing part of this product is the device classifier functionality; it analyzes the signals it hears and tells the operator the type of device, such as microwave, Bluetooth, or cordless phone. In general, here are the primary distinguishing factors in PC-based spectrum analyzers:

- Ease of use
- Richer user interface
- RF signature detection—device classifier
- Speed
- A number of different and customizable views
- Integration with other wireless network management system (WNMS) platforms

Other PC-Based Spectrum Analyzers   Others have also entered the market with similar products of varying capabilities and other form factors.

AirMagnet (`www.airmagnet.com`)   AirMagnet is a division of Fluke Networks and has several products that also perform spectrum analysis. Figure 9.2 shows a USB form factor that can also be used on laptop computers. Because laptop computers no longer use CardBus or PC Card technology, USB form factors have become a must until PC Card Express adapters become more common.

FIGURE 9.2   AirMagnet Spectrum XT

Courtesy of AirMagnet

Wi-Spy (`www.metageek.net`)   Metageek also offers a USB-based spectrum analyzer, called Wi-Spy, which has gained a great deal of popularity. This product has traditionally been the lowest cost Wi-Fi spectrum analyzer that is popularly used. An example is shown in Figure 9.3.

Berkeley Varitronics Systems (`www.bvsystems.com`)   Berkeley Varitronics also manufactures a handheld and tablet form factor spectrum analyzer that includes a full software suite such as the one shown in Figure 9.4. The benefit of this unit is that it is a dedicated device used primarily for spectrum analysis, but also has other Wi-Fi related utilities that assist in field troubleshooting and analysis.

FIGURE 9.3   Wi-Spy USB Spectrum Analyzer

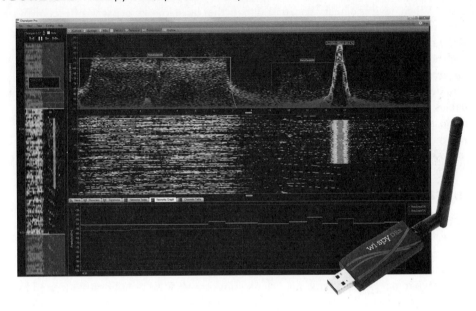

Courtesy of MetaGeek, LLC

FIGURE 9.4   Berkeley Varitronics Systems YellowJacket Tablet

Courtesy of Berkeley Varitronics Systems, Inc.

Some of these products even integrate with survey mapping software or WNMS products. When devices detect abnormal signals that have known negative effects on Wi-Fi, they can send email or other alerts to staff.

Many full-featured spectrum analyzers often come with other important capabilities. One of the next most important features is *network signal analysis*, also referred to as a *vector network analysis (VNA)*. It is beyond the scope of this text to discuss this topic in detail, so just keep in mind that a VNA becomes incredibly valuable in analyzing RF cables and antennas. A VNA will provide details of RF transmission lines, including return loss, impedance measurements, and detailed information to quantify antenna tuning characteristics. With the use of a VNA, you can quickly determine whether you have a bad antenna, RF cable, or connector.

Integrated Spectrum Analysis

In the past, Wi-Fi radios were not capable of capturing or reporting many meaningful RF statistics. The radio would detect and receive RF signals and report decoded information to the operating system of the host device. In that sense, WLAN chipsets were generally designed to transmit and receive IEEE 802.11-compliant transmissions.

That is what makes a spectrum analyzer so important. WLAN radios are affected by interference of non-802.11 transmissions but previously couldn't report them, so without a spectrum analyzer you would be blind to RF interference.

WLAN chipset manufacturers are starting to incorporate spectrum analysis into their chipset designs. As of this writing, it is too early to speculate on the full capabilities that will be provided by integrated spectrum analysis. In the meantime, the feature quality looks very promising, though only a few vendors have implemented these solutions. Because WLAN radios are price sensitive, it is likely that dedicated spectrum analyzers will still be one of the critical items in a WLAN survey team's arsenal. Without question, spectrum features in WLAN radios will never compare to the capabilities of the best dedicated, full-purpose spectrum analyzers. However, for many use cases, integrated spectrum analysis will provide a great deal of value.

The Physical Layer of Wireless

If you have a networking background, you are familiar with the OSI model. Layer 1 of the OSI model—in wired networking—refers to the physical cabling that is used between networked devices. In wireless, the physical layer is the wireless medium.

The use of "physical" might be a difficult concept to compare RF transmissions to. Just because humans cannot detect them doesn't mean that they are any less real or physical in nature. In fact, in terms of thinking about RF and how important it is, *physical* is probably the best term to use in order for wireless professionals to grasp RF topics.

It is important to understand this concept as you will hear the wireless medium referred to as the physical layer in this book and other industry-related materials.

 Real World Scenario

Interference with Patient Care

A hospital contracted for a new WLAN to be installed in their new expansion. This new area also incorporated the use of a patient telemetry system. As the new hospital wing was about to open and all the furnishings were installed, the WLAN team performed a survey to determine each AP's placement. During that time no interference was detected when a spectrum analysis was performed.

The hospital continued to install and test each of the other systems for this expansion. As the new WLAN was installed, the IT team began to test the network performance and received incredibly poor performance. Their client devices kept disconnecting and they could hardly pass any data. After a great deal of lost time (several days), they called the site survey team back in and another spectrum analysis was performed.

What the spectrum analysis showed was an incredible amount of interference across the entire 2.4 GHz ISM band where their new 802.11g network operated. After tracking down the source of the interference, the team identified the culprit as the patient monitoring system (a.k.a. the telemetry system). The type of interference the system was transmitting was so severe that it would be impossible for a 2.4 GHz Wi-Fi system (or any 2.4 GHz system for that matter) to co-exist in the same area reliably.

The hospital staff then determined that the telemetry system they purchased was different than that used elsewhere in the hospital. It was the "new" version of the product, but unfortunately the staff didn't realize this until it was too late.

In this case, one system had to move away from the 2.4 GHz band. The hospital decided to deploy an 802.11a solution operating at 5 GHz. However, this is a severely limiting factor for Wi-Fi and not all hospitals would have chosen this path. In fact, many Wi-Fi clients are not 802.11a or 802.11n (5 GHz) capable. The best solution for some would have been to return the telemetry system to the manufacturer for a system that doesn't use 2.4 GHz.

When to Perform a Spectrum Analysis

Any time WLAN analysis or site surveys are being performed, spectrum analysis provides critical data about RF health that leads to WLAN performance. At least a minimal spectrum analysis provides a great insurance plan.

Some larger companies who depend heavily on their WLANs even install sensors that have incorporated spectrum analysis into their feature set. This provides a constant, 24/7/365 monitoring of their RF environment and can quickly report troubles to an operations team. Cisco's 3500 series APs were the first on the market with an integrated spectrum analysis chip, which Cisco calls CleanAir technology.

Integrating spectrum analysis functionality with the AP radio might appear to have some limitations. This technology bets on your 802.11 network not being overutilized. In fact, most of the time APs are not transmitting and are able to collect a great deal of information and report the findings to a centralized database for later reference. One of the most notable benefits is having the ability to rule out highly impacting spectrum problems during troubleshooting events. If interference events are recorded in a database when they occur, this might also prove highly beneficial in determining the root cause after a WLAN outage has occurred.

Documenting Your Data

Whenever you perform a spectrum analysis, you always need to record the location where the measurements were taken, the local time, and any other activity or purpose of the scan. If a non-PC-based spectrum analyzer is being used, the screen shots tend to show the configuration of the instrument without having to record them manually. PC-based spectrum analyzers are generally nonconfigurable. Therefore, documenting analyzer settings for these devices is largely irrelevant unless you are using an external antenna.

Remember, spectrum recordings are location and time dependent. For example, looking at a recording a month later that simply says ACME Corp Recording 1 has much less value than one labeled as ACME-Location3-StaffBreakRoom-2.2dBiOmni-20100816-1454. In the second example, you know the location, which may even refer to a documented map indicating Location 3, the antenna type, and the date and time.

Locations can be documented in a column and row fashion by taking a floor plan and overlaying a labeled grid using letters on one axis and numbers on the other. In this case, you could label the previous example recording as LocationB3.

Regardless of the method you use, it is important to capture this information in order to make it useful when viewing recordings at a later date.

Some PC-based spectrum analysis products integrate with survey mapping software so that you can recall this data based on the exact location it was gathered from. The person performing the survey simply clicks on a map location and keeps moving. This process allows for the engineer to walk through a large area in a very short amount of time. An example is shown in Figure 9.5.

FIGURE 9.5   AirMagnet Survey PRO

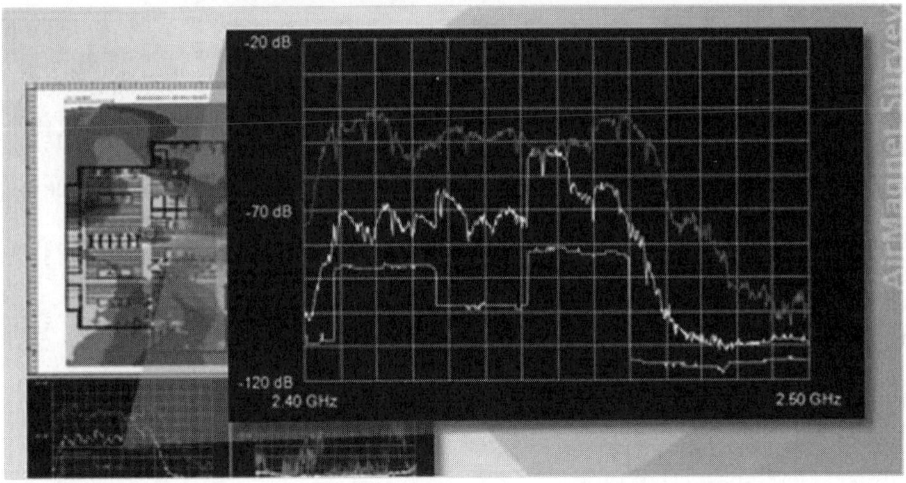

Courtesy of AirMagnet

Configuring Your Wi-Fi Adapter When Performing Spectrum Analysis

One of the most common mistakes people make when performing a spectrum analysis is not disabling their WLAN radio from transmitting. While several PC-based spectrum analysis products rely on a laptop's WLAN radio to detect 802.11 transmissions, the WLAN radio only needs to perform that task in listen-only mode. Some WLAN client utilities allow you to instruct the radio to not attempt to connect to any network, which essentially places the WLAN radio in listen-only mode.

If this is not performed, you will find very high-powered wireless transmissions in your spectrum recordings. The fact that a PC-based spectrum analysis chip is in such close proximity to the WLAN radio's antennas explains why signal levels are registered at such high levels. When observing these high transmissions, it is not always obvious that they are coming from their own analysis station.

Disabling the WLAN radio on your laptop, for example, would also disable the ability to detect 802.11 transmissions for the spectrum analysis product.

Investigate the proper settings with your WLAN client adapter that enable you to suppress connecting to WLANs without actually disabling the adapter.

Using a PC-Based Spectrum Analyzer

Let's now explore how to use a PC-based spectrum analyzer to analyze Wi-Fi frequencies; note that the base concepts are the same for all spectrum analyzers. We are focusing on the PC-based models in lieu of the others because they are the most commonplace and affordable varieties for design and survey tasks. Other types of spectrum analyzers certainly have their value, but for a field analyzer, there is nothing better than simply slipping an adapter onto your laptop to get you up and running. Many of you might even already be taking one of these with you just about everywhere you go.

In this section we will explore the types of measurements that you should pay the most attention to.

FFT

Fast Fourier transform (FFT) is a method of showing RF power as a function of frequency. FFT is the most commonly used function of a spectrum analyzer of nearly any kind. Any type of transmission that is heard on a specific frequency will be reported based on the actual signal level that was recorded.

FFTs are built by sweeping the frequency band. Usually three traces of particular significance are shown in an FFT:

Current   The current trace is usually the default when a spectrum analyzer is launched. It is the maximum signal level reported over the measurement or display interval. For example, if a signal is transmitted at 2454 MHz, the analyzer reports the maximum signal level heard on that measurement interval even if the transmitter of the 2454 MHz signal only transmits once. If the analyzer swept that same frequency 10 times in a second and that was the highest RF signal it heard out of all 10 times, it would report that value on the FFT plot.

Average   The average plot is an averaging of all the data points the spectrum analyzer recorded over a measurement interval. For example, using the same scenario as mentioned earlier, all the signal readings would be averaged and displayed in the same plot as the Current FFT trace, but usually as a different color for clarity.

Max Hold   When viewing an FFT plot over time, the signal levels constantly change when viewing Wi-Fi network transmissions. Max hold is a trace that will keep a visual indicator of the maximum RF signal strength per frequency within a real-time FFT plot. It is a great method for viewing interfering RF signals in addition to Wi-Fi transmissions.

Figure 9.6 shows a PC-based spectrum analyzer using all three traces.

FIGURE 9.6   Real-time FFT from Cisco Spectrum Expert

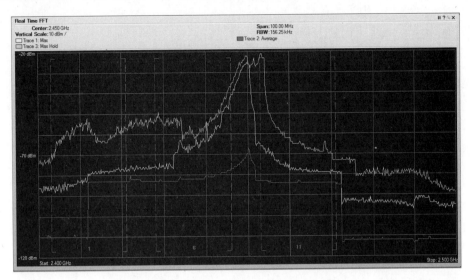

Duty Cycle

When wireless devices transmit, they may do so in very short bursts like a Wi-Fi network, or worst case, they can send a continuous transmission such as with certain wireless video cameras. The amount of time a device occupies the wireless medium is measured in terms of *duty cycle*. In other words, duty cycle is a measurement of RF transmissions in the time domain (at a specified amplitude threshold or higher) rather than by signal strength, like with the FFT measurement.

Devices that use a 100 percent duty cycle are the worst types of wireless devices if you would like to share the same frequencies with other wireless systems. When a device transmits at a 100 percent duty cycle, you can also refer to it as a continuous duty transmission. This is important as a device occupying a specific range of frequencies that never stops transmitting makes it impossible for other devices to use those same frequencies. Remember, the 802.11 protocol utilizes a collision avoidance mechanism whereby it detects if the medium is available before it transmits. If the medium isn't available, then a compliant device shouldn't transmit.

Duty cycle plots can also incorporate the same current, average, and max hold traces that an FFT plot uses. Figure 9.7 shows an illustration of a duty cycle plot from a PC-based spectrum analyzer.

FIGURE 9.7 Duty cycle from AirMagnet Spectrum XT

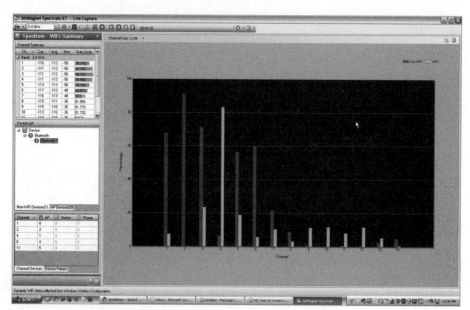

Measurement Variables

Many PC-based spectrum analyzers on the market today have limitations on how the analyzer can be configured. Nearly all have fixed scanning behavior and bandwidth settings that cannot be adjusted. If you are not using a PC-based spectrum analyzer or one that may be adjustable for different measurement variables, you need to understand how they will affect the data values. Even if you are using an analyzer that has fixed settings, you should also know how to relate the output to other spectrum analysis measurements.

Sweep Times When a spectrum analyzer scans the RF medium, it begins at the start frequency and measures the RF in chunks of frequency as specified by resolution bandwidth, which we will discuss next. The analyzer continues to measure new chunks of frequency until it reaches the stop frequency. The elapsed time to scan a frequency range in chunks starting from the start frequency and ending with the stop frequency is called a *sweep time*. A slow sweep time will not provide reliable duty cycle measurements because it doesn't get enough data samples of each frequency. It is important to understand sweep time when using any spectrum analyzer, whether or not it can be adjusted, in order to interpret the data properly.

In PC-based spectrum analyzers the speeds at which sweeps are accomplished are quite fast—so fast, in fact, that you can truly get a good gauge of duty cycle across a wide range of RF frequencies. This is something that is difficult to achieve across a wide frequency width with traditional spectrum analyzers.

Resolution Bandwidth   Spectrum analyzers will measure RF in specific frequency widths. Therefore, when a spectrum analyzer is sweeping the RF medium it is reading the RF medium in chunks of RF as specified by a value known as the *resolution bandwidth* value. Resolution bandwidth is the actual frequency width that is used during a sweep cycle and affects the granularity of the RF information displayed to the operator.

Resolution bandwidth is usually not controllable in PC-based spectrum analyzers. In traditional spectrum analyzers, resolution bandwidth can be adjusted so that finer and finer frequency widths are used to provide a higher resolution of RF medium transmissions.

Dealing with Intermittent Interference

There are two kinds of RF interference that some would classify as the worst kind:

Continuous Duty   The most notorious kind is one that is in continuous duty (it never stops transmitting) and therefore knocks out everything around it on that frequency.

Intermittent Interferer   The other kind is the one that shows up unexpectedly and unpredictably, has a high enough severity to impact performance or reliability, and then goes away until yet another unexpected and unpredictable occasion. This type of interferer is called an *intermittent interferer.*

Months can go by when you are dealing with an intermittent interferer and you never find the source. This can drive you batty. One of the best methods to handle intermittent interferers is by using *triggers*. Triggers are configurable thresholds from which a spectrum analyzer will trigger a series of actions.

For example, assume an environment has an intermittent interferer and a spectrum analyzer is brought onsite. The spectrum analyzer can be configured to start a recording and perhaps even send an alert to the IT administrator when the duty cycle reaches past 50 percent for a duration of 5 seconds. Once that condition is met, the action is kicked off.

Triggers can be quite helpful in allowing an IT administrator to monitor an environment without having to sit and wait for the event to recur.

Survey Types

There are several types of surveys that you can perform. Some are better suited for certain environments or for obtaining different types of data. You will find that some people have strong feelings about one survey method versus another. At the same time, what you lose or gain from one method isn't always self-evident. We will explore the different types in this section, starting with choosing the right client to perform a survey.

Choosing a Survey Client

Not all clients are created equally. If you've read Chapter 2, you should have a firm understanding of just how much clients differ from one another. When performing a WLAN survey, choosing the wrong client may yield an unusable WLAN design for inferior-performing devices in comparison to the client used for designing the WLAN. Grasping this fact is a critical requirement to be able to design enterprise WLANs.

It's a good idea to make a list of all the critical and widely deployed client devices that will be supported on the WLAN. Next, try to obtain some data from spec sheets or other forms of documentation that detail transmit power and receive sensitivity. These two factors are the biggest variables in client device performance.

Of the clients that are to be deployed, the device with the lowest transmit power and worst receive sensitivity would be the best choice. Transmit power is more of a function of determining what the AP transmit power will be. However, assuming the AP's power and client's power matches, the receive sensitivity of the client makes the next biggest difference.

Detailed client specifications like these aren't always easy to obtain. It is more likely that transmit power will be easier to obtain than receive sensitivity. If that is the case, a benchmarking exercise would yield the best results.

To benchmark your client devices, take an AP and set up a new SSID just for testing. This effort doesn't require sending any data, so it can be an open SSID that isn't even connected to a distribution system like an Ethernet network. Next, take each of your client devices to a fixed location that isn't immediately next to the AP. In fact, we recommend that you have clear line of sight with minimal multipath and obstructions that produce RF signal reflections. This often means that an elevated position is desirable. For example, mark a spot where the client device reports approximately −60 to −65 dBm from one of the test clients. Going upward or near −70 dBm will likely kick off the roaming algorithm of the device and unpredictable behavior may occur, so it is best to not go where the signal is that weak.

Next, take a spreadsheet and record each of your devices at that same location in a similar orientation. Each client device data should be recorded in their normal use case. That means if it is a phone, place it on a person's head. If two different laptop models use the same WLAN chipset, it is possible that the antenna design may be different, so it is best to also include device variations.

We also recommend that you record client uplink RSSI information, which is the value that the AP reports the client is connected at. Be aware that some APs average this value over a long period of time and you might need to wait a while in order for the averaging algorithm to weed out outlying data points. Consult your equipment vendor's documentation to make the reporting value as real time as possible for this exercise.

When a device is connected to the test SSID, it is also important to turn off automatic RF management features so that the AP never changes power or channel. In fact, you should not use dynamic transmit power control (DTPC) if you also want to record uplink RSSI information. DTPC causes the client to change its radio transmit power based on information that the AP tells it. For example, if the AP reports that it is configured at

14 dBm, clients that support DTPC will also turn their transmit power levels to be in parity with the AP.

It's a good idea to check each client device at different angles to the AP. For example, if you are using a laptop, stand in front of it to simulate how the device will be used in its real deployment scenario, and then rotate your orientation to the AP so that the laptop has a different orientation to the AP. Ninety-degree increments should do the trick. This way, you can help determine orientation variance to the AP.

Once this step is done, you should know your client device population quite well. When comparing the results of all your client devices, it should be apparent just how different their performances are from each another. Hopefully these client data measurements illustrate just how important selecting the right client is and how using different devices will result in very different survey data results. The best recommendation is to choose the worst performing client device that is supported by your survey application with which to perform surveys. This way you ensure that the network will support all of your client devices.

Keep in mind that most survey software packages do not allow you to use application-specific devices like VoWiFi phones, though basic surveying applications for some mobile platforms are currently available. You should also include in this client analysis a list of supported adapters that your survey software of choice also supports. Doing so will help you baseline your survey client adapter to the rest of your device population.

Survey Mapping Software

Until the day that glasses are invented that allow humans to see RF signals, we will need to visualize RF propagation using other methods. One of the best methods for visualizing RF data is to use a *survey mapping software* tool. This approach will import a scaled floor plan or map where the user can then associate RF data points to. Before these products existed, large CAD drawings were often used and RF values were handwritten manually onto these maps. That is a time-consuming process and makes it hard to visualize the results.

One of the first things you must do is calibrate the map. *Calibration* requires the user to measure a distance from two known points that are also identifiable on the map. The distance is then entered into the software to calibrate the entire map based on the known distance between those locations. Indoor environments that use drop ceilings are great because you can usually simply count the number of ceiling tiles and then multiply by the width of the tile. We recommend calibrating using long distances if possible, because the margin for human error is far less. Regardless of your method, once that is done the entire map should have dimensions true to real-world conditions that will allow the software to perform RF calculations.

 Before data collection—the time-consuming part of a survey—we highly recommend that you confirm that the calibration was performed correctly. Take two other measurements and compare the results. If a calibration error occurred and it wasn't caught, it is likely that the data gathered with an improperly calibrated map will be largely unusable.

Survey mapping software allows you to show a color overlay that corresponds to actual data measurements on top of a map, similar to what is shown in Figure 9.8. Maps showing a graphical representation of RF signals on top of a floor plan or map are also called *heat maps*.

FIGURE 9.8 Example of a heat map

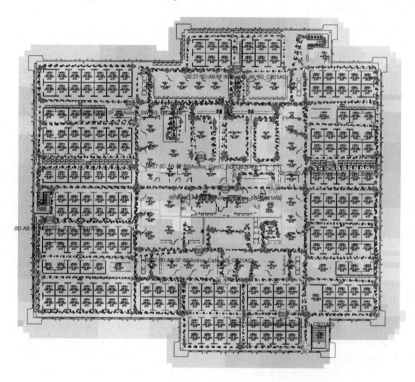

When you are analyzing RF survey data, heat maps serve an incredibly valuable purpose for visualizing the RF environment as an overlay on a map. This allows you to quickly see where signal levels do not meet certain design specifications.

Propagation Assessment

In addition to the data points that will be taken during the surveying process, survey mapping software commonly uses RF algorithms in order to calculate an area around the measurement points and for other visualization purposes. In fact, there may be no algorithm involved at all and the survey software simply draws a bubble of information around each data point that matches the actual measured data. It is important to realize that it is the survey software's guess. Some programs allow you to adjust the amount of guessable distance from each data point. If you are the one setting up the survey software parameters, you must determine how big this "guess zone" should be.

Keep in mind that the size of this zone in no way changes the actual data measurements. It is a visualization feature that makes the map look prettier. Improperly set propagation assessment distances lead more uneducated users of the heat map to assume that coverage might or might not be present in specific locations where no data was recorded, as shown in Figure 9.9.

FIGURE 9.9   Potentially misleading propagation assessment

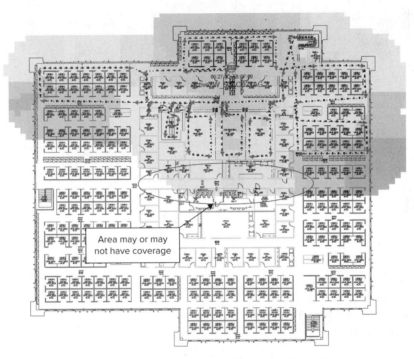

The area circled in Figure 9.9 is a hallway and the AP being measured is at the top of the map. The actual data measurements are based on the walking path where the dashed lines and arrows are indicated. In this case the propagation assessment was set to 25′. That means that in this case the SNR visualization will extend a bubble of color in a 25′ radius from a given data point.

Perhaps that hallway was made of a different building material or floor-to-ceiling metal filing cabinets full of paper were located against these walls. Would the signal propagate based on this assessment of 25′ as the survey software might predict? Assume that it will not. Unless a data measurement is made in a location, you cannot assume it will be covered unless you measured that location, which is why it is important to collect as many data points as possible for maximum accuracy. Minimize software guesswork when you can.

Compare this to the same survey, but when rendering the map using a 15′ propagation assessment, as shown in Figure 9.10.

FIGURE 9.10   Shorter propagation assessment

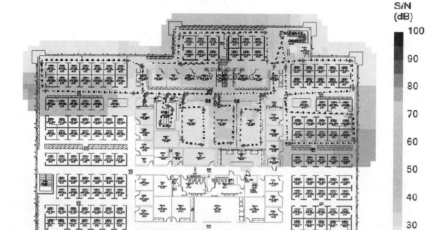

Spatial Orientation

Using survey mapping software requires a high degree of spatial orientation. When performing a manual site survey, some people struggle with tracking to the correct place on a map far more than others. You may find that you are one of those people. To complicate matters further, floor plans and maps aren't always up-to-date and that can cause disorientation. This has nothing to do with technical competency. For people who fall into this group, it may take more time to perform a survey of this type than others.

Some devices aid with overcoming disorientation. Tablet PCs that can use pen-based input can be rotated as the surveyor turns in different directions while keeping the tablet in the same orientation as the physical environment.

Simulations

Some survey mapping software packages also have simulation tools that incorporate the known data points as well as the map calibration in order for WLAN designers to test modifications to their designs. These tools are particularly helpful in augmenting an existing design in which you were able to measure RF data points.

To gather data points, the surveyor will need to start in one area of a map and begin moving. As the surveyor walks, they click the mouse where they are walking on the map. Most mapping software automatically samples data points at regular intervals between mouse clicks. Therefore, every time the surveyor's velocity or direction changes, they must click the mouse at those points in order for the automatic samples to be accurate. A good general rule is to record a manual data point approximately every 15′ or so. It is a general guideline, but realize that this is a safeguarding measure in case the surveyor has to retrace steps from an erroneous click, they are stopped in the hallway, or for a variety of other reasons. That means a minimal amount of resurveying will need to be done if steps have to be retraced.

Not all simulation tools are created equal—you usually get what you pay for in this category. To be clear, when we refer to the "wireless industry" it means more than just the 802.11 WLAN community. As a reminder, there are many other types of wireless communication, and some software is better suited for some technologies and use cases more than others. Simulation software is known to employ advanced RF calculations with a great deal of variable elements that an RF designer can tweak.

Passive Surveys

Passive surveys are surveys that are performed using a listen-only method. The survey client never associates to the AP. Such surveys can be quite helpful when you are looking for rogue devices or you want a good gauge of downlink RF coverage from the infrastructure devices. By downlink coverage, we mean the range of RF coverage that comes from AP transmissions. Passive surveys will be able to report downlink coverage and do not factor in any client uplink information.

Specifically, passive surveys listen for 802.11 beacons that come from infrastructure APs. Beacon frames are always sent at the lowest basic rate. Therefore, choosing 54 Mbps as the lowest basic rate on your survey APs will yield different results and range than a rate set to 2 Mbps. Lower data rates can be understood (decoded) at much further distances. We highly recommend that you use the same radio settings that you would in your production network.

Again, it is important to remember that passive surveys only provide information of downlink coverage from your WLAN infrastructure. APs that are set to very high or very low transmit powers can provide a skewed perspective of the network.

Convenience is your biggest gain when conducting passive surveys. There is less complication, and regardless of the security policy used, you will be able to perform a site survey.

Use passive surveys when you are trying to accomplish the following:

- Find rogues
- Locate RF trouble zones quickly
- Validate final RF settings
- Validate a network that uses enterprise security
- Perform initial surveys (caveats apply)

Methodologies of a Passive Survey

Passive surveys are used for a variety of purposes. Analyzing an existing network is one of the most common use cases. Passive surveys can quickly reveal areas of low or too much signal based on current settings. As mentioned earlier, the results can be dangerously misleading if the transmit power of the infrastructure is unknown or improperly configured.

Another common use of passive surveys involves the use of finding rogue APs. In this approach, configure the survey software to scan all possible 802.11 channels. That way, if a rogue AP was installed, a passive survey will most certainly catch at least one beacon from the AP when it scans each RF channel.

If you are using passive surveys to perform site surveys for new WLAN deployments, pay careful attention to detail. First, the transmit power of the survey AP must be reasonably low. We recommend that you use a transmit power that is close to or at the lower range of what you will want to support in your production environment. Specifically, this means that the AP transmit power should not exceed the maximum transmit power of your least powerful client devices. Another consideration is to not misconfigure your AP to exceed regulatory power constraints for the area where you will be operating your WLAN.

Client *channel scan settings* are another area where mistakes are commonly made when performing site surveys for new WLAN designs. If your survey AP is on channel 1 and your survey client is scanning all channels, you will not have usable results with which to gauge your WLAN deployment.

Optimizing Channel Scan Settings

When performing a passive site survey, usually the default settings are to scan all 802.11 channels. To help quantify this, assume that all 14 channels for 2.4 GHz ISM are scanned, plus all of the 24 channels for 5 GHz UNII and ISM. Next, the dwell time the survey radio will spend on each channel is configurable. The default in AirMagnet Surveyor is 250 ms because it needs to pick up at least one beacon for each AP on that channel, which is usually a default interval of about 100 ms. Ideally, more than one data sample is preferred before changing to the next channel in order to help mitigate against multipath and RF nulls.

In this case, that means a total of 38 channels are scanned. Therefore, only 1/38th, or 2.6 percent, of the time is spent analyzing a given channel. In other words, assuming 250 ms is spent on each channel, that would yield a total of 9.5 seconds to sweep through all the configured channels. A lot of physical ground can be covered within about 10 seconds. Assuming that your environment doesn't use all these channels and you are not looking for rogue devices, you will need to optimize the survey software to eliminate looking at those channels. In other words, if you are trying to analyze your WLAN infrastructure and it only operates on a subset of those channels (usually a small subnet), you will not achieve the results you might expect.

Another consideration when performing a passive survey is that you want to turn off automatic RF management features at least during the survey—that is, unless you want to validate that the automatic RF features are doing their job correctly. The reason you might want to turn off automatic RF management features is because you do not know what the AP transmit power is set to. Even if you recorded a snapshot of the network's values, they can still change at any time. Regardless, it is still an exercise to manually determine the AP transmit power when you have to analyze the survey results.

If you surveyed an environment, say, at 25 mW and based your AP placements using sound methodologies, it is hard to imagine that it would ever make sense for an AP to go down to 1 mW or perhaps even up to 100 mW. In both of these cases, problems will likely occur. Specifically, if coverage is based on 25 mW and you measured that it provided coverage into nearby rooms and areas where clients will reside, turning it down to 1 mW made your network unusable at the extents of its original coverage. Conversely, if the AP went to 100 mW, it is likely that you may have WLAN clients that aren't capable of that power. So, you get the megaphone on the hill analogy where clients can hear the AP, but the AP can't hear the clients back. Remember, transmit power doesn't change receive sensitivity; it only changes downlink coverage and what you are striving to achieve in WLAN designs is symmetry in the RF link. Of course, high transmit power could also create a co-channel interference problem too.

The point should be clear here that passive surveys can get you into trouble if you do not consider these variables.

Most site survey software packages do not work with enterprise WLAN security. While some offer support for certain EAP types, we highly recommend that you avoid all forms of WLAN security. It complicates the initial configuration of your survey and you are only concerned with RF coverage. If you need to analyze WLAN security, make that a separate task so it doesn't complicate the RF analysis. Furthermore, WLAN security should only be tested on the actual clients that your network will use.

Greenfield Deployments

One method of performing site surveys for designing new, or Greenfield, installations is to use a passive survey. If done correctly, this survey can result in time savings. In this approach, the survey AP is placed where the surveyor believes an optimal location is and the survey utility is configured to scan only that channel. The AP is configured to broadcast a survey-specific SSID regardless of the security type being used. Without even concerning yourself with security settings of the AP, as long as the AP is broadcasting an SSID, the client will be able to gather what it needs. Remember, beacon intervals are set to approximately 100 ms, so that will yield approximately 10 data samples per second, which is pretty darn good.

It is possible to expand this process to multiple APs. This means that you can take a second AP and configure it for the same or perhaps a different channel. It is usually best to use the same channel so the survey client never needs to change its channel. If another channel is used for the new AP, you should set your survey utility to scan *only* the two channels the survey APs are configured for. Failure to do so will result in the channel scanning phenomenon mentioned earlier where it will receive only a small fraction of information from the APs you are surveying.

This method requires caution. Placing APs either too close or too far away might not be evident until you have started or even finished your survey process, which would require you to start the survey all over again. If you choose to use this method, it is very important to walk to the extents of where you are trying to obtain coverage with your survey client to determine if any location changes are required before you begin to record data. Doing this for two APs certainly will add some time to each initial AP setup, but you need to take this into account if you believe it will save you time in the end. For those who do not have a lot of experience performing surveys, we don't recommend this method. In fact, there is a lot of room for error using this approach, but it is still a viable alternative.

What You Lose When Using Passive Surveys

The most significant loss of information with passive surveys is uplink information, PHY rate boundaries, and retransmissions. As you have already learned, PHY rates are generally based on RF signal and noise levels. A passive survey will only report signal propagation for beacons measured by the particular client device used to perform the measurements.

PHY rates can only be measured by sending actual data to and from an AP. PHY rates are also good indicators of RF signal health and balanced link budgets. For example, if an AP's transmit power is set at the maximum level, the passive survey will show a very large coverage area. What it wouldn't show is the usable subset of that coverage area by your least capable client devices. If a client device can only transmit at half the range of the AP, it will result in a client's inability to connect reliably to the infrastructure. PHY rates and retransmission information can be a useful gauge in comparison to purely downlink information.

Active Surveys

Active surveys are surveys performed with the survey client associated to the APs used during the survey. When a client is associated, it performs all the tasks a typical 802.11 client performs, which includes shifting data rates as RF conditions change and performing retransmissions when it determines that the AP did not hear the transmission. This information is incredibly valuable in order to highlight network problems.

Active surveys are commonly used for new WLAN deployments because they provide the most amount of detail to base a design on. Unless you are doing multiple APs at a time, it takes roughly the same amount of time to perform an active survey as compared to a passive one. Active surveys also benefit from reducing human error during the survey process. When performing an active survey, the only critical component to the survey equipment configuration is AP transmit power settings.

Use active surveys whenever you are looking to understand more information from your surveys. Having PHY rate and retransmission information tells you much more about the environment and the ability for a client to communicate back to the AP. Additionally, knowing how far your APs will propagate is useful information for a variety of purposes.

Active surveys are also recommended for less experienced survey teams because they can reveal and help to eliminate human error. They allow the person performing the survey to see the full coverage that a single AP provides that will most easily guide them in placing the next AP.

Some people refer to active surveys as "AP on a stick" surveys.

Methodologies of an Active Survey

There are two main methods for performing active surveys: the BSSID method and the SSID method.

BSSID Method

The BSSID method of an active survey is the most common of the two methods. This method locks a client into an AP's radio MAC address and prevents the client from roaming. This gives you a full picture of an AP's connectivity zone along with a rich amount of performance detail.

When this method is used, each individual AP can be analyzed, allowing a surveyor to show the complete RF propagation pattern and PHY rate zones. This information is, of course, based on the survey client type being used for the survey.

In Figure 9.11, a map of an active survey using the BSSID method was used. As you can see, different aspects of the data can be viewed—in this case, the actual PHY rate measured by the survey client.

FIGURE 9.11 PHY rate map

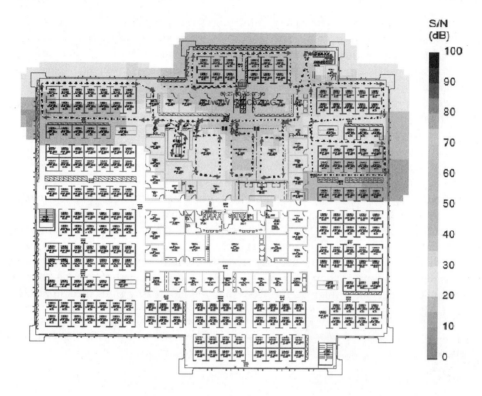

In Figure 9.12, the same map is shown but this time retransmission data was used. This map is a good gauge of performance and of spectrum interference. You would expect to see a large amount of retransmissions at the edges of coverage when using the BSSID method. By definition, you are asking your survey client to forcefully lock into the AP you are surveying, so it will continue to retry each data transmission until it is successfully heard or the client disconnects. It is likely that standard 802.11 clients will trigger the roaming process if excessive retransmissions occur. This map usually indicates the areas where clients will roam away from the AP being surveyed. Note that PHY rate shifting usually occurs once an 802.11 station starts to experience retransmissions. Therefore, you can expect to see an increase in retransmissions at rate shift boundaries.

Human error may also be reduced when compared to passive surveys. In an active survey, the surveyor does not need to pay attention to channel scan settings in the surveyor client. The software will find the AP and stay there until the survey is stopped.

FIGURE 9.12   Retransmission rate map

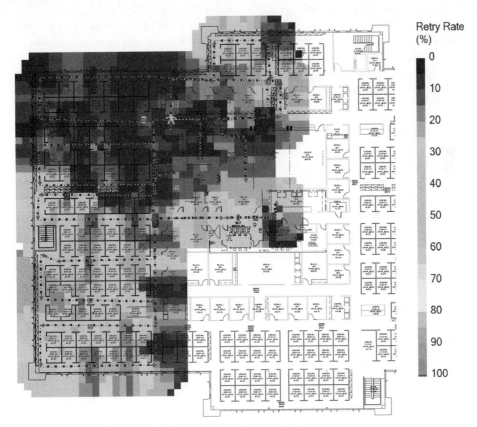

SSID Method

The SSID method of an active survey is used for surveying multiple APs and is more commonly used for postdeployment scenarios. This method enables the survey client to associate to an SSID where the client will roam between multiple APs. Some survey clients let you adjust the roaming thresholds for when the client will decide to roam. The SSID method is the closest example to real-world client roaming conditions of all the survey methods.

There are some limitations to using this method, including the loss of some visibility to the full RF propagation of each AP. In other words, you lose visibility to where acceptable coverage might begin and end for each AP. This is due to the fact that when the client leaves an AP and roams to another, it loses all visibility to the one it just left. Furthermore, if a client has acceptable coverage from an AP it is already associated to and it moves into a zone of another AP that is spaced too closely, it will likely not roam to that new AP until acceptable coverage degrades past the point where the surveyor client has instructed it to roam.

Another limitation to using this method is that roaming triggers used in the surveyor client likely do not mimic real-world conditions with standard WLAN clients. Therefore, it is not necessarily an accurate gauge of how your network and client devices will perform.

Conceptually, this method does have some value in helping to see how certain client roaming settings might perform on your network. Therefore, this method is largely used to augment other survey methods used, but usually does not serve as a replacement.

Security Limitations

Performing active surveys involves a full 802.11 association, which includes needing to configure WLAN security. This may be a problem when performing postdeployment coverage validations. Some survey software packages allow you to configure WLAN security, but often there are severe limitations on EAP types and compatibilities.

Simply put, it is best to avoid all security configurations when performing surveys using survey mapping software packages. The best option is to configure a temporary SSID or use a guest SSID (if one exists). On this temporary SSID, you can usually add a firewall rule to prevent all traffic from hitting the Ethernet network, if the AP is connected to the network. Otherwise, depending on the survey software package, using a WPA PSK key might be an option.

What You Lose When Using Active Surveys

With active surveys, the only thing you really lose is rogue or misconfigured AP information. Because the 802.11 client is actively associated to a BSSID it is not constantly changing channels hunting for APs that might be misconfigured or considered rogue.

Depending on what you are trying to achieve, it is usually best to perform a quick passive scan of all channels before performing an active survey. Passive scans of this nature consist of simply walking major areas of a coverage area. For example, if the environment is a university, it would be sufficient to walk the hallways doing a passive scan of all available channels. This process will find any AP that is transmitting beacons.

Virtual or Predictive "Surveys"

In the 802.11 industry, there are certainly a variety of contentious topics that are debated among professionals, not the least of which is the topic of virtual, or predictive, surveys. A *predictive survey* is a survey performed using a software program and an operator that is programming the tool with information about the coverage area in order for the software to perform AP placement based on RF algorithms. These surveys are typically void of any type of field measurement. From a business perspective, the gain is obvious: time and money. The problem is that if a predictive design is a bad design, the upfront savings of time and money are lost. In fact, recovering from a bad design can result in a substantial amount more money, and time, than would have been the case had the design been done right from the start.

Using the term *survey* for a completely software-based exercise is a play on words to some extent. Webster's Dictionary defines the word *survey* essentially as the act of taking measurements using analytical and mathematical methods. Predictions, although based on mathematic principles, do not factor in the unknown and real-world variables that exist. Many have argued the use of the word *survey* related to this method.

Environments that have critical dependencies on WLANs should not employ predictive surveys. This method should be reserved for environments where best effort performance is required. Predictive surveys also have value for budgetary planning purposes.

Another use of this method is when the building does not yet exist. In other words, you cannot survey an environment that hasn't been built, so you essentially have no alternative other than to perform a predictive survey—that is, unless you can wait until after the environment is built. If the target environment will critically rely on the WLAN for certain activities, including a heavy reliance on seamless roaming, it is indeed recommended to wait. Examples of these types include areas where VoWiFi will be deployed and places like hospitals with highly mobile devices and staff members with mobile devices. Otherwise, a predictive survey can get you mostly there and you can later perform a postanalysis of the network once it is installed and the environment is fully populated with furniture and other items that might affect RF propagation.

It is often best to pull additional cable drops and purchase additional APs whenever a predictive survey is used. This will more easily allow for altering the design based on the postvalidation survey.

The best times to incorporate a predictive survey are as follows:

- When the deployment environment hasn't yet been built
- To obtain a budgetary estimate for WLAN-related hardware
- When roaming requirements are less stringent
- When tolerance for less-than-perfect coverage is less critical

There is value to a predictive survey, but in practice, few environments have reliable enough information to base a predictive survey on. In addition, many facilities have less-than-accurate CAD drawings, a fact that adds even more complexity to the equation.

Approaches to Conducting Predictive Surveys

Predictive surveys involve complex software tools that are designed to import CAD drawings of the intended deployment environment. The basic concept is that you inform the software about certain characteristics of the environment based on the imported drawing. For example, you would specify the type of walls that are in the environment and the type of construction used. Walls that are made of concrete have higher attenuation than do walls made of sheetrock with wood or metal studs. Effectively, the knowledge of the person (operator) informing the predictive software tool about the environment is the single biggest factor for success. If there is a lack of detailed information available to the operator, then the results will be less reliable.

Calibration of a predictive modeling tool is absolutely essential. The software uses algorithms based on *free space path loss (FSPL)*, the information that the operator provides to the software, antenna type, and transmit power to predict locations for each AP.

The operator must also have knowledge of the deployment environment—perhaps even more so than someone who has the ability to visit onsite. For instance, the software tool might not be able to factor in atriums, areas of high aesthetic concern, mounting options, mounting height, antenna types, cable length limitations, and many other factors that can render certain locations not deployable.

It's possible for a predictive survey tool to incorporate measured RF propagation information in the environment. If you place a single AP in an environment and then walk the area and measure using a survey client, your software could incorporate that information into its prediction process. In fact, this method would be much less of a prediction because it incorporates this *RF fingerprinting* data.

If predictive modeling will be used, this is the recommended method. Take actual data samples from the deployment environment and use those RF propagation characteristics to calibrate the modeling software. In other words, use the real-world measured data to recreate the propagation characteristics in the software. This is a useful method for large deployment environments and allows for semi-accurate calculations. The actual deployment will require fine-tuning, if not more substantial changes, of AP placement, but the predictive approach will provide a useful framework. This survey method is often paired with dynamic RRM functionality.

What You Lose When Using Predictive Surveys

Whenever you are asked to perform a predictive survey and the use case doesn't fall into the categories we discussed earlier, you should ask your customer to reconsider.

When deciding to use a predictive survey for a WLAN design, you generally get exactly what you set out to achieve: a prediction. Nearly all WLAN experts with a respectable amount of field experience would agree that nothing beats actual field measurements and data on which to base a WLAN design.

There are so many variables that will affect RF propagation. Anybody who has performed a substantial number of surveys in a variety of environments can probably tell you a number of stories of just how hard it was to get ample coverage in certain parts of their projects. How RF will perform in a real environment is not easy to predict.

In short, you can lose a lot with a predictive RF survey, but these surveys still have their place and value proposition. Consider your choices wisely and *predict* what the consequences would be in both time and money (and to your reputation) if the design doesn't meet the requirements for proper performance, up to and including VoWiFi applications.

You must inform and educate your customer accordingly when you are asked to perform a predictive survey by using the information and caveats listed here.

Postverification

Based on the proper applications of when to use a predictive survey, you should also include a thorough postverification analysis of the network once it's installed. Chapter 14, "Post-Installation Validation," delves into methods for properly performing this task. Post-installation surveys are probably the most important aspect to all surveying approaches. You must verify that your design and deployment actually works for the actual clients that will be used. This is key.

Dealing with Multiple Floors

The interesting part of RF is how it penetrates through opaque materials. As humans, we tend to think about things in terms of light and how light stops when anything opaque stands in front of it thus creating a shadow. For example, television remote controls use Infrared light, which is why they do not work when pointed away from the television. While some good analogies of light may be used when discussing RF principles, it fails to compare on many other aspects. RF is vastly different from light because it has the ability to pass through walls, floors, and a variety of other objects. This includes in two-dimensional spaces as well as three dimensions. Three-dimensional RF propagation can be both a hindrance and a benefit.

RF can reflect, refract, and scatter off a variety of materials. Placing antennas near certain objects can change the tuning characteristics of the RF performance of those antennas—in a two-dimensional as well as a three-dimensional plane.

Simply put, RF propagates between floors—so much so in some environments that an AP on the floor above (although usually below) can provide enough coverage to service a sizable area of floor space below. It all depends on the building construction, the antenna types used, the mounting location, and antenna placement. Older construction techniques have tended to use strong and thick interior walls in multistory buildings for additional structural integrity. This type of construction limits a company's ability to reconfigure the floor based on its business needs. Architects and builders have learned this over the years and generally use building techniques that have strong floors with lightly constructed walls to allow for reconfiguration of the space based on future business needs.

From an RF coverage perspective, you may find yourself seeing much more floor-to-floor propagation in older construction than you see in newer or similar construction techniques. Floor-to-floor propagation will, without question, affect performance of the final design solution. For example, if you were to stack APs on top of each other from floor to floor, that arrangement will usually maximize the stacked APs' ability to hear one another. Configuring these APs for the same RF channel can have a significant impact on performance. This is not a desirable outcome.

What is likely to occur is the APs hear one another's transmissions to their associated client stations, but they do not hear the client station return transmissions especially if a client is directly above or beneath an AP on a different floor. This situation will usually invoke a common RF phenomenon called *hidden node*. Hidden node is most commonly drawn from a 2D perspective, but when you consider it from a 3D perspective, it makes the possibilities for hidden node even more real. Figure 9.13 shows a simple illustration of an AP that is able to communicate with a mobile device on the same floor using the same channel as an AP placed on the floor below it. The transmissions from the AP back to the client are also heard by the AP below it, resulting in interference and corruption from hidden node transmissions.

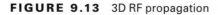

FIGURE 9.13   3D RF propagation

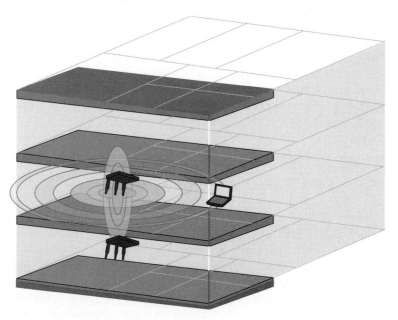

Understanding RF Propagation

Passive surveys are excellent for helping you gain a solid understanding of RF propagation between floors. Of course, they will only work if the APs are installed, which is arguably too late in many cases. Therefore, multifloor RF propagation needs to be factored in, and quantified, during the initial RF survey designs.

In general, you should take spot measurements at different locations in a facility from the floors above and below an AP placement. Because it is cost prohibitive to perform this measurement for every AP placement, and you are hoping to gain a perspective of the propagation between floors, you should perform this activity only where construction methods and periods are different. For example, parts of a facility that have been expanded over the years most likely have different floor-to-floor signal bleeding than parts constructed during earlier periods. This information, in essence, tells you to what extent you need to worry about floor-to-floor stacking of APs. Alternatively, this information might help you design for signal propagation in some parts of a facility.

In general, signal bleeding through floors produces a small geographical area of acceptable signal coverage. In this case, you should not rely on this coverage for applications like VoWiFi or where devices are highly mobile. When in motion, a client device might roam to the floor above or below, and as the device continues to be in motion, it will then quickly roam out of its acceptable coverage area. The result would be two quick roaming events, which might cause a perceptible delay in service. This same phenomenon is similar to APs that are powered down to the lowest of extremes.

In other instances where roaming activities are minimal or devices are stationary, this 3D bleeding might be factored into a design. Multifloor coverage applies in certain situations where two AP coverage patterns meet and a device is stationary. We don't recommend that you rely on multifloor coverage, but it is just another tool in the toolbox for certain corner cases.

The important thing is to familiarize yourself with the negative effects of multifloor propagation and be able to quantify how much it needs to be factored into your design. It is always best to quantify this aspect by performing at least a few measurements. Special areas like atriums, outdoor areas adjacent to multifloor buildings with deployed APs, and similar types of cases are obvious areas of concern.

RF Propagation in Atriums

A good rule of thumb when dealing with atriums is to not place APs too close to the walls of the atrium when providing coverage to adjacent (non-atrium) areas. APs placed in an atrium will usually propagate quite far, and if the signals of APs placed in other parts of the coverage area do not propagate into the atrium, this means that explicitly placed APs in the atrium can provide the best, contention-free coverage to clients also located in the atrium. We generally recommend that you use directional antennas in atriums to maximize the coverage in the atrium while also minimizing the propagation into the adjacent areas.

Floor-to-Floor Placement

In general, avoid stacking APs directly on top of each other between floors. Depending on the type of antenna used, the propagation pattern might be minimal directly above and below, and in those cases it is certainly acceptable. In some cases it may be unavoidable due to mounting or cabling restrictions.

It is best to place APs in a staggered fashion between floors. Where two AP cell edges meet on one floor, you should place an AP directly above and/or below that spot on neighboring floors. Doing so can help protect against coverage gaps should construction or other factors change in the environment that affect the original propagation from APs. In this case, 3D RF propagation can help a design be more resilient to changes over time.

Most enterprise APs that incorporate internal antennas tend to be designed to be mounted to a ceiling and provide coverage somewhat similar to a low-gain patch antenna. The signal is somewhat of a carotid pattern from back to front. Figure 9.14 is an example of an enterprise AP coverage pattern that is heavily used in the enterprise.

FIGURE 9.14   Elevation plane (2.4 GHz) propagation pattern of a Cisco 1142 AP

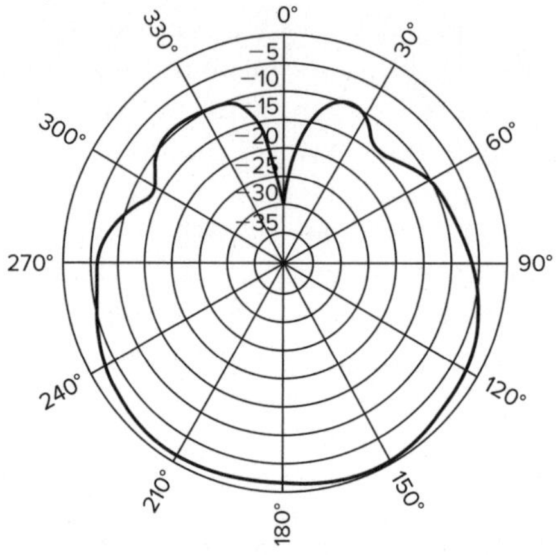

Channelization

As you may have already determined at this point in the chapter, channelization should be based on floor-to-floor propagation from all the APs in an environment. If you are not planning on using an automatic channel assignment algorithm, you will need to rely on your survey information to best assign channels based on multidimensional information.

Most new deployments of any scale will likely have automatic RF algorithms built into the infrastructure. If this is the case, you may find that you might experience some unexpected results. In some cases, you might find that several immediately adjacent APs on the same floor use the same RF channel. Although this situation may not seem ideal, it is often likely due to multifloor RF propagation. What the channelization algorithm is likely doing is configuring different channels for each of those APs based on its hottest RF neighbors. Therefore, from the perspective of each of these APs it is likely that they are hearing APs from floors above and below hotter than the adjacent APs on the same floor.

This arrangement yields, from the perspective of the AP, too many RF neighbors for the channels it has available. Too many neighbors and too few channels to pick from is especially true when you're using the 2.4 GHz ISM band where only three nonoverlapping channels are available. In this scenario, it is important to either trust the algorithm or consider redesign efforts. After all, the algorithm is based on the most important metrics.

Utilizing Infrastructure Links

Infrastructure links in the context of this discussion pertain to *point-to-point (PTP)*, *point-to-multipoint (PtMP)*, and *mesh* AP RF links. Typically these are APs installed in outdoor environments that bridge computer networks or devices in multiple locations. Mesh links, in particular, are generally used to extend the range of an RF coverage area where a network backhaul connection is not feasible.

These types of infrastructure links can often travel great distances. The following is usually the case: the longer the distance that needs to be covered, the higher the antenna gain that must be used at each side of the link. As you increase the amount of antenna gain in an infrastructure link, the alignment of these antennas can be quite a challenge. Let's now discuss infrastructure links in detail.

Point-to-Point Links

PTP links usually travel the farthest distances of any of the infrastructure links we've mentioned. By definition, they involve a device dedicated to each end of the RF link that speaks to one and only one RF peer. Because of this fact, you will find a special breed of APs, called *bridges*, that are designed and marketed specifically for these applications. The term bridge is overused and can be interpreted as many different technologies in computer networking. In the wireless world, using the word bridge by itself is usually interpreted as a PTP link device, but we recommend that you refer to them as a PTP bridge in order to be more specific.

Because PTP links are designed to speak with only one peer, it is quite common to see them sold or packaged in pairs. When they are not, it is often because the manufacturer has a variety of options for each bridge, such as internal or external antenna ports, different types and quantities of wired ports, powering options, and so forth. It is not uncommon to have to spec different, but compatible, model numbers for each end of the PTP link.

Compatibility is an interesting topic when it comes to PTP bridge links. A standards-based, multivendor protocol is not required. When you are using a device for such a specific use, a manufacturer tends to optimize a standards-based protocol like 802.11 with certain proprietary tweaks to gain performance and stability. Such tweaks may include delaying the standard ACK times because of the time involved for RF propagation to occur over distances and the response to be provided back to the transmitter. If you need to travel far distances, it takes longer and longer for the RF transmission to travel that distance. Channel bonding (increasing the frequency bandwidth) is another common technique by PTP bridge manufacturers to gain more data throughput. Other areas of tweaking include different modulating and coding schemes, contention algorithms, and QoS prioritization. The PTP link doesn't even have to use RF at all—some companies use lasers and other mediums as a form of optical, long-range communication for the same purpose. We always recommend that you avoid mixing different vendors with PTP links.

PTP links are often used as a replacement for a physical data circuit that comes with a high monthly recurring price tag. They are also used as a means of increasing data throughput to an existing set of circuits where IP routing protocols can load-balance traffic across. Using PTP links for this purpose usually provides a great deal of cost savings and perhaps a big increase in speeds with reduced latency. Even buildings that may be located close to each other may use PTP links in lieu of trenching the ground, running conduit, and installing fiber-optic or copper cabling. A great deal of labor and cost is involved in this effort. While wired connections have some benefits, using PTP links provides a cost benefit and they can even be used for relatively temporary installations.

What if you don't have LOS between the two PTP links? Usually no LOS spells disaster. Many RF links have still been made even with this deficiency. Typically success is achieved only by using the lowest frequencies possible—which explains why you still see many 900 MHz ISM band PTP products on the market. The speeds that are possible using 900 MHz are less than the higher frequencies, but the lower frequency can penetrate through many more obstructions, and therefore products using this band still have their niche in the marketplace.

Alignment

One of the hardest tasks when dealing with PTP links is getting the proper alignment. While this is usually a problem attributed to longer-range links, sometimes even shorter-range PTP links present a challenge. As you'll recall from our discussion of antennas in Chapter 7, "RF Hardware and 802.11n," achieving higher antenna gain means that the RF signal is reduced for other directions. So, the higher the antenna gain, the higher that directionality of the antenna. Additional RF isn't manufactured from higher-gain antennas; it is just that higher-gain antennas shape the RF signal to the particular antenna pattern.

When using high-gain antennas for PTP links, you'll find it difficult to align over long distances where you may not even be able to see the other end of the link. Here's a good parallel: pretend you are five miles away from a colleague at the other end of a communication link and you are both holding a laser beam. Imagine trying to align both laser beams at each other perfectly. Both sides must be properly aligned for a functional communication link.

This is only an analogy and no antenna gain manufactured at this time has a *beamwidth* that small. However, a 24 dBi parabolic dish or grid antenna only has a horizontal and vertical beamwidth of approximately 10°. That is an extremely tight beamwidth to align over long distances.

One way to get around this issue is to use a high-gain antenna on one end of the link and a lower-gain antenna (15–19 dBi) on the other, as shown in Figure 9.15. This method allows for very high gain in the link budget without complicating the installation and tuning process.

FIGURE 9.15   PTP link with lower gain antenna on one side

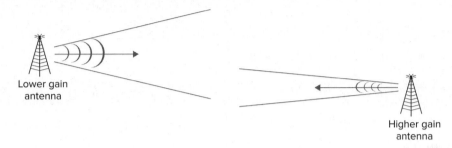

Lower gain
antenna

Higher gain
antenna

In fact, there are many stories of installation professionals who have spent a day or more trying to align very high-gain antennas at each end of a link where they knew RF LOS was possible.

When you use a lower-gain antenna on one side, it may only reduce the overall link budget by a number in the single digits. At the same time, the antenna can move due to wind (on top of a tall mounting pole or radio tower) and will still maintain a solid link.

Another point to keep in mind is that, by definition, using a lower-gain antenna has a wider propagation pattern. The result may be that other unwanted RF transmissions that are in range of the lower-gain antenna are introduced. For example, if the lower-gain antenna is mounted on top of a roof where APs using the same channel are installed, the lower-gain antenna's pattern may include these APs in its primary propagation pattern. That will cause transmission hold-offs on PTP links transmissions because, as you'll recall, we are using CSMA/CA or collision avoidance techniques.

If that is the case, you should consider on which side of the link it may be best to place the lower-gain antenna. Perhaps only one side of the link has this issue. An example of this technique would be to use a 24 dBi high-gain parabolic dish on one side of the link but a lower-gain 15 dBi yagi antenna on the other.

Polarization

The polarization of an antenna is defined as the *E field*, or electric field. When the E field is vertical, the polarization is said to be vertically polarized. Alternatively, if the E plane is parallel to the ground, the polarization is said to be horizontal. If you look on the back of most directional antennas, the direction of the E field is usually marked with an arrow. For additional clarity, refer to the manufacturer's documentation for the antenna you are using.

Antenna polarization becomes much more of a design factor over longer distances. If antenna polarization is incorrect, the signal may not be strong enough to maintain a reliable signal for the PTP link. Be certain to use the same polar alignment for both sides when using PTP links. Figure 9.16 illustrates one antenna using horizontal alignment and another using vertical alignment.

FIGURE 9.16   Antenna polarization misalignment

Antenna polarization might be a technique you want to use when trying to avoid interference from other RF transmissions. One polarity might be better than the other and you can make this determination during a PTP site survey.

Survey Methods

The first step in a PTP link survey is to get absolutely everything working perfectly in the comfort of an office with the equipment placed nearby each other. Doing so saves you a great deal of time in the field configuring the units and eliminating configuration from the troubleshooting equation. Even after doing so, you must *save* the configuration to the flash memory or equivalent of the radio and perform a full power-down and power-up to ensure the changes stuck.

While you may need to change RF frequency of the link during the survey depending on RF conditions, this task is extremely minor in comparison to configuring everything from scratch.

When performing a survey for a PTP link, come prepared with an entirely different arsenal of tools than you might need for an indoor survey. You will need the following:

- A variety of gain and types of antennas, including very high ones
- Antenna cables and connector adapters
- Binoculars, a spotting scope, or a telescope
- Mirrors
- Accurate GPSs
- A compass or sighting compass
- A level
- A protractor
- Tape or chalk for marking alignment
- Mobile phones
- A laptop computer
- A Wi-Fi radio or PC-based spectrum analyzer with an external antenna connector (if applicable)

A common technique is to start with lower-gain antennas and build your way up. For example, one side of the link can start with a 15 dBi antenna coarsely pointed using GPS coordinates and a compass for alignment. The other side of the link can also use a 15 dBi antenna using the same technique for coarse alignment. This method allows for a very wide tolerance of error usually in both the vertical and horizontal alignment.

Always perform a PTP RF survey using two teams of people. One team (or person) needs to be at each end of the PTP link.

Assuming you've done your homework and you have the coarse alignment correct, you may be able to establish a link. In situations such as longer-range PTP links, you may need higher-gain antennas to establish a link. Lower gain antennas will steal signal from the RF link budget. In that case, you may have to start with a higher-gain antenna at one side of the link. If you need it for both, perhaps a PTP link is questionable to begin with because you shouldn't be operating with such a small margin in your link budget.

Remember, even a low-quality RF link from the PTP peers is enough to start optimizing the alignment and antenna choice.

The coarse tuning method is sometimes referred to as *prealignment*. Prealignment may also be performed using other techniques incorporating the materials we've mentioned. For example, mirrors have traditionally been used to reflect the sun from one side of the link to the other. You've likely experienced the bright sun reflected back to you from a mirror. It is quite noticeable even from very far distances.

Other methods include using binoculars, spotting scopes, or telescopes to see the other end of the link to get coarse alignment. Spotting scopes and telescopes can be quite nice when used with tripods because they provide a visual point of reference for the coarse antenna alignment.

 Real World Scenario

Using Optical Scopes

One of the authors received a phone call from a colleague who was performing a PTP radio installation at a job site. The colleague, Joe, said that he had an interesting story to relate. So, he began to explain by describing the environment and the fact that the antennas were separated by a distance difficult to determine by the naked eye. He commonly carried a spotting scope for such purposes.

In order to perform the work, Joe explained to the employees of the facility that he would need to be on the roof of the area, and he asked the employees to alert the security staff. But during his coarse alignment activities, Joe was interrupted by a team of officers with armed weapons pointed directly at him. Because the environment was an airport, the use of the spotting scope on top of a roof overlooking a runway of taxiing aircraft while he was in a prone position didn't sit well with the airport police.

Hopefully you will never find yourself in this predicament, but be aware that it might be best to request an escort for some environments.

After the coarse alignment is performed, you can then start to fine-tune the alignment. One technique is to find the center of the pointing direction. Here's where marking tape and chalk come in handy. Take one end of the PTP link and, reading signal levels from the PTP radio, move the antenna all the way to either the left or the right until the signal degrades rapidly. Repeat this exercise several times to make sure there weren't other factors temporarily contributing to the signal degradation. Once you determine the pointing direction where the signal rapidly degrades, mark the pointing direction on the floor or other surface using tape, chalk, or other means. Take the midpoint of the left and right markings, and this should be near the optimal pointing location for the *azimuth*. Once you determine the azimuth, record an exact compass reading along with a GPS coordinate.

You can perform the same general marking process for the vertical pointing, otherwise known as the *elevation*. Instead of using a GPS and a compass, use a level and a protractor. Even if the mounting survey for the antenna isn't perfectly vertical from the perspective of a level, you can still establish the elevation pointing direction by measuring the angle using a level to determine an exactly vertical reference point. Next, perform the same exercise for the other end of the link. In general, it is best to start with a zero elevation for coarse tuning, which you can usually obtain by using a level.

Once pre-alignment and some fine-tuning are completed, you now have a clear angle to position different antenna types. For example, if you want to increase the signal quality of the RF link, you can now attempt a higher-gain antenna, starting with only one side of the link. It is recommended to start with only one side of the link at a time. Remember to check for proper antenna polarization and verify that your cables are tightly secured each time you use a different antenna.

Performing PTP antenna alignments can be extremely time-consuming. It is not uncommon for a full day to be consumed aligning two high-gain antennas. Increasing distances add to the difficulty.

Point-to-Multipoint Links

PtMP links can be very different design scenarios compared to PTP links. PtMP links often involve employing traditional APs using bridge link modes, but you may use products from PTP bridge manufacturers as well. PtMP links are often used when access to network resources from one location needs to be given to several remote locations. These remote locations may be relatively adjacent buildings or perhaps even separated by some distance.

Let's start with a simple scenario. Consider a central office building with two remote locations that are at completely different pointing directions. Figure 9.17 shows what this design scenario may look like.

FIGURE 9.17   PtMP design scenario

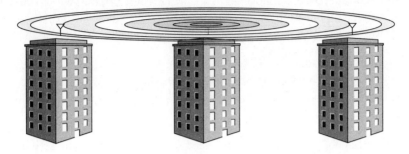

The central location has a single *root bridge* and several nonroot bridges joined to the bridge. The antenna for the root bridge is an omnidirectional antenna because each building has an opposite pointing direction. Perhaps if the buildings were separated by an angle of only 60° or so from the central location, a higher-gain antenna could have been chosen.

Regardless of whether the central location uses an omnidirectional antenna or not, the RF channel will be the same for all communication. Depending on the technology used, the maximum bandwidth possible that a single RF channel can provide will vary. The other challenge is that in PtMP links, the nonroot bridges may not be able to hear one another's transmissions to the root bridge. In this scenario, hidden node problems occur, and if the nonroot bridges communicate at the same time, collisions take place. Once this happens, the total throughput of the link drastically decreases in addition to increasing latency.

PtMP links using standard 802.11-based protocols are usually not recommended due to these effects. Some PTMP vendors provide their own proprietary protocol where timing techniques can be used when nonroot bridges have dedicated time slots for communications or a different medium reservation protocol is used.

If standard 802.11-based APs are used, it is best to use dedicated radios for each remote location back to the central location using different RF channels along with high-gain antennas at the central site. The high-gain antennas allow for better isolation from adjacent channel interference between the other radios used for the other PTP links. Even when you use high-gain antennas at the central location, you may not be able to separate the mounting locations very far from each other. When this happens, using nonadjacent RF channels is always the best route.

The other benefit of using this technique is increased bandwidth and elimination of contention from other remote link transmissions. In essence, each PTP link pair will have its own RF domain to manage. This arrangement increases the amount of throughput by what a single channel capacity can bear depending on the technology used. It also nearly eliminates the amount of contention and RF collisions for the channel, thereby reducing the latency problems inherent in a standard PtMP link.

Mesh

Mesh networks gained a great deal of steam when more and more interest in outdoor metropolitan networks began. The concept of a mesh network is that you put up a series of APs, called *root nodes*, that are connected to an Ethernet or other type of backhaul network. You then add APs not connected to a backhaul network that will result in a self-formed, multilink RF connection network between the root nodes. The benefit of mesh networks is that you can save money in metropolitan deployments by not supplying a backhaul connection to each and every AP.

Mesh network APs come in two forms: single- and multi-radio mesh APs. Single-radio mesh networks use a single RF channel between all mesh nodes. After all, how could an AP serve traffic to clients and then communicate with other mesh nodes at the same time? That is why a single channel is used. The problem with a single-radio design is that the same radio is used to provide access to client devices and to provide backhaul connectivity.

Multi-radio mesh nodes usually use a different, dedicated radio for the actual backhaul connection. For example, one radio uses the 2.4 GHz band to service wireless clients in a full-time fashion whereas a second radio uses the 5 GHz band to communicate with other mesh nodes. The benefit to this design is that latency is greatly reduced. Whereas in single-radio mesh APs the only radio has to service clients and then transmit it again to another mesh node, a dedicated backhaul radio can perform this operation in a parallel fashion. There are mesh AP designs that use more than one backhaul radio and perhaps even more than one access radio. Other frequency bands such as 4.9 GHz (in the United States only) or even multiple channels at 5 GHz can be used.

With mesh networking, all APs are required to see each other at fairly high signal levels. Recall our discussion of SNR and how that affects data rates. For example, if a mesh AP has to communicate to another mesh AP and the signal level is weak, it can only use PHY rates applicable to signal and noise values. This can easily lead to a mesh AP serving wireless clients who are connected at high PHY rates while the mesh node can only forward traffic at lower PHY rates. If that same mesh node was also serving other mesh APs that need to forward traffic through it, you would have even more congestion on the backhaul link.

Mesh networks also benefit from highly optimized traffic distribution algorithms that can self-heal. The concept is that if a mesh network is designed so that it can see more than one mesh node, the backhaul network can recover from a single-mesh node failure. Of course, clients located where the mesh node failed would have no connectivity (unless cell overlap was planned for), but the backbone network should survive.

Designing a mesh network requires careful attention to backhaul connections just as with client connections. In order for the backhaul network to properly operate, it requires high PHY rates, ideally using separate radios designated for backhaul connections.

Antenna gain is important in the backhaul connection. Mesh nodes might be 90° separated from each other or in a 360° pattern. Although you would want to use antenna gain, the downside of using it would be that it makes adding to the mesh more difficult. Suppose your mesh node uses a directional antenna and points back to the rest of the mesh network; if you add another mesh AP to that network, it would likely point to the back of the antenna it needs a mesh connection with. This is why many mesh networks use omnidirectional antennas for backhaul.

Regardless of whether single- or multi-radio mesh nodes are used, the big challenge with mesh is latency. Because not every mesh node has a wired backhaul connection, mesh

APs need to relay traffic back to root nodes. In ideal RF conditions the transmission might arrive rather quickly, but since we are using unlicensed frequencies, RF congestion and interference often occur where traffic needs to be retransmitted, creating a variable amount of latency.

Several mesh networking vendors originally showed interest in a standardized mesh platform from the IEEE under the 802.11s task group. As of this writing, 802.11s was subject to abandonment because of the lack of vendor cooperation and limited appeal in real-world environments.

Handling Critical Findings

This section explores dealing with situations or findings that require immediate escalation to your point of contact. The important point to remember is that it sometimes is better to escalate an issue during the survey process itself rather than wait for a later date (such as simply including the issue in the documentation).

Bad Interference

When you are performing an RF site survey, one of the biggest areas of concern is bad RF interference. If you recognize areas where substantial RF interference exists, you should immediately escalate this issue to your point of contact.

Once you encounter bad interference, quantify what it is and locate the source. It is not always possible to identify the source, but you can usually identify the location. At the same time, identifying the source can indicate where the transmitter is located. Of course, this may not be possible if the spectrum analyzer doesn't have a device classifier or you can't manually identify the signal.

Some spectrum analyzers have an equivalent of a Geiger counter to assist with these efforts. Figure 9.18 shows that type of feature from a PC-based spectrum analyzer.

FIGURE 9.18   PC-based spectrum analyzer device finder

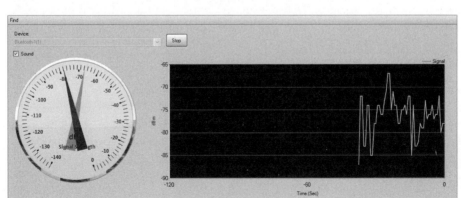

Directional antennas can also be helpful coupled with a spectrum analyzer. The directional antenna can be used to stand in a single location and point the antenna in different directions to see where signal levels peak. Be aware that in indoor environments the source may be originating from a different floor and that signal reflections and multipath effects are more common.

Specifically, the types of bad interference you should watch for are ones with very high duty cycles. A list of APs that you picked up at about −90 dBm and with duty cycles of less than 10 percent is not something that generally requires immediate attention unless the environment or your customer warrants it.

Interference from intermittent, non-Wi-Fi transmitters can be quite troublesome and frustrating to deal with. Intermittent interferers are often the most difficult to identify and locate. It is comparable to a person experiencing problems with their PC and an IT person is called over to resolve the conflict but the problem does not occur; when the IT person leaves, the problems start to occur again. With RF interference it is worse because unless a spectrum analyzer is used at the time, it is often hard to determine whether it is an equipment problem, a network problem, or an application problem. Trigger features that automatically initiate data gathering come in handy in this situation.

Whenever an RF survey is performed, each microwave should be checked for interference severity. As you've read repeatedly in this book, microwave ovens will interfere with Wi-Fi, but some are drastically worse than others. Microwave ovens use a variety of types of shielding to keep the microwave signals used to cook the food from escaping the oven. The fact is that some manufacturers do a far better job than others. What's more, the shielding can deteriorate over time after repeated use.

When the shielding deteriorates, the microwave needs to be replaced. Fortunately, microwaves are cheap and their cost pales in comparison to the cost involved in troubleshooting incidents related to microwave oven interference. Microwave ovens most certainly fall into the category of intermittent RF interferers.

Suspicious Rogues

Rogue APs come in a variety of forms. Rogues may be neighboring APs that you can't do anything about, or perhaps they are APs within the same deployment area of your target location that you are surveying. Here are some examples of rogue APs that should be escalated upon discovery:

- An AP connected to the wired LAN with no security
- An AP that is consuming a great deal of channel capacity that is affecting performance
- Non-802.11 network devices, such as frequency hopping (FH) APs

The benefit of using unlicensed frequency bands is that you do not have to purchase a license to operate in that band. Because the band is unlicensed, the sales volume of manufacturers is exponentially higher and therefore the costs are low and fiercely competitive among equipment manufacturers. On the other hand, the problem with unlicensed frequencies is just that—they are unlicensed. Anybody can use the spectrum and there isn't much you can do about it.

Rogues are considered a fact of life in many environments. However, rogue APs deployed against policy by employees or hackers on your network are nearly always within the purview of the design team. Regardless, it is best to quantify the effects of each rogue AP and locate each one within the coverage area of your network design.

For 802.11a/b/g/n radios, this task can be fairly simple. Performing a passive site survey scanning all available channels using a dual-band 802.11 radio will usually uncover all of them. Assuming the surveyor wasn't sprinting through areas, a rogue AP should be caught. Survey mapping software often has filtering options that display in a map the signal strengths of each unique AP that was found during the survey, clearly indicating areas of the highest signal strength.

Finding IEEE 802.11 FH devices is more difficult. The reason is that the narrowband spikes of each FH transmission can travel for quite a distance. Here again you'll want to use a directional antenna to help determine the direction of the device.

It is sometimes possible to find APs that have been hidden by employees providing their own Wi-Fi service. This is most common in areas where Wi-Fi hasn't already been deployed. Hidden APs are difficult to find. They can be located above drop ceiling tiles or mounted to the bottom of desks. Figure 9.19 shows a heat map of a rogue AP discovered during a passive scan of a facility.

FIGURE 9.19   Heat map of a rogue AP

A list of rogue APs that have signal strengths stronger than –80 dBm should be escalated to your project team or customer immediately. Chapter 15, "Design Troubleshooting," describes troubleshooting techniques for handling rogue devices.

Mounting Restrictions

One of the challenges of designing WLANs is that you can't always place an AP or antenna where you need it. Placement limitations are common and although they can be frustrating, they are a reality of the job. This challenge is particularly evident when you're placing outdoor APs.

You will usually find that there are relatively painless solutions available to overcome outdoor placement limitations, but in some cases the problem affects the design of the WLAN in a particular area. When this is the case, you need to alert the stakeholders of the WLAN. Suppose you have to cover a long, narrow walkway and you cannot place equipment down the middle (due to a variety of reasons). As the tunnel fills up with people, equipment, or other things that affect RF propagation, the signal degrades in the middle of the tunnel to an insufficient level.

Various mounting restrictions include the following:

- You are unable to install an AP or antenna in the most convenient location.
- You are unable to get unshielded twisted pair (UTP) cabling or power into a specific location.
- The WLAN exceeds the cable length limitations.

Ceilings

High ceilings are a common trouble spot for AP placement for two primary reasons. First, it is difficult to install the AP because you might need a man lift. In general, if something is difficult to install, consider the effectiveness of that solution and use locations where access to that placement at a later date will be less burdensome. If you can't survey in that location, that's a hint that you might want to reconsider the placement. Second, high ceilings may not provide the best RF coverage to your WLAN clients; the signal may not have enough vertical gain in order to provide sufficient coverage.

Hard and decorative ceilings can also be tricky locations to install APs or antennas. We forget how spoiled we are when using drop ceilings with removable tiles whenever we have to run additional cable. With hard or other types of permanent ceiling construction, installing an AP may be unrealistic. But although hard ceilings are a requirement for some facility locations for a variety of business reasons, in order to maintain a sufficient level of serviceability to the building, access panels are often installed in these rooms, allowing you to pull your cable through.

Even with a drop ceiling with removable tiles, cable runs might not be easily achieved. You never know what is above the ceiling tiles, and you always need to confirm with the proper personnel.

Ceiling challenges aside, there may be areas where running cable presents a formidable challenge for other reasons—too many to mention here. The point is that, ironically, it takes a lot of wire to design and deploy a wireless network.

Proximity Limitations and Obstructions

Proximity restrictions to other hardware or systems can also pose a challenge. These include minimum distance requirements from fire suppression systems like sprinklers, sensors of various types, and other types of RF devices.

Mounting an AP near a sprinkler head that is used in the case of a fire will restrict the spray pattern of the sprinkler. This is just an example, but other systems have proximity restrictions, so you want to check local building codes or a licensed authority.

Co-locating other RF systems immediately adjacent to each other is not a good idea. Examples include some cellular systems (like distributed antenna systems), two-way radio, telemetry, and similar systems. Even though those systems may not be operating on the same RF channel, there are sometimes side effects like intermodulation. Generally speaking, do not mount an AP within 1 meter of another antenna system. The farther away the better you are.

Always consult local, state, or federal regulatory building codes whenever installing an AP. As we've mentioned in other parts of this book, a variety of industry vertical regulatory requirements come into play, depending on the type of venue.

Materials that have been commonly used for construction have changed over the years. Most of you may have heard of asbestos, which is an insulation material that was commonly used for a number of years. Asbestos is now banned and considered highly hazardous, and you may face it in a future design. If the building where you are installing looks old, you should ask whether asbestos was used in the building's construction. If that is the case, it might drastically change the locations available to you for your design. Costs can also greatly increase when you have to run cables in a building that contains asbestos.

If you are installing equipment or cabling indoors, you may have *plenum* requirements to deal with. A plenum space is an area, usually above a ceiling or below a floor, that is used for air circulation in inhabited areas. The concern over plenum spaces is related to fire. When higher air circulation is available, so is the availability of oxygen that will make a fire grow stronger. Whenever plenum requirements are present, you have to factor in every component of an AP installation—including the cabling, the AP itself (not all APs are plenum rated), and antenna cables.

There are other mounting concerns that may seem like common sense, but it is still quite common to see mistakes made. Be cognizant of mounting locations that affect door openings, roll-up doors, or other facility materials.

When you are faced with mounting APs that have high security access restrictions, determine whether performing maintenance or troubleshooting will be possible. This caveat also applies to certain areas like hospital operating rooms (ORs). ORs have highly erratic schedules and may completely restrict any IT personnel from doing anything with the AP while operations are in progress.

Cable Length Limitations

Copper twisted pair cabling is commonly referred to as UTP, CAT5, CAT6, and so forth. This cabling has length limitations when used with Ethernet networks. The distance is approximately 100 meters, or approximately 328 feet, and PoE requirements follow the same limitation. You need to consider the entire cable length required from the switch port to the AP, which may also include one or more patch cable lengths. The entire length has to be less than 100 meters.

If length is not an issue, it is always best to install *service loops* at the ends of cable runs. A service loop is excess cable neatly looped at the end of a cable run. The service loop allows you to move the cable if you have to relocate an AP in the future.

When cable runs get too long, it usually gets expensive. Fiber-optic cabling is usually the only way to run cable from one central place without adding another Ethernet switch. If there are a lot of runs that will be over the 100 meter limitation, it might be best to install another PoE switch. You can then place the switch in a location central to all the cable runs and run a fiber-optic line to it.

Not everyone realizes that it is possible to order pre-terminated fiber-optic cables to different kinds of lengths. This also may be the cheapest, fastest, and simplest option in some cases. Fiber-optic cable has a reputation for being expensive because of the equipment and specialized labor required to terminate the cable, but fiber-optic cable is the most cost-effective and efficient option for some environments.

If you do not install a new Ethernet switch and are planning on running fiber-optic cable to the AP locations, you will likely have to factor in two things: powering the AP via a nearby electrical receptacle and having to convert the fiber-optic line back to UTP. Often running a new electrical circuit in itself can be a costly situation and also adds points of failure to the equation.

The important point is that you will need to factor in all these costs and design considerations. The best advice we can give you is to present all the options to your customer and let them decide. Some customers may prefer the more expensive alternatives based on other projects or situations they have been working around.

Asbestos also comes into play again when considering cable length limitations. It may be logical to run cable around an area where an AP needs to be installed, thereby requiring more length of cable to place an AP where you want it. All aspects of cabling need to be considered.

Changes to Coverage Area

Part of the challenge of planning surveys is dealing with out-of-date maps of WLAN coverage areas. It is important to ensure that you are dealing with accurate maps. CAD drawings and maps are one of the most critical components in a WLAN design planning effort. If they are not accurate, change orders may be necessary, resulting in extra cost and perhaps time overruns.

CAD drawing accuracy is important for your survey because if you are performing an active survey and walking through an area, you are basing your map location on the current physical location while constantly comparing your real environment to the CAD drawing. When you click on the map, a data measurement is recorded at that position. If the map is not accurate, from the perspective of the CAD drawing it might appear that you are walking through walls or, worst yet, the representation of your data will be inaccurate.

When you encounter this situation, the worst thing you can do is pick spots on the map that aren't to scale with the rest of your data points. Survey mapping software relies on distance calculations in addition to measured data, and if your data points are not accurate in 2D space, the survey results will not be accurate.

If it is possible, attempt to click on the map based on the location where you think you are standing relative to the map you are dealing with. Doing so can provide some data to analyze at a later date even if the map isn't accurate. The main risk involved in this process is human error in recording data points at the actual locations.

Predictive surveys will be inaccurate when CAD drawings are out-of-date. If walls and rooms with large furniture are installed where the drawing shows open space, the prediction will be useless.

When you find yourself in this situation, you must escalate the problem to the project manager immediately. Sometimes it may be so minor that it doesn't affect the design, but in other situations it might drastically change the schedule and costs.

Notifying Personnel

During the course of your work, employees will stop you for various reasons. Some are simply inquisitive whereas others are disruptive. For example, if you are performing a survey or spectrum analysis and enter an area where employees are present, they may not have been told that visitors would be performing work. Reactions will vary, but be prepared in case someone has a negative reaction.

Some people simply react a certain way because management or business policy requires them to do so. This is why the proper preplanning steps must be taken in order to ensure local procedures are followed and policies are being adhered to. A good rule of thumb is to request a company escort so they can explain your presence to anyone who hasn't been notified.

Another option is to use the presurvey walkthrough to identify locations where employees may not know of your presence. Because this walkthrough is almost always done with an escort, it is also a good opportunity to introduce yourself to local management and security personnel.

Obviously, a security badge or other identifying information is an excellent safeguard that can also prevent uncomfortable situations.

 Real World Scenario

The Spies Are Among Us

When performing a site survey in a large enterprise facility, this author was stopped by an employee who was greatly concerned about what was going on. Picture me standing there with a tripod with a bunch of antennas, electronic devices, a power supply, and laptop computers. A local employee who noticed me was convinced that management had sent me in to spy on their department and that we were planning to install surveillance equipment. The employee caused quite a ruckus.

Unbeknownst to me, there had been a tenuous situation only a few days back between management and the local department that resulted in some friction. My project was delayed several hours by the time management was called in and we demonstrated the equipment and project details.

Designing for Dual Spectrums

Designing a WLAN to support both 2.4 GHz and 5 GHz from the same AP infrastructure can be quite a challenge considering the two frequencies propagate differently. Also, APs and clients can behave or perform differently at different bands and even channels within the band. This calls for extra attention to the type and configuration of survey equipment being used.

Antennas are one of the biggest areas of concern. In Figure 9.20 you see an indoor AP with an omnidirectional antenna pattern for 2.4 GHz and 5 GHz. This AP clearly has a different propagation pattern between 2.4 GHz and 5 GHz. Some external antennas to dual-band APs also exhibit these characteristics. You must be careful about your antenna and other design choices that exhibit these types of characteristics if your design calls for dual-spectrum deployments.

FIGURE 9.20   Enterprise AP azimuth pattern

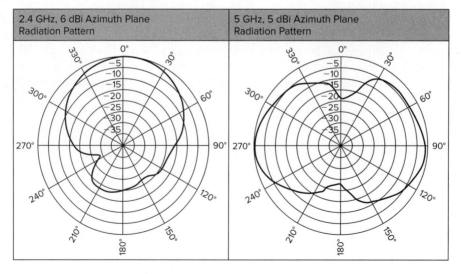

As you can see, if your antenna pattern is different, there is nothing you can do about gaps (or overlaps) in signal. In this case, you should seriously reconsider your options.

For APs with internal antennas, it is uncommon to see this kind of irregular pattern between bands. Equipment manufacturers are getting more experience every day making products with internal antennas and the antenna designs are improving with this collective experience. Large variations in antenna performance seem to be fewer nowadays, making our job as designers even easier.

If you take the time to look at antenna patterns between different manufacturers' products (or even products from a single manufacturer), you will see a great deal of variability in antenna and radio performance. This is why you should survey using the vendor's equipment that you intend on deploying. Changes to antenna types and orientation will render a survey null and void.

You must also determine transmit power differences both within a single band, but also across any other bands the device operates at. Regulatory domains play one of the biggest roles in this equation. A radio that's capable of higher transmit power may limit output because you have configured the AP in a regulatory domain where transmit power in all or part of a frequency band is required.

The 5 GHz UNII bands used in the United States and other regulatory domains fall into this category. According to FCC part 15.407, UNII-1 (5.15–5.25 GHz) transmitters should not exceed 50 mW (17 dBm) EIRP. There are cases that are outside the scope of this section that can reduce EIRP to 40 mW (16 dBm). For example, assuming 50 mW max with a 6 dBi antenna, the transmitter output cannot exceed 12.5 mW (11 dBm).

Granted, a single dBm difference isn't going to make the spectrum police knock on your door, but the difference is when an AP is designed with internal antennas. Because the antennas are fixed, the AP will be designed to operate safely within this spec, so you might even expect this to be the lesser value.

Understanding Client Support

Whenever you plan to operate at two bands simultaneously, pay close attention to your client device configurations. You must also include capabilities in your assessment.

Most older 802.11a adapters will not operate in the UNII-2 extended (2e) band that was opened up for use after they were manufactured. The same goes for infrastructure devices. You can't blame the equipment vendor of the devices; it is a fact that technology changes, and in this case, there was a change in the fundamental factors that equipment manufacturers designed to.

Intel's 3945 and earlier adapters, for example, were based on regulatory and certification requirements at the time. Therefore, when the FCC later opened up additional frequencies at 5 GHz, the Intel devices were not certified to operate in that space. Keep in mind that manufacturers have to get their devices tested by independent testing laboratories. The tests at that time didn't address those frequencies and therefore the manufacturer had to recertify those devices with the FCC—which proved to be a costly expense (assuming a device was even capable of the new frequency operation). We aren't picking on Intel in this case; all 802.11a devices certified in that era fall into the same category.

It's likely the adapter can operate at those frequencies, but it is not *certified* to do so. Therefore, it would be a legal concern should a new firmware package be available to enable its use.

Why is this important? Think about the scenario of deploying a new infrastructure product that is capable of operating at UNII-2e. If you have a legacy client that doesn't support UNII-2e and it roams to an area where the AP is configured for a UNII-2e channel, guess what would happen. The client would be disconnected from the network if it didn't drop down to 2.4 GHz operation. Effectively, the service area provided by that AP operating at UNII-2e would be a black hole to those older client devices.

If you have older client devices that you must support at 5 GHz, you unfortunately need to disable UNII-2e channels in order to avoid disruption to those client devices.

Utilizing Dual-Band Antennas

Another area that has gained a lot of attention for designers is dual-band antennas. These antennas primarily come in two forms.

Single Antenna   The first is a single antenna with a single antenna connector that is tuned for both frequencies. This type of antenna is most appropriate for radios that can be software configured to operate in multiple bands.

Single Antenna Enclosure Housing Multiple Antennas   The second type, as shown in Figure 9.21, is a single antenna enclosure that houses multiple antennas dedicated to different frequencies using different antenna connectors. In this case, the antenna connectors are marked to indicate which antenna connector goes to which radio.

FIGURE 9.21   Dual-band omnidirectional antenna in a single enclosure

Courtesy of TerraWave Solutions

In the first scenario, where a single antenna element is used for multiple bands, you usually have to sacrifice some performance. Antennas are optimized for specific frequencies or frequency ranges. When you have multiple channels and frequencies you have to support, it is usually the case that some channels do not perform the same as others.

This would cause an inconsistent performance of the AP based on what channel the AP is currently set to. Assuming the antenna has been designed sufficiently, the penalty might not be that noticeable.

Consider for a moment how client device antennas are designed. Specifically speaking, we are talking about the dual band–capable clients. The same problem exists for the antennas used in these devices. If performance on a particular channel is deficient at the AP but slightly better on that channel at the client device, the impact will be less perceived. The problem is when *both* sides have deficiencies on that same channel. In such cases, you may very well notice that your signal coverage is not as good on one channel as it is on another.

This is not a common scenario, but it is important to point out the most fundamental aspects that affect WLAN performance. When troubleshooting, thinking all the way down to the physical layer is very important.

Survey Client Considerations

When choosing a WLAN client to survey with, it is important to consider the target client population. As we've stated elsewhere in this book, you do not want to pick a high-performing WLAN client to perform your surveys because the data will not be consistent with your lower-performing devices.

The following is a minimal list of criteria that you should consider when selecting a survey client:

Diversity   Diversity helps mitigate the negative effects from multipath. Diversity will even out signal strength hysteresis of reported measurements. Not using diversity in your survey client will result in more irregularity in the RF signals it reports, and you may experience more retransmissions and cyclic redundancy check (CRC) errors. This issue may or may not reflect your client conditions.

MIMO   The use of MIMO in a survey client is another worthwhile consideration. Specifically, a MIMO client will exhibit signal processing improvements as compared with an 802.11a/b/g client. Again, the important factor here is to match the survey client with the lowest common denominator of your intended client population. MIMO is an excellent technology for 802.11 performance enhancements, but the improvements may not reflect the expected behavior of your actual client population. If MIMO is in use by your clients, choose an adapter that supports the MIMO configuration (number of transmit and receive radio chains) and 802.11n features that are present in your client devices.

Polarity   Polarity enters into the equation when you're performing outdoor installations or you are operating a client device at a farther distance from an AP than with typical indoor situations. In outdoor or very large, open indoor environments, use higher-gain antennas that allow clients to connect from farther distances. The polarity of the RF signal has a greater effect in these situations. That means that when performing a survey in these situations, consider your client population and mimic the real-world conditions.

Frequency and Band Support   Remember that not all clients support multiple bands. Some client devices that support these different bands can be configured to not utilize the additional frequency real estate.

Some client devices may even differ in their performance within a single frequency band. There has been more than one defective adapter. You need to test your client device across several different channels and ensure that you have a properly performing adapter across all the survey channels.

Figure 9.22 illustrates an approximate frequency bandwidth comparison between 2.4 GHz and 5 GHz. There is a marked difference in how an antenna manufacturer will design something for 2.4 GHz versus 5 GHz. Using the same antenna for both frequencies is yet another challenge. Not all channels will perform equally across multiple bands. This will affect the channels that you use to perform your site survey.

FIGURE 9.22   Relative frequency bandwidth comparison

Another important point to remember is the survey client settings. You must prepare your survey client to ensure that device behavior is what you want to observe. Pay specific attention to transmit power settings, roaming thresholds, and channel bonding.

Frequency Band–Specific Considerations

We have already discussed a great deal of detail related to frequency bands and considerations when performing a survey. For reference, here are a few details that need to be discussed:

- Transmit power and modulation type
- Regulatory channel and transmit power restrictions

- Band support
- 20/40 MHz channels
- Benefits and challenges of more channels

Transmit power and modulation type are pretty straightforward topics and have been discussed elsewhere in this text. In short, transmit power usually is not equal across frequency bands and even more so across modulation and coding types. For example, DSSS and OFDM usually do not have the same maximum transmit power for many APs and nearly all client devices. Also, as PHY rate increases, transmit power also backs off for various technical constraints.

Regulatory domains will further limit transmit power and even operational modes in different bands. Different regulatory domains also limit the bands that are available for use.

Spectrum band support includes not only the 2.4 GHz ISM and 5 GHz UNII bands but also the 4.9 GHz band. This is especially true for outdoor operation for municipal customers. Even within 5 GHz, the UNII-2e band was added after many client devices were sold. While operation in the UNII-2e and the 4.9 GHz bands will add some complexity to the survey, the process isn't any different than designing for 2.4 GHz and 5 GHz. The same steps must be followed.

Channel bonding as used with 802.11n is also not consistent across all hardware. Even though 802.11n supports channel bonding at both 5 GHz and 2.4 GHz, it is not recommended to support channel bonding at 2.4 GHz.

Even though it might be possible to configure 40 MHz channels at 2.4 GHz on an infrastructure product, you will find that many client devices do not support 40 MHz mode at 2.4 GHz. In fact, the 802.11n standard built in a feature to advertise "intolerance" for 40 MHz operation to the infrastructure, as described in IEEE 802.11n-2009.

Having more channels is a double-edged sword. The more channels an infrastructure operates at, the more channels a client device will need to scan when roaming. If voice is used at 5 GHz, for example, its quality may be affected whenever the handset has to roam. Unfortunately, no Information Element (IE) with beacons and probe responses advertises the list that the collective infrastructure operates at.

PHY Rate Support

When designing a new WLAN, you must determine the applications that will need to be supported. For example, if voice is a target application, supported PHY rates in most enterprise deployments should not include the lower DSSS rates such as 1, 2, and 5.5 Mbps.

Whether these rates should be supported or strictly disabled is a contentious topic. Every voice vendor uses different techniques and differs at least slightly in their design recommendations. Regardless of which side of the fence you sit on, the most benefit is gained by making a higher data rate a *basic rate*. As you may recall from Chapter 3, "Designing for Applications," where we discussed voice and real-time applications in depth, the lowest basic rate is the PHY rate at which an AP sends all its management frames. Making 11 Mbps the lowest basic rate means that 11 Mbps will be the PHY rate at which beacons and other management frames will be transmitted.

Having to support applications that require higher PHY rates means that you must design the network to support RF conditions to ensure the lower data rates will not be needed. Outside of the basic rate factors, lower rates are needed only when RF conditions warrant their use—when RF signal quality is at its worst.

When you design a network with those PHY rates disabled, make sure cell edges have a sufficiently high SNR to make higher dates possible. For example, voice deployments use a value effectively equating 25 dB of SNR, which will ensure enough RF signal quality to support very high PHY rates.

If you are designing a network that will have minimal usage, such as for handheld computers that only use Telnet or similar types of low-bandwidth applications, you can use fewer APs and support lower PHY rates to enable connectivity at longer distances.

Lower PHY rates travel much farther distances than higher PHY rates . . . well, actually, they travel the same distances but their modulation is simple enough that their signals can be decoded from much farther away. Using lower PHY rates also means more contention to the medium because they travel much farther and likely will cross over into nearby same-channel APs. That means channel 1 clients and APs using lower PHY rates will affect other channel 1 APs in relatively close proximity.

The other problem with lower PHY rates is that your applications will be bandwidth restricted. If higher PHY rates are supported and used for the vast majority of the traffic, bandwidth would not be a problem. However, even a single client device at a cell edge sending a large amount of data would be doing so using a low PHY rate. That would result in very high channel utilization, penalizing other users of that same channel within earshot of the transmissions.

Once you have factored in your client devices and applications, you need to decide whether you will be designing your WLAN for high PHY rates and thus installing a higher number of APs, or designing for range and thus trying to maximize the coverage of each AP.

Designing for Rates

Designing for rates means that you are trying to design for higher PHY rates. Higher PHY rates require high signal strength in order to support the higher modulation and coding schemes. The closer you are to the AP, the better the signal quality is, assuming that transmit power is balanced on both sides of a link. This usually requires that you place APs closer together.

When APs are spaced closer together, you have to deal with the negative side effects of co-channel interference. Figure 9.23 depicts a highly simplified AP deployment using three different channels. Keep in mind that this type of simple RF propagation plan never exists in real life and is used for illustrative purposes only.

FIGURE 9.23   Three-channel design

When designing for high PHY rates with densely located APs it is important to also reduce transmit power to avoid co-channel interference. It is often mistakenly thought that simply disabling lower rates will suffice to prevent interference and excess contention to neighboring cells. In reality, the AP's transmissions at higher rates will still travel the same distance, but the usable range of those transmissions will be shorter. The RF amplitude of those signals will not change as a result of supported data rates. Even so, it is important to disable the lower rates in this design scenario so that clients can only connect within the intended high rate area, and not at great distances from the AP, which could add contention problems for neighboring cells.

Lower data rates also require more time to transmit the same amount of information. When any device transmits using lower PHY rates, it penalizes the other stations also operating nearby on the same channel by bringing down the total amount of throughput the medium would normally allow. That means that other higher-speed devices will have to wait until the slower-speed transmission is finished. Potentially, if other higher-speed devices were to use the wireless medium at the same time, the total amount of throughput the AP would be able to sustain would be far greater.

When designing for rates, you must strongly consider the negative effects of co-channel interference when using the lower data rates.

Real World Scenario

Hospital VoWiFi Deployment Gone Bad

A large hospital purchased a VoWiFi solution and deployed its Wi-Fi network based on the vendor's best practices. APs were spaced quite closely, and the hospital was told that automated RF management would resolve all the RF configuration and tuning. The entire infrastructure was installed and turned on, and the network sat overnight in order for the automatic RF management algorithm to fully tune the large, multifloor hospital facility.

The phones were configured and deployed to the staff, but the phone performance was very poor. IT staff from the hospital worked for many days performing tests and checking signal strength in order to figure out what was happening.

Finally, the hospital IT department resorted to bringing in a consultant and demanded that the person be a Certified Wireless Network Expert (CWNE). The consultant arrived at the hospital and after interviewing the staff they went to visit an area of the hospital where the phones were deployed.

The CWNE noticed that APs were spaced very closely to one another and that they all were placed in the hallways. The consultant used a Wi-Fi analyzer to measure the VoWiFi phone conversation and noticed that RF channel utilization was at about 50 percent of capacity. Worse yet, the VoWiFi phone hadn't even dialed and nobody else was using the network.

Immediately the CWNE noticed that all the data rates that were occupying the channel were at 1 Mbps. Each AP was serving six SSIDs for various purposes. The CWNE then noticed that all the 1 Mbps transmissions were beacons from the APs. The number of APs that were seen from a single location totaled over 100.

The problem was that with a highly dense deployment, six SSIDs, multiple floors, and 1 Mbps enabled, 1 Mbps transmissions can be heard from very far away. The CWNE informed the IT department that disabling 1, 2, and 5.5 Mbps would not negatively affect client connections because of the density of the AP deployment throughout the coverage area. After reviewing all the facts, the IT staff disabled two of the SSIDs that weren't being used at the time and turned off the 1, 2, and 5.5 Mbps data rates. The channel utilization went down to 6 percent.

Once that was done, the performance of the wireless network skyrocketed and phone operation met the original expectations.

Designing for Range

When you design for range, you are making a conscious decision to leverage lower data rates and seeking to maintain client connections at maximum distance. This method is commonly used for outdoor environments and sometimes for warehouse environments.

By choosing to design for range, you are also consciously giving up WLAN capacity. Capacity, in this situation, can be considered in speed and number of clients. When using lower data rates, the same packets that need to be transmitted over the wireless medium simply take longer. That means the rate at which the transmissions are sent is lower. Therefore, the effective throughput of the WLAN is decreased.

The other area of capacity relates to the number of client devices. When lower data rates are supported, assuming the same types of applications are being run on each client, each client produces additional load on the wireless medium. Assuming that each client device behaves in a similar way, each client represents a finite amount of contributed traffic to the overall workload on the WLAN. This means that fewer wireless transmission opportunities exist and therefore the number of wireless clients is decreased. The amount of traffic in a wireless medium is inversely proportional to the number of new client devices that the WLAN will support.

Updating an Existing Design

Not all Wi-Fi network deployments are Greenfield. Nowadays, chances are a Wi-Fi network already exists and the design needs to be upgraded. Sometimes only a few APs might be deployed. Or perhaps the entire network needs to be augmented, analyzed, or even replaced with an 802.11n network.

Performing work on an existing WLAN can present some unique challenges in comparison to designing a new network from the ground up. Active surveys, for example, can be more difficult if the only SSIDs are 802.1X/EAP enabled. The existing network might also incorporate automatic RF management and transmit power might be highly variable on an AP-to-AP basis. Finally, some companies take issue with survey APs using the same channels during hours of normal operation.

Technology Upgrade

One of the most common reasons for updating an existing design is that the equipment is getting old and is no longer supported. Another reason is that the business is relying on the WLAN more heavily than ever before and requires a technology upgrade to support higher speeds, more spectrum, or specific features.

When technology changes, the existing AP layout may not provide a baseline for the new technology. One example involved the earlier 802.11 FH systems. FH APs could travel quite some distance, but the speeds were limited. Warehouse environments in particular were heavy users of FH technology and found themselves adding a much higher number of

DSSS- or OFDM-based APs when replacing the older FH-style APs. Therefore, you may not be able to leverage the existing Ethernet cable runs and mounting locations. Be sure to inform your customers if that's the case.

Customers found themselves in a similar predicament when upgrading from 802.11b AP technology using 2.4 GHz only to 802.11a/g-based APs using dual spectrums. Designers found that usable 802.11a cell sizes were often smaller than the previous 802.11b cell sizes, and they needed to factor in more APs and tighter spacing.

Technology will continue to evolve. In fact, the IEEE is working on a gigabit PHY technology under two different standards called 802.11ac and 802.11ad. It's premature to discuss the details of those standards, but when this technology arrives there will yet again be more design challenges involved in technology upgrades. In the meantime, it is best to focus our efforts on 802.11n and associated design strategies.

It took many years for 802.11n to arrive as a fully ratified standard. Business and consumers were eagerly anticipating the benefits of better radio technology along with an increase in transfer speeds. Now that 802.11n is fully ratified and every equipment manufacturer has an offering, WLAN designers are finding that many of their efforts are centered on moving from 802.11a/g technology to 802.11n.

Several things changed with 802.11n from a design perspective. These include the following:

Multiple Antenna Elements   Using multiple antenna elements is an important improvement in order to gain most of the advantages of MIMO and throughput speeds.

Heavy Focus on 5 GHz   The primary benefits of 802.11n rest in the 5 GHz UNII bands, so most designs are now primarily focused on 5 GHz.

Cell Sizes   Cell sizes aren't necessarily a 1:1 ratio to existing 802.11a/g designs. And for a variety of contributing factors, external and directional antennas tend to be less common.

Nobody likes the expense and labor involved in performing site surveys, and several manufacturers have claimed that you can perform a 1:1 swap of existing 802.11a/g APs with 802.11n APs. Then, in a different white paper or marketing bulletin, they may claim a 20–30 percent increase in range. Which is true? Should you simply take an existing 802.11a/g design and swap the APs with 802.11n models?

Before you begin, critique the existing design and understand how it was designed. This process includes interviewing users on how well the existing network has been performing for them. Here are some questions you should ask:

- Is the existing network too dense to begin with? Is the AP placement too sparse?
- Are all the required coverage areas for the new design covered in the previous?
- Was the existing network designed using directional antennas?

A good technique is to experiment a bit. Using a good survey mapping software package (or using other, manual methods), perform a survey of an installed AP. Is the transmit power reasonable? If not, set the transmit power of your test AP to the proper level before performing the survey. Once that is done, place an 802.11n AP in the same location and perform a survey using that AP. If they are roughly equivalent, that is a good start.

Next, perform a passive survey of the entire coverage area. Before performing the survey, consider these important factors:

The Survey Client   Is the performance of the existing client devices similar to the devices that you plan to deploy in the upgraded network? If it isn't representative, then you should use the lowest common denominator of device that will be around for the foreseeable future.

Transmit Power of the Existing APs   Because a passive survey is a downlink-only measurement, it is critical to normalize power across the entire environment. Ensure the transmit power is known and ideally consistent across the entire network.

Optimized Channel Scanning   Whenever analyzing an existing network using known channels, you should configure your survey client utility to scan *only* those channels. This gives you more information regarding the channels that you are operating on and provides you with a better basis for analysis.

One of the benefits of a passive survey is that it can be performed quickly. Once that process is finished, take a look at the survey data and review the results. Are there coverage gaps in the existing design? If so, the new design may need to incorporate more APs than the current one has. However, if the existing network is already too dense, you might need fewer APs.

Another factor that is important to analyze in an existing design is AP placement. You have already seen how AP placement affects location accuracy if RTLS will be used. Different placement might be recommended in some areas regardless of whether RTLS is used.

Existing designs might also have all the APs down the center of long hallways and not into the rooms where users are located. Depending on the facility, the APs in the hallways usually hear one another loudly, which usually causes channel contention. At the same time, if automated RF management algorithms are used, this might cause the APs to automatically power down their transmit power to a point where the users in the rooms have limited or poor connectivity. In situations like these, some might argue that the original design was flawed.

Phased Upgrades

Sometimes it can be difficult to update a large WLAN deployment in one single event. In such cases, from a business perspective it might be best to phase in the upgrades.

Phasing in upgrades sometimes has its own unique challenges. Upgrading from one technology to another might not seem disruptive to client applications, but sometimes it is. For example, an existing design might use a specific VLAN for all users and the new design uses another. If the same SSID is used for the old and new infrastructure and they will be adjacent to each other, a client device will roam between the two without knowing that it will be placed on a different VLAN. This will likely cause disruption in user applications.

Another example is when fast secure roaming is enabled, but not functional between the old and new environments. Even if the two WLANs are on the same VLAN, roaming between the two environments might require clients to perform a full 802.1X/EAP authentication on every roam between each other. Remember, the client device seeks any

AP that matches its configuration profile for SSIDs. If another AP is a suitable match and the RF signal is better, the device will roam there.

Perhaps 802.11 technology is changing from 802.11g to 802.11n at 5 GHz. Does the client driver and AP firmware allow state to be flipped back and forth seamlessly between the two technologies? Bugs may be revealed when moving between the two in one or both environments.

Phased upgrades are best performed in geographically segregated areas, perhaps one building at a time. One floor at a time in a multifloor building is not the same thing—clients often jump between APs on different floors in most multifloor AP deployments.

Upgrading Clients

When upgrading an existing design, take another hard look at the client devices. When mobile carriers upgrade their networks, phones often need to be upgraded as well. Many of you know from experience the benefits of updating your mobile phone at times.

WLAN client devices are no different. When a newer AP technology is deployed, client devices will have to be programmed to take advantage of new features. Perhaps the driver is old and would benefit from an upgrade anyway.

The point here is that whenever you upgrade your WLAN infrastructure, you must perform some level of upgrade, or at minimum, some level of monitoring, to your client devices. Even if that involves a simple driver update, this step usually provides results with a high payback.

Interpreting Survey Results

After performing a site survey, you have a lot of data to look at and make sense of. It may feel like a daunting task reviewing all the information in detail.

One of the first things that you should do when reviewing survey data is to look for common problems that surveyors make. Performing an 802.11 RF survey isn't exactly a science that has been around for a long time. And not everybody gets to attend expensive training programs.

A nice side effect of reviewing site survey data is that you can often filter on rogue APs. Looking for interference issues is also important when viewing survey results.

In this section we will explore the common problems with interpreting survey results and looking for key findings from the data gathered in the coverage area.

Common Problems to Look For

Let's assume that you are looking at a site survey that was performed by a third party. The survey file says that it was a passive survey. You learned several attributes of passive surveys earlier in this chapter, so you know that when performing a passive survey a WLAN client doesn't associate to the AP. The benefit of this approach is that you can see richer data about all the APs in an environment. The problem is that the survey client constantly scans a preconfigured set of RF channels.

Configuring these channels appropriately for the type of analysis that needs to be performed is critical to providing the type of data required. For example, assume the survey client was configured to scan all 2.4 GHz channels and the network being surveyed was an SCA using only channel 6. In this case, the client constantly scans all the other channels using a dwell time of 250 ms. That would mean that scanning 2.4 GHz channels 1–14 would take 3.5 seconds to complete. If the surveyor was walking at a brisk pace, the data resolution may not be as fine as desired because channel 6 data samples were not frequent enough.

When reviewing survey information, try to interpret the information being presented to ensure the scan settings were properly configured for the statement of work required.

Another common problem is erroneously reporting interference. The interference in this scenario is what the interference analysis modules of survey mapping software programs report. Suppose you are analyzing an existing WLAN deployment and device to use a passive survey to perform a downlink coverage assessment of the WLAN. When you review the results of the survey using the survey mapping software package, it provides an interference analysis report. If the network being surveyed was running multiple SSIDs, it is highly likely that the survey mapping software would see each SSID from each AP as individual APs. When multiple SSIDs are used, a different BSSID (MAC address) is used on the AP. When this is the case, the survey mapping software sees a unique BSSID and assumes that it is a stand-alone AP. Therefore, the survey mapping software interprets this as multiple APs deployed in the same spot using the same channel. You will need to filter the data from the passive survey so that the interference analysis report includes only a single BSSID from a single AP that was surveyed.

One of the most common problems is improperly scaled maps. When maps are imported into survey mapping software packages, the graphic file is scaled to the screen. Each pixel has no relevance to real-world dimensions because graphic files do not contain this information about dimensions. Survey files might be skewed in one dimension more than another when they are first imported. You can usually tell this by looking at text and doorways between the x and y dimensions. Doorways of similar type are usually exactly the same. Using that information to your advantage will allow you to quickly determine whether the surveyor scaled the map before performing the survey. Another method is to use a measuring tool in the survey mapping software to measure points on a map and confirm to known, real-world dimensions.

Another common problem is insufficient walking paths. When a surveyor walks a map to analyze RF coverage, they must click locations on the map within the software where they are standing in real time. The tricky part is that they must also click on the map when they change directions (every time) as well as speed (every time). If that step isn't followed, the survey software package keeps recording data at predetermined intervals and spaces the data points equal distances apart between the two mouse clicks. If a change of direction isn't recorded and the survey mapping software isn't stopped, paths might appear to go through walls. When you see walking paths do this, it is a clear indication that the data points do not reflect real-world conditions and that the data is likely unusable. Similarly, the surveyor's walking path should not be limited to hallways and common areas. It is important that accurate coverage maps be obtained by gathering data samples from as many points on the map as possible (or reasonable, within the constraints of the project). As data samples increase, so does the accuracy of the heat maps.

Locating and Quantifying Rogues

Rogue devices or networks can impact the performance of your network. Rogue devices from company personnel usually can be quickly remedied, but rogue devices from neighbors can't. Part of the challenge of using unlicensed frequencies is that as long you are staying within the regulatory transmission limits, people are free to utilize that frequency. That means you have little to no recourse to do anything about it.

When performing a site survey you can locate rogue devices quickly, but passive surveys are the best way to locate rogue devices. Most survey mapping software allows you to filter the survey results to show the rogue devices individually, by channel, by SSID, and more. Figure 9.19, earlier in this chapter, is an example of a passive survey that was filtered to show where a rogue device was found during the course of a survey.

When viewing site survey results, always communicate to the proper personnel the survey findings of rogue APs that were discovered during the survey process. In particular, rogue APs that have minimal security policies are ones that require immediate escalation.

Interference Mitigation

Interference from non-802.11 sources is one of the single biggest factors that can wreak havoc on a WLAN. Certainly not all interference is created equal, but by performing a spectrum analysis, you can quantify the impact to the RF spectrum as well as the connection quality (if an active survey was performed). Negative effects from interference include higher retransmission rates while even in an area of strong signal quality, lost 802.11 frames, higher reported noise floor, and connection drops.

Survey results will show symptoms of interference. These symptoms include elevated noise floor, high retransmission rates, and usually lower PHY rates than what would be expected for a given signal strength. You can view the recorded data rom a site survey using several methods. One of these methods includes looking at noise levels across the entire surveyed area. If this area is several floors of a large multistory building, seeing an elevated noise floor is a sign that some form of interference is likely present.

This same information can help you pinpoint where the interference is located. Once a location is loosely determined, taking a spectrum analyzer using a directional antenna can be a helpful method of finding the problem device.

MCA vs. SCA

Performing a survey for a single-channel architecture (SCA) versus a multichannel architecture (MCA) theoretically isn't that different. Sure, you do not worry about the channel settings of the final AP configuration, but you still have to concern yourself with pure RF propagation. Without proper RF propagation, it doesn't matter what channel one or all of the APs are on.

It seems that SCA vendors more commonly deploy a higher density of APs than do MCA vendors. Because the RF algorithms are intended to be more coordinated between APs in SCA systems, the logic for some is that deploying a higher density of APs with SCA deployments has fewer side effects than with MCA deployments.

While many WLAN professionals debate this topic, APs placed closer together will still have to contend for airtime. When a device transmits on a particular channel, the wireless medium may be occupied. The distance of impact to adjacent devices is one of the biggest differentiating factors. Keep in mind that we are speaking of transmissions from both clients as well as APs.

Simply put, all of the same logic still applies to AP placement regardless of what type of technology you intend to deploy, though the surveying process for an SCA should be slightly simplified because channel and transmit power settings do not need to be carefully managed for contention planning. In SCA networks, transmit power is usually set to max power (usually 100 mW).

Summary

One of the most fundamental steps in WLAN design is ensuring proper RF propagation. Without proper RF propagation, the WLAN performance and user experience will be poor. The analogy is equivalent to faulty cabling in wired network design.

In this chapter we reviewed many types of survey methods you can use in order to accomplish a thoughtful and effective RF design. Some are more effective and applicable to certain situations than others. Just as with many things in life, one size doesn't fit all. It is important that you understand these survey methods and when to best apply them.

Survey mapping software can be a useful asset for performing RF surveys and are a valuable visualization tool for you as the designer as well as the customer of the network. Predictive design software packages are also valuable in some situations, but they can provide inaccurate results if not used properly or if the input and assumptions for the design are not accurate.

Infrastructure links such as PTP and PtMP links have their own unique set of survey requirements and the design techniques are quite different from indoor designs.

When you update existing WLAN designs, you're interested in leveraging existing assets, but you need to be cautious about utilizing bad elements of existing designs to base a new WLAN design on. Furthermore, when updating the WLAN infrastructure, you should always look to upgrade or update the client devices that will also utilize the new network.

Finally, once all the RF measurements are taken, an analysis process must be performed. You need to be on the lookout for common mistakes people make when analyzing survey output before drawing any specific conclusions.

All in all, RF design is one of the most important factors to a successfully operating WLAN. Without sufficient RF performance, everything that depends on it will be affected. Hopefully this chapter has provided you with a good foundation for improving your future designs.

Exam Essentials

Explain differences between survey methodologies and when best to apply different ones. Know the differences between active and passive surveys as well as predictive designs, including different modes of each one.

Describe why a spectrum analysis is important in RF design. Be able to explain the major measurement types of spectrum analysis methods and how to interpret results.

Understand the factors involved in designing for multiple spectrums. Explain the various details involved in designing WLANs for more than one spectrum.

Define techniques for designing for rates versus range. Describe details of design techniques for a variety of business requirements that may affect AP placement and high-level design factors.

Understand important factors in updating existing WLAN designs. Understand the important aspects of updating an existing WLAN design and how that will affect client connectivity.

Review Questions

1. Before performing a pre-deployment passive RF survey of a new deployment using survey mapping software, which of the following must be performed?

    A. Determining AP transmit power

    B. Checking client DTPC settings

    C. Scaling the map

    D. Selecting antennas

2. When you're performing a passive survey and channel scan settings are set to all available 802.11 channels, what information will you gain? (Choose all that apply.)

    A. SSIDs of all APs

    B. Rogue APs

    C. AP channel and power settings

    D. BSSIDs of known APs

3. Passive surveys performed using only the channels on which an existing WLAN is operating have which of the following benefits?

    A. Longer scan times

    B. Same as default scan settings

    C. More information per channel

    D. Less roaming delay

4. You are being consulted to observe a spectrum analyzer recording and you notice strong RF transmissions in narrow spikes across the entire band. What type of measurement have you been shown?

    A. Swept spectrograph duty cycle

    B. Real-time FFT

    C. Return loss S12

    D. Max Hold

5. Active surveys benefit from what additional information versus a passive scan? (Choose all that apply.)

    A. RSSI

    B. Signal to noise

    C. PHY rates

    D. Retries

    E. Loss

6. NicoCo is building a new facility and would like to install a WLAN for primary connectivity of all clients. The requirements are dual-spectrum 802.11n supporting voice and location tracking. What type of pre-deployment survey should be performed?

    A. Passive, using optimized channels

    B. Active, using a voice handset

    C. Active, using a lowest common denominator client

    D. Predictive

    E. Passive, all channels

7. You are being asked to perform a survey in a multifloor building. The building has very thick walls that you know are going to highly attenuate signal propagation. When performing some analysis onsite you notice fairly strong propagation between floors. What two factors should you be very aware of? (Choose all that apply.)

    A. Channel planning

    B. Transmit power

    C. Hidden node

    D. Multi-path

    E. Stacking APs

8. Assume Inc. is doing a point-to-point (PTP) network installation and has asked you to be onsite to consult for the alignment and tuning effort. The equipment has been installed and powered, but no link is being made. You can see that the antennas are a short distance away and RF line of sight should not be an issue. What is the first question you should ask?

    A. Is your antenna polarization aligned?

    B. Did you test configurations before installing?

    C. What is the transmit power at each end?

    D. What are the channel settings?

9. You are being asked to design a solution for a long-range PTP link using 5.8 GHz. While the distance is well within the link budget, the other end of the links will be difficult to see for alignment. What initial consideration could you factor into your design to ease the alignment process?

    A. Additional antenna gain

    B. Receive sensitivity adjustment

    C. Lower antenna gain

    D. Antenna polarization

    E. Frequency choice

10. Four buildings are located in a square orientation to each other. Fisch Stix Food Company is requesting a PtMP link between the buildings. On the building with the root bridge link, what type of antenna is the best choice?

    A. Vertically polarized omni

    B. 60° yagi

    C. Parabolic dish

    D. 100° sector

    E. Horizontally polarized omni

11. You are viewing a site survey report from a vendor who provided spectrum analysis readings. The report show screen shots of the real-time FFT chart where non-802.11 RF interference is seen. When interpreting this data to grasp the impact on the performance of the new WLAN, what can you say?

    A. Since other devices are using the medium, it will impact performance.

    B. You ask the vendor to include duty cycle before providing any feedback.

    C. You ask the vendor to include device classifier information before providing any feedback.

    D. Since other devices are present on those channels, you should avoid known bad channels.

12. MUG Inc. has installed a large mesh network in a large convention facility. The mesh APs installed at the farthest end of the building have received a large number of user complaints. What design information should you immediately ask for? (Choose all that apply.)

    A. Topology of the network showing root mesh nodes

    B. RF signal readings between mesh nodes

    C. The number of radios used on mesh nodes

    D. The types of applications the network supports

13. Lace Doily Company is highly concerned about aesthetics and you are being asked to keep APs from being visible on the ceiling. What best practice option should you explore as a first step?

    A. Install APs with internal antennas above the ceiling.

    B. Investigate using small external antennas that can be mounted to the ceiling and walls.

    C. Paint the APs or antennas using the same paint used for walls or ceilings.

    D. Point out that there are smoke detectors, sprinklers, lighting fixtures, speakers, and other existing items and the APs will hardly be noticed.

14. What factors can prevent mounting APs where your design may call for placement? (Choose all that apply.)

   A. Maximum Ethernet cable distance versus maximum PoE distance

   B. UTP cable distance

   C. Power availability

   D. Installation/maintenance labor costs

   E. Plenum rating

15. When designing for dual-spectrum AP deployments, what design planning exercise should you perform before starting the full survey?

   A. Matching propagation patterns on both bands

   B. Normalizing transmit power

   C. Telling the customer to use it as an excuse to buy new laptops

   D. Infrastructure-based load balancing, which will free up 2.4 GHz

16. Schembs MMA Inc. just installed a brand-new 802.11n network and they have asked your help in determining why legacy clients are having performance problems. You determined the following: 40 MHz channels are in use, all UNII bands are being used, an 802.11n client was used for the survey, 2.4 GHz is not being used, all MCS rates are enabled, and lowest basic rate is 9 Mbps. What items are you most concerned about? (Choose all that apply.)

   A. Lowest basic rates

   B. No 2.4 GHz is being used

   C. MCS rate selection

   D. 40 MHz channel settings

   E. 802.11n client used for survey

   F. All UNII bands are used

17. Sandlin Sandwich Company has asked you to consult on their WLAN upgrade that will be performed in phases. They plan on updating a floor at a time, adding 5 GHz, and would like to change IP subnets. What recommendations do you offer?

   A. Change the SSIDs on the new network.

   B. Using the same SSID is OK because clients will only connect to the APs on the floor they are located on.

   C. Existing client drivers will perform equally.

   D. Existing Ethernet uplinks will suffice.

18. You are being asked to design a WLAN for a number of WLAN clients that will use Telnet as the primary application. The customer has asked that you use only the number of APs necessary because of the complex installation and construction costs each AP installation will incur in this particular environment. What design factors do you consider?

    A. Use 11 Mbps as the lowest basic rate.

    B. Omnidirectional antennas should be used to maximize cell overlap.

    C. AP transmit power should be turned down to minimize co-channel interference.

    D. Clients could benefit from RTS/CTS mode for all transmissions.

19. Head Thinkers Inc. is asking you to consult on a WLAN upgrade where each AP will be upgraded from a dual-band 802.11a/g version to a dual-band 802.11n AP. When you review the design, what critical factors are you looking for? (Choose all that apply.)

    A. Antenna patterns

    B. Usage statistics of current network

    C. Ethernet uplink speeds

    D. 802.11n SGI setting

20. You have been asked to review a predictive design that was performed by a third party. You notice an abnormally high quantity of APs used for a small office building. What might be the root cause?

    A. VoWiFi is a design requirement.

    B. The network will support a high number of client devices.

    C. The design calls for 5 GHz.

    D. Map scaling was done improperly.

Answers to Review Questions

1. C. Survey mapping software uses FSPL calculations in addition to recorded data. An improperly scaled map will alter the results provided by the software.

2. B, D. When performing a passive survey using all channels, you gain optimal visibility of all APs that can be heard. That includes all known and all unknown APs.

3. C. When you're performing a passive survey to analyze an existing WLAN, it is best to configure a passive survey client to scan only the channels that the WLAN operates on in order to have more data points for each AP. Channel scan settings set to their default values can spend too much time off channel and create gaps in data that can skew final results.

4. B. The spectrum plot showing signal strength across a frequency range (frequency domain) is called an FFT.

5. C, D, E. Since active surveys associate to an AP, data can be recorded consistent with actual associated stations.

6. D. If the building hasn't been built, then unfortunately an active or passive survey cannot be performed. However, since the requirements are so great and the WLAN will be used for primary network connectivity and voice, a full active survey should be performed once the facility is built and populated with all furniture and other items that can affect RF characteristics.

7. A, E. Every building and construction method will affect RF propagation differently. It is important to consider three dimensions when planning channels and co-channel interference introduced by stacking APs on top of each other between floors. Staggering, rather than stacking, APs can sometimes provide better long-term coverage at RF cell overlap zones as changes to a facility alter RF coverage patterns, causing weaker overlapping signals at cell edges.

8. B. Installing PTP links require attention to detail in the preparation and testing before actual installation. When on a radio tower or 10+ story rooftop building, all testing needs to be performed prior to installation, such as using multiple power cycles to ensure configuration settings have been properly saved.

9. C. When installing long-range PTP links, antenna gain that's too high will get you into trouble when you attempt to align the antennas. At least one end of a PTP link should have a lower antenna gain in order to aide in the antenna alignment process. Once proper alignment is achieved during the coarse tuning effort, high-gain antennas can replace the lower-gain antennas after the final pointing direction is determined.

10. D. If all four buildings are in a perfect square orientation to each other, that means they are an angle of 90° apart. Installing a 100° sector antenna on the root node building will provide enough azimuth to reach all three other buildings while rejecting other RF interference in the areas where no buildings are present. Using a sector antenna also minimizes elevation antenna gain (again, where no other building PtMP antennas will be installed).

11. B. Duty cycle will provide the most useful information regarding how existing RF interference will affect a WLAN. You can have very low signal levels but have very high duty cycle, which might hardly register on the FFT plot. Options A and D are cop-outs; 802.11 uses unlicensed frequencies and there will always be some form of interference. Option C may not be possible depending on the spectrum analyzer the vendor used. Worse yet, there may not be classifiers for some forms of interference and, regardless, you can obtain the information you need from the Duty Cycle plot.

12. A, B, C, D. The two top questions should be how many mesh nodes have backhaul connections to the wired network and how many radios are being used in the mesh design. If mesh nodes are several hops away from a root node, it will take several mesh hops before traffic hits the network. This adds latency and congestion from many mesh APs backhauling all their data to a limited number of root mesh nodes. Other factors that will affect performance are signal readings between mesh nodes and the types of applications the network must support.

13. B. Some external antennas are quite small and may still provide good coverage without compromising performance. Installing APs above ceilings will affect signal propagation and is never recommended. Painting APs or antennas must only be done using specific types of paint that will not affect RF propagation. While pointing out existing installed items may seem pertinent, the company likely already knows this and do not want to continue to add to the clutter.

14. B, C, D, E. Ethernet and PoE run off UTP (a.k.a. CAT5 or CAT6) cabling and both have the same maximum usable length (100 meters). If total length between an Ethernet switch and the AP exceeds that length, the AP may not work. Installation and labor costs are a big factor in total WLAN budget planning. Plenum requirements will also limit certain AP and antenna choices if all components are required to be plenum.

15. A. When planning a dual-spectrum WLAN design, one of the hardest parts is having consistent performance between 2.4 GHz and 5 GHz propagation patterns. Transmit power adjustments should be made to optimize propagation patterns while not exceeding link budget transmit power. Spectrum load balancing features may not perform as expected if clients are not capable or not configured to use both bands.

16. E, F. If clients are connecting at all, it means that all legacy clients are 802.11a capable since 9 Mbps is enabled as a basic rate, so that would not be an area you focus on first. MCS rate selection only affects 802.11n clients. 40 MHz channel operation still provides full connectivity for legacy clients using the primary channel. The fact that an 802.11n client was used for the survey is an indicator that legacy clients might not be able to match the same performance and the network might be inadequate for some legacy clients. Since all UNII bands are used, which includes UNII-2e, it is highly possible that some legacy clients do not support UNII-2e channels and the network would have dead spots from the perspective of those clients.

17. A. The most correct answer is A. Since IP subnets will be changed, you do not want clients changing subnets when they roam to APs on different floors, which is likely to happen. Client drivers should not be assumed to perform equally and an upgrade should be investigated. Ethernet links might want to be upgraded to gigabit if 802.11n is being used.

18. D. None of the available options were that compelling, but out of the list, RTS/CTS mode can provide some benefits from hidden node interference if a large coverage area is provided by each AP. Since bandwidth is not a concern, this option can cut down on collisions.

This scenario is a typical *rates versus range* design situation where you have to design a WLAN to support a particular application and you have design and budget constraints that must be considered. In this case, Telnet is the WLAN application that will be used, which requires very little actual throughput to operate. Therefore, speed of the WLAN is not a requirement, but budgetary constraints are the biggest consideration. Basic rates and other data rates lower than 11 Mbps should be enabled because range is your highest design requirement. AP transmit power has little to do with co-channel interference in this particular design scenario.

19. A, C. Changing out a legacy AP type with an 802.11n AP cannot be assumed to provide equal coverage. Existing APs might use external antennas that are directional in nature. Unless the new APs provide a similar coverage pattern, coverage holes may exist. Uplink speeds are another area for which you might recommend a new 802.11n network.

20. D. One of the most common mistakes people use when performing site surveys is not properly scaling maps. Unless the map is scaled properly, the predictive design software will not be able to determine AP placement adequately.

Chapter 10

MAC Layer Design

THE FOLLOWING CWDP EXAM TOPICS ARE COVERED IN THIS CHAPTER:

- ✓ Demonstrate a detailed knowledge of WLAN architectures and solutions. Identify best practice design concepts for each architecture including the following considerations:
    - Management solutions
    - Protocols for communication and discovery
    - Data forwarding models
    - Scalability and bottlenecks
    - Redundancy Strategies
    - Device location in the network
    - Encryption and decryption
    - VLANs
    - QoS
    - Roaming considerations
    - Architecture-specific security considerations
    - RF and channel planning
    - Capacity planning
    - AP-Controller associations
    - Licensing
    - Advantages and limitations
- ✓ Explain best practices for common WLAN feature support, configuration, and deployment strategies.
- ✓ Demonstrate a detailed understanding of the role that the wired network infrastructure plays in WLAN design.
- ✓ Explain design approaches related to specific layers of the OSI model.

✓ **Explain the significance of QoS in multi-service WLANs and illustrate a comprehensive understanding of the following:**

- WLAN arbitration
- WMM and EDCA operations and parameters
- Policy-based queuing
- 802.1p (802.1D/Q) CoS priority tagging
- Differentiated Services Code Point (DSCP)
- Admission control
- End-to-end QoS
- Airtime fairness mechanisms

✓ **Understand and describe VLAN use in wired and wireless network segmentation.**

✓ **Describe load balancing, what purpose it serves for the network, and when and how it should be implemented.**

✓ **Describe common design practices for high availability and redundancy.**

✓ **Illustrate best practices for roaming support in a WLAN.**

✓ **Understand the basics of 802.11 arbitration processes and wireless contention domains, and describe how these factors influence network design.**

✓ **Discuss design concepts related to frequencies and bands used for WLAN communications.**

✓ **Demonstrate a detailed knowledge of the common problems related to high user densities and describe effective strategies to address them.**

✓ **Illustrate best practices for data rate/MCS configurations to manage client connectivity.**

✓ **Describe the role of Transmit Power Control (TPC) in WLANs and explain when and how it should be implemented.**

✓ **Demonstrate the importance of, and design considerations related to, Fast BSS Transition (Fast/Secure Roaming).**

Application performance demands are continuing to increase, and new efficacious features are required to keep pace. The aim of this chapter is to highlight proper network design and feature selection as it relates to the many MAC technologies and protocols that have propelled Wi-Fi as a convincing access technology.

As you probably know already, the 802.11 specification addresses WLAN protocols and operation at the MAC and PHY layers of the OSI model, so it should come as no surprise that MAC-layer design will be a major focus in the deployment of an 802.11 WLAN. A stock set of standardized MAC functionality will often serve adequately for simple Wi-Fi networks, but optimization for high-performance multiservice networks usually requires additional features and design considerations at this level.

Quality of service (QoS) is possibly the most important MAC feature in use today, largely because QoS is usually required to support sensitive applications like voice and video. Wi-Fi protocols use QoS at the MAC layer, but QoS functionality also depends on reliable RF handling at the physical layer (layer 1), infrastructure support at the MAC and Network layers (layers 2 and 3, respectively), as well as data classification from layers 4–7. This chapter will look at the many details of QoS design and will include a discussion about *airtime fairness*, a proprietary feature that fits generally into the category of QoS-like features.

With VoWiFi phones, tablet computers, handheld devices, and other battery-sensitive devices requiring service from wireless networks, power conservation features have become very significant. There are currently a few power-saving methods available, and network designers should understand how each one works, why they are significant, when they should be used, and what other power save considerations should be made. This chapter will address deployment considerations and best practices for power save features.

Many battery-sensitive devices are also highly mobile and pose other challenges to network design. Mobile devices supporting session-based applications like voice and real-time client/server applications have also gained popularity on Wi-Fi-capable devices, which adds a new emphasis on minimizing latency during inter-AP roaming. With a litany of different network architectures with proprietary and standardized roaming features, network designers must stay abreast of the technical merits, limitations, and functionality of each roaming method. We will cover this topic here as well.

Understanding Quality of Service

If we look at changes in network uses over the course of the last 10 years, it is quite clear that simple, data-only networks are a thing of the past. In an effort to maximize efficiency, mobility, and productivity, competitive businesses are continuing to adopt wireless technologies to support mission-critical, high-performance, and often sensitive applications. Although this trend toward wireless mobility has motivated the progress of Wi-Fi standards and proprietary feature development by Wi-Fi vendors, it has also created new burdens that were previously only experienced by a select few enterprises at the leading edge of the technology. Enterprise network applications have never been more demanding, and as the role of wireless changes from convenience to mission-critical, network design must change with it.

Generally speaking, QoS is a network function designed to optimize application performance by providing differentiated services to devices, users, applications, or service sets. In other words, applications vary in their performance requirements, and QoS helps control the distribution of resources to meet application-specific needs. For example, some applications, devices, or service sets require more bandwidth than others. At the same time, some applications require less latency than others. Some applications are tolerant to low bandwidth and low latency, but require little or no loss. To meet these varying application needs in a network with limited resources, you need differentiated services.

Application Performance Requirements

Chapter 3, "Designing for Applications," addresses the details of application-specific design requirements, so we will not cover them in detail here. But QoS design is dependent on an intimate understanding of the applications that will be supported on a network. Each application requires a certain performance commitment from the network, and MAC design must take these performance requirements into consideration. Bandwidth, *latency*, *jitter*, and *loss* are all important performance factors that may be directly correlated to, and dependent on, properly provisioned networks. Understanding application performance requirements is the first step to planning the resources that will meet the application's needs.

Bandwidth

Some applications demand a lot of throughput. However, high bandwidth usage does not necessarily make an application demanding. In most cases, high throughput is only challenging when it is paired with a requirement for low latency and low jitter. For example, an application like FTP file transfers may be somewhat bandwidth hungry, but FTP is tolerant to high latency and jitter, so the throughput requirement can be spread across a longer period of time, which preserves precious bandwidth for other applications. HD video teleconferencing is a good example of an application that can require high throughput while also requiring low latency, low jitter, and low loss. This type of application is more sensitive to properly provisioned and controlled network throughput.

One simple way to protect the bandwidth of a WLAN is to configure rate limits for devices or service sets that do not require special priority handling. Traffic control has many relevant uses in WLANs, and when network congestion is causing higher-priority traffic streams to experience performance problems, rate limits may be an effective way of managing excess traffic.

Latency

Latency is the same as delay and is a measurement of the time it takes for a frame to reach its destination (end-to-end delay). Or latency can be measured in the time it takes a frame to reach its destination and the response to be sent back to the original transmitter (round-trip latency). In any case, there are generally two contributors to latency: fixed and variable factors.

Fixed Latency   This includes static elements that do not change, such as preparing a signal for transmission), encoding/decoding, and translation.

Variable Latency   This is often the most important type of latency and includes queuing delays, errors and retransmissions, contention and congestion, and more.

Voice and video are two of the most common applications that are sensitive to latency. In an optimum deployment, total end-to-end delay for voice would be less than 150 ms.

Jitter

Jitter is the variation in latency between packets. When jitter is high, an application's jitter buffer may not be large enough to maintain a steady supply of data for application delivery. This may lead to choppy voice calls, abnormal pace in audio delivery, or video delays or quality impairment. Some applications provide adaptive jitter buffers that change along with jitter conditions. Some applications have a user-defined jitter buffer, which can be helpful if jitter is a suspected cause of poor application performance. For voice, less than 5 ms of latency is typically optimal.

Loss

Loss is a measurement of the difference between packets transmitted and packets received by the destination. Loss can be caused by channel congestion, poor signal quality (low SNR, excessive multipath, collisions), buffer overflow, normal routing procedures, and more. 802.11 MAC protocols provide a resiliency to packet loss by virtue of acknowledgments and retransmissions. Of course, this applies only to unicast traffic. Multicast and broadcast traffic are not acknowledged, so higher levels of loss are far more likely.

As most networking folks already know, use of TCP or UDP at the transport layer also makes a difference here. With TCP, loss is less significant because TCP accommodates loss with acknowledgments and retransmissions, but with UDP, no provision is made to recover lost frames. With UDP, if network conditions are creating loss, no recovery is provided and application quality can suffer. While TCP does minimize loss, acknowledgments and retransmissions may also impact performance. The application in use will determine whether to use group addresses or a unicast address, and it will also determine the transport-layer protocol.

Real World Scenario

Identifying Application Requirements for Video

As we discuss application requirements and network provisioning, let's quickly look at the example of video over wireless. You might be tempted to think that video streams on the Wi-Fi network have a pretty standard set of performance requirements, characterized by moderate bandwidth, low latency, low jitter, and low loss. In some cases, this assumption would be right, but not all video is the same.

Wireless users are consuming different kinds of video media all the time, and companies are relying on wireless connectivity to serve varying video needs, such as:

- Streaming video (e.g., surveillance or webcasts)

- On-demand video sources (e.g., Internet-based media or locally hosted media)

- Interactive video (conferencing and collaboration)

Each of these categories of video includes several subtypes, and each subtype of video delivery has a unique traffic fingerprint. Many require moderate to high bandwidth, but some are low-quality video streams, demanding only small amounts of bandwidth. Some applications can tolerate high latency or jitter, whereas others are very sensitive to high latency or jitter.

As an example, consider the differences between consumption-based video such as YouTube and collaboration-based video like video teleconferencing. Though both of these applications fall under the category of video, the application requirements are completely different. On-demand video like YouTube requires moderate bandwidth, but since these videos are buffered, they can tolerate high latency and jitter. Conversely, teleconferencing applications are real-time, demanding high bandwidth as well as low delay, jitter, and loss. These are stringent demands, but the demands must be known if the network is to be properly provisioned.

Table 10.1 shows a common set of applications along with their typical performance requirements. As a disclaimer, it can be a challenge to identify an application with a specific set of performance requirements because some application types have many variant implementations. It is also often difficult to obtain specific information about the application's network requirements from the application vendor for a variety of reasons. For clarification, Table 10.1 uses the terms Low, Medium, and High to refer to the application's needs or tolerances. For example, low throughput indicates that the application does not require much throughput. Low jitter, latency, or loss indicates that the application requires low jitter, latency, and loss. High jitter, latency, or loss means the application is tolerant to high jitter, latency, or loss.

TABLE 10.1   Application Performance Requirements

Type of Application	Throughput	Latency	Jitter	Loss
Email	Low	High	High	High
Web browsing	Low	High	High	High
Chat	Low–medium	Medium	Medium	Medium
File transfer	Low–high	High	High	High
VoIP	Low	Low	Low	Low
Videoconferencing	Medium–high	Low	Low	Low
Video streaming	Low–high	Low–medium	Low–medium	Low-medium
Video on demand	Low–high	High	High	Low

Application requirements are an important determining factor in QoS design. Some applications are tolerant, and others are demanding. Understanding the application's needs is a proper first start to deploying network resources and ensuring that those resources will yield a pleasurable end-user experience.

End-to-End QoS Flow

Very few applications are initiated on a wireless station, cross a wireless medium, and terminate on a wireless station without also traversing a wired medium somewhere along the way. For that reason, WLANs that support sensitive applications usually depend on systemwide QoS support, which is also known as *end-to-end QoS*, by all networking systems from endpoint to endpoint.

However, before application data makes it onto the wireless medium, it must first be classified and prioritized within the initiating station. Intra-station QoS begins at the application itself (layer 7) and must continue, without disruption, all the way down the protocol stack (in OSI speak) and onto the outgoing transmission interface. Preserving QoS within a station requires that classifying traits are passed between management layer entities. Similarly, QoS protocols at each layer within the station have internal contention and collision procedures that serve to maintain priority between different transmission queues within the station.

After the data is transmitted onto the carrier medium, it must also be classified (identified as traffic requiring QoS prioritization) and honored (scheduled or queued) with the proper QoS parameters across all network links. There may be several links in the transmission path, and prioritization must usually occur across switched (layer 2) and routed (layer 3) network hops, sometimes including the public Internet, where service is unpredictable. WLAN specifications (*802.11e* and *WMM*) define how QoS works within and between wireless stations, but in most cases, the wireless frame is translated by the AP and/or WLAN controller to a wired networking format (Ethernet), as shown in Figure 10.1.

FIGURE 10.1 Demarcation of wireless and QoS

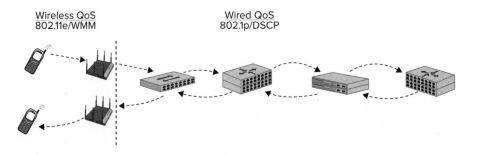

Wireless QoS
802.11e/WMM

Wired QoS
802.1p/DSCP

In other words, QoS is an end-to-end endeavor and must be planned as such. One weak link (no QoS or poorly implemented QoS) in the network path can ruin the service quality that network designers work so hard to protect.

It is also important to consider that QoS is dependent on reliable and highly available carrier mediums. There are several places in this book where we discuss the dynamic and unstable nature of the wireless medium, and for good reason. The RF domain is an important foundation on which wireless technologies are built. QoS protocols is not an adequate answer to an unreliable RF domain. If all the proper classification, queuing, and prioritization occur within stations and on the wired network but the wireless domain is unreliable (high collisions/retries, low bandwidth, interference, etc.), QoS won't be effective for ensuring application performance. For that reason, it is important that wireless designers ensure optimum planning and use of the RF medium so that applications can use the wireless resources effectively and end users can keep smiling. QoS is end to end, or it is nothing at all.

Classifying and Marking

Classifying and *marking* are two terms related to the way in which packets are identified as needing differentiated treatment across network hops. *Classification* is generally considered to be the interpretation of QoS settings for incoming packets. *Marking* is generally considered the designation of QoS parameters for outgoing packets. So, you classify incoming traffic, and you mark (or tag) outgoing traffic.

There are a number of ways to classify QoS data, and these methods largely depend on the medium type of the network, the protocol in use, and the capabilities—and configuration—of the infrastructure equipment. In some cases, application data can be classified on a per-hop basis by some characteristic of the data (i.e., IP addresses, MAC addresses or OUIs, or network service), but it is more common (and often easier) to rely on trusted markings in frame or packet headers as specified by a common MAC- or IP-layer protocol, such as DSCP. After classifying data, appropriate QoS policies can be applied to the data.

Queuing and Scheduling

Queuing and *scheduling* refer to the way in which classified data is handled and the order in which it is processed for outgoing transmission. In other words, how is priority actually provided? There are several techniques designed to facilitate priority. Among others, these include:

- Scheduled polling

- Weighting mechanisms

- Round-robin

These are generic types of QoS scheduling, and there are many different variations on these types. Data arrives at a station, is classified into a queue, and is then selected from queues in accordance with the scheduling or queuing algorithm or mechanism. A queue is sometimes called a bucket, where frames wait to be processed for transmission by a network node.

In accordance with the network medium type, networking protocols, and QoS method(s) in use, network nodes perform frame and/or packet translation (conversion from one type to another). As a part of translation, stations must take the incoming data classification and convert that classification into an outgoing QoS marking or tag. This translation and conversion process facilitates the end-to-end QoS at each hop in the data's transmission path. In some cases, translation will convert one type of classification and convert it into another type of marking. In other cases, the same protocol(s) may be in use on the incoming and outgoing interfaces, so the classification translation is a direct transfer.

In the next sections, we will look at the intricate details of WLAN QoS as well as some of the most common wired QoS protocols. As we flesh out the details of these protocols, it will help us to discuss network design practices from a technical perspective.

WLAN Arbitration

If we compare wired and wireless technologies today, it becomes apparent fairly quickly that wired networking technologies generally offer greater capacity and performance than wireless networks. Wireless networks come with many benefits as well—such as mobility and low cost—but their primary drawback is the constraint of a shared wireless medium. As 802.11n has demonstrated, wireless technologies are always improving and capacity is increasing, but resources remain limited.

In this section, we will take a deeper dive into WLAN QoS by looking at the technologies, processes, and protocols that are used on WLANs. The foundational element to this discussion is WLAN arbitration and 802.11 channel access. This is a hefty topic by itself, but we will attempt to truncate it to the most essential components for this treatment and to tease these design applications out in a following section.

Our intention here is not to bog you down with the details but to provide the details that any professional WLAN designer should know. An understanding of 802.11 arbitration is fundamental to proper network design and QoS provisioning.

Channel Access Methods

The 802.11 specification defines a MAC architecture for 802.11 channel access. This architecture includes four different channel access methods that dictate how wireless stations should use the shared wireless medium in a "good neighborly" way.

These channel access methods (or functions) dictate the rules or patterns in which a wireless station can access the wireless medium. Each method has different rules for different network environments. In general, they are designed to facilitate relative "fairness" or to create statistical priority for devices or applications to access the wireless medium. Here's a description of each:

Distributed Coordination Function (DCF)   The *Distributed Coordination Function (DCF)* is the fundamental, required contention-based access function for all networks. DCF does not support QoS.

Point Coordination Function (PCF)   The *Point Coordination Function (PCF)* is an optional, contention-free function, used for non-QoS STAs. PCF is not currently implemented in the market.

Hybrid Coordination Function (HCF) Enhanced Distributed Channel Access (EDCA)   *Hybrid Coordination Function (HCF) Enhanced Distributed Channel Access (EDCA)* is optional, but it is the method used to provide prioritized contention-based QoS services. EDCA is *the* way to provide QoS for modern WLANs.

Hybrid Coordination Function (HCF) Controlled Channel Access (HCCA)   *Hybrid Coordination Function (HCF) Controlled Channel Access (HCCA)* is optional, and provides parameterized contention-free QoS services. HCCA is not currently implemented in the market.

Of the four channel access methods, only two (DCF and EDCA) are used today. The other two access methods, PCF and HCCA, have not been implemented by WLAN vendors, so we will avoid discussing these coordination functions here. The MAC channel access architecture is shown in Figure 10.2.

FIGURE 10.2 802.11 MAC architecture

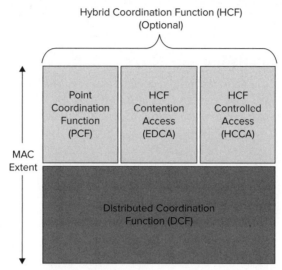

The foundational access method is called Distributed Coordination Function (DCF). In DCF, the coordination function logic is generally the same in every station (STA) in a *basic service set (BSS)*—except PHY-specific parameters, such as slot times. Stated differently, each station within a DCF follows the same channel access rules. DCF is contention based, which means that each device "competes" with the other devices to gain access to the wireless medium. After contention is won, the STA can transmit a frame, or series of frames, depending on the access rules. Then the contention process resumes. As the original 802.11 network access method, DCF is the most simple channel access method; however, being the first access method, it lacks support for QoS. To maintain support for non-QoS devices in QoS-enabled networks, support for DCF is required in all 802.11 networks.

As an optional access method that may be used in addition to DCF, HCF was introduced to support QoS. HCF EDCA offers prioritized contention-based wireless medium access. In other words, EDCA provides a way to prioritize 802.11 traffic so that certain traffic types are statistically more or less likely to be transmitted first. This is done by classifying 802.11 traffic types by user priorities (UP) and access categories (AC), which are associated with more or less aggressive contention parameters, depending on the desired priority.

A *user priority (UP)* is a value associated with a medium access control (MAC) service data unit (MSDU) that indicates how the MSDU is to be handled. The UP is assigned to an MSDU in the layers above the MAC. There are eight UPs, and these eight UPs map to four WMM access categories.

An *access category (AC)* is a label for a set of parameters used by QoS stations to contend for priority access to the medium. There are four ACs.

Contention Mechanisms

Both DCF and EDCA use the same basic contention mechanisms to arbitrate access to the wireless medium. We will look at these mechanisms in greater detail in this section, and we will discuss how differentiated priority is provided within EDCA.

Carrier Sense

To be friendly users of the shared frequency space in which they operate, Wi-Fi devices listen before transmitting. This process of listening is called *carrier sense*, and as the term implies, it is a way for stations to sense the activity on the medium. There are two modes of carrier sense: physical and virtual. Carrier sense works the same way with all channel access mechanisms.

Physical Carrier Sense—CCA   There are actually two subtypes of *Clear Channel Assessment (CCA)*—carrier sense (CS) and energy detect (ED):

Carrier Sense (CS)   The first type is simply called carrier sense (CS). CCA's CS mechanism is used to monitor the RF domain for incoming WLAN traffic. In other words, when a STA is not transmitting, its receiver is always listening and ready to process modulated WLAN frames, beginning with the PHY preamble (the start of a WLAN frame). If a STA detects an incoming WLAN frame at an RF amplitude above its CCA CS threshold, the STA will identify the RF medium as "busy" and it will not contend for the medium or transmit a frame. If there are no incoming frames or the amplitude of an incoming frame is lower than the CCA CS threshold, the STA will perceive the wireless medium as "idle" and continue to freely contend for the medium and transmit frames if it wins contention.

Energy Detect (ED)   The second type of CCA is called *energy detect (ED)*. ED is similar to CCA CS, but instead of listening for WLAN frames, the ED busy/idle state is dependent on raw RF energy. For ED to indicate a "busy" medium, the RF energy on the wireless channel must be pretty substantial.

With either method (CS or ED), a "busy" medium will prevent the STA from attempting to win contention. During a busy medium, WLAN stations sit quietly and wait to begin "contending" again. As you can see, CCA is a bit like a permission slip for WLAN transmissions. When the medium is idle, STAs can contend and transmit frames. If the medium is busy, they must wait. CCA is a critical aspect of WLAN arbitration.

⊕ Real World Scenario

Physical Carrier Sense Threshold Values

As an example of the CCA thresholds for a specific PHY, let's look at 802.11a details in Clause 17.2.10.5 (CCA sensitivity) of the 802.11-2007 specification:

CCA CS   CCA indicates a busy medium when the start of a valid OFDM transmission is received at a level equal to or greater than the minimum modulation and coding rate sensitivity (–82 dBm).

CCA ED   If the PHY preamble of the frame is missed, the CCA holds a busy medium for any signal 20 dB above the minimum modulation and coding rate sensitivity, which equates to –62 dBm.

Clause 17's CCA sensitivity is much higher (meaning the signal can be lower power) when the frame header is received and processed correctly. The sensitivity threshold for RF noise, including 802.11 frames whose header was not processed, as well as non-802.11 RF sources, is much lower, at –62 dBm. Thus, it takes a much stronger signal to indicate a busy medium when CCA ED is used instead of CCA CS.

A real-world example of this would be if an 802.11b/g/n client station were attempting to transmit a frame and a microwave oven in the area caused the 802.11 station to indicate a "busy" medium and cease transmitting. That is, if the microwave oven's amplitude was measured by the wireless station at a level above its ED threshold, the station would not be able to transmit on the affected channel.

Virtual Carrier Sense—Network Allocation Vector (NAV)   In addition to the physical carrier sense mechanisms, the 802.11 specification also defines a virtual carrier sense. Within the MAC header of WLAN frames is a field called the Duration field. This field carries a value that is used to indicate the duration of time before STAs can contend for the wireless medium again. To be completely accurate, the duration value covers the interframe space (required quiet period) after the frame in which it resides, as well as all remaining frames and interframe spaces that are a part of the current frame exchange or transmission opportunity. Figure 10.3 shows a simple frame exchange and the values that are used by the STA to virtually identify the busy/idle state of the wireless medium.

When STAs process the Duration value, they set a *network allocation vector (NAV)* timer, and count down that timer until the duration value reaches zero. The NAV timer must equal zero for a STA to contend for the wireless medium and transmit a frame. The NAV timer is used in concert with the CCA to inform the STA of the status of the wireless medium, whether busy or idle.

FIGURE 10.3 Purpose and location of the Duration field

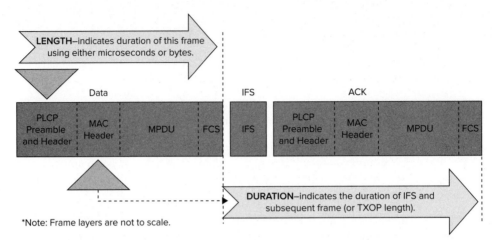

Interframe Spacing

Interframe spaces are an important part of channel access rules that dictate when a STA can access the medium, or when they can begin contending for access. After a frame has been transmitted on the wireless medium, there must be a short idle period before another frame may be transmitted by any station. This idle period is called an *interframe space (IFS)* and is measured in microseconds (μs). Interframe spaces are used to provide granular controlled access to the wireless medium. For example, some frames must be immediately acknowledged. Thus, before an ACK frame is transmitted, a short IFS (SIFS) is observed by the transmitter. This ensures that the ACK frame takes priority over other frames, which require longer IFS intervals before transmission.

The length of an IFS depends on the frame being transmitted and the access method in use. There are six types of IFS:

- Short interframe space (SIFS)

- PCF interframe space (PIFS)

- DCF interframe space (DIFS)

- *Arbitration interframe space* (AIFS)

- Extended interframe space (EIFS)

- Reduced interframe space (RIFS)

For our discussion here, we will only look at three of the interframe spaces: SIFS, DIFS, and AIFS.

The basic concept of an IFS is shown in Figure 10.4, which shows a data frame, SIFS, and ACK. Following the ACK frame, a DIFS would be observed (assuming DCF); then contention would continue until the next station transmits a frame.

FIGURE 10.4   The basic concept of an interframe space

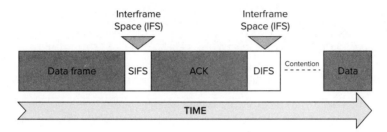

SHORT INTERFRAME SPACE (SIFS)

SIFS are used within both DCF and EDCA. For 802.11-2007, SIFS is the shortest of the IFS values and is used prior to ACK and clear to send (CTS) frames. However, with 802.11n, a shorter IFS (RIFS, which we will not discuss here) was introduced. The purpose of SIFS is for stations to maintain control of the wireless medium during a frame exchange sequence that warrants priority. By using SIFS, which is a small amount of time, no other stations (which would use other, longer IFS) will be able to win contention and disturb an ongoing exchange.

In other words, SIFS is used as a priority interframe space once a frame exchange sequence has begun. It allows the participants of a frame exchange sequence to complete their conversation uninterrupted. This is true when multiple frames are transmitted within a transmission opportunity (TXOP) (as with frame bursting), and it is also true when a single frame is transmitted (as with typical Data-ACK exchanges).

DCF INTERFRAME SPACE (DIFS)

When a STA desires to transmit a data frame (MAC protocol data unit, or MPDU) or management frame (MMPDU) for the first time (not a retry) within a DCF network, the duration of a DIFS must be observed after the previous frame's completion. As the IFS for DCF, a DIFS does not provide QoS differentiation. To provide relative equality in channel contention, DIFS values are the same for all STAs with similar PHY capabilities. The DIFS values are shown in Table 10.2.

TABLE 10.2 Calculations for IFS Values

PHY	SIFS	Slot Time	PIFS	DIFS
HR/DSSS (802.11b)	10 µs	20 µs	30 µs	50 µs
ERP (802.11g)	10 µs	Long = 20 µs Short = 9 µs	Long = 30 µs Short = 19 µs	Long = 50 µs Short = 28 µs
OFDM (802.11a)	16 µs	9 µs	25 µs	34 µs
HT (802.11n)	10 µs – 2.4 GHz 16 µs – 5 GHz	Long = 20 µs –2.4 GHz Short = 9 µs – 2.4 GHz 9 µs – 5 GHz	Long = 30 µs – 2.4 GHz Short = 19 µs – 2.4 GHz 25 µs – 5 GHz	Long = 50 µs –2.4 GHz Short = 28 µs – 2.4 GHz 34 µs – 5 GHz

ARBITRATION INTERFRAME SPACE (AIFS)

With EDCA, the basic contention logic is the same as with non-QoS networks, but in order to facilitate QoS differentiation, some notable differences are provided. While DCF designates a single DIFS value for each PHY to use for contention, as shown in Table 10.2, EDCA establishes unique IFS durations for each AC within a BSS. These unique IFS values are called AIFS, and because an AIFS is unique for each AC, an AIFS is notated as an AIFS[AC]. QoS STAs' TXOPs are obtained for a specific AC, so each STA is simultaneously contending for medium access with multiple ACs. An AIFS interval is used by QoS stations when attempting to transmit data frames, management frames, and some control frames.

For improved control of QoS mechanisms, AIFS values are user-configurable. By default, QoS APs announce an EDCA parameter set in the Beacon frame that notifies stations in the BSS about these QoS values. When you change these values in the AP configuration, the AP will broadcast a different set of parameters to the BSS. These parameters have a direct impact on the amount of priority given to a specific AC.

Figure 10.5 shows a Beacon frame that includes the AIFSN value for the Best Effort AC. As in the figure, these values can be found for each AC in the EDCA Parameter Set Element within a Beacon frame. In Figure 10.5, a highlight shows that this is the best-effort AC and the second highlight shows that the AIFSN is currently set to 3, the default setting. The AIFSN value determines the duration of the AIFS[AC], as we will discuss next.

FIGURE 10.5 Default AIFSN value as seen in a Beacon frame

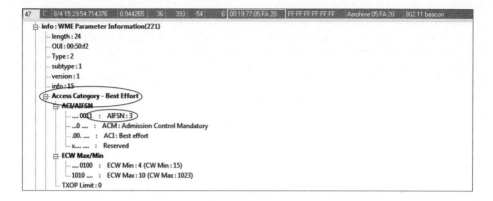

As a quick disclaimer, some of the calculations related to IFS values can be a bit intimidating at first. Other materials are available for the same topic, and we highly recommend that you look at these topics in greater depth.

For a more thorough and in-depth treatment of this topic, refer to the whitepaper titled "802.11 Arbitration," authored by Marcus Burton, which is available at http://www.cwnp.com/pdf/802.11_arbitration.pdf.

An AIFSN is a number (AIFS number) value that is user-configurable and determines the brevity (or length) of an AIFS interval. AIFSN values are set for each access category, giving the AIFS[AC] a shorter or longer duration, in accordance with the desired priority of the AC. This is demonstrated by the formula used to calculate an AIFS[AC]:

$$AIFS[AC] = AIFSN[AC] \times aSlotTime + aSIFSTime$$

These calculations can be made using the Slot Time and SIFS values from Table 10.2. The default values for each AIFSN[AC] are shown in Table 10.3 along with the resulting AIFS[AC] value for each PHY. By modifying the AIFSN[AC] shown in Table 10.3, administrators can manipulate the AIFS[AC] duration.

TABLE 10.3 Default AIFS Parameter Set

AC	AIFSN	802.11b AIFS[AC]	802.11g AIFS[AC]	802.11a AIFS[AC]	802.11n 2.4 GHz AIFS[AC]	802.11n 5 GHz AIFS[AC]
AC_BK	7	150 μs	Long = 150 μs Short = 73 μs	79 μs	Long = 150 μs Short = 73 μs	79 μs
AC_BE	3	70 μs	Long = 70 μs Short = 37 μs	43 μs	Long = 70 μs Short = 37 μs	43 μs
AC_VI	2	50 μs	Long = 50 μs Short = 28 μs	34 μs	Long = 50 μs Short = 28 μs	34 μs
AC_VO	2	50 μs	Long = 50 μs Short = 28 μs	34 μs	Long = 50 μs Short = 28 μs	34 μs

In comparison with Table 10.2, which shows the fixed SIFS and DIFS values, you can see in Table 10.3 that AIFS values are always longer than a SIFS for a given PHY. This ensures that SIFS-separated frame exchanges take priority.

Although much of this discussion about IFS has been academic, understanding these principles is relevant to network design. Figure 10.6 shows how the IFS values differ, and how a change in these values is directly related to a device's ability to win contention and transmit frames.

FIGURE 10.6 Relationship of interframe spaces in contention framework

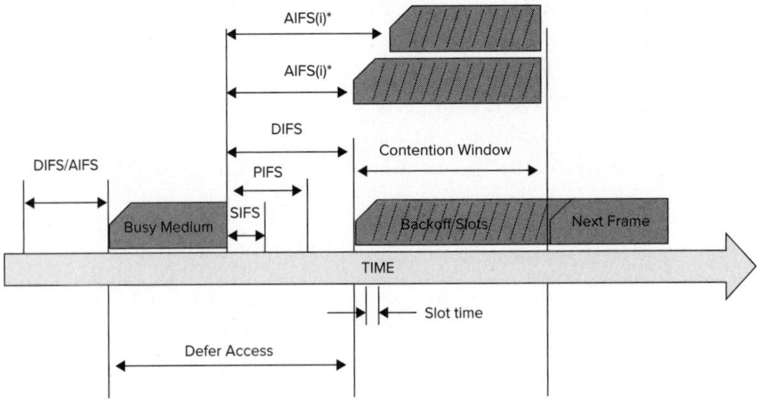

*Note—AIFS(i) refers to the AIFS values specific to an access category (AC).

IEEE Std 802.11-2007, Copyright 2007 IEEE. All rights reserved.

Backoff Timers

The concept of a *backoff timer* is fairly complex, and we will avoid all of the intricate details for this discussion. Instead, we will focus on the simple purpose of a backoff timer, some basics on its functionality, and how it is relevant to network design.

A random backoff timer is a way to add randomness to the 802.11 contention process to minimize collisions between competing stations. The backoff timer is a value that is randomly selected from a range of values called the *contention window (CW)*. The CW is based on EDCA parameters specified by the 802.11 standard and are user-configurable for QoS control. Here's how it works.

A STA randomly selects a backoff value from the CW. The backoff value represents the number of slot times (we will discuss this value in the next section) that must be observed with the wireless medium remaining idle before a STA can transmit a frame. So, if a STA selects a random backoff value of 7, it must wait seven slot times. The size of the CW varies in accordance with the PHY technology in use on a STA as well as the AC for QoS STAs. As you might guess, higher-priority ACs have smaller CWs, which gives them a higher probability of selecting a lower backoff value. For example, if you have a voice AC with a CW from 0–7 and you have a best-effort AC with a CW from 0–31, the voice AC is far more likely to select a lower backoff value than the best-effort AC. Lower backoff values represent a greater likelihood to win contention and transmit a frame.

The lower range of the CW is always 0. The upper range of the CW is based on one of two values: the CWmin and the CWmax. For the first attempt at a frame transmission, the CWmin value is used as the upper limit of the CW. For example, if the CWmin is 15, the CW for the first attempt at a frame transmission would be 0–15. If a collision occurs and a frame must be retransmitted, the upper limit of the CW increases exponentially for each retry until this value reaches the CWmax, as shown in Figure 10.7. In other words, collisions and retries are bad. Collisions require that STAs wait longer (statistically) for each subsequent attempt at a frame transmission. This helps us to see why high retry rates in latency-sensitive environments can be problematic for application performance.

FIGURE 10.7   Relationship between retries and a CWmax

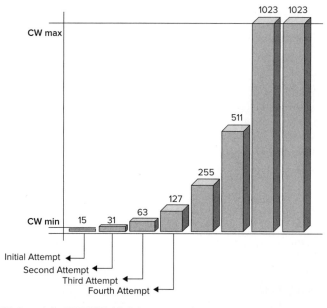

Just to reiterate, the CW is the range of values from which a STA randomly chooses a backoff value. This backoff value is equal to the number of slot times the transmission medium must be idle before the STA can transmit a frame.

So, as we mentioned in passing before, the CW represents a statistical probability for priority. ACs or STAs with lower CW values are more likely to select lower backoff timers, and thus, win contention more frequently. Higher-priority ACs, such as for voice and video, have small CWs. To make this concept more tangible, the CW parameters are shown in Table 10.4 for an 802.11n STA using default EDCA parameters.

TABLE 10.4   802.11n STA Default Contention Window Values

AC	AIFSN	CWmin	CWmax
AC_BK	7	15	1023
AC_BE	3	15	1023
AC_VI	2	7	15
AC_VO	2	3	7

As you can see from Table 10.4, AC_VO and AC_VI have a significantly higher priority than AC_BE and AC_BK due to a lower AIFSN[AC] and smaller CWmin and CWmax values. As this plays out in the arbitration process, high-priority ACs are far more likely to win contention than low-priority ACs and STAs.

Slot Times

As we discussed previously, a slot time is a PHY-specific time value, measured in microseconds (μs), that is used as a part of the arbitration process. Specifically, the random backoff value reflects the number of slot times that must be observed before a frame may be transmitted. So, a lower slot time reflects a contention advantage over other devices with higher slot times. Refer to Table 10.2 to see the slot times for each PHY. As you can see from Table 10.2, legacy PHYs have higher slot times than modern PHYs.

Implications for WLAN Design

Let's now look at some of the ways in which we can apply this knowledge at a high level:

Contention Domains and Probabilistic Contention   The first obvious fact about wireless networks is that they operate within a shared contention domain. Contention domains can be segmented—generally speaking—by isolating devices physically, by using nonoverlapping channels, and by shaping RF propagation with antennas and transmit power configurations. Operating within the constraints of 802.11 arbitration, we must use these controllable design elements to maximize capacity and minimize contention within the RF domain. As the number of devices within a contention domain increases, collisions will inevitably increase. Of course, a modest number of collisions and retries is acceptable and normal, but in excess, collisions and retries can bring application performance to unacceptable levels.

Standardized WLAN arbitration is probabilistic. This means that QoS only provides a statistical advantage for some devices to access the network; it does not provide a guaranteed priority. Based on that knowledge, you should approach network design by assessing the load that will be placed on your network and the mission-criticality of sensitive applications. If voice is the most important application on your WLAN, you may want to consider taking extra steps toward isolating VoWiFi to its own contention domain or ensuring that the statistical priority is sufficient for application performance requirements. Many experts in the field recommend deploying latency-sensitive applications like voice in an entirely different frequency band than data. This is an option, but it may lead to other problems, such as what to do with devices that are both data and voice devices (such as smartphones and laptops with softphones). Similarly, the advances of 802.11n in 5 GHz are most beneficial to data applications, whereas voice applications enjoy only a modest benefit. Further, if you prioritize voice applications by supporting them in 5 GHz, your data applications will likely see a performance impact if they are relegated to 2.4 GHz. If there is a clear priority for one application over another, this may be a viable option, but in most cases, several applications are mission-critical, which prevents complete isolation of contention domains by application.

SSIDs and Contention Domains   As you assess the options for segmenting applications into different contention domains, remember that SSIDs do not divide a network into different RF domains. All SSIDs supported on a radio operate within the same contention domain. SSIDs are one way to control the access rules by which client devices compete for the medium (such as by preventing certain access categories, or by supporting proprietary access control mechanisms like airtime fairness), but SSID "segmentation" has limited benefit to wireless contention.

Customizing EDCA Parameter Sets   While the standardized set of EDCA parameters is usually sufficient for WLAN QoS, some networks may require fine-tuning of these parameters. Thankfully, most WLAN infrastructure vendors allow administrators to change these settings, so you can provide greater differentiation between low- and high-priority access categories.

Channel Capacity and User Density   Designers should also consider AP-to-client load expectations with arbitration in mind. When there is a high number of high-priority devices (such as VoWiFi phones), designers may do well to attempt to minimize the load on each AP by decreasing AP coverage areas, performing load balancing, or using other load management practices. The traffic patterns of some low-latency, high-priority applications can be somewhat demanding when there are high user densities. This is often because these applications must transmit frames frequently, and they observe short contention periods. For this reason, a fewer number of devices can typically be supported by a single AP. When CWs range from 0–3 (default for AC_VO) and devices are attempting to access the medium frequently, the statistical likelihood of two devices transmitting at the same time increases dramatically. This may lead to a significant number of collisions when client density is too high. For this reason, WLAN voice client vendors typically have a recommended maximum client density for each AP.

WLAN QoS: WMM and 802.11e

The WLAN QoS mechanisms described in the previous section and later sections were introduced to 802.11 WLANs by the 802.11e amendment, which is now a part of 802.11-2007. However, in the real world, only a subset of 802.11e functionality has been implemented by vendors. The Wi-Fi Alliance introduced a specification based on 802.11e QoS, called Wi-Fi Multimedia (WMM). WMM represents the functionality we see in the real-world implementations.

 The Wi-Fi Alliance's WMM knowledgebase can be found at www.wi-fi.org/ knowledge_center/wmm. Some of this content requires a Wi-Fi Alliance membership.

As a subset of 802.11e, WMM makes implementation of WLAN QoS easier for infrastructure and client vendors. As with other Wi-Fi Alliance specifications, a certification program is in place to validate device compliance with WMM functionality. Device certification is an important insurance for device selection and planning of QoS-enabled WLANs. Today, all 802.11n certified devices support WMM.

In the wireless domain, WMM is a feature that should be supported by both the AP and the client for maximum effectiveness; however, WMM does not have to be supported by both. In a QoS BSS, non-QoS traffic is assigned best effort (AC_BE) priority. Most WLAN vendors' APs can still perform downstream QoS, even if the recipient client does not support WMM. Remember, 802.11 QoS is largely designed to provide prioritized access to the transmission medium, so even if QoS is only downlink, it will still be helpful for some applications. If an application requires bidirectional prioritization, as with most voice implementations, performance will suffer if the client does not support WMM. Applications like unidirectional video will not be as noticeably impacted if WMM is only supported on the downlink. For WMM *admission control*, WMM is mandatory on both the client and the AP. Similarly, there are many facets to WMM that are lost when both the client and the AP do not support WMM.

In many client devices supporting WMM, very few configuration parameters are provided. In some cases, there aren't any client configuration variables. In others, configuration is limited to enabling or disabling WMM, as is shown in the Vocera badge configuration utility in Figure 10.8. In that regard, the client application and software driver dictate the operation of a specific NIC.

FIGURE 10.8   WMM configuration options for Vocera VoWiFi badges

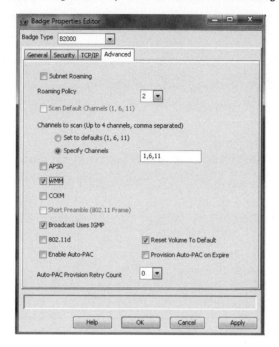

There are many important aspects to WMM operation, so we will explore them in the following sections.

WMM QoS Classification

In our introduction to QoS in the WLAN arbitration section, we mentioned that there are eight user priorities (UPs) and four access categories (ACs). As data is passed from an application down the protocol stack within a STA, it is classified with a UP in accordance with the coding of the application. This UP is passed to the MAC layer for classification and queuing.

Because of the relationship between WLANs and Ethernet LANs, WMM classification is correlated with *802.1p* (now part of *802.1D*) UPs. We will look briefly at 802.1p UPs later in the section entitled "QoS in Wired Networks." In WMM, these UP classifications are mapped to four ACs, which possess their own queues and access parameters. The UP to AC mapping and naming conventions are shown in Table 10.5. To preserve the UP value for a frame when it is translated to different media types, WMM stations also include the UP (which is more granular than the AC) in the QoS Control field of transmitted QoS frames—802.11 management frames do not include the QoS Control field, so they are treated with AC_VO access parameters on the wireless medium, and they are not forwarded to the wired interface. The QoS Control field enables the receiving STA (usually an AP) to read the UP classification and then properly mark the frame when it is translated and transmitted onto the wired medium.

TABLE 10.5   Relationship Between 802.11 Access Categories and 802.1p User Priorities

Priority	UP	802.11 AC	802.11 AC Designation	802.1D Designation
Lowest Priority	1	AC_BK	Background	BK
	2	AC_BK	Background	--
	0	AC_BE	Best Effort	BE
	3	AC_BE	Best Effort	EE
	4	AC_VI	Video	CL
	5	AC_VI	Video	VI
	6	AC_VO	Voice	VO
Highest Priority	7	AC_VO	Voice	NC

Note:UP values are identical to 802.1D UPs.

Each of the four ACs specified by WMM has its own contention parameters and frame queues. The intra-station contention and queuing concept is shown in Figure 10.9.

FIGURE 10.9   WMM queuing within a STA

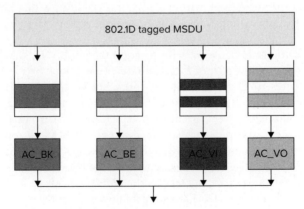

Admission Control and Traffic Streams

Admission control is a configurable option in which stations must request permission prior to using an AC. Support for admission control is indicated by use of an "admission control mandatory" bit, so you will often see the abbreviation ACM referring to admission control. In busy network environments, when too many users are attempting to access the network resources at the same time, quality will suffer for everyone. The purpose of admission control is for the AP to maintain control of the use of network resources so as to preserve application quality for the maximum number of stations. Clients must check in with the AP to see if an acceptable amount of resources are available. The AP's admission control algorithms are vendor specific and are dependent on channel capacity, RF link conditions, network performance indicators (errors, retransmissions, etc.), and other criteria. Some user-defined admission control parameters are also commonly used, such as the number of permitted calls and maximum bandwidth allocation; these configuration elements are shown for a Cisco 5508 WLAN controller in Figure 10.10. Figure 10.11 shows a Beacon frame with admission control disabled for all ACs.

FIGURE 10.10 Cisco admission control settings for voice traffic

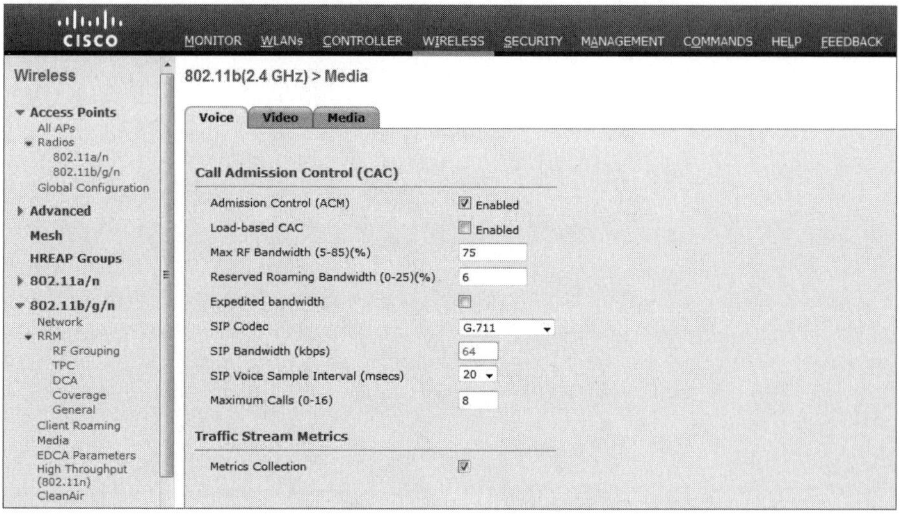

If admission control is enabled, associated clients seek the AP's permission to use a network resource by sending an ADDTS (short for Add Traffic Stream) Request Action frame to the AP. ADDTS frames are designed to create new *traffic streams (TSs)* with custom service parameters. Within an ADDTS is a *TSPEC* (short for *Traffic Specification*) element, which is a set of parameters that classify the performance requirements of a traffic stream. A sample ADDTS Request frame is shown in Figure 10.12.

FIGURE 10.11   Admission Control disabled for all ACs

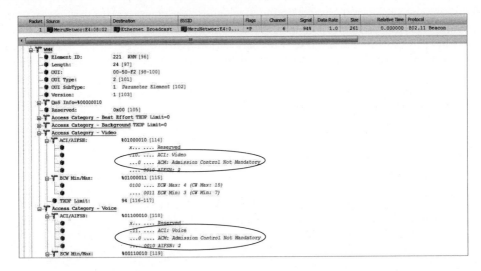

FIGURE 10.12   ADDTS Request frame

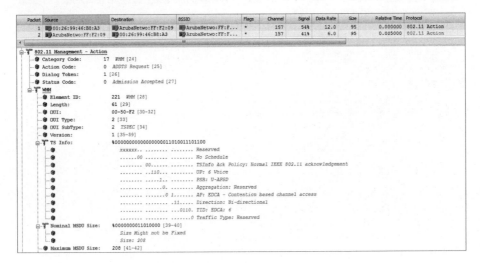

The AP processes the ADDTS Request (by using the information in the TSPEC element), compares it with the admission control algorithms, and either accepts, rejects, or modifies the TSPEC information. The AP's response is sent in an ADDTS Response frame, which informs the client how to proceed. A sample ADDTS Response frame is shown in Figure 10.13. If clients are joining a BSS, a TSPEC can be established by means of a TSPEC element in (re)association request frames. The AP's response to the TSPEC comes in the (re)association response frame. The details of admission control processes are beyond the scope of the CWDP exam, but proper design always requires that designers understand the technology and processes that underlie the deployment.

FIGURE 10.13 ADDTS Response frame

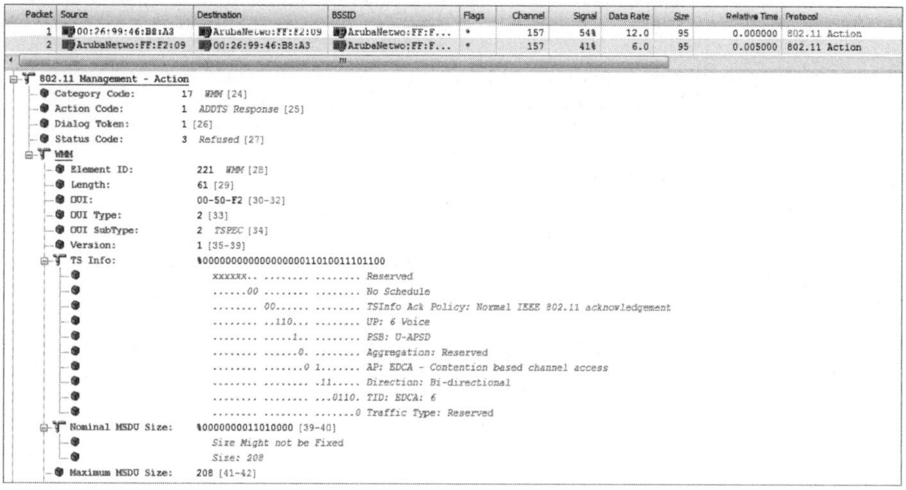

Packet	Source	Destination	BSSID	Flags	Channel	Signal	Data Rate	Size	Relative Time	Protocol
1	00:26:99:46:B8:A3	ArubaNetwo:FF:F2:09	ArubaNetwo:FF:F...	*	157	54%	12.0	95	0.000000	802.11 Action
2	ArubaNetwo:FF:F2:09	00:26:99:46:B8:A3	ArubaNetwo:FF:F...	*	157	41%	6.0	95	0.005000	802.11 Action

```
802.11 Management - Action
  Category Code:      17  WMM [24]
  Action Code:         1  ADDTS Response [25]
  Dialog Token:        1  [26]
  Status Code:         3  Refused [27]
  WMM
    Element ID:      221  WMM [28]
    Length:           61  [29]
    OUI:              00-50-F2 [30-32]
    OUI Type:          2  [33]
    OUI SubType:       2  TSPEC [34]
    Version:           1  [35-39]
    TS Info:         %00000000000000000110100011101100
                       xxxxxx.. ........ ........  Reserved
                       ......00 ........ ........  No Schedule
                       ........ 00...... ........  TSInfo Ack Policy: Normal IEEE 802.11 acknowledgement
                       ........ ..110... ........  UP: 6 Voice
                       ........ .....1.. ........  PSB: U-APSD
                       ........ ......0. ........  Aggregation: Reserved
                       ........ .......0 1.......  AP: EDCA - Contention based channel access
                       ........ ........ .11.....  Direction: Bi-directional
                       ........ ........ ...0110.  TID: EDCA: 6
                       ........ ........ .......0  Traffic Type: Reserved
    Nominal MSDU Size: %0000000011010000 [39-40]
                       Size Might not be Fixed
                       Size: 208
    Maximum MSDU Size: 208 [41-42]
```

Even when admission control is not required, traffic streams with custom TSPEC parameters may still be established. If the upper layers of a STA determine that a set of frames requires some specific treatment beyond the basic set of contention parameters defined for an AC, the upper layers can indicate this requirement in the instructions to the MAC. The STA then follows the same steps described in the previous paragraph to set up a TSPEC to meet the traffic stream's performance requirements.

Identifying Traffic for Prioritization

When the upper layers of a station have data to send, they send the data down the protocol stack with instructions to the MAC layer with information about the data to be transmitted. In the instructions from the Logical Link Control (LLC) to the MAC, each MSDU includes a traffic identifier (TID), as determined by the upper layers. The TID indicates the type of treatment desired for a specific MSDU. TID values range from 0–15; however, only TID values 0–7 are currently used with EDCA. TID values 8–15 correspond with HCCA (or HEMM) traffic streams. The information sent from the upper layers also indicates whether additional prioritization measures are required for the set of MSDUs. These additional measures would call for a unique set of traffic requirements, as defined within a TSPEC.

Assigning QoS Policies

Within a typical WLAN infrastructure, QoS policies may define traffic classifications, admission control parameters, bandwidth contracts, scheduling policies, and more. These QoS policies are then tied either to SSIDs for ESS-wide QoS policy enforcement or to groups and users for more granular QoS. AAA attributes, or other user-based authentication methods, are typically used to assign a QoS profile to a user or group. As you plan your method of QoS application, realize that user-based QoS is far more granular and allows for more differentiated services within a service set. However, applying QoS directly to a WLAN profile (SSID) may reflect an easier administrative approach. The decision ultimately comes down to the way in which you are dividing your traffic and service types up within the WLAN profiles.

QoS in Wired Networks

After all of our discussion about WLAN QoS, we must remember that WLAN QoS is useless if it isn't translated to the wired network. For that reason, if we're to understand wireless QoS, we must also understand at least the basics of wired QoS.

In general, WLANs are an extension of 802.3 Ethernet LANs that support the IP protocol at Layer 3. With that in mind, we will provide a quick overview of the predominant QoS protocols and considerations that are relevant to those medium types.

The Difference Between Wired and Wireless QoS

We should point out one significant difference between wired and wireless QoS. It is a common practice in wired network design to gratuitously overprovision networks so that there are enough resources to accommodate the expected traffic load without stressing the network's capacity. In any network with sufficient resources, throughput, latency, jitter, and loss requirements are likely to be met for most applications if the network is not being overly taxed. In practice, overprovisioning usually adds cost to a network deployment and is embraced as a tactic to avoid the complexities of configuring systemwide QoS. Unfortunately, overprovisioning is not an option with WLANs, as bandwidth is limited by virtue of a crowded, shared contention domain; therefore, end users are forced to use the available resources with utmost discrimination. That discrimination leads us to the necessity of QoS.

802.1D, 802.1Q, and 802.1p Standards

802.11 WLANs may be deployed into many different types of wired networks, and the overwhelming majority of deployments are as an extension of 802.3 Ethernet LANs. End-to-end QoS implementations are heavily dependent on compatibility of standardized

QoS protocols between different media types, so the IEEE 802.1 working group specifies standards that are intended to facilitate compatibility between different 802.*x* mediums, such as 802.11 and 802.3. 802.*x* standards are primarily MAC-layer protocols, and these protocols are an important part of QoS homogeneity across an enterprise. For the wired QoS discussion with Ethernet, 802.1p UPs are our primary topic of interest, but we should briefly discuss 802.1D and 802.1Q before looking specifically at 802.1p.

802.1D   The 802.1D standard defines IEEE MAC bridging. The original 802.1D standard did not specify a way for bridged networks to signal user priority within a frame, so 802.1p was specified as an addition to 802.1D for that purpose.

802.1Q   802.1Q is a standard that defines virtual LANs within the context of the bridging framework defined by 802.1D. At this point, you may be asking what VLANs have to do with QoS. The answer is that they don't really have much to do with QoS, but 802.1Q modifies MAC frame formats in such a way that 802.1p user priorities can be included in the modified frames. 802.1Q provides VLAN support by extending the MAC header of 802 frames with a 4-byte (32-bit) field, which includes a VLAN identifier. 802.1p was developed separately from 802.1Q, but 802.1p is used as a part of 802.1Q frame expansion. Specifically, 3 of the 32 bits that are added to an 802.1Q-expanded frame are used for the 802.1p user priority, also known as a priority code point (PCP). For a reference, the 802.1Q expansion field is shown in Figure 10.14.

FIGURE 10.14   802.1Q frame expansion

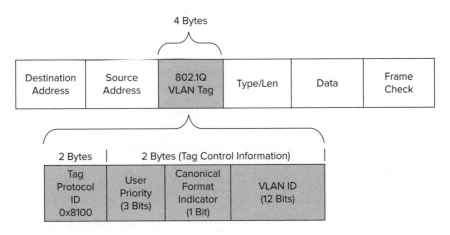

802.1p   As you can see in Figure 10.14, the PCP (User Priority, in the figure) subfield is 3 bits in length, which accommodates values from 0 to 7. The eight PCP subfield values are 802.1p UPs, and correspond to different *classes of service (CoSs)*, which are also known as traffic categories. These eight UPs are shown in Table 10.6 with their corresponding traffic type. As we discussed earlier, these eight UPs are mapped to 802.11 AC classifications.

TABLE 10.6 802.1p User Priority Classifications

User Priority	Acronym	Traffic Type
1	BK	Background
2	--	Spare
0 (Default)	BE	Best Effort
3	EE	Excellent Effort
4	CL	Controlled Load
5	VI	Video
6	VO	Voice
7	NC	Network Control

IEEE Std 802.11-2007, Copyright 2007 IEEE. All rights reserved.

Keeping 802.x Standards Organized

It can be a challenge to keep the myriad 802.x standards organized. The numbering and lettering formats can get confusing. While we don't have a quick and easy way to keep it all organized, repetition may be helpful. As it relates to 802.x standards, let's review:

802.1D Specifies IEEE MAC Bridging. 802.1p was added to the 802.1D standard.

802.1Q A standard that defines virtual LANs within the framework of the 802.1D Bridging standard.

802.1p Defines eight UPs, which are signaled in a 3-bit priority field that is a part of 802.1Q-tagged Ethernet frames. Despite its relationship to 802.1Q, 802.1p was written as an addition to the 802.1D standard, and was rolled into 802.1D in 1998.

802.3ac An amendment to the Ethernet (802.3) working group that expanded the maximum frame size from 1518 to 1522 bytes. This change accommodates the 4 additional bytes from 802.1Q expansion, which includes the 3-bit PCP (802.1p) CoS field.

802.11e An amendment to the 802.11 standard; defines QoS for WLANs. 802.11e was rolled into 802.11-2007.

DiffServ Protocols

All of the QoS protocols we've discussed thus far have been MAC-layer protocols. At the network layer, DiffServ is the primary QoS mechanism used in today's IP-based networks. To meet the needs of a highly divergent set of IP networks, DiffServ is a highly flexible QoS mechanism.

DiffServ Resources

The IETF defines DiffServ and provides additional help in a number of RFCs, as the following list shows. A simple Internet search will also yield a number of informative articles and links about DiffServ.

RFC 2474 Definition of the Differentiated Services field (DS field) in the IPv4 and IPv6 headers

RFC 2475 An architecture for Differentiated Services

RFC 2597 An assured forwarding PHB group

RFC 3140 Per-hop behavior identification codes (obsoletes RFC 2836)

RFC 3246 An expedited forwarding PHB (obsoletes RFC 2598)

RFC 3260 New terminology and clarifications for DiffServ

RFC 4594 Configuration guidelines for DiffServ service classes

---

DiffServ classification can be performed in a number of ways, including the IP source or destination address, the network service, or more commonly, *Differentiated Services Code Point (DSCP)* bits in the IP packet header. Classification results in an assignment of each packet to a traffic class, which is associated with policies that determine the services provided to that traffic class. The frame handling policies for a traffic class are referred to as per-hop behaviors (PHBs). The IETF provides recommended PHBs for each traffic class and DiffServ is designed to be highly flexible and granular, so network designers may also apply other traffic engineering policies, such as rate limiting and traffic shaping, to IP traffic.

Within an IPv4 packet header, there is an 8-bit differentiated services field. Six of these bits are the DSCP values used for classification, which provides a total of up to 64 different traffic classes. Half of the DSCP values are designated for specific services, but the other half are open for user-defined services.

Each implementation is tailored to the needs of a specific network, which makes its relationship to wireless networks slightly more flexible and fluid. In other words, the DSCP policies that are applied at the network layer do not have a fixed correlation to the policies on the 802.11 MAC. Whereas 802.1p and WMM share a common mapping of 3-bit UP values, DSCP and WMM do not share a consistent one-to-one priority mapping for all networks. However, the IETF does provide fairly extensive documentation and deployment recommendations for DSCP traffic classes, services, and code-point assignments, and these recommendations pave the way for a reasonable amount of consistency across different networks. This allows WLAN vendors to use some consistent UP-to-DSCP conversion.

Instead of using 1:1 UP to DSCP conversions—because there are so many DSCP traffic classes—UP to DSCP classifier maps may translate a range of DSCP values to a single UP value for 802.1p or WMM. For example, DSCP values 40–47 may all be mapped to a UP value of 5 (which maps to WMM AC_VI), and vice versa. To demonstrate how this might look in an actual implementation, Table 10.7 shows Cisco's suggested DSCP to 802.1p and 802.11e UP baseline conversion maps, and Figure 10.15 shows Aerohive Networks' default classifier map policy, which maps DSCP ranges to UP values.

TABLE 10.7 Cisco's Suggested DSCP Conversion Map

QoS Baseline – Traffic Type	DSCP	802.1p UP	802.11e UP
Network Control	--	7	--
LWAPP/CAPWAP Control – 802.11 Management	48	6	7
Voice	46 (EF)	5	6
Video	34 (AF41)	4	5
Voice Control	26 (AF31)	3	4
Background (gold)	18 (AF21)	2	2
Background (gold)	20 (AF22)	2	2
Background (gold)	22 (AF23)	2	2
Background (silver)	10 (AF11)	1	1
Background (silver)	12 (AF12)	1	1
Background (silver)	14 (AF13)	1	1
Best Effort	0 (BE)	0	0, 3
Background	2	0	1
Background	4	0	1
Background	6	0	1

Courtesy of Cisco, Copyright 2010

FIGURE 10.15:   Classifier map configuration menu

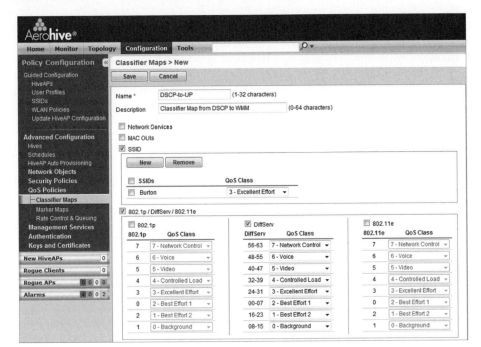

Used with permission from Aerohive Networks

Network Control Priority

You may notice from Table 10.7 that Cisco's baseline QoS mapping reserves the highest priority 802.1p value for Network control. This traffic type is necessary for maintaining functionality and availability of network resources, so it takes precedence over all types of user traffic. For that reason, it is assigned the highest priority and all other services (such as voice and video) are assigned the next lower priority class to accommodate. This illustrates that vendor-specific design practices are an important part of network design, as is integration of the WLAN into the wired LAN.

Integrating WLANs into Wired Networks

There are several considerations to make as you design the wireless network's integration with the wired network. Many are architectural in nature and relate to translation of frame markings from one protocol or OSI layer to another. Also, many others are related to integrating with existing wired QoS practices and configuring QoS trust on infrastructure devices.

There are two primary models for data forwarding at the AP: distributed and centralized. When distributed forwarding is employed, APs must have sufficient processing and memory capacity to apply sophisticated QoS scheduling and queuing policies to each frame. This was previously a limitation for some deployments because of underpowered APs. Today, many vendors are moving intelligence into the AP to accommodate this need. QoS configuration on the WLAN will largely depend on the QoS policy on the wired LAN. Some WLAN infrastructure vendors provide granular control of classification and marking maps. In other cases, these maps are fixed and are based on common mappings. If these maps don't coincide with the desired QoS policy for the network, the wired infrastructure will have to be configured to reclassify traffic that originated from the WLAN or is destined for the WLAN. Let's look more closely at QoS design considerations for distributed and centralized forwarding models.

Distributed Forwarding   One of the first design practices for QoS in distributed forwarding situations is to ensure that the AP is configured to translate between WMM (L2) and 802.1p (L2) and DSCP (L3). In addition to this, the AP's Ethernet switch must be configured to support and honor the same QoS priority sent by the AP. If the network is using 802.1p CoS bits to provide QoS at the MAC layer, the switch should be configured with appropriate L2 trust and 802.1Q should be enabled on the switch port. On the other hand, if network layer QoS (DSCP) is preferred, the switch should be honoring the DSCP values provided by the AP, and 802.1Q becomes arbitrary for QoS. Depending on the systemwide approach to QoS, the network infrastructure may be applying its own QoS classification policies aside from, or in addition to, code-point values, which may mean that the DSCP values are ignored or changed in favor of new markings. These QoS actions are likely already defined within the company by routing and switching policies, and the primary responsibility of the WLAN is to get the WMM classifications translated to 802.1p and/or DSCP. The wired infrastructure will do the rest.

When a WLAN client constructs an MPDU, the DSCP values are marked in the IP header, encapsulated into an 802.11 header, and passed to the AP. In normal L2 operations, the AP does not inspect DSCP values sent from the wireless client. Thus, in a distributed forwarding model, when the AP forwards the frame on to the wired network, the original DSCP markings from the 802.11 client remain intact.

Centralized Forwarding   However, in a centralized forwarding model (frames are forwarded through the WLAN controller), the AP encapsulates the original 802.11 MPDU with new IP and Ethernet headers (with L3 tunneling to the WLAN controller) and marks the new headers in accordance with values derived from the MAC header of the 802.11 frame and the AP's QoS translation table. In other words, the AP takes the UP from the 802.11 frame, and converts it into 802.1p for the new MAC header and DSCP for the new IP header (assuming 802.1p is marked on the new MAC header, which it may not be). Then these encapsulated frames are sent through the network to the WLAN controller. The original DSCP markings from the wireless client are left intact. When L3 tunneling is used between the AP and WLAN controller, DSCP classification is favored and 802.1p may not be marked at all.

When the WLAN controller receives these encapsulated packets, the outer L2 and L3 headers are removed and the original 802.11 frame is handled by the WLAN controller. In accordance with the QoS policy for that frame, the WLAN controller will apply the appropriate 802.1p and/or DSCP markings on the outgoing frame if it is not destined to return to the AP.

If a frame is destined to go from the WLAN controller to the AP, the controller will encapsulate that frame with an outer MAC and IP header (again, if L3 tunneling is used), marking 802.1p and/or DSCP on the outer headers for proper handling through the network to the AP.

When a centralized forwarding model is used, the network switch to which the WLAN controller is connected must also be properly configured to handle QoS tags from the WLAN controller. This switch port, or combination of switch ports, must be designated with QoS trust in accordance with the desired L2 or L3 QoS policy for the network. If the WLAN controller marks 802.1p and DSCP, the switch may only use 802.1p (CoS trust), or it may strip off and ignore the MAC header CoS bits and rely on the WLAN controller's DSCP markings. Yet another option is that the Ethernet switch would reclassify the traffic and mark it with new QoS tags to comply with the rest of the wired network configuration.

QoS Challenges

It is difficult to cover the full scope of challenges that may arise with Wi-Fi QoS, but here is a short list of the most high-level headaches:

RF is an unstable and dynamic medium.   First, the RF medium is inherently unstable and dynamic. New RF obstructions are introduced and removed. RF interference comes on and goes off. New office partitions are built, removed, or otherwise modified. Doors open and close. Furniture is rearranged. The RF environment is the foundation on which upper-layer protocols and mechanisms, like QoS, are built. If the RF environment is unstable or unreliable, upper-layer features that are built on it will also be unreliable. Stability at this level will generally improve application performance.

Users are mobile and user populations are dynamic.   Similarly, users are mobile and are constantly moving throughout a service set. Laptops and other Wi-Fi devices are coming and going, being turned on and off. Legacy devices—with legacy PHYs or no QoS support—join and leave. Neighboring networks are installed, removed, or modified. For many reasons, data rates are always changing. All of these changes affect network capacity and contention.

WLAN QoS is largely probabilistic.   We've already mentioned it, but it bears repeating that WLAN QoS is probabilistic. Contention mechanisms are designed to provide statistical priority based on a device or access category's contention parameters. This is not a service guarantee. One of the ways to combat this is to attempt to isolate high-priority devices into their own contention domain. However, when you use separate SSIDs to differentiate between different services, what do you do with devices that don't fit entirely into a specific service category (e.g., data or voice)? Many end users are using voice services on their laptops along with interactive video, email, and web browsing. Similarly, smartphones, tablet devices, and other similar electronics require many different types of applications. Restricting services to a specific band is becoming increasingly difficult.

Standardized QoS may be insufficient.   Standardized QoS mechanisms are usually adequate for maintaining service quality in most WLANs; however, they also fall short in some areas, such as balancing airtime usage among clients with high or low data rates so as to maximize efficiency. For this purpose, proprietary features may be required.

Application-Specific Challenges

For some networks where standardized QoS falls short, we must often turn to proprietary solutions implemented by WLAN vendors.

Increased Demand for Video

One of the hot topics of modern WLANs is the increased demand for video consumption. Video raises a unique challenge for WLANs because some video applications rely on multicast traffic. In fact, any application that relies on multicast for sensitive traffic may pose problems, because wireless multicast has some significant QoS drawbacks, such as:

- Multicast traffic is assigned to AC_BE. Network administrators cannot designate a higher-priority access category for multicast and broadcast (MC/BC) traffic. This is a major drawback, because contention management is the primary QoS mechanism in WLANs.

- All WLAN traffic with an MC/BC destination address must be transmitted at a rate in the Basic Rate Set. This often constrains multicast and broadcast traffic to low data rates, such as 1, 2, 5.5, 6 or 11 Mbps.

- MC/BC traffic in a WLAN is not acknowledged, which paves the way for high loss and low reliability.

- When power save functionality is supported within the BSS, power save operation can severely delay the delivery of MC/BC traffic. Specifically, MC/BC traffic is buffered at the AP until after *Delivery Traffic Indication Message (DTIM)* Beacons, at which point all stations awake to receive these frames. Even if every Beacon is a DTIM, this is still a problematic amount of delay for sensitive traffic.

- Multicast group subscription is not easily determined by the AP unless the AP snoops client traffic for multicast join requests. It is quite possible that all members of a multicast group (for whom the multicast stream is still active) would be disconnected from an AP, but the AP would still be transmitting a multicast data stream, taking up valuable network airtime.

To address some of these concerns, vendors have responded with proprietary solutions. The primary way to address many of these multicast-related problems is to convert multicast traffic into unicast traffic. This addresses many of the problems in the previous list and allows these data flows to be given proper treatment. As a word of caution for multicast to unicast conversion, if there are a lot of client subscriptions to the multicast flow in a BSS, network capacity can quickly become overwhelmed when a single multicast flow is transferred into many high-priority unicast flows. If all unicast flows are at a high data rate, the adverse affect may be minimized, but if a few clients are connected at low data rates, the impact to network utilization could be severe.

Other Demands

In addition to multicast related problems, some applications have other demands that are difficult to meet with standardized QoS. For example, some applications are sensitive to latency and loss. It may be advantageous to intentionally transmit these application flows at a lower data rate to ensure signal reception with lower loss and lower retries. Similarly, with video applications, some of the data frames are more significant than others; these frames should also be prioritized in a way that reduces retries and maximizes efficiency, but this type of functionality requires application-level insight by the WLAN infrastructure. These types of application-specific hurdles are minor, but many networks can benefit from any and all QoS improvements that are available. To offer these types of advanced QoS features, application and network infrastructure vendors will either have to be tightly integrated or these products will have to be provided by the same vendor.

Time Sensitivity

With voice and video, the time sensitivity of some data is a higher priority than loss. If there are high retries, at some point, a specific frame should be dropped because it may no longer be valid for the application flow. This can be user-defined with retry count limits and CWmax settings, but in an ideal world, the WLAN infrastructure would be aware of application requirements and could adjust its behavior accordingly. Proprietary features are required to address these custom application optimizations.

Basic QoS Troubleshooting

When application performance isn't meeting expectations but QoS is enabled and configured, what do you do?

First, consider all the factors that impact network traffic from start to finish, among them:

- Proper marking and tagging
- The maintaining and honoring of classification across all network hops
- QoS trust
- Transport delays
- Translation delays
- Queuing delays
- Utilization of network links (congestion)
- End-to-end bandwidth resources
- RF interference
- Data forwarding models
- Roaming

As you encounter specific problems and try to isolate the root cause, it may help to consider each of these variables and how they may affect the network.

Keep in mind that many WLAN QoS problems are also caused by poor RF design and resource management. A simple analysis of channel traffic may help to identify if the wireless medium is saturated, if RF interference is causing issues, if clients with sensitive applications are roaming excessively, or if the wireless domain is operating as it should be. Is there too much management traffic (too many SSIDs?), are you supporting the lowest basic rates (try disabling 1, 2, and 5.5 Mbps), are there too many errors and retries? Look for indicators that would help you isolate the problem to the wireless or wired domains.

You should also consider whether other applications are functioning properly. If so, you're likely looking at an issue of sensitive application requirements and insufficient resource provisioning. Ensure that your application's traffic is being marked and prioritized properly (on transmit *and* receive). Analyze latency and jitter if the flow is bidirectional. If bandwidth is being consumed by other lower-priority devices, explore ways to limit bandwidth consumption—move some stations back to the wired network, use rate limiting or service level agreement (SLA) policies, and so forth—and free up resources for the sensitive applications.

Another issue you may observe is one-way QoS—for instance, your phone is sending properly tagged and prioritized upstream traffic, but downstream traffic from the AP is not being prioritized. This is often an issue of improperly planned end-to-end bidirectional QoS. Since there are several potential points of failure along the end-to-end QoS link, you should reassess your APs QoS configuration, including conversion of markings. Also, ensure that your access switches are configured with proper trust. There are many other considerations here as well. One way to test proper end-to-end QoS in a site assessment is to initiate a voice call to another voice station in the same BSS. If frames are transmitted and received by both clients with proper markings, your end-to-end QoS should be intact.

Finally, what if your wireless station isn't sending properly tagged frames? Begin by ensuring that your device supports QoS. Is it WMM certified? Is WMM enabled on the client and infrastructure—for VoIP, check the VoIP server as well. Is your application properly tagging the data? Does your driver support WMM?

Airtime Fairness

In the "WLAN Arbitration" section, we discussed the standardized methods by which wireless contention is managed. Standardized contention parameters were specified by the IEEE to handle normal traffic loads and to provide priority to some devices or access categories, but new network technologies demand new network solutions. In many cases, standardized arbitration mechanisms are not enough to provide the type of differentiated service that many enterprises require for the network, and other solutions, like airtime fairness, are needed.

Airtime fairness is a proprietary feature offered by a number of vendors to bridge the gap between the standardized contention processes and the requirements of modern WLANs. Specifically, airtime fairness addresses a significant problem that occurs when some devices within a network use low data rates and take up a disproportionate amount of airtime as compared with devices that use higher data rates. When this occurs, devices using high data rates suffer the consequences of the slow devices consuming too much precious airtime.

The concept of airtime "fairness" is raised here because devices that operate with low data rates—either because they use legacy PHYs that only support legacy rates, or because they are at the edge of a service area and may only communicate with low data rates—can ruin WLAN performance for an entire BSS.

Since standardized features do not yet address this problem, proprietary features are required. As you might guess, this problem has become commonplace in the enterprise with the advent of 802.11n. For a visual demonstration of the problem, see Figure 10.16.

FIGURE 10.16   Equal contention opportunity for slow and fast STAs

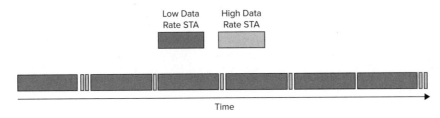

Figure 10.16 shows two stations contending for access to the wireless medium. One station is operating at a high data rate and the other is operating at a low data rate. In this scenario, both stations will statistically win contention a similar number of times. They may be transmitting the same amount of data during each transmission opportunity, but the amount of time it takes to transmit that data is highly divergent. The 802.11 arbitration protocols are designed to create relative equality in contention, but the use of airtime in this example is hardly "fair." The station operating at a low data rate is taking up about 20 times more airtime than the station operating at a higher data rate, but they both transmit the same amount of data. In the real world, you may have an 802.11n AP that supports client stations operating at 300 Mbps, and you may have stations in the same service set operating at 1 Mbps. It's simple math, but that's a 300:1 difference in airtime for the same amount of data.

To eliminate this unfairness, vendors use proprietary scheduling and queuing mechanisms that seek to balance the airtime usage on a PHY-specific—or data rate–specific—basis, which improves aggregate performance for the entire network. In fact, airtime fairness improves performance for stations operating at high data rates, and the impact on stations operating at low data rates is very minimal. So, it is a win-win for the entire BSS. Figure 10.17 shows the same two stations from Figure 10.16, but this time they are using the airtime more efficiently.

FIGURE 10.17 Airtime fairness in action

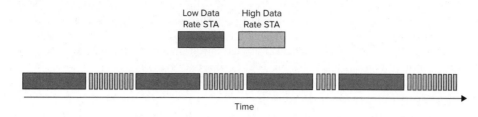

The basic logic behind airtime fairness is that stations connecting with higher data rates should be afforded more opportunities to transmit data because they are using the wireless medium much more efficiently than stations operating at low data rates.

For the most part, airtime fairness is a downstream technology performed by the AP. It is important that the AP be the decision maker because fairness scheduling algorithms can be applied to data more effectively with a holistic, BSS-wide perspective of data flow. This prevents latency-sensitive traffic from being under-prioritized in favor of high bandwidth data at higher rates, and it also prevents a few stations with low data rates from crippling the network's performance.

Though airtime fairness is not yet a ubiquitous feature, many vendors have assimilated it into their products. If you are supporting lower data rates and have clients with highly divergent speeds within your WLAN, airtime fairness can be a helpful tool to avoid some problems. In a typical configuration, the administrator can specify a priority or a weight to be applied to user groups, SSIDs, or WLAN policies—specific configuration steps and procedures will vary by vendor. The complex scheduling algorithms do the rest.

Protection Modes

As you can see from the long discussion about QoS, QoS is an important topic. Since the 802.11 protocol is primarily a MAC protocol, there are also several other topics to consider in the network deployment. Protection mechanisms are an important feature for networks with diverse client populations because there are many ways in which legacy clients can impede network performance. As we discussed in the "Airtime Fairness" section, one of the most harmful impacts of legacy clients is inefficient use of the airtime. Legacy clients also impact WLAN performance by requiring extra control overhead in the form of protection mechanisms when modern PHYs are used and backward compatibility is desired.

There's no need to repeat the technical reasoning for protection mechanisms from CWNA, but we should discuss design practices related to their use. After many new PHY enhancements within the 802.11 standard, there is now a long line of backward compatibility. 802.11n is backward compatible with 802.11a/b/g and DSSS, 802.11g is backward compatible with 802.11 (DSSS) and 802.11b, and 802.11b is backward compatible with 802.11 (DSSS).

One of the big problems with backward compatibility, as prescribed by the standards, is that protection may be required when legacy devices are present, regardless of whether they are yours, your guests, or your neighbors. For that reason, protection mechanisms can be minimized but rarely avoided altogether.

At some point, network deployments must move past the model of backward compatibility in favor of higher-performance LANs. When standards bodies aren't forcing this progress, it is up to network designers to influence this change. There are two ways to manage the use of protection mechanisms in a wireless environment:

- Configuration-related parameters that dictate how protection mechanisms are used and what mechanisms are supported
- The process of physically controlling the types of devices and PHY technologies in your network environment

Physical device control is a necessary, albeit limited, option because this type of control requires a lot of administrative work and authority. However, you can establish a baseline for device support on the network. For example, you may wish to remove all company-owned legacy (802.11b or earlier) APs and client devices.

In all up-to-date enterprise networks today administrators have the option to control the types of devices that access their network. This can be done by disabling or enabling certain data rate sets. If you'd like to prevent the oldest and slowest clients (802.11 DSSS) from joining your network, disable 1 and 2 Mbps data rates. To disallow 802.11b as well, disable 1, 2, 5.5, and 11 Mbps. Some vendors simplify this configuration step with an operability mode selection (e.g., 802.11g/n only; no 802.11b) for a BSS. Ideally, modern networks would eliminate all 802.11b and earlier devices, but this is not economically feasible or practical for many companies.

Further, some client devices rely on low data rates (like 1 and 2 Mbps) for essential functions. Some VoWiFi phones require these rates for broadcast frames, and some RFID tags also transmit "beacons" at these rates. So, even if you wanted to disable these rates to prevent other legacy clients, you could not.

On the client side, adapter capabilities and drivers vary in configurability; most client adapters have a limited set of user-defined protection parameters. In many adapters, nothing is user configurable. However, some adapters allow the user to configure the PHY mode, such as 802.11a/b/g, 802.11a only, and 802.11b only. The wireless PHY mode configuration option is shown in Figure 10.18 and may impact the AP's protection response. In real-world networks, there's no reason to support 802.11b but not 802.11g. However, this parameter can be helpful if you'd like to restrict a device to a certain frequency band. In addition to the operational mode, some adapters allow you to configure the type of protection used, such as *request to send/clear to send (RTS/CTS)* or *CTS-to-Self*. This option is shown in Figure 10.19 for a popular Intel adapter.

FIGURE 10.18 Setting the PHY operation on a client STA

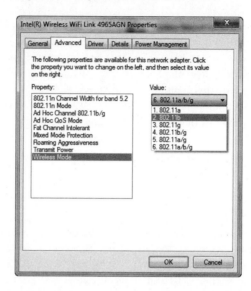

FIGURE 10.19 Configuring the protection mechanism on the client STA

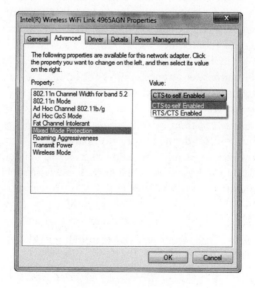

802.11n introduces many new interoperability mechanisms and requirements as well. Many of these mechanisms are automated (not user configurable) and are simply a result of your chosen deployment model (such as 20 or 40 MHz channel widths) and supported features (like spatial multiplexing, Space-Time Block Coding [STBC], or short guard intervals [GI]). The primary design consideration here is to weigh the benefit of new 802.11n features against the drawback of protection mechanisms. Most 802.11n features are valuable enough to justify their use, but some may not be.

For example, as you entertain the idea of 40 MHz channels, you should consider how many 20 MHz-only devices (802.11a/b/g) will be present in the same frequency space. In the 5 GHz spectrum, you are more likely to get clean 11n 40 MHz operation with few protection requirements for 802.11a devices. However, in the 2.4 GHz spectrum, there are so many 802.11b/g devices in most environments that your 40 MHz channel will almost always be using some type of protection, thus nullifying any potential benefit from a 40 MHz channel. In fact, a 40 MHz channel may cause interference in the rest of your 2.4 GHz network and be more of a problem than a benefit. To that end, any 802.11n deployment or migration strategy should include a discussion of protection mechanisms, such as feature selection and configuration based on client PHY population, removal of legacy devices, and techniques to maximize the investment. With that in mind, network engineers should properly set expectations in accordance with the decision to support or not support legacy devices.

Power Management

Power management is another one of those topics that becomes increasingly important with the proliferation of mobile Wi-Fi devices. As with protection mechanisms, many power management features are not user configurable and power save functionality is transparent to the end user. Because of that, the primary responsibility of network designers is to properly plan a deployment by ensuring that the infrastructure and client devices both support the intended power management features, the AP and client devices interoperate properly, the power management functionality doesn't impact performance to unacceptable levels, and the desired amount of battery preservation is achieved.

There are two primary power management techniques:

802.11 Power Save (a.k.a. legacy power save)   Legacy power save has been around for many years, and was a somewhat fundamental approach to conserving battery life. Client devices that support legacy power save functionality alternate between awake and dozing states and wake up to check in with the AP at regular, predefined intervals (DTIM Beacons) to see if the AP has frames buffered for it. If it does, the client requests delivery of those frames by transmitting a PS-Poll frame to the AP. This process continues until the buffer is empty.

WMM Power Save   *WMM Power Save (WMM-PS)*, which is the power save extension of the Wi-Fi Alliance's WMM specification, is a more effective and important power save technique today. It works essentially the same way as legacy power save stations, but it is more flexible and efficient for a few reasons:

- First, WMM-PS stations can request frames from the AP at any time by sending trigger frames (if the AC is trigger enabled), which allows for more efficient and timely delivery of buffered frames.

- Second, WMM-PS is derived from WMM, so it provides a way for the client to request data for specific ACs instead of requesting any and all data destined for the client.

- Third, WMM-PS has different modes of traffic delivery, including scheduled and unscheduled; these delivery policies can be negotiated separately for each AC.

- Fourth, when the client station requests buffered data, the AP can empty the buffer in a burst; legacy PS required a separate poll frame from the client for each buffered frame.

As a Wi-Fi Alliance–certified feature, WMM-PS support can be identified for both client and AP devices by looking at the Wi-Fi Certified certificates found on the Wi-Fi Alliance's website. The core functionality of WMM-PS is called Automatic Power Save Delivery (APSD), so you will often find that WLAN vendors use this term in configuration menus instead of WMM-PS. U-APSD refers to the unscheduled mode of APSD, which is the most common implementation. Most WLAN infrastructure configuration for WMM-PS is limited to enabling or disabling support for it on an SSID profile.

Power save features are directly correlated with performance. Dedicated devices like voice phones don't use power save during an active call, but will enter power save mode whenever there is not a call, so this is not a big deal for voice performance during a call. For multifunction devices, like laptops or PDAs, power save functionality occurs during normal traffic flows, so it may add delay and jitter while reducing throughput, especially for downlink traffic. This is because the AP buffers the traffic until the client requests it, or until the scheduled delivery period. For uplink traffic, the client station can control awake and dozing states in cooperation with the flow of its data from the application layer. When your client devices support high-performance features like frame aggregation, channel bonding, spatial multiplexing, and Multiple Ratio Combining (MRC), you will notice that battery life will be shorter. Usually, there's not much you can do about this from the client side unless the client driver or provisioning utility allows you to enable or disable specific features. Most devices today are not quite this granular.

However, there are client-side configurations that can improve battery life. In addition to standardized power save features, transmit power has a direct relationship to battery life. If mobile devices are transmitting at maximum power, more battery life will be used; if you find that devices are quickly running out of juice, consider modifying the transmit power settings. TPC may also help to control optimal client transmit power so that clients aren't unnecessarily using battery life with excessively high transmit power. As you weigh the output power of client devices, remember to seek a balanced power ratio between the client and AP. So, you won't want to configure the client for low transmit power if this has a negative impact on the link balance.

As you research client device capabilities, you will find that manufacturers of battery-sensitive devices make most of the battery conservation decisions as a part of engineering, and they remove these decisions from the customer. Case in point, VoWiFi phone manufacturers are highly conscious of battery life. For that reason, as of this writing, only one dedicated VoWiFi phone manufacturer has made an 802.11n phone because 802.11n is usually a higher-performance protocol that requires more battery life. Many manufacturers also restrict their voice devices to 2.4 GHz to conserve power—because 5 GHz requires larger antenna elements or more power to collect the same amount of signal as in 2.4 GHz. Similarly, manufacturers of mobile devices (mobile phones, tablet computers, netbooks, etc.) that support Wi-Fi are also limiting the capabilities of their devices. For those that do support 802.11n, they're usually 1x1 or 1x2 MIMO only.

Power save can also have BSS-wide performance implications for broadcast and multicast traffic. Specifically, when a power save device is dozing, the AP buffers unicast traffic to that station. It also buffers all group addressed traffic to the BSS because at least one member of the BSS is incapable of receiving it. At each DTIM interval, the dozing station(s) wakes up to receive frames buffered for it, and also for the delivery of group addressed frames to the BSS. The problem with this is that some latency-sensitive applications natively use multicast traffic for delivery. Multicast video streaming and multicast voice sessions are example applications that would be impacted by power save functionality.

In most cases, even if the DTIM interval is set to 1 (every Beacon is a DTIM Beacon), latency-sensitive multicast applications still won't function properly. Some vendors have sought to remedy this by translating multicast traffic for some applications into unicast data streams, but not all vendors have such a solution. This means that either power save functionality must be disabled, power save devices must have their own SSID (without sensitive multicast applications), or latency-sensitive multicast applications simply won't work.

802.11n also introduces new power save modes called *Power Save Multi-Poll (PSMP)* and *Spatial Multiplexing Power Save (SMPS)*. For the purposes of network design, these power save modes have not yet become significant as selection criteria or device configuration options. 802.11n chipsets have not reached full maturity, so spec sheets tend to be slim on 802.11n power save details. Even if devices do support SMPS and PSMP, there are not likely to be any configuration parameters for client devices.

The details of these operational modes are covered in the *CWNA Certified Wireless Network Administrator Official Study Guide: Exam PW0-104,* First Edition, by David D. Coleman and David A. Westcott (Sybex, 2009).

Roaming and Mobility

Mission-critical applications, real-time applications, and latency-sensitive applications have specific and demanding network service-level requirements. So that users of these applications have acceptable performance, you need to ensure the following:

- Application performance levels are maintained as clients move throughout an ESS.

- Roaming occurs with low latency and is fully transparent to end users.

- Security, data reliability, and low retransmission rates are maintained for mission-critical applications.

This combination of requirements demands that network designers focus on roaming and mobility in a secure network.

As we will discuss in Chapter 12 ("Advanced Enterprise WLAN Security Design"), 802.1X/EAP authentication can take more than a full second to complete. During a client reassociation, this amount of delay will cause a noticeable service outage for most latency-sensitive applications. For some real-time applications, this much delay can cause a timeout to the application's session, forcing users to manually reconnect a phone call or initiate a new client/server session. This is a considerable problem for application performance, as illustrated in Figure 10.20.

FIGURE 10.20   The 802.1X/EAP slow roam process

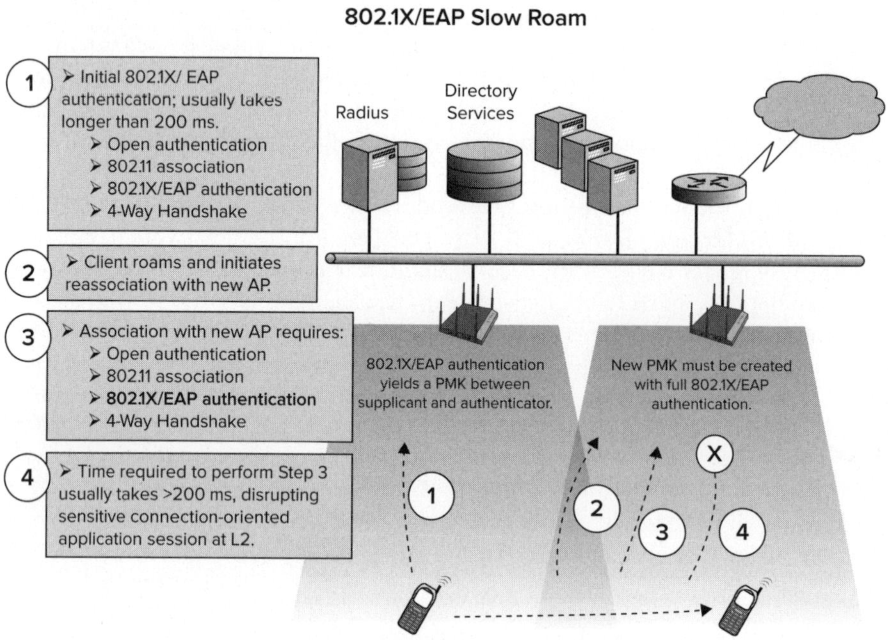

There are several technical ways to address this problem when 802.1X/EAP is required, but most of them have limitations. In this next section, we will look briefly at the technical approach to each *fast secure roaming*—often abbreviated as FSR, mechanism and discuss their strengths and weaknesses. We will then discuss roaming optimization and finally cover other roaming considerations.

Layer 2 Roaming Methods

As a MAC protocol, the 802.11 standards bodies have provided several options for fast secure roaming at Layer 2. In addition, proprietary solutions have been introduced to improve on the MAC framework offered by the 802.11 protocol.

PMK Caching

PMK caching (a.k.a. fast roam-back) is defined in 802.11-2007. How does PMK caching work? In short, an 802.1X/EAP authentication yields a pairwise master key (PMK), which is used as an input for dynamic encryption key generation at the supplicant and authenticator. Instead of discarding the PMK after the association is destroyed (e.g., disassociation, reassociation, or deauthentication), the PMK is cached on both devices and a PMK identifier (PMKID) is calculated as a reference to that specific PMK. So, when the client roams back to that AP, it looks for a valid PMK for the AP, and if it finds one, it references the PMKID in the reassociation frame. The PMK is reused instead of re-creating one with a full 802.1X/EAP authentication.

While helpful, PMK caching is limited in that it only helps a client "roam back" to an AP to which it has previously performed a full 802.1X/EAP authentication. This means that every time the client roams to a new AP, it will be a slow roam—full 802.1X/EAP authentication. This has limited effectiveness and benefit. PMK caching is shown in Figure 10.21.

FIGURE 10.21 How PMK caching works

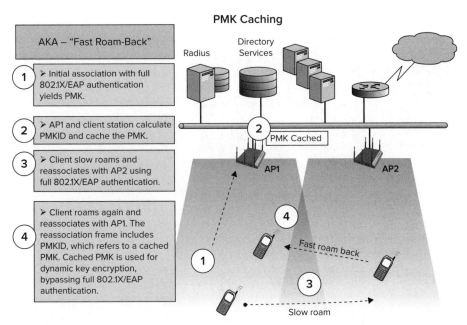

Preauthentication

The other 802.11-standardized method, *preauthentication*, takes a different approach. To address the obvious flaw with PMK caching, preauthentication seeks to preestablish a PMK between the client and all APs to which the client may roam in the future. Before roaming, the client initiates an 802.1X/EAP authentication with other APs through its current AP via the wired network. PMKs are created and then stored on both the client and potential future AP with a PMKID to reference that PMK. When the client roams to a new AP, it references the previously created PMKID in the reassociation request frame, thus allowing a fast roam.

While helpful, the problem with preauthentication is that the implementation is limited for various reasons:

- It causes extra traffic on the network

- It puts extra and unnecessary load on the authentication server and user databases.

- It is essentially a "cover all the bases" approach that is highly inefficient.

For preauthentication to be successful, clients must accurately know and predict the APs to which they may roam or they must roam with every AP in the vicinity. Preauthentication is shown in Figure 10.22.

FIGURE 10.22 The preauthentication process

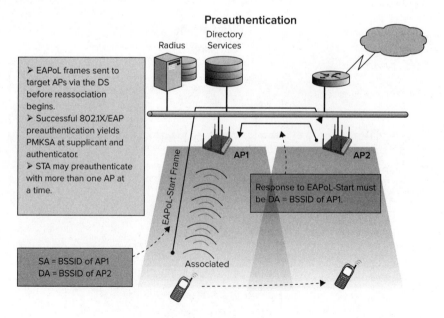

Opportunistic Key Caching

One of the best solutions to-date is *opportunistic key caching (OKC)*. In its simplest form, OKC is a hybrid between PMK caching and Cisco's proprietary method, *Cisco Centralized Key Management (CCKM)*. OKC takes PMK caching a step further and "opportunistically" shares cached PMKs with other APs within a mobility domain or RF neighborhood. Thus, when a client roams, a PMK is already present on the target AP and the client only needs to reference the PMKID in the reassociation request frame. The PMKID value comes from a formula that includes the client MAC address as well as the BSSID, which allows for unique per-AP and per-client combinations. Seems simple, right?

Unfortunately, OKC suffers the ill fate of nonstandardization. Symbol and Microsoft were co-creators of OKC, but it is not well documented or standardized anywhere. For that reason, not all implementations of OKC are compatible or consistent. By now, most infrastructure vendors are supporting OKC except those with a vested interest in a proprietary solution. But many client vendors have been slow to adopt OKC, so client support is sporadic. OKC is shown in Figure 10.23.

FIGURE 10.23   The opportunistic key caching (OKC) process

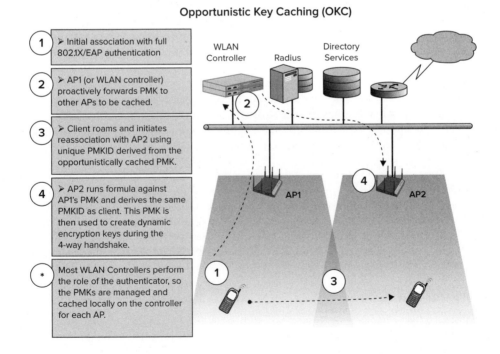

Of these three previously mentioned roaming mechanisms, a consistent problem is client support. Most enterprise networks support many different client types, but client vendors have been highly inconsistent in their support of fast roaming methods. Additionally, even when a client supposedly supports one of these mechanisms, the implementations are often quite poor. For example, with OKC, clients may only send a PMKID in the reassociation request half of the time. This causes a number of problems and does not lead to administrator confidence or user satisfaction.

802.11r Fast BSS Transition

The most promising solution for fast secure roaming is 802.11r *Fast BSS Transition (FT)*, which is defined by 802.11r. The technology that comprises FT is far more complex than the previously discussed roaming methods. The intricate details of its operation are not pertinent to the purposes of this book, so we will spare the details for this discussion. At present, FT is not supported by any AP or client vendors, and its support will largely be postponed until the release of the *Voice Enterprise* certification by the Wi-Fi Alliance. The Voice Enterprise certification has been in progress for multiple years now and is finally reaching maturity. It is reaching the final stages of the Wi-Fi Alliance's testing and support process and should be released sometime in the middle of 2011. In addition to 802.11r, Voice Enterprise is based on functions introduced by 802.11k and 802.11v.

In short, FT works in a similar way as OKC, but it is more efficient. FT seeks to modify the frame contents of the reassociation request/response exchange as well as the 4-way handshake to make them more efficient. FT introduces new keying concepts, key holders and distributors, and other ancillary information about mobility domains and groups that is relevant to mobility transitions.

You should know that FT is a promising set of protocols that will drastically improve on client roaming methods. FT is standardized (by IEEE) but is not yet a certified roaming platform (by Wi-Fi Alliance); however, it is an efficient, resourceful, and effective method that looks to be a de facto solution for years to come. For now, we must simply await its acceptance and proliferation, which will not happen overnight.

For more information and a deep technical dive on Fast BSS Transitions as well as any of the other roaming mechanisms discussed in this section, see the Robust Security Networks (RSN) Fast BSS Transition (FT) whitepaper authored by Devin Akin. This whitepaper is offered free of charge by CWNP and can be obtained at http://www.cwnp.com/pdf/802.11_RSN_FT.pdf.

Proprietary Solutions

In addition to the previously mentioned fast secure roaming methods, we have proprietary mechanisms from Meru and Cisco. Other vendors also offer proprietary enhancements to the previously mentioned protocols, but no other vendors have comprehensive solutions like the two offered by Meru and Cisco.

Single-Channel Architecture   Meru pioneered the single-channel architecture (SCA), which uses a single BSSID (per-SSID or per-client) across all APs on a given channel. Client devices interpret the single BSSID as a single large AP, and the WLAN infrastructure takes care of transparently optimizing the client's association by quickly transferring the client's association to different APs. It is probably safe to say that this method is the most efficient and effective form of roaming available today, but it is proprietary and limited to a single vendor. Also, this solution requires support for the much contested single-channel architecture. We discuss the SCA approach to roaming in greater detail in Chapter 5, "Vendor and WLAN Architecture Selection."

Cisco Centralized Key Management (CCKM)   We also have CCKM, which has received pretty good market penetration due to Cisco's market share leadership. With CCKM, a WLAN controller or AP provides WDS (Wireless Domain Services) functionality within an ESS. WDS functions consist of caching and forwarding PMKs to other APs within the ESS. CCKM is basically a Cisco-specific version of OKC. CCKM requires client support and participation (CCKM compatibility) as a part of the Cisco Client Extensions (CCX) program. This limits the supplicant selection and may add cost to the supplicant deployment. As with Meru's proprietary option, CCKM locks a customer in with a single vendor.

Overview of the Roaming Landscape

Among these options, no single approach will work for all occasions. Although they each have drawbacks, the network designer should evaluate which of the drawbacks are tolerable for the deployment scenario. Both of the proprietary solutions have strengths, but so does OKC. Client support will be a major part of the final decision. When the Wi-Fi Alliance releases the Voice Enterprise certification and vendor adoption is pervasive, Voice Enterprise will be our best choice in most cases. As of this writing, it is difficult to know how far in our future this will be.

If these options do not meet your business or application needs, other security solutions, such as WPA2-Personal, or per-user preshared keys (PPSK) are recommended. We will discuss this further in Chapters 11 ("Basic WLAN Security Design") and 12 ("Advanced Enterprise WLAN Security Design").

Roaming Optimization

In all roaming methods except Meru's proprietary technology, client devices are the decision maker when it comes to roaming. The roaming algorithms of client drivers dictate when and where a client will attempt to reassociate with a new AP. In general, client roaming algorithms initiate a roam when signal quality (as determined by RSSI, SNR, data rate, collisions/retries, and/or dropped frames) changes below a certain threshold. For this reason, RF design techniques should account for the types of client devices—and resultant roaming behaviors—that will be present within the network.

Proper site surveying should indicate typical roaming boundaries for client devices, and designers should attempt to plan these boundaries strategically. Of course, you can't be expected to control every roaming boundary all the time, but you can reduce pain points by monitoring roaming boundaries in popular user congregation or transitional areas.

A common example for user congregation is nurse stations within a hospital. Nurses commonly gather in these areas with voice phones in tow, and you do not want the phones to be encountering a roaming boundary right in this area. That may cause the phones to perpetually roam back and forth while nurses remain in the same location. By the same token, if you can't eliminate "slow roams" from your network, try to plan the slow roam boundaries at natural transition areas, such as between buildings on a campus.

You will also want to consider the role of WLAN controllers in the roaming process. We will talk more about intercontroller roaming in the next section, "Other Roaming Considerations," but the key point here is that you want to avoid intercontroller roaming where possible. In other words, if half of your APs are homed to one controller and the other half are homed to another controller, you do not want to stagger these APs in the deployment so the clients are walking down the hall and continuously roaming back and forth between APs on different controllers. This has been referred to as a salt and pepper approach (which has the appearance of RF coverage resiliency if a controller fails), and it is not optimal.

There are many other fine points of consideration for optimizing roaming, but one final suggestion is to carefully set your 802.1X key timeout intervals (or rekeying interval). This value will determine when the client will be required to create a new key by means of a full 802.1X/EAP authentication. Some companies with aggressive security policies set this value to 15 minutes, but this is not usually advisable. This value should be set to coincide with times that the client device is not likely to be in use, such as at break times or shift changes. This will prevent an application session from being terminated as a result of forced rekeying.

Other Roaming Considerations

In addition to the mobility topics discussed thus far, there are several other issues to think about, such as the difference between inter- and intracontroller roaming, Layer 2 and Layer 3 roaming, and the distinction between mobility groups. We will discuss these topics next.

Centralized Architecture Roaming

There are two general types of roaming in a centralized architecture:

Intracontroller Roaming   In intracontroller roaming, clients are roaming between APs managed by the same controller. Intracontroller roaming is a simple process because WLAN controllers are typically managing client security keys, QoS and security policies, and more, and can easily move them from one AP to another within the controller itself.

Intercontroller Roaming   In intercontroller roaming, clients are roaming between APs on different controllers. Controllers must transfer client state information, keys, buffered frames, and policies, which requires more time, coordination, and traffic overhead. When possible, limit the amount of intercontroller roaming. Controller-to-controller handoffs rely on proprietary communication that is usually transparent to the network administrator, but for those vendors that provide configuration parameters for controller-to-controller communication, it is important that settings be optimized for roaming. Generally, it is required that controllers be assigned to the same mobility group for intercontroller roaming to occur seamlessly.

L3 Roaming

In our roaming discussion thus far, we've been primarily concerned with moving a client association at Layer 2. However, Layer 3 roaming also occurs and requires additional techniques. Different WLAN controllers/APs within the enterprise are often on different VLANs. When a client roams from a controller/AP on one VLAN to a controller/AP on another VLAN, this would normally require that the client obtain a new IP address for the new subnet. This is known as Layer 3 (L3) roaming. If the client must obtain a new IP address, this means that all sessions above the IP layer will be terminated, which is bad.

Most vendors handle the problem of L3 roaming by forming an IP tunnel between the new controller/AP and the old controller/AP. The client traffic is thus sent to the new controller/AP, encapsulated in the tunnel, and forwarded to the old controller/AP for processing. In this way, the client's association is transparently maintained at the old controller/AP and on the old subnet. This allows the client to maintain its IP address on the old subnet, thus preserving application sessions. This concept is often referred to as anchoring, and you will find this term in the configuration menus of some vendors.

Tunneling is generally a good thing because it maintains the flow of application data. However, one problem with L3 tunneling is that it adds latency and additional network hops to network traffic. Depending on the type of application in use, it may be desirable to force the client to obtain a new IP address on the new subnet so as to avoid the extra latency incurred from tunneling. In an ideal world, this would be delayed to a time after the application session has ended. In most cases, the WLAN infrastructure will force the client to obtain a new IP address after a certain interval.

Mobility Groups and Domains

The terms *mobility group* and *mobility domain* vary from one vendor to the next. Commonly, the term mobility group refers to a set of WLAN controllers or APs within which mobility messages are shared and roaming is expected to be commonplace. Mobility domains, on the other hand, are sets of mobility groups within which roaming is supported but is not expected to happen as frequently. The implementation of mobility groups and domains is dependent on the vendor, and designers should understand how mobility is, or is not, supported or required between groups and domains.

WLAN Configuration

In addition to the larger topics we've already addressed in this chapter, you need to take into account more subtle MAC configuration parameters when deploying a WLAN. These parameters will vary from one vendor to the next, but there are many consistencies. They usually fit within the realm of a "WLAN profile," which may be called a *WLAN* or a *virtual AP*. We will discuss the most common of these parameters in the following sections.

SSID

We've already discussed some of the basic SSID configuration suggestions in other areas of this book, but we'd like to include a brief discussion of SSID conventions here as well. At the most basic level, an SSID should be configured in accordance with the policies and intentions of the company. When multiple SSIDs are supported by each AP, SSID naming conventions should facilitate end users in their discovery and selection of a network. Network designers will want to minimize help-desk calls by making network selection clear and easy.

We discuss the topic of SSID hiding in Chapter 11, so we will not go into great detail here. There may be administrative reasons to hide the SSID, but it is not recommended as an effective security tactic. The same logic applies to AP configurations that allow the AP to ignore broadcast probe responses.

The most important aspect of SSID design is deciding how many SSIDs to support on each AP. The answer to this question will largely depend on the types of services supported on the WLAN as well as the expected traffic load. Many network administrators go about the SSID creation process somewhat haphazardly, adding new SSIDs as they see a need for a new service. However, too many SSIDs can quickly cause an excess amount of management overhead on the wireless channel.

Every SSID must transmit a Beacon stream to broadcast its presence, and Beacons are usually transmitted every 100 ms by default. Consider for a moment that you have enabled eight SSIDs on each AP and you have four visible APs in a given area on a specific channel—32 Beacon streams. Then remember that broadcast traffic is transmitted using a basic data rate. So, you have 32 Beacons every 100 ms transmitted at a low data rate. Given the size of 802.11n beacons, that is a lot of airtime being used up for beaconing. In some network environments with many SSIDs and densely deployed APs, management traffic alone can account for 30–50 percent (or more) of a channel's capacity. This is often referred to as management frame poisoning because this much management traffic will severely impact application performance when any amount of load is placed on the network.

If you notice that your beacon traffic is reaching unacceptable levels, one simple remedy would be to combine like services onto a single SSID. Then take advantage of user-based or group access control assignments to differentiate the allowed services within a single SSID. This can be done with RADIUS return attributes or by other authentication methods supported by most vendors.

There are other considerations as well. Most WLAN vendors employing the centralized architecture (WLAN controller and APs) are creating L3 tunnels between the AP and WLAN controller. However, in a few vendor implementations, we're not talking about a single L3 tunnel for an AP to a controller. We're talking about a single L3 tunnel for each SSID on each radio for each AP. In other words, if you have a dual-band AP with four SSIDs in each band, there would be eight separate L3 tunnels between the AP and the WLAN controller. Many WLAN designers can be myopically focused on the wireless side of the network without considering the implications this will have on the wired side. While these tunnels may not create an extraordinary amount of traffic on the Ethernet switches, they do put a lot of stress and strain on the CPU of the WLAN controller. If you have a WLAN controller that supports 250 APs and you load it down with eight SSIDs per AP, you may quickly realize that WLAN performance suffers as a result of excess tunneling.

Each vendor does tunneling a bit differently, so you should find out how your vendor tunnels traffic between the AP and WLAN controller. This topic has not been widely publicized and is unknown to many administrators, but it has severe implications for WLAN design. As a best practice, when possible, limit the number of SSIDs on each AP to four or less. Monitor the amount of management traffic required to sustain your SSIDs, and this will help you identify if it is becoming problematic to your applications.

Beaconing

As we think about SSIDs and management traffic, the Beacon interval becomes an important parameter. Every vendor has standardized on a default Beacon interval value of 100 ms (actually, it is 100 Kμsecs, which is often rounded to 100 ms for simplicity), but this is usually a configurable parameter. If you must support a high number of SSIDs, you can modify the Beacon interval to a higher value (such as 200 ms), but this approach is generally not recommended. Some client device drivers begin to display aberrant behaviors when they do not see a Beacon every 100 ms. Similarly, some client devices are configured to passively scan a channel for 110 ms before moving on to another channel. This allows them to catch a Beacon, interpret the information, and move on to the next channel. If the Beacon interval is higher than the default 100 ms, you may have client connectivity issues (creating or maintaining a connection).

The DTIM interval is a value that determines what Beacon frames are DTIM Beacon frames. In power save operation, dozing stations must awake for every DTIM Beacon. After a DTIM, all buffered multicast and broadcast traffic is delivered to the BSS; following that, power save stations can request their buffered frames from the AP. In general, a DTIM between 1 and 5 is normal, but traffic requirements will dictate this need. Some WLAN client vendors suggest configuring every Beacon as a DTIM (value of 1) to minimize delay in the delivery of multicast and broadcast traffic. This is especially true of mildly latency-sensitive applications that rely on either multicast or broadcast traffic for some function. The DTIM interval configuration parameter is shown at the top of Figure 10.24.

FIGURE 10.24   DTIM, data rates, and other configuration parameters

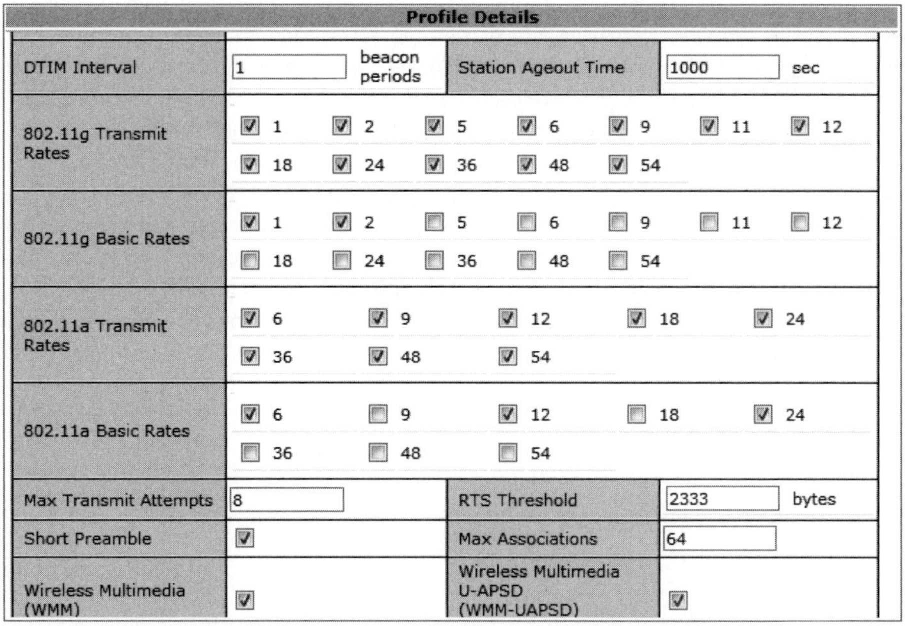

Profile Details						
DTIM Interval	1	beacon periods	Station Ageout Time	1000	sec	
802.11g Transmit Rates	☑ 1 ☑ 2 ☑ 5 ☑ 6 ☑ 9 ☑ 11 ☑ 12					
	☑ 18 ☑ 24 ☑ 36 ☑ 48 ☑ 54					
802.11g Basic Rates	☑ 1 ☑ 2 ☐ 5 ☐ 6 ☐ 9 ☐ 11 ☐ 12					
	☐ 18 ☐ 24 ☐ 36 ☐ 48 ☐ 54					
802.11a Transmit Rates	☑ 6 ☑ 9 ☑ 12 ☑ 18 ☑ 24					
	☑ 36 ☑ 48 ☑ 54					
802.11a Basic Rates	☑ 6 ☐ 9 ☑ 12 ☐ 18 ☑ 24					
	☐ 36 ☐ 48 ☐ 54					
Max Transmit Attempts	8		RTS Threshold	2333	bytes	
Short Preamble	☑		Max Associations	64		
Wireless Multimedia (WMM)	☑		Wireless Multimedia U-APSD (WMM-UAPSD)	☑		

Supported and Basic Data Rates

Another important step in deploying a WLAN profile is to enable or disable data rates for the BSS. The primary purpose of this step is to maximize the efficiency or availability of the WLAN channel. As legacy clients join a service set or associated clients move to the edge of the service area, their data rate will naturally drop as a function of dynamic rate switching. These slower devices will then have an adverse impact on channel utilization. So, the enabling or disabling of specific rates is largely a balance between availability and broad client support on the one hand and performance and efficiency on the other hand.

If you intend to support legacy devices (802.11 DSSS or 802.11b), you will have to leave some legacy rates (1, 2, 5.5, or 11 Mbps) enabled. However, when you allow clients to connect at low data rates, you leave the door open for a single client to severely impact channel utilization by taking a long time to transmit a small amount of data; this impacts everyone.

In most multiservice WLANs, it is advisable to disable support for at least the lowest data rates (1 and 2 Mbps) in favor of higher rates. Some engineers may prefer to be more aggressive in their data rate support by also disabling 5.5 Mbps within the BSS. If you are providing backward compatibility for 802.11b, 11 Mbps could still be supported. Or, if you prefer to disallow DSSS and 802.11b devices, you can simply disable all of these legacy rates. These configuration parameters are shown in Figure 10.24.

The Basic Rate Set for a BSS is a set of data rates that must be supported by all stations in the BSS. So, if you desire to support 802.11b, you will want your Basic Rate Set to reflect 802.11b capabilities (e.g., make 5.5. and 11 Mbps a basic rate but not 6, 12, 24, etc.). When selecting a basic rate, the important thing to know here is all devices must support these rates, and frames with multicast or broadcast addresses, as well as some control frames, are always sent using a basic rate. So, if 1 and 2 Mbps are your basic rates, you will see a lot of traffic at these low rates. This will adversely impact utilization of the wireless medium.

However, as you will find as you begin testing your data rate configurations, client drivers are sometimes unpredictable. For no apparent reason, some client devices will not function properly if certain data rates are not supported. Thus, you should monitor your data rate selection carefully and keep these parameters in mind if you find connectivity problems after changing the supported or basic rate set. Of course, disabling lower data rates is an effective way to ensure that your WLAN channel is being used efficiently, and this tactic is becoming increasingly common, especially in environments with high user densities and latency-sensitive applications. Many VoWiFi design guides encourage engineers to disable lower data rates.

Band Steering

In the wake of dual-band 802.11n APs and the continued desire to maximize wireless capacity, WLAN infrastructure vendors have sought proprietary ways to make maximum use of the unlicensed frequency spectrum. By now, readers of this book should be familiar with the differences between the 2.4 GHz and 5 GHz frequencies, including the number of channels and common uses for these bands. 2.4 GHz has only three nonoverlapping 20 MHz channels and is typically pretty saturated with Wi-Fi and non-Wi-Fi interference sources. The 5 GHz bands offer up to 24 nonoverlapping 20 MHz channels (depending on regulatory domain)—or fewer bonded 40 MHz channels—and are typically much "cleaner" RF bands. In other words, far fewer devices are currently using the 5 GHz bands, which makes their use for Wi-Fi far more desirable.

To take advantage of the highly available 5 GHz bands, some vendors have introduced a proprietary feature called *band steering*. The simple goal with band steering is to attempt to move 5 GHz-capable client devices into 5 GHz bands and out of the 2.4 GHz band. Each vendor's version of band steering works a bit differently, but the basic functionality is generally the same.

Almost every Wi-Fi device that is 5 GHz capable is also 2.4 GHz capable. Unfortunately, client software drivers are not consistently implemented to prefer the 5 GHz band and to use the congested 2.4 GHz band as a last option. So, the WLAN infrastructure must attempt to simulate this priority by selectively responding to, or avoiding response to, the client's active scanning attempts. The intention is to make the client think that a service set is only present in the 5 GHz spectrum, which would cause them to initiate authentication in 5 GHz instead of 2.4 GHz.

Because of its efficiency for scanning a large number of channels, most client devices prefer active scanning over passive scanning. This is a good thing for band steering, because clients could always use Beacon streams to identify a BSS. Unfortunately, the biggest problem with band steering is that client drivers are all different. Some devices that are 5 GHz capable are still very reluctant to associate in the 5 GHz band, so they will continue scanning the 2.4 GHz band despite the presence of 5 GHz networks. In most implementations of band steering, the AP will ignore the clients' first several (usually two or three) probe requests in the 2.4 GHz band, and if the client does not join in the 5 GHz band, the AP will eventually begin responding to the client's probes in the 2.4 GHz band as well. This concept of band steering is shown in Figure 10.25.

As you have probably gathered, band steering isn't effective for every client, or in every circumstance. However, it does work for many client devices and is a highly valuable feature, especially for high-density deployments. If you have ever sought an automated way to maximize the 5 GHz bands while providing the same service sets to 2.4 GHz and 5 GHz devices, band steering is the answer.

FIGURE 10.25 Typical implementation of band steering

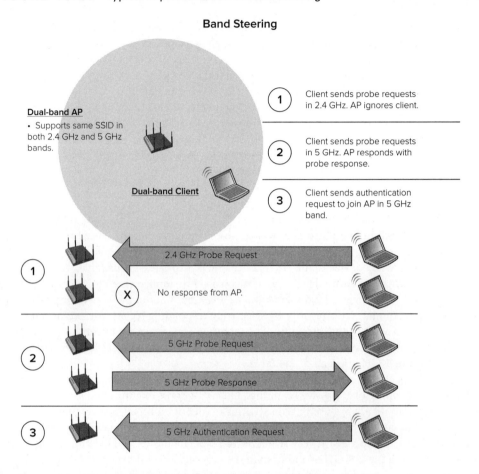

Band Steering

Dual-band AP
• Supports same SSID in both 2.4 GHz and 5 GHz bands.

Dual-band Client

1   Client sends probe requests in 2.4 GHz. AP ignores client.

2   Client sends probe requests in 5 GHz. AP responds with probe response.

3   Client sends authentication request to join AP in 5 GHz band.

1   2.4 GHz Probe Request

X   No response from AP.

2   5 GHz Probe Request

  5 GHz Probe Response

3   5 GHz Authentication Request

While band steering is largely an automated process that is configurable within the WLAN infrastructure, the same net effect can often be achieved with some careful network planning and provisioning. The simple principle here is to configure similar service sets for 2.4 GHz and 5 GHz bands, but to use different naming conventions for the SSID.

For example, the SSID for the 5 GHz service set may be "FastWiFiAccess," and the SSID for the 2.4 GHz service set may be "SlowWiFiAccess." When end users scan for available networks, they see these two options—fast and slow Wi-Fi—and end users will likely choose the fast option. If the client device is not 5 GHz capable, a network scan will only discover the 2.4 GHz network, and the user will have no choice but to join the "slow" network. This type of SSID naming is a manual way to offload network traffic from 2.4 GHz and put it on 5 GHz. This is sometimes jokingly called poor man's band steering.

Both manual and automated band steering methods can be effective ways to optimize the client load across the spectrum. Simple configuration options like this can go a long way toward alleviating congestion from high user densities in the crowded 2.4 GHz band.

Frame Aggregation and Fragmentation

802.11n introduced a new efficiency mechanism called frame aggregation, which enables a transmitter to combine multiple MSDUs or MPDUs into a single frame for transmission. You may remember that in years past, the opposite trend, called frame fragmentation, was more popular.

In most of today's networks, aggregation is more useful than fragmentation. The purpose behind fragmentation was to split large frames into multiple smaller frames so as to minimize collisions on heavily utilized WLAN channels. The problem with fragmentation is that it was not beneficial in many environments and it added management overhead. However, it was useful in some environments, largely because legacy RF handling mechanisms (like simple diversity) were not robust enough and data rates were not efficient enough to combat environments with high multipath and dense user populations.

Frame aggregation is made possible by 11n's superior signal transmission and reception technologies as well as the higher data rates that are supported. Higher data rates allow more data to be transmitted in a shorter amount of time. By aggregating multiple MSDUs (*A-MSDU*) or MPDUs (*A-MPDU*) into a single frame transmission, you improve channel efficiency by reducing management overhead. However, aggregating data frames is not always beneficial to a service set.

First, frame aggregation is great for cramming a lot of data on the wireless medium. However, throughput is not always the most important metric for application performance. When throughput takes priority and individual frame transmissions take a longer amount of time to complete, less airtime is available for other devices, like voice phones, that must access the medium frequently and consistently to transmit small amounts of data. In networks with a high number of voice clients, frame aggregation can be harmful to voice flows.

Both A-MSDU and A-MPDU can be supported at the same time. Aggregation configuration is usually made at the radio level of a WLAN, but it is a MAC-layer feature. In configuration menus, you will often find configuration options to enable or disable each type of aggregation as well as a maximum A-MSDU or A-MPDU size. In almost every case, you will want to keep the default size configuration. One vendor's configuration parameters for frame aggregation are shown in Figure 10.26.

FIGURE 10.26 Frame aggregation parameters for Motorola

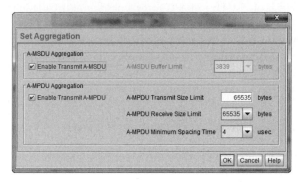

Additional Configurations

In addition to the previous list of common WLAN profile configuration parameters, every vendor has their own list of additional configurations. These include options like the following:

Client Timeout (or Ageout) Values The length of time a client can be idle before its association is destroyed.

RTS Thresholds The maximum value of an RTS control frame.

Client Limits The number of clients that can be supported on a specific SSID or AP at a time.

Proprietary Optimization Features These are various as there are many different proprietary features that may enabled on a WLAN. Consult vendor documentation for details.

Peer-to-Peer (P2P) Blocking Prevents clients within a BSS from communicating directly with one another through the AP.

Protected Management Frames These enable protection for some management frames so that attackers cannot conduct certain types of attack.

Fragmentation Thresholds If *fragmentation* is in use, frames larger than the fragmentation threshold are divided into multiple separate frames. In many legacy networks with high utilization, frame fragmentation was helpful for minimizing collisions and maximizing channel efficiency.

IDS Behaviors There are many IDS behaviors that may be tied to a WLAN, such as channel scanning behaviors, client or rogue priorities, and many more.

These are just a few. A sample set of these advanced configuration parameters is shown for two different vendors in Figure 10.27 and Figure 10.28. Because we can't address each configuration option exhaustively, our best approach is to defer to vendor documentation. Often, feature naming conventions vary from vendor to vendor, so it is always helpful to consult the documentation. Similarly, many of these features are offered by most vendors, but the exact implementation or configuration parameters vary.

FIGURE 10.27 Advanced configuration parameters

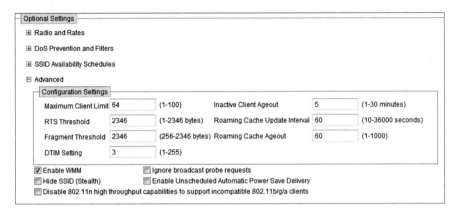

FIGURE 10.28 More advanced configuration parameters

Summary

In this chapter, we looked at many of the features and technologies that take a WLAN from a base set of functionality to high-performance, mission-critical, multiservice functionality. There are many aspects to a high-performance WLAN deployment, but since the 802.11 protocol is primarily a MAC-layer protocol, it should come as no surprise that MAC-layer considerations are absolutely essential. More and more enterprise companies are turning to the WLAN to meet the connectivity needs of increasingly mobile clients, and MAC-layer features accommodate this demand.

With this new emphasis on WLAN usage, the shared contention domain of unlicensed frequencies is becoming increasingly crowded. Unfortunately, bandwidth resources on Wi-Fi networks are limited, and as more devices contend for this resource, it is important to allocate these resources properly. That is the role of QoS. While QoS doesn't add any more bandwidth, it does provide more discriminating use of the available bandwidth. With such a diverse set of applications on the WLAN, end-to-end QoS is absolutely essential for creating priority for some applications. Wireless QoS is a unique challenge by itself. But in addition to wireless considerations, the wired network must be provisioned properly. Then the WLAN must integrate properly with the wired network. It's a large hurdle but a necessary one. Without QoS, many mission-critical applications won't live up to their intended uses.

Many of the same mission-critical applications that require QoS are also power sensitive. Mobile devices are a new breed of network-connected electronics, and there is always a balance between performance and power conservation. In this chapter, we looked at important design considerations for protecting battery life while maintaining optimum performance levels. Power-saving protocols, like WMM Power Save, are an important piece to this puzzle.

Roaming is also an important part of mobility in the enterprise. With so many options for roaming protocols, it is important for us to understand the options as well as the strengths and limitations that come along with each protocol. There are many detailed design considerations to facilitate effective roaming.

In addition, you must take into account many other MAC-layer configuration options and deployment considerations. As devices with different PHY capabilities populate the airwaves, MAC-layer protocols are left to help everyone play nicely together. Protection mechanisms serve this purpose, and their use has many implications.

No MAC design discussion is complete without talking about the many checkboxes and custom fields that are a part of any WLAN infrastructure and client solution. There are so many common vendor-specific MAC features that we couldn't possibly address them all. To that end, we will defer to user guides and vendor-specific implementations.

Exam Essentials

Identify the need for QoS and explain its significance.   Recognize why QoS is necessary and understand how application requirements and limited network resources demand it. Also understand how it benefits application performance.

Demonstrate a thorough knowledge of WLAN arbitration.   Understand the relationship between WLAN arbitration and application performance, particularly as it relates to QoS.

Illustrate a comprehensive understanding of QoS technologies.   Illustrate the technical intricacies of wired and wireless QoS as well as integration of WLANs with the wired network.

Explain the benefit and operation of proprietary optimization features.   Understand the purpose, functionality, and benefit of proprietary optimization features like airtime fairness, band steering, and others.

Illustrate best practices for roaming support in a WLAN.   Understand the technologies and protocols related to roaming in a WLAN. Explain different types of roaming, challenges related to roaming, vendor-specific processes to handle roaming, best practice for client roaming, and the limitations and benefits of specific roaming methods.

Explain best practices for deployment of power management features and PHY protection mechanisms.   Understand the technologies related to power management in WLANs and illustrate when and how they should be implemented. Understand how different PHY technologies interoperate and how to properly plan for their presence in a network environment with protection mechanisms.

Explain best practices for common WLAN feature support, configuration, and deployment strategies.   Demonstrate a thorough understanding of common WLAN configuration parameters and identify when and how to configure them.

Review Questions

1. What parameters are included in the EDCA parameter set? (Choose all that apply.)

    A. CWmin

    B. CWmax

    C. AIFSN

    D. Slot time

2. A MAC frame is marked with a UP value of 6. To which WMM access category (AC) would this frame be mapped?

    A. AC_VO

    B. AC_VI

    C. AC_BE

    D. AC_BK

3. What new power management mechanisms were introduced with 802.11n? (Choose all that apply.)

    A. PSMP

    B. WMM PS

    C. SMPS

    D. MRC PS

    E. MIMO PS

4. According to industry best practices, what is the recommended maximum number of SSIDs that should be supported on each AP radio?

    A. 1

    B. 2

    C. 4

    D. 8

    E. 16

5. How does band steering typically work?

    A. Band steering is a client-side feature that allows the client device to measure channel utilization and select an AP and operating channel based on frequency congestion.

    B. Band steering forces clients to join in the 5 GHz band by stopping an AP's Beacon stream when the client load threshold is reached.

    C. Band steering is a load-balancing mechanism used by WLAN controllers to move a client association from the 2.4 GHz band to the 5 GHz band using channel switch announcement messages.

    D. Band steering attempts to move 5 GHz–capable stations to the 5 GHz band by withholding probe responses when the client sends a probe request in the 2.4 GHz band.

6. Why is end-to-end QoS important? (Choose all that apply.)

   A. All applications requiring QoS need bidirectional uplink and downlink priority.

   B. Failure to prioritize traffic on any single hop within a frame's data path may negate QoS provided on all other hops.

   C. Evaluation of admission control criteria should account for all resources from the data source to the network destination.

   D. If QoS markings are not preserved across all links on the network, data authenticity calculations will fail on the wireless endpoint.

7. What is the basic problem with Layer 3 roaming?

   A. Standardized 802.11 roaming mechanisms at Layer 3 are not typically supported by all clients.

   B. The Wi-Fi Alliance has been slow to create a specification for Layer 3 roaming based on 802.11r.

   C. Layer 2 QoS and security policies cannot be maintained across Layer 3 links.

   D. Roaming between different subnets normally requires the client to obtain a new IP address, which can stop active applications.

8. How many Differentiated Services Code Point values are available in an IP header?

   A. 8

   B. 16

   C. 54

   D. 64

9. What statements are true regarding jitter and latency? (Choose all that apply.)

   A. Latency is a measurement of the time required to transmit two subsequent frames.

   B. Jitter is a measurement of average latency based on a sample of >100 frames.

   C. Jitter is a measurement of latency variability from one frame to another.

   D. Latency is a measurement of the time delay experienced in the delivery of a frame.

   E. Jitter is a measurement of the variance of the number of frames received from an application for a specific time interval.

10. Which of the following reflect accurate application performance requirements for VoWiFi phone calls? (Choose all that apply.)

   A. High bandwidth

   B. High latency

   C. Low jitter

   D. Low loss

11. As a wireless engineer, you are asked to research the ways in which QoS can be marked in Ethernet networks. You have previously read about Ethernet frame expansion to allow for an 8-bit CoS priority field, and you want to go to the source standard to collect the details. What standard specifies Ethernet frame expansion to include a VLAN ID and CoS markings?

    A. 802.1D

    B. 802.1p

    C. 802.3ac

    D. 802.11e

    E. 802.1Q

12. Your company supports non-QoS client stations in a QoS BSS. To what WMM AC is non-QoS data traffic mapped when it is sent by a wireless client station?

    A. Non-QoS traffic is not supported in QoS BSSs, so it is dropped by the AP and is not mapped to an AC.

    B. AC_VO

    C. AC_VI

    D. AC_BE

    E. AC_BK

13. When some stations are operating within a BSS at low data rates and other stations are operating within a BSS at high data rates, the stations operating with lower data rates consume a disproportionate amount of wireless resources on the time domain. What proprietary feature, supported by many WLAN vendors, may be implemented to address this problem?

    A. Band steering

    B. Airtime fairness

    C. RTS thresholds

    D. Round robin queuing

    E. WMM

14. What is the most significant drawback of PMK caching?

    A. It is not standardized.

    B. Most client vendors do not support it.

    C. It only allows "fast roam-back."

    D. It requires costly add-on client software.

15. What MAC features were discussed in this chapter that are, or will be, certifications offered by the Wi-Fi Alliance? (Choose all that apply.)

A. 802.11 Power Save

B. Wi-Fi Multimedia

C. Opportunistic key caching (OKC)

D. WMM Power Save

E. PSMP

F. Voice Enterprise

16. Your wireless network designer has dictated that 802.11b devices should be prevented from associating to your WLAN. To implement this policy, what data rates should not be supported by your APs? (Choose all that apply.)

A. 5.5 Mbps

B. 6 Mbps

C. 11 Mbps

D. 12 Mbps

E. 13.5 Mbps

17. In your company's WLAN, you expect to have a mixed client PHY environment and plan to use protection mechanisms. The protection mechanism used by your client devices is configurable. What is the best protection mechanism for backward compatibility of 802.11n devices with 802.11b devices?

A. WMM Protection

B. RTS/CTS

C. CTS-to-Self

D. Dual-CTS

E. SMPS

18. What three 802.11 amendments are being used as contributing data for the Wi-Fi Alliance's Voice Enterprise certification? (Choose all that apply.)

A. 802.11r

B. 802.11D

C. 802.11k

D. 802.11w

E. 802.11v

F. 802.11n

19. What is the purpose of the clear channel assessment (CCA) function of WLAN arbitration?

    A. CCA predicts the busy state of the wireless medium by means of the Length and Duration fields in the PHY and MAC headers.

    B. CCA adds an element of randomness to the arbitration process by means of a contention window so as to minimize collisions.

    C. CCA measures and detects Wi-Fi and non-Wi-Fi transmissions on the wireless medium to determine whether a station can contend for access to the medium.

    D. CCA values are PHY-specific parameters that dictate the number of CCA intervals a station must wait after it has chosen a random backoff value.

20. For what purpose is SSID hiding generally useful? (Choose all that apply.)

    A. Obscuring the network name from potential attackers

    B. Preventing guests from attempting to join the secured corporate network

    C. Preventing legitimate corporate users from finding the guest network

    D. Minimizing help desk calls from users and guests attempting to join the wrong network

Answers to Review Questions

1. **A, B, C.** Along with other parameters, the AIFSN, CWmin, and CWmax are included in the EDCA parameter set. These parameters dictate the contention behaviors of EDCA client stations in a QoS BSS. A slot time is a fixed, PHY-dependent value that applies to all stations regardless of the channel access method in use.

2. **A.** 802.1p user priority (UP) values are mapped to WMM access categories. While these mappings are customizable, default configurations usually map UP 6–7 to AC_VO. UP 4–5 maps to AC_VI. UP 0, 3 maps to AC_BE. UP 1–2 maps to AC_BK.

3. **A, C.** To maximize power efficiency with 802.11n's new performance features, Power Save Multi-Poll and Spatial Multiplexing Power Save features were introduced. WMM PS is also a power save mechanism that will be supported by most 802.11n stations.

4. **C.** The recommended maximum number of SSIDs for an AP radio is dependent on a number of factors, such as channel utilization, the purpose and/or need for multiple service sets, and the Beacon interval settings, among others. In the enterprise, a maximum of four SSIDs is widely accepted as a best practice. Beyond four SSIDs, management traffic can begin to reach problematic levels for channel contention.

5. **D.** Band steering is a feature designed to offload WLAN traffic from the 2.4 GHz band by "steering" clients to 5 GHz. This is accomplished by the AP by withholding probe response frames when a client sends a probe request in the 2.4 GHz band.

6. **B, C.** It is commonly said that QoS is end-to-end or it is not at all. Priority handling must be applied across all hops of a network. If data is prioritized throughout the network but then hits a bottleneck that adds significant latency because the data is not properly prioritized, the priority provided in the rest of the network will be moot. Similarly, when admission control is required, resources should be evaluated from start to finish. This will ensure that application data will be successfully supported on the network.

7. **D.** Most WLAN vendors implement proprietary tunneling protocols to facilitate Layer 3 client roaming. When a client roams between subnets, it would normally require a new IP address on the new subnet. With most WLAN implementations, the client's association is anchored at the original AP/controller and is tunneled from the new AP/controller to the old AP/controller.

8. **D.** DSCP supports up to 64 traffic classes by means of 64 different code point values.

9. **C, D.** Explanation: Jitter is the measurement of latency variability from one frame to another, and latency is the measurement of time delay experienced in the delivery of a frame.

10. **C, D.** VoWiFi calls require low jitter and low loss to achieve call quality, which is rated with high Mean Opinion Scores (MOS). MOS is a subjective perception of the quality of a call.

11. **E.** 802.1Q defines a 4-byte expanded Ethernet header to accommodate a VLAN ID. 802.1p defines a 3-bit CoS value to identify frame priority within the 802.1Q-expanded Ethernet header. In WLANs, the 3-bit 802.1p UP values are mapped to four WMM ACs.

12. D. Data traffic sourced from, and destined to, non-QoS stations operating in a QoS BSS is mapped to AC_BE.

13. B. Airtime fairness is a proprietary feature that seeks to balance airtime usage by client stations in accordance with the efficiency of their modulation and coding scheme. When slower stations in a BSS are not regulated, performance for the entire BSS suffers.

14. C. PMK caching is standardized by the 802.11 specification. As an early solution to the problem of roaming with 802.1X/EAP, PMK caching is a limited implementation. Specifically, PMK caching is often referred to as "fast roam-back" because it does not provide fast roaming to new APs; it only facilitates efficient roaming when a client roams back to an AP with which it has previously had an association.

15. B, D, F. The Wi-Fi Alliance has become an important standardization body within the Wi-Fi industry. WMM is an important QoS certification; WMM Power Save is also an important certification related to WMM for power conservation. Voice Enterprise is a certification based on 802.11r, 802.11k, and 802.11v that is currently in development by the Wi-Fi Alliance.

16. A, C. 802.11b uses 1, 2, 5.5, and 11 Mbps data rates. To prevent 802.11b devices from joining your network, your network administrator can simply disable support for these rates.

17. B. For client devices, RTS/CTS is the preferred protection mechanism for backward compatibility with 802.11b devices. With RTS/CTS, client devices begin a frame transmission by sending an RTS control frame to the AP. The AP then transmits a CTS frame back to the client. The purpose of these frames is to reserve the medium for the data transmission, which will occur at a data rate that is not understood by the legacy device. Because client devices are not typically centrally located in an AP's service area, CTS frames transmitted by the client may not be heard by all stations in the area. For that reason, the AP should be the one to transmit a CTS after the client sends an RTS.

18. A, C, E. The Voice Enterprise certification being developed by the Wi-Fi Alliance is designed to implement technologies and protocols derived from the 802.11k, 802.11r, and 802.11v amendments to the 802.11 specification. 802.11k defines radio resource measurement enhancements. 802.11r defines RSN fast BSS transition (FT) enhancements for roaming, and 802.11v contributes features related to wireless network management as it relates to mobility transitions.

19. C. The Clear Channel Assessment (CCA) function is a way for a Wi-Fi radio to physically sample the wireless medium to detect both Wi-Fi and non-Wi-Fi transmissions. PHY-specific rules dictate how a transmitter should respond in the event that the wireless medium is busy or idle.

20. B, D. Removing the SSID from Beacons was an early attempt at "security through obscurity." However, this should not be viewed as a valid approach to network security. On the other hand, SSID inclusion or removal may have administrative benefits related to minimizing the number of help-desk calls from users who are attempting to join the wrong network. This is done by hiding the SSID of networks where the clients are automatically configured. By so doing, guests will not likely discover and attempt to join the wrong network.

Basic WLAN Security Design

**THE FOLLOWING CWDP EXAM TOPICS
ARE COVERED IN THIS CHAPTER:**

✓ Identify weak security solutions and protocols, and
provide acceptable alternatives.

✓ Recommend appropriate authentication solutions and
explain design concepts related to their use.

✓ Recommend appropriate data encryption solutions and
explain design concepts related to their use.

✓ Identify the role and limitations of client capabilities in
security planning.

Wi-Fi networks are becoming increasingly important to a broad range of users. For home users and the smallest companies who want simple Internet access to the largest corporations and governments with stringent network demands, every wireless network requires some level of security. Yet the impressive growth of the Wi-Fi industry and the amazing demand for mobile technologies have been consistently met with a barrage of bad press and confusing marketing proclaiming that Wi-Fi networks are inherently insecure. This, as you'll see, can be an unfair assessment. In an exploration of security technologies and best practices for security design, this chapter will introduce some of the basic, common elements of WLAN security that are relevant for networks of all sizes. Along with Chapter 12, "Advanced Enterprise WLAN Security Design," we will demonstrate that security can be a fun topic, and WLANs can be secure if proper design techniques are followed. Technologies and protocols are in place for end users to establish secure networks, but education is a necessary first step to help drive adoption of these technologies. Many enterprises are deploying more secure WLAN security technologies, but many also remain unaware of the risks of outdated solutions.

In this chapter, we will take a look at some of the best and worst security strategies for WLANs. We will discuss the best ways to implement security to maintain network integrity and privacy, to control access, and to protect all of the valuable resources that are contained within a network, while maintaining the required level of application performance and network service. We will also note the common missteps of many network security designers.

A General Overview of WLAN Security

As a blanket statement, wireless networks of all kinds require security. The tools we use to help protect our networks from intrusion fall under several broad elements. Here are some of the most important elements of network security:

- *Authentication*, or proof of identity
- *Confidentiality*, or encryption; also called privacy, ciphering, obfuscation, or cryptography
- *Integrity*, or protection from tampering
- *Authorization*, or what a user is allowed to do

- *Accounting*, or usage tracking
- *Availability*, or protection from service disruption
- *Nonrepudiation*, or auditable proof of activity or inactivity

As a quick overview, let's look at some basic examples of what is at stake with a wireless network:

Data Privacy and Integrity Assurance   User data is traversing the wireless medium. If important and private information is being transmitted across the shared wireless medium, the data must be protected in some way by preventing unauthorized eavesdropping and providing assurance of the data's source. Privacy and data integrity are necessary.

Controlling Access to Network Services   Wireless devices connect to a network that provides services and maintains resources. Each network has its own important information, which could include passwords, user databases, sensitive files, trade secrets, services, and devices that are important for network functionality. For this reason, it is important that access to the network and its resources is controlled. These tasks of validating users and assigning permissions are often known as authentication and authorization.

In addition to the valuable resources that are stored within the network, each network is typically a portal to other networks, including the Internet. Even if no services or resources are provided directly by the local network, there may be a liability in providing an open portal for wireless users to perpetrate IT crimes against other networks or users.

Maintaining Service Availability   The wireless network exists to provide some business service to its owner. It costs money to operate and usually provides an important business function that keeps the company operational. The cessation of wireless services is never desired, so part of the goal of security is to prevent disruption. This task is often referred to as maintaining availability.

Monitoring and Auditing   Even the best security—whether wired or wireless—may be subject to a breach. In the unfortunate event that security is compromised, it is important that the network owner can account for the damages done, identify the perpetrator, and hopefully defend this information legally. These processes are a part of accounting and nonrepudiation.

There are several ways—and reasons—to implement security within an 802.11 WLAN. The strengths and weaknesses of the various 802.11 security methods have received widespread attention in numerous books, articles, and discussions, but for this book we will focus on simplifying the details and providing concise directives that help users make decisions in accordance with best practices. Each network environment is unique, but there are many consistencies within the selection and deployment of security models that, with a little logic, can be applied to the enterprise.

We understand that it is one thing to prescribe the best and most secure security model for all situations, but it is quite another to select a security solution when you have a limited budget, limited staff, specific hardware requirements, inflexible applications and infrastructures, and many other limitations. With those constraints in mind, we will attempt to stay balanced and offer insight for these limitations while promoting the most secure solutions.

Basic WLAN Security

Many sources claim that Wi-Fi networks are inherently insecure. They have a point—sort of. Of course, we all know that the wireless medium is unbounded and can be seen (received) by anyone within listening range with some basic WLAN hardware. Radio waves propagate outside of building walls, which makes the fundamental access principles of Wi-Fi different from wired networks. Five years ago, we don't think anyone could argue that Wi-Fi was inherently insecure because the security protocols designed to protect the network were weak. However, the demands of secure end-user mobility in the enterprise have reached the ears of standards and interoperability organizations as well as vendors, making current Wi-Fi security very robust. In fact, you could easily argue that many Wi-Fi networks are more secure than wired networks by simple virtue of the fact that the vulnerability of wireless has been highly publicized and network designers have responded by battening down the hatches. In other words, attention en masse has heightened awareness and improved security stances on the WLAN.

Weak legacy security protocols and highly publicized security breaches have also played a big part in the perception that wireless is insecure. Yet these breaches and vulnerabilities largely boil down to design flaws that could have been prevented. So now that you know what not to do, let's review some basics about 802.11 operations and then discuss legacy security protocols and design philosophies.

Review of 802.11 Association Procedures

Before discussing the actual security mechanisms for WLANs, let's take a minute to review the fundamental connectivity mechanisms of the 802.11 protocol. The 802.11 connectivity paradigm includes three basic procedures that are part of a wireless connection—properly called *association*:

1. Client stations must *discover* the network of which it desires to be a part. WLAN discovery is often divided into two separate types: *active discovery* and *passive discovery*. With either type, the purpose of discovery is for the client device to ascertain certain parameters, supported features, operating modes, and security settings of a BSS. This information is used by the client in the association process.

2. The 802.11 specification defines a basic two-frame handshake called authentication—often called 802.11 or *open authentication*. Not to be confused with the type of authentication that provides robust identity validation, open

authentication is more of a handshake formality that lays the groundwork for creating a network association between two stations.

3. Following authentication, the final step in creating network connectivity is *association*. In this step, the client device issues an association request message to the AP. Association requests contain the capabilities and data rates supported by the client station as well as the SSID of the WLAN. In reply, the AP will transmit an association response message. The association response message carries network functionality parameters, the status code, and, if successful, an association ID (AID), which is used during power save operations.

Unless additional security procedures such as 802.1X have been enabled, once the client station has achieved an association it can begin to transmit and receive data frames. At this point, the confidentiality and integrity security elements become an important factor. For modern WLAN security solutions, the actual user/device authentication (validating that users are who they say they are) occurs after 802.11 association. In that sense, discovery, 802.11 authentication, and 802.11 association are intended to create an operational framework on which robust security solutions are built.

You can think about these three steps as a means by which a client and AP establish a communication link where an enterprise security authentication (802.1X/EAP) can then take place. Without this step, the mobile device and infrastructure would not be able to communicate authentication information. We will elaborate on this topic as we explore reliable security mechanisms.

Weak Security Methods

Several aspects of the 802.11 protocol are considered legacy from a security design perspective. However, there are various instances when weak security might be acceptable. For instance, you may use open authentication with a guest access network because the priority of simplicity and ease of use outweighs the necessity for security—although usually a web-based captive portal mechanism, segmentation and filtering, and other security fail-safes are also implemented in that scenario. Similarly, some companies still use WEP encryption for legacy VoWiFi phones because the phones are incapable of being upgraded to a better security solution and the data crossing the wireless medium (voice calls) is not thought to need strict protection. In that scenario, the trade-off is financial savings, ease of use, and even fast handoffs in exchange for weak security. Again, layered security like segmentation and filtering would also be used. With these layered mechanisms in place, end users are able to minimize the risk of weak security solutions. The use of legacy security is somewhat common in many network environments because the benefit of simplicity and cost savings seems to outweigh the risks presented by weak security.

As we look at legacy security, let's start at the beginning with the early years of 802.11. Two basic authentication modes were built into the original 802.11 standard: open authentication (a.k.a. *802.11 authentication*) and shared key authentication.

Open Authentication

As we discussed earlier in this chapter, open authentication consists of a simple two-way handshake and is normally successful. It does not actually "authenticate" the user or client device aside from ensuring that the client station has the ability to transmit a properly formed authentication frame. Open authentication, by itself, does not provide any security, and it was not designed to do so. Rather, open authentication was designed as an introductory framework as an alternative to *shared key authentication.* Now that robust security mechanisms are mature and pervasively supported, open authentication is used in almost every WLAN in existence to provide a gateway for more sophisticated security solutions, such as *802.1X/EAP*, which we will discuss in Chapter 12.

Shared Key Authentication

The alternative to open authentication is a primitive authentication mechanism called shared key authentication. The IEEE has officially deprecated this authentication mechanism, and it is not recommend for use. In fact, it is difficult to find support for it in client supplicants anymore, and it is infrequently used in network deployments.

Pursuing RF Obscurity

It is common to see industry articles and press in which the unbounded RF medium is blamed for Wi-Fi's security woes. As we discussed earlier, an unbounded medium does change the fundamental access principles of the network, but it does not mean that the responsive security solution should be to attempt to hide the network. This is often referred to as security through obscurity. The technique here is essentially to limit the transmit power, choose low-gain and perhaps directional antennas, and strategically place access points so that the RF waves are not transmitted outside the building (to be exact, RF waves will always travel outside the building, but the idea is to minimize the signal strength at the building's perimeter so that the signals are unusable), and thus, not available to attackers for exploitation.

Some highly secretive and ultra-security-conscious facilities may employ special means of RF protection, such as an EMF (electromagnet field) barrier around the perimeter of a building or room, but this is very rare. In most cases, organizations desiring this much security should not employ Wi-Fi technologies in the first place. For most Wi-Fi networks, controlling the RF medium like this is impractical and ultimately not a good security solution. If you are attempting to provide reliable Wi-Fi connectivity throughout your building, Wi-Fi signals will inevitably "bleed" outside the building. Even if you are able to limit the RF propagation outside your building's perimeter, potential attackers can use high-gain antennas to amplify their reception. Thus, if you measure low signal amplitude at the building's edge with standard Wi-Fi client devices with internal antennas, high-gain antennas can still pick them up. Instead of attempting to hide the network, robust security, such as WPA2 with AES-CCMP, should be implemented.

Other than for those few highly secretive deployments, we do not recommend RF obscurity because it is cost prohibitive to do effectively and it does not provide security against inside attacks. In addition to these reasons, better security is available. At the same time, we encourage that RF signal coverage and proper contention planning be the primary determinants of AP location, transmit power settings, and antenna selection.

 Real World Scenario

RF Obscurity: A Contentious Topic

Many people in the Wi-Fi industry have recommended designing networks to contain RF signals for security purposes. RF signals can always be heard from a distance at some level except for facilities that have perimeter fences, security gates with armed security guards, and a 5-mile border around your facility. Facilities such as those can generally afford to implement a strong enough security protocol. WLANs are often deployed in public facilities. Any facility using this technique for security purposes should place their energy into more fruitful activities.

There are, however, better uses for RF obscurity. Focusing your antenna's propagation pattern where your actual client devices will be placed is a good RF design principle. For example, placing an AP with an omnidirectional antenna in the corner of a building would not necessarily be a good design practice. Perhaps a low-gain patch antenna on the wall focusing its energy inward would yield better performance with the unintentional side effect of RF obscurity to outside parties.

SSID Hiding

As we mentioned previously, two types of scanning techniques may be used to discover a WLAN. Both of these methods are used by clients to discover basic parameters of the BSS, including the SSID—the network name. The SSID is a requisite parameter that is necessary for a client association to an AP. For this reason, some have surmised that *SSID hiding* would be a practical method of securing the WLAN. This is another type of security through obscurity, which is a weak solution, but this method may hold slightly more design value than hiding the WLAN via RF control.

For security purposes, SSID hiding may prevent some basic client utilities from discovering the network name. However, any protocol analysis tool can easily identify the SSID by capturing a frame that mandatorily contains the SSID field, such as an association request frame, which is shown in Figure 11.1. The SSID cannot be removed from these frames, which is why SSID hiding has limited effectiveness. For security purposes, hiding the SSID is not recommended.

FIGURE 11.1   The association request always includes the SSID.

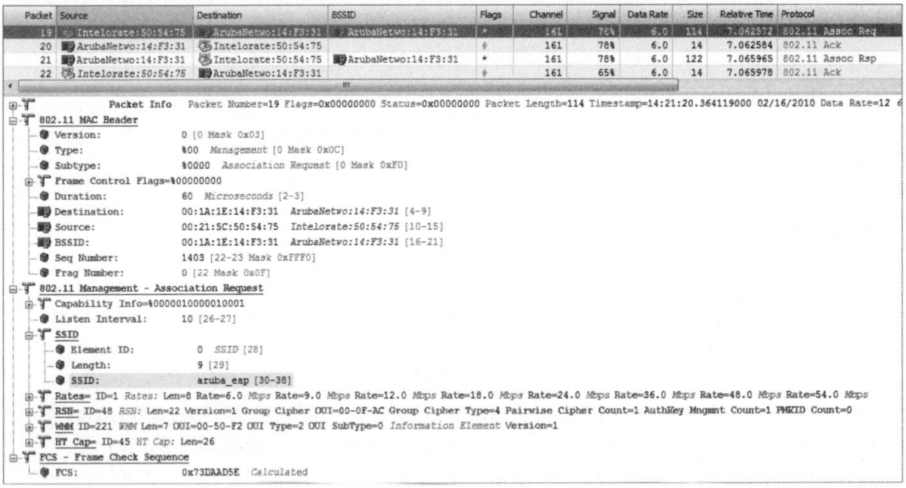

Despite this fundamental limitation in the effectiveness of SSID hiding as a security mechanism, SSID hiding may be valuable for other purposes. Specifically, it is common for enterprise companies to broadcast multiple SSIDs from each AP. This setup allows differentiated services for each ESS and may be used to segment specific applications, network uses, or security requirements.

For example, one SSID may be for corporate data usage, another SSID may be for VoWiFi, and a third SSID may be for guest users. Of course, you want your guests to be able to identify the network that is designed for them, so you might label it with an SSID like "FreeGuestWiFi." When guests are visiting your facility and attempting to connect to your guest network, you want them to be able to clearly identify the intended SSID for connection, and you do not want them to attempt to connect to your corporate SSID. You may facilitate this design approach by "hiding" the SSID of your corporate networks so that your guests are not attempting to connect to, and failing authentication on, your corporate network and then contacting your help desk because they cannot connect to the network. Of course, hiding your corporate SSID may provide help desk–related problems for your legitimate corporate users as well, but for those environments where user devices are controlled by the IT department, SSID hiding may be a worthwhile configuration option.

The decision to broadcast the SSID depends entirely on the end users and client devices that are used with the network. If there is a clear administrative and support advantage to hiding the SSID, then by all means, hide it. But remember that for security purposes, this solution is easily defeated.

MAC Filters

Another legacy security mechanism that is still found in the market today is *MAC filtering*. As with other weak security techniques, MAC filtering was an attempt at security before the IEEE and Wi-Fi Alliance introduced legitimate, robust security protocols to market. We should all remember from our network fundamentals education that each network interface card (NIC) is hard-coded with a supposed-to-be-unique MAC address. The manufacturing and MAC address assignment process is designed to prevent more than one NIC from having the same MAC address. Thus, the uniqueness of a MAC address was supposed to be an opportunity to provide or restrict network access based on this address.

Despite the intention for each device to possess a unique MAC address, there are several utilities and command-line tools that allow users to easily modify the MAC address of a NIC. For wireless networks with MAC filtering, users can simply observe the frames that are successfully transmitted and received on the wireless medium, copy the plain-text MAC address of the legitimate client, and modify their client device with the same MAC address. This is a simple workaround that easily defeats MAC addresses.

So, our instinct would be to prescribe total abandonment of MAC address filtering, right? Well, it's not quite so cut and dry. On the one hand, MAC filtering is not a robust security solution. Additionally, the administrative overhead of collecting user MAC addresses, maintaining a list of allowed or denied devices, and managing filters—also called *whitelists* or *blacklists*—on the infrastructure can be imposing. However, not all networks or client devices are capable of supporting robust security, so MAC filtering can be an alternate plan.

For example, consider the overwhelming task of managing client connectivity at a large university. Students come to school with a large array of Wi-Fi devices, from computers and phones to printers and gaming consoles. Now, for universities that are proactive about protecting student connectivity, 802.1X/EAP with PEAPv0/EAP-MSCHAPv2 is a common user-based authentication mechanism for most student connectivity. Unfortunately, many Wi-Fi devices are not capable of using 802.1X/EAP, and—although rare—some may not even support PSK-based authentication such as WPA-Personal or WPA2-Personal. So, instead of implementing WEP, which requires static keys and adds configuration steps, the networking department at the university will often provide a separate SSID for student connectivity to serve devices with limited security capabilities. Then, they'll require that students register the MAC address of their device (usually gaming consoles), and a simple MAC filter (along with appropriate segmentation and filtering) will serve as basic network security. It's a fairly primitive solution, but even a weak MAC filter is better than no security at all. If nothing else, it keeps most illegitimate devices off the network.

To turn this example around, blacklisting certain devices can have its merit. If a WPA-Personal PSK was configured into a VoWiFi handset device, for example, and it was stolen, one method that can provide some value is to blacklist that device. Ideally, this approach is coupled with a monitoring tool that will alert administrators in the event that the device showed up, but you will at least be able to prevent it from joining the network.

In addition to blacklisting or whitelisting for simple access control, MAC filters can be used to assign some basic security policies. MAC addresses for large universities and enterprise organizations are usually stored as a part of a large user database. Upon authentication, the access controller can also use the MAC address to assign basic user privileges. Again, you wouldn't want to rely on MAC addresses in a user database to provide robust access control for important network resources, but for simple Internet access, rate limiting, or other tasks, it may be useful.

 Real World Scenario

Unsuspected Processing Delays

A large enterprise network had deployed a VoWiFi solution many years ago, and the handsets were only capable of weak security protocols. MAC filtering was chosen to be used as one of the added measures to deter users from using the WLAN.

As time continued and new devices were added and replaced, the list of MAC addresses became quite large. When users roamed from AP to AP in the WLAN, a noticeable audio clip would occur. Months of troubleshooting ensued to find the problem. A test was made from a VoWiFi handset using a different SSID that did not incorporate MAC filtering, and the audio clip went away.

It was later determined that the MAC filtering list had grown so large that the time involved in looking up the MAC address of roaming users was long enough that it caused perceptible problems for the users.

Most people would not consider this seemingly simple process to query and compare a list much to worry about. However, realize that human beings write software code to perform every task that an AP does and not always the most efficient computing method may be used. This is especially true when it comes to legacy security methods. With any feature, the amount of testing involved prior to deployment is usually respective to the popularity and intended use of the feature.

Wired Equivalent Privacy

Wired Equivalent Privacy (WEP) is a legacy encryption protocol that was originally introduced by the IEEE to provide wired-like data privacy against casual eavesdropping on the wireless medium. WEP has been at the forefront of much of the industry discussions about Wi-Fi security, and by now, everyone knows that WEP is a deprecated security protocol. At its inception, WEP was a valuable protocol for data privacy because it is a fairly simple encryption process and does not have much processing overhead. Of course, this simplicity is also an indicator of WEP's strength. Due to several published weaknesses, WEP is not suitable in the enterprise. Even so, it is still very common to see WEP deployed in homes, small businesses, and, unfortunately, the enterprise.

Due to its relatively low processing overhead, many legacy devices that had minimal processing capabilities were capable of performing the WEP computations. In fact, most 802.11 radio implementations included an on-board chip designed to offload all of WEP's processing. Because legacy devices were manufactured before AES-CCMP became standardized, this is why these devices cannot be upgraded to support AES.

When the 802.11 designers wanted to move to AES-CCMP, backward compatibility was critically important. This is why TKIP was introduced (as a part of WPA-Personal and WPA-Enterprise) as a temporary cipher protocol that improved upon the weaknesses of WEP. TKIP, in most cases, allowed for legacy devices to be software upgraded because like WEP, TKIP also incorporates the *RC4* encryption cipher. TKIP does so in a much more secure manner. Therefore, most legacy WEP-only devices were capable of being upgraded to TKIP with a simple firmware upgrade. Even today, there is a massive difference in the security afforded by TKIP, as compared with WEP.

CWNP's Certified Wireless Security Professional (CWSP) certification addresses the many weaknesses of WEP in greater detail, but for the purposes of network design and the CWDP exam, it is sufficiently important to understand that WEP is not typically recommended for use in enterprise networks. It still only affords protection against "casual eavesdropping."

Similar to many passphrase-based security solutions, WEP has the drawback of high management overhead and static keys. When WEP is used, all clients and APs within an ESS share the same static WEP key. If the key is compromised, all data and network access is compromised. If you desire to change the static WEP key, all keys on all devices must be changed. This is a management problem.

As you research WEP implementation options, you will find that there are several variations on WEP, such as WEP-40 (also known as WEP-64), WEP-104 (also known as WEP-128), dynamic WEP, and other proprietary versions. In most cases (such as with WEP-40 and WEP-104), static keys are used as inputs to the RC4 (the encryption algorithm used with WEP) function. However, in some early instances of 802.1X/EAP implementations, dynamic keys that were exported from 802.1X/EAP authentication were used as inputs to the WEP protocol. While dynamically rotating keys may be helpful for minimizing the likelihood of exploitation of WEP, the same weaknesses—short and plain-text IV, weak ICV, etc.—are still found in dynamic WEP. All versions of WEP should be avoided in favor of new, reliable security protocols.

Shared Key Authentication and WEP

Shared key authentication is a frame exchange handshake consisting of four frames: an initialization, challenge, challenge response, and notification. In order to use shared key authentication, the legacy encryption protocol known as Wired Equivalent Privacy (WEP) is required. WEP's weaknesses have been highly publicized, and it can be easily defeated with publicly available software. While you might think that shared key authentication adds a modicum of reinforcement to WEP, it actually exacerbates the problems of WEP, making its flaws more pronounced.

Since WEP is required for encryption with shared key authentication, the challenge and challenge response frames used during the authentication exchange are generated by the WEP algorithm. Interestingly enough, the AP's challenge data (second frame) is sent in clear text to the client device, and the response (third frame) is encrypted by the client station with the same static WEP key that is subsequently used to encrypt data after successful shared key authentication. If an attacker captures these frames, they can more easily and quickly obtain the WEP key. Success or failure of shared key authentication depends on both the client station and the AP having exactly the same static WEP key manually configured on both devices. For this reason, shared key authentication is not a recommended option if network protection is desired. Even if your network consists of legacy devices that cannot support modern security mechanisms, you are better off configuring your network to use WEP encryption without shared key authentication.

Similar to the qualifications we made with MAC filtering, we would also like to include a few provisions about WEP's use. Let's reiterate that we strongly recommend that all efforts be made to avoid using WEP when any amount of wireless security is desired; however, we understand that there are always extenuating circumstances and other technical hurdles that prevent forward progress. In these cases, we concede that WEP is better than no security at all. Some applications may not require data privacy. Similarly, some network segments may not contain any important network resources. In these cases, WEP should only be used as a worst-case scenario, and additional layers of security—such as MAC filtering, ACLs, and VLAN segmentation—for these networks are highly recommended.

EAP-MD5

In Chapter 12, we'll address Extensible Authentication Protocol (EAP) types in some detail, but we want to briefly mention that *EAP-MD5* is one EAP type that certainly falls under the category of legacy security. EAP-MD5 was initially designed for wired networks and to test basic connectivity between the supplicant, authenticator, and authentication server in wireless networks, but EAP-MD5 was never intended as a robust authentication protocol for wireless networks. More pointedly, EAP-MD5 has the following limitations:

- It does not support mutual authentication.
- It does not export dynamic keys.
- Its authentication exchange is subject to dictionary attacks.
- It does not support any modern, secure encryption protocols.

For this reason, we do not recommend the use of EAP-MD5 for wireless networks in any case. What's more, you will find extremely limited support for EAP-MD5 in most client and infrastructure products.

VPN

While VPN security is not necessarily a legacy security method, it should be noted that many legacy Wi-Fi networks depended on VPN security for data privacy. Generally speaking, VPNs were effective in securing WLANs; however, the IEEE 802.11 specification was never intended to be secured primarily by a VPN. For that reason, VPNs introduced additional network overhead and connectivity requirements that were only tolerable when robust standardized 802.11 security was not available.

In today's networks, VPNs are useful for remote connectivity across unsecured networks as well as for proprietary solutions, such as bridging. They may also be used as an added layer of security in addition to standardized WPA/WPA2 methods, but this additional layer of security adds overhead and is rarely necessary. In today's networks, VPNs are rarely used as the exclusive method of Wi-Fi security, and when WPA/WPA2 can be used, VPNs are almost never recommended unless it pertains to the data path the traffic will use, such as on a wired or WAN connection. Even then, those connections are better secured by infrastructure network devices.

Recommendations and Best Practices when Using Legacy Methods

Before we move on and begin discussing robust security mechanisms, it is important that we rehash some of the basics of weak security approaches. Most important, we want to reinforce that legacy security mechanisms are never recommended when better security can be used. When a security solution is suspected of vulnerabilities, seek out a migration path to more secure mechanisms as soon as possible. If your hardware does not currently support acceptable security protocols, check with the hardware manufacturer for firmware or driver upgrades that may provide better security options. Of course, in the best-case scenario, legacy hardware would be replaced with new, better-performing equipment that supports all the best in modern WLAN security. When in doubt, seek input from the equipment manufacturer, and always double-check for Wi-Fi Alliance certifications to ensure that your equipment is certified.

Wi-Fi Alliance Security Certifications

The Wi-Fi Alliance offers security certification programs for both clients and infrastructure devices. Among the Wi-Fi Alliance's security certification programs are WPA and WPA2 Personal and Enterprise, as well as seven different EAP types, including the following:

- EAP-FAST

- PEAPv0/EAP-MSCHAPv2

- PEAPv1/EAP-GTC

- EAP-TLS

- EAP-TTLS/MSCHAPv2

- EAP-SIM

- EAP-AKA

Wi-Fi Protected Setup is another security feature that is tested, but it is for SOHO networks and has not been widely used in the industry.

In any case, you can search Wi-Fi-certified products at http://www.wi-fi.org/search_products.php to ensure that your products have passed basic interoperability testing. If so, they will receive a certificate showing their certification criteria, as shown here:

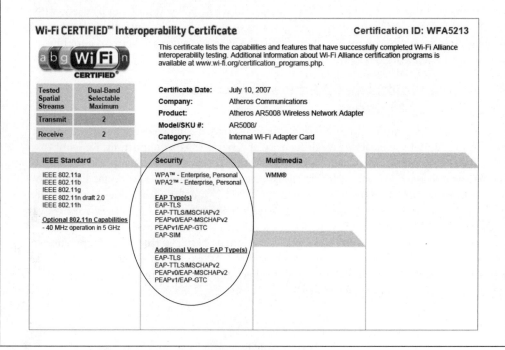

When legacy security solutions must be used, we recommend the use of security layering to maximize protection. For example, if you must use WEP, consider also using MAC filtering and VLAN segmentation along with firewalls. The wireless segment of the network may not necessarily be "secure," but every additional element of protection may help. In all cases where legacy security is used, it is paramount that appropriate firewalls, ACLs, and segmentation be used to minimize the risk of an unsecured network.

Also, always consider the traffic traversing your wireless network, the devices that are accessible via the wireless network, and the network resources that are behind a poorly secured wireless network. Performing a proper risk assessment, asset inventory, and impact analysis is incredibly important in this phase of a design. This step cannot be understated. Risk assessments, asset inventories, and impact analyses are always important factors in selecting security solutions, but they are especially critical when legacy mechanisms are knowingly used.

WPA-Personal and WPA2-Personal

As the Wi-Fi industry continues to move away from legacy security protocols, it is moving toward Wi-Fi certified security solutions based on 802.11i, such as *WPA-Personal* and *WPA2-Personal*. As you likely remember from your CWNA studies, the *802.11i* task group (TGi) had two primary purposes:

- Bridge the gap of weak security by addressing the weaknesses of WEP and shared key authentication.
- Introduce a new, more robust security solution that would be future proof for many years to come.

While the Wi-Fi Alliance awaited the 802.11i amendment from the IEEE, the Wi-Fi Alliance released the Wi-Fi Protected Access (WPA) certification as a stop-gap solution to address the weaknesses of WEP with *TKIP*. This provided a secure alternative to WEP and shared key authentication while the IEEE was completing work on *AES-CCMP*, which was the foundation for Wi-Fi Protected Access 2 (WPA2).

TGi also defined the idea of a *robust security network (RSN)* and made allowances for the continued use of pre-802.11i security methods in conjunction with TKIP or AES through the use of a *transition security network (TSN)*. At first, AES-CCMP capable equipment was rare and expensive, but all new Wi-Fi certified equipment is capable of supporting CCMP. In fact, 802.11n requires that AES-CCMP be used for encryption between 802.11n stations in an RSN supporting 802.11n MCS rates, and the Wi-Fi Alliance now mandates that all new devices be WPA2-certified.

Of course, 802.11n devices can still use open or WEP security modes, but in an RSN, AES-CCMP is required. If you find that this is confusing, you are in good company. In fact, 802.11n Draft 2.0 had more strict guidelines on encryption between 802.11n devices. Since many of today's products were released when Draft 2.0 was the latest version of 802.11n, you will find that some 802.11n devices will not support 802.11n MCS rates unless AES-CCMP is used. In other words, if you attempt to use open authentication or WEP the AP will default to only 802.11a/g data rates. This is a significant, though common, software problem that should have been updated with the final release of 802.11n. Check your vendor's implementation to be sure.

As security certifications, WPA-Personal and WPA2-Personal include both authentication and encryption requirements. The authentication portion of WPA-Personal and WPA2-Personal operates exactly the same way. However, the encryption specifications differ.

PSK Authentication

The authentication portion of WPA-Personal and WPA2-Personal relies on a *preshared key (PSK)* or *passphrase* that is entered on both the client and infrastructure devices. After the 802.11 association that we discussed earlier, the PSK is converted into a PMK, which is used as an input to the encryption key generation process during the four-way handshake. We will not go into details about the four-way handshake (for more information on these details, see *CWSP Certified Wireless Security Professional Official Study Guide* by Coleman et al., published 2010 by Sybex), but you should know that this four-frame exchange verifies mutual possession of the shared key. There are several important design elements to consider as a part of WPA/WPA2-Personal security implementation. First among these considerations is a determination of proper use cases for PSK-based security. WPA/WPA2-Personal can be a secure solution, but it is not well suited to all network needs. Along these lines, we will also discuss some of the benefits and limitations of an ESS-wide static PSK. Also, selection, management, and secrecy of the PSK are important factors to consider.

Preshared Key (PSK) or Passphrase?

When using WPA/WPA2-Personal, there are two terms that are frequently misused that can lead to confusion among administrators. The two terms are preshared key (PSK) and passphrase. These terms are not synonymous. The PSK is a 256-bit character string that, in WPA/WPA2-Personal networks, is used as the PMK. The PMK is subsequently used to derive encryption keys.

However, there are different methods of entering the PSK into a system. In WPA/WPA2-Personal networks, the PSK can be entered directly as a 64 hexadecimal (256 bits) preshared key. Or, the PSK can be mapped from a shorter, easier-to-remember, but less secure, ASCII passphrase (8–63 characters). The PSK is always 64 hex characters. The reason for the passphrase entry method is to make it easier for administrators to configure the keys. People (normal people) find it difficult to remember and work with long strings of characters, and especially with hexadecimal characters. So the 802.11 standard makes this passphrase provision to allow an admin or end user to enter a shorter word or phrase and allow the protocol to convert the passphrase into a 256-bit PSK for them.

However, you will find limited or no support for entering 64-bit PSKs into client and infrastructure products. While it may be possible to enter a PSK on one end of a link, entering a passphrase might be the only option on the other endpoint, resulting in an inability to connect.

It is largely an academic topic, but since it is used in other industry documents, it is important to mention it from a design perspective. For this reason, many industry documents will typically use the terms interchangeably as do the authors of this text.

Ideal Use Cases

There are several network uses and benefits for WPA/WPA2-Personal, and we will discuss them here.

Simplicity in Small Offices   One of the great benefits of WPA/WPA2-Personal is that it is simple. You select a passphrase, enter it on your infrastructure, and enter it on your client. That's it. This makes the solution great for home networks or small companies in which a single passphrase and network access mechanism is required. Everyone shares the simple passphrase, everyone respects the privacy of the network, and everyone is happy with relatively simple, though effective, security.

Clients Lacking 802.1X/EAP Support   There are many devices that still do not support 802.1X/EAP. Many new consumer devices are being built with Wi-Fi enabled radios, and some of these devices, like printers, smart phones, gaming consoles, and more, do not yet support 802.1X/EAP. For these device types, WPA/WPA2-Personal is the next best thing.

In addition, many legacy devices are not capable of supporting 802.1X/EAP, but many of them can support WPA-Personal with TKIP. This paves the way for short-term security until these devices can be upgraded or a new solution can be implemented. Either way, the enterprise is often handcuffed to PSK-based security due to the requirements of legacy hardware, although many of these legacy devices are being phased out of the enterprise.

Centrally Provisioned Client Devices   Some enterprise devices support 802.1X/EAP but are still provisioned centrally in a way that favors PSK. For example, Vocera voice badges are configured with SSID and security parameters by means of a centralized provisioning utility. When deploying the network, you configure the badge configuration utility (BCU) with a single PSK once, and you don't have to worry about it again. All devices share the same PSK, but end users can't recover the PSK (because they can't access that part of the device's configuration), and a single network profile can be applied to all phones within the network. It's secure, simple, and effective for that purpose. Vocera does support 802.1X, but all voice badges share a user profile for 802.1X/EAP, which minimizes some of the security advantages provided by 802.1X.

Application Performance Requirements   Some other situations that may call for WPA/WPA2-Personal include support for devices (like voice phones) with sensitive applications that require low-latency roaming times. The short authentication exchange used with WPA/WPA2-Personal is usually more than adequate to maintain sessions for sensitive applications while roaming from one AP to another. In cases where adequate fast secure roaming (FSR) features are not available with 802.1X/EAP, a PSK-based security method may be the only option to maintain acceptable application performance along with security. This is common for handheld barcode scanners, VoWiFi phones, mobile client-server applications (as with electronic medical records on tablet computers), and other applications.

Limitations

WPA/WPA2-Personal also has some limitations in many applications. For starters, standardized WPA/WPA2-Personal uses an ESS-wide security parameter, meaning that every user shares the same passphrase. If any end users are aware of the passphrase, you must trust that they will not share this access credential with users who are not supposed to have it. Further, by sharing a passphrase across an entire ESS, it becomes more difficult to provide user-level or group-level access control, authorization, and accounting. Each user authenticates with the same password (no username); thus, it is more difficult for the system to assign custom privileges to each user.

Similarly, WPA/WPA2-Personal may introduce a moderate, if not excessive, amount of management overhead for IT staff. If end users are not trusted with the passphrase, then IT staff must manually configure the passphrase for each client device. Sometimes this is not a problem, but in other cases, the task is overwhelming. This may be a significant limiting factor when it comes to large-scale networks.

In addition to the management overhead of initial device configuration, the shared PSK poses a risk of requiring network-wide reconfiguration. For example, let's say that a disgruntled employee who knew the passphrase was fired and vowed harm to the company. What now? Well, you now have to change the passphrase on every device in the network. Several months later you then find out that a member of the IT staff leaked this information to a user who was not supposed to know the passphrase. What now? Well, you change the passphrase on every device in the network again.

It is also generally recommended that static passphrases be changed at consistent intervals (such as biannually or quarterly), which requires device reconfiguration. All of requirements should make it fairly clear that shared passphrases can be problematic.

Finally, as we'll discuss briefly in the next section, passphrases are not impervious to network attack. For a passphrase to be memorable, it must be short and simple, which means it runs the risk of being too short or simple to stand up to brute-force dictionary attacks. Difficult-to-remember passphrases may mitigate some of the advantages related to the simplicity of WPA/WPA2-Personal networks.

Creating a Passphrase or PSK for WPA/WPA2-Personal

As we previously discussed, there are different ways of implementing the PSK/passphrase. We don't want to dwell on this topic, but it bears stating that the use of passphrases may introduce security risks. The purpose of a passphrase is almost always ease of use. We want to remember it, right? Unfortunately, the problem is that short, simple passphrases, while tempting to use, are subject to exploitation. While WPA-Personal and WPA2-Personal are generally perceived as modern, reliable security solutions, the authentication process may be subject to brute-force dictionary attacks if the selected passphrase is not long or complex enough.

WPA/WPA2 passphrase policies should dictate that passphrases contain 13 or more (some suggest using no less than 20) characters that incorporate mixed alphanumeric and special characters. The passphrase is case sensitive; thus, a long, complex passphrase such as `Je&83Keios)jd23*(&` would be acceptably secure in most networks. Of course, most people couldn't remember that passphrase without a lot of mental anguish, so passphrases may end up being something long and memorable that wouldn't be in a dictionary file, such as `CWNProcksthehouseallthetime`. It is even more common, unfortunately, to have long, complex passphrases pasted on user desktops for easy reference. The selected password may be robust and effective, but the method for managing, storing, and referencing the passphrase may introduce vulnerabilities.

Regardless of the password policy in effect, WPA/WPA2-Personal solutions often require a delicate balance between simplicity and security. Passphrase or PSK selection and management is a major part of that formula.

When in doubt, select a long and ugly passphrase with highly random mixed character strings; or better yet, use utilities such as Password Amplifier from Funk (now Juniper) Software. This tool converts an easy-to-remember phrase (with optional "salt" for additional mixing) into a fairly long and complex password that can be repeated. Figure 11.2 shows the Password Amplifier utility.

FIGURE 11.2 Password Amplifier

For single-use PSKs or complex ASCII passwords, other tools are available, such as Gibson Research Corporation's Perfect Password feature, which can be found on their website at `https://www.grc.com/passwords.htm`. If your AP or client devices require the use of a PSK, you can convert a passphrase into a PSK using a helpful tool provided by Wireshark that is available at `www.wireshark.org/tools/wpa-psk.html`.

IT staff should ensure that the supported client devices support both passphrase and/or PSK entry before settling on a solution. All devices support passphrases, but not all devices support entry of a 64-character (256 bits) hexadecimal PSK.

Per-User Preshared Keys

To date, two wireless vendors (Aerohive Networks and Ruckus Wireless) have introduced proprietary WPA/WPA2-Personal solutions to address some of the inherent drawbacks of ESS-wide PSKs. As we've already established, some of the problems related to PSK usage are that a single access credential is shared by all devices/users across the entire ESS. However, both of these vendors offer *per-user preshared keys (PPSKs)*, which is a novel way of providing each user or device with a distinct access credential that is not shared by others. This is accomplished within the framework of standardized, certified WPA/WPA2-Personal.

There are several benefits to this approach. First, by providing a unique passphrase to each user, authorization to network resources can be controlled more granularly. The unique passphrase identifies the user, and the user can be assigned permissions in accordance with their policy or their group's policy. Individually assigned PSKs also allow for quick and easy deletion or addition of a single user. As in the example we used earlier in this chapter, if an employee leaves the company and the knowledge of the PSK goes with them, IT staff would not be forced to reconfigure each and every device. They could simply delete (or disable) that user along with that user's PSK. Nothing else needs to be done. Figure 11.3 shows the configuration GUI for Aerohive's Private PSK™.

FIGURE 11.3 Aerohive Private PSK™

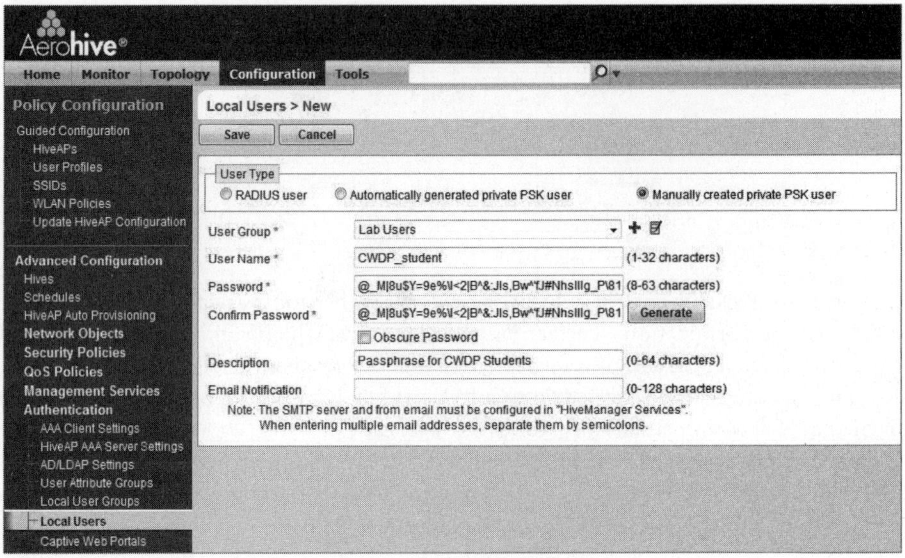

In summary, PPSK solutions simplify management, reduce security risks, and provide individualized access control and authorization while maintaining simplicity. PPSK represents many of the advantages of 802.1X/EAP, without many of the drawbacks. Of course, neither Aerohive nor Ruckus would recommend that PPSK be perceived as a sufficient replacement to 802.1X/EAP, but rather as an improvement to WPA/WPA2-Personal. This feature may work quite well in some industry verticals like higher education.

Dynamic PSK vs. Private PSK

Ruckus pioneered the concept of a per-user PSK and introduced the concept as Dynamic PSK™. Aerohive also introduced a unique version of per-user PSKs, and their implementation is called Private PSK™. In essence, both versions of the technology represent the same concept: providing each user or device with a unique access credential, instead of sharing a passphrase or PSK across all devices. CWNP chose the neutral term per-user PSK (PPSK) to reflect the fundamental technical principle at play within these technologies. Although both Aerohive and Ruckus employ the same general concept, their implementations do have some fundamental differences, which are primarily related to the way in which the PSK is distributed to end users as well as the extent of control provided to the administrator for creating or manipulating each PSK.

Encryption

When any WPA or WPA2 (Personal or Enterprise) solution is to be used, the encryption strength is an important consideration. Modern 802.11 encryption methods provide assurance of data privacy, integrity, and data authentication. Since we've already established that WEP is deprecated and not recommended, we'll focus only on TKIP and CCMP in this section.

 You will commonly see abbreviations for RC4-TKIP and AES-CCMP. When speaking of Wi-Fi data encryption, TKIP and CCMP are the only encryption methods that are used with WPA-based operation. AES is also used synonymously with CCMP because it is the base cipher that CCMP was built on.

As for Wi-Fi Alliance certifications and encryption, WPA (Personal and Enterprise) supports TKIP and TKIP only. WPA2 requires support for CCMP, but it also includes a provision for simultaneous support of TKIP. Some proprietary implementations allow for the use of CCMP with WPA, but this is nonstandard and, technically speaking, does not differ from using WPA2 with CCMP. In the following sections, we'll elaborate on these security mechanisms and discuss recommendations for their use.

TKIP

Since WPA was introduced as a temporary solution to replace WEP, even from its inception, TKIP was known to have limitations that could be exploited. As an update to WEP, TKIP was designed with certain constraints in mind, such as the use of the same RC4 encryption algorithm that is used with WEP. In other words, TKIP was never meant to be a long-term solution—it was intended to serve as a patch for the leaking dam of WEP.

As of this writing, TKIP has stood up fairly well to the scrutiny of security researchers, and no severe exploits are currently publicized. However, since TKIP was designed to operate within a limited computing budget (for backward compatibility with legacy hardware), TKIP's message integrity check (MIC) function (a.k.a. Michael) has only 20 bits of effective security and is subject to vulnerability. For that reason, TKIP was also introduced with "countermeasures." When two MIC failures are detected within 60 seconds of one another, TKIP-enabled STAs cease receiving frames for 60 seconds. As a denial-of-service attack, TKIP countermeasures are somewhat difficult to produce, and other easier attacks are more likely.

In the latter half of 2009, much was made of new attacks to exploit the MIC integrity function of TKIP. None of the attacks have exposed TKIP encryption keys or encrypted data, but these attacks are indicators that the timeline for TKIP as a recommended solution is coming to a close. In fact, both the IEEE and Wi-Fi Alliance are in the beginning stages of designating TKIP as a legacy encryption mechanism. In the future (beginning with changes in January 2011), the Wi-Fi Alliance will stop certifying clients and APs that support TKIP at all. In the meantime, TKIP is still an acceptable encryption solution, but CCMP is superior by far.

Encountering MIC Countermeasures on Your WLAN

Some Wi-Fi products have been discovered to have a MIC calculation error in their algorithm for certain kinds of transmissions. While firmware upgrades are available for these products to correct the flaw, you might encounter them in the daily operation of your WLAN. If you happen to see an error message indicating a MIC error, you should first look at the MAC address of the device that transmitted that frame and look at the release notes for that client radio device.

Due to this fact, several infrastructure equipment vendors have allowed the ability to disable MIC countermeasures.

CCMP

Back in 2004, the IEEE completed the task of replacing WEP with TKIP as well as specifying a robust, long-term encryption solution that would stand up to security scrutiny for many years to come. AES-CCMP was introduced with the 802.11i amendment as the long-term solution, and thus far, it has lived up to its billing.

Counter Mode with Cipher Block Chaining Message Authentication Code Protocol (CCMP) is quite a mouthful, which is why we use the CCMP acronym. CCMP is a block cipher protocol that is paired with the AES encryption method specified by the National Institute of Standards & Technology (NIST) in 2001. The IEEE specified that for 802.11 WLAN encryption, CCMP shall only be used with AES with a 128-bit key and a 128-bit block size. This security implementation is very secure and is thought by security researchers to remain secure for many years to come.

The Wi-Fi organizations that are primarily responsible for forward momentum of the technology are all beginning to take a stronger stance in support of AES-CCMP and against TKIP. Specifically, all modern Wi-Fi equipment that is Wi-Fi Alliance certified must support AES-CCMP. Further, the IEEE specified (in 802.11n-2009) that in order to use 802.11n MCS rates for communication in an RSN, AES-CCMP encryption is required. These are pretty strong messages coming from the Wi-Fi Alliance and IEEE. The point is becoming clear that all modern networks desiring robust privacy, integrity, and data authentication should use AES-CCMP.

The IEEE's implementation of AES-CCMP has few, very minor published security weaknesses. Of course, selection of a security method is always a trade-off between convenience, cost, industry availability, performance impact, and actual security. For that reason, AES-CCMP may not always be an option, especially with legacy hardware. As we've already touched on many times in this chapter, one of the biggest hurdles with the adoption of robust encryption is the additional processing requirements. Many legacy devices can be software-upgraded to support TKIP, but the additional processing overhead of AES-CCMP without hardware acceleration is too much of a performance impact. For new devices, support for AES-CCMP is assumed, so hardware provisions accommodate this processing requirement without a noticeable difference in cost or performance.

To drive home the point, let's be clear in stating that in all possible cases, AES-CCMP is the recommended encryption solution for Wi-Fi. If you are using TKIP with 802.11n in an RSN, MCS rates are not allowed, and you will not be able to gain any speed advantages over the legacy protocols; CCMP is required for 802.11n MCS rates in this situation. It is the best solution for Wi-Fi encryption for the foreseeable future.

Supporting Multiple Ciphers

In some cases, it may be advantageous to support multiple encryption algorithms within an ESS to accommodate devices with different capabilities. It is important to understand that when multiple ciphers are used within the same ESS, only unicast data traffic is encrypted with each client's negotiated encryption mechanism.

If you have a CCMP-capable device, it will use CCMP to encrypt unicast traffic if it is supported in the BSS. Similarly, a TKIP-capable device will use TKIP to encrypt unicast traffic. However, encrypted group (broadcast or multicast) traffic is encrypted using the weakest encryption mechanism that is supported in the BSS. In other words, if both CCMP and TKIP are supported, group traffic will be encrypted with TKIP. Therefore, it is important to consider the potential impact of supporting multiple ciphers.

Summary

In this chapter, we looked at several critical components related to the deployment of a network security solution. As we look at these different elements of a holistic security posture, it becomes clear that there are many layers to proper security planning. It is important to consider authentication (proof of identity), confidentiality (encryption), integrity (protection from tampering), accounting (usage tracking), availability (protection from service disruption), and nonrepudiation (auditable proof of activity or inactivity) as a part of security planning.

We looked at legacy security mechanisms that are not generally recommended for use. We also investigated security solutions that may be relevant in the enterprise as well as the SOHO market. Finally, we discussed encryption selection, which is relevant for networks of all types. In the next chapter, we will look at many more advanced topics that are specific to enterprise WLAN security.

Exam Essentials

Identify weak security solutions and protocols.   Recognize weak security protocols and deployment models and be able to recommend acceptable alternatives.

Recommend appropriate data encryption solutions and explain design concepts related to their use.   Understand the strengths, weaknesses, and design best practices for WLAN encryption protocols, including WEP, TKIP, CCMP, and proprietary solutions.

Review Questions

1. You are tasked with selection and configuration of a security credential for your organization's WPA/WPA2-Personal WLAN. By what methods can the WPA/WPA2-Personal client credentials be configured on client devices and APs?

   A. As a 256-bit ASCII passphrase

   B. As a 64 hexadecimal character PSK

   C. As an ASCII passphrase at least six characters long

   D. As a 256-bit PMK

2. In the enterprise, when is WPA/WPA2-Personal generally a recommended solution? (Choose all that apply.)

   A. When client devices do not support 802.1X/EAP

   B. When mobile device applications require high-latency roaming times between APs

   C. When client devices are provisioned in bulk and would otherwise share 802.1X credentials

   D. When the network security policy demands that each user have unique access credentials

3. What are some common problems with short (12 or fewer characters) ASCII passphrases in WPA/WPA2-Personal networks?

   A. They are more susceptible to dictionary attacks than longer passphrases.

   B. They lead to weak group keys in a BSS.

   C. They only produce a 64-bit PMK instead of a 256-bit PMK.

   D. Very few AP and client vendors support entry of an ASCII-based passphrase.

4. What term refers to the security practice of obfuscating actual data from unintended receivers as the data crosses the transmission medium?

   A. Authentication

   B. Confidentiality

   C. Integrity

   D. Accounting

   E. Nonrepudiation

5. What security function falls under the classification of *availability*?

   A. Protection from data tampering

   B. Usage tracking and monitoring

   C. Protection from service disruption

   D. Proof of an entity's identity

   E. Determining a user's permission

6. The 802.11 connectivity paradigm includes three basic procedures that are part of a wireless connection. In the order in which they occur for an initial 802.11 connection, what are those three basic procedures?

    A. Active Discovery, Passive Discovery, Association

    B. Discovery, Association, Authentication

    C. Authentication, Authorization, Association

    D. Discovery, Authentication, Association

    E. Identification, Authorization, and Association

7. When a client successfully associates to an AP, the AP assigns the client with a unique parameter so that the client can identify when it has frames buffered at the AP during power save operations. What is this unique client-specific parameter called?

    A. Attribute Value Pair

    B. BSSID

    C. PPSK

    D. Association ID

    E. Identity MIC

8. Which of the following security solutions provides the most robust protection against network attacks?

    A. WEP

    B. Shared key authentication

    C. MAC filtering

    D. SSID hiding

    E. WPA-Personal

9. What two authentication types were specified in the original 802.11 specification? (Choose all that apply.)

    A. 802.1X/EAP

    B. WPA/WPA2-Personal

    C. Open authentication

    D. WEP authentication

    E. Shared key authentication

10. What is the best encryption method specified for use with 802.11 Wi-Fi networks?

    A. WEP

    B. TKIP

    C. RC4

    D. RC5

    E. CCMP

11. What security-related certification programs are offered by the Wi-Fi Alliance for an AP or client device certificate? (Choose all that apply.)

   A. WMM

   B. WPS

   C. EAP types

   D. WPA-Personal

   E. WPA2-Enterprise

12. SSID hiding is not generally recommended because some frames require inclusion of the SSID. In what frames is the SSID always included?

   A. Beacon

   B. Association request

   C. Probe response

   D. Probe request

   E. Authentication response

13. For what reasons is "security by obscurity" not generally recommended? (Choose all that apply.)

   A. Even if the signal strength at the edge of a building is fairly low, attackers could use high-gain antennas to pick up a weak signal from a significant distance.

   B. Many network applications have stringent RF requirements for proper functionality. By planning power settings, antenna selection, and AP locations for the purpose of "obscurity," some applications may not work properly in parts of the building.

   C. Obscuring the network via RF propagation control is both practically difficult and cost prohibitive. Other security solutions are generally more effective and less expensive.

   D. This deployment practice is only achievable with a few select vendors with unique antenna technologies. While this solution is acceptable for those vendors, it does not work well with other vendors.

14. Why is EAP-MD5 not used as an acceptable EAP type? (Choose all that apply.)

   A. It does not support mutual authentication.

   B. It does not export dynamic keys.

   C. Its authentication exchange is subject to dictionary attacks.

   D. It does not support secure encryption protocols.

   E. It requires use of the weak RC5 encryption algorithm.

15. What are some of the limitations that exist with WPA/WPA2-Personal? (Choose all that apply.)

   A. Secure passphrases or PSKs can be difficult to remember.

   B. Network-wide passphrase/PSK change management procedures can be cumbersome.

   C. Encryption ciphers are less robust than with WPA/WPA2-Enterprise.

   D. User-specific policies are more difficult to apply when shared access credentials are used.

16. What EAP types are certified by the Wi-Fi Alliance? (Choose all that apply.)

   A. EAP-PSK

   B. EAP-MD5

   C. EAP-TLS

   D. EAP-FAST

   E. PEAPv2

17. Due to budget limitations, the network manager has decided that some WEP-only devices will not be replaced this year. For that reason, you have to deploy a BSS that supports WEP. What are some practical security-related fail-safes that should be implemented for the WEP BSS? (Choose all that apply.)

   A. Apply ACLs to the traffic on this BSS so that it is limited to the necessary network services only.

   B. Segment this BSS with VLANs so that it is logically separated from important network resources.

   C. If available, layer the wireless security solution with MAC filters and other pseudo-security methods.

   D. Implement a 512 kbps rate limit policy for users of this BSS to mitigate the speed in which a network attack can be conducted.

18. What are the two types of WLAN discovery/scanning?

   A. Manual

   B. Automatic

   C. Passive

   D. Active

   E. Probe

   F. Hidden

19. What encryption method is required when shared key authentication is implemented?

   A. None

   B. Static WEP

   C. Dynamic WEP

   D. TKIP

   E. AES

   F. CCMP

20. What advantages are provided by per-user PSKs when compared with ESS-wide PSKs? (Choose all that apply.)

A. Per-user PSKs allow easier user-based access control with WPA/WPA2-Personal security.

B. Per-user PSKs are easier to manage if a PSK is compromised or an employee leaves a company.

C. Per-user PSKs are standardized and certified by the Wi-Fi Alliance.

D. Per-user PSKs are more secure than ESS-wide PSKs because they support mutual authentication.

Answers to Review Questions

1. B. WPA/WPA2-Personal supports authentication credentials in the form of passphrases or PSKs. A passphrase must be 8–63 ASCII characters long, and the passphrase must undergo a conversion process before it becomes a PSK. This process is called passphrase-to-PSK mapping. Alternatively, you can select a PSK directly by using a string of 64 hexadecimal characters.

2. A, C. WPA/WPA2-Personal can be an effective security selection for the enterprise in the right situations. Some client devices do not support 802.1X at all, which leaves WPA/WPA2-Personal as the next best solution. Also, due to the relatively short authentication and key derivation process for WPA/WPA2-Personal, this solution provides fast roaming times between APs. This is good for applications that are sensitive to high latency. In addition, some clients are configured and deployed in bulk and would share 802.1X/EAP authentication credentials. For these devices, 802.1X may be more work than it is worth.

3. A. When a security policy allows ASCII passphrases instead of 64-bit hexadecimal PSKs, the ASCII should be sufficiently long to prevent dictionary attacks. Most experts agree that 20-character ASCII passphrases are sufficiently strong to prevent dictionary attacks.

4. B. Confidentiality is also known as encryption, privacy, ciphering, obfuscation, or cryptography. This is the practice of changing the plain-text data so that it is not perceptible to unintended receivers. This is an especially important aspect of security for wireless networks since the wireless medium is unbounded and accessible to all.

5. C. Availability is the practice of maintaining the functionality of network service. While availability is a design goal that permeates many areas of network design, the security aspect of availability is related to the task of preventing (or at least detecting) denial-of-service attacks and other security-related issues that could cause service outages.

6. D. Prior to a client device's attempt to join a network, the client must "discover" the network. Discovery is the first stage in the 802.11 connectivity process. The 802.11 protocol specifies an association state machine that has three states: unauthenticated, unassociated; authenticated, unassociated; and authenticated, associated. So, 802.11 authentication occurs after discovery; then association occurs after authentication.

7. D. When a client associates to an AP, the AP assigns the client a unique identifier known as an association ID (AID). During the power save operation, the AID is used by the client station to determine if the AP has frames buffered for it. If so, that client's AID will be set to 1 in beacon frames.

8. E. There are many cases where legacy security mechanisms are the only option for WLAN security. Of the options listed, WPA-Personal is still an acceptable security solution for many applications for the near future, but it is on its way to becoming a deprecated solution. WEP, shared key authentication, MAC filtering, and SSID hiding are all weak security solutions that are highly vulnerable to exploitation by attackers.

9. C, E. In the original 802.11 specification, 802.11 authentication (a.k.a. open authentication) and shared key authentication were defined. This is prior to 802.11i, which introduced the use of passphrase/PSK-based authentication as well as 802.1X/EAP authentication. WEP is an encryption method and is not an authentication method.

10. E. AES-CCMP is currently the strongest encryption suite specified for use with 802.11 WLANs. The IEEE specifies that CCMP be used with AES using a 128-bit block size and 128-bit keys. This solution is thought to be secure for many years to come.

11. B, C, D, E. The Wi-Fi Alliance certifies APs and client devices in several areas of Wi-Fi security. WPS is a SOHO solution designed to make security setup easier for most consumers. Additionally, the Wi-Fi Alliance maintains certification programs for both WPA and WPA2 in Personal and Enterprise modes. Finally, they also certify seven different specific EAP types.

12. B. The association request frame always carries the actual SSID. Some vendor implementations allow administrators to remove the SSID from beacons and probe response frames, but this is not an effective security tactic for hiding the network.

13. A, B, C. Security by obscurity refers to the practice of attempting to hide a wireless network by means of RF control. In most cases, the cost and effort required to achieve actual RF obscurity outweighs the actual benefits achieved. Network designers are better off selecting robust security protocols.

14. A, B, C, D. EAP-MD5 was not designed for use in enterprise WLANs and has several flaws. In reality, EAP-MD5 was designed for wired networks and to test basic connectivity between 802.1X participants. It should never be used for wireless networks.

15. A, B, D. Due to its simplicity and intended design, WPA/WPA2-Personal security poses some drawbacks for use in the enterprise. First, secure passphrases must be sufficiently long to prevent dictionary attacks, but then they become difficult to remember. Also, since the passphrase or PSK is generally shared among all users in a BSS, change management can be a problem when the passphrase is compromised.

16. C, D. The Wi-Fi Alliance certifies APs and client devices for seven different EAP types, including EAP-TLS and EAP-FAST. In addition, they certify PEAPv0/MSCHAPv2, EAP-TTLS/MSCHAPv2, PEAPv1/EAP-GTC, EAP-SIM, and EAP-AKA. The latter two are used primarily in cellular networks.

17. A, B, C. Some legacy security mechanisms, like WEP, are still used in many network environments due to budget or hardware limitations. In those situations, WEP is better than nothing and should be deployed along with other layered solutions. WEP-protected networks should be deployed with access only to the network services required for that application, such as a voice server (when used with WEP VoWiFi phones). Rate limiting would not likely prevent or mitigate an effective network attack.

18. C, D. Both active and passive scanning are specified by the 802.11 specification for discovery of service sets. With passive scanning, stations listen for AP beacons, which are transmitted at regular intervals by the AP. With active scanning, stations send broadcast probe requests and receive directed probe responses from the AP.

19. B. Shared key authentication was specified in the original 802.11 specification, but it is now deprecated. Shared key authentication requires static WEP encryption, and makes WEP's flaws more pronounced and more readily exploitable. For that reason, it should never be used.

20. A, B. Per-user PSKs (PPSK) are a unique feature offered by a few WLAN vendors. PPSK solutions have many advantages over classic ESS-wide, shared PSKs. Namely, PPSKs provide more secure user-based access control, and they are more friendly to management staff when keys must be reconfigured or changed. There are other benefits provided by PPSKs as well.

Chapter

12

Advanced Enterprise WLAN Security Design

THE FOLLOWING CWDP EXAM TOPICS ARE COVERED IN THIS CHAPTER:

- ✓ Recommend appropriate authentication solutions and explain design concepts related to their use.

- ✓ Illustrate common deployment and design strategies for AAA, especially RADIUS.

- ✓ Consider the following network services and protocols as they relate to wireless interaction with the wired network:

    - RADIUS

    - Directory Services (LDAP)

    - Certificate Authority (CA)

- ✓ Understand design strategies for integration of client authentication with directory services.

- ✓ Identify the role and limitations of client capabilities in security planning.

- ✓ Describe the methods of designing a secure network with segmentation and filtering.

- ✓ Explain best practice security design concepts for guest and public access Wi-Fi networks.

- ✓ Describe and implement common VPN uses with WLANs.

- ✓ Describe deployment and design strategies for Wireless Intrusion Prevention Systems (WIPS).

✓ Identify and explain factors that motivate AP and WIPS sensor placement.

✓ Demonstrate the importance of, and design considerations related to, Fast BSS Transition (Fast/Secure Roaming).

As with the SOHO market, Wi-Fi networks are becoming increasingly important to enterprise companies. Home users have experienced the benefits of wireless and mobility, and they now bring the same expectations for productivity to work. The benefits of Wi-Fi are easy to see, but enterprise deployments also have stringent network performance, ease of use, and security demands. These competing requirements make the network designer's job, as it relates to security design, more difficult.

In an exploration of security technologies and best practices for security design, this chapter will demonstrate that WLANs can be very secure if proper design techniques are followed.

In this chapter, we will take a look at the best security strategies for WLANs in the enterprise along with some common challenges. We will discuss the best ways to implement security to maintain network integrity and privacy, to control access, and to protect all of the valuable resources that are contained within a network, while maintaining the required level of application performance and network service.

All of these steps require some strategic planning as well as an intimate knowledge of the network user population, client and infrastructure devices, existing security resources (such as user databases and *public key infrastructure [PKI]*), client applications, and many more factors.

If you have previous experience with the breadth of topics within WLAN security, you're probably wondering how we will address enterprise security design in a single chapter. Our answer to that question is that, in some instances, we will defer to more exhaustive resources, such as the *Certified Wireless Security Professional Official Study Guide: Exam PW0-204* (Sybex, 2010), on some topics. However, we will attempt to address the most important security *design* strategies from head to toe. With that challenge ahead, let's get going.

WPA-Enterprise and WPA2-Enterprise

As we discussed in Chapter 11, "Basic LAN Security Design," the Wi-Fi Alliance introduced WPA and WPA2 for different reasons. WPA includes support for TKIP encryption for backward compatibility with legacy devices, whereas WPA2 includes support for both CCMP and TKIP for future-proof and backward-compatible encryption. There are a few significant differences between WPA/WPA2-Personal and WPA/WPA2-Enterprise—the most important difference is the method and strength of authentication. We will focus on that here.

As we discussed in the previous chapter, WPA/WPA2-Personal employs passphrase or PSK authentication in an attempt to maintain simplicity. In some instances—such as for devices with limited authentication support or for those requiring fast secure roaming—WPA/WPA2-Personal may be useful in the enterprise, but where possible, WPA/WPA2-Enterprise is preferred because of its superior security.

WPA-Enterprise and *WPA2-Enterprise* employ the *802.1X port-based access control* authentication standard along with the Extensible Authentication Protocol (EAP).

802.1X-2004

The 802.1X-2004 standard defines a framework for authentication in which access to network resources is managed via controlled and uncontrolled authentication ports (port-based access control). During a client authentication, the *802.1X/EAP* exchange is permitted on the uncontrolled port of the authenticator (i.e., the AP or WLAN controller). When a successful authentication completes, the controlled port is unblocked, providing client access to network resources. A conceptual rendering of port-based access control within the authenticator is shown in Figure 12.1.

FIGURE 12.1 802.1X port-based access control

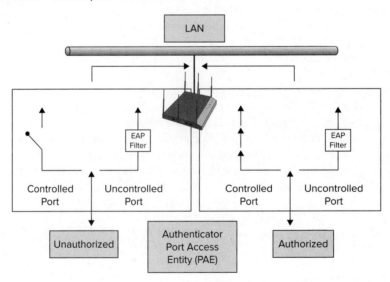

802.1X-2004 also defines *supplicant, authenticator,* and *authentication server (AS)* roles for the devices participating in an 802.1X authentication exchange. These roles and devices are shown along with the generic 802.1X/EAP framework in Figure 12.2.

FIGURE 12.2   802.1X EAP framework

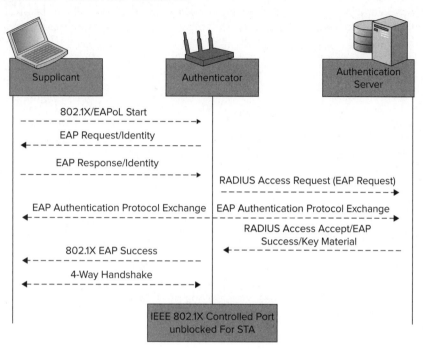

WPA/WPA2-Enterprise security introduces the requirement of an authentication server (as prescribed by 802.1X-2004), which is usually a RADIUS server. The authentication server (AS) must also query a user database of some type for user authentication. These AS and user database requirements are not present in WPA/WPA2-Personal networks, which is why WPA/WPA2-Enterprise is significantly more complex than WPA/WPA2-Personal. Integration, availability, and configuration of the AS and user database plays a large part in this complexity.

Extensible Authentication Protocol

The *Extensible Authentication Protocol (EAP)* is a generic authentication framework defined by IETF (RFC 3748) that provides flexibility for different implementations that serve specific needs. Specific EAP types—such as PEAP or EAP-TLS—are based on the EAP framework and have been created by various organizations (infrastructure, client, and supplicant vendors, neutral industry organizations, etc.) to meet market demands. The generic EAP framework is shown in Figure 12.2. We will discuss the most common EAP types later in this chapter with a focus on their strengths, weaknesses, and ideal use cases.

As we mentioned, 802.1X introduced several roles that are important for enterprise authentication. The supplicant and authenticator are the entities within the endpoints of the

Wi-Fi connection—that is, the client device and the Wi-Fi infrastructure, respectively. Since 802.1X/EAP authentication relies on an additional component called the authentication server, we must look at the backend infrastructure entities that facilitate this function.

AAA

To perform the role of the AS, an *Authentication, Authorization, and Accounting (AAA) server* is typically used. AAA is defined by the IETF in a number of different RFCs (see the sidebar "More Information about AAA"). These three services are essential for user-based access control in the enterprise.

More Information about AAA

For more information about the AAA protocol, in addition to the CWSP study guide, check the Wikipedia entry at http://en.wikipedia.org/wiki/AAA_protocol. While this Wikipedia entry is fairly short, it does include a helpful set of links to IETF RFCs relevant to AAA. These documents detail the guts of the AAA protocol.

Here's a description of each of the three components of AAA:

Authentication   *Authentication* is the process by which a user's or device's identity is verified against a trusted, reliable database. In other words, authentication validates that you are who you say you are. The process of validating an identity usually comes in the form of comparing user-provided access credentials, such as username/password combinations, digital certificates, one-time passwords (OTP), smart cards, and/or biometrics, with the same credential stored in the database.

Authorization   The next step in the AAA process is *authorization*. After a user or entity is positively identified (authentication), they are allocated or restricted from network resources in accordance with the privileges of their role, as defined by a user or group policy. In other words, the user's role is associated with permissions, and these permissions dictate how a user's connection is handled within the network. This application of a policy often comes in the form of specific ACLs, firewall rules, bandwidth restrictions, VLANs, as well as other permissions like time of day, length of connectivity, and physical location restrictions. Policies can be as simple or complex as necessary, but the assignment of these policies is a function of authorization.

Accounting   The third function for an AAA server is *accounting*. Once resources have properly been authorized and a user has performed actions while connected to a network, it is important to track and log those actions so that an accounting trail is available. General accounting functions include monitoring and logging of events, behavior analysis, and reporting of network threats/events. AAA server accounting reports the who, what, when, and where of network use, and may be used to generate alarms or notifications. Accounting records aren't very detailed, but they at least give enough information for an investigation to be performed based on specific time events and other useful information.

The basic function of an AAA server is that of an access controller. *AAA clients* (e.g., Ethernet switches, APs or WLAN controllers, guest access controllers, or VPN servers) provide services to end users on a network. However, most AAA clients do not maintain local user databases with lists of permissions and access rules. Therefore, AAA clients often defer authorization of end user devices to an AAA server, which acts as a middleman between the AAA client and user database to control authentication and authorization for network services. End user devices request access to network services, the provider of the network service (i.e., the AAA client) proxies the request to the AAA server, and the AAA server validates the client's authentication and authorization status by checking against a user database—or by validating a specified condition, such as username, MAC address, password, VLAN, time of day, etc. Once the AAA client receives a user's permission rules, it can apply the policy to actual data traffic as necessary.

Selection

In most cases, enterprise networks will already have a fully operational and interoperable (with a user database, that is) AAA server in the network. For this reason, wireless design professionals may have little or no control or input regarding the AAA server that is used for Wi-Fi authentication. This is also true of user databases. In most cases, services for the Wi-Fi network are added onto existing infrastructure solutions. This may limit the scope of the wireless professional's selection tasks to that of integration with existing infrastructure and does not typically require selection or configuration of these platforms. That being said, it is not against best practices to use a different AAA server for wireless authentication. Since it may be a different server anyway, using a different server product is possible.

Every small-medium business (SMB) and enterprise network has a user database, and most databases are compatible with the *Lightweight Directory Access Protocol (LDAP)* retrieval protocol. In fact, some enterprises have more than one user database, which will add complexity to the design. However, not all networks use LDAP, so it is important to know what is and what isn't supported by the user database. The AAA server must use a protocol that is capable of exchanging authentication, authorization, and accounting information with the existing user database(s). Generally speaking, the AAA server's role is as a middleman between the WLAN authenticator and the user database. This functionality is provided by means of a common protocol between the authenticator and AAA server (usually RADIUS) as well as the AAA server and user database (often Microsoft Windows Active Directory or LDAP). The AAA server takes requests from the authenticator and queries the user database for information. For most networks, this exchange is not just about validating a username and password, but may also include the assignment of user or group privileges based on attributes held in the user database. Figure 12.3 illustrates how an AAA server will have to proxy authentication requests to many different databases, including a PKI infrastructure, which we will talk about later in this chapter.

FIGURE 12.3   Authentication server proxy

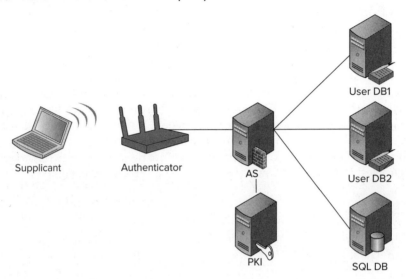

Beyond integration and compatibility with existing infrastructure components, one of the most important features for an AAA server may be support for information attributes, which are parameters that may be used as a method of assigning network privileges to users or devices. For example, RADIUS supports something called RADIUS attributes or *attribute-value pairs (AVPs)*, which can be used for many purposes, including client assignment of user groups, VLANs, IP addresses, throughput limitations, as well as many other functions. If this type of granular control is desired, RADIUS is usually the best AAA server implementation because it is well supported by WLAN infrastructure vendors and is a flexible protocol. We'll discuss RADIUS more in the next section.

However, not all network configurations will provide this type of granular user authorization from the AAA server. More to the point, some enterprises assign network permissions by providing multiple SSIDs at each AP and configuring each SSID with the relevant privileges for that group of users. This allows for the network service level to be defined within a WLAN profile—sets of parameters that apply to the service set. When users are authenticated to a specific WLAN profile, they are automatically subject to the restrictions or privileges of that service set. The AAA server's role is simply to ensure that they are permitted to be a part of that service set.

Using SSIDs as a method of differentiating user groups is an inefficient use of the wireless medium, thus posing scalability problems when multiple different levels of service are desired. Unless specific 802.11 operational parameters, such as authentication or encryption methods, need to be different for each client device set, we highly recommend that you merge services to fewer SSIDs and assign client device authorization using the authentication identity of the supplicant.

Of course, the method of applying user-specific privileges depends on many factors. Some WLAN vendor equipment does not have robust support for return attributes from the AAA server, so policies are assigned by the WLAN profile within the WLAN infrastructure. Most enterprise vendors support the full gamut of AAA server authorization parameters as well as many proprietary ones, which allows for more flexibility in the assignment of user permissions as well as better integration with an array of preexisting user databases and group policies. In most enterprise deployments, the WLAN profile provides the primary policy and performance set for users, while the AAA server provides additional user-specific authorization criteria.

Another important selection criterion for AAA servers and user databases is support of EAP, and more important, the specific EAP type that will be used for authentication. As we will discuss later in this chapter, some EAP methods have received more widespread acceptance than others. If a specific EAP type is required, ensure that your AAA server supports it and that the user database can return the required credential to the AAA server.

It is possible to replace an external AAA server altogether by enabling the authenticator to query the user database directly. For example, an AP or WLAN controller can authenticate directly to Windows Active Directory's LDAP implementation. Some vendors are beginning to build Windows Active Directory support into their WLAN infrastructure products. Because of Active Directory's popularity and the fact that it is built on a framework that can include a great deal of information about users and devices, the equivalent of AVPs can be achieved through this method. For smaller and simpler WLAN designs, this might be a valuable option to explore if your equipment vendor supports it. The primary problem with using a direct LDAP query model is that it may limit the EAP type support and communication protocols used for authentication; for that reason, few enterprises currently use this model.

RADIUS is by far the most common and best supported AAA server in use today, and most of this book is based on RADIUS as the AAA server. Before we do that, let's clear up some basic terminology.

Authentication Roles and Terminology Within 802.1X terminology, the wireless client station is called the supplicant, the AP or WLAN controller is referred to as the authenticator, and the RADIUS server is called the authentication server (AS). A bit confusingly, with RADIUS terminology, the AP or WLAN controller may be called the network access server (NAS) or even the RADIUS client. The wireless client station is called the user. To add just a tad more complication, with generic AAA terminology the AP or WLAN controller is the AAA client. Table 12.1 shows this terminology in a more organized fashion.

TABLE 12.1   802.1X, RADIUS, and AAA terms

Technology Reference	Client Device	AP or WLAN Controller	Backend Authentication Server
802.1X	Supplicant	Authenticator	Authentication server
RADIUS	User	Network access server (NAS) or RADIUS client	RADIUS server
AAA	User	AAA client	AAA server

RADIUS

Most EAP types used with WLANs rely on *RADIUS* to perform the AAA functions of the AS. The 802.11 and 802.1X standards don't require this, but in practice, RADIUS is the method of choice.

RADIUS is an application-layer protocol that provides User Datagram Protocol (UDP)-based client/server AAA services across an IP network. RADIUS servers come in many different form factors, and are commonly deployed as a service running on a server cluster, as a dedicated RADIUS appliance, or even as a service within an 802.11 access point or WLAN controller.

There are also many different ways to implement RADIUS within a network architecture, including:

- Local RADIUS with internal user database(s)
- Local RADIUS proxying to external user database(s)
- Distributed RADIUS with internal user database(s)
- Distributed RADIUS proxying to external database(s)
- RADIUS proxying to other RADIUS servers
- RADIUS integrated into the WLAN infrastructure

The most common method in the enterprise is to provide local RADIUS services that proxy to a local user database. However, distributed RADIUS with an internal or external user database is also common for some networks that span many campuses and remote offices. Distributed RADIUS architectures will help lighten the processing demands on a single, centralized RADIUS server and will increase availability.

Deciding on a RADIUS Architecture

The location of the RADIUS server(s) within the network architecture can have a massive impact on network performance, especially when there is significant latency and many network hops between the RADIUS server and WLAN infrastructure devices. This delay will also be increased if even more latency is added between the RADIUS server and the user database(s).

Each time a client station authenticates (during initial association or reassociation) to the WLAN, it will have to communicate many authentication messages (depending on EAP type and roaming enhancements) to the RADIUS server. If the RADIUS server is separated from the local LAN over a WAN link, you will often see severe latency and performance degradation for roaming users for some applications. Applications such as video and voice over Wi-Fi are the most notable, but any real-time application will suffer the same results. Further, since RADIUS is a critical component in allowing new users onto the network, remote RADIUS can be a major problem if the WAN link is prone to outages, or if the link is commonly saturated with traffic. Similar drawbacks exist if the RADIUS server—even a local one—is querying a remote user database for client authentication.

Providing Redundant RADIUS Servers

Regardless of the way in which RADIUS is deployed, providing redundant RADIUS servers is a strongly recommended practice to protect against a single point of failure. Redundancy is often accomplished via replication strategies. One RADIUS server may be designated as the primary server, and the primary RADIUS server's configuration may be replicated to other RADIUS servers to maintain consistency of configuration. If the primary RADIUS server fails, the same configuration is present on all of the slave or secondary RADIUS servers, providing the same authentication experience as the primary server.

Similarly, in the interest of providing maximum network uptime, RADIUS failover configurations within the WLAN infrastructure should also be provided. For example, if your primary RADIUS server is in your local office, what happens if that RADIUS server fails? Or, if your primary RADIUS server is across a WAN link, what happens when the WLAN can't reach that RADIUS server? In highly available designs, a failover RADIUS server will be designated in the WLAN configuration so that a single RADIUS failure or even a WAN link failure will not cripple network access. Most WLAN vendors provide an option for at least a primary, secondary, and tertiary RADIUS server.

Understanding Attributes

One of the major strengths of RADIUS is that it has been very widely accepted and implemented. This allows for pervasive and extensive support of RADIUS attributes, also known as AVPs. RADIUS attributes are parameters within RADIUS frames that contain specific data elements for communication between the authenticator and RADIUS server. Each specified attribute has a specific function, and there are more than 100 attributes.

For example, the RADIUS EAP-Message attribute carries the EAP-specific data from the authenticator to the AS, and vice versa. So, this attribute would be used to carry EAP-Success or EAP-Failure messages. Many of the attributes are used for normal RADIUS services, such as the User-Name attribute, the User-Password attribute, and the NAS-IP-Address (authenticator's IP address) attribute. These three refer to the client username, the client password, and the authenticator's IP address, respectively. However, RADIUS attributes can also be used for other purposes, such as dynamic VLAN assignment, QoS settings, bandwidth constraints, or WLAN group assignment.

Due to its widespread use and applicability to many different network services, RADIUS also supports something known as *vendor-specific attributes (VSAs)*. As you might guess, these are vendor-proprietary attributes that serve a special function to the vendor that defines it. An example of a VSA used for a particular equipment vendor's product might be to enable or disable a proprietary feature based on individual user/machine authentications.

Configuring RADIUS

There are some basic configuration processes with RADIUS that we would like to mention. Each version of RADIUS will differ in features and configuration options, but there are many similarities across platforms. Generally speaking, RADIUS must be configured with RADIUS clients (AAA clients), user databases, and specific EAP and RADIUS authentication parameters.

Configurations of RADIUS servers for each AAA client are generally fairly minimal. The AAA client (AP or WLAN controller) must be added to a list on the RADIUS server. Configuration of each AAA client includes the IP address, *RADIUS shared secret*, authentication protocol, communication ports (usually UDP 1812/1813 or 1645/1646), and a handful of other parameters. In some instances where multiple AAA clients are being added—as with clusters of WLAN controllers, or when large populations of APs are the AAA clients—entire subnets may be added to the RADIUS configuration profile to ease the management overhead of manually entering tens or hundreds of IP addresses. The RADIUS shared secret is used for authentication of the AAA client to the RADIUS server. It is also used in some RADIUS frames as an input to a hash function to convert elements of the RADIUS message into a hashed message digest.

In addition to configuring AAA clients, RADIUS must also be configured with a user database. When a local/native RADIUS user database is implemented, users and groups can be created and configured with very detailed access policies that are assigned to users as a part of the authorization process. When external databases are used, configuration varies in accordance with the type of database in use and the retrieval protocol. As an example, when LDAP compatible databases are used, the RADIUS configuration includes the LDAP hostname, port number, protocol version, security parameters, directory-specific details, server timeout values, and many more parameters. Figure 12.4 shows Cisco's ACS RADIUS configuration menu for querying an external LDAP database.

FIGURE 12.4   Sample Cisco ACS LDAP configuration

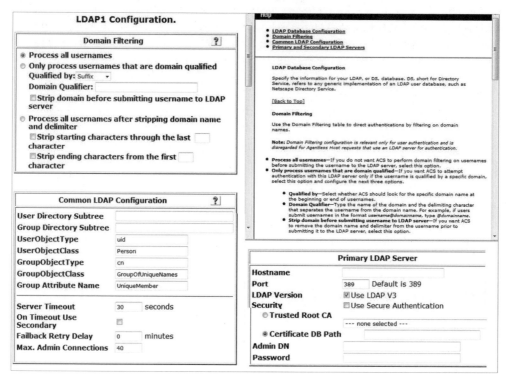

In addition to more traditional centralized user databases such as Windows AD or Novell eDirectory, RADIUS may also proxy authentication requests as a client to other types of user databases, such as token servers. We will discuss token authentication in a later section, "Authentication Form Factors," where we look at specific EAP types. In brief, token servers are user databases that are synchronized with the RADIUS server. The token server maintains a continually incrementing token value (e.g., it may increment every 60 seconds) that stays synchronized with the hardware token possessed by a user. In order for the client to be authenticated to the network, it must demonstrate possession of the hardware token by referencing the current value that is displayed on the hardware token, which should match the value calculated in the token server. This type of authentication adds a layer of security in the form of a hardware token (something the user must possess).

Finally, there are many other parameters that are configured on the RADIUS server. These include RADIUS authentication protocols (PAP, CHAP, etc.) for AAA client authentication, management of certificates, administration management, activity logging and accounting, replication, enabling of specific EAP types and configuration of relevant parameters, and much more.

There are many popular versions of RADIUS on the market today, including Microsoft's Internet Authentication Service (IAS) and Network Access Protection (NAP), Cisco's ACS, Juniper's Steel-Belted RADIUS, FreeRADIUS, Open System Consultants' Radiator, and Periodik Labs' Elektron, to name a few. In addition, APs and WLAN controllers often have limited-feature RADIUS servers built into them.

Server Selection

In the section discussing AAA servers, we mentioned that you should consider the EAP type desired for use when selecting a AAA server. To take that point a little further here, you will find that some RADIUS servers are highly limited in their EAP support. Some organizations may want to deploy multiple EAP types; sometimes even multiple EAP types on the same SSID. Perhaps those different EAP types require separate user databases or authentication backends. You will find that, unfortunately, not all RADIUS servers allow this type of implementation. Some RADIUS servers are more flexible than others, whereas some RADIUS servers are easier to use than others. You should define your WLAN security needs before selecting a RADIUS server when at all possible.

User Databases

We've already discussed a few of the topics related to user databases in WLANs. In many cases, WLAN designers won't have any influence in the selection or configuration of a user database, but this doesn't mean that user databases are an irrelevant topic.

Predominantly, RADIUS servers will proxy to existing centralized user databases. In some smaller businesses, user databases are not centralized and remain local to the server providing services. For example, a network access storage (NAS) server may have an internal database with groups and users. Similarly, FTP or VPN servers may have their own user databases that are used to control access to FTP and VPN services. As you might imagine, in this type of network with distributed user databases for each service, wireless network access will rely on a dedicated user database within the WLAN infrastructure itself or possibly within the RADIUS server.

Local RADIUS or WLAN databases are scalable to a certain limit within small and medium businesses, but at some point, centralizing the user database for network privileges in enterprise networks makes far more sense. The point at which these native databases become problematic is not really clear-cut. It will vary for each network, and will depend on the types of services provided on the network, the capabilities of the native RADIUS or WLAN infrastructure database, and the management burdens that come from multiple disparate user databases.

All of the most popular RADIUS on the market include local user databases. RADIUS servers that are designed for the enterprise include configuration options to apply authorization parameters to the user. Basic user authorization parameters include IP address assignment, ACLs, group assignment, and more. Of course, most configurations also employ group policy settings that might include IP address pools, ACLs, RADIUS return attributes, time of day restrictions, and more.

Similarly, enterprise-class WLAN infrastructure vendors have also incorporated native user databases into their products as a standard feature. In some cases, user-based management within the WLAN infrastructure provides a robust enough feature set that there may not be much need to depend on a centralized user database for WLAN authorization in smaller environments. The caveat is that most of these integrated RADIUS offerings are limited in options and what EAP types are supported. However, if a simple authentication is all that is desired, then it may suffice for some.

Some WLAN infrastructure products with built-in firewalls and granular user policy engines provide additional filtering and access restriction capabilities. In this model, you may authenticate users against a centralized user database, and configure a RADIUS return attribute to assign a WLAN user to these groups defined within the WLAN infrastructure configuration. In other words, you configure the WLAN infrastructure with the authorization parameters for a user and/or group. When many of the performance- and security-related parameters are already defined by an SSID, this may be a nice option for some design scenarios.

Extensible Authentication Protocol

The Extensible Authentication Protocol (EAP) is used with all WPA/WPA2-Enterprise deployments. EAP is the authentication protocol used between the supplicant and authenticator, and is defined in RFC 3748. EAP is also encapsulated in RADIUS messages between the authenticator and RADIUS server.

As of this writing, the Wi-Fi Alliance certifies devices for support of up to seven EAP types:

- PEAPv0/EAP-MSCHAPv2
- PEAPv1/EAP-GTC
- EAP-TTLS/MSCHAPv2
- EAP-TLS
- EAP-FAST
- EAP-SIM
- EAP-AKA

Of these, there are several popular EAP types available, each with their own strengths and weaknesses. Some are very secure at the expense of high management overhead or high cost, whereas others are easy and cost effective to implement but may not provide the preferred level of protection or the desired authentication form factor. These and other trade-offs must be factored into the selection and configuration of a specific EAP type.

In fact, one of the primary advantages of EAP is choice. By definition, it is extensible, so designers have a wide range of options to meet their deployment needs. If broad client support is important, there's an EAP type for that. If simple client configuration is important, there's an EAP type for that. If utmost security is important, there's an EAP type for that.

Thankfully, some EAP types provide a suitable balance between these variables, which makes their use much more prolific. Before selecting a specific EAP type, let's discuss a few more considerations that are relevant to this decision.

Choosing an EAP Type

As just discussed, there are various EAP types and your needs will determine which one is best for you. Here's a list of the main topics to consider:

Determining Authentication Strength   Authentication strength is probably a priority for most companies. Some EAP types are stronger than others, but with only a few exceptions—*EAP-MD5* and EAP-LEAP—most EAP types are sufficiently strong to be unequivocally recommended for the enterprise—perhaps excepting government-level security. Mutual authentication is an important piece to the security puzzle, and nearly all of the modern EAP types support it.

Understanding Tunneling   Another important factor related to authentication strength is that of tunneling. With most secure EAP methods, a *Transport Layer Security (TLS)* tunnel is created using the server's X.509 certificate. This is much like a web-based e-commerce transaction where your web browser uses the web server's SSL certificate to send your credit card securely in an encrypted tunnel. For EAP, within the TLS tunnel, the client's authentication credentials are passed across the wireless medium and then across the wired network within this secure tunnel to the authentication server. This is a strong way to protect client credentials from exploitation. In fact, this is the very reason that relatively weak client authentication protocols—such as MSCHAPv2—can be securely used. EAP-TLS does not require tunneling because both client and server certificates are used for authentication. Since certificates are inherently resilient to compromise, there's no need to build a TLS tunnel, though there is an option for it.

In the original EAP specification, there is a requirement for the client's username to be passed at the beginning of the EAP exchange. Legacy EAP types, such as LEAP, send the client's actual username in clear text at the beginning of the authentication exchange. This information exposure is a major contributor to LEAP's weaknesses. For tunneled EAP types, there is a provision for the client to provide a bogus username in this initial "outer identity." Then, inside the TLS tunnel, the real username is transferred. For that reason, the most secure EAP types—with the exception of EAP-TLS—require tunneling.

Considering Ease of Use and Management Overhead   Ease of use and management overhead are two additional considerations when choosing an EAP type that are also very important for most companies. These two qualities are often dependent on the method for client authentication that is specified by an EAP type. For example, simple username/password pairs are fairly easy to implement and control. On the other hand, client-side certificates and client smart cards, while secure, often add a significant amount of complexity to the deployment.

Evaluating Cost   Cost is another important factor. As in the previous discussion about simplicity, usernames and passwords are easy to implement and don't require additional infrastructure, so they're inexpensive. However, client smart cards and *one-time password (OTP)* tokens require additional infrastructure components, such as card readers, token servers, and the like. This adds cost in the form of hardware, service contracts, electrical power, and additional possibly staff resources. Some models require client-side certificates, which may require the purchase of client-side certificates for each client device. Even if a private PKI is used, it also comes at a significant cost.

Accommodating Your Current Infrastructure   Another important consideration is that of existing infrastructure. What is required to implement a specific EAP type? If a PKI is required, is one already in place? If not, that may eliminate it from contention. What about requiring smart cards or security tokens? Are these infrastructure components already in place for other network technologies? If so, adding Wi-Fi authentication will be much easier. If not, perhaps other solutions with lower cost, lower management overhead, and quicker deployment cycles would be a better fit.

Similarly, your existing RADIUS server may not support all flavors of EAP. Some RADIUS servers are very limited in this realm, so you should evaluate the existing services before deciding on an EAP type—or multiple EAP types—that may ultimately require new servers.

Determining Client Support   Finally, everything else aside, one of the largest considerations for EAP selection is client support. Some EAP types are proprietary and are limited to a small subset of client devices. Other EAP types have not been widely embraced by the industry; thus the EAP types are not supported in many client supplicants. Some client devices support only a few EAP types.

Thankfully, many of the most useful EAP types have received widespread support—or maybe they're useful because they've received widespread support—and are available across a broad range of client supplicants and operating systems. In any case, this requirement is very important. Designers must understand the EAP types that are supported by the client devices within the network. PEAP is one of the most popular EAP types for this reason. It is almost ubiquitously supported.

Interestingly enough, EAP selection has very little to do with the WLAN infrastructure in use. In essence, EAP is passed from the supplicant to the authentication server through the authenticator, so the WLAN infrastructure is typically an irrelevant variable in the selection of a specific EAP implementation—that is, unless the WLAN infrastructure is not the RADIUS server as mentioned earlier. For the sake of this discussion, we are considering the traditional design of 802.1X authentication.

Frankly put, there is no perfect EAP solution that fits every scenario. However, there are popular, secure, cost-effective, and relatively easy-to-implement EAP methods. With a focus on the previous list of design considerations, we will explore specific EAP types in the following sections. For reference, Table 12.2 provides an organized overview of the most common EAP types and their features.

TABLE 12.2   EAP Types and Features

	EAP-MD5	EAP-LEAP	EAP-TLS	EAP-TTLS (MSCHAPv2)	PEAPv0 (EAP-MSCHAPv2)	PEAPv0 (EAP-TLS)	PEAPv1 (EAP-GTC)	EAP-FAST
Defined	RFC-3748	Cisco	RFC-5216	RFC-5281	IETF Draft	IETF Draft	IETF Draft	Cisco
Digital Certificate (Client)	No	No	Yes	No	No	Yes	No	No
Digital Certificate (Server)	No	No	Yes	Yes	Yes	Yes	Yes	No
Client Password	No	Yes	N/A	Yes	Yes	No	Yes	Yes
PACs (Client)	No	No	No	No	No	No	No	Yes
PACs (Server)	No	No	No	No	No	No	No	Yes
Credential Security	Weak	Weak (Depends on password strength)	Strong	Strong	Strong	Strong	Strong	Strong (If Phase 0 is secure)
Encryption Key Management	No	Yes	Yes	Yes	Yes	Yes	Yes	Yes
Mutual Authentication	No	Yes	Yes	Yes	Yes	Yes	Yes	Yes
Tunneled Authentication	No	No	Yes (optional)	Yes	Yes	Yes	Yes	Yes
User identity exposed	Yes	Yes	Yes	No	No	No	No	No

EAP-LEAP

EAP-LEAP is a popular, proprietary EAP type that was created by Cisco and is used primarily in Cisco implementations. Because of LEAP's previous market success, it was licensed by several other vendors. Due to Cisco's market influence, many customers deployed LEAP in the early stages of their autonomous WLAN deployments. For that reason, LEAP is still fairly common in the enterprise. However, a well-known vulnerability exists for LEAP whereby attackers can recover the client username and hashed password of LEAP supplicants using brute-force dictionary attacks—made popular with a tool called ASLEAP. For that reason, LEAP has been deprecated by Cisco and is no longer recommended for use. It has also been deprecated by the Wi-Fi Alliance.

LEAP performs no validation of the authentication server. The supplicant provides the client-side username/password in a modified version of the MS-CHAPv2 protocol to authenticate the client. Other EAP types use similar credentials in a secure way.

Because of LEAP's vulnerability, it is recommended that users of LEAP migrate to a more secure solution as soon as possible.

Protected EAP

The most popular EAP type in use today is a version of *Protected EAP (PEAP)*. PEAP is often referred to as "EAP-in-EAP" because it prescribes the creation of a TLS tunnel— which is made possible by requiring server-side X.509 certificates—and then uses variant EAP types (such as EAP-MSCHAPv2, EAP-TLS, and EAP-GTC) to authenticate the client within the tunnel. These two steps are often referred to as phases:

Phase 1   This includes the client authenticating the server (by validating its certificate) and the construction of the TLS tunnel.

Phase 2   This is the EAP-in-EAP client authentication within the TLS tunnel. Phase 2 is different for each version of PEAP.

There are two primary types of PEAP, referred to as PEAPv0 and PEAPv1. Unlike most protocol versions within the information technology security industry, these version numbers have no bearing on their relevancy or security merits.

PEAPv0

There are two common subtypes of PEAPv0. *PEAPv0/EAP-MSCHAPv2* is the most widely implemented EAP type in use today. *PEAPv0/EAP-TLS* is a very strong EAP type but has not received widespread use. In fact, you will find it rare to encounter in the real world. This is largely due to the fact that it requires client-side TLS certificates and is not widely supported by RADIUS servers.

PEAPv0/EAP-MSCHAPv2

PEAPv0/EAP-MSCHAPv2 uses an MS-CHAPv2 challenge/response within the TLS tunnel, providing client authentication via a username and password pair. As with all versions of PEAP, the server is authenticated with an X.509 certificate, assuming the client is configured to do so. Validating the reliability of the server's certificate is an optional step and at the full discretion of the supplicant.

PEAPv0/EAP-MSCHAPv2 has been very well adopted within the industry, and is supported by almost every client device and operating system on the market. Similarly, all RADIUS servers support it. It is easy to configure because the client only requires a username/password pair, and it is highly secure. As with any EAP implementation requiring a server-side certificate, the biggest challenge is configuration and generation of the server certificate as well as distribution and installation of the server certificate on the client device. We will discuss certificates in a later section, but in the meantime, it is important to know that X.509 certificates are very secure and are pretty much a way of life within 802.1X/EAP.

Due to all of these factors, PEAPv0/EAP-MSCHAPv2 is a highly recommended and very popular EAP type. Because of its advantages and relative lack of weaknesses, it is the go-to EAP method in most deployments. The only way PEAP lacks strength is how it is implemented. Poor password policy is one method and the supplicant failing to validate the authentication server's certificate is the other.

PEAPv0/EAP-TLS

PEAPv0/EAP-TLS has not seen anywhere near the same widespread use as PEAPv0/EAP-MSCHAPv2. This is largely due to the use of EAP-TLS for client authentication. Furthermore, it offers little benefit to what EAP-TLS already offers by itself, though it does hide the client ID in the TLS tunnel. As you already know, the server requires a certificate with PEAP; however, with PEAPv0/EAP-TLS, client authentication is also performed with a client-side certificate. This means that every client device using the network must have its very own certificate. For that reason, this EAP type requires a PKI for certificate creation, management, distribution, and storage. Otherwise, a very large budget would be necessary to purchase client certificates from a third-party PKI vendor. That aside, distribution and installation of these certificates on client devices is a burden in itself. In other words, complexity and overhead increase significantly.

Despite the management drawback of PEAPv0/EAP-TLS, this EAP type is very secure. In fact, along with EAP-TLS (non PEAP), PEAPv0/EAP-TLS is thought to be the most secure EAP type in common use. However, EAP-TLS (non-PEAP) has many of the same advantages and drawbacks as PEAPv0/EAP-TLS, which is why PEAPv0/EAP-TLS has not been widely used in the marketplace. EAP-TLS is already well supported, but PEAPv0/EAP-TLS is only sparsely supported. Thus, companies tend to adopt EAP-TLS before PEAPv0/EAP-TLS.

To avoid confusion, we should also point out that EAP-TLS in PEAP has recently been submitted as PEAPv2. So, you may see that nomenclature instead of PEAPv0/EAP-TLS.

PEAPv1/EAP-GTC

PEAPv1/EAP-GTC follows the same basic constraints of PEAPv0 mentioned previously, but uses an inner-EAP type following the *Generic Token Card (GTC)* method prescribed in the original EAP RFC (RFC 3748). In this mode, again PEAP uses a server-side certificate to establish the tunnel. Within the tunnel, the authentication server sends an authentication message to the client and the client responds with virtually any generic token that may be a username and password. It also may generate a response based on a hardware token. In this case, the user manually enters the information shown on the hardware token. With EAP-GTC, the authentication server acts as a client to a backend token server that maintains synchronization with the end user's token hardware.

PEAPv1 had a divisive beginning, as Cisco was attempting to slow the use of PEAPv0 (created in part by Microsoft) in favor of its own method. PEAPv1 has received pretty widespread use in the marketplace, largely since it actualizes the advantages of multifactor authentication, but *multifactor authentication* is possible via other EAP methods as well. Specifically, users must both know something (a pin) and possess something (a hardware token) in order to be authenticated. One of the drawbacks of this method is that it does require additional infrastructure and end user hardware as well as additional configuration and maintenance.

EAP-TTLS

EAP-TTLS (Tunneled Transport Layer Security) represents another secure tunneled EAP type that is fairly common. EAP-TTLS shares many qualities with PEAPv0/EAP-MSCHAPv2, but has not been adopted quite as widely. However, it has gained some popularity and is supported by all major third-party supplicants.

One of the unique characteristics of EAP-TTLS is that it supports many inner authentication protocols. Some of these include legacy authentication modes. Inner authentication options include PAP, CHAP, TLS, MS-CHAP, and MS-CHAPv2, within the TLS tunnel. For that reason, you will often see EAP-TTLS notated as EAP-TTLS/MSCHAPv2, which is the most common implementation, and is the only EAP-TTLS method certified by the Wi-Fi Alliance.

Similar to PEAP, EAP-TTLS uses a server-side certificate for server authentication and TLS tunnel creation. It also uses simple username/password pairs for client authentication. EAP-TTLS is relatively easy to configure, cost effective, and highly secure. Assuming all clients within the network support it, EAP-TTLS is a good option and is a recommended EAP choice.

EAP-TLS

Sharing many of the strengths and weaknesses already mentioned with PEAPv0/EAP-TLS, *EAP-TLS* is a very secure EAP type that is well supported by infrastructure and client manufacturers. Due to the added complexity of a PKI, many companies opt not to use EAP-TLS, instead favoring more user-friendly methods.

Despite this, many companies and government organizations desiring maximum security will use EAP-TLS. As we've seen in the previous set of EAP types, tunneling is pretty common. However, EAP-TLS supports both non-tunneled and tunneled modes. Most implementations opt for non-tunneled mode because tunneling is simply unnecessary. Since the client uses a certificate just like the server, there's no need to transport it within a TLS tunnel. The only value tunneled mode provides for the client certificate is obfuscation of the clear-text owner of the client in the client certificate response. That being said, PKI is already inherently secure, based on the fundamental principles of certificate trust and asymmetric cryptology (we will discuss these later).

To add an element of security, parts of the US government use *Common Access Cards (CAC)*, which are a specific type of smart card. Essentially, the CAC card contains user-specific data and an embedded client certificate, which is read by a card reader and can be used for client authentication. As with EAP-GTC, this method add an authentication form factors, providing more dimensions to the security process. It requires the user to know something and possess something. A sample CAC card is shown in Figure 12.5.

FIGURE 12.5 Common Access Card (smart card)

When a PKI is already in place or high security is a primary concern, EAP-TLS is a good choice. For most enterprises, the additional security is unwarranted, given the additional management overhead and cost.

EAP-FAST

EAP-FAST represents another Cisco-proprietary EAP type. EAP-FAST was marketed and positioned as the successor to LEAP. It was released around the same time that the LEAP vulnerabilities were made public, providing a recommended transition for existing LEAP users. Instead of using certificates for tunneling, EAP-FAST uses something called *protected access credentials (PACs)*. We could extend this section by looking at the many details of a PAC card, but we'll defer that topic to other texts, such as the CWSP study guide.

For this text, it is important to know that a PAC shares elements of both digital certificates and shared secrets. The PAC must be generated and installed on the server side and then each client must also receive an individual PAC, which adds a bit of management overhead. Depending on the method for provisioning PACs to clients, security vulnerabilities may be present. Specifically, EAP-FAST supports either automatic or manual PAC provisioning. The automatic method is much easier from an administrative perspective, but it introduces the possibility, though minimal, of attacks. This is because automatic PAC provisioning can be anonymous (meaning the provisioning agent is not authenticated or otherwise validated), which enables exploitation of clients while they are "open" to automatic PAC provisioning.

An EAP-FAST client can also be vulnerable to man-in-the-middle attacks unless it is configured to speak only to a specific authentication server. For example, an EAP-FAST client that is configured for anonymous PAC provisioning may erroneously trust an attacker's device, provision a PAC, and subsequently use that PAC to transmit its credentials to the attacker.

EAP-FAST is gaining in popularity, though it is not extremely common. Assuming manual PAC provisioning is used, EAP-FAST is highly secure, but, in the management overhead realm, it starts to look a bit like EAP-TLS at that point and therefore exhibits the same drawbacks. EAP-FAST may be less recommended than other EAP types, but can be quite easy to deploy.

Failed Authentication when PAC Provisioning

When a supplicant gets provisioned an initial PAC file, it will appear to have failed authentication to the network. In fact, client and RADIUS server logs might even indicate as such. However, the supplicant will usually install the new PAC and then use it to properly authenticate briefly thereafter. It is important to remember this fact if you plan on deploying EAP-FAST with automatic PAC provisioning.

Other EAP Types

Of the seven EAP types, we've already discussed five. As Wi-Fi and cellular technologies continue to converge, we are beginning to see broader use of EAP types that are used in the cellular space. EAP-SIM and EAP-AKA represent these options. Though they are not currently deployed as primary Wi-Fi EAP types, EAP-AKA will likely begin to see more use along with better fixed mobile convergence (FMC) adoption.

Authentication Form Factors

As you may have noticed in our previous discussions, there are several different authentication form factors to choose from. From username/password pairs and X.509 certificates to OTP tokens and PACs, there are many different choices with varying strengths and weaknesses. In some networks, multiple form factors may be layered to provide additional security. This is often known as multifactor authentication. Authentication factors are often broken down into three components:

- Something you are
- Something you know
- Something you have

Most Wi-Fi networks are not currently using biometrics (something you are) for authentication, but this is certainly a potential option. Similarly, some authentication methods require users to log into a computer, then enter a pin number to launch network authentication (something you know). Following that, the user may be prompted for a smart card (something you have). This type of layering, as usual, adds overhead and complexity, but it also adds security. In the next section we will focus on machine authentication.

Machine Authentication

Machine authentication is a way of authenticating the *device* through which a user will connect to the network. It is used for two primary use cases.

First, machine authentication facilitates an active network connection for devices that require a user login before the user desktop environment is loaded, such as the case with Windows-based computers. A machine authentication will provide a network connection to validate the username and password entered at the operating system login prompt, behaving much like the machine is wired to an Ethernet network. More to the point, many networks provide services to computers by virtue of domain connectivity via the network. With Wi-Fi connectivity, these services are very difficult to provide without the use of machine authentication. These services include remote desktop access, software upgrades, roaming user profiles, noncached user profiles, OS patches, or the like. Upgrades, patches, and other remote administration tasks can be accomplished by authenticating a machine to the network even when a user is not directly authenticated to the WLAN.

The other use case is related to ensuring people only use the network from enterprise assets. In other words, a user authentication might be forbidden unless a machine authentication has been performed first. For user-driven network use, user-specific authentication (what we've been describing thus far in this chapter) usually follows machine authentication but is not necessary.

There are a handful of design considerations that are relevant to machine authentication, but the first requirement is that your client supplicant support it. Furthermore, it is only relevant for computers that require login to a centralized user database prior to allowing users to access the desktop environment. For more information on machine authentication, see the CWSP study guide.

PKI and Certificates

In the previous section, we looked at authentication form factors for the 802.1X/EAP supplicant. We also noted that the most popular EAP types employ X.509 certificates for secure server authentication and TLS tunnel creation. In addition, EAP-TLS, PEAPv0/EAP-TLS, and a mode of EAP-TTLS use client-side certificates. For secure environments, certificate selection, management, assignment, and installation is important; we will look at this topic in greater detail in this section.

Public Key Infrastructure

With most of the popular EAP types, the EAP protocol requires a trusted X.509 digital certificate to be assigned to the authentication server. Digital certificates can come from many places, and the source of a digital certificate will often impact the cost, the distribution method (getting it to the proper device), the management overhead, as well as the certificate installation method. Digital certificates may be purchased from a trusted, third-party *certificate authority (CA)*, such as VeriSign, Thawte, or Entrust, or they may be issued by an organization's internal CA.

Digital certificates (X.509) are a component of a PKI. In a PKI, digital documents are created and securely assigned to an owner. Using highly sophisticated hashing algorithms, digital signatures are created that are extremely difficult to duplicate or change without detection. This digital document is then prescribed as authentic by the issuing agent (i.e., the CA). Inherent in the reliability of a PKI system is trust in the CA. In other words, we will be taking the word of the CA that a certain digital certificate is valid, was securely distributed, and is possessed only by the proper device; it is critical that we be able to trust the reputation of the CA.

All modern computer operating systems have the ability to use PKI, which was made quite popular to allow safe e-commerce transactions. They do this by providing a preinstalled list of CAs called the *certificate trust list (CTL)*. A CTL is queried by Secure Sockets Layer (SSL) or Transport Layer Security (TLS) protocols during security transactions. The CTL contains a listing of all trusted root certificates known to that PC. The entries on the CTL point to validations (root digital certificates) for the globally trusted CAs. When a digital certificate is received as part of an authentication exchange (such as with the 802.1X/EAP authentication), the SSL/TLS protocol consults the CTL to verify that the issuer of the current certificate is trusted by the CTL. In the case of e-commerce with a web browser, if the issuer of the certificate is not listed on the CTL, then the security protocol will issue a warning to the end user stating that this is an invalid certificate and that it should not be trusted.

For our purposes with WLAN authentication, a nontrusted certificate will cause an 802.1X/EAP authentication to fail. If the certificate is trusted, the client station may reliably use the public key that was provided to it, and this key will facilitate encryption. We will discuss the technical mechanics of this process in a following section.

X.509 Certificates

In most cases, it is easier to implement a PKI by using publicly trusted, third-party CAs because their trustworthiness has been established and confirmed by virtue of being listed on the CTL. For e-commerce and other secure HTTPS login requirements, this is the only recommended method for establishing PKI. But, when using a PKI to perform 802.1X/EAP authentication for a private group of users that are known by the organization, it may not be necessary to purchase the needed digital certificates from a *third-party CA*. If an organization has a need to create and manage their own digital certificates, they can set up their own certificate-issuing agency by running a private CA application.

CA applications may be included as part of a server operating system, purchased separately as a stand-alone third-party application, integrated with AAA services, or downloaded for free as an open source offering. The certificates created by a private CA are called *self-signed certificates*, and are perfectly serviceable in every way, for many types of private use. Since you will be the issuer and user of the certificates, you should know whether or not you can trust yourself. In this case, not using a third-part PKI can be considered more secure.

The problem comes when you try to use the certificate. Since your private CA will not be recognized by end user devices because it does not yet have the self-signed certificate in its CTL, your self-signed user certificates will fail the trust test. To address this you will need to distribute this self-signed certificate and install it onto the CTL on every device that will require trust of that certificate. Once that has been done, your self-signed user or AS certificates will perform exactly like the ones purchased from globally trusted CAs.

Selection

Now that we've provided some technical background regarding the use of X.509 certificates, let's look some of the selection criteria for self-signed versus third-party certificates.

Ease of Use   First on the list of selection criteria is ease of use. Maintaining self-signed certificates and an internal PKI requires a lot of effort, time, and cost. Many enterprises don't have a specific need for an internal CA; thus it is much easier to purchase third-party CAs. Internal PKIs can be complex and resource intensive to manage. When a PKI is already in place within an organization, its adoption for use with WLAN authentication may be a bit easier. However, if one is not already in place, most companies will opt for third-party CAs if only server-side certificates are required. The other side benefit of third-party CAs is that once a certificate is purchased, the issuer of the certificate or the root authority of the issuer is already in each client's CTL. This usually eliminates the need for adding the certificate to each client as would be required with a self-signed method.

EAP Security Requirements   Part of the ease-of-use requirement must be weighed against security requirements. As we discussed in the prior EAP section, some EAP types use server-side certificates and client-side certificates. If your organization has many thousands of client devices requiring certificates, it becomes unrealistic to use third-party certificates because there are so many certificates to manage and the cost of purchasing third-party certificates will become exorbitant. In this case, an internal CA and PKI would be recommended. However, enterprises requiring this added security often already have a PKI in place, so the only challenge is adopting the technology for WLAN clients.

Cost and Quantity   If a PKI is not in place but is desirable for the WLAN, it can be an expensive proposition. In addition to the cost of infrastructure equipment required to perform the functions, companies must also hire or train staff resources to manage it. Granted, thousands of third-party certificates can become extremely expensive as well, so the cost/benefit analysis must weigh the number of devices requiring certificates. Generally, for fewer certificates, third-party CAs are more appropriate.

Client Installation and Configuration   Finally, installation of certificates and client trust configurations are important considerations. For enterprises with managed end user stations, it can be a chore to update certificate trust lists for self-signed certificates (server-side certificates) on each client device. Of course, there are several ways to automate this process so that a domain-wide Group Policy configuration update also updates certificate trust lists. Alternatively, some security companies offer specialized software designed to provide an installation file that configures client devices appropriately. However, this step requires extra time and resources. With third-party CAs, client operating systems receive certificate trust updates via regular OS updates. Assuming that organization's operating systems are already up-to-date or regularly do OS updates, this is a slightly easier way to manage trust lists. In some environments, such as universities, this may be the preferred way to manage certificate trust since the IT staff does not manage end user devices.

There are many variables in this process, but the important thing is that when designing the network, the client population is considered as a part of certificate administration.

Public and Private Key Cryptography

We've already discussed certificate signing, but let's take a step back to see why this is important. Certificate signing is the process where a CA binds a public key to an organization (DNS name, email address, etc.). This binding process relates to the public key, which is part of a public/private key set. When the public key is signed, the certificate is created, then distributed. This is an important process because the two keys are used for *asymmetric key encryption* during the PKI session. Most of the confidentiality types we have discussed to this point (WEP, TKIP, and CCMP) use a form of computer security known as symmetric key encryption, which uses the same digital key for encryption and decryption. Management and distribution of symmetric keying material (e.g. PSKs) is left to the IT staff. With asymmetric key encryption, which is shown in Figure 12.6, one key is used for encryption and a different key is used for decryption.

FIGURE 12.6   Asymmetric encryption principles

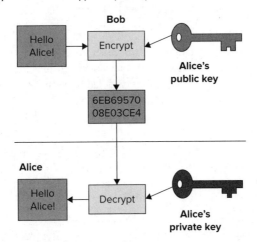

If using an EAP type that uses digital certificates at the AS, the AS will transfer its digital certificate, containing its public key, to the supplicant through the authenticator. This step occurs over an unsecured wireless connection. Since this link is unencrypted, it is quite possible that an unauthorized intruder may intercept the plain-text transmission and recover both the digital certificate and the public key. That's OK. In fact, that's how the entire PKI system works.

The supplicant, after validating the server's digital certificate, will then encode all subsequent responses to the authenticator using the server certificate's public key to perform the encryption. The encrypted data is then transmitted back to the AS. This is referred to as tunneling.

Since the public key was used to encrypt the supplicant's traffic, only the *private key* can be used to decrypt those messages. Public keys can't be used to decode messages encrypted with public keys—only the private key. If the intruder tries to intercept and decrypt the encrypted transmissions from the supplicant to the authenticator, the intruder will fail. Therefore, it is safe to send the public key out over an unprotected network since it can only be used to encrypt messages intended for viewing by the holder of the private key. Likewise, the digital certificate verifies the identity of the sender and is meant to be publicly transferred, so it is of little use to an intruder. However, it is important that the private key be safe and secret.

Asymmetric key encryption is a safe and well-supported security platform, but because the computations used during these procedures are somewhat intensive, with standardized WLAN security, asymmetric keys are only used temporarily to establish a symmetric key. Once the entities have been authenticated and keying material has been exchanged, the asymmetric key encryption techniques are suspended in favor of faster, less processor intensive symmetric key cryptography.

For WLANs, the 4-way handshake takes the keying material that was exported from the 802.1X/EAP authentication and creates *symmetric encryption* keys on both the authenticator and the supplicant used for data communications with CCMP/AES and TKIP/RC4.

Segmentation and Filtering

Most of the security methods we've talked about thus far have focused on WLAN-specific security. However, it is important to consider that Wi-Fi traffic is just a part of an entire network ecosystem. Certain rules must apply to WLAN traffic, and for this reason, enterprise networks segment and filter WLAN traffic according to its use within the network. Both segmentation and filtering are interrelated, and the goals are generally the same. That is, by applying specific policies and access privileges to WLAN users and devices, you can limit vulnerabilities from the wireless medium, wireless users, and traffic originating from the wireless network. The reverse of that is also true in order to protect wireless devices from network traffic.

The following sections will address specific types of and best practices for segmentation and filtering.

VLANs

Virtual LANs (VLANs) are a popular wired network segmentation method that allows a single hardware network domain (e.g., a switch or a switch port) to be divided into multiple broadcast domains. More simply, VLANs create Layer 2 segments that operate independently from each other. This allows network administrators to keep broadcast traffic on one network segment from interfering with another. Traffic from different VLANs can flow across the same network medium, but it will be handled differently based on the VLAN to which it belongs. There are many technical documents on the Web discussing VLANs. Aside from this brief introduction, we are assuming that our readers already possess a modest technical understanding of VLANs. Otherwise, this information is sufficient preparation for the CWDP exam.

In wired networking, VLANs serve many purposes, such as:

- Minimizing the size of broadcast domains
- Creating segmented network boundaries for security
- Maximizing the flexibility of existing hardware
- Differentiating the services provided to users via a shared medium

Wireless VLANs are used for many of the same purposes, and simply extend the VLANs from the wired network into the wireless medium. However, we should point out some VLAN principles that are unique to the wireless network:

Managing Broadcast Domains   One of the primary differences between wired and wireless networks is related to broadcast and collision domains. While traffic from different VLANs can traverse the same network medium on the wire, the same holds true for the wireless medium. The major difference is that in the wired domain the switch is able to selectively forward broadcast traffic to endpoints based on the VLAN assignment of each switch port. In the wireless domain, the AP can do something similar by only forwarding broadcast traffic from applicable BSSIDs, but it is important to differentiate that wireless users share the same collision domain so bandwidth cannot be protected by VLAN segmentation. Also, wireless clients check the BSSID of transmitted broadcast traffic to see if they should process those frames, though this is only effective if there is a one-to-one relationship with BSS and VLAN, which is not always the case.

An important note to consider is that just as multiple VLANs may share a common network medium like a trunk link from one switch to another on the wire, all of the VLANs sharing that link will impact performance of other VLANs. In other words, the medium has a certain, limited capacity and is shared among the VLANs. Broadcast traffic for one VLAN, while destined only for members of that one VLAN (and possibly SSID), will still impact wireless performance equally for all wireless clients.

Maximizing the Usefulness of a Single Infrastructure   The use of VLANs in wireless networking does allow for some helpful capabilities within the wireless domain. For example, VLANs provide a way for the users of the wireless domain to be divided into different virtual domains on the wired network. Since the wireless network is shared and APs can't isolate RF transmissions for a specific VLAN, the AP or WLAN controller acts as the VLAN traffic cop and will translate a VLAN assignment so that a client device's traffic is placed in the appropriate VLAN on the wired network.

In other words, a single wireless radio can advertise and provide services for multiple WLANs simultaneously by monitoring the traffic. As with Ethernet switching equipment, the use of VLANs with WLAN infrastructure devices greatly increases its flexibility and usefulness in the enterprise.

Limiting Services and Creating Layer 3 Boundaries   In the enterprise, each wired network VLAN will provide certain resources, such as Internet access, printers, and databases, in accordance with ACLs and other filtering that may be placed with the network serving those VLANs. With WLANs, segmentation is often provided by mapping VLANs directly to an SSID. When the wireless client successfully associates to that SSID, they inherently become part of the VLAN. For greater flexibility, VLANs can be assigned to users or groups dynamically via RADIUS attributes or WLAN user/group policies.

VLAN Encapsulation

Although there are still examples of earlier, proprietary, VLAN encapsulation protocols in use (e.g., Cisco Inter Switch Link [ISL]), most current VLANs make use of IEEE 802.1Q encapsulation. 802.1Q inserts a 32-bit VLAN tag, of which 12 bits are used as the VLAN ID, on the Ethernet header to map individual VLANs to and from the wired side of the network. The VLAN tag identifies the Ethernet frame's VLAN membership to the switch, which then sorts it onto the correct VLAN. Once a frame arrives at its destination or is directed to a nontrunked port, the VLAN tag is stripped away from the Ethernet header.

Wireless VLANs in Practice

By using 802.1Q tagging, we can construct logical segmentation in our wireless network to provide discriminating services to wireless users (again, this does not segment contention in the wireless domain). In the enterprise, most VLAN rules will already be provided by virtue of an existing Ethernet infrastructure. Many wireless users will already have specific network privileges based on their role in the company. In these cases, the WLAN must make sure that users are provided with correct VLAN assignments and filtered onto the wired network accordingly.

To be clear, VLANs are not normally transmitted as a part of 802.11 frames. Instead, the WLAN infrastructure is responsible for determining the VLAN to which a specific user's data applies and keep them there. Once the WLAN places the wireless traffic onto the wired medium with appropriate VLAN tags, existing wired policies will take care of the rest.

It is quite possible to restrict network access to certain locations by removing support for certain SSIDs/VLANs from certain APs. For example, if a public access SSID/VLAN is offered to guests for simple Internet access, it is fairly easy to remove this SSID from APs outside of the desired service area. Perhaps you only want to serve guests in a lobby or conference areas, but not in areas where you don't expect guests to be. The benefit is that all of this can be done without having to add additional hardware to the network. In some ways, this is more a function of SSID broadcasting, but it is a way of segmenting service.

When designing a network for VLANs, it is important to consider the network architecture and forwarding model as well as whether the Ethernet access layer switch to which an AP is attached is a trunked port or an access port. With these considerations in mind, the following section discusses VLAN design principles for different data forwarding architectures.

Centralized Forwarding

When WLAN controller-based architectures are used with centralized forwarding, the AP may be connected via an Ethernet access or trunked port, and the WLAN controller is always connected via trunked ports.

When an AP processes a data frame destined to the wired network, the actual 802.11 frame is encapsulated inside an IP packet (assuming L3 connectivity between the AP and WLAN controller) and transmitted on the wire to the WLAN controller; thus, the original frame is preserved between the AP and the WLAN controller.

When the WLAN controller receives the packet and views the original 802.11 frame to determine how to process it, the VLAN assignment is made, and the outgoing frame (from the WLAN controller) is tagged appropriately for wired network transport.

This is fairly standard, assuming the WLAN controller is trunked. If the WLAN controller is not trunked, all traffic will be placed on the default VLAN of the access port and all traffic must be assigned to the same VLAN.

Distributed Forwarding

When distributed forwarding is implemented in any WLAN architecture, it is important that the switch ports to which APs are connected are trunked with support for all VLANs necessary for the clients associated to that AP. If the switch port to which the AP is connected isn't trunked, the AP will not be able to deliver traffic to the appropriate destination for multiple VLANs—unless a tunneling protocol is used on a VLAN that is shared by the two APs. Access switch ports will limit the AP to the single default VLAN that is provided by that switch. In other words, distributed forwarding may demand that access layer switches support trunk ports to APs. This is sometimes necessary to support QoS requirements at the edge anyway, but current infrastructure configurations may not support it. This will add some configuration steps, and possibly a re-architecting of the switching infrastructure.

Role-Based Access Control

In enterprise networks, authorization to network resources is typically controlled on a per-user or per-group basis by assigning permissions (security policies composed of access rules) to user or group entities. As we discussed earlier, this functionality is provided by means of user-based 802.1X/EAP authentication (or PPSKs), and typically, RADIUS return attributes. It is fairly common for the WLAN infrastructure to maintain group, or role, permissions and rules. This allows the WLAN infrastructure to receive a group assignment for a user from RADIUS and then apply policies and filters accordingly.

When the WLAN infrastructure has limited support for user or group access policies, filtering is usually provided by a combination of WLAN profile parameters, RADIUS return attributes, VLANs, and authorization applied by the wired infrastructure.

In any case, *role-based access control (RBAC)* follows a basic logical flow:

- You create users with specific parameters.

- Users are assigned to groups that contain certain parameters.

- Security policies (VLANs, ACLs, time restrictions, etc.) are applied to groups.

In this way, users inherit policies by virtue of being a member of a certain group. When maximum granularity is desired, policies can be applied directly to users, though this is often unnecessary and creates significantly more management overhead.

Wireless Firewalls

While the use of VLANs allows us to control the subnet on which the WLAN is accessed, they cannot control the types of traffic that are allowed on the network. To do that, firewall rules are used and are assigned along with other permissions in the 802.1X authorization process. Firewalls filter traffic based on policies composed of rules. Simple firewall rules consist of a few basic elements:

Source   The origin of the traffic determined by an IP address or MAC address

Destination   The delivery point of the traffic determined by an IP address or MAC address

Service   The type of traffic, determined by TCP or UDP protocols and port assignment, or by application-layer protocols or behaviors

Action   Reject, Drop, or Permit

The combination of source, destination, and service determine which action is to be taken. For a secure approach to policy design, any services that do not have a specific reason to be used should be blocked. This can be done easily by following the same element order above (source – destination – service – action): a single "any – any – any – drop" rule located as the final rule in the policy list. This rule means that by default, the firewall will drop all packets from any source to any destination. Since firewalls read and act upon rules in top-to-bottom order, this rule must be placed as the last one in the list. After this default rule has been inserted, you can define additional rules inserted above the "drop all" rule to specifically allow the types of traffic that are to be allowed.

Additionally, some WLAN infrastructure vendors offer application-layer firewalls. These firewalls tend to require significantly more processing cycles, but they also add another element of security for network protection.

Captive Portals

Open authentication is very common with guest networks. However, most WLAN hosts do not want to simply open up their network to any user that may want to use it. The primary way to control access to the wireless network in this case is to provide a *captive web portal* that requires users to first identify themselves with preassigned credentials, by filling out a form or simply accepting a usage agreement before assigning them to a user/group profile and granting them network access. The captive portal acts as a containment area for unregistered users while granting registered users varying levels of network privileges. In this way, anonymous users can be allowed network access on demand without the need for a network administrator to become involved.

Guest access was discussed in Chapter 3, "Designing for Applications," where the concept of a captive web portal was introduced. However, in this case the base technology of a captive portal is leveraged for a larger context, as mentioned earlier.

To configure a captive web portal, a VLAN with limited privileges such as Internet-only access is created and assigned to a unique SSID such as "Guest." As users attempt to join the network, they follow a number of typical steps, as follows:

1. Once a previously unregistered visitor associates with the Guest SSID, using open authentication, the captive portal will allow only basic services, such as DHCP and DNS, to pass. This allows the unknown client to receive an IP address and resolve domain names, but any additional traffic is restricted and redirected.

2. To complete the registration procedure, the end user must open a web browser on the client station. The captive portal intercepts all of the unknown clients' HTTP and HTTPS packets and redirects the client's browser to a visitor registration web page, discarding any additional traffic from that user.

3. Once the user completes the online registration form, the captive portal stores the client station's MAC address and applies an appropriate user profile, then stops redirecting the user's HTTP and HTTPS (as well as all other denied services) traffic. At this time the user will have full access to the privileges of that WLAN.

The registration process can be used to force a user to perform a complete registration, including a requirement of personal identification or financial information. In addition, you may enforce a requirement for end users to accept a network use policy before being allowed on the network. This can be a good choice if it is not known who will be using the WLAN. An appropriately designed acceptable use policy may also limit your liability as the network service provider. For known users, a simpler authentication screening may require only a username and password to gain access through the captive portal. Another option might be to only require acceptance of the network use policy before proceeding to full access privileges.

From a security viewpoint it should be remembered that the gathering of personal or financial information over an unsecured web interface (HTTP) can be vulnerable to eavesdropping by unauthorized intruders. Only a protocol analyzer is needed to capture and view the unprotected user information unless a secure web connection (HTTPS) has been provided.

Similarly, most captive portals by themselves are only for basic authentication. They do not provide encryption and should be used cautiously. In most cases, captive portals are employed for public access networks and hotspots. Vendor implementations are fairly divergent, and your specific use will dictate how to configure the captive portal features, such as user screening and authentication requirements, security roles, firewall rules, bandwidth limits, usage limits, billing information, and activity logging.

Endpoint Security

Thus far, we've looked predominantly at infrastructure-side security. While client feature support is important when planning infrastructure features, there are several client-specific security requirements. These are just as important as infrastructure security. Here's a list of some common client-side security considerations to make before putting your devices on a wireless network:

Personal Firewalls It almost seems silly to mention personal firewalls as a client security mechanism. Most client operating systems have personal firewalls enabled by default, and when they're not enabled, the OS persistently nags you about it. This is a good thing for end users who accidentally turn their firewall off. Firewalls are especially important when users are on unsecured public networks, which are networking environments that represent low-hanging fruit for potential attackers. It's simple really. Unless an application needs permission through the firewall, the personal firewall should block inbound traffic. Firewalls should be updated as new OS patches and updates are made available. Firewalls should always be on.

Antivirus Software Similar to personal firewalls, the need for antivirus software is pretty much ubiquitously understood in today's IT landscape. Except with home users and small offices, most companies maintain security policies for antivirus use and updates. Again, it's simple. Update antivirus software with the latest threat signatures as often as possible. This is especially important when using public access networks where the infrastructure security solution—or lack thereof—provides little protection against probing attackers.

Endpoint Agents If, like most companies, you don't trust your end users to always know and uphold wireless security policies with their computer, *endpoint agents* can be invaluable. The purpose of an endpoint agent is to monitor and manage client network connectivity and ensure that the conditions for WLAN connectivity meet the defined policy requirements. Endpoint agent software is installed on the client device and IT staff configures the wireless connectivity policy that should be maintained.

As an example, imagine that your network policy forbids the end user from connecting to networks that are unencrypted. Or perhaps you want to restrict the device even further by allowing only corporate SSIDs. If the user takes the laptop home, perhaps they have a remote AP that broadcasts the corporate SSID and tunnels the traffic back to the company via a VPN. This is all well and good. But let's say the user violates company policy (due to ignorance or disobedience to a known policy) and goes to the local coffee shop and attempts to check their email there. If configured correctly, the endpoint agent will prevent the client supplicant from connecting. In cases where administrative rights are granted to end users, endpoint agents can add a layer of protection by simply restricting the networks to which users can connect.

VPN Software One of the most common IT challenges for companies with traveling users is enforcing the use of VPNs. Because VPN technology may be confusing and cumbersome for typical end users, there must be a policy that enforces their use. For traveling users, connectivity to a corporate network resource should be done through a secure VPN, such as one created using IPSec tunneling. In deployments requiring maximum security for traveling users at unencrypted networks, VPNs that tunnel to the corporate network and then back out to the Internet may be the only way to provide secure services.

Depending on the assets stored on traveling users' computers and the security staff's tolerance for risk, split tunneling may be used to provide access to corporate resources while preventing unnecessary traffic bottlenecks at the VPN concentrator. Many companies disallow split tunneling because the secondary network can become an attack vector or entry point to gain access down the established tunnel of the client device.

Network Access Control (NAC)   In addition to all of the policies we've discussed so far, *network access control (NAC)* can be a great way to maintain client security posture. In fact, that is its purpose. NAC solutions are designed so that after a client authenticates to the network, the client must be screened to ensure compliance to a minimum set of security or even software patch-level requirements. A NAC server queries and isolates the end user device (facilitated by a client NAC application) to ensure that it is compliant with the company IT policies, which usually includes up-to-date antivirus software, enabled personal firewall, operating system patches, and other similar security checks. If a device connects that is not compliant with the NAC's policy, devices can be quarantined for a short period of time with limited access so they can complete the requisite upgrades or configuration changes to conform to policy. NAC ensures that client devices are consistently maintaining the appropriate security posture. NAC implementations have not really received standardization within the industry, but as a general concept, NAC can be a helpful way of enforcing yet another layer of security for client access.

NAC has traditionally fallen short when it comes to application-specific devices with proprietary or closed operating systems. If a NAC agent cannot run on a host device, it cannot determine these critical factors for network admission. Administrators typically opt to have devices such as these placed on a separate, locked-down VLAN only for these devices. Therefore, if a virus outbreak or other compromising event occurred with these devices, the impact would be minimal.

The challenge is determining which VLAN to place them in if there are multiple device classes. Determination might be required to be based on the MAC address of the client radio (or Ethernet port if NAC is used on wired devices). Some forms of NAC might even base a policy decision on the MAC address of the client and then wait for certain types of network activity in order to make a VLAN assignment decision.

When devices simply do not comply, they are typically placed on a quarantined VLAN where their network communication might be suppressed until the required remediation activity occurs.

OS Permissions Control   One of the best ways to enforce security policy on client devices is via OS user account control. When a company standardizes with specific client devices or client device operating systems, it is fairly common to deploy computers with limited user account permissions. By doing so, you can effectively prevent the end user from making changes that will create security vulnerabilities. This often includes restrictions in the ability to install software. Malicious software that is installed on one computer can quickly make its way throughout a network, especially if it is installed on the computer of a user with high levels of authorization to other machines or file shares.

Some OS permission control can prevent users from changing wireless network supplicant settings. Usually this is only made possible using the built-in wireless utility/supplicant included with the operating system. This feature restricts users from inadvertently disabling security features and also allows administrators to enforce consistency across the entire network.

Virtual Private Networking

The use of *virtual private networking (VPN)* protocols in a wireless network was once a very popular security tactic. This was mostly due to the inadequacies of the legacy 802.11 security methods such as WEP. Today, it is still possible to use VPN applications for WLAN security, but it is not a common practice and is typically not an ideal implementation.

In most modern networks, VPNs may be useful to wireless networking for a handful of reasons, including:

- Remote APs that tunnel to a corporate WLAN controller or other VPN concentrator
- Connectivity of branch offices to corporate datacenters for centralized WLAN management, authentication servers, user databases, or other related services
- AP or other WLAN device connectivity to cloud-based management solutions
- Secure client connectivity to corporate resources across unsecured networks, often provided via public access Wi-Fi hotspots
- Proprietary point-to-point or point-to-multipoint bridging

For any of these uses, a few salient considerations should be made. Of course, the VPN protocol should be evaluated for proper security. Of the commonly used protocols, IPSec is highly secure and is well supported in most environments. SSL-based VPNs have taken over a lot of IPSec's domain and are also a commonly used method for VPN. On the other hand, PPTP is widely supported but is subject to brute-force dictionary attacks.

In addition to security strength, VPNs should be evaluated for performance-related criteria. Some VPNs introduce a fair amount of cryptographic processing overhead, which can decrease throughput and increase latency, both of which may cause a noticeable impact on the application. Further, VPNs should be evaluated for ease of use, support within the industry (especially if clients must support a specific protocol or implementation), compatibility with existing hardware/software, and cost.

WIDS/WIPS

By virtue of the "visible to all" nature of the wireless medium, even the most secure WLAN deployments may need an additional layer of protection in the form of wireless monitoring and intrusion protection. *Wireless intrusion detection systems (WIDSs)* and *wireless intrusion prevention systems (WIPSs)* are gaining in popularity and are intended to provide that extra layer of protection for monitoring the airwaves against network threats.

WIDS or WIPS

Initial WLAN monitoring efforts included the use of passive sensors that identified threats and reported them to the WIPS server. Alerts were sent to appropriate IT staff, threats were investigated, and manual action was taken. This type of monitoring and reporting is often known as a wireless intrusion detection system (WIDS). As wireless security has become more sophisticated, the traditional WIDS has been upgraded with automated response tactics in which a normally passive sensor goes active and mitigates the impact of a network threat.

A wireless intrusion prevention system (WIPS) is used in many different ways, but the key point is that the sensor is not just detecting a threat; it is also acting upon the threat and preventing it. Of course, this gives us the name wireless intrusion prevention, which is a step up from WIDS. In today's marketplace, almost all enterprise vendors offer some amount of built-in WIDS or WIPS functionality; there are also several third-party vendors that have purpose-built WIPS solutions as an overlay product. The WIDS is largely becoming obsolete as enterprises are favoring the feature capabilities of automated response.

The typical architecture of a WIPS implementation includes a WIPS server, WIPS sensors, and a WIPS management console. WIPS sensors are deployed much like access points (though not as densely) and are the wireless data collection points. The sensors scan the air and gather the data, then forward the collected data to the WIPS server for aggregation. The WIPS server utilizes the network-wide data and compiles it for monitoring, auditing, and forensics. A WIPS management console is then used to retrieve the data from the WIPS server, usually via a graphical interface with a web browser.

There are several functions of a WIPS, including:

- Identification, classification, and prevention of WLAN security threats
- Security posture evaluation, auditing, and reporting
- Regulatory compliance auditing and reporting

- Performance monitoring, assessment, and reporting
- Network configuration continuity monitoring
- Forensic data analysis
- Distributed protocol analysis
- Distributed spectrum analysis
- Rogue device location services

This is a somewhat high-level list, but it should serve to demonstrate that a WIPS is designed to monitor the air for any network events that could adversely impact the WLAN. Monitoring is not relegated to security; it includes performance, regulatory compliance, location-based services, and more.

Many WIDS/WIPS products have troubleshooting features that also double as protocol analyzers that can cost-effectively assist IT support desks, especially in remote locations.

The first step in designing a WIPS deployment is to identify the goals of the WIPS. You may want casual monitoring to identify rogue APs and to attempt to identify other network attacks. Or you may want some basic security audits to ensure that your network complies with regulatory requirements, such as PCI-DSS v2.0. More secure network environments may want full-time monitoring and threat prevention, rogue device triangulation, and daily, customized vulnerability reports. Each of these three use cases represents a different approach to WIPS deployment. For that reason, it is difficult to prescribe all the ins and outs of how to deploy a WIPS. There are many consistencies that we can explore to help provide the big picture regarding how to deploy a system in your environment. First, let's look at the basic differences in WIPSs.

Integrated vs. Overlay

There are two primary ways to deploy a WIPS:

Integrated   In integrated systems, the WIPS functionality is integrated with the hardware of the access points.

Overlay   With overlay systems, dedicated WIPS sensors are overlaid onto the existing WLAN infrastructure.

Many WLAN vendors are now integrating WIPS functionality into the AP, so it is becoming a common practice to deploy additional APs in a sensor-only mode for scanning. Third-party vendors also make dedicated overlay sensors that can perform the same functionality.

When comparing a third-party solution to an integrated option, one significant difference is the purpose-built nature of third-party overlay systems. Because WIPS vendors specialize exclusively in intrusion prevention and security threats, they are usually at the forefront in terms of in-depth wireless intrusion detection, automated intruder mitigation, threat assessment, and auditing/reporting functions related to legislated compliance.

On the other hand, integrated WIPS functionality (even when deployed as dedicated sensors) is handy because these sensors integrate with the existing WLAN management hardware—as a caveat, some WLAN infrastructure vendors may require additional hardware or feature licenses for WIPS services. Overlay systems require additional hardware and added learning curves that typically come along with new vendor solutions. This comparison comes down to the customer's needs and the functionality offered by third-party WIPS products as compared with the WLAN infrastructure's offering.

Dedicated vs. Part-time

With integrated WIPS sensors, there are two basic operating modes:

Dedicated   Dedicated WIPS sensors are full-time radios dedicated exclusively to WIPS functionality.

Part-time   Part-time scanners are AP radios that also serve clients. At regular intervals, the AP radio will stop serving clients for a short time in order to scan surrounding channels for security threats.

Neither of these options is necessarily right or wrong, but there are obvious trade-offs between the two.

With dedicated radios, the commitment to threat detection is much better. Remember that APs typically transmit beacons every 100 ms, or ten times per second. In order for a WIPS sensor to scan through all 14 of the channels in the 2.4 GHz band (depending on regulatory requirements), dwelling on each channel for at least one beacon interval, it would take over a full second. This assumes that it scans a channel for 100 ms and then hops to the next. Now, add into this equation all twenty-four 20 MHz channels (again, depending on regulatory domain) in 5 GHz, and you've exacerbated the problem even more. This doesn't even consider that you must now also scan 40 MHz channels, at least in 5 GHz. This doubles the list of channels, at a minimum (remember, 40 MHz channels are 20 MHz channels with 20 MHz extension channels *above or below*). Long story short, there are a lot of channels to scan, and it will take a lot of time.

Dedicated sensors will not be able to catch every frame on every channel, but they will tend to catch a greater percentage of network threats than part-time sensors because they are scanning each channel for longer periods of time, more frequently, or possibly both.

Now, consider that part-time sensors must serve clients on a specific channel, and at regular intervals, scan all of these channels for threats. How long would it take to scan each of these channels in the list, and what is the penalty to WLAN client performance when this happens? In most cases, when latency-sensitive traffic (like VoWiFi) is supported, part-time sensors can't abandon the client traffic flow to scan off-channel. What if a voice call lasts 20 minutes? That's 20 minutes of time in which no off-channel scanning is taking place, no rogues are detected, and no threats are intercepted.

As we discuss the efficiency of dedicated versus part-time sensors, we should also discuss what a WIPS sensor does when it discovers a threat. Dedicated sensors can remain on a specific channel, preventing the offending device from exploiting the network (in many cases). Part-time sensors are torn between an obligation to serve clients and an obligation to prevent threats. Client service may take priority here, leaving manual threat mitigation by IT staff as the only option. Alternatively, nearby sensors might also be able to hear the activity and be able to help mitigate the threat.

Configuring Policies

When you are designing and deploying a WIPS solution, the wireless security policy is an important tool. In effect, the WIPS should be configured to maintain compliance to the security policy and attempt to prevent behaviors that interfere with compliance. To that end, configuration of an acceptable wireless policy is typically a first step in preparing a WIPS. This includes parameters such as authentication, encryption, SSID usage, and other related criteria. These criteria are a configuration baseline for the WIPS to enforce.

After WIPS sensors are online and have populated a list of visible APs and clients, administrators will assign classifications to those devices. Usually, there are a handful of device classification categories. Known, unknown, friendly, neighbor, and rogue are all common classifications. This is an important step, especially if automated threat mitigation will be enabled. For example, if you configure the WIPS to automatically contain threats from rogue devices, it is critical to ensure that your "rogue" devices are actually offending rogues. You may inadvertently label your neighbor's AP as rogue, and your WIPS would proceed to cause a denial of service (DoS) to your neighbor's network. This represents a legal liability, so great care needs to be taken.

 Real World Scenario

Inadvertent Threat Mitigation

One wireless infrastructure vendor recently reported another vendor's abuse of WIPS threat mitigation. The vendors shall remain nameless here, but it is important to recognize the potential problems that may occur when WIPS products are configured haphazardly.

The reporting vendor received customer complaints that their product was not working as expected. Since it was an unusual problem, the vendor sent engineers to the customer's site to help troubleshoot and remedy the issue. After a fair amount of investigation, including extensive spectrum and protocol analysis, they discovered that spoofed management frames were being sent by a nearby station that did not belong to the customer. As they followed the RF evidence, they discovered that an AP from a neighboring network was the transmitting culprit. After further investigation with the neighboring company, they realized that the AP was misconfigured (possibly by the vendor itself) to perform automated threat mitigation against all "rogue" APs. Unfortunately, the legitimate APs of the customer were being mislabeled as offending rogue APs, and an intentional DoS was being performed.

This type of misconfiguration and absent-minded network design is fairly dangerous. On the one hand, it could be interfering with the mission-critical services of neighbor networks. That could lead to a costly lawsuit. On a lesser scale, the affected customer could force the offending neighbor to pay for the consulting services of the engineer who discovered the problem.

At the end of this investigation, the affected customer didn't press charges, and their providing vendor also took the high road by keeping the other vendor undisclosed. However, the point should be clear that automated WIPS response should be taken seriously, both by the vendor itself as well as the customer.

WIPS products generally come preconfigured with numerous alarm and threat signatures that can be used to automatically detect suspicious activities and compare them to a database of attack sequences. When the WIPS finds a match between the detected activities and an attack scenario, it will generate an alarm or other automated response. Once an intrusion has been identified and the threat level determined, the WIPS can trigger notification (e.g., email, SMS, hardcopy reports, or detailed forensics logging) and responses. You may choose to have the WIPS perform automated mitigation on the wireless medium (often called rogue containment), or you may wish to block the wired port to which the rogue device is attached (often called port suppression). Either of these actions can be launched as an automated procedure or can be configured to wait for final approval from an administrator before beginning the mitigation actions.

In addition to alarms, responses, and notifications, WIPS policies are often paired with risk assessments, vulnerability reports, logging, and forensics. Modern WIPS products are becoming more sophisticated, allowing for automation of most of these functions. For example, you can configure the WIPS to generate a monthly report showing all alarm activities as well as a prolific subset of information relevant to each alarm. Similarly, you can configure the WIPS to generate a monthly report showing your network's compliance with an industry regulatory policy, such as PCI, HIPAA, or other similar requirements. This provides verifiable and traceable evidence in the event that a network audit is performed.

WIPS policy configuration could easily represent an entire chapter in this study guide, but we will defer to the CWSP study guide and WIPS product user guides on this topic. In short, your configuration will depend on the goals you are trying to achieve with the WIPS platform. If you are looking to maximize automated response, even at the risk of false positives, you should set aggressive WIPS policies. However, if you want to prevent all false positives, you may want to use alarm and reporting functions more heavily and rely on manual investigation and verification to contain potential threats.

Advanced Performance Monitoring and Reporting

A WIPS is generally purchased with the intention of providing a perimeter security envelope around the WLAN. But, in addition to providing constant 24x7x365 monitoring of the security metrics of a WLAN, most WIPSs are also able to track key performance indicators, such as misconfiguration, saturated channels, or heavily utilized APs. As with security events, alarms, notifications, and reporting actions, performance criteria can also be acted upon.

As new types of communication services such as voice and video applications grow more popular on the WLAN, additional expectations for quality of service become more common. As this happens, it will become increasingly important for the network administrator to be able to proactively determine when and where service disruptions are occurring in order to correct those problems in advance of a service level agreement (SLA) violation. Full-time monitoring and enforcement of expected service levels is a capability of the WIPS that may prove to be invaluable.

WIPS Sensor Placement

The WIPS system is a critical piece of the WLAN deployment. It provides the final ongoing monitoring and enforcement of perimeter security and performance. For best results, the placement and number of WIPS sensors should be carefully considered during the design phase of the WLAN. Although it may be tempting to "eyeball" the locations and numbers of WIPS sensors, just as with trying to guess the number of APs needed to meet customer expectations this method seldom results in a well-designed sensor network.

All WIPS vendors have recommendations on how to design the sensor network, and this documentation should be consulted for optimum performance. However, in order to determine the optimal placement of sensors in your network design, you should consider the type of monitoring services that will be required and plan accordingly. Beginning with the vendor's recommended AP-to-sensor ratio, look at some of the selection criteria we have mentioned previously, such as:

- Will you be scanning all channels, or just the primary channels within a band (e.g. 1, 6, 11)?

- Do you intend to provide full-time, automated threat mitigation if the need arises?

- Will you be attempting to locate rogue APs or clients with triangulation, RF fingerprinting, or time difference of arrival (TDoA) techniques?

These services all impact the number and placement of sensors. Specifically, as you desire better scanning coverage, higher resolution in rogue location tracking, or better dedicated threat prevention, more sensors are usually warranted.

To provide the best sensor platform for these additional applications, it is usually necessary to configure the WIPS sensor deployment with greater attention than would be needed for basic security monitoring. Some WIPS vendors also offer a site survey mode in which the sensor begins actively transmitting data, facilitating a manual site survey. With this method, network designers can collect actual data to gauge the sensor's effective range, which ultimately helps determine proper placement.

Do You Need a WIPS?

There's no hard and fast rule to indicate whether you should or shouldn't have a WIPS in place for your wireless network. As with most security-related decisions, this assessment results from a comparison of security importance, cost, and complexity. Generally speaking, WIPS are the only real way to discover some of the potential vulnerabilities in a WLAN. Often times, it is not enough to support robust authentication and encryption mechanisms. You must also monitor the airwaves around you for potential threats.

In fact, some companies for whom a WIPS may be most useful are those companies with a "no Wi-Fi" policy. When network-wide security visibility is important, WIPSs are quite helpful and highly recommended. If your only goal is to identify and manually remove potential rogue APs, part-time WIPSs usually work just fine. If you want the best of the best, dedicated overlay WIPSs add a significant final layer of security to the network. There are many options to meet the various security needs of companies.

Fast Secure Roaming

As we've already discussed throughout this chapter, the strongest security solutions may come with trade-offs to cost, ease of use, management overhead, and possibly performance. One of the major performance-related drawbacks that may come along with robust security is high latency during roaming due to long 802.1X/EAP authentications. As you might expect, simple authentication protocols, such as 802.11 authentication (a.k.a. open authentication) and WPA/WPA2-Personal require a minimal number of frame exchanges to complete authentication and begin passing data traffic. More complex and stout authentication mechanisms, such as 802.1X/EAP, require much more time to complete, thus delaying the application's data flow during this time.

During a reassociation in an open network (no security), roaming times are very short—usually less than 15 ms. This amount of delay will not have a noticeable impact on modern applications. WPA/WPA2-Personal authentication with a PSK or passphrase takes slightly longer than open authentication—usually around 25 ms or less—but this is also a fairly nominal amount of delay. Assuming channel utilization is not causing excessive retransmissions, roaming in open networks or WPA/WPA2-Personal networks will be transparent to the end user.

However, when we compare these simple authentication solutions to 802.1X/EAP authentication, the problem becomes clear. During normal 802.1X/EAP reassociations, assuming no *fast secure roaming (FSR)* mechanisms are in place, all of the following events are required:

- Open authentication
- 802.11 association
- 802.1X/EAP authentication

- 4-way handshake

With WPA/WPA2-Personal, all of these steps are required except the 802.1X/EAP authentication component. As we think about what is required during an 802.1X/ EAP authentication, it is easy to see why this phase of the roaming process becomes problematic. Each EAP implementation varies, but in most cases in the enterprise, there are many reasons for delay at this stage. First, the AP proxies authentication requests to an AAA server. Then the AAA server must query a separate user database for user credentials. This process goes back and forth for the duration of the 802.1X/EAP authentication exchange and can take a significant amount of time with a great deal of frame exchanges to complete. Add to this equation the delay that occurs at each hop in the network from the client to the AP to the AAA server to the user database, then back from the user database to the AAA server, back to the AP, and then back to client. This multihop, multidestination exchange process happens many times during the authentication. Figure 12.7 provides a simplified visual reference for this process. Note that Figure 12.7 shows the simplest arrangement of 802.1X/EAP infrastructure. In real-world deployments, these devices may cross many L2 or L3 hops, including remotely hosted AAA servers or user databases. Also, to demonstrate the amount of frames traversing and processes occurring across the wireless and wired medium at this stage, Figure 12.8 shows only the exchanges that are

FIGURE 12.7   Simple illustration of 802.1X/EAP participants

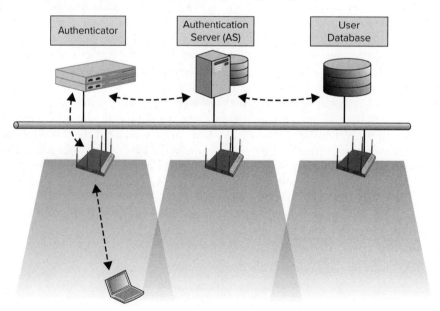

FIGURE 12.8 Frames and processes required for a PEAPv0/EAP-MSCHAPv2 authentication

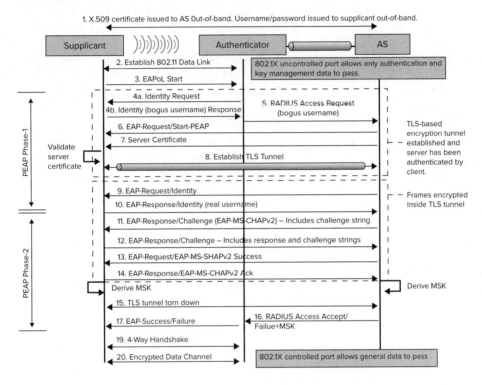

1. X.509 certificate issued to AS Out-of-band. Username/password issued to supplicant out-of-band.

| Supplicant | Authenticator | AS |

2. Establish 802.11 Data Link

802.1X uncontrolled port allows only authentication and key management data to pass.

3. EAPoL Start

PEAP Phase-1

4a. Identity Request
4b. Identity (bogus username) Response

5. RADIUS Access Request (bogus username)

6. EAP-Request/Start-PEAP

7. Server Certificate

Validate server certificate

8. Establish TLS Tunnel

TLS-based encryption tunnel established and server has been authenticated by client.

PEAP Phase-2

9. EAP-Request/Identity

10. EAP-Response/Identity (real username)

Frames encrypted inside TLS tunnel

11. EAP-Response/Challenge (EAP-MS-CHAPv2) – Includes challenge string

12. EAP-Response/Challenge – Includes response and challenge strings

13. EAP-Request/EAP-MS-SHAPv2 Success

14. EAP-Response/EAP-MS-CHAPv2 Ack

Derive MSK

Derive MSK

15. TLS tunnel torn down

17. EAP-Success/Failure

16. RADIUS Access Accept/Failue+MSK

19. 4-Way Handshake

20. Encrypted Data Channel

802.1X controlled port allows general data to pass

performed between the supplicant, authenticator, and AS for the most common EAP type, PEAPv0/EAP-MSCHAPv2.

You also need to factor in the amount of time it takes the client to validate a server certificate, the time it takes the AAA server to validate client credentials, and the time it takes the AAA server and client devices to export keys. Then add to this mix 802.11 frame contention on a busy wireless medium, frame retries, and any other variables that create additional delay. Finally, AAA servers and user databases may also be serving other authentication requests at the same time, so an additional delay may occur when the authentication infrastructure is heavily utilized. Needless to say, 802.1X/EAP authentication can take a long time to complete. Depending on the network configuration, this process can take more than a full second to complete for the first authentication—though, in simple networks, it can take less than 150 ms. In an ideal world, reassociations would take approximately 150 ms or less to complete, depending on the EAP type.

Many of today's applications are highly sensitive to long delays like this. Large amounts of delay can take a noticeable toll on voice, video, and other sensitive session-based applications. In many cases, the application's session will actually terminate, requiring end user intervention to reinitiate the flow of data. If we apply this information to a real-world scenario, it's easy to see why this is problematic. Imagine a nurse who is walking through the hospital hallway, being briefed on her way to assist a patient in need. The phone's supplicant initiates a roam,

---

Calculating Roaming Times

When we discuss the topic of roaming delay, it is often unclear what constitutes the beginning of a roam and the end of a roam. Since the user's experience is based on application performance, roaming times are usually measured in terms of application data. Specifically, a roaming event begins when a client station leaves its current operating channel and transmits its first frame to the new AP on the new channel. To be clear, we are assuming that in a properly designed multiple channel architecture (MCA) network, roaming events will occur across two nonoverlapping channels. So, the roam begins when the application's data flow is stopped (the client leaves its current channel, or when it begins the 802.11 authentication with the new AP if on the same channel). As you might guess, the roaming event ends when the last frame of the reassociation process is received, encryption keys are installed, and data traffic is ready to resume.

In modern networks, this last frame is usually the fourth frame of a 4-way handshake; however, this depends on the authentication method and the FSR protocol in use. After this frame is received, the application flow can resume. During the roaming process, the application is prevented from delivering or receiving new data to or from the AP.

---

and the voice call abruptly ends. With this and other frustrating scenarios, it's important to realize that businesses are increasingly relying on their WLAN for mission-critical business goals. This can be a very painful problem for businesses.

In some cases, the solution to long roaming delays is simply to use less complex authentication mechanisms. This is an example where PPSKs can be very useful. However, there are many times in which 802.1X/EAP is the only acceptable authentication mechanism, and roaming times must be decreased. Enter fast secure roaming.

There are many different types of FSR, including a few proprietary solutions. Unfortunately, FSR has not been perceived as a high priority by some industry organizations or vendors, and protocol development and certification adoption has been slow and sporadically embraced. The two early standardized FSR methods (*PMK caching* and *preauthentication*) both have notable limitations. IEEE 802.11r also introduced a complete solution to *Fast BSS Transitions (FT)*, but industry adoption of FT has been delayed because the Wi-Fi Alliance and participating vendors have not prioritized their *Voice Enterprise* certification program. Other FSR methods like *opportunistic key caching (OKC)* are available, but OKC is not defined by any central, authoritative standards body, which means that implementations vary from one vendor to the next. In addition, OKC has been limited by slow and inconsistent client vendor adoption.

In short, 802.1X/EAP authentication is robust and is highly recommended, but is not always practical. It is possible to make 802.1X/EAP perform well, but it usually takes tuning client devices and enabling certain features. In Chapter 10, "MAC Layer Design," we discuss configuration and support for FSR mechanisms in greater detail.

As it pertains to security, it is important to understand that, as of this writing, industry support for FSR is still not terribly mature. The ratification of 802.11r is frankly a game changer and it will soon change. It is coming along, albeit slowly. The best current estimates indicate that the Voice Enterprise certification will be available in mid-2011.

The possibility of performance degradation should be factored into a security design in which robust authentication is desired along with high-performing, session-based, sensitive applications. Testing and tuning your client devices and infrastructure settings will have a significant payoff.

Summary

In this chapter, we looked at several critical components to securing a WLAN in the enterprise. As you explore these various elements of a holistic security posture, it becomes clear that there are many layers to proper security planning.

While we have not covered all the technical nuances and options related to WLAN security, we have discussed many of the most important issues. There are always limitations when a vendor-neutral approach to security planning is taken, but this information will provide the necessary framework for Certified Wireless Design Professionals to pass the exam and to make informed and educated decisions as you evaluate the many security options that are available.

For more detailed information on WLAN security, please refer to the *CWSP Certified Wireless Security Professional Official Study Guide: Exam PW0-204.*

Exam Essentials

Recommend appropriate authentication solutions and explain design concepts related to their use.   Understand the appropriate deployment scenarios and best practices for WPA/WPA2-Personal, WPA/WPA2-Enterprise, captive portal, and proprietary authentication solutions.

Understand the 802.1X and EAP protocols and their use in WLANs.   Demonstrate an intimate knowledge of how the 802.1X protocol works, what makes it secure, and how it is used in WLAN security. Understand the common EAP types in use today, their advantages and disadvantages, and best practices for EAP selection and deployment.

Illustrate common deployment and design strategies for AAA and RADIUS servers.   Be able to show a thorough understanding of the use of RADIUS in network deployments, including RADIUS deployment models. Understand the components of the AAA framework.

Understand design strategies for integration of client authentication with directory services.   Demonstrate how to integrate authentication services with existing user databases for client authentication. Understand common deployment practices and recommended best practices for user databases.

Explain best practice security design concepts for guest and public access Wi-Fi networks.   Understand how to deploy a guest network using common features like captive portals, network segmentation, content filtering, and access control.

Describe deployment and design strategies for wireless intrusion prevention systems.   Demonstrate the purpose and features of a WIPS and explain proper design techniques for WIPS deployments. Be familiar with WIPS architectures, WIPS selection criteria, and common configuration tasks.

Demonstrate the importance of, and design considerations related to, fast secure roaming.   Understand why FSR protocols are necessary and what security factors impact their use.

Identify the role and limitations of client capabilities in security planning.   Know how client devices impact and limit security implementations.

Describe the methods of designing a secure network with segmentation and filtering.   Understand common segmentation and filtering protocols, approaches, and best practices.

Review Questions

1. What differences exist between VLANs in wireless and wired domains?

   A. Wireless VLANs do not always segment traffic into separate broadcast domains on the wireless medium. Wired VLANs do segment broadcast domains on the wired network.

   B. Wireless VLANs are not effective for segmenting the available services and network permissions available to clients. Wired VLANs are effective for this purpose.

   C. Wireless VLANs are not an effective way to utilize a single set of infrastructure equipment to provide different services to different client groups. Wired VLANs are effective for this purpose.

   D. Wireless VLANs are never carried in 802.11 frames that cross the wireless medium. VLAN identifiers are always carried in Ethernet frames to indicate the proper VLAN.

2. You have been asked to select a secure EAP type for your organization's upcoming WLAN deployment. In addition to a requirement for robust security, you were given three requirements for the EAP type:

   ▪ Must support server X.509 certificates

   ▪ Must support usernames/passphrases for client authentication

   ▪ Must support TLS tunneling

   What EAP type could you recommend that would meet these criteria?

   A. PEAPv1/EAP-MSCHAPv2

   B. PEAPv1/EAP-GTC

   C. EAP-LEAP

   D. EAP-TLS

   E. EAP-TTLS/MSCHAPv2

3. For what purposes are VPNs typically used in modern WLANs? (Choose all that apply.)

   A. Remote AP tunneling to a corporate WLAN controller or VPN concentrator

   B. Client device connectivity to corporate resources from unsecured public networks

   C. Initial 802.11 authentication with the AP and subsequent data encryption

   D. Tunneling APs and WLAN controllers to cloud-based management platforms

   E. Tunneling APs and WLAN controllers to RADIUS and token servers

   F. Bridging client connectivity in ad hoc networks

4. What are some significant drawbacks that are present with WPA/WPA2-Enterprise that are not present with WPA/WPA2-Personal? (Choose all that apply.)

  A. WPA/WPA2-Enterprise often requires more administrative overhead for configuration than WPA/WPA2-Personal.

  B. WPA/WPA2-Enterprise does not provide a way to perform per-user authorization and access control.

  C. WPA/WPA2-Enterprise does not support the use of usernames/passwords for client authentication.

  D. WPA/WPA2-Enterprise always requires X.509 certificates for server authentication.

  E. WPA/WPA2-Enterprise often requires additional backend infrastructure components that are not required with WPA/WPA2-Personal.

5. What design architectures are commonly available for wireless intrusion prevention systems (WIPSs)? (Choose all that apply.)

  A. Dedicated overlay

  B. Part-time overlay

  C. Dedicated integrated

  D. Part-time integrated

6. What WIPS deployment model represents the lowest-cost option with the lowest added security for enterprise networks with an existing WLAN deployment?

  A. Dedicated overlay

  B. Part-time overlay

  C. Dedicated integrated

  D. Part-time integrated

7. What are some of the common ways by which WLAN users receive network permissions? (Choose all that apply.)

  A. RADIUS return attributes

  B. WLAN profile settings

  C. WLAN infrastructure group profiles

  D. LDAP database WLAN plug-ins

8. What functions may be performed by a WIPS? (Choose all that apply.)

  A. Automated threat mitigation

  B. Data forensics and analysis

  C. Distributed protocol analysis

  D. Performance monitoring and response

  E. Client access to the distribution system

9. When are self-signed X.509 certificates and an internal PKI generally recommended?

    A. When the selected EAP type requires X.509 certificates

    B. When the client population on the network is not owned or managed by IT staff

    C. When there is a requirement for a large number of X.509 certificates for client devices

    D. When e-commerce is an important business function and many X.509 certificates are required for web servers

10. What is another name for an AAA client?

    A. Supplicant

    B. Network access server (NAS)

    C. RADIUS server

    D. Authentication server

    E. User database

11. What are the two ports specified by 802.1X-2004 port-based access control? (Choose all that apply.)

    A. Supplicant port

    B. Controlled port

    C. Uncontrolled port

    D. Authenticator port

    E. RADIUS port

    F. LDAP port

12. What statements are true of PEAPv0/EAP-MSCHAPv2? (Choose all that apply.)

    A. Allows X.509 client certificates

    B. Is widely supported by client supplicants

    C. Has relatively high management overhead compared with other EAP types

    D. Has a tunneled and an untunneled mode

    E. Protects the supplicants actual username inside a TLS tunnel

    F. Specifies three EAP phases: Phase 1, Phase 2, and Phase 3

13. In a network supporting WPA/WPA2-Enterprise, what authentication protocol is used for communication between the supplicant and authenticator?

    A. EAP

    B. LDAP

    C. RADIUS

    D. 802.1X

14. In an RSN requiring low-latency reassociations and no fast secure roaming protocols, what security solutions are ideal for protecting VoWiFi communication? (Choose all that apply.)

  A. WPA2-Personal

  B. WEP

  C. 802.1X/EAP

  D. WPA2-Enterprise

  E. WPA-Personal

15. What is the purpose of role-based access control?

  A. To control network permissions by managing multiple WLAN profiles (SSIDs)

  B. To ensure that all users within a WLAN have equal authorization privileges

  C. To offload traffic from RADIUS servers and user databases by incorporating user and group policies within the AP

  D. To provide unique network access privileges to users in accordance with group or policy assignments

16. Why is RADIUS ubiquitously used as an AAA server for WLANs? (Choose all that apply.)

  A. It is a flexible protocol that can serve many purposes.

  B. It is pervasively supported by user databases and AAA clients.

  C. Native RADIUS services are always provided within WLAN infrastructure devices.

  D. RADIUS adds encryption strength to the 802.1X/EAP protocol.

17. What solutions are important endpoint security practices to maintain a wireless security policy? (Choose all that apply.)

  A. Endpoint software agents

  B. Network admission control

  C. Virtual private networking

  D. PMK caching

  E. Captive portals

  F. Walled gardens

18. What term refers to a RADIUS attribute that is specified by a specific vendor for the vendor's own use?

  A. Vendor-specific attributes (VSA)

  B. Virtual RADIUS attributes

  C. Proprietary return attributes

  D. Vendor attribute-value pairs (AVPs)

19. What is a primary difference between VLANs used on the wireless and wired domains?

   A. VLANs on the wired network segment users into different IP subnets, whereas VLANs on the wireless network do not.

   B. VLANs on the wired network allow IP-level ACLs to be applied to data traffic, but VLANs on the wireless network do not.

   C. VLANs in the wired domain segment collision domains and broadcast traffic, but VLANs in the wireless domain do not segment collision domains and broadcast traffic.

   D. VLANs are an effective way to provide secure network segmentation in the wired domain, but VLANs do not provide secure segmentation in the wireless domain.

20. What is the highest amount of delay that is typically acceptable for a roaming event in an 802.1X/EAP network supporting VoWiFi?

   A. 15 ms

   B. 50 ms

   C. 150 ms

   D. 500 ms

   E. 1 second

Answers to Review Questions

1. A. VLANs have many similarities and differences on wireless and wired domains. The primary difference is that VLANs do not always segment broadcast traffic into different contention domains on the wireless medium. All devices on all VLANs (for a given AP radio) share the same contention domain.

2. E. Of the five EAP types listed, only EAP-TTLS/MSCHAPv2 would meet the criteria provided. PEAPv0/EAP-MSCHAPv2 would be a common EAP type to use in this scenario, but the answer options didn't include this EAP type. PEAPv1 always uses EAP-GTC, which employs token cards for client authentication. EAP-LEAP has known security weaknesses and is not recommended for modern networks, and EAP-TLS requires X.509 certificates for the server and clients.

3. A, B, D. VPNs are used for many purposes in modern WLANs. Tunneling remote APs back to a corporate VPN concentrator is becoming more common as workforces become more mobile. Similarly, end users are taking advantage of working in remote locations and often require secure VPN technologies to access corporate resources across unsecure connections. In some cases, VPNs are also used to tunnel APs or WLAN controllers to cloud-based management appliances. In the past, VPNs were used as the primary authentication and encryption mechanism for WLANs, but with modern security, this is no longer required or recommended.

4. A, E. WPA/WPA2-Enterprise is generally the recommended solution for client authentication in enterprise WLANs. However, this does not mean that WPA/WPA2-Enterprise is not without its drawbacks. Added security with WPA/WPA2-Enterprise usually comes with the compromise of added management overhead and configuration complexity. It also typically costs more to implement and requires additional backend infrastructure components, such as an AAA server and user database.

5. A, C, D. There are two primary architectures for WIPS deployments: overlay and integrated. With overlay deployments, WIPS sensors are always dedicated to full-time scanning and are not deployed as part-time scanners. With integrated WIPS deployments, the sensor radio can be deployed as a dedicated, full-time sensor or a part-time sensor.

6. D. Part-time integrated WIPS deployments take advantage of WIPS functionality built into an existing WLAN architecture. WLAN radios are configured as part-time scanners, which means they serve clients on a channel part of the time and they scan off-channel part of the time. Because the radio has two distinct responsibilities, the security benefits are limited. However, this represents a low-cost option if the currently deployed WLAN infrastructure supports integrated WIPS functionality.

7. A, B, C. There are several ways to apply network permissions to WLAN users. In most cases, enterprises use a combination of WLAN profile settings and user database parameters that are specified during 802.1X/EAP authentication. Also, many WLAN infrastructure vendors provide local user groups with specific network privileges. LDAP databases are often queried during authentication, but they do not use WLAN plug-ins.

8. A, B, C, D. WIPSs serve many different purposes, mostly related to security and performance monitoring and response. While they may be configured to actively transmit to mitigate a wireless threat or for site surveying processes, they do not service client access to the network.

9. C. For most EAP types where the server requires X.509 certificates but the client does not, third-party certificate authorities are generally very useful. This offloads some complexity, infrastructure equipment, and management overhead from the company implementing EAP. With some of the most secure EAP types, such as EAP-TLS, clients also require certificates. For these EAP solutions, a PKI and self-signed certificates are required. In these cases, certificates must be installed on each individual client device, so it is preferable that the IT staff have control of client devices. In other words, this type of solution would not be good for a university with student-owned and controlled laptops.

10. B. In the 802.1X/EAP authentication framework, there are many different terms used to reference the same entities. RADIUS is a form of AAA, so a RADIUS server and an AAA server are the same thing. Within the AAA framework, an AAA client is often referred to as a network access server (NAS) since it is providing access to a network service that requires authentication.

11. B, C. The 802.1X-2004 standard specifies three roles for authentication: supplicant (the client), authenticator (the AP or WLAN controller), and the authentication server (usually a RADIUS server). The authenticator controls the flow of authenticated and unauthenticated traffic by means of controlled and uncontrolled ports. The uncontrolled port is blocked until the client successfully authenticates using the controlled port.

12. B, E. PEAPv0/EAP-MSCHAPv2 is the most common EAP type in use today because it has many strengths and very few, if any, weaknesses. PEAPv0/EAP-MSCHAPv2 is widely supported by client supplicants, requires server certificates, uses client username/password credentials, is relatively easy to implement, requires TLS tunneling, protects the supplicant's actual username inside the TLS tunnel, and has two phases.

13. A. When WPA/WPA2-Enterprise is the chosen security solution, the EAP protocol is used between the supplicant and authenticator.

14. A, E. An RSN requires either TKIP or CCMP encryption. For reliably fast reassociations, WPA/WPA2-Personal is generally the best option. WPA/WPA2-Enterprise can also be used to meet the requirements of FSR, given that FSR protocols (like preauthentication, OKC, or proprietary methods) are used.

15. D. Role-based access control (RBAC) is a general concept by which each user receives specific network authorization in accordance with the user's group or policy assignment. RBAC can be performed in many different ways, such as user/group configurations native to the WLAN infrastructure, RADIUS return attributes, and other methods.

16. A, B. RADIUS is by far the most common AAA protocol in use today. RADIUS is popular because it is ubiquitously supported by user databases and AAA clients and because it is a flexible protocol that can adequately serve the needs of many enterprises. In some cases, WLAN infrastructure devices have native RADIUS services, but this is not necessarily a part of all WLANs. Similarly, the strength of 802.1X/EAP is not dependent on RADIUS and is not innately improved with RADIUS.

17. A, B, C. Endpoint security is an important step in maintaining a corporate security policy. Endpoint security generally includes personal firewalls, antivirus software, endpoint agents, network admission control (NAC), VPN software, and OS permission control.

18. A. In some cases, vendors create their own vendor-specific RADIUS attributes to perform a specific function. These are called vendor-specific attributes (VSAs).

19. C. VLAN operation is largely the same on wired and wireless networks, but the primary difference is that VLANs do not segment the collision and broadcast domain in wireless networks. Broadcast traffic in one VLAN will create contention for all devices in a service area on the wireless network.

20. C. Option D, 150 ms, is typically thought of as the highest amount of acceptable delay for a roaming event in an 802.1X/EAP network. It is not uncommon to see roaming times above 1 second, which will cause noticeable problems for latency-sensitive applications like VoWiFi.

Chapter

13

Documentation and Finalizing the Design Solution

THE FOLLOWING CWDP EXAM TOPICS ARE COVERED IN THIS CHAPTER:

- ✓ Implement and understand the role of documentation in network planning and design.

- ✓ Describe processes and best practices related to documenting collected survey data and generating a deliverable report.

One of the most important deliverables to your customer or upper management (if you are designing a WLAN for your own company) is the design documentation. In this chapter, we will focus on the different types of documentation deliverables that need to be produced for any WLAN design effort.

In Chapter 9, "Site Survey RF Design," we discussed the RF survey process and generating data on which to base your final design. This chapter addresses how to take that information and provide a documentation set that includes the design decisions for AP placement. As you'll see, not all projects are created equal; some can be very large in scope and some can be very small—even consisting of just a single AP. When the scope of the WLAN increases, the amount of documentation that is required usually increases along with it. Regardless of size, documentation is still needed. The size of your documentation and how it fits your project is also an important topic and one we'll cover in this chapter.

Other common design documents we will explore include the high-level design (HLD), low-level design (LLD), and operational and maintenance planning documents. This chapter will discuss each of these documents and what type of content needs to be included in each.

Design Documentation

There aren't many people who actually like to create documentation. It is an arduous and often time-consuming task. What's more, a variety of factors, including customer preference, seem to often necessitate a need to revise. Yet, it's critical to create reliable documentation for your project. In fact, in regard to success factors, it is second only to making sure the product, a WLAN design in this case, accomplishes what it sets out to do and effectively *works*.

 Real World Scenario

The Importance of Documentation

When I (Shawn) was 18 years old and attending my first year as a computer science major at Cal Poly San Luis Obispo, my professor, who was one of the most senior members of the department staff, stood up in front of the class and said, paraphrasing of course, "The goal of all computer programs is, one, that it is *correct*. Two, that it is *documented* very well." I can't even remember what the third item was anymore, but what I do remember is that she never said *efficient*, *fast*, or anything even related to that. I was 18 years old then, and she was nearing retirement age and I thought to myself, "Geez, she doesn't have a clue." I agreed with her assessment that it is important for the code to be correct. After all, a software program that provides erroneous results is useless. It's like a calculator that doesn't divide properly. But I couldn't understand her reasoning for placing documentation second on the list. After spending over 15 years in the professional world, I now know that the professor was right and I, the know-it-all 18-year-old freshman, was the one who didn't have a clue.

When all is said and done and any project is complete—especially a project that results in a complex technical system—documentation is essentially all that there is to leverage in group discussions, troubleshooting efforts, and just about any activity that involves any number of interested parties in any part of the life cycle of the product.

For example, if you design a solution and one of your colleagues has to work on it while you are away on vacation, you will experience the importance of documentation. Similarly, what would happen if you left the company? Documentation is also critical when dealing with an older project, even if it was your own project that you designed. There are simply too many details that can be lost if they aren't put into some form of documentation that can be referenced later.

Hopefully these points have sold you on the value of providing good documentation. Maybe we have even inspired you to author *great* documents. Documentation comes in many forms; there isn't a single format that we can prescribe for all WLAN designs. What we do aim to accomplish in this chapter is to provide a solid and flexible foundation that should suffice in the smallest of projects to even the largest of them. In general, the larger the scope of a project, the more people are involved and the greater amount of documentation needed.

For example, a single WLAN installation at even a large enterprise facility may not require a large amount of documentation, relatively speaking. However, if the documentation is a template for a new WLAN standard that will be deployed across many locations in a variety of environments that may involve multiple teams, you can bet that a solid base of documentation will be one of the single most important fruits of your labor.

Let's now discuss the different audiences of your documentation and also specify a minimum set of requirements that should be included in a WLAN documentation set regardless of size and complexity.

Audience

When writing documentation, have an audience in mind. Each audience will require different data sets and presentation styles, so you will often find that, as the designer, you will have to put yourself in many different people's shoes as you create documentation. Management and end users require a different set of information than IT support staff who will be maintaining the design in the operational phase of the life cycle. To provide some guidance on how to address each of these audiences for your documentation, we will discuss each audience type below. Most of this chapter focuses on the technical audience, as these are the people who will implement, operate, and make future revisions to your network design.

Management

This audience demographic usually requires the smallest amount of documentation for direct consumption. Their support staff may be involved in the detailed components of the design, but usually management requires simply an overview.

Communication goals that need to be addressed to management are usually included in an executive summary. You typically summarize design requirements and how they are met by the proposed design.

Management will also usually be looking for a high-level diagram of the WLAN design and how it fits into an existing diagram or framework with which they are already familiar (ideally). It is advisable to look for existing diagrams that may fit this bill instead of creating something from scratch. If nothing currently exists, you can use a baseline diagram to illustrate the current environment and then display the same diagram with the proposed WLAN design changes.

Even though we will focus on technical design documentation in this chapter, it's important to note that whenever talking with management, you should explain the virtues of the design and any benefits that are worth repeating or referencing. This strategy is helpful whenever management plans to speak with other colleagues and interested parties of various types.

Engineering

Engineers can fall into multiple categories depending on the size of the IT team and the organizational structure. In some smaller organizations, engineers may be the architects and planners for new standards as well as the people creating the detailed design. Yet larger organizations usually have separate roles for each of these tasks.

The task of engineering in a larger organization enters into the equation after a product direction and a design standard have been chosen. Usually, engineering leads are consulted for the standard development, but they are usually the main consumers of the high-level design. Specifically, engineering will take the design standard and develop a low-level design (LLD) for a particular site. Therefore, project documentation is key to the engineering staff where they, in turn, further develop documentation for their implementations.

Implementers

When a design has been created and detailed specifications exist that define a new deployment, the role of the implementer is to facilitate getting the design installed. An implementer is often a field engineer, a network technician, or the like. Some organizations combine the role of the implementer and the engineer, though they are usually separate roles in larger organizations. Implementers are typically responsible for racking/mounting, labeling, and cabling equipment, whether the equipment is in closets or throughout the facility, as with APs. Engineers can provide preconfigured devices for the implementers or, depending on the organization, provide configurations or detailed instructions for the implementer to configure themselves.

If implementers will be involved in designs you are developing, consult with them to see what documentation items would be helpful to them. Perhaps they may have a request for specific fields and nomenclature that you should include.

Support Staff

Once a design is installed and is being used, a different team of people provides support. They are the first line of defense for the end users who are the consumers of your new WLAN design. Operational support usually leverages a help desk ticketing system where end users can generate problem reports and the resolution can be tracked. Software and driver updates, patches, and onsite troubleshooting and analysis typically start with the operational staff.

Operational support teams are also the ones who may suffer from bad design decisions. It is important that a feedback loop be created to allow for problem reports to make it back to the designers of the WLAN. When problem reports become larger issues, it is also important that they be able to escalate issues back to engineering and maybe even designers of the WLAN if the problem is significant enough.

Minimum Requirements

WLAN designs may be anywhere from a few APs all the way to multiple sites spanning international boundaries that support thousands and thousands of devices with large numbers of technical staff involved in the process. Regardless of size, there is a minimum set of documentation that is always necessary.

Documentation for WLAN designs is different from other types of networking designs. You can say that WLAN designs are network designs with an additional component: RF. There might be unique construction elements as well, but largely the primary difference is the RF factor. From a network perspective, usually the minimum level of network documentation is a low-level network design document that provides the following:

- Some form of RF documentation that illustrates why APs were placed where they were and what the signal coverage was at the time of the survey

- Logical representation of the network

- A physical network design that shows cabling, mounting locations, and other details

RF Design

One of the most important details when troubleshooting a WLAN is documentation of AP locations and the RF environment. This information is the result of the site survey process as defined in Chapter 9.

Once an RF design is determined, final selection of exact AP placement as well as antenna choices and mounting methods need to be documented. Each AP placement should minimally include the following information:

- A description of AP locations—a text description of where the AP is placed, including nearby rooms, markers, or other identifiable sources
- A map of AP locations
- The AP make and model
- Mounting details
- Antenna selection and orientation (if applicable)
- The power level used in the original survey
- RF channel (only when automated channel management isn't used or specific channels need to be avoided, such as when interference was found)
- Cabling and power considerations, such as cable media type, termination, origination source, and power source

Including Photos in Your Documentation

Photos are often a debated topic with AP placement documentation. They can be incredibly valuable to installation teams to identify exact AP location, mounting considerations, or any other detail that needs to be called out. On the other hand, they may provide very little value and unnecessarily bloat the size of the document.

Two problems are often found with photos included with site survey documentation. The first problem is when no identifiable markers are included in the photo. For example, let's say that an AP is supposed to be mounted in an indoor location from a suspended T-bar ceiling. T-bar ceilings often look in one place just like every other place where a similar ceiling is installed. When these photos are taken, be sure to include some identifiable characteristic of the area that is unique.

The second common problem is just the opposite. That is, instead of focusing too closely on one area with no distinction, photos of distant locations are submitted. Without adequate zoom into the specific area of interest, the photo provides no additional value to the audience of the document.

The bottom line is that if photos are included for AP placement, you should make certain they have an explicit purpose and provide value to the installation team.

AP locations also need to be very clearly documented on maps. A single, clean map with AP locations, their labels, and even the base radio MAC address for each radio can greatly enhance troubleshooting efforts. A second map that also shows signal coverage from an actual site survey is valuable as well. Ideally, the final coverage map is one that is based on a post-validation survey—one that is performed after all APs and antennas have been placed.

Logical Network Design

Logical network designs show all of the system components and the path by which data flows in the system. As opposed to a physical topology, a logical network design is independent from the physical interconnections made between network components. During documentation, each system component should be labeled along with its network addresses. Often icons are used to represent system components with lines in and out of them to represent links between components, such as the one shown in Figure 13.1.

FIGURE 13.1   Sample logical network design

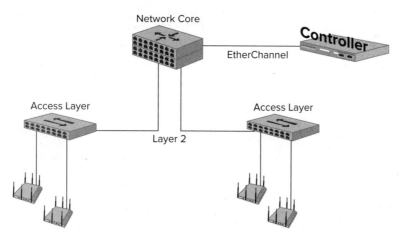

The WLAN controller as shown in Figure 13.1 shows a connection to the network core. The physical connection(s) to the WLAN controller can be any type of EtherChannel link that can be configured in a variety of ways. For example, two, four, or more physical Ethernet links can be used in an EtherChannel configuration and bonded together to obtain greater bandwidth and redundancy.

The logical network design documentation is one of the most important documents to convey your design to a large audience. Showing network devices, where they are located in the network hierarchy and logically how they are connected, abstracts the finer details that do not matter to a larger audience.

When drawing links between systems in logical network designs, you should provide only enough detail to convey the medium, such as Ethernet and wireless, and include information such as the VLAN number or the SSID.

Some logical designs go as far as providing device names and IP addresses, but this may not always be necessary to convey logical design concepts.

Physical Network Design

Because logical network design documents do not explain details of how network devices are connected to each other, we usually place that detail into *physical network design* documents. Physical network documentation should specify the following:

- Actual ports used on the local network device

- Ports used on the peer endpoint from the local device

- The media type by which the devices are connected

- MAC addresses, IP addresses, and/or actual device names, in order to clearly identify which device is being referred to

Eliminating as much ambiguity as possible is one of the major goals of physical network design documents.

An example of a physical network design appears in Figure 13.2.

FIGURE 13.2 Sample physical network design

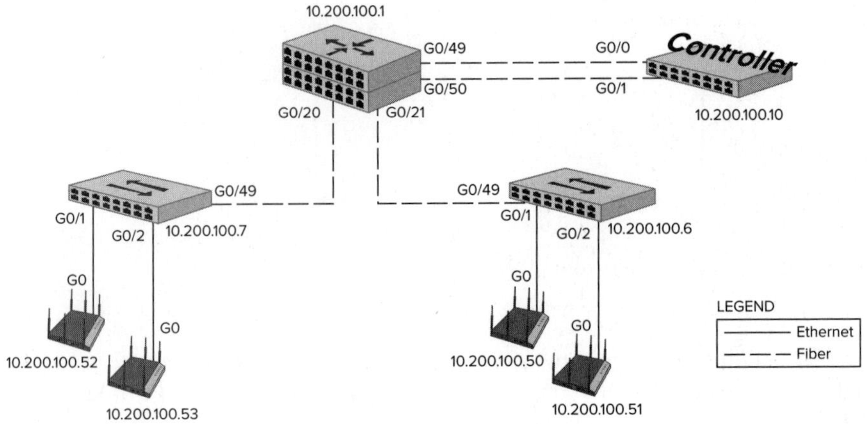

Notice that each device shown in the design has each physical connection to other devices clearly documented. The physical port that each cable is plugged into is shown in the document along with the media type of the connection. Furthermore, each device is shown with the specific IP address it has been assigned. Your organization or customer may prefer to use a device name that will also be entered into the DNS server.

Physical network designs should also have a spreadsheet of the network devices and important information documented such as IP addresses, VLAN assignments, MAC addresses, serial numbers, and other important details.

High-Level Design

High-level designs (HLDs) are primarily used to provide an overview of a WLAN design solution. As it fits into the larger documentation scheme, the HLD is like a general design framework around which specific design components can be built. It provides a set of standards (such as vendor selection and deployment architecture) that facilitate a certain amount of design continuity across the enterprise. The importance and extent to which HLDs are used in some organizations will vary. HLDs are often included to convey a network design standard that can be used in a number of network implementations. Larger networks of significant cost usually incorporate HLDs because of the amount of attention paid to larger projects by upper management and other key stakeholders.

Single implementations usually do not produce a separate HLD document. These installations may simply combine elements from an HLD into a low-level design (LLD) document, which we will discuss later in this chapter.

If you're in a larger organization and deploying a new WLAN technology, you can create an HLD document that discusses the following:

- Details of the design that relate back to business and technical requirements.

- Services that are provided by the new design standard

- An architectural overview

- Specific mention of the primary WLAN applications of data, voice/video, location, and guest network services

If you are deploying a number of sites based on a single design methodology, you should develop an HLD that will then be used to help encourage conformity to the design team's goals.

We will now review the various document sections that you should include in an HLD document. Use these sections as a starting point and include or omit specific sections based on your audience, organization, and design needs.

Executive Summary

An *executive summary* is used in a variety of business documents and serves the purpose of summarizing the entire document at a high level so that a busy executive need only read that single section to understand the core concepts of the design. It is possible that an executive will skim the rest of the document, but many do not get past the executive summary.

Executive summaries should include the following:

- Business objective mapping that discusses how the design meets major business requirements
- A description of the other goals of the project and how the design meets them
- A section that highlights any concerns the client should be aware of and how they can support addressing them
- A brief illustration of other important benefits of the solution that may not have been covered by the business requirements and goals

Engineering Summary

HLD documents for larger WLAN designs can be quite long. Engineers and implementers who are producing individual designs based on them do not always want to or have time to read a lengthy document. Ideally they will read the entire document, but you should also include a summary section for engineers that includes hard-hitting and design summary information that they can quickly reference. This section should clarify details that may not be easily picked up in a large document.

Any type of design information that can be summarized into tables and cheat sheets should be included in the engineering summary section. Examples may include, but are not required or limited to:

- Decision criteria for device placement
- Decision criteria for subnet sizing
- Decision criteria for VLAN numbering
- Decision criteria for redundancy

Background and Goals

This section of the document addresses background and goals and should at least include a review of the business and technical project requirements. It may be important to also summarize the business driver for WLAN design and certain information that might be important to a designer.

Some organizations also have to adhere to regulatory policies or their own internal standards. When this is the case, you should reference these policies and discuss how the design addresses (or does not address) concerns related to these policies.

Services and Applications

In Chapter 3, "Designing for Applications," we discussed several types of WLAN application types: data, voice/video, location services, and guest access. In this section, you should call out specifically which type of applications the WLAN is being designed to accommodate. You can go into detail under each of these categories if there are additional details that you think your audience will be looking for.

If voice and video are applications that your design will be supporting, you should detail the QoS design and features you are specifying in the HLD. This must include both wireless and wired QoS configurations. Guest networks may also have QoS markings in order to place that traffic into the lowest possible QoS queue.

Architecture

In this section that covers architecture, it is a great opportunity to indicate the specific platform(s) the design is based around, which includes the vendor and make and model. You should mention specific components of the overall solution and their function within the design.

For each type of make and model, it is important to describe the type of data forwarding model. Chapter 5, "Vendor and WLAN Architecture Selection," discussed several types of WLAN architectures and modes of data forwarding.

Redundancy design is another important topic to include in this section. Include design details about the WLAN equipment itself as well as other elements of your design that address redundancy elements related to LAN connectivity, power supply, or other areas.

Diagrams are another important element to include in this section. Diagrams should only be logical network diagrams in an HLD document. They should detail the topology of the network and where the WLAN components reside in the overall LAN hierarchical design.

Finally, include a section on security design. It's important to document where the authentication server fits into your network design. If possible, the network distance from the 802.1X authenticators (APs or WLAN controllers) should be apparent from the diagram.

Low-Level Design

If you've ever heard the saying "The devil is in the details" and it didn't fully sink in, it will once you've authored a *low-level design (LLD) document*. This document takes the design that has been outlined by the HLD document and fleshes out all the intricate details that are required to successfully deploy the design. It's essentially the DNA of a network design and should give any engineer who reads it a solid understanding of how the design is or will be deployed and the configurations that make it work.

LLD documents are usually based on implementations of a single WLAN installation. The LLD documents the actual configuration and implementation choices made for a specific installation.

When approaching the creation of the LLD, there are generally two trains of thought:

Straw Man LLD   For some installations it might make more sense to put together a *straw man LLD*. A straw man LLD means that you have the basic configuration details but there are several unanswered configuration details that you will document as you go. The LLD will then be completed as the actual installation ends up in the final state.

Full LLD   Alternatively, you can do the *full LLD* from the start and make incremental updates as changes occur.

In either instance, it's important to realize that the document is only as good as it is accurate. The "details" described earlier tend to change frequently as things like scope creep and previously unknown requirements surface later in the deployment.

You'll find that there are trade-offs in the two LLD approaches. The straw man LLD is more process driven and is updated in stages, requiring less dedicated, up-front commitment. However, if you aren't persistent and committed to making updates during the installation, you can end up with an incomplete document. On the other hand, the full LLD requires a lot of up-front planning and documentation, but it lends itself toward more thorough preparation and completeness. Whichever camp you're in, you should develop as detailed an LLD as possible before stepping into any installation. You can always modify an LLD during the course of an installation with information such as the switch port you used for an AP.

Once you're finally at the point where you are ready to create your LLD, you need to decide where to start. While there is certainly some room for interpretation and creativity, most LLDs will have sections covering the following topics:

- About This Document
  - Document Purpose
  - Intended Audience
  - Scope
  - Assumptions and Caveats
  - Related Documents
- Network Overview
- Network Architecture
- Technology areas
- Software Summary
- Installation Requirements
- Equipment List – BOM
- History/Review/Document Acceptance

About This Document

Every professional document requires a bit of overhead in order to provide context to all audiences whether or not they are familiar with the project. Every LLD should start with a short section detailing who the author(s) are and the document reference numbers will be used for revision control tracking. Contact information should be included for each document author to facilitate revisions and to address questions to.

Document Purpose   This section should be short and to the point. Essentially you are making a statement that the document is a representation of a design and the relevant design decisions that were made along with their configurations. Don't go overboard on this section—just a simple statement reflecting what the LLD contains and why is all you need.

Intended Audience   This section is another short, direct section. It should be no more than a sentence or two describing who the document is aimed at—typically the network planning and engineering personnel responsible for the day-to-day maintenance and troubleshooting of the network.

Scope   This section of your LLD should describe the bounds for the document. Describe what technologies the LLD is covering. If some things are purposely left out, this is a good place to describe what is not covered and why. Stating what is not included is just as important as stating what is included.

Assumptions and Caveats   Assumptions about the detailed requirements should be documented in the customer requirements document (or CRD, discussed in Chapter 1, "Gathering and Analyzing Requirements"). If for some reason a CRD does not exist, the Assumptions and Caveats can be listed in this section; however, it is ideal to have the CRD created early and point to it as a reference from this section of the LLD.

Related Documents   This section should contain a list of documents that are referenced in the design. Documents such as the previously discussed CRD and HLD should be listed here as well as any other configuration guides, IP addressing spreadsheets, configuration templates, diagrams, and policies.

Network Overview

This section should contain a high-level overview of the entire design. The content from this section can be easily pulled from the HLD and only needs to introduce the design without going into details about any specific component or technology. Those specifics will be addressed directly in the following sections. This section should include a high-level network diagram. If the WLAN will be integrated to a LAN, which is typical, the LAN architecture should be shown in this section.

Network Architecture

At this point you are starting to get into the meat of the document. The Network Architecture section should contain details of the WLAN component devices and how they are physically connected to one another. From there it should go into the configuration specifics for each device and provide an explanation of the services it provides. This information should include the logical flow of information during both the steady-state operation as well as when failover scenarios occur.

This section is typically focused primarily on the routing and switching core network components. It should describe where other advanced technology components are located within the network, but the specifics for those technologies are typically explained in a section dedicated to that particular technology.

If you are only responsible for the wireless portion of the design, then you will likely be writing the wireless LLD as a portion of the overall LLD. On the other hand, if you are in a situation where the wired network infrastructure already exists prior to your engagement with the project, you can reference the LLD that should have been created when the original network was deployed.

Logical and Physical Designs

LLD documents need to include a logical and physical diagram of the network design. The details surrounding accomplishing this were discussed in the beginning of this chapter. In the LLD, provide both a Layer 2 and a Layer 3 design.

IP Addresses, Names, Interface Details

Create a table or spreadsheet that provides a central reference for all IP addresses and DNS names for each network component. A single network component might have several interfaces and all need to be included in this table.

It's a good idea to include a table of VLANs in this section as well. Each VLAN should have a description of how it is used and what device(s) provide routing for each VLAN.

Technology Areas

If your design encompasses more technologies than just wireless (yes, that is the norm), then from this section forward all of those technologies should be broken out into sections. If, however, you are only responsible for adding wireless to an existing wired network, this section should contain only information on the specifics of the network as they pertain to the wireless implementation.

From here on out, each section of the LLD will be focused on the specific technologies used in the design. The following sections give guidance on what areas are typically included in the wireless section of an LLD:

Hardware Selections There should be a section that has vendor and model information on every device being used. It's also a good idea to include links to the product documentation and configurations guides from the website of the vendor(s) involved. This information comes in handy both in the deployment phase and in the future when you need to know whether things like a particular feature, RF channel, or power setting are supported on a particular device.

SSIDs Dedicate a section to explaining the details about each SSID implemented in the design along with its function. You can pull many of the details for this section from the CRD and HLD as a start, but the specific settings for each particular SSID need to be documented here. In terms of specifics, the amount of documentation can be quite large for each SSID. To help with this, it's generally accepted that any nondefault configuration needs to be documented and explained.

You can expect this section to get quite large as there will likely be lots of details depending on the complexity of the design. A data, voice–video, location, and guest design will generate significant configuration details that need to be documented. Remember, details are important at this stage.

Mobility Design   This section should explain how clients will roam from location to location throughout the network. This includes explanations of IP subnet sizing and their related addressing boundaries. Explain where Layer 2 versus Layer 3 roams will occur and provide details regarding the traffic flow of each scenario.

Failover Design   This section should explain how the devices are connected and configured to provide redundancy. Give details on what the network should look like in steady state, as well as in a failure scenario. Outline how the network will be configured to balance the load under normal conditions as well as how it will handle failures and what the failure scenarios will be.

Security   Enterprise security (802.1X/EAP) requires infrastructure components in order to provide functionality to the WLAN. Locations of authentication servers (ASs) and information regarding their redundancy configuration should also be included. Also include the EAP types that are supported by the ASs, particularly specific configuration details that are important for each WLAN component. This includes the order of the servers within each WLAN controller or AP.

Authenticator devices (WLAN controllers and APs) sometimes have specific features regarding AS failover, timers, and other information. Any of these features or details should be included in this section as well.

Software Summary

Software versions used for network devices may change over time, but it is imperative to document the software version that the design is to be deployed with. Only once a new software version is tested should a device run anything other than what the LLD specifies. At that point, the LLD should be revised specifying a new software version that all devices need to incorporate along with any other features that may be implemented at the time of the upgrade. When the LLD document is referenced at a later date, it can clear up questions as to why a particular feature was or wasn't used.

Installation Requirements

AP placement may not always dictate a uniform installation method. Some APs require special consideration for installation even when used in indoor environments. In contrast, outdoor AP installations tend to have unique installation requirements for each AP. This can include how the APs are powered; the type of antenna, orientation, and polarization; physical mounting; and housing. We recommend that you include details on every outdoor AP if there are unique elements for each of them.

Equipment List – BOM

Each LLD that is developed is unique. LLDs, by definition, are site specific and usually have differences from site to site. This can include items such as access switches and uplink capacity. It can sometimes be as simple as mounting brackets and patch cable lengths.

Bill of materials (BOMs) should include all components needed to implement an entire location where a WLAN will be installed. Design approval should be based on a full solution implementation to bring the network from an existing state to the final state with all details. Include in the BOM anything needed to connect and power each network component that doesn't already exist.

The BOM will minimally include the product name, part or ordering numbers, quantity, description, and optionally price.

History/Review/Document Acceptance

Finally, be sure to conclude the LLD document with a page that provides a means to document the history of the LLD. Keep in mind that an LLD is a living document and as changes are made to the network over time, those changes have to be incorporated into the existing LLD with the dates that the changes were made. These updates don't always happen, but for the diligent customers who do keep their documentation up-to-date, future changes and modifications will be made easier.

In some organizations, maintaining an accurate LLD is coincident with any and all network updates. In that sense, management will require that the LLD be reviewed and updated prior to approval of network updates. For that reason, keeping up with the history of revisions is important for document acceptance by management.

Operational and Maintenance Plan

It is hard enough to fully design, engineer, and implement a new technology system. Many believe it can even be harder to operate and maintain one. So although a relatively small number of people are typically involved in the design and engineering processes, don't be surprised that the operational and maintenance phase has the largest number of people interacting with the new system. The diversity and quantity of the additional people involved with a design introduces an entirely new complexity. The operation and maintenance stage requires extensive documentation if support services, change management, network continuity, and workflow processes are to be maintained with consistency.

Whenever a new system is designed and placed into a production environment, it shouldn't be considered complete without thoughtful consideration as to how it will be operated and maintained. This includes system administration, monitoring and maintenance, troubleshooting procedures, staff preparation and role definition, and much more. These processes can be documented in a manual that defines operational processes. You may see a master document that defines operational and maintenance procedures, and then some subdisciplines of operation (such as help desk) will also have their own documentation policies.

System Administration

Whenever referring to the role involved with operating and maintaining a technology system, the term *system administration* is often used. The system administrator performs updates to the system once the system is in production. Administrators also monitor the health of the infrastructure and even the end user devices in some organizations.

Every technology system requires an administrator of some sort. The role of the system administrator from a WLAN point of view is usually assigned to perform all day-to-day infrastructure management activities.

Network Monitoring

There are a variety of methods organizations can use to perform network monitoring. Most of the time, a monitoring server is installed that uses a wide range of means to obtain device status. This can include SNMP protocols or even HTTP and other types of application protocols that the system uses. Many WLAN systems today have built-in monitoring and reporting capabilities that implement dashboard overviews as well as detailed menus. These systems often also include automated alarms.

Larger organizations usually have some sort of *network operations center (NOC)* that receives monitoring alerts from monitoring software systems and can make a decision on how best to respond to the alarm.

Your design should include detailed information about how the new network will be monitored on an ongoing basis. This can be a manual process or it may be automated. Someone will be responsible for performing these functions or ensuring that the system is functioning as designed, and these processes should be documented in the LLD. Monitoring encompasses performance as well as security monitoring.

Maintenance

Maintenance activities involve performing necessary updates to systems as well as regular procedures that ensure the continued operational health of all the system components. This includes backing up configurations and message logs, managing storage space, or just about any other activity that a system requires to remain in a healthy operational status.

Change control procedures should be followed whenever maintenance activities occur, which include documenting the activities and having backup plans in case something goes awry. This section should also cover device failure and repair or replacement processes. Vendor or reseller service contact information could be useful in the documentation here as well.

Troubleshooting

We hope that troubleshooting will never be necessary, but inevitably it always is. When users encounter problems with their wireless connectivity, they need to know how to obtain support and troubleshoot their issues.

Specify the roles and means by which users will contact the proper personnel to obtain support. In addition to including this information in the operations documentation, these processes will often be defined in help desk manuals that designate troubleshooting policy. This can include calling a manufacturer help desk number or opening a trouble ticket using a software ticketing system. The ticketing system in turn instigates a process by which all of the proper staff are contacted and the response can be recorded and measured for service level agreements.

The tools the staff will use should be described in this document. You should also specify which troubleshooting procedures should be followed by the staff. I'm sure all of us can recall phoning a large company's help desk number and getting someone who asks a series of highly structured questions following a script. The script that the phone support personnel use is constantly updated with the most common problems based on incoming incidents and are designed to resolve operational problems as quickly as possible.

Feedback to Engineering

One of the most common problems larger organizations have when operating a system that is in production is how the information gets fed back to engineering and the design personnel who developed the initial system design. Larger organizations often repeat similar design methods from site to site, and it is critically important that feedback from each implementation make it back to the engineering and operational teams.

Call centers and software ticketing systems are some methods that can make this possible. There are certainly others, but the preferred method should be specified in your design documentation.

Procedures

To make changes to any existing system, change management procedures should always be followed. Smaller organizations often do not have clear or documented procedures when changes may be performed. Describe in this document what procedures should be followed in order to perform any type of configuration change or maintenance operation that can affect the stability and continued operation of the system. This includes having other staff members review the changes that are to be performed and limiting change windows to specific times of day.

Some changes to WLAN infrastructure components do not affect the experience for end users, whereas others may cause a complete system outage for a period of time. Regardless of the change, document it and have a colleague review your changes before they are performed on the production infrastructure.

Staff

Installing a new WLAN will affect the day-to-day lives of two primary groups: the end users and the IT staff who support the WLAN. Each group should also have some form of training that covers how the WLAN will affect their job. You will find that some of these processes are defined in employee manuals, but for this discussion, we are primarily focused on defining training processes in a network operation manual. In that manual, there should be a staff and an end user training section. We will discuss some basics for preparing these two groups in the following section.

IT Staff Preparation

Wireless technology is a fairly new technology for most people, even IT staff. While many of us have wireless networks at home, there are many differences in enterprise hardware to consider. Here are some examples:

- The need for roaming is much greater.
- The security model is different.
- The size of the network is different.
- The usage policies are stricter and have bigger implications.

We recommend that you provide some type of training program and set of operational tools to help ensure the success of the overall WLAN implementation. One thing is certain: without any form of training or tools for IT staff to assist with troubleshooting, problems encountered with the system will likely continue to extended periods of time that will most certainly affect productivity of all users of the system. You should compare the cost of the loss of productivity to the cost of the training and tools for the IT staff.

In this section includes the types of training as well as the tools that are to be used. If the network is sufficiently large, it is possible that there may not be enough staff to support the WLAN at all. If this is the case, you should explain this to management.

End User Preparation

End users who will be using the WLAN will usually be required to perform their daily functions in a different manner. The effect on the workers' daily functions should be conveyed to them, usually via regular training sessions, in operational manuals, or through employee handbooks. New expectations may also be required of the end users, and these should also be included in a training program.

Training can be provided via in-person or instructor-led methods, or it may be incorporated into an electronic method that can be provided to a large audience in geographically dispersed areas. Electronic methods also benefit from the ability to score the comprehension of the audience to ensure a minimum baseline is met.

The Handoff

Once an operational plan has been made, the support systems and procedures are in place, and all the staff are trained, you can begin handing off the system to the operations team. Often there are limited periods of time that engineering will partner with operations in order to jointly provide service to end users. This phase allows for a seamless handover to the operations team.

Summary

Producing good documentation is hard work. However, as we discussed in the beginning of this chapter, it should be clear just how important it is to facilitating sustained and healthy operations for a WLAN design.

In this chapter you learned how to produce documentation for the smallest of WLAN designs as well as the largest. We discussed the minimum requirements to document any WLAN design, regardless of size.

Especially with larger WLANs, it's critical to base your installation on high-level design (HLD) documents. When a large number of staff members are involved in deploying and supporting installations of each WLAN, the stakes are even greater.

We also reviewed low-level design (LLD) documents and the different types of sections that should be included in them. Operational documents also need to be created to aid in the long-term support and maintenance of the WLAN. Once a design is implemented and all the documentation exists to support it, it can then be handed off.

Exam Essentials

Understand the components of and critical factors for network design. Be able to identify, explain, and interpret network design deliverables.

Understand the components of an RF site survey. Be able to explain what details need to be included in survey documentation and what data to use.

Explain documentation best practices for the high-level design. Understand the purpose behind HLDs and how to best utilize best practices in your design.

Explain documentation best practices for the low-level design. Understand the purpose behind LLDs and how to best utilize best practices in your design.

Describe design reports and their sections. Understand what documents should be included in design documentation reports.

Explain how operational documents are used and what they should contain. Discuss the value and contents of operational documentation and their value to end users and IT support teams.

Review Questions

1. What level of documentation do large enterprise deployments require that the network designer provide?

   A. Depends on complexity and scope

   B. Always requires HLD, LLD, operation and maintenance manuals, employee handbooks, and help desk manuals

   C. Requires at least an HLD and an LLD

   D. Enterprises may not require any documentation.

2. Name the audience type not addressed in this chapter for HLDs.

   A. Engineering

   B. Executives

   C. Operations

   D. Designers

3. Young Kimball Corp. is designing a WLAN for their new billiard hall. The number of APs required for full facility coverage was determined to be four APs, but they would like to do data and voice applications. What design documents would you recommend at a minimum? (Choose all that apply.)

   A. Logical network design

   B. Physical network design

   C. High-level design

   D. RF design

4. You work at a university and need to cover indoor spaces. A colleague of yours wants every desired AP location from the RF site survey to have a photo, but she has asked for your input. What considerations can you offer? (Choose all that apply.)

   A. All AP locations need to have close-up photos to determine mounting hardware.

   B. Photos taken at a distance illustrate AP placement relative to other locations.

   C. Photo file sizes add to the document file size and should have an explicit purpose.

   D. Photos can be taken with average cell phones for nearly all photos.

5. You are creating a logical network design for a large WLAN implementation. What information should be included in the deliverable? (Choose all that apply.)

   A. Number of interfaces

   B. Icons of network devices

   C. Physical interfaces

   D. IP addresses

6. In what design document deliverable is a logical network design usually found?

    A. HLD

    B. LLD

    C. Operational and maintenance plan

    D. RF design

7. Your company, Tom's Transmission Lines, requires a WLAN at 15 locations around the globe for a single application and has a centralized support department. What design document is not needed?

    A. LLD

    B. RF design

    C. HLD

    D. Operational and maintenance plan

    E. None of the above

8. An engineering summary is helpful in what type of document?

    A. Site survey document

    B. LLD

    C. Logical network design

    D. HLD

    E. CRD

9. What design document should specify redundancy criteria for WLAN designs?

    A. HLD

    B. LLD

    C. Business requirements document

    D. CRD

10. You are an engineer for Mark Us Burnt On T-shirt Design Company and are responsible for a WLAN design at a single production facility. What document will you be most likely required to produce?

    A. Operational and maintenance plan

    B. HLD

    C. CRD

    D. LLD

11. What type of design document usually results in a BOM?

    A. HLD

    B. RF Survey

    C. LLD

    D. CRD

12. What element is typically not detailed in an LLD security section?

   A. EAP types

   B. Authentication server order

   C. Security policy

   D. AS redundancy

13. A table of VLANs in a _____ document should include what device performs _____ services. (Fill in the blanks)

   A. LLD, bridging

   B. LLD, routing

   C. HLD, QoS

   D. HLD, routing

14. The installation crew for your WLAN project wants to install a few APs to locations nearby the ones specified in the RF design document. What next step should occur?

   A. Consult the RF designer.

   B. Confirm the mounting hardware.

   C. Choose a different AP model.

   D. Update the documentation.

15. What might happen if the following information is provided to install a PTP root bridge in an LLD?
Antenna type, azimuth angle, RF channel, and mounting hardware and location

   A. Power mismatch

   B. Channel mismatch

   C. Improper alignment

   D. Vertical standing wave ratio

16. You are reviewing an LLD document and you come across configuration items for radio settings. Several settings are specified, but several others are not. What should you do?

   A. Implement the specified settings.

   B. Use settings complementary to the ones specified.

   C. Ask the document author to finish the document.

   D. Some settings are obvious and don't always need to be specified.

17. You are being asked to author an HLD for a WLAN design. You come to the Network Overview section. What should you include in this section?

   A. Requirements review

   B. Physical design

   C. AP placement

   D. Logical design

18. All of the design documents and network assurance steps are completed and the handoff is ready to occur when somebody calls to your attention that something was forgotten. At this stage of the deployment, what important business objective may still need to be accomplished?

    A. Post-deployment validation

    B. Staff training

    C. Pilot testing

    D. Firmware updates

19. What important item is often left out of operational and maintenance plans?

    A. Network overview

    B. Syslog analysis

    C. Configuration backups

    D. Engineering feedback

20. You are part of the implementation team and you notice the equipment arrived with a newer firmware than the one specified in the design documentation. What course of action do you choose?

    A. Use the newer software version.

    B. Let the document author(s) know a new one is available.

    C. Downgrade it to the one specified.

    D. Assume the design document is out of date.

Answers to Review Questions

1. **A.** Even large enterprise deployments may not require a lot of documentation. Large deployments can have highly repetitive components that do not need a lot of detailed explanation. Therefore, the amount of time required for documentation may not be extensive.

2. **C.** High-level design documents are not geared toward operations teams. They primarily provide information for engineering teams to base individual designs on and/or address major design decisions.

3. **A, B, D.** Small networks do not typically require high-level design documents. Usually low-level design documents can address any design-related questions without requiring a separate document.

4. **B, C.** Photos should only be included when they offer information that can be valuable to each placement. Design documents are typically printed out on black and white printers and are often illegible. If you decide to include a photo, it should have easily identifiable markers of surrounding objects to aid in placing APs.

5. **B, D.** Only high-level details need to be included in logical network designs. The number of interfaces as well as which physical interfaces are used is usually too detailed for logical network designs.

6. **A.** The high-level design (HLD) should always include a logical network design.

7. **E.** For a deployment of this scale, you should produce all of the documents listed in A through D.

8. **D.** HLDs should contain summary information for engineers to base design decisions on.

9. **C.** Business requirement documents specify the criteria on which design parameters need to be based.

10. **D.** Often, for single-facility network designs, a more detailed design document, the LLD, is required. Since the high-level design will not be reused by the business, it is important to specify all the intricate details of the network so that the LLD can be referenced for troubleshooting or future design changes.

11. **C.** Low-level designs produce the information necessary to order project materials for WLAN design implementations.

12. **C.** Security policy is typically referenced by LLD and even HLD documents. HLDs usually address how the security policy is satisfied by the chosen design approach.

13. **B.** LLDs should include documentation of VLANs being used along with what device provides the routing for the VLAN.

14. **A.** Before making any changes to antenna orientation and placement, the RF design team needs to be consulted. If a decision is made to change the placement, then and only then should the documentation be updated.

15. C. The elevation angle was not specified in the included list. Elevation plays a big role in PTP antenna alignment, especially for high-gain antennas.

16. A. In LLDs where some configuration details are specified but others are missing, it should be assumed that other unspecified settings are default values.

17. D. Logical network designs are commonly included in the section that provides an overview of the network design.

18. B. Documents help a great deal, but in order to hand off a WLAN design to support staff, some form of training needs to occur.

19. D. One of the most common yet critical components of operational and maintenance plans is feedback of common and frequent support events to engineering and design staff.

20. C. If specific software revisions are specifically called out for network devices, you should always use the one specified in the documentation with no questions asked.

Chapter

14

Post-Installation Validation

THE FOLLOWING CWDP EXAM TOPICS ARE COVERED IN THIS CHAPTER:

✓ Describe common design practices for high availability and redundancy.

✓ Illustrate best practices for roaming support in a WLAN.

✓ Illustrate a comprehensive understanding of the role of channel planning and usage in network design.

✓ Describe the role of load balancing in RF spectrum management.

✓ Explain how to conduct a proper WLAN site survey according to industry best practices.

✓ Demonstrate a detailed and thorough understanding of surveying types and methodologies.

✓ Explain the metrics, data, and other information collected and reported during a site survey.

✓ Describe how channel planning and output power configurations are determined by an RF site.

✓ Identify the purpose and methods of post-installation site surveys.

✓ Perform and interpret an RF analysis for an existing WLAN deployment.

✓ Illustrate the use of a protocol analyzer and interpret the results to identify problems with the following aspects of network design:

  ▪ Security setup and configuration

  ▪ Roaming

  ▪ PHY rate analysis

- MAC feature parity
- QoS
- Client (including drivers) and infrastructure compatibility

✓ **Understand proper WLAN functionality, including wired infrastructure connectivity and services, and identify problematic characteristics in network design.**

✓ **Demonstrate a detailed knowledge of common client-side and application problems and isolate unexpected client behavior.**

Once a WLAN is finally installed, it is usually the result of a great deal of planning and preparation. Nonetheless, after all of this preparation there are still areas where the design needs to be tweaked. Depending on how much time has passed since the original WLAN survey, the RF design might need to be adjusted after everything is installed. Sources of RF interference might have cropped up since the original survey that should be mitigated before going live. Infrastructure and client feature configurations are also a common last-minute configuration item that may require further validation before the WLAN is turned to a production state.

WLAN infrastructure and client devices alike do not behave perfectly either. There are reasons why firmware and drivers get updated, and it is not always done just to enable new features. Humans write software and humans also make mistakes. In general, any sufficiently complex system will not be without bugs and certain features that do not behave equally in all deployment environments.

Security is an important factor to validate in a post-installation exercise. After all, the customer of the WLAN design is expecting that necessary security precautions were considered in the WLAN design, and without verifying their existence and proper behavior, you are not secure.

Finally, whenever deploying a new WLAN, you must thoroughly test applications. Even after everything is validated before this point, other issues may arise. Sometimes it may simply be a firewall rule or perhaps a real-time application like voice or Voice Over Wi-Fi (VoWiFi). The bottom line is that you must properly test a network and correct any and all forms of human error, design flaws, and software bugs before placing a WLAN into production use.

Post-Installation RF Assessment

Before assessing any other part of a new WLAN deployment, always start with the physical layer. As you've learned, the physical layer in WLANs is RF. Without a solid RF foundation in the design, support staff will constantly be chasing problems related to connectivity and performance, and they may look for a solution in many areas other than RF. That is why it is crucial to validate the performance of the most basic element of wireless communication: RF propagation.

The primary areas that we will focus on include transmit power and channel plans. Once you confirm that the configuration of these items is in line with your design plan, you will then confirm signal quality, otherwise known as signal-to-noise ratio (SNR).

After you perform that analysis, we will show you how to review those results and deal with areas that you determine to be trouble spots, should any exist.

Transmit Power

When a WLAN is surveyed, it is done so based on a specific transmit power on the APs used during the survey. Generally speaking, when you deploy the network, it should be configured in line with the original survey. If you plan on using automatic RF management features that are built into WLAN infrastructure products, you must ensure that the algorithm doesn't vary too far from this originally surveyed transmit power value.

Consider a WLAN that was surveyed for 25 mW, but the automatic RF management feature changed power down to 5 mW. What do you think will happen to the total cell size that you originally designed for? The same goes for automatically setting this value too far in the other direction. Perhaps the infrastructure automatically configured 100 mW as the transmit power. The cell size would be too big in comparison to the original survey, resulting in a lot of co-channel interference.

Sometimes when an automated RF management algorithm uses such radical values, it is an indicator that you might have a design problem, such as too many or too few APs or poorly planned mounting locations.

 Real World Scenario

AP Locations and Automated Radio Management

Consider a design where many APs are placed in a long hallway, such as the one shown here:

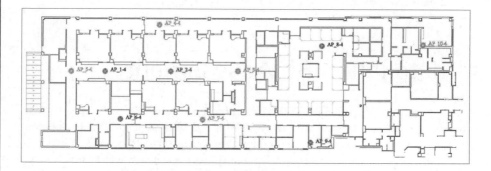

If your design requires that the APs be placed in the hallways as shown in the graphic and they cannot be placed in the rooms, automated RF management algorithms can go haywire. What happens is that the APs can hear one another very loudly. The automated

RF algorithms likely do not take into account that they are placed in a hallway in a straight line. In other words, a computer algorithm is not like human beings; after all, we can *see* the spatial orientation of APs placed in particular locations on a map. A computer algorithm is much simpler than that. WLAN systems usually look at raw received signal strength indicator (RSSI) values measured by each AP (while including other sources of RF and an overall SNR value) and then try to adjust each AP so that output power and channel settings are balanced across the system. The end goal here is to ensure that nearby APs are not talking too loudly over one another's coverage area. The only thing to do in this case is to lower the transmit power.

The computer algorithm may not take into account that lowering the transmit power too much just brought the downlink coverage from an AP below adequate levels. If an AP is advertising its power level—which most APs do by default in modern WLANs—the client devices will typically reciprocate power levels to match the power of the AP. Granted, this isn't always the case because the client device may have to support *Transmit Power Control (TPC)*.

The same scenario is also common in warehouse installations where higher gain omnidirectional antennas are placed on the ceiling above the inventory shelves. In this situation, all the APs hear one another very loudly.

It could be said that the AP layout, density, or mounting locations are flawed, which is why the algorithm is making those choices. As presented in the hallway case study, it might just be that there was a design constraint preventing the placement of APs in the rooms and not in the hallway. Remember, we cannot always place APs exactly where we want to place them.

The point of this explanation is that you should confirm the decisions a computer algorithm is making with your WLAN design. There are a variety of scenarios like this that may warrant disabling the automated RF management features. It doesn't mean that these features are all bad, but there are many times that the default settings for these features cause more problems than they solve. As these features become more sophisticated and WLAN designers adopt them more readily, most vendors are also adding better configuration options to tailor these features to your AP layout. This often includes sensitivity settings for power changes as well as scan intervals.

There is another point you should understand before performing an RF analysis of a new network. If an automated RF management system is in use and transmit power settings between APs are widely variant, you will also likely find that the actual transmit power settings vary considerably from the original, intended design. If a passive manual site survey was conducted to perform a coverage analysis, the site survey data will not likely reflect the currently configured transmit power. The settings and resultant coverage are dynamic. Therefore, you end up with a survey of how that network was dynamically configured at the moment you were surveying that particular area of the WLAN. For that reason, the data holds little long-term value. Transmit power settings change and the RF environment changes; application performance may change with them. Such an approach to RF validation confirms how the automated RF management algorithm performed at original deployment.

We recommend that you configure a WLAN infrastructure to the power levels that you originally surveyed for before performing an analysis of a new WLAN infrastructure. For example, if you originally surveyed the environment using 25 mW of transmit power, we recommend configuring all of the WLAN infrastructure APs for that same transmit power. This allows you to see a baseline of how the final installation varies from the original survey. It will also more readily point out where you are likely to have performance problems with your new WLAN.

Remember, automated RF management algorithms cannot manufacture RF. Furthermore, they cannot completely compensate for a bad design. However, they may be used to fine-tune your WLAN using empirical and mathematical models, assuming that they do not have known software bugs.

Channel Plan

One of the most beneficial features of automated RF management algorithms is channel planning. When new networks are brought online, turning on this one feature can save a lot of manual configuration. If you do plan on using dynamic channel assignment features on a brand-new network, the system will require a fair amount of time to perform this optimization. A good rule of thumb on a larger WLAN that uses a hundred APs or more is to allow at least 12 hours for the automated settings to tune, adjust, and eventually reach a state of relative balance. Waiting longer may be necessary in some cases depending on the infrastructure product.

If you plan on configuring a manual channel plan, that is fine, too. It might even be easier for smaller networks to configure channels manually rather than waiting for the algorithm to optimize the network over a long time period. For systems that do not have dynamic channel assignment algorithms, you have no choice other than to configure them manually.

Remember, channel changes are disruptive events to client devices. There better be a good reason for an AP to change channels if it is currently serving client devices. When an AP changes channels, it may use channel change announcement messages that are designed for 5 GHz radar detection and avoidance. However, this solution wasn't specified as an all-around way to dynamically change AP channel settings, so it may be insufficient for most scenarios, especially for 2.4 GHz networks. In some cases, the AP may simply deauthenticate all associated clients, change its channel, and then wait for clients to reassociate after rediscovering the AP. Ideally, any AP channel change would incorporate application-aware intelligence, which would prevent disruption of any important WLAN services.

Poor vendor implementations of dynamic channel setting features have caused some APs to change channels for no reason or to change channels at an inopportune time. It is somewhat funny how heavily these features have been marketed for so long, and now that they are beginning to incorporate spectrum-level intelligence, they are starting to work more or less as initially advertised when these features first came to market. Suffice it to say that these features are getting much better in the newest hardware and software products.

If dynamic channel assignment is a feature that you will be using, you may have to adjust the algorithm in order for the feature to function in your new WLAN. These adjustments may include minimum and maximum transmit power settings, scan intervals and lengths, data error thresholds, application awareness settings, and many other parameters that will impact channel (and transmit power) settings. Keep in mind that if you do not see the results you might expect—such as a group of APs staying on the same channel—you may have to adjust these default values.

Regardless of the method that you choose, ensure that the channel plan looks as you might expect to see in an optimized WLAN. Until this is done, you should make the proper adjustments before continuing with your post-assessment.

Signal Quality

In an RF assessment, simple RSSI measurements are not enough. You must also evaluate a more aggregate signal level, which is called signal-to-noise ratio (SNR), or, when interference is included in the metric, signal-to-interference and noise ratio (SINR). When a signal is received by a radio, the amplitude of the signal is important, but the usefulness of that signal is measured relative to its distinction from the noise floor and other RF interference. Just like when you are having a conversation in a busy restaurant, the background noise causes one of two things: you increase your own volume or you misunderstand what you hear and ask for it to be repeated. I suppose a third possibility is that you have exceptional hearing, but even still, the noise will likely affect your conversation. The same applies when dealing with RF networks.

If there are areas in your new WLAN deployment that have traditionally adequate signal levels but are accompanied by a high noise floor, performance will suffer. For example, if signal levels from an AP are measured at −67 dBm and the noise floor in the same location is −92 dBm, the SNR is 25 dB. If the same signal level was measured but the noise floor was elevated to −87 dBm, the signal quality would be worse at 20 dB. This difference might cause more transmission errors, resulting in a rate shift that decreases the PHY data rate.

If your site assessment reveals high noise levels in some areas, you need to investigate its source(s).

One of the best methods to assess your new WLAN for real-world traffic conditions is to perform a survey using a survey mapping software package. Once the RF data is gathered, you can view the results of the data in terms of signal quality (e.g., SNR), instead of raw signal amplitude, as shown on the coded heat map in Figure 14.1. In survey software, these maps are color-coded, which makes the data easier to read. In the same way, you can also view the data only showing signal or noise levels.

FIGURE 14.1 Illustration of signal quality

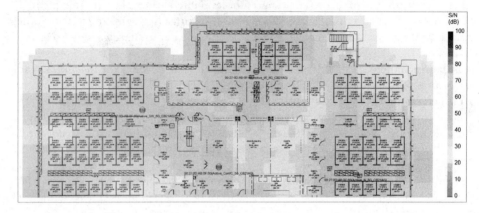

Assessing SNR by filtering out levels below, say, 25 dB of SNR should yield where VoWiFi handsets are likely to have performance problems. For an RF assessment, you should not simply look at received signal amplitude alone.

It is important to note that some WLAN clients do not properly display noise levels to WLAN analysis software. Check the client's reporting capabilities, which may be available from the WLAN analysis vendor. In a "quiet" RF environment in the Wi-Fi frequencies, you will likely see noise levels between –95 and –100 dBm.

Trouble Spots

Upon analyzing the RF of a new network, you may have found some areas where the network needs to be augmented. Keep in mind that dynamic external factors, such as construction, furniture additions or removal, stock changes (as in a warehouse), and more can affect your design. Additionally, a network installer could have mounted an AP improperly because of carelessness or poor site survey documentation and AP mounting descriptions.

APs are sometimes mounted in strange places. Any number of variables could cause an AP to be mounted in the wrong place or way. In fact, many installation crews make mounting decisions independent of RF propagation behavior. For example, it may be difficult for an installation crew to access the ceiling in an area where the design has specified; in response, the AP may be mounted elsewhere, despite the fact that installation documentation is provided and that documentation is based on some form of predeployment site survey.

Another common issue is improper antenna orientation. If a survey was performed using an antenna pointed in one direction but installed in another, RF propagation will be different than the original design specification. Antennas may also be moved, causing improper polarization, after installation for many untold intentional or unintentional reasons.

Suffice it to say that a number of factors can come into play that will compromise a design between the time it was surveyed and specified and the time it was installed. Even if there was an error in the original design, it is best to handle it during the validation period before production use of the WLAN begins.

For designs that were based on predictive surveying methods, it is likely that there will be areas that need to be tuned for optimization. Whenever you are using predictive designs, it is likely that APs will need to be moved, added, or even removed. When adding APs after the initial installation, don't forget to weigh the cost of changes in time, labor, and hard costs (cabling, power, etc.).

Interference Mitigation

Before a new WLAN is rolled into a production state, it is always best to sweep the environment using a spectrum analyzer one last time. In new buildings where WLANs are just being installed along with other new systems purchased for the facility, there may be a source of unplanned RF interference.

If interference is found, the first challenge is identifying its sources and evaluating its potential impact on the WLAN. The second challenge is locating the source and determining an action plan to remove it if possible; if it cannot be removed, the action plan should specify how to mitigate its impact on the WLAN and design around it, as necessary.

Identifying Interference

Because we are only concerned with frequencies where 802.11 devices operate, PC-based spectrum analyzers are not only cost-effective in comparison to traditional spectrum analyzers, but they also have interference identification features that other spectrum analysis systems do not have. These features were discussed in Chapter 9, "Site Survey RF Design," but we now need to focus on utilizing specific features of these products for the purpose of identifying and mitigating RF interference.

One of the most important tools for gauging the severity of an interference source is by looking at duty cycle measurements. As you learned in Chapter 9, duty cycle is a measurement of the amount of time the transmitter is utilizing the RF medium above a specified threshold. When interference is found, you should obtain a baseline by allowing the spectrum analyzer to collect data over a moderate period of time (this will vary with the type of interference discovered and the mission criticality of the network). After all, you're only going to be able to quantify interference when the interferer is transmitting. It is very possible that an intermittent source of interference may be missed by simply walking through an area where the interference source is located.

Locating and Removing

After you discover interference, you can choose from many techniques, listed next, to locate the source device. Features are built into most spectrum analysis products that can filter the display to focus on a specific interference source and show a gauge of signal strength that aids location discovery.

Walking the Area   With omnidirectional antennas, discovery of source devices usually means that you must walk a fairly large area in order to locate where stronger signals are present and focus more attention there. This is a time-consuming task. Sometimes the source may not even be on the floor of the building where you are walking.

Directional Antennas   Directional antennas can be used as well. Keep in mind that within indoor buildings, signal reflections and other RF signal multipath may not lead you in the right location, but this is generally an accurate technique. If you decide to use a directional antenna, you may need to take signal readings from several areas (ideally spaced very far apart) to triangulate the strongest direction of the interference source. With directional antennas, lower antenna beamwidths (higher gain) provide greater location accuracy.

Survey Mapping   Some survey mapping software packages also have spectrum analyzer integration features. That means that you can walk a facility using only a spectrum analyzer and click on a map where each data point is taken. Then, you can view the recorded data after walking the area in order to help determine where the strongest signal is coming from. This technique is shown in Figure 14.2, where spectrum analysis measurements are taken as a part of a manual site survey.

FIGURE 14.2   AirMagnet Surveyor Pro spectrum integration

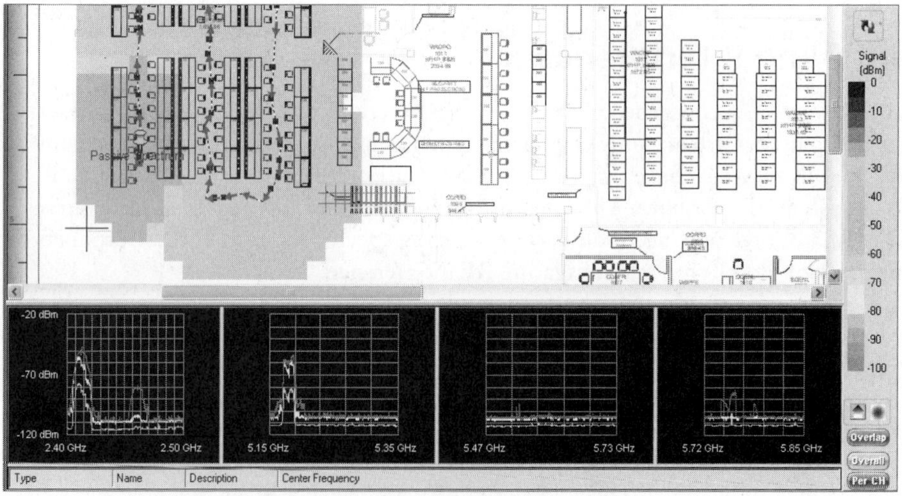

Integrated Spectrum Analysis   Most enterprise infrastructure AP products are starting to incorporate spectrum analyzer features into the WLAN. This allows a WLAN controller or management server to report the strongest signal source of the RF interference. Figure 14.3 shows an integrated spectrum analysis platform that is showing multiple interferers and identifying their locations. With this technology, narrowing the search down to a single AP is an incredible gain of efficiency when you are trying to seek out interference sources.

FIGURE 14.3   Cisco interference mapping features

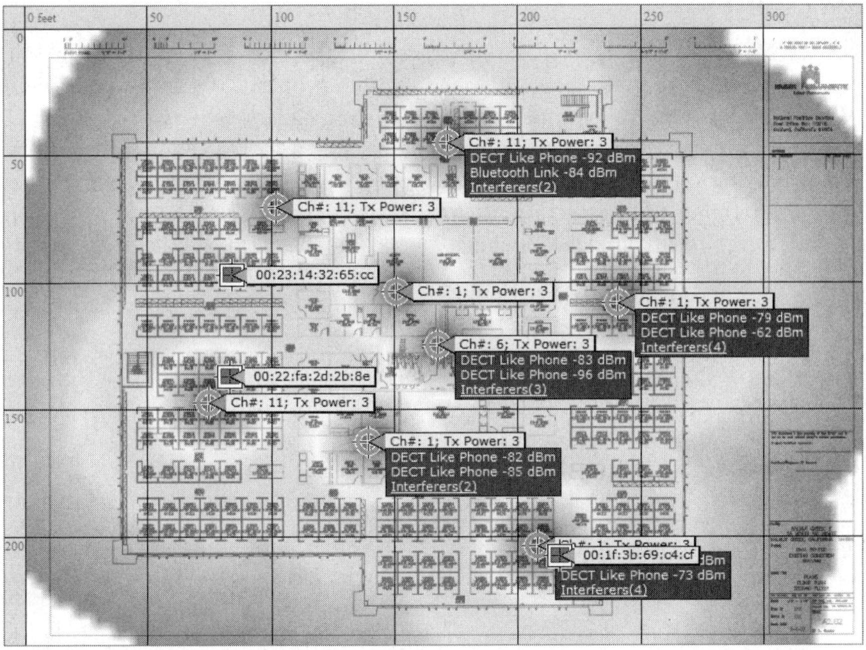

As you discover interference sources that cannot be removed, you also need to ask yourself if it is possible to work around the channels affected by the interference. If the source is a spread-spectrum signal, which may be transmitting across an entire frequency band, there is nothing you can do about it. However, if the device uses a specific, narrow frequency, it might be possible to change the frequency used by the interference source. In areas where it is not, perhaps the zone of impact is small enough that you can simply channel-plan around it. Yes, that means that you will have a heavier use of a few channels within that area (at least, this is true in the constrained 2.4 GHz band), but this drawback may be better than a complete denial of service (DoS) to your WLAN. If at all possible, it is usually best to simply remove the source altogether.

Design Validation

Once you have validated the design and implementation of all RF-related components of the WLAN (or at least have plans to resolve all known problems), you should begin to validate the other aspects of your new WLAN. These areas include wired components, 802.11 configuration parameters, and last but not least, security. Next to RF, these are the most fundamental components of WLAN design.

Wired Analysis

In most WLANs, APs are connected via Ethernet links. Especially in controller-based architectures, if these Ethernet links are not configured properly, the entire performance of the WLAN will suffer. For example, Figure 14.4 shows a simple network diagram of a controller-based architecture configured in a campus-based LAN. Redundancy has been removed for illustration purposes, but this diagram shows that the wireless network is not on an island. It requires tight integration with, and is dependent on, the wired network infrastructure. Each of the links between network components plays a critical part of our WLAN design validation.

FIGURE 14.4 Sample campus LAN

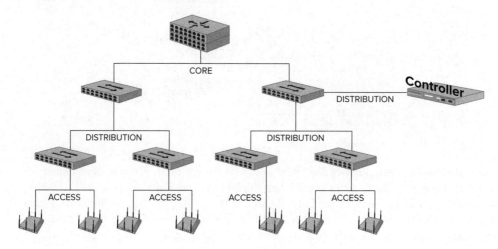

Link Metrics

Two important factors to consider when validating the wired network are speed and duplex, which should be familiar terms. Unfortunately, Ethernet links do not always negotiate *speed* and *duplex* settings properly. Speed in this case refers to the LAN PHY (or signaling) rate of the wired Ethernet link. Examples of common speeds are 100 Mbps, 1 Gbps, and 10 Gbps. Duplex settings refer to how transmissions are sent over that link, such as half duplex or full duplex. Half duplex will allow only one wired peer to transmit at a time while full duplex allows each side of the link to transmit simultaneously. Unfortunately, it is far too common to have mismatched speed and duplex settings between hardware devices, even from the same manufacturer. Always confirm each of these factors, at least between common congestion points in the network.

Along the same lines as speed and duplex, another important part of the validation process is interface health analysis. Each interface in an enterprise networking device will maintain individual statistics on Ethernet links. An example of interface statistics is as follows:

```
FastEthernet1/0/11 is up, line protocol is up (connected)
  Hardware is Fast Ethernet, address is 0022.9077.e18d (bia 0022.9077.e18d)
  Description: LAP in MBR
  MTU 1500 bytes, BW 100000 Kbit, DLY 100 usec,
     reliability 255/255, txload 1/255, rxload 1/255
  Encapsulation ARPA, loopback not set
  Keepalive set (10 sec)
  Full-duplex, 100Mb/s, media type is 10/100BaseTX
  input flow-control is off, output flow-control is unsupported
  ARP type: ARPA, ARP Timeout 04:00:00
  Last input 00:00:46, output 00:00:00, output hang never
  Last clearing of "show interface" counters never
  Input queue: 0/75/0/0 (size/max/drops/flushes); Total output drops: 0
  Queueing strategy: fifo
  Output queue: 0/40 (size/max)
  5 minute input rate 2000 bits/sec, 2 packets/sec
  5 minute output rate 3000 bits/sec, 3 packets/sec
     26653941 packets input, 9734676602 bytes, 0 no buffer
     Received 167656 broadcasts (0 multicasts)
     0 runts, 0 giants, 0 throttles
     0 input errors, 0 CRC, 0 frame, 0 overrun, 0 ignored
     0 watchdog, 55882 multicast, 0 pause input
     0 input packets with dribble condition detected
     36014622 packets output, 28644188103 bytes, 0 underruns
```

```
0 output errors, 0 collisions, 1 interface resets
0 babbles, 0 late collision, 0 deferred
0 lost carrier, 0 no carrier, 0 PAUSE output
0 output buffer failures, 0 output buffers swapped out
```

You will notice that there are no interface counters for input errors, CRCs, output errors, collisions, and other statistics that indicate poor interface performance. Also notice in the beginning of this interface status output are a few bold items that can be used to verify the state of the link. In this case, the design was intended to be for 100 Mbps full duplex. This output verifies this fact.

Another common point of failure to consider in wired LANs is removable interface modules such as Gigabit Interface Connector (GBIC), Small Form-Factor Pluggable (SFP), and now SFP+ and 10 Gigabit Small Form Factor Pluggable Module (XFP) modules. It is usually more common that these modules fail before typical, built-in Ethernet switch ports. The problem is that they do not always fail completely. "Failure" could mean that they drop or corrupt some packets that traverse through them. Always confirm interface statistics thoroughly before placing the WLAN into full production.

IEEE 802.1Q Trunk Ports

When connecting two network devices together and multiple VLANs are being used, a common practice is to send traffic from multiple VLANs between network devices using 802.1Q tagging. IEEE 802.1Q tagging allows Ethernet frames from multiple VLANs to traverse a single Ethernet link while traffic is kept secure and logically separate. Ethernet frames will have a VLAN identifier, indicating their VLAN membership so the receiving device can segment the traffic back into its appropriate virtual network.

VLAN tagging can be a complex configuration process, leading to many misconfigurations. For example, let's say you are adding 3 VLANs to an existing wired LAN design that already has 25 or more VLANs operating on it. It is a good network design principle to enable a feature called *VLAN pruning* to improve bandwidth across trunk links. In essence, VLAN pruning allows each switch to notify neighboring switches which VLANs it is supporting on its ports; this information allows switches to disable unnecessary VLANs on the trunk port if the peer switch doesn't need that VLAN. Without VLAN pruning, broadcast traffic from unnecessary VLANs would cause added congestion for all trunk links in the network, thus impacting performance.

If the VLAN pruning implementation is misconfigured, or if the pruning process is done manually, adding or removing VLANs on switch ports could cause WLAN performance issues. It is particularly important to make certain that all trunk ports are not filtering out wanted VLANs, but also allow only the VLANs that are needed on each side of a trunk link.

> ### 🌐 Real World Scenario
>
> #### VLAN Support and L3 Roaming
>
> Consider a WLAN situation in which VLAN support is misconfigured on Ethernet switches. Perhaps all switch ports but one support the appropriate VLANs for wireless clients. The client associates to an AP and is placed on VLAN 54. All switches that have APs connected to them are designed to be a member of this VLAN. When the WLAN client roams onto an AP connected to a switch that cannot pass traffic for VLAN 54, all traffic for that client is dropped at the switch. No error is presented; it is simply a condition where the user of that device thinks that the network has sustained a temporary outage or they are having a problem with their client device.
>
> Of course, it is also quite possible that the client would associate to an AP that does not support the required VLAN, in which case there will be no client service. Also, it is important to remember that some networks are designed so that clients will roam to APs that do not support the requisite VLANs. In this case, the WLAN must support a tunneling model that allows the client's traffic to be tunneled back to the WLAN controller to be placed on the appropriate VLAN.

QoS Configuration

QoS is a big and complicated topic to address, which is why it shows up numerous times in this book. In this chapter, we will simply focus on the process of validation of QoS markings, which is important for end-to-end QoS across the wireless and wired domains. QoS isn't supported by all devices in a consistent way. Even if a device supports QoS, it doesn't mean that all traffic from the device will be prioritized.

For example, let's use a QoS-capable VoWiFi phone to explore what this looks like. When a VoWiFi phone registers with its gateway, it is sending data frames that have no need to be prioritized. Therefore, the phone sends the data frames just like any normal device would send best effort data frames. Now, let's assume a call is initiated from the phone. When a phone is instructed to dial a number, it sends this information to the voice gateway using a protocol like Session Initiation Protocol (SIP), H.323, or even a proprietary protocol. This traffic is considered *call signaling* traffic. Usually, a higher QoS class than data is given to this traffic. In 802.11, this is usually a UP (user priority) of 4. In 802.3 Ethernet it is a CoS (class of service) of 3. Once the call is initiated, the actual voice stream is encoded using a voice codec like G.711, G.729, or a variety of others. The voice stream is more commonly referred to as the *media stream*. The term "media" is used because voice isn't the only real-time information that a communication device can send. Videoconferencing systems also send video in the media stream just as they do audio. For the media stream, the higher QoS classes are typically given, which are a UP of 6 or 7 for voice and a UP of 4 or 5 for video.

Therefore, a QoS-capable device isn't always sending time- or bandwidth-intensive traffic that is marked for QoS. This is important to realize when you are analyzing applications and devices that support QoS.

This may seem like a lot is going on, but fortunately there is a simple way of validating both the WLAN and the LAN at the same time. The assumption here is that all of the LAN and WLAN devices actually are QoS capable and the devices honor QoS-marked traffic. With that assumption in mind, if a Wi-Fi device (such as a phone) sends QoS-marked traffic to another QoS-capable device (such as another phone) and the frame arrives to the receiving device with all of the QoS markings intact, then the WLAN and the LAN are likely configured properly.

The easiest way to do this is to use two VoWiFi phones that you know are 802.11e or WMM QoS compliant and initiate a phone call to each other while connected to a single AP. Once the call is under way, you should look for QoS markings, as shown in Figure 14.5.

FIGURE 14.5 QoS marking example to distributed system

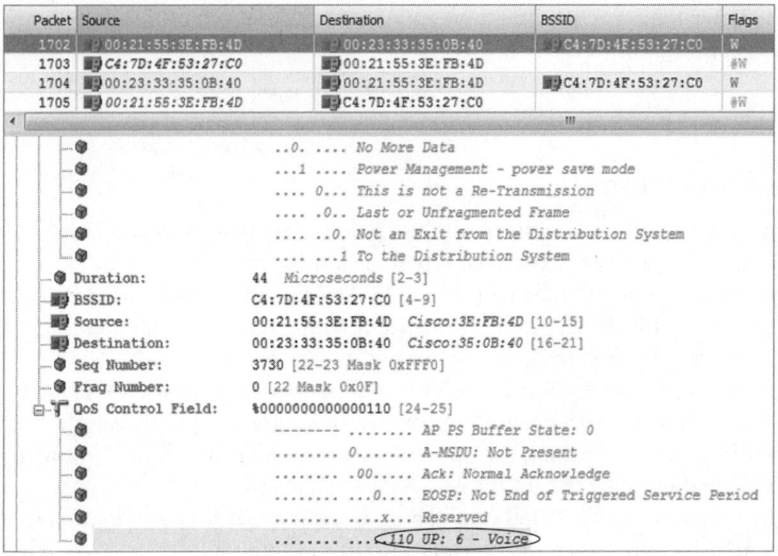

Packet	Source	Destination	BSSID	Flags
1702	00:21:55:3E:FB:4D	00:23:33:35:0B:40	C4:7D:4F:53:27:C0	W
1703	C4:7D:4F:53:27:C0	00:21:55:3E:FB:4D		⊕W
1704	00:23:33:35:0B:40	00:21:55:3E:FB:4D	C4:7D:4F:53:27:C0	W
1705	00:21:55:3E:FB:4D	C4:7D:4F:53:27:C0		⊕W

```
                        ..0. .... No More Data
                        ...1 .... Power Management - power save mode
                        .... 0... This is not a Re-Transmission
                        .... .0.. Last or Unfragmented Frame
                        .... ..0. Not an Exit from the Distribution System
                        .... ...1 To the Distribution System
  Duration:        44  Microseconds [2-3]
  BSSID:           C4:7D:4F:53:27:C0 [4-9]
  Source:          00:21:55:3E:FB:4D  Cisco:3E:FB:4D [10-15]
  Destination:     00:23:33:35:0B:40  Cisco:35:0B:40 [16-21]
  Seq Number:      3730 [22-23 Mask 0xFFF0]
  Frag Number:     0 [22 Mask 0x0F]
  QoS Control Field:  %0000000000000110 [24-25]
                        -------- ........ AP PS Buffer State: 0
                        ......... 0........ A-MSDU: Not Present
                        ......... .00...... Ack: Normal Acknowledge
                        ......... ...0..... EOSP: Not End of Triggered Service Period
                        ......... ....x.... Reserved
                        ......... .....110 UP: 6 - Voice
```

In Figure 14.5, the QoS Control Field is highlighted with the frame marking of an 802.11 frame using the G.729 codec. The frame is encrypted, so we would not have known the codec if we didn't take the capture ourselves or were given the trace with that information provided. The next frame, #1703, is an 802.11 ACK to the previous frame. Frame #1702 was a frame originating from a phone to the distribution system (DS), as we can see just above the Duration field. We need to start with a frame originating from a device with a known marking and then follow its path back down to the receiving device. In this case, this involves two phones on the same AP. We can then see in frame #1704 that the 802.11 frame is transmitted back to the receiving device by the AP. If we look at the QoS Control Field in this frame, as shown in Figure 14.6, we see that it also has an 802.11 UP of 6.

FIGURE 14.6   QoS marking example from distributed system

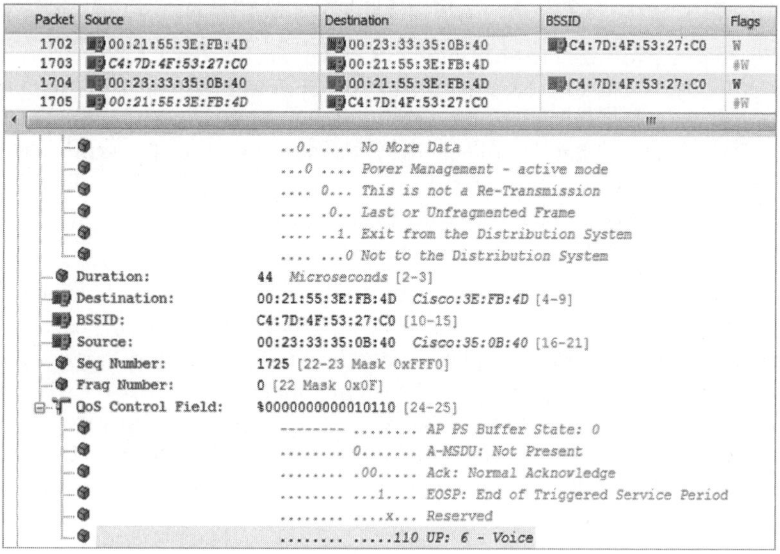

This is a rather simple method, but it means that the frame was sent from the VoWiFi device, in this case, and the AP sends it back to the other VoWiFi phone with a proper 802.11 marking. The frame has to be relayed minimally by a single AP, but in a controller-based architecture the fact is that the original frame has to be received by the AP, transmitted via the LAN to the WLAN controller, back down a tunnel to the same AP, and transmitted back to the receiving phone. In a controller-based architecture (which is what this capture was taken from), this validates that the entire network has end-to-end QoS integrity; otherwise we would have seen frame #1704 without a proper 802.11 UP marking. The UP would be 0 if something was wrong.

Next, we recommend that in this case you take one of the handsets and move to another AP on the same switch, then to another AP on another switch and any other part of the network where the network architecture might be different, and continue to validate the same information. You will not see the transmission from the original handset, but you already know it is properly marking the traffic because you verified it once. You would simply look at a frame from the same MAC address also marked from the DS with an 802.11 UP of 6. A good hint to make sure you are dealing with a voice frame is to record the frame size from the original capture and look for a frame that meets the previous criteria that also matches the same frame size.

IP and Ethernet Services

There are many network services that are used by WLANs. Although they are traditionally thought of as wired services, or they are at least services that originate on the wire, it is important that we explore the ways that WLANs use these services and depend on them:

IP Routing   IP routing is usually only a wired issue in most networks. While some WLAN controllers can perform routing functions, most WLANs solely leverage the same IP routing framework as the rest of the LAN and simply add VLANs for the wireless devices.

In validating routing, you are largely looking to make certain that VLANs are routing to each other properly. When VLANs are added, it is important to make sure that you can route to all the networks that you need access to. If you find that you are not routing as you would expect, first try pinging the gateway for the network you are connected to. If you can ping the gateway, chances are that you have a routing problem. This assumes that you have not enforced any firewall rules or access control lists (ACLs) that would prevent traffic from passing.

DHCP   DHCP is another area that needs to be validated. You should not only confirm that DHCP is working for WLAN clients, but also for APs that might be using DHCP. Controller-based APs are typically deployed using DHCP and may use special DHCP options as well. These options are usually to help brand-new, unconfigured APs to find a WLAN controller to join. In that case, you need to verify that DHCP options are provided back from the DHCP server that you require. One of the simplest methods to accomplish this is to do a packet capture and look for a DHCP offer in response to a DHCP request. From a packet capture utility, you can look at the DHCP offer and you can view all the DHCP options specified.

DHCP options are also used for certain WLAN clients. It is quite common to see devices request the use of DHCP options to specify a TFTP server to pull down a configuration file or other information. If your design calls for configuring these options, you need to validate the functionality of these features by using a packet capture utility once everything is deployed. In this case, you can run a packet capture utility on a laptop computer, associate to the WLAN, and then view the DHCP offer you receive after joining the WLAN.

EtherChannel   One option when connecting Ethernet switches and WLAN controllers to each other is using a link aggregation protocol like *EtherChannel*. In simplest terms, EtherChannel takes two separate physical links and virtually bonds them together to form one aggregated link. In WLANs, ten 802.11n APs could easily saturate a single gigabit (Gb) uplink to the controller, so it may be useful to bond multiple Gb uplinks using EtherChannel. By taking two Gigabit Ethernet links and configuring them into an EtherChannel, the switch effectively has a 2 Gb uplink capacity. For example, you can configure EtherChannel in a variety of ways, and some WLAN products traditionally have not worked well with all modes. You must validate the following when using EtherChannel:

- Utilization and load balancing
- Failover
- Traffic corruption

EtherChannel functionality can be tested using multiple clients configured with load generation utilities. Send traffic in excess of a single port's capacity across the EtherChannel link and confirm that bandwidth is greater than a single port's capacity. You should also look at traffic counters or bandwidth statistics on the LAN switch ports before and while traffic is being sent to confirm that both links are getting their equal share of load. That is a good way of validating link utilization.

Confirming that the failover feature is working properly is fairly easy. Using the same load generation utility, simply unplug one of the links; if the failover process works properly, the link should continue to allow traffic to pass. If disconnecting one of the links drops the entire connection, that is an indication that there might be a misconfiguration or bug.

Spanning Tree Protocol (STP)   *Spanning Tree Protocol (STP)* is a loop prevention and link failover protocol; many of those who have used it in the past would like to forget it ever existed. It has been notorious for bringing down entire LANs largely due to erroneous configuration changes. Nonetheless, it is still a commonly used protocol. It has a faster, newer cousin called *Rapid Spanning Tree Protocol (RSTP)*, which has better failover performance than its older cousin. We will simply refer to both protocols for the remainder of this discussion simply as STP, which you can infer as STP or RSTP.

STP is still a commonly used protocol to gain link failover between LAN switches—usually from the access layer to the distribution layer or directly to the core if a distribution layer doesn't exist, such as with smaller LANs. A common practice is to use two Ethernet links that connect two Ethernet switches with STP enabled; one of the switch ports will be blocked, which prevents the traffic loop. Should the primary link go down, the other link is enabled and the LAN stays functional.

The problem with STP is that it blocks the use of an entire Ethernet link until a failover occurs. When STP is used, the only way to prevent that is to use a proprietary method that allows the use of separate STP instances for each VLAN (PVST) or each group of VLANs (MSTP). Then, you can assign half of the VLANs to one link, where the other link is blocked for those same VLANs, and then assign the other link for the other half of the VLANs, where the first one is blocking for that set of VLANs.

As with EtherChannel, you will want to use similar methods to confirm that the STP configuration is working properly, including performing failover testing of the links to ensure that the redundancy configuration is working properly.

Power over Ethernet (PoE)   *Power over Ethernet (PoE)* is also an item that requires validation. You might say that it is something that requires proper power budgeting within your LAN. In the design phase, you should have calculated the load that each AP will require for power; simply multiply that by the number of APs and then confirm that this total load is within the PoE supply capacity of the switch that the APs will plug into. One consideration here is that the same switch that supports APs may also support other PoE endpoints that are outside of your realm of influence. For example, perhaps the telephony team requires PoE for the wired VoIP phones. If your power budget maxes out the switch, this leaves no power capacity for the phones or for some of your APs. Needless to say, someone must ensure that the total PoE power budget is within the capabilities of the switch; you should confirm this in your design validation.

A common symptom of going over budget with PoE is when WLAN radios do not turn on. The AP might power up, but the radios do not turn on because the switch port that the APs are plugged into will not grant enough power for the AP to fully power up with functional radios. Another problem with PoE is improper negotiation. Some equipment vendors may use a slightly different PoE protocol or may have incompatibilities with PoE endpoints.

Configuration Validation

Now that some of the RF and LAN variables are out of the way, we need to turn our attention to the configuration of the WLAN equipment. There isn't a particular order for the parameters that should be validated, nor is there a definitive list of items. As per your design, you should have specified configuration items that must be enabled, and therefore validated, in the post-validation analysis. Minimally, you should validate settings like the following:

- 802.11 authentication methods (Open, WPA, and/or WPA2)
- PHY and MCS rate settings
- VLAN assignment
- Short/long preambles (for 802.11b legacy clients)
- Protection mechanisms
- Dynamic Transmit Power Control (DTPC)
- Power saving features (DTIM and U-APSD)
- Rate limiting/traffic policing
- User policy enforcement

It is out of scope of this book to discuss the processes for validating each one of these items and their functions, but we recommend that you at least verify that each of these settings is configured and working according to the design specification.

Security Testing

Security testing is an important topic and one that can take a fair amount of time to validate. Depending on the network security policies, a variety of security aspects should be validated. It is tough to provide a list of exactly what to do for WLAN validation because every design is different. However, in the following sections we will list the broader topics and specific validation options to consider.

EAP Types

Some WLANs support multiple EAP types whereas others support only one. Regardless, you should confirm several items before configuring and testing a single WLAN client to connect to the WLAN. These include the following:

- RADIUS server is online and functioning.

- All APs or WLAN controllers are added to the RADIUS server as RADIUS clients.

- RADIUS servers are configured on the APs or WLAN controllers.

- RADIUS servers and APs or WLAN controllers are using the correct UDP ports and shared secret.

- RADIUS server is configured to support the EAP type(s) that WLAN clients will use. Also, ensure that only the EAP types you want to support are enabled and nothing more.

- 802.1X is enabled on the APs or WLAN controllers for each of the SSIDs that will use 802.1X/EAP.

- Clients are properly configured with proper EAP types and related settings.

These items should always be validated before attempting to connect any WLAN client. If you have validated each of these items and a WLAN client still won't connect using one of the allowed EAP types, you should refer to debug logs, system logs, vendor-specific messages, or other similar troubleshooting options provided by the equipment vendors in order to determine your next steps.

Authentication and Accounting

When using 802.1X/EAP, confirm that authentication is being logged properly on the RADIUS servers along with the associated accounting information for each WLAN client. Most WLAN equipment vendors allow for configuration of authentication servers separate from accounting servers. It is important to verify that both are functioning as expected.

You should also configure a log file or database backup or archiving scheme for these log files. Some organizations require retention of these log files for a certain period of time.

Encryption

Whenever a WLAN is deployed, 802.11 encryption should be a requirement. Perhaps the only exception would be for guest networks. However, some organizations even use a WPA PSK for their guest networks as a deterrent to keep neighbors from using the guest WLAN.

To determine if encryption is being used properly, use a WLAN packet capture utility. Configure the packet capture software to capture data frames that are supposed to be encrypted and validate that no upper layer data is visible. You could also confirm this by checking specific information elements and fields in certain management fields. For more information on those details, refer to the *CWAP Certified Wireless Analysis Professional Official Study Guide* by David Coleman (Sybex, 2011).

Wired encryption is also an option with some enterprise equipment manufacturers. For encryption protocols supported over the wire, such as for VPNs, tunneling to a controller, or tunneling between APs, a simple wired Ethernet capture of the traffic will verify data privacy as well.

Device Management

Once a WLAN is configured and is ready to be placed into operation, management capabilities should be locked down with an appropriate accounting trail. You have a variety of factors to consider here, including VLAN segmentation, firewalls, ACLs, administration credentials and privileges, and access protocols.

First, management interfaces of WLAN equipment should only be placed on specific firewalled or ACL'd network segments. This prevents infrastructure equipment from even seeing any requests to manage the equipment from unauthorized users or subnets.

Next, login authentication methods may be used, such as a RADIUS server, a built-in database, or a different user authorization management system such as TACACS+. The benefit of an authorization management system is that individual user logins can be allowed or denied the use of certain configuration commands with the WLAN infrastructure devices. In other words, your organization may require layered administrative access in which different members of the IT team are granted scalar configuration and monitoring permission. The same system also logs all of the activities users perform in an accounting database. These accounting databases can be helpful to use for security forensic purposes. Needless to say, all default manufacturer credentials need to be changed or deleted.

Protocols used for management may include Telnet, SSH, HTTP, HTTPS, SNMP, and more. Telnet and HTTP are protocols that do not use encryption. When a user logs in via one of these protocols, the username and password can be seen in clear text if the packets are captured. For this reason, these protocols should be disabled. As an alternative, SSH or HTTPS should be used; both offer strong encryption.

SNMP is often enabled on infrastructure equipment by default. Worse yet is that the SNMP strings and login information are parameters that can be easily obtained from a user manual that is public domain. All default logins and SNMP community strings should be changed or deleted. Some equipment vendors allow the use of ACLs that prevent any device from performing SNMP requests to an infrastructure device. Where possible, newer versions of SNMP, such as v3, should be implemented for best security practices.

Traffic Filtering

A variety of features fall into the traffic filtering category. Some equipment vendors offer more features than others, so this may be a quick exercise depending on the equipment manufacturer and/or the configuration complexity of your WLAN design. Yet whatever equipment you are using, there are a few things that you should confirm in a WLAN post-validation effort, assuming these options are present.

Some WLANs can block some or all peer-to-peer traffic. Sometimes this blocking is a good idea, but in other instances, it can be a serious problem depending on the applications being used. For instance, a voice SSID using peer-to-peer traffic blocking would be disastrous. However, we usually recommend enabling this feature for a guest WLAN. Always validate this feature to make sure it is configured properly.

As you test devices for basic connectivity, watch for firewall software that is enabled on PCs. If you attempt to ping another WLAN device from a different WLAN device, the receiving device may have firewall software enabled and might block all ICMP traffic, thus preventing an ICMP response. Confirm that firewall software is not enabled on the test devices.

Another form of traffic filtering is URL filtering. This form of traffic filtering is commonly used in enterprise and guest networks. Many enterprises filter out the use of social networking sites, media streaming sites, and other web destinations known to host malware, illegal content, or other illicit material. For guest networks, the worst thing a company needs is to provide guest access to somebody viewing inappropriate material and another guest user to witness it. This is the reason many organizations use some form of URL and content filtering.

There are many other types of filters, such as time-of-day restrictions for certain users and rate control filtering. It is a good practice to test such mechanisms by attempting to violate them.

Rogue Detection

Rogue detection and mitigation features are becoming more sophisticated for WLAN equipment, and some of these features may be enabled by default. Depending on your organization's security policy, you may have a simple and minor detection policy, or you may have a sophisticated one. In either case, it is important to test and confirm that detection, reporting, and mitigation features are all working as desired. Test this capability by installing a rogue AP and confirming that an alarm is triggered and logged, or a report is generated, or possibly that the AP responds with appropriate active containment measures. Each policy will differ, but the same principles apply across all networks. Make sure the features are working before you set them loose and trust that they are providing the desired protection.

Client Device Validation

Once you know the infrastructure design is validated at a fundamental level, you must investigate the other end of the RF link—clients. This step needs to be done before you proceed any further in the validation process because if the client devices are not configured properly or there is an unforeseen incompatibility, the subsequent validation phases would need to be performed all over again.

Configuration parameters selected between infrastructure components and client devices must be in parity. If devices are not in parity, you can not only expect poor performance, but you may also experience more severe problems that affect reliability as a whole. For example, a client device that is not configured to use the right frequency bands or 802.11 parameters may not associate to the WLAN how you intend. If your network uses 802.11n at 5 GHz, you must ensure that you are enabling 802.11n and that you have also enabled 5 GHz. All client driver and supplicant settings need to be validated in this step.

Using a survey client equipped with special analysis software can only provide one perspective of the WLAN installation. A survey client is usually a specific laptop and radio card that the IT staff or an outside vendor uses where the survey analysis software is exclusively licensed to. The perspective from these devices is nearly always not quite the same picture that your actual client devices will see. More specifically, special survey clients do not tell you how the actual devices the network must support will *actually* behave. Different WLAN radio cards, antennas, driver software, configuration parameters and many other factors influence how different devices behave differently. Therefore, you must perform a validation using a representative sample of the actual supported WLAN devices. This may seem logical, but this is usually the most underperformed design validation step.

Ideally, your design should have already dictated specific client driver versions that were tested to be compatible with WLAN infrastructure firmware that you have deployed at this stage. WLAN client drivers may have substantial compatibility and performance issues with certain infrastructure software versions. Therefore, at this stage, you want to check to see what drivers your clients have deployed in addition to configuration parameters.

One product used to perform client testing is WaveDeploy from VeriWave. WaveDeploy provides the ability to perform a battery of tests using the actual client devices configured for your network. WaveDeploy places a small software agent on each client device you would like to test. The software agent then checks in with a central software console that usually resides on an Ethernet network. The central software console can then command each client device to perform a specific test plan. This is done by the test conductor clicking on a map location where client devices are physically located. If several client devices are used, the tests are performed serially, which may take some time to execute depending on the configured test plan. The devices are then moved to a new location, and this process is repeated. The final result it a series of heatmaps that show how each client device performed at each location. This not only includes RF coverage information, but also throughput in uplink and downlink with a variety of application protocols, MOS score for voice clients, latency, and more. This process can allow for fine tuning of infrastructure and client device parameters by making software and/or configuration tweaks and executing the process again.

Another product that has been used to test network devices is IxChariot from Ixia. IxChariot is more suited for performance and application testing on Ethernet networks rather than RF and 802.11 testing, but nonetheless provides a great deal of valuable data to validate against.

When recording results from client devices, you need to record at least the following information along with the test data set:

- WLAN client device make and model
- Make and model of the WLAN radio card
- Antenna details if external antennas were used
- WLAN driver or device firmware versions
- Complete documentation of all client driver, supplicant, and any configuration parameter that will affect radio behavior

Depending on how the test is performed, other information may also be required, but this list should provide a valuable baseline. It is also assumed that you have already captured a snapshot of the infrastructure equipment and infrastructure RF state prior to client testing. If you do not have both sets of information, interpreting the data is left to a great deal of guess work.

Frame and Channel Analysis

We recommend that you perform some form of frame and channel analysis during a post-validation. It can be a highly definitive way of capturing important metrics that indicate a properly functioning WLAN.

An 802.11 frame capture utility will need to be used for these purposes. While Linux has a few basic utilities to perform some analysis, most of the Windows utilities are more sophisticated. Some are free (though you must purchase supported adapters), and others come in a range of cost. If they can be justified for your organization, these tools can be well worth the money. Some popular examples include Wireshark, CommView for WiFi, WildPackets' OmniPeek, and AirMagnet Analyzer.

As you analyze your network at Layer 2, there are a lot of details. Let's look at some of the most important areas to focus on at this stage of the deployment.

Important Metrics

Some analysis tools report so much data that it can be confusing. Certain metrics provide the best insight into the network's health, and we will focus on these in the following sections. Since most networks use encryption (which obfuscates Layers 3–7), frame analysis is primarily done at Layer 2. We will focus on networks that use encryption because that is (and should be) the most common method.

Retransmissions

In RF communications, especially ones that use unlicensed frequencies, retransmissions are simply a fact of life. You'll never see a network completely rid of them. Whenever a frame isn't heard or cannot be decoded as transmitted, the frame isn't acknowledged (ACK'd) by the receiver (assuming some acknowledgment is expected). This informs the transmitter that it must retransmit the frame.

Retransmissions in WLANs are the frames that are picked up by a protocol analyzer that have the retry bit set to 1 in the 802.11 frame header. A good general rule of thumb in large WLAN deployments is for retransmissions to be approximately 5 percent or less of all of the frames transmitted. More than 10 percent retransmissions is usually a sign that the network is experiencing poor RF performance. Also, it is important to realize that as higher signaling rates are utilized on the WLAN and overall capacity and throughput increases for a cell (such as with 802.11n), retransmissions may actually increase, and this is normal. With more PHY rates, the more rate shifting will occur as the RF link between the client and AP changes. Clients and APs usually change PHY rates after they have to retransmit frames. With more rate shifting, there should be more retransmissions by definition. There is still a NET gain because the time it takes to transmit the same information at a higher PHY rate is less.

Keep in mind that if a single device is communicating, and it has a very low signal or is not sending much traffic, the data sampling may not be representative of real-world conditions. It is always best to have clients deployed in their intended use case and have people use the devices as they would normally be used. A data sampling of that type should be the only type used for this analysis.

CRC Errors

When 802.11 frames are received by a frame analyzer but cannot be properly decoded for one reason or another (usually low SNR or interference), this is usually characterized as a CRC error. A valid CRC error count is similar to the retry count in its indication of network health, but it is important to understand the difference. That is, retries indicate that the intended receiver did not correctly receive a frame and that the transmitter resent it. CRC errors only indicate that the network analyzer did not correctly receive a frame. This difference cannot be understated. The significance here is that a protocol analyzer typically uses a client adapter and antenna, which are typically inferior to AP radios and antennas. Similarly, the receiving capabilities of the analyzer software are dependent on location. In other words, you are collecting network statistics at a point in space, and that point in space may not be representative of the entire network. Weigh the CRC error count as a performance metric with those considerations in mind. When possible, obtain the CRC error count from the WLAN infrastructure platform itself, and this will give you a better sense of performance.

It is important to understand that some clients will be communicating with the AP at high PHY rates. The ability for those devices to use high PHY rates is a function of the RF quality between them. If your analyzer is not in the same vicinity to hear the communication at the same RF levels, your analyzer may not be able to understand the full conversation. For example, if you are analyzing communications between client(s) and an AP that are on the other side of an RF coverage cell, there is a strong chance you will not pick up all of the traffic. It is quite common that your protocol analyzer will report the frames it did not fully receive intact as CRC frames. The preambles sent at the beginning of each 802.11 frame are always done so at a low PHY rate and the rest of the frame is usually sent at a higher PHY rate (in most circumstances). Therefore, your analyzer's radio can usually decipher that a frame is being transmitted (because it heard the preamble), but it cannot decipher the payload sent using a higher order modulation of a high PHY rate. Keep this in mind when reporting on CRC errors.

Similarly, keep in mind that not all client adapter drivers are equal. Some drivers filter out traffic so that it is not reported to the operating system (and therefore the analyzer) if signal levels are really low. It is a best practice to use drivers that are designed specifically for the analysis software.

CCA Congestion

Wireless medium contention practices can also be helpful for indicating when an 802.11 network becomes overloaded. IEEE 802.11 is, by design, a listen-before-talk protocol. If the wireless medium is busy and the device needs to transmit, it will wait to use the medium until the medium is idle. This process is called clear channel assessment (CCA), and a saturated RF medium is often referred to as *CCA congestion*. Some infrastructure devices report this information in statistic counters, which provides incredible insight to the inner workings of the AP in the RF environment.

One interesting thing to observe in large WLAN deployments is variance in this statistic between APs. Areas where there is a high amount of busy time can indicate areas of RF interference and/or very high traffic usage that might warrant further investigation.

Highly Variable RF Signals

In some network deployments, a dynamic RF environment with excess multipath can cause highly variable signal amplitude at the location of a specific receiver. If the variance in signal amplitude of successive signals at a receiver is too large, it might be an indicator that too much multipath is present or possibly that diversity isn't working properly on the client or AP device. As you measure signal strength, a range of 10 dB isn't uncommon. However, greater variations in devices with simple diversity may represent an issue with excess multipath. 802.11n MIMO can utilize this phenomenon for signal processing gains, but legacy 802.11a/b/g devices cannot cope as well with multipath.

If you are experiencing this issue with 802.11n, you may have an issue with MIMO diversity. If you see this problem with 802.11a/b/g, try moving a few inches or so and repeat the analysis. You would be surprised how much difference there can be in RF sampling with even small location changes. If the same problem is still being seen, you should investigate if antenna diversity is working properly, if the device supports it.

There have been several installations that have benefited from AP relocation even to within several feet from the original location. This issue is even more critical for PTP or PTMP RF links.

Channel Performance

Ultimately, much of the performance of a WLAN depends on available channel capacity. When channel capacity is used up, there is no opportunity for a performance increase. We have already discussed in this book the effect that low PHY rates can cause on large WLAN deployments. Low PHY rates can be decoded much further than higher PHY rates. To make matters worse, an 802.11 frame sent at a low PHY rate occupies the wireless medium much longer than the same frame transmitted at a higher PHY rate. Effectively, channel capacity is reduced simply from 802.11 management frame overhead sent at low PHY rates, even when the network is not transferring data traffic.

To prevent this from crippling the network, PHY rates should be appropriately configured in the WLAN based on a proper RF site survey. Usually, even a data grade network with APs spaced further apart than WLANs providing real-time services should normally not need PHY rates lower than 11 Mbps. There are cases where stations can benefit from lower rates, depending on where they are connecting from, but in general, PHY rates lower than 11 Mbps will do more harm than good in the vast majority of large WLAN deployments.

To measure channel performance, use a professional WLAN analyzer. One that performs exceptionally well in this use case is AirMagnet WiFi Analyzer, shown in Figure 14.7.

FIGURE 14.7   AirMagnet WiFi Analyzer channel analysis

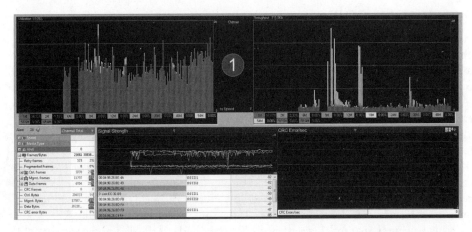

The graphs in Figure 14.7 show channel utilization (top left) and bandwidth (top right). On the left, not only do you see how high the utilization is for each measurement interval, but you also see a breakdown of the PHY rates that contributed to that channel utilization. This is a powerful graphic because it correlates transmitted data in the same interval and allows you to see the inversely proportional effect that lower PHY rates have on performance and channel utilization. You can also see that when high PHY rates are in use, a substantial amount of traffic can be sent with low channel utilization.

The AirMagnet WiFi Analyzer is notoriously colorful. Unfortunately, including screenshots that are printed in grayscale does not do justice to the capabilities of this platform. On a computer monitor, this data is very useful and tangible for analysis and design experts.

Roaming Analysis

Today's wireless networks are increasingly supporting mobile devices and applications. For that reason, it is important to validate client roaming functionality before turning the network loose.

An important fact about the 802.11 protocol is that clients make the decision when and where to roam. Because clients are the ones that are mobile, this makes sense. The problem is that client roaming algorithms are all different, meaning each client device (driver, really) behaves differently. Chapter 2, "Designing for Client Devices and Applications," goes into great detail about client roaming issues and how to properly design for them. This section will cover how to assess client roaming behavior as well as the impact that 802.1X/EAP security can play in the roaming process.

Assessing Client Roaming

The IEEE 802.11 standard does not currently specify any details about when and why clients should roam to another AP. This is up to client device manufacturers to implement as they see fit. Because clients make the decision to roam and there are a variety of WLAN chipsets, driver versions—along with configuration options—control roaming processes. For that reason, each client type should be assessed independently.

The method for doing this can be as minimal or extensive as your organization requires. It can be as simple as walking around the WLAN deployment with the client device running an application and gauging performance purely from an end-user perspective. This method is certainly sufficient for some situations, but if you would like to know more information about device behavior, you might also run a program, if available on the client device, that displays connection status and performance metrics. Specifically, we are looking for RF metrics like RSSI and/or SNR metrics, and ideally application metrics as well, such as errors, retries, round-trip delay and jitter, and loss. Another important piece of information is the MAC address of the AP that the device is connected to. This information is helpful in determining the location and RF signal levels when devices will roam.

If you have designed your network properly, you should have cell sizes that do not have too much co-channel interference. RF cells should have some level of overlapping coverage to facilitate a seamless roaming experience without too much signal degradation, but not so much coverage that you still have high signal strength while standing underneath an adjacent AP. This is a sign that the APs are placed too closely together or perhaps that transmit power is set too high. Usually it is the former because if transmit power is set too high—implying that transmit power on the AP is higher than what is capable from the client device—the uplink transmissions from the client device may not be heard by the AP with the same reliability as downlink transmissions from the AP. In this case, the client device would look to roam when traffic conditions degrade beyond a certain threshold. Keep in mind that not all clients will do so because some client vendors simply key the roaming process from RF signal levels alone. That is not optimal.

Roaming between frequency bands may also be an important requirement for your WLAN. The reasons for this vary, but sometimes it is solely due to being resilient to RF interference on one band. Should a device roam between frequency bands, we need to observe that the roaming process is not disruptive and the client device doesn't disconnect in such a way that end users will notice the effect. This also means that the infrastructure does not place the client on a new VLAN (or if it does, it uses tunneling to maintain IP connectivity) and the mobility and authentication state is kept seamless during a roam between bands.

802.1X/EAP Roaming Performance

There are several items to examine when analyzing 802.1X/EAP performance. First, an important statistic to measure is the time it takes for initial association and authentication using the 802.1X/EAP protocol(s) that will be used on the WLAN. This includes the total time to perform a full authentication beginning from the initial 802.11 association request and ending with the WPA four-way handshake completion. Ideally, we would like it to be 250 ms or less in good RF conditions. If the RADIUS server is located over a WAN link, this will certainly add time to the authentication process. Keep in mind that in poor RF conditions, retransmissions and added latency from slower PHY rates are likely to increase this time substantially. First test the initial authentication in good RF conditions.

By definition, the authentication time for the first authentication cannot be using a previously authenticated session. If it is, try fully rebooting the WLAN client or forcing a client off the AP or WLAN controller using an appropriate command based on the equipment vendor's product. Usually, what you want to see is a full 802.1X/EAP authentication using a strong EAP type.

Next, you want to measure roam times to other APs. When 802.1X/EAP is run with fast secure roaming (FSR), opportunistic key caching (OKC), 802.11r Fast BSS Transition (FT), or vendor proprietary features, you should see substantial improvement on roam times. WLAN controllers can track clients using the same credentials when roaming between APs that are under its control. Even when you are using the strongest of EAP types, roam times can be as little as 20 ms. Generally speaking, roam times less than 50 ms are considered very good with 802.1X/EAP; in fact, that's the target metric used for the IEEE 802.11r standard.

Performing a roaming analysis is challenging using a single WLAN radio with a WLAN capture utility. If you do not have the ability to perform a multichannel capture using multiple WLAN adapters on your analyzer, you can lock in your analyzer to the RF channel of an adjacent cell to which you will roam the client device you are analyzing. Then, associate to an AP and walk toward the AP whose channel you configured your analyzer to capture and you should capture a full roaming event beginning with the reassociation request.

Channel Support

It is critically important to ensure that client devices support all the channels that are used by the WLAN infrastructure. Years ago, the 5 GHz UNII bands were expanded to include more channels in a frequency range called the UNII 2 extended (2e) band. Almost all 5 GHz–capable client devices that are several years old were only certified and designed to support the 5 GHz UNII 1, 2, and 3 bands. Therefore, if you configure the WLAN infrastructure to support a UNII 2e channel you could be creating dead spots in your network for some WLAN clients.

Load and Performance Testing

When you're buying a new sports car, it's easy to feel like a teenager again as you drive off the lot, thinking "What can this thing *really* do?" Testing a WLAN deployment can be a similar experience. You've spent an incredible amount of time and money planning, installing, and configuring your new WLAN. Now, wouldn't you like to know what kind of maximum speeds and client density numbers can be expected?

While there is more than one method to accomplish just about any type of test, this section will provide methods and criteria for performing a thorough load and performance evaluation process. You may ultimately decide to implement your own method based on your customer or deployment environment, but the concepts in the following areas will still apply.

Throughput

Performance doesn't always boil down to throughput, but it is important to know what bandwidth limitations exist. If performance is really poor, it might point to another problem somewhere in the WLAN infrastructure, the clients, the wired infrastructure, or elsewhere.

As wireless technology is becoming increasingly faster, it can become harder to generate enough load from a single client for an adequate throughput test. Therefore, several clients may need to be used. In fact, it is a far more realistic test to perform load testing using several WLAN clients. This approach allows for completely separate 802.11 state machines, (ideally) different RF conditions, different PHY rates, and medium contention processes to be evaluated in the test.

Throughput Performance Checklist

When you're performing throughput testing, the following is a good checklist of areas to consider:

Different Clients   It's best to understand the impact of mixing legacy and 802.11n adapters. You should also understand the impact of mixing different types of chipsets and even software versions that you will have in production. However, keep in mind that you are validating your network for the real world, so attempt to mimic your native client population as closely as possible.

RF Conditions   Place clients in different physical locations, testing varying RF signal qualities. Do not place clients in poorer conditions than what you would encounter in your production environment.

PHY Rates   Ensure the proper PHY rates are enabled before testing, confirming that the lowest basic rate is properly set.

Bands Run tests with clients on different bands. This information can help you determine if you want to force specific clients to use only a specific band. Not all clients perform equally on different bands for a variety of reasons.

Protocols Certain application protocols have more overhead than others, so test using different types of protocols, minimally to include TCP and UDP.

Applications

When you're performing network performance tests, several free and fee-based utilities are available. We have listed a few popular ones with enough information to get you started using them quickly.

iPerf

iPerf is arguably one of the most common command line-based network performance testing applications available. iPerf is a free, open source software utility. Many first-time users complain that they are unable to achieve the performance results they were seeking. jPerf is a derivative from iPerf that adds a graphical UI, making some functions easier to use.

 You can download iPerf at http://sourceforge.net/projects/iperf/.

The following syntax should produce good results over 802.11 wireless networks:

Measuring TCP Throughput Run the following command on the server with a 256 k TCP window size:

```
Iperf −s -w 256k
```

Run the following command on the client with six simultaneous client threads, also with a 256 k TCP window size, and perform bidirectional tests individually for a total time of 60 seconds:

```
Iperf −c <server IP address> -P 6 −w 256k -r −t 60
```

Measuring UDP Throughput Run the following command on the server with a 56 k buffer length:

```
Iperf −s -u −l 56k
```

Run the following command on the client with a 56 k buffer length, 50 Mbps of bandwidth, and six simultaneous client threads:

```
Iperf −c <server IP address> -u −b 50M −l 56k −P 6
```

nuttcp

nuttcp is a command line-based platform for TCP or UDP network performance testing and is a free, open source utility.

 You can download nuttcp at http://www.lcp.nrl.navy.mil/nuttcp/.

The preferred setup for nuttcp is to configure one host to run in server mode (-S) and a second host to either transmit or receive data from the server by specifying a -t or -r, respectively. One of the nice features of nuttcp is the amount of options it provides. You can specify details such as QoS values, window sizes, frame sizes, and others.

The following syntax should produce good results over 802.11 wireless networks:

Measuring TCP Throughput   Run the following command on the server:

```
nuttcp -S
```

Run the following command on the client to receive traffic, reporting data in one-second intervals, with a socket buffer window size to 8 MB:

```
nuttcp -r -i1 -w8m <server IP address>
```

Measuring UDP Throughput   Run the following command on the server:

```
nuttcp -S
```

Run the following command on the client to transmit traffic using UDP, reporting data in one-second intervals:

```
nuttcp -t -u -i1 -l512 <server IP address>
```

IxChariot by Ixia

IxChariot is a test tool for simulating real-world applications to predict device and system performance under realistic load conditions. The IxChariot product family offers thorough network performance assessment and device testing by simulating hundreds of protocols across thousands of network endpoints. IxChariot lets you confidently assess the performance characteristics of any application running on wired and wireless networks. IxChariot is a fee-based software product.

 Find information on IxChariot at www.ixchariot.com.

WaveDeploy by VeriWave

WaveDeploy is a site assessment and readiness solution for IEEE 802.11a/b/g/n networks. It provides deep insight into the behavior of live networks while consuming a minimal amount of time to conduct a survey. WaveDeploy is a panoramic solution that offers passive, active, and mobility measurements by client during a single pass through the surveyed facility. It delivers true end-user Quality of Experience (QoE) measurements based on the nature and behavior of client devices and applications running on these devices as well as the interaction between those devices and the network infrastructure.

 WaveDeploy Basic and other information on WaveDeploy products can be found at www.wavedeploy.com.

WaveDeploy offers a free version, called WaveDeploy Basic, which provides TCP Downstream, RF Signal, and Co-Channel Interference heat maps. VeriWave also offers a Pro and Expert version with expanded features.

Jitter and Latency

The concepts of jitter and latency have been discussed at various places in this book and should be well understood at this point, so we will not review them again. Yet the question of how to measure these metrics still remains. These are important metrics for latency-sensitive applications, so you should validate them during your WLAN assessment.

Measuring Latency

It is usually more important (and easy) to measure latency for round-trip times than for one-way times. If an 802.11 frame is sent to a particular destination, measuring the time it takes to receive a response from the destination device is the key metric because it mimics the end-user experience more accurately.

Basic latency is usually measured by sending a ping packet because the receiving device doesn't perform any processing on the packet, so there is no processing delay. This makes measuring latency more accurate. However, because 802.11 WLANs are encrypted, this is hard to measure with a protocol analyzer. Therefore, it is usually best to perform from the actual devices operating on the WLAN. Also remember that ICMP will not be prioritized with QoS, so this is a somewhat barbaric measurement of latency. For truer measurements, you will have to implement a software test solution that performs this measurement with two endpoints.

It is quite common to see some 802.11 devices that have more latency than others when using ping, for example, for measuring latency. The root cause of this added latency may be the power save settings on the client devices themselves. Therefore, you should test with these settings on and off if you are experiencing higher-than-expected delays and most certainly if it is only with some devices versus others. If you do not see any differences between devices, the issues likely are network related. When using a QoS-based method of testing latency, you may find that high latency points back to a QoS confirmation problem.

Measuring Jitter

Jitter is a little trickier to analyze. To measure jitter, you must have a constant stream of traffic with frames of similar size transmitted at regular intervals. Without that, transmission times from the source itself are variable and will always result in variable timing differences between responses. Therefore, only real-time protocols like voice or video media streams are the focus of jitter measurements.

Many protocol analyzers offer "voice" versions that are usually upgraded versions of standard or professional offerings. In these products, a variety of tools are available for performing this analysis. Unfortunately, in the WLAN industry, they don't offer as much value. The reason is because nearly all of the voice and video traffic that is sent on a WLAN is encrypted. Sometimes this encryption is in very weak forms that can allow someone to use a protocol analyzer to decrypt the traffic if the encryption key is known (such as with WEP and WPA-PSK). However, this is not possible with 802.1X with strong EAP types. Therefore, you have to dig a bit deeper to ascertain which set of frames you captured are actual voice or video frames that need to be analyzed for jitter.

Some voice and video devices themselves can report jitter. It makes sense to capture this from the devices themselves because they certainly know which traffic to rule out of measurement calculations. The problem arises when the devices report a high degree of jitter and you are then faced with figuring out the root cause. Devices simply report the presence of jitter. The analysis involved in this process is beyond the scope of a design book and better left to an analysis discussion. This topic is addressed in the *CWAP Certified Wireless Analysis Professional Official Study Guide* by David Coleman (Sybex, 2011). Beyond using the actual 802.11 client devices themselves, using one of the voice analysis products on the market can assist with this process. The other most common root cause is wireless medium contention due to high channel utilization, lack of end-to-end QoS integrity, or the traversal of a large number of network hops by traffic.

Application Testing

We have focused most of this chapter on analyzing OSI Layers 1 and 2 because unless those two layers are healthy, the entire foundation of the network is on rocky footing. However, this is not enough; we also recommend that you test primary applications that will operate over the WLAN. These may include a wide variety of applications such as general email and web browsing applications, guest access features, and many others.

You will hear the term *Quality of Experience (QoE)* used when referring to application performance. Effectively, QoE is a term used to quantify the end-user experience of the person using an application on the WLAN. In the next section, we will discuss some basic administrative considerations for network application usage as well as for guest networks.

General Data

In the general data application category, we are generally talking about non-real-time applications, like email, web browsing, and others. Real-time applications require their own set of tests that will vary depending on the application requirements and perhaps the application manufacturer. Since we have already covered many of the topics relating to performance metrics, we will not go into more detail for real-time applications.

When you're performing tests for general data applications, it is important to perform these tests using the devices that will be deployed over the WLAN. Use credentials and security authorization privileges that general users will be using. This will help you validate that not only the 802.11 security authentication is performing as expected, but that the entire end-user experience is satisfactory.

Often, administrators test their own laptops and user accounts on any type of network and subsequently feel that everything is working as expected. They often forget that other users do not have the same level of elevated authorization privileges or that the device they are testing may have been altered in other ways. Administrators usually tinker with their devices and have increased security privileges that common users don't have. Testing the lowest common denominator in this fashion will help validate various firewall policies and other features as well.

In short, perform testing using devices and accounts of end users in order to gauge real-world application performance. This may even mean that several different types of devices may need to be tested with different user credentials, depending on your design.

Guest

Guest networks work by performing some sophisticated interception and processing of client device traffic. Guest networks have several areas that can go awry, such as the following:

- How guest users are filtered and walled off prior to authentication
- What services may be available immediately
- How browsers are redirected for acceptance of usage terms
- How the entire guest authentication application operates

Guest networks are a combination of OSI Layer 2 interception, protocol and service filtering, and browser-based applications; each portion needs to be tested thoroughly.

When providing wireless guest access, usually the first requirement is to keep guest users from accessing important network resources that only authorized users should access. Therefore, the first test you should perform is to ensure that all types of traffic, including non-web-based traffic, cannot reach any internal network resources. If resources can be reached, there is a problem either in the design or implementation of the guest solution.

It's also important to perform valid and nonvalid authentication of the guest application from a variety of end-user devices. These include laptops, mobile phones with 802.11 radios, and personal tablet devices. Also, test devices with different operating systems, browser types and versions, and WLAN adapters.

Common features used in guest network applications include rate limiting and time-based deauthentication. You should test each of these processes in turn by attempting to generate large traffic loads and then by attempting to remain connected beyond the time restriction value. Ensure that clients are properly rate and time limited. Of course, you should also test any other features you are implementing, such as secure captive portal authentication, collection of payment for charged services, and any others.

Failover and Redundancy Testing

What happens when a component of your WLAN design fails or goes offline? The answer to that question is important, and it depends on your redundancy and failover strategy. This is one of the most important facets of all modern networking in business environments, as most networks are mission critical for business functions. It is best to quantify the outcome of failure events before a WLAN is placed into production, which includes documenting the results for future reference. That is especially true if you are not the one who will be operating the WLAN on a day-to-day basis. In the next section, we will discuss many aspects to the redundancy and failover strategy.

Network Switch Failover   APs are usually powered by PoE sourced from a network switch. This means that in the event of a total switch failure the APs will power down and RF coverage, along with all wireless service, will be lost. Some organizations choose to install multiple switches in equipment closets and alternate placement of APs between different switches. This helps minimize the impact of a switch failure and prevents huge sections of RF coverage from being lost.

Router Failure   In the event of a router failure, most network designs incorporate some form of redundancy. Because routing is such a critical function and typically performed at the distribution or core of a LAN, if the device failed without any redundancy then it can not only take out the entire WLAN but the entire LAN as well. For this reason, redundant routers are usually deployed using Hot Standby Router Protocol (HSRP), Virtual Router Redundancy Protocol (VRRP), or other mechanisms to perform automatic failover in the event of a single router failure. Router failover testing should also be performed for a new WLAN install, and it is smart to perform some testing on a regular basis—at least annually.

WLAN Controllers   WLAN controllers present a critical failure point in many WLAN designs. Sometimes hundreds of APs can be serviced from a single WLAN controller, and losing one can be a catastrophic event if redundancy is not accounted for. WLAN controllers should be deployed with some level of failover. Perform several types of failure testing with WLAN controllers before going live with a new WLAN deployment. Test Ethernet link failure and then perform complete controller failover testing. Depending on the equipment vendor, there may be specific features that govern the behavior of devices in the event of certain failure events, and this is also a good time to test them outside a lab environment.

The severity of a WLAN controller failure depends on the architectural model in use. If all data is forwarded through the controller, a failure is catastrophic if a backup is not in place. For distributed forwarding, the controller may be providing some authentication and Radio Resource Management (RRM) services, so the immediate failover is slightly less significant. In either case, you should know what services are lost in the event of a controller failure.

Link Failures   In the earlier section "Wired Analysis," we discussed link failures, but it is worth mentioning again. Regardless of whether you're using EtherChannel, test Ethernet link failure and bring the Ethernet link back online to ensure the network will recover from a failure. If you're using EtherChannel, test each link of the EtherChannel configuration, and when you restore the link, full service should commence. Alternatively, you can use other forms of link redundancy that is vendor proprietary.

RADIUS Failover Testing   RADIUS failover testing is an important core component of a WLAN that should be well tested. Failover can happen as a result of various reasons. Failover decisions are controlled by the authenticator role in the 802.1X process. You can't expect the reasons for a RADIUS failover to always be what you expect. Even once a failover happens, does the authenticator fail back to the RADIUS server that you expect? It isn't sufficient to only cause a failover and test whether failover properly occurs; you must also test whether the authenticator will fall back to the originally designated authentication server if that is what your design intends in the event that the primary configured server is restored to a normal operating state.

DHCP Failure   DHCP failure can cause disastrous effects to network operations. Nearly all WLAN client devices used in the majority of network designs rely on DHCP. If DHCP isn't fully reliable, client connectivity will be stopped short, preventing any real use of network services. It isn't just important to test the affected client devices that use the WLAN—you must also test APs that operate using DHCP. APs that use DHCP are typically controller-based APs, but some network designs incorporate DHCP reservation for all network devices in order to allow for easier network address management from a centralized location. IP helper commands are also administered on routers that redirect DHCP requests to these central servers. Ensuring that backup addresses are configured and properly redirecting traffic is also important.

Network Approval

Before we complete this chapter, it is important to wrap up all the technical discussion with a business reminder. As you perform this validation assessment for the WLAN, it is important to ensure that you are measuring and meeting the customer's (or your company's) requirements. These requirements should be documented in the early stages of the network design process. However, it is not enough to document that you have met the requirements. It is important to create a document that defines the measured criteria, evaluates the network's performance according to those objective criteria, and demonstrates that the network is ready for use. A representative from the customer's company should sign off on this documentation to confirm that you have validated your design work and that the network is ready for real-world use.

Summary

When you're performing a post-analysis of a new WLAN installation, a number of things can go wrong. RF propagation and link budget balancing usually has the highest payoff. No configuration option or automated RF management algorithm can resolve a bad design, so it makes sense to start with a physical layer analysis first.

Once the RF environment is deemed healthy, the low-level design and configuration options should be validated across several categories, including security, radio settings, QoS configuration, and wired network settings. Applications and end-user devices should also be thoroughly tested using as close to real-world usage patterns and actual user security credentials as possible to ensure the end-user experience is as designed.

The time invested during a post-installation validation has huge payoffs because it allows new networks to be fully analyzed and remediated prior to any production use where users might be negatively affected. Once the network is placed into a production state, it can be difficult to address issues and may even cost a great deal of money if users experience problems. Therefore, performing a thorough assessment should save a great deal of time and money.

Exam Essentials

Understand the methods for assessing RF performance.   Be able to validate and improve channel plans, signal quality, and transmit power implementations, and also identify and fix RF trouble spots.

Quantify and validate RF interference.   Understand methods for properly surveying for, identifying, locating, quantifying the impact of, and removing sources of RF interference.

Perform an analysis of wired components to a WLAN deployment.   Analyze common components of a wired network design integrating with a WLAN, including wired links, 802.1Q, QoS, and IP and Ethernet services.

Validate common WLAN configuration options.   Perform a thorough assessment to validate proper configuration and operation of common WLAN parameters, such as SSID settings, power save, and optimization features.

Confirm proper design and implementation of security.   Test all the functional areas of WLAN security to ensure the network is protected as desired. These areas include EAP;

authentication, authorization, and accounting; encryption; device management; traffic filtering; and rogue detection and threat mitigation, at a minimum.

Measure common metrics that indicate a design problem.   Analyze the network with common performance metrics in mind, including errors, retries, congestion, and common RF problems.

Perform a roaming analysis.   Validate roaming operations by testing how and when clients roam to identify trouble spots as well as to verify fast secure roaming operation with 802.1X.

Analyze frame and channel information.   Use a protocol analyzer in order to obtain and quantify frame and channel performance issues and metrics.

Perfom load and performance analysis.   Be able to perform application performance testing and know what information is important to obtain.

Ensure proper operation of failover and redundancy strategies.   Test failover and redundancy strategies to ensure that the inevitable failure has a minimal and short-lived impact on network operations.

Review Questions

1. The first part of a post-installation RF assessment should begin with which of the following? (Choose all that apply.)

    A. Link budget

    B. Channels

    C. Multipath analysis

    D. Signal quality

2. You are reviewing a new network installation for Coleman Cogs, Inc. and you notice that automatic transmit power configuration is averaging 5 dBm for all APs. What document should you ask for in order to check whether network coverage gaps exist?

    A. Survey AP config

    B. RF survey data

    C. Low-level RF design

    D. Transmit power threshold plan

3. You are reviewing a new WLAN install for a multifloor hospital scheduled to open in two weeks. The RF design was based on a predictive RF assessment. You notice that the automatic RF management system is configuring AP transmit power levels at the highest and lowest possible values. A passive survey was performed and the RF levels look OK. What concern should you have, if any?

    A. Areas with low power might have coverage holes.

    B. Some clients might experience a link budget imbalance.

    C. None. The passive survey showed ample coverage.

    D. The seed value to the channelization algorithm is too large.

4. You were just hired at a new company with an existing WLAN that has no automatic RF management capability. There are a large number of reports of connectivity problems. The company told you that they intend to add a WLAN controller to the network and let the controller fix the RF issues with the existing APs. What is an important message to convey to them?

    A. Automatic RF management cannot manufacture RF.

    B. You should try upgrading the clients first.

    C. You have already done that previously.

    D. A WLAN controller's self-healing capabilities will fix it.

5. You are reviewing a recently installed WLAN network and users are sporadically reporting disconnected sessions and dropped voice calls. Automatic RF is enabled. What might you review? (Choose all that apply.)

    A. Transmit power change history

    B. Whether 802.11h is enabled

    C. 802.11e roaming reports

    D. Channel change history

6. You are troubleshooting poor throughput performance in an area of a new WLAN deployment. Whenever clients are in that area, they have very low data throughput, but outside of that area they are fine. RSSI looks fine in the trouble area. What else should you consider?

    A. Client orientation to AP

    B. Radio frequency noise levels

    C. Whether the AP power needs to be raised

    D. Channel scan settings on clients

7. You are asked to analyze a spectrum analysis capture that was taken during a post-installation assessment. You notice a sawtooth pattern in the real-time FFT display peaking at –25 dBm and a duty cycle percentage of 5 percent. What analysis can you offer?

    A. Signal levels are high and will always cause a significant impact on performance.

    B. The source is likely a wireless video camera and should be eliminated.

    C. It is likely a DECT phone and only 5 percent of airtime is left.

    D. The duty cycle is still very low and not a big concern.

8. You're performing a throughput test using a 3x3 802.11n AP capable of up to 450 Mbps PHY rates using a three spatial stream capable client. When testing throughput running at signal quality more than necessary to support maximum PHY rates, you are unable to achieve throughput beyond 90 Mbps. What might be wrong?

    A. You are only running 802.3af and not all radios are powered.

    B. Ethernet link speeds need to be verified.

    C. MCS rates 0 through 7 are not enabled.

    D. The radio is not operating using 5 GHz.

9. You have just installed a WLAN controller and no traffic is traversing the VLANs that are configured on the WLAN controller because no wireless clients are connected yet. However, you are noticing a lot of link activity. Which of the following should be verified? (Choose all that apply.)

    A. VLAN pruning on the WLAN controller

    B. 802.1p broadcast suppression

    C. EtherChannel configuration on the Ethernet switch

    D. Whether APs are downloading configuration

10. You are performing a post-validation survey with an autonomous AP network. You pass traffic fine until reaching a small group of APs. You are associated and fully authenticated, but you cannot obtain an IP address. What should you investigate as a potential concern?

    A. 802.1X is failing the four-way handshake.

    B. The APs have an incompatible basic rate enabled.

    C. An AP might not be properly configured for all VLANs.

    D. A switch might not be properly configured for all VLANs.

11. You are performing a wired assessment during a post-validation survey and notice that a WLAN controller has interface errors on one of the links. The stats show CRCs and collisions. What should be immediately suspected as a concern?

    A. This is normal when large amounts of data are transferred.

    B. A bad cable is installed on that port.

    C. 802.3at negotiation has likely failed on that port.

    D. There is a duplex mismatch on that port.

12. Early tests during a post-deployment assessment reveal poor audio quality. What steps should be taken to determine whether QoS is configured end to end?

    A. Ensure uplink UPs are enabled and the AP is using the proper EDCA Tx timing.

    B. Ensure uplink UPs are enabled and the ingress switch port trusts DSCP values.

    C. Ensure uplink UPs are enabled and downlink UPs are present.

    D. Ensure uplink DSCP values are enabled and downlink DSCP values are present.

13. When validating an EtherChannel configuration, which criteria should be considered? (Choose all that apply.)

    A. Failover

    B. Link errors

    C. Utilization

    D. 802.3at values

14. You have plugged your APs into a PoE-capable switch, but only a certain number of APs are fully powering on and the order is random. What should be validated?

    A. 802.3at power negotiation failure

    B. Whether PoE crosstalk is present

    C. The power budget of the PoE switch

    D. Whether 802.11ac is negotiating at full power

15. You are analyzing client roaming performance of a new WLAN install and the client is connected to one AP, walks past another AP without associating, and connects to another AP altogether. Which of the following are possible causes? (Choose all that apply.)

   A. The client roaming threshold is set too low.

   B. The RF channel is not supported by the client.

   C. Cells are overlapping too much.

   D. The AP is not roaming the client properly.

16. During a post-validation assessment, you have configured a client for 802.1X/EAP but it is not passing authentication. Which areas should you check in the WLAN configuration?

   A. Whether the RADIUS server is online and configured for the matching port on the APs and WLAN controllers

   B. Whether the authenticator is configured to support the EAP type(s) your client is configured for

   C. Whether the RADIUS shared secret is properly configured on the supplicant and authentication server

   D. Whether the client has a fully valid certificate

17. Default configurations of enterprise networking equipment may pose security vulnerabilities. On most enterprise network devices, what actions should be performed to avoid vulnerabilities that result from default settings? (Choose all that apply.)

   A. Disable open authentication.

   B. Change the default administrator username and password.

   C. 802.1X authentication database specification so all user authentications aren't automatically accepted.

   D. Change the default SNMP strings.

18. When performing frame and channel analysis during a post-installation assessment, which of the following is important to validate about retransmissions?

   A. CRC error values seen using an analyzer should be less than 5 percent.

   B. The CRC error average should be no more than 10 percent.

   C. Signal quality should be within transmitter specs.

   D. Retransmissions should only rarely occur.

19. When viewing channel utilization information from a protocol analyzer, if high channel utilization is occurring, what should you ensure does not exist?

   A. A high percentage of low PHY rates

   B. An RF signal generator causing an RF DoS

   C. High levels of workload

   D. High frames per second

20. What type of tool is best to have when performing a roam time analysis?

    A. Multi-channel capture utility

    B. 802.11h channel switch announcement

    C. WIDS/WIPS

    D. A protocol analyzer that is scanning all channels

Answers to Review Questions

1. **B, D.** The first part of a post-installation assessment should start with the physical layer, which primarily includes channel and transmit power.

2. **B.** The data generated during the original RF survey using a survey mapping software program will help you determine whether transmit power is set drastically lower than the original RF design. If transmit power is set too low, outer edges of originally intended AP coverage patterns might not have enough coverage.

3. **B.** APs whose transmit power is too high will cause a perception that proper RF coverage exists, but weaker powered clients may not be able to communicate well at the cell edges of high-powered APs. This is a common misperception with passive surveys where transmit power levels are not in balance with clients.

4. **A.** Automated RF management cannot fix a bad design.

5. **A, D.** When an AP changes channels when automatic channel management is enabled, it usually causes clients to disconnect. Sometimes it can be a disruptive disconnection, causing clients to drop sessions. Reviewing whether APs have changed channels might help you understand the root causes.

6. **B.** Even though RSSI levels may be sufficient, higher noise levels might exist that can degrade signal quality, resulting in lower PHY rates.

7. **D.** Even though signal levels are high, only 5 percent of the available spectrum is being used by the interference source and all other transmitting devices.

8. **B.** Ethernet links speeds need to be verified in post-validation assessments. An 802.11n AP requires greater than Fast Ethernet link speeds in order to achieve high throughput.

9. **A, D.** All VLANs that are not used by the WLAN controller should be pruned from the configuration of the Ethernet switch for all VLANs that are not used by the WLAN controller and wireless clients. APs that might be already online searching for a controller may have found it and have already started downloading its configuration.

10. **D.** Since the question pertained to more than one AP, the problem is likely the Ethernet switch that serves the group of APs that is not properly configured with the user VLAN used for that wireless client authentication.

11. **D.** On wired Ethernet, seeing interface errors such as CRCs and collisions are likely indicators that an Ethernet link is improperly negotiated.

12. **C.** By taking two properly configured QoS devices and initiating a QoS-applicable application session, traffic marked on the uplink should remain intact on the downlink to the other device anywhere the device may roam. For 802.11, only Layer 2 UP values are of any significance in order to gain QoS over the wireless medium.

13. **A, B, C.** Failover should be tested along with confirming no traffic corruption is occurring that results in link errors. Also ensure all links involved in the EtherChannel configuration are servicing their fair share of traffic.

14. C. PoE switches are capable of distributing a finite amount of power. You need to validate that you are staying within your allotted power budget.

15. A, B, C. The only invalid option is D because APs do not participate in client roaming in a standard 802.11 architecture.

16. A. Only A is a fully correct answer. The authenticator does not restrict or allow EAP types. RADIUS shared secrets are only configured on the AS and authenticator. Client certificates are only applicable with certain EAP types.

17. B, D. Failing to change default usernames and passwords as well as default SNMP strings is a huge security vulnerability that needs to be validated during a post-installation assessment.

18. B. Frame retransmissions of a heavily used network during a post-validation would be a concern if the rate approached 10 percent. Normally, retransmission rates should be very low, but large volumes of traffic and RF interference will elevate retransmission levels with a greater quantity of devices and in the presence of mild RF interference.

19. A. Low PHY rates will consume nearly all the available channel capacity while only allowing a small amount of throughput for network applications.

20. A. A single WLAN radio cannot capture traffic off a configured channel and see all the traffic a roaming client is sending on different channels. Using a multichannel capture utility will allow you to see all the client behavior on multiple channels simultaneously.

Chapter

15

Design Troubleshooting

THE FOLLOWING CWDP EXAM TOPICS ARE COVERED IN THIS CHAPTER:

- ✓ Illustrate a comprehensive understanding of the role of channel planning and usage in network design.

- ✓ Describe the role of load balancing in RF spectrum management.

- ✓ Explain the metrics, data, and other information collected and reported during a site survey.

- ✓ Identify the appropriate uses of spectrum analysis in network design and troubleshooting.

- ✓ Perform and interpret an RF analysis for an existing WLAN deployment.

- ✓ Illustrate the use of a protocol analyzer and interpret the results to identify problems with the following aspects of network design:

  - Security setup and configuration

  - Roaming

  - PHY rate analysis

  - MAC feature parity

  - QoS

  - Client (including drivers) and infrastructure compatibility

- ✓ Understand proper WLAN functionality, including wired infrastructure connectivity and services, and identify problematic characteristics in network design.

- ✓ Demonstrate a detailed knowledge of common client-side and application problems and isolate unexpected client behavior.

Regardless of how well a network is planned, designed, and implemented, there will always be a troubleshooting component involved. Even if you have a newly deployed network, you'll likely need to complete some troubleshooting to iron out the kinks (i.e., minor mistakes that no one caught during the deployment) and ensure the network is performing as expected. If you have a network that has been around for a year or more, it's a safe bet that something has changed since the time it was deployed. Such changes can be related to configuration of a new feature, firmware updates, hardware failure, or physical tampering (intentional or accidental). More commonly for WLANs, changes are environmental in nature and impact the RF medium. The impact may be related to a building renovation that has changed the building layout; the addition, removal, or rearrangement of furniture; and other factors. In any of these scenarios, the functionality of the wireless network is subject to change.

Troubleshooting wired networks can often be viewed as systematic and methodical (assuming you have the background to troubleshoot the protocols in use). Wireless troubleshooting, however, tends to have an added complexity in that there are many aspects that cannot be easily "seen" that can impact how well the network operates. This chapter will address not only wireless network issues, but also traditional wired network issues that affect the wireless network. After all, in the vast majority of cases, a WLAN is merely an extension of a wired LAN.

Troubleshooting Steps

The first step in any troubleshooting effort is to figure out what you are troubleshooting in the first place. Begin by asking lots of questions, such as:

- What is working?

- What is not working?

- Does this problem happen all the time or just sometimes?

Troubleshooting needs to be systematic and iterative in nature. The goal is to eliminate possibilities. Think of it as equivalent to peeling away the layers of an onion, except you are instead removing the layers of complexity.

The next step is to start with the very basics of wireless communication. Again there is a list of questions you should ask:

- Is the wireless card on and working?
- Do you have a quality signal available?
- Are you able to join the wireless network?

If your wireless card is working and you have a quality signal, the client could potentially be failing during the security challenge process. The next step is to try removing security as a quick test. Does it work then?

The same logic applies for non-coverage-related issues. Suppose you have a client that fails when roaming from one AP to another in a controller-based environment. At this point you should ask yourself, "Does this happen if APs are on different controllers or the same controller?" Assuming different controllers, does it still happen if the APs are on the same controller?

A good rule of thumb for troubleshooting is to reference the *OSI model* (shown in Table 15.1) and move from Layer 1 (this is a good time to recheck your signal) up through Layer 7. Check now to see if your application works. By systematically removing complexities and retesting a scenario over and over again, you can eliminate possibilities and move further down the path to resolution.

One thing that should *not* be a part of your troubleshooting methodology is to make multiple changes at once. Avoid doing this if at all possible as you may not know which change either fixed things or made things worse. Try to always test one item at a time and document the result.

TABLE 15.1   The OSI model

	Data unit	Layer	Function
Host layers	Data	7. Application	Network process to application
		6. Presentation	Data representation, encryption/decryption
		5. Session	Interhost communication
	Segments	4. Transport	End-to-end connections, flow control and reliability
Media layers	Packet	3. Network	Path determination (routing) logical addressing
	Frame	2. Data Link	Physical addressing
	Bit	1. Physical	Media, signal, cabling, binary transmission

Coverage Analysis

When it comes to troubleshooting a wireless network, validating coverage is typically one of the very first things to take place. This makes sense, as without a quality signal, you can't expect to have high-quality wireless communication between the client and the AP. And without good communication, operations *always* begin to break down. We will now explore how to troubleshoot signal problems by expanding on the information you learned in Chapter 8, "Site Survey Preparation," which covered methodologies for performing RF site surveys. Topics we'll cover include considerations for site surveying with troubleshooting in mind.

When dealing with a problematic wireless network you're likely in one of two categories:

- You are familiar with the network and may have been involved in the design and/or implementation.

- You know nothing or very little about the network.

The interesting thing about being an effective troubleshooter is that you should treat any network as if you don't know much about the network, even if you do. Why take that approach?

The proper mindset should be to leave no stone unturned. Let's say you did design the network, but perhaps that was 18 months ago. While it is indeed helpful to be familiar with aspects of the network environment, it can also be a detriment. After all, with familiarity come assumptions, and assumptions often lead you to overlook network elements because you "know" it wasn't deployed that way. Yet it's easy to forget that if you're being called on to troubleshoot the network, obviously something has changed, and the WLAN is no longer working as well as it was before. The main point here is that the network isn't performing adequately now, and you need to figure out why.

Collecting RF Data

When surveying in a troubleshooting scenario like this, you should strongly consider setting up your survey tool to scan all the channels in the band you are concerned with (using Passive Survey mode). This is because you can potentially miss interfering networks that are operating on those off channels, which could be contributing to the issue you are trying to identify. The downside to doing this is that you have to move *very* slowly due to the amount of time it takes to cycle through the channels. This is directly related to the amount of time the software listens on each channel prior to moving to the next channel. As we've already covered in Chapter 9, "Site Survey RF Design," the time it takes to perform this work may be time prohibitive. Sometimes, it is safer to perform a passive scan of all channels to discover all devices and then follow it up with a passive survey using only the channels that your WLAN uses.

You do not need to be close to an AP in order to catch at least one beacon to know approximately where it is. Even walking fairly fast or covering hallways or major walking areas only will provide enough information for a more targeted revisit in order to pinpoint a device.

Analyzing RF Data

Once you've collected the RF data, it's time to begin analyzing it. The first thing to do is filter the data to display only the targeted RSSI or SNR level. Anything that falls outside that targeted level should be clearly indicated, as shown by the darker color in Figure 15.1. This configuration setup is shown for a popular surveying utility in Figure 15.1.

FIGURE 15.1 Survey with cutoff

This configuration setup makes it easy to spot coverage holes. The coverage-hole journey is just beginning at this point. Next you have to figure out why you have this gap in coverage or signal quality. Oftentimes, the collected survey data may help expose the real issue. One of the first steps is to review the transmit power settings for the APs servicing that area.

First, check to see if the transmit power is statically set, or if it is set using an automatic power and channel algorithm. Also, note whether the surrounding APs are at full power. If they are, this can be bad for several reasons. First, if they are already at full power and you still have areas that lack the proper coverage, you may need additional APs or new antennas. Even if your coverage is sufficient, APs operating at maximum power may still be a problem. Many clients have maximum transmit power values that are much less than what the AP is capable of. If you have an AP that is at maximum power and a low-powered client that is at the edge of that cell, you will likely experience a "one-way" situation where the client can hear the AP well but the AP is not able to hear the client well. For that reason it's generally recommended that you have the maximum AP transmit power not exceed the least common denominator of transmit power among your set of clients. Most vendors that have implemented auto channel and power algorithms have also realized the need to have a maximum transmit power setting for their algorithms.

Another thing to check for is channelization problems. In general these are less common than transmit power issues; however, one common channelization problem exists in the 5 GHz band. Many of today's enterprise-class APs support the UNII-2 extended band. Yet not nearly as many clients currently support these channels (100–140). When troubleshooting the network for issues, make sure that the channel set in use matches the capabilities of the clients or your "holes" might not be holes after all. The issue could merely be a mismatch in channel capabilities.

Spectrum Analysis

Although the topic of spectrum analysis could fill a book, the discussion in this chapter will focus on the common scenarios you are likely to encounter when troubleshooting a wireless network and when taking the certification exam. Interference to Wi-Fi networks can generally be broken down into two categories:

- Non-Wi-Fi
- Wi-Fi interferers

Things such as wireless phones, microwaves, video cameras, and Bluetooth devices are examples of non-Wi-Fi interferers and are commonly seen in network environments. Wi-Fi interferers are interference sources that are coming from other Wi-Fi transmitters and can be further broken down into Wi-Fi that is a part of your network and Wi-Fi that is not a part of your network.

All of these different interference sources can seem a bit daunting. Fortunately for us, a large majority of the non-Wi-Fi interferers have been fairly well identified by user-friendly, mobile spectrum analysis tools (as opposed to the bigger, bulkier spectrum analyzers that cover much more spectrum than just bands where Wi-Fi lives). We refer to the user-friendly tools as the ones that are Wi-Fi specific and give you alarms and information based on a set of signatures it has in its database that catalogs most of the offending devices commonly found.

Are there signatures for all potential offending devices? Unfortunately no, but the ones that do exist are helpful. For the ones for which there aren't reliable signatures, the spectrum analyzer still does a great job of showing interference sources and can be critical in tracking those sources down. As for the Wi-Fi interference, the spectrum analyzer is helpful here as well; it can show you the number of stations it is detecting, the operating channel and power level of those stations, and general channel usage statistics, like duty cycle. In addition to a spectrum analyzer, protocol analysis tools such as AirMagnet WiFi Analyzer are particularly effective at showing how much bandwidth is being consumed on a channel.

Non-Wi-Fi Interference

It should be clearly understood that the possibilities for non-Wi-Fi interference are great, due to the fact that WLANs operate in an unlicensed spectrum. Therefore, it's not against the law to use these frequencies for other devices like video cameras, phones, headsets—the list goes on and on. Fortunately, you do have spectrum analyzers available to help you "see" what is happening to the spectrum. This section covers two popular non-Wi-Fi interferers: microwave ovens and Bluetooth devices.

> As you are troubleshooting an issue that manifests itself as a non-Wi-Fi interferer, it is helpful if you can identify common characteristics of the interfering device. Chief among these common signature characteristics are wideband versus narrowband, high amplitude versus low amplitude, and continuous transmitters versus intermittent transmitters. Even if you can't identify the specific type of device that is interfering, if you can identify some of these characteristics, you will be able to understand the impact on the network and more rapidly "fix" the problem.

Microwave Ovens

Microwave ovens are one of the most common non-Wi-Fi interferers you will come across because they are present in just about every home and business and for the most part they operate in the 2.4 GHz band. Due to their usage characteristics, microwaves can be particularly destructive to a Wi-Fi network. Picture this: a hungry employee walks into the break room and puts his cold pizza in the microwave. He sets it to heat the pizza for 60 seconds. During that 60-second period, an assault is occurring on the Wi-Fi network, and the impact is typically across multiple channels in the 2.4 GHz band. Users in the vicinity are experiencing this disruption in the form of slow or no connectivity, dropped voice calls, dropped VPN connections, and more. Then, just as abruptly as it started, it ends. The hungry person has hot pizza, the wireless network stabilizes, and applications resume again. The users may call tech support to complain of this intermittent problem, but every time someone shows up, the hungry people are nowhere to be found. It's this type of dilemma that makes microwaves a thorn in a wireless designer's side.

Are all microwaves created equally? Not exactly. In addition to the intermittent nature of microwave oven usage, not all microwave ovens emit the exact same RF signature. Although most of them stay within the same relative frequency range (usually around channels 6-11), some have more of a wideband impact than others. Keep this in mind if you have a large environment where microwaves are in use, especially near break rooms. Sticking with the same make and model microwave would at least ensure you that you are affecting perhaps only one channel, whereas if you were to mix and match you have the potential to impact more than one. Another thing to note about microwaves is that they tend to have higher RF "leakage" properties over time. Over the years, that door will open and shut thousands of times (think of all those breakfast burritos!), and as seals experience wear and tear, the result is poor RF isolation and thus higher amplitude interference impacting your WLAN.

Bluetooth

Bluetooth devices are just as common today as microwave ovens. More and more devices are taking advantage of Bluetooth technology due to the increasing demand for wireless as a cable replacement technology. While Bluetooth and Wi-Fi can coexist, there is a minimal cost to the Wi-Fi network. Stations in close proximity to active Bluetooth devices generally see slightly less throughput due to higher retransmissions. The latest Bluetooth specs use avoidance technologies that minimize interference with Wi-Fi. For this reason, if Bluetooth coexists with Wi-Fi in small quantities, it won't cause problems. A large number of Bluetooth devices will begin to impact WLAN performance.

For the purposes of this book, it is not necessary to delve into Bluetooth specifics too deeply but rather to recognize it as an interference source, to understand its impact on the WLAN, and to know what it looks like in a spectrum analyzer trace. Bluetooth is easily identified in a spectrum analyzer by looking for the very high spikes (in a real-time FFT display) that cross all channels (since it's a frequency hopping technology). Figure 15.2 shows an example taken from a Cisco Spectrum Expert card with the Max Hold setting enabled. You can see the unique Bluetooth signature in the Real Time FFT chart, but in areas with heavy usage and a busy RF medium, the Swept Spectrogram chart may be more useful for identifying Bluetooth. As you can see, there is a characteristic set of "dots" across the entire band.

FIGURE 15.2   Bluetooth as seen from Cisco's Spectrum Expert

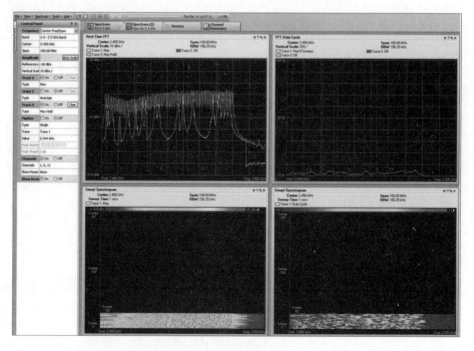

Wi-Fi Interference

One of the most commonly overlooked WLAN troubleshooting topics is the impact that Wi-Fi can have on itself. Many engineers tend to gravitate and stick to the search for non-Wi-Fi interferers, when in reality a large majority of issues are caused by Wi-Fi interference, which can be minimized with proper design techniques. As explained earlier, there are two main types of Wi-Fi interference. There's the Wi-Fi interference that's created by your own APs on your network. Then there's the Wi-Fi interference that's caused by either rogue APs on your network or a neighboring network that is in close proximity. The following sections cover the most common sources of Wi-Fi interference.

Co-channel Interference

Co-channel interference occurs when you have more than one AP on the same channel within RF range of one another, meaning the APs and either all or some of their associated clients are able to "hear" one another's transmissions. Why is this bad, you might ask? Well, remember that wireless is a polite protocol and is based on the CSMA/CA principles of listen before talk. If you have multiple APs that are able to clearly "see" neighbor stations on the same channel, essentially what you have is all those clients plugged into a hub. They are all sharing the same channel, commonly called a contention domain.

Now suppose you have three APs on channel 11 and each AP has 10 clients and all of these APs and clients can clearly decipher one another's transmissions (most importantly, the Duration/ID field in the MAC header). The net result is that only one out of 30 of those clients can talk at a time. Now imagine those same three APs but this time their output power is reduced and their spacing or channel assignment has been changed so that their transmissions are either not heard by one another (or associated clients), or, if they are heard, the amplitude is near the noise floor. By separating them into different contention domains, the result is that 3 out of 30 can transmit at the same time. With this basic example, you can see what impact co-channel interference can have on cell capacity and the overall throughput of your wireless network. Although 3 out of 30 may not seem like much, this is triple the previous capacity.

So where did all this co-channel interference come from? Two places: either your own network or someone else's!

Operator-Owned Wi-Fi Interference

Let's talk about co-channel from your own network first. Over the past few years, wireless networks have been making a fundamental shift from *coverage-based networks*—meaning a network that was designed to cover as much area as possible with as few APs as possible— to *capacity-based networks,* which essentially means you're trying to cram as many APs into an area as you can to increase your capacity. Let's be clear here: designing for a capacity-based network is no easy chore. Many engineers make the mistake of thinking they can increase capacity by simply adding more APs to the network. This is not so. What they end up doing is adding more co-channel interference to their already stressed network.

There are specific factors that should be planned for when attempting to increase capacity. Some of these methods are as follows:

- Adjusting transmit power
- Using more directional antennas as opposed to using omnidirectional antennas
- Disabling lower data rates
- Placing APs so that you utilize a building's natural RF characteristics to provide isolation between APs (APs in rooms versus hallways, etc.)

And even with these techniques, there is always a capacity limit. Smaller AP cells with lower transmit power will eventually cease to yield gains because an unwanted signal (usually between –75 dBm and –90 dBm) also increases outside the desired basic service area (BSA).

Neighboring Network Interference

The second source of co-channel interference is from networks that are not under your control. These can be from rogues (either infrastructure or ad hoc) that are within your building, or from APs that are simply neighboring Wi-Fi networks that could be from a tenant occupying space within nearby RF range of your building. The challenge here is that it's easy to fail to realize that you have a neighboring network that's impacting yours.

 Real World Scenario

The Not-So-Friendly Neighbors

A customer calls you and requests assistance with troubleshooting what they describe as a performance issue on their wireless network. This is a network you designed and deployed, and you're shocked to hear this since you are confident the network has properly placed APs and correct antenna alignment, that channel and power settings are optimal, and that you've disabled lower data rates (1, 2, and 5.5 Mbps). Yet you are now getting complaints of poor throughput and poor user experience. You tell the customer you will visit this problematic area and see what you can figure out.

When you get to the client site, you go to the problematic area and perform basic protocol analysis. You see a rogue network occupying the same channel as your AP (e.g., channel 1). Next you check the per-channel utilization and throughput for channel 1, as shown in Graphic 15.1. You are shocked to see that nearly 90 percent of your channel is being consumed by 1 MB traffic even though you have that data rate disabled and you are beaconing at 11 MB. What is happening here?

What you find is a busy neighboring network, one that is broadcasting several SSIDs with the lower data rates enabled. Remember, just because the hardware will let you configure a high number of SSIDs, that does not make it a good idea. The AP has to send beacons

---

for each one of those SSIDs, and with the lower data rates enabled, it's sending those beacons at 1 Mbps. Now let's factor in user traffic, both from your own network and from the neighboring network.

If you're in a situation where you have a neighboring network that's doing something like this, the best defense is good social tact. The neighbors aren't doing anything legally wrong, but they are being a bad RF neighbor. The best you can do is find where this traffic is coming from, approach the person responsible for that network, and kindly suggest that they take some action to help alleviate the situation.

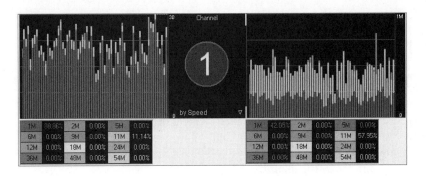

Adjacent-overlapping Channel Interference

Adjacent-overlapping channel interference occurs when you have an AP that is on a channel that is overlapping with another channel. Its effects are somewhat similar to co-channel, but they may be worse. In the United States, for example, the three nonoverlapping 2.4 GHz channels are 1, 6, and 11. So, assuming you have APs using those three channels, if you were to have a rogue AP operating on a channel other than those three, it would impact two of those three channels. The 2.4 GHz ISM band channel plan shown in Figure 4.1 earlier in this book helps illustrate this problem.

In the 5 GHz spectrum, all of the 20 MHz channels are natively considered to be nonoverlapping since the channelization pattern was specified for easier configuration. However, since there are far more available channels in the 5 GHz bands, we recommend that you try to space at least one channel between adjacent cells. Even though the primary OFDM signals don't overlap on the main channel, the secondary "shoulder" may overlap at a lower amplitude. At high transmit powers, this could have a negative impact on adjacent channels. Figure 15.3 illustrates UNII 1 and 2 frequency bands.

As a general recommendation, when troubleshooting performance issues on your wireless network, pay close attention to both co-channel and adjacent-channel interference sources.

FIGURE 15.3 UNII 1 and 2 channel usage.

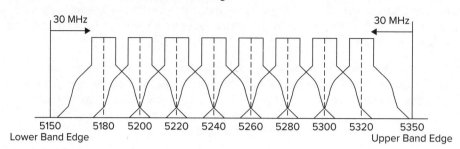

Security Model Analysis and Troubleshooting 802.1X Authentication

To troubleshoot client authentication using 802.1X, you should break down the key components of the end-to-end infrastructure and follow a modular troubleshooting approach. The three key components involved in 802.1X authentication are the *supplicant,* the *authenticator,* and the *authentication server.*

Authentication failures are generally caused by misconfigurations, certificate provisioning errors, or a credential mismatch between the supplicant and the authentication server. In Figure 15.4 you see an entire EAPOL exchange between the supplicant and the authenticator that results in a failure.

FIGURE 15.4 EAPOL exchange between supplicant and authenticator from start to failure

No.	Time	Source	Destination	Protocol	Info
1	16:27:48.180853	Intel_01:07:b2	Cisco_35:77:af	EAPOL	Start
2	16:27:48.182053	Cisco_35:77:af	Intel_01:07:b2	EAP	Request, Identity [RFC3748]
3	16:27:48.311615	Intel_01:07:b2	Cisco_35:77:af	EAP	Response, Identity [RFC3748]
4	16:27:48.318875	Cisco_35:77:af	Intel_01:07:b2	EAP	Request, EAP-Cisco wireless (LEAP) [Norman]
5	16:27:48.319567	Intel_01:07:b2	Cisco_35:77:af	EAP	Response, Legacy Nak (Response only) [RFC3748]
6	16:27:48.327715	Cisco_35:77:af	Intel_01:07:b2	EAP	Request, PEAP [Palekar]
7	16:27:48.332140	Intel_01:07:b2	Cisco_35:77:af	TLSv1	Client Hello
8	16:27:48.339898	Cisco_35:77:af	Intel_01:07:b2	TLSv1	Server Hello, Change Cipher Spec, Encrypted Handshake Message
9	16:27:48.345881	Intel_01:07:b2	Cisco_35:77:af	TLSv1	Change Cipher Spec, Encrypted Handshake Message
10	16:27:48.351286	Cisco_35:77:af	Intel_01:07:b2	TLSv1	Application Data
11	16:27:48.356475	Intel_01:07:b2	Cisco_35:77:af	TLSv1	Application Data
12	16:27:48.360856	Cisco_35:77:af	Intel_01:07:b2	TLSv1	Application Data
13	16:27:48.362100	Intel_01:07:b2	Cisco_35:77:af	TLSv1	Application Data
14	16:27:48.368346	Cisco_35:77:af	Intel_01:07:b2	TLSv1	Application Data
15	16:27:48.381476	Intel_01:07:b2	Cisco_35:77:af	TLSv1	Application Data
16	16:27:48.446512	Cisco_35:77:af	Intel_01:07:b2	TLSv1	Application Data
17	16:27:52.719892	Intel_01:07:b2	Cisco_35:77:af	TLSv1	Application Data
18	16:27:52.765430	Cisco_35:77:af	Intel_01:07:b2	TLSv1	Application Data
19	16:27:56.343753	Intel_01:07:b2	Cisco_35:77:af	TLSv1	Application Data
20	16:27:56.389171	Cisco_35:77:af	Intel_01:07:b2	TLSv1	Application Data
21	16:28:00.074053	Intel_01:07:b2	Cisco_35:77:af	TLSv1	Application Data
22	16:28:00.080358	Cisco_35:77:af	Intel_01:07:b2	TLSv1	Application Data
23	16:28:00.081102	Intel_01:07:b2	Cisco_35:77:af	TLSv1	Application Data
24	16:28:00.086123	Cisco_35:77:af	Intel_01:07:b2	EAP	Failure

```
⊞ Frame 24: 22 bytes on wire (176 bits), 22 bytes captured (176 bits)
⊞ Ethernet II, Src: Cisco_35:77:af (00:17:0f:35:77:af), Dst: Intel_01:07:b2 (00:18:de:01:07:b2)
⊟ 802.1X Authentication
    Version: 2
    Type: EAP Packet (0)
    Length: 4
  ⊟ Extensible Authentication Protocol
      Code: Failure (4)
      Id: 15
      Length: 4
```

Knowing that the authenticator is simply a pass-through device, you can work your way back to the authentication server where the failure message originated. Figure 15.5 displays the RADIUS exchange between the authentication server and the authenticator.

FIGURE 15.5   RADIUS exchange between the authentication server and the authenticator

No.	Time	Source	Destination	Protocol	Info
1	16:38:33.145751	192.168.1.100	192.168.1.250	RADIUS	Access-Request(1) (id=180, l=142)
2	16:38:33.150817	192.168.1.250	192.168.1.100	RADIUS	Access-challenge(11) (id=180, l=70)
3	16:38:33.153478	192.168.1.100	192.168.1.250	RADIUS	Access-Request(1) (id=181, l=149)
4	16:38:33.159745	192.168.1.250	192.168.1.100	RADIUS	Access-challenge(11) (id=181, l=73)
5	16:38:33.166322	192.168.1.100	192.168.1.250	RADIUS	Access-Request(1) (id=182, l=272)
6	16:38:33.171499	192.168.1.250	192.168.1.100	RADIUS	Access-challenge(11) (id=182, l=207)
7	16:38:33.179902	192.168.1.100	192.168.1.250	RADIUS	Access-Request(1) (id=183, l=221)
8	16:38:33.183211	192.168.1.250	192.168.1.100	RADIUS	Access-challenge(11) (id=183, l=110)
9	16:38:33.190595	192.168.1.100	192.168.1.250	RADIUS	Access-Request(1) (id=184, l=203)
10	16:38:33.192835	192.168.1.250	192.168.1.100	RADIUS	Access-challenge(11) (id=184, l=102)
11	16:38:33.196052	192.168.1.100	192.168.1.250	RADIUS	Access-Request(1) (id=185, l=203)
12	16:38:33.200204	192.168.1.250	192.168.1.100	RADIUS	Access-challenge(11) (id=185, l=134)
13	16:38:33.215571	192.168.1.100	192.168.1.250	RADIUS	Access-Request(1) (id=186, l=251)
14	16:38:33.278073	192.168.1.250	192.168.1.100	RADIUS	Access-challenge(11) (id=186, l=206)
15	16:38:37.554370	192.168.1.100	192.168.1.250	RADIUS	Access-Request(1) (id=187, l=251)
16	16:38:37.597209	192.168.1.250	192.168.1.100	RADIUS	Access-challenge(11) (id=187, l=206)
17	16:38:41.178400	192.168.1.100	192.168.1.250	RADIUS	Access-Request(1) (id=188, l=251)
18	16:38:41.221070	192.168.1.250	192.168.1.100	RADIUS	Access-challenge(11) (id=188, l=206)
19	16:38:44.909043	192.168.1.100	192.168.1.250	RADIUS	Access-Request(1) (id=189, l=251)
20	16:38:44.912676	192.168.1.250	192.168.1.100	RADIUS	Access-challenge(11) (id=189, l=110)
21	16:38:44.915706	192.168.1.100	192.168.1.250	RADIUS	Access-Request(1) (id=190, l=203)
22	16:38:44.918137	192.168.1.250	192.168.1.100	RADIUS	Access-Reject(3) (id=190, l=56)

```
⊞ Frame 22: 98 bytes on wire (784 bits), 98 bytes captured (784 bits)
⊞ Ethernet II, Src: ViaTechn_e6:b3:95 (00:40:63:e6:b3:95), Dst: Cisco_91:38:60 (00:1a:6c:91:38:60)
⊞ Internet Protocol, Src: 192.168.1.250 (192.168.1.250), Dst: 192.168.1.100 (192.168.1.100)
⊞ User Datagram Protocol, Src Port: radius (1812), Dst Port: filenet-rpc (32769)
⊟ Radius Protocol
     Code: Access-Reject (3)
     Packet identifier: 0xbe (190)
     Length: 56
     Authenticator: 0a0dc643ef807e567e602a3ec313ce6e
     [This is a response to a request in frame 21]
     [Time from request: 0.002431000 seconds]
   ⊟ Attribute Value Pairs
     ⊟ AVP: l=6  t=EAP-Message(79) Last Segment[1]
         EAP fragment
       ⊟ Extensible Authentication Protocol
           Code: Failure (4)
           Id: 15
           Length: 4
     ⊞ AVP: l=12  t=Reply-Message(18): Rejected\n\r
     ⊞ AVP: l=18  t=Message-Authenticator(80): 34525031347c7173d75e7433b89c5001
```

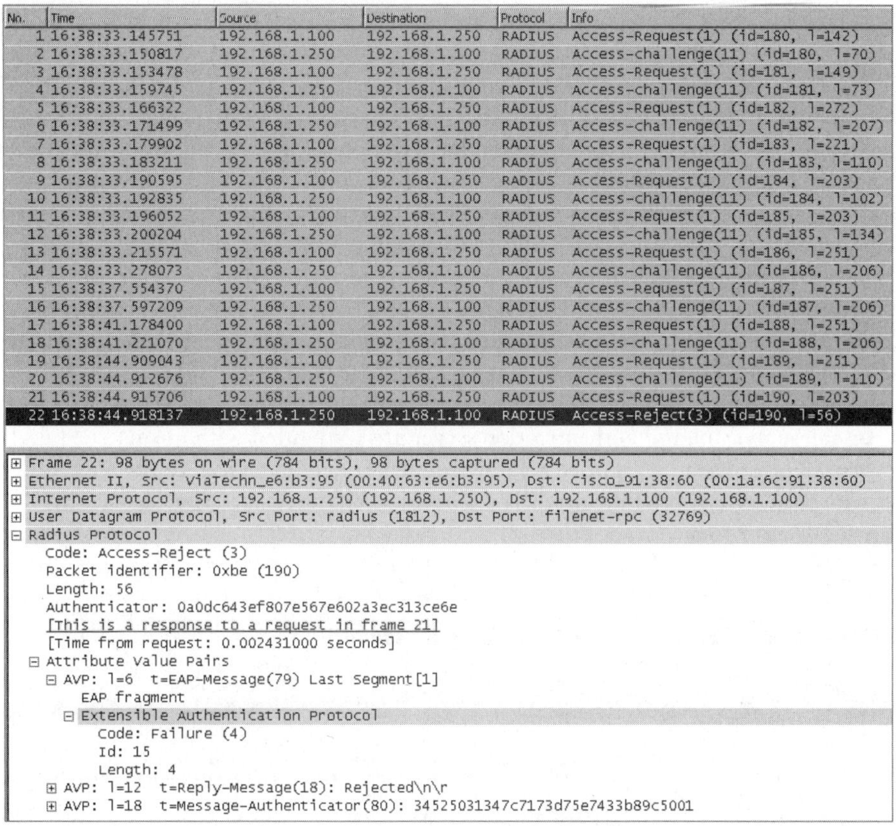

The EAP identifier (Id: 15) and code (Code: Failure) within the EAP message of the RADIUS packets are the same as the EAP values in the EAPOL trace (Figure 15.4) that is used to match up the EAPOL and RADIUS packets. To identify the root cause of the failure, you must understand why the authentication server rejected the client authentication. You can do this by checking the authentication server logs during the time period of the failure and searching based on the supplicant's MAC address or *calling-station-id (RADIUS attribute 31)*.

The most common causes for an Access-Reject from the authentication server are mismatched credentials, protected access credential (PAC) or certificate failure, and EAP type mismatches. In scenarios where the supplicant has an invalid certificate or PAC, the supplicant may not respond to the EAP identity request sent by the authenticator, and the process will not result in an Access-Reject and will not typically show up as a failure in the authentication server failure logs. However, you should see these types of failures in the authenticator logs as a message indicating an EAP timeout where the client failed to respond within the appropriate amount of time.

EAP timeouts can also occur when the authenticator's EAP timers are set too aggressively. This issue occurs in scenarios where supplicants installed on older client devices take a long period of time to respond, especially during EAP-Fast PAC provisioning or during the EAP-TLS certificate key exchange. Other causes may be if the supplicant is waiting for user input and has prompted the user to select a certificate, enter a username and password, or change their password. If the EAP timeout on the authenticator is too short, the user will not have time to take the appropriate action on the supplicant.

When a certificate expires or becomes invalid on the authentication server, the server should immediately stop using the EAP types that are tied to the expired certificate. This will result in an Access-Reject and a failure message on the authentication server stating that the EAP type is not allowed or no longer configured (unless the supplicant and authentication server are able to negotiate a different EAP type).

When the supplicant and authentication server are configured with mismatched EAP types, the client will send a negative acknowledgment (NAK) message to the authentication server with the desired authentication type that it is configured for. You can see this exchange in Figure 15.6.

FIGURE 15.6 Packet #5 showing the NAK message

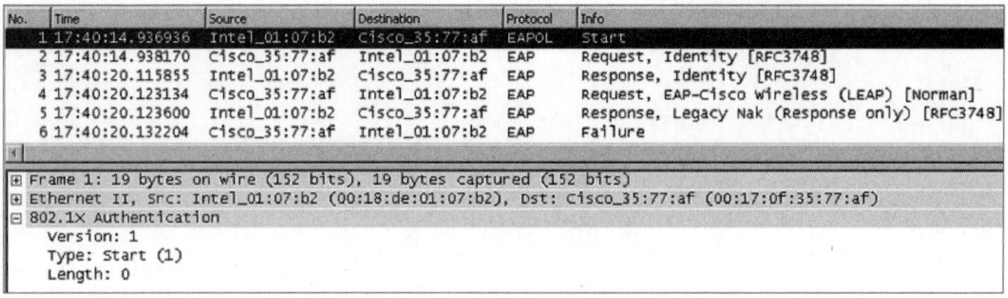

In Figure 15.7, the supplicant responds with an EAP NAK message with a desired EAP type of 25, which is PEAP.

```
⊞ Frame 5: 24 bytes on wire (192 bits), 24 bytes captured (192 bits)
⊞ Ethernet II, Src: Intel_01:07:b2 (00:18:de:01:07:b2), Dst: Cisco_35:77:af (00:17:0f:35:77:af)
⊟ 802.1X Authentication
    Version: 1
    Type: EAP Packet (0)
    Length: 6
  ⊟ Extensible Authentication Protocol
      Code: Response (2)
      Id: 16
      Length: 6
      Type: Legacy Nak (Response only) [RFC3748] (3)
      Desired Auth Type: PEAP [Palekar] (25)
```

As you can see from Figure 15.6, the authenticator sends an EAP failure message to the supplicant indicating the authentication server is not configured to allow PEAP.

Failures can also occur between the authenticator and the authentication server where you do not see any response coming back from the authentication server. To identify the root cause of the failure, you will need to check the logs on the authentication server to see why it is not sending a response back to the authenticator. You may have to use a network sniffer to ensure that the RADIUS packets sent by the authenticator are being received by the authentication server. Typically this behavior is caused by:

- The authenticator's IP address is not configured as a NAS or AAA client device on the authentication server.

- A shared secret mismatch has occurred.

- Communication ports (usually 1812 or 1645) are mismatched or otherwise incorrect.

- There is a key wrap configuration mismatch.

- The RADIUS service has stopped running on the authentication server.

- General network issues exist that prevent the authenticator and authentication server from communicating.

The authenticator should be configured to send SNMP or syslog alerts when the authentication server is unreachable as this type of failure will prevent the authenticator from allowing any users to authenticate.

Quality of Service Analysis

Quality of service (QoS) allows the wireless LAN system to prioritize selected network traffic over other types of traffic. Without QoS, all user traffic will have the same priority and will be transmitted using a best effort, "listen-before-talk" algorithm where each device waits for a random backoff time and then transmits only if no other device is transmitting at that time. During times of congestion, delay-sensitive traffic such as voice and video can suffer from degraded quality as traffic load increases.

As a quick rehash from Chapter 10, "MAC Layer Design," *802.11e* uses Enhanced Distributed Channel Access (EDCA) traffic classes to provide multiple traffic classes and queues for transmission. Each traffic class can have its own AIFS, CWmin, and CWmax values, which are used to help determine the wait period before transmission. Traffic classes with the smallest AIFS, CWmin, and CWmax values have statistically the best chance to get access to the RF media.

Wi-Fi Multimedia (WMM) is a traffic prioritization method created by the Wi-Fi Alliance, which is based on the 802.11e standard that is used to determine the assignment of traffic classes based on four access categories (ACs):

- Voice
- Video
- Best effort
- Background

The WMM ACs are designed to easily map to 802.1p, also known as class of service (CoS) and IP Differentiated Services Code Point (DSCP) priorities for interoperability with the wired network. Non-WMM-capable clients that are not assigned to a specific AC are categorized by default as having best effort priority.

To ensure end-to-end QoS priority, inspect the proper QoS priority markings at each endpoint. This can be an arduous task, but it is important to identify where the problem breaks down if you are to preserve application performance. Figure 15.8 shows a packet from a WME-capable wireless device.

FIGURE 15.8   Packet from a WME-capable device

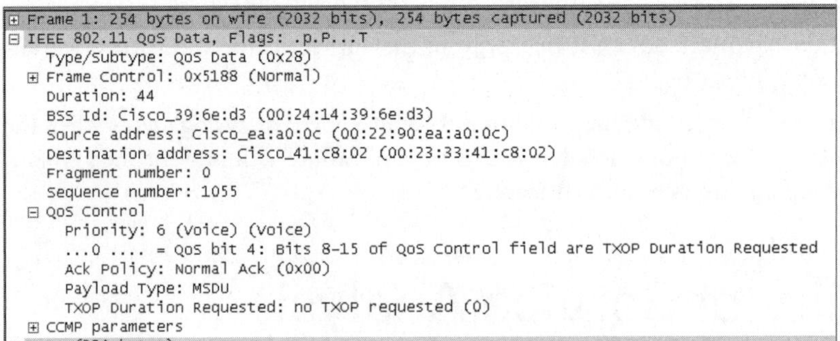

```
⊞ Frame 1: 254 bytes on wire (2032 bits), 254 bytes captured (2032 bits)
⊟ IEEE 802.11 QoS Data, Flags: .p.P...T
     Type/Subtype: QoS Data (0x28)
  ⊞ Frame Control: 0x5188 (Normal)
     Duration: 44
     BSS Id: Cisco_39:6e:d3 (00:24:14:39:6e:d3)
     Source address: Cisco_ea:a0:0c (00:22:90:ea:a0:0c)
     Destination address: Cisco_41:c8:02 (00:23:33:41:c8:02)
     Fragment number: 0
     Sequence number: 1055
  ⊟ QoS Control
       Priority: 6 (Voice) (Voice)
       ...0 .... = QoS bit 4: Bits 8-15 of QoS Control field are TXOP Duration Requested
       Ack Policy: Normal Ack (0x00)
       Payload Type: MSDU
       TXOP Duration Requested: no TXOP requested (0)
  ⊞ CCMP parameters
⊞ Data (220 bytes)
```

You can see the 802.11e UP value is marked at 6. If your client devices are WME capable and configured for a specific AC and you are not seeing the 802.11e AC marking, you will need to check to make sure the WMM parameter information element is set in the beacon, probe response, and association response frames from the AP radio. Also ensure that WMM is enabled on the WLAN that the client is associated to.

In Figure 15.9, you see a packet from the AP to a wireless IP phone.

FIGURE 15.9   Packet from AP to wireless IP phone marked as Best Effort

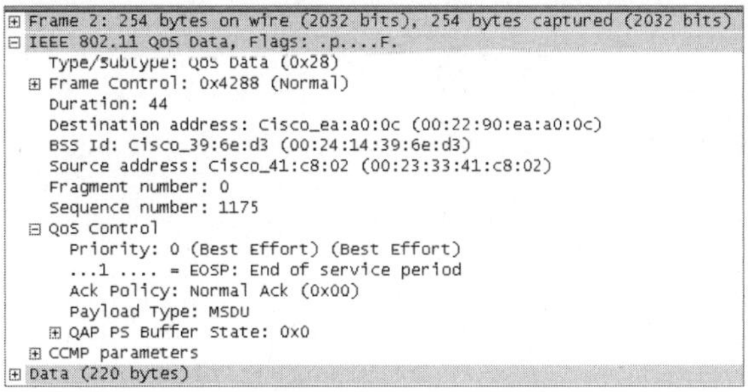

```
⊞ Frame 2: 254 bytes on wire (2032 bits), 254 bytes captured (2032 bits)
⊟ IEEE 802.11 QoS Data, Flags: .p...F.
    Type/Subtype: QoS Data (0x28)
  ⊞ Frame Control: 0x4288 (Normal)
    Duration: 44
    Destination address: Cisco_ea:a0:0c (00:22:90:ea:a0:0c)
    BSS Id: Cisco_39:6e:d3 (00:24:14:39:6e:d3)
    Source address: Cisco_41:c8:02 (00:23:33:41:c8:02)
    Fragment number: 0
    Sequence number: 1175
  ⊟ QoS Control
      Priority: 0 (Best Effort) (Best Effort)
      ...1 .... = EOSP: End of service period
      Ack Policy: Normal Ack (0x00)
      Payload Type: MSDU
    ⊞ QAP PS Buffer State: 0x0
  ⊞ CCMP parameters
⊞ Data (220 bytes)
```

In this voice packet you see the packet is marked as Best Effort. You can work your way back to the sending IP phone to see where the QoS marking is dropped. We recommend that you perform end-to-end QoS tests for devices that are using delay-sensitive applications such as voice and video by verifying that the proper QoS classification is set at each end station:

Wireless Devices   For wireless devices you must verify the proper 802.11e value is set. If the value is not set properly, it is important to understand the packet flow between the two wireless devices. Also note the direction of the traffic when the QoS marking is set improperly.

Stand-alone APs   For stand-alone APs, the wired 802.3 Ethernet frames will be transmitted and received locally at the Ethernet port and separated with the use of 802.1Q VLAN tags. The stand-alone AP should be configured with proper 802.11e-to-802.1p mappings. If the 802.11e value is not marked properly for downstream traffic for wireless clients associated to different APs, you will need to ensure the proper 802.1p and DSCP markings are set and trusted on each Layer 2/Layer 3 hop between the two APs. Do so by reviewing the switch and router configurations or using a network sniffer at each hop to verify the 802.1p and DSCP markings. If you are seeing the improper marking directly at the AP port, there is most likely an improper 802.11e-to-802.1p mapping configured on the AP.

In Figure 15.10 you see the voice packet on the wired network is properly marked for a configuration where the 802.11e UP value is mapped to an 802.1p value of 5 and the switch is configured with a CoS-to-DSCP map where the CoS of 5 is mapped to a DSCP value of 46. We see the traffic is tagged with an 802.1Q VLAN tag of 111 with an 802.1p marking of 5 (shown as "PRI: 5" and encoded as 101, which equates to a UP of 5). The IP DSCP marking is also properly set to 0x2e (the "2e" here is the hexadecimal representation of the decimal number 46), as shown in Figure 15.10.

FIGURE 15.10   Packet with properly marked DSCP

```
⊞ Frame 2: 78 bytes on wire (624 bits), 78 bytes captured (624 bits)
⊞ Ethernet II, Src: Cisco_84:7f:85 (00:11:92:84:7f:85), Dst: Cisco_58:b6:3b (00:1b:d4:58:b6:3b)
⊟ 802.1Q virtual LAN, PRI: 5, CFI: 0, ID: 111
    101. .... .... .... = Priority: Video, < 100ms latency and jitter (5)
    ...0 .... .... .... = CFI: Canonical (0)
    .... 0000 0110 1111 = ID: 111
    Type: IP (0x0800)
⊟ Internet Protocol, Src: 10.10.111.18 (10.10.111.18), Dst: 10.10.111.44 (10.10.111.44)
    Version: 4
    Header length: 20 bytes
  ⊞ Differentiated Services Field: 0xb8 (DSCP 0x2e: Expedited Forwarding; ECN: 0x00)
    Total Length: 60
    Identification: 0x8ea0 (36512)
  ⊞ Flags: 0x00
    Fragment offset: 0
    Time to live: 64
    Protocol: UDP (17)
  ⊞ Header checksum: 0xf906 [correct]
    Source: 10.10.111.18 (10.10.111.18)
    Destination: 10.10.111.44 (10.10.111.44)
⊞ User Datagram Protocol, Src Port: 18324 (18324), Dst Port: 21872 (21872)
⊞ Data (32 bytes)
```

For APs that operate in a centralized, controller-based system, the wireless traffic is typically tunneled between the AP and wireless LAN controller. The outer IP header of this tunneled traffic should also be marked properly for end-to-end QoS.

For tunneled traffic that is sent upstream from the AP to the controller, the 802.11e UP value is typically used to determine the value of the DSCP marking in the outer IP header and the DSCP marking in the inner packet is left intact; the DSCP in the outer header is typically used by the controller to mark the 802.1p value for the de-encapsulated traffic going out to the wired network. For traffic that is received at the controller from the wired network, the controller typically uses the original DSCP value of the received packet and marks the DSCP of the outer IP header with the same marking, which is then used by the AP for 802.11e. In Figure 15.11, you see a packet that is captured from a CAPWAP-based wireless LAN controller. The inner CAPWAP packet carries the original wireless data with a source IP of 10.10.111.18 that is marked with a DSCP value of 0x2e; the outer IP header is also marked with a DSCP of 0x2e. When the wireless controller de-encapsulates the packet and sends the traffic out to the wired network, the 802.1p value should be marked with the appropriate value based on the configured 802.11e-to-802.1p mapping and the IP DSCP marking of the inner packet is typically left intact.

In Figure 15.12 you can see the same packet (with the same IP DSCP of 0x2e) when it is de-encapsulated from the tunneled CAPWAP packet, which carried the original IP DSCP of 0x2e. The controller is configured to mark this traffic with an 802.1p value of 5, which you see is properly marked. You can confirm this is the same packet because the IP Identification of 0x2fe8 (12264) matches in both traces.

FIGURE 15.11   Packet from a CAPWAP-based wireless LAN controller

```
⊞ Frame 3: 142 bytes on wire (1136 bits), 142 bytes captured (1136 bits)
⊞ Ethernet II, Src: Cisco_cc:72:64 (00:24:97:cc:72:64), Dst: All-HSRP-routers_00 (00:00:0c:07:ac:00)
⊟ Internet Protocol, Src: 10.10.100.151 (10.10.100.151), Dst: 99.99.99.61 (99.99.99.61)
    Version: 4
    Header length: 20 bytes
  ⊞ Differentiated Services Field: 0xb8 (DSCP 0x2e: Expedited Forwarding; ECN: 0x00)
    Total Length: 128
    Identification: 0x95b7 (38327)
  ⊞ Flags: 0x02 (Don't Fragment)
    Fragment offset: 0
    Time to live: 255
    Protocol: UDP (17)
  ⊞ Header checksum: 0xafbb [correct]
    Source: 10.10.100.151 (10.10.100.151)
    Destination: 99.99.99.61 (99.99.99.61)
⊞ User Datagram Protocol, Src Port: capwap-data (5247), Dst Port: 39695 (39695)
⊞ Control And Provisioning of Wireless Access Points
⊞ IEEE 802.11 Data, Flags: ......F.
⊞ Logical-Link Control
⊟ Internet Protocol, Src: 10.10.111.18 (10.10.111.18), Dst: 10.10.111.44 (10.10.111.44)
    Version: 4
    Header length: 20 bytes
  ⊞ Differentiated Services Field: 0xb8 (DSCP 0x2e: Expedited Forwarding; ECN: 0x00)
    Total Length: 60
    Identification: 0x2fe8 (12264)
  ⊞ Flags: 0x00
    Fragment offset: 0
    Time to live: 64
    Protocol: UDP (17)
  ⊞ Header checksum: 0x57bf [correct]
    Source: 10.10.111.18 (10.10.111.18)
    Destination: 10.10.111.44 (10.10.111.44)
⊞ User Datagram Protocol, Src Port: 31458 (31458), Dst Port: 20048 (20048)
⊞ Data (32 bytes)
```

FIGURE 15.12   De-encapsulated CAPWAP packet

```
⊞ Frame 2: 78 bytes on wire (624 bits), 78 bytes captured (624 bits)
⊞ Ethernet II, Src: Cisco_84:7f:85 (00:11:92:84:7f:85), Dst: Cisco_58:b6:3b (00:1b:d4:58:b6:3b)
⊟ 802.1Q Virtual LAN, PRI: 5, CFI: 0, ID: 111
    101. .... .... .... = Priority: Video, < 100ms latency and jitter (5)
    ...0 .... .... .... = CFI: Canonical (0)
    .... 0000 0110 1111 = ID: 111
    Type: IP (0x0800)
⊟ Internet Protocol, Src: 10.10.111.18 (10.10.111.18), Dst: 10.10.111.44 (10.10.111.44)
    Version: 4
    Header length: 20 bytes
  ⊞ Differentiated Services Field: 0xb8 (DSCP 0x2e: Expedited Forwarding; ECN: 0x00)
    Total Length: 60
    Identification: 0x2fe8 (12264)
  ⊞ Flags: 0x00
    Fragment offset: 0
    Time to live: 64
    Protocol: UDP (17)
  ⊞ Header checksum: 0x57bf [correct]
    Source: 10.10.111.18 (10.10.111.18)
    Destination: 10.10.111.44 (10.10.111.44)
⊞ User Datagram Protocol, Src Port: 31458 (31458), Dst Port: 20048 (20048)
⊞ Data (32 bytes)
```

In Figure 15.13 you see a correct IP DSCP of 0x2e, but the 802.1p value is set improperly to 0.

FIGURE 15.13   802.1p value incorrectly set to 0

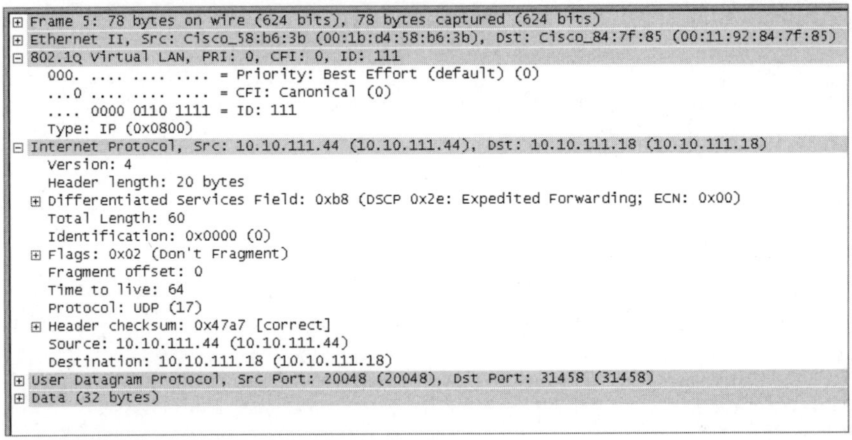

```
⊞ Frame 5: 78 bytes on wire (624 bits), 78 bytes captured (624 bits)
⊞ Ethernet II, Src: Cisco_58:b6:3b (00:1b:d4:58:b6:3b), Dst: Cisco_84:7f:85 (00:11:92:84:7f:85)
⊟ 802.1Q Virtual LAN, PRI: 0, CFI: 0, ID: 111
      000. .... .... .... = Priority: Best Effort (default) (0)
      ...0 .... .... .... = CFI: Canonical (0)
      .... 0000 0110 1111 = ID: 111
      Type: IP (0x0800)
⊟ Internet Protocol, Src: 10.10.111.44 (10.10.111.44), Dst: 10.10.111.18 (10.10.111.18)
      Version: 4
      Header length: 20 bytes
   ⊞ Differentiated Services Field: 0xb8 (DSCP 0x2e: Expedited Forwarding; ECN: 0x00)
      Total Length: 60
      Identification: 0x0000 (0)
   ⊞ Flags: 0x02 (Don't Fragment)
      Fragment offset: 0
      Time to live: 64
      Protocol: UDP (17)
   ⊞ Header checksum: 0x47a7 [correct]
      Source: 10.10.111.44 (10.10.111.44)
      Destination: 10.10.111.18 (10.10.111.18)
⊞ User Datagram Protocol, Src Port: 20048 (20048), Dst Port: 31458 (31458)
⊞ Data (32 bytes)
```

This improperly set 802.1p mapping is typically caused by a router or switch between the AP and the wireless LAN controller that was not properly configured to trust the DSCP in the outer IP header (which was set by the AP based on the wireless client's 802.11e UP value). We recommend that you use a network sniffer to verify the DSCP marking in the outer IP header at the controller port. If the DSCP in the outer IP header is marked improperly at the controller port, there is most likely a QoS misconfiguration on the controller, or perhaps the switch port that the controller is attached to is not properly configured to trust the 802.1p value being sent by the controller. If the outer IP header DSCP value is not marked properly, we recommend that you sniff the AP port to verify the AP has set the correct DSCP value in the outer IP header. Then verify each L2/L3 hop from the AP to the controller to find where the DSCP value is being re-marked by checking the router and switch configurations or by using a network sniffer.

Whenever critical real-time traffic is deployed in a wireless LAN, you should always verify at each endpoint that you are seeing the proper QoS markings. It is important to understand the QoS translations between 802.11e, 802.1p, and IP DSCP to pinpoint where the classifications are being lost.

Network Analysis

When it comes to troubleshooting enterprise wireless networks, you cannot rely solely on the wireless components as the focus of your troubleshooting effort. The clients and the wired network can often be the cause of the issues that occur on the wireless network. In this section, we'll dig into some common causes of issues on the wired and client side.

Controller and AP Provisioning

APs that operate in a controller-based environment need to be provisioned to discover a wireless controller to operate properly and pull down the proper configuration and software version. Typical controller-based APs will use the IP protocol to communicate with the wireless controller. For controller discovery, the controller-based APs generally use DHCP options that carry the wireless controller's IP address. To ensure the AP can join the wireless controller, check that:

- The AP obtained a proper IP address on the correct VLAN and IP subnet
- The AP can contact its default gateway
- The AP can discover the wireless controller IP address
- Communication is not blocked by access lists or firewalls

For normal troubleshooting, you can verify IP reachability by issuing `ping` and `traceroute` commands from the wireless controller to the AP. You can also sniff the AP and wireless controller port to ensure proper communication. Examine the Address Resolution Protocol (ARP) cache on the default gateway of the controller to check for a duplicate IP address where another wired device is using the same IP address as the controller. The ARP cache on the controller's default gateway should map the controller's IP address to its MAC address. You can also sniff the wireless controller VLAN and clear the controller IP address from the ARP cache. Then ping the controller IP; if you see more than one device respond to the ARP request, you can track down the MAC address of the other devices that respond to the ARP request to the controller IP.

Client IP Provisioning

For client IP provisioning, the wireless client will send a DHCP discover/request as an all-subnets broadcast. If the DHCP server is across a Layer 3 boundary, the first hop router must be configured as a DHCP relay to forward the broadcast to the DHCP server. Also you must ensure there is IP reachability between the DHCP server subnet and the client subnet. The DHCP server should be able to get a ping response from the default gateway of the client subnet. The first hop router for the client subnet should have an entry in its routing table that includes the DHCP server subnet, and vice versa. If the routes exist and you are unable to ping and ICMP is allowed end to end, you should verify there is IP reachability via a traceroute to identify the last Layer 3 hop in the traceroute. In the case of a routing loop, you will see the traceroute bounce between the same two Layer 3 hops until the time-to-live (TTL) expires.

Trunking and Pruning

For APs where wireless traffic is locally switched on the AP, the client traffic is separated on the wired network using VLAN tags. You will need to ensure that all the necessary VLANs are allowed over each trunk link. For controller-based deployments, the wireless traffic on the AP may be centrally switched back to a wireless controller. In these deployments, the APs are typically connected on access ports with the VLANs trunked to the wireless controller. To avoid unnecessary VLAN traffic, you will need to prune all the unnecessary VLANs from each trunk link. Also be aware that most APs and wireless controllers do not participate in VLAN Trunk Protocol (VTP) or VTP pruning, so it will most likely be necessary to manually add and remove VLANs from each trunk link. You will also need to verify that the necessary VLANs are in a spanning tree forwarding state.

MAC Address Tables

When a wireless client is able to authenticate and associate to the wireless network but is unable to obtain a DHCP address or obtains an IP address on the wrong VLAN/subnet, it is a good idea to verify whether the wired network properly learned the client's MAC address. To do this, check the switch's MAC address table on the AP port for stand-alone APs and the controller port for controller-based environments. The MAC address table should include the client MAC address, ingress port, and VLAN ID.

General network troubleshooting requires you to be aware of how the client traffic is forwarded onto the wired network to verify that Layer 2 forwarding and Layer 3 routing is properly configured.

Pesky Clients

During the process of troubleshooting wireless LAN-related issues, a large amount of attention is often so focused on the underlying infrastructure that client-related issues are ignored or overlooked. In many cases, it is difficult to troubleshoot client-related issues due to the lack of control you may have over the client devices. Specifically, many enterprises don't own all the clients on the network, and they have no authority to perform the necessary troubleshooting steps. Similarly, there is typically only one infrastructure vendor in operation on a network, but there are many different client devices with different capabilities, management utilities, drivers, and applications. However, client devices are responsible for a significant number of WLAN problems, and more times than not, the issue can be related to an old driver version or a low-quality radio in general. Not all radios are created equal; low-cost clients tend to be low cost because the hardware they use is cheaper. You can bet that it's cheaper for a reason. For example, radios with low receive sensitivity are cheaper than radios with high receive sensitivity, but this parameter is important to communication fidelity. The following list examines common client-related problems:

Data Rates   802.11 WLANs support multiple data rates to allow clients to adapt to the diverse nature of the RF environment. Typically clients will downshift due to multiple 802.11 retries that are not ACK'd (or changes in RSSI, SNR, etc.) and upshift after multiple successful 802.11 transmissions. The method and rate at which the client downshifts and upshifts can vary between vendors and clients; some older driver versions may never rate switch properly. You must identify this behavior because clients that are stuck using lower data rates can cause an overall throughput drop to all stations associated to the same access point.

Sticky Clients　While the wireless LAN infrastructure can influence a client's initial association behavior, the roaming decision is made by the client device (except in the SCA architecture). Older client driver software is typically less optimized for modern, highly mobile enterprise environments because they were designed for early networks without fast roaming or only a single access point. In this scenario, the client will continue to stay connected to the associated AP until a wireless signal is no longer detected. In an enterprise environment, this will cause a significant delay when roaming between access points. This will often lead to scenarios where the client is associated to an access point with a poor signal in areas where there is strong coverage that is being provided by other access points. This situation poses a problem for both this and other stations in the same BSS since the "sticky" client will most likely stay associated using lower data rates and experiencing retransmissions, impacting performance for everyone. Certain client adapters may have settings that allow you to adjust the rate and signal level threshold (or general roaming aggressiveness level) where the client will attempt to scan for and roam to a better access point.

Bad Drivers　We've already mentioned that drivers can have a significant impact on client performance. This impact comes in the form of poor roaming, low data rates, frequent disassociations, inconsistent protocol implementations, and other unexpected behaviors. In many cases, there's no immediate explanation for a client's erratic behavior other than a poor driver build or feature implementation. In these cases, the best approach is to test different driver builds or client software utilities, and attempt to identify the most stable combination. Depending on your infrastructure solution, you may also find that there is an outstanding bug or feature incompatibility with the infrastructure and client firmware. For client devices with modular WLAN adapter slots, replacing the radio hardware with a higher quality product with better driver builds may also be recommended.

The key takeaway for this section is that poor client behavior on a single client can affect the overall performance of all the clients on the BSS. It is important to ensure that all clients have current driver builds installed and are optimized to operate properly in an enterprise WLAN environment. Though this section makes up only a small part of this chapter, client troubleshooting is probably more common than any other type of troubleshooting because client devices are usually the guilty party when new, unwanted WLAN behaviors occur.

Common Troubleshooting Mistakes: What Not to Do

Over the course of troubleshooting wireless networks, you will begin to notice that sometimes things just didn't go as they should have. As you'll see in the following sections, things can go wrong during the installation process. How does this happen, you might ask? Well, it depends on the situation, but it's easy to see that at times there's a disconnect between the wireless engineer indicating where to place an access point and the person who actually places it. Some companies have special contracts in place when it comes to any and all equipment installation. In times like those, the technicians who install the AP might not understand how the technology works—and that can turn out to be a disastrous arrangement.

Figure 15.14 illustrates an AP mounted inside a metal enclosure with the dipole antennas turned flat against the metal enclosure.

FIGURE 15.14 An AP in a metal enclosure with dipole antennas touching a metal door

In this configuration, the omnidirectional dipoles act more like a directional patch as they have a large reflective object on the back side of the antenna. To make things worse, up to 50 percent of the energy is reflected back toward the radio, making the efficiency of the AP itself much less than its true capabilities. Finally, you should notice that it's mounted up in the ceiling *above* metal water pipes and other metal objects. Always try to keep the AP closer to the clients when possible and away from materials that will block RF propagation. When APs must be mounted above the ceiling, make every effort to keep them as close to the ceiling tile or other ceiling material as possible. The further the AP goes into the ceiling, the higher the chance of excessive reflection, multipath, and signal attenuation due to ceiling tile grids, air ducts, cable trays, and so forth.

Figure 15.15 illustrates what can happen when an AP is installed and someone follows up after the installation and, without knowing what the AP actually is, creates a new problem.

FIGURE 15.15   Wall-mounted AP hidden behind new piping

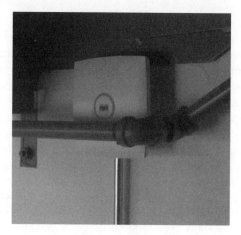

To complicate matters further, this particular AP is designed to be ceiling mounted. That's not to say it cannot be mounted vertically, but you must take into consideration that the RF propagation is not the same as it would be on the ceiling due to the large metal cooling plate that is on the back of the unit. Therefore, when wall mounting an AP, as seen in Figure 15.15, focus most of the energy away from the wall. Any intended coverage behind that wall will likely be inadequate.

Figure 15.16 is an example of a poor above-ceiling installation. The clients are obviously below this ceiling, and the combination of the AP in a metal enclosure, above the ceiling, and surrounded with metal ductwork and I-beams, is a multipath nightmare at best. At worst, it's a black hole for signal penetration. So what can be done to remedy a situation like this one? You can leave the AP above the ceiling in the box then mount external antennae on the underside of the ceiling tile. Problem solved!

FIGURE 15.16   Example of a poor above-ceiling installation

Summary

Throughout this chapter you've learned various troubleshooting techniques associated with some common problems to wireless networks. As stated at the beginning of this chapter, there will always be a troubleshooting component for wireless networks. That being said, being proficient at solving complex issues will set you apart from your peers if you're able to carefully dissect and solve problems.

When approaching a new issue, remember to be systematic: start at Layer 1 of the OSI model by checking physical connections. Ask yourself if power is being supplied and if antennae, cables, connectors, and adapters are connected and oriented properly. From there move through the model to determine if you have Layer 2 connectivity or if other problems are occurring with the protocols at this layer. You then should check Layer 3 connectivity and stability. Collect as much information and diagnostic material as possible, target common problems, find the consistencies in the problem, and take advantage of professional troubleshooting tools. Remember: debugs, protocol and spectrum analyzers, support forums, and surveying tools are your friends, so leave no stone unturned.

Exam Essentials

Use a systematic approach to troubleshooting.   Reference the OSI model and start with Layer 1 before moving on to higher layers when eliminating potential causes for problems. Avoid making multiple changes at once as it is difficult to distinguish which change had which effect when multiple changes occur in unison.

Be able to validate coverage.   Ensure the coverage area is receiving a quality signal that meets the design requirements. Use site survey software to analyze and spot problematic areas.

Understand the importance of quality of service.   Be able to identify different methods commonly used to give preference to high priority traffic. Understand what happens on both the wireless and wired side of QoS markings.

Know how to troubleshoot security.   Be able to troubleshoot the common failures that can occur during 802.1X/EAP exchanges.

Know how to avoid common mistakes.   Be able to spot mistakes that happen during installations. Ensure that the design has been deployed as it was intended.

Identify sources of interference.   Be able to identify sources of interference that are impacting the wireless network. Those may be Wi-Fi or non- Wi-Fi; understand the impact of each.

Validate the wired infrastructure.   Not all wireless issues are purely wireless. Be able to troubleshoot common wired network issues such as DHCP and basic routing that can cause issues on the wireless network.

Review Questions

1. Which of the following is an example of non-Wi-Fi interference?

   A. Co-channel interference

   B. Bluetooth

   C. Thunderstorms

   D. Cosmic rays

2. Your company is located in a downtown high-rise building. You've configured your network so that your lowest mandatory rate is 12 Mbps. Users are complaining about poor throughput. Upon inspection, you notice that over 90 percent of the traffic is being sent at 1 Mbps. What is most likely the cause?

   A. A software bug on the network

   B. An AP that has lost its connection to its controller and is repeatedly sending management frames

   C. Neighboring networks from above and/or below that are very busy and have the lower data rates enabled

   D. Nothing, since this is normal

3. What are the key entities in the 802.1X architecture model?

   A. Supplicant, authenticator, authentication server

   B. Client, domain server, RADIUS

   C. EAP, EAPOL, RADIUS

   D. Authentication, authorization, accounting

4. What type of device is classified as an authenticator? (Choose all that apply.)

   A. Access point

   B. Radius server

   C. Wireless LAN controller

   D. TACACs server

5. When troubleshooting coverage issues for a wireless network as it appears to new client associations, you should perform which type of survey?

   A. Active survey

   B. Passive survey

   C. Predictive survey

   D. A survey is not necessary.

6. Which of the following are examples of Wi-Fi interference for channel 6? Assume all access points are within RF range of one another. (Choose all that apply.)

   A. Other access points on your network that are on channel 6

   B. Other access points that are not on your network but are on channel 11

   C. Other access points that are on your network but are on channel 1

   D. Other access points that are not on your network but are on channel 3

7. WMM prioritizes traffic across which four access categories?

   A. Voice, video, best effort, background

   B. CWmin, CWmax, TXop, AIFS

   C. 802.11e, 802.1p, EDCA, CoS

   D. EF, AF41, AF31, BE

8. Which of the following devices determine when a client will roam from one AP to another?

   A. The access point

   B. The wireless LAN controller

   C. A combination of the wireless LAN controller and the client

   D. The client

9. CAPWAP uses which of the following port(s) for discovery?

   A. UDP 5246

   B. UDP 12222 and 12223

   C. TCP 5246 and 5247

   D. TCP 12222 and 12223

   E. UDP 1812

10. What protocol is typically used by the authenticator to communicate with the authentication server?

    A. EAP

    B. EAP over LAN

    C. RADIUS

    D. MD5

11. In general, troubleshooting should always start at what layer of the OSI model?

    A. Layer 7

    B. Layer 6

    C. Layer 2

    D. Layer 1

12. What QoS marking is set in the packet's IP header?

    A. 802.1P

    B. EDCA

    C. WMM

    D. DSCP

13. How are EAP messages transported over 802.11 wireless LANS?

    A. EAP-Fast

    B. PEAP

    C. EAPOL

    D. EAP_TLS

14. To increase capacity in a coverage-based wireless network, which of the following techniques are typically recommended? (Choose all that apply.)

    A. Turn up power on the access points.

    B. Lower power on the access points and, after careful planning, add more APs.

    C. Maximize airtime usage by disabling lower data rates.

    D. Add additional APs and use directional antennas.

15. A wireless network with fewer APs at higher power levels to cover a large area is said to be which of the following?

    A. Coverage based

    B. Ideal for roaming

    C. Capacity based

    D. Destined for failure

16. Identify two types of key caching used for fast secure roaming. (Choose all that apply.)

    A. PMK caching

    B. 802.11N

    C. EAP

    D. CCKM

17. At which layer of the OSI model does ARP operate?

    A. Layer 2

    B. Layer 3

    C. Layer 4

    D. Layer 6

18. Where can you check to identify a duplicate wireless controller IP address?

    A. IP routing table

    B. CAM table

    C. ARP cache

    D. Spanning tree state

19. What are the four main EAP codes?

    A. Request, Response, Success, Failure

    B. Code, Identifier, Length, Data

    C. Version, Packet Type, Body Length, Packet Body

    D. Identifier, Length, Authenticator, Attributes

20. Which EAP type does the supplicant send to request a different EAP type?

    A. Reject

    B. Logoff

    C. NAK

    D. EAPOL Start

Answers to Review Questions

1. B. Bluetooth operates in the 2.4 GHz band, and although it is not Wi-Fi, it interferes with Wi-Fi since it shares the same frequency.

2. C. While it could potentially be a software issue on an AP, there's a much higher likelihood that the traffic is coming from a neighboring network. Given that the question includes "a high-rise building," option C is the best answer.

3. A. The three key entities are the supplicant, authenticator, and authentication server.

4. A, C. Access points and wireless LAN controllers act as the authenticator in an 802.1X network.

5. B. When troubleshooting, a passive survey is used to get a holistic view of the RF environment.

6. A, D. Access points that are either on channel 6, or are on a channel that overlaps with channel 6, will interfere with one another regardless of which network they belong to.

7. A. WMM access categories are voice, video, best effort, and background.

8. D. While the wireless network can have an impact on initial associations (such as with band steering or load balancing techniques), the actual roaming decision is made by the client.

9. A. CAPWAP uses UDP 5246 for discovery as defined by RFC 5415.

10. C. EAP messages are transported between the authenticator and the authentication server using the RADIUS protocol.

11. D. Troubleshooting should always start at Layer 1 (the physical layer). By troubleshooting from Layer 1 to Layer 7, you have a systematic approach for eliminating possible causes of the problem.

12. D. The IP DSCP marking is set in the IP header.

13. C. EAP messages are delivered over 802.11 wireless LANs using the EAPOL protocol.

14. B, C, D. Increasing power is not often an effective means of increasing capacity. To increase capacity, you must usually isolate contention domains. This is done through use of lower-power APs, directional antenna use, and the disabling of low data rates.

15. A. Fewer APs at higher power is indicative of a coverage-based network.

16. A, D. PMK and CCKM are two key caching schemes used for Fast Secure Roaming.

17. A. ARP is a Layer 2 protocol that maps Layer 2 hardware addresses to a Layer 3 address such as an IP address.

18. C. Check the ARP cache on the default gateway of the wireless controller to identify a duplicate controller IP address.

19. A. The four main EAP codes are Request, Response, Success, and Failure.

20. C. The supplicant sends a type 3 NAK response to request a different EAP type.

Appendix

About the Companion CD

IN THIS APPENDIX:

✓ What you'll find on the CD

✓ System requirements

✓ Using the CD

✓ Troubleshooting

What You'll Find on the CD

The following sections are arranged by category and summarize the software and other goodies you may find on the CD. If you need help with installing the items provided on the CD, refer to the installation instructions in the "Using the CD" section of this appendix.

Some programs on the CD might fall into one of these categories:

Shareware programs are fully functional, free trial versions of copyrighted programs. If you like particular programs, register with their authors for a nominal fee and receive licenses, enhanced versions, and technical support.

Freeware programs are free, copyrighted games, applications, and utilities. You can copy them to as many computers as you like—for free—but they offer no technical support.

GNU software is governed by its own license, which is included inside the folder of the GNU software. There are no restrictions on distribution of GNU software. See the GNU license at the root of the CD for more details.

Trial, demo, or *evaluation* versions of software are usually limited either by time or by functionality (such as not letting you save a project after you create it).

Sybex Test Engine

The CD contains the Sybex test engine, which includes all the assessment test and chapter review questions in electronic format, as well as two bonus exams located only on the CD.

Adobe Reader

We've also included a copy of Adobe Reader so you can view PDF files that accompany the book's content. For more information on Adobe Reader or to check for a newer version, visit Adobe's website at www.adobe.com/products/reader/.

Electronic Flashcards

These handy electronic flashcards are just what they sound like. One side contains a question and the other side shows the answer.

System Requirements

Make sure your computer meets the minimum system requirements shown in the following list. If your computer doesn't match up to most of these requirements, you may have problems using the software and files on the companion CD. For the latest and greatest information, please refer to the ReadMe file located at the root of the CD-ROM.

- A PC running Microsoft Windows 98, Windows 2000, Windows NT4 (with SP4 or later), Windows Me, Windows XP, Windows Vista, or Windows 7
- An Internet connection
- A CD-ROM drive

Using the CD

To install the items from the CD to your hard drive, follow these steps:

1. Insert the CD into your computer's CD-ROM drive. The license agreement appears.

Windows users: The interface won't launch if you have Autorun disabled. In that case, click Start ➤ Run (for Windows Vista or Windows 7, Start ➤ All Programs ➤ Accessories ➤ Run). In the dialog box that appears, type D:\Start.exe. (Replace *D* with the proper letter if your CD drive uses a different letter. If you don't know the letter, see how your CD drive is listed under My Computer.) Click OK.

2. Read the license agreement, and then click the Accept button if you want to use the CD.

The CD interface appears. The interface allows you to access the content with just one or two clicks.

Troubleshooting

Wiley has attempted to provide programs that work on most computers with the minimum system requirements. Alas, your computer may differ, and some programs may not work properly for some reason.

The two likeliest problems are that you don't have enough memory (RAM) for the programs you want to use, or you have other programs running that are affecting installation or running of a program. If you get an error message such as "Not enough memory" or "Setup cannot continue," try one or more of the following suggestions and then try using the software again:

Turn off any antivirus software running on your computer. Installation programs sometimes mimic virus activity and may make your computer incorrectly believe that it's being infected by a virus.

Close all running programs. The more programs you have running, the less memory is available to other programs. Installation programs typically update files and programs, so if you keep other programs running, installation may not work properly.

Have your local computer store add more RAM to your computer. This is, admittedly, a drastic and somewhat expensive step. However, adding more memory can really help the speed of your computer and allow more programs to run at the same time.

Customer Care

If you have trouble with the book's companion CD-ROM, please call the Wiley Product Technical Support phone number at (800) 762-2974. Outside the United States, call +1(317) 572-3994. You can also contact Wiley Product Technical Support at http://sybex.custhelp.com. John Wiley & Sons will provide technical support only for installation and other general quality-control items. For technical support on the applications themselves, consult the program's vendor or author.

To place additional orders or to request information about other Wiley products, please call (877) 762-2974.

Glossary

Numbers

802.1Q An IEEE standard that defines virtual LANs.

802.1X A port-based access control standard, 802.1X provides an authorization framework that allows or disallows traffic to pass through a port and thereby access network resources. An 802.1X framework may be implemented in either a wireless or a wired environment. The three main components of an 802.1X framework are the supplicant, the authenticator, and the authentication server.

802.1X/EAP A term used to specify an 802.1X authentication using an EAP authentication protocol.

802.1X supplicant There are three roles in the 802.1X process: supplicant, authenticator, and authentication server. The supplicant is the 802.1X software agent residing on the device wishing to authenticate using the 802.1X protocol.

802.11 authentication The service used to establish the identity of one station (STA) as a member of the set of STAs authorized to associate with another STA.

802.11e An amendment to the original IEEE 802.11 standard that defined QoS enhancements. 802.11e was integrated into 802.11-2007.

802.11i An amendment to the original IEEE 802.11 standard that specifies enhanced security mechanisms. 802.11i was integrated into 802.11-2007.

802.11r-2008 An amendment to the 802.11-2007 standard that specifies roaming enhancements.

802.1D An IEEE standard, part of the 802.1 family, that defines MAC bridging.

802.1p An IEEE standard that defines a 3-bit priority code point (PCP) user priority (UP) value for QoS support within the 802.1D bridging framework. 802.1p has been rolled into the 802.1Q standard and is a legacy term, but is still commonly used to refer to OSI Layer 2 QoS markings.

A

AAA Authentication, authorization, and accounting (AAA) is a security concept involved in proving the identity of supplicants, granting them authorization to network resources, and properly accounting for their activities. The term *AAA server* is often referred to as the authentication server in the 802.1X process.

AAA client An AAA client is a RADIUS or authentication server term for each configured authenticator that is allowed to request authentications for supplicants.

acceptable use policy (AUP) An AUP is a legal document that is provided by the operator of a network that outlines the restrictions that a user of the network must abide by.

access category (AC) A label for a set of contention parameters used by QoS stations to contend for prioritized access to the wireless medium.

access control gateways Devices that are commonly used in guest networks that force users to a captive portal (web page) to perform a set of actions that may eventually result in access to the network. Until access control is granted to guest users, all traffic is usually completely restricted to only the access control gateway itself. While these devices may perform many different functions, they are referred to in this book as the device that performs at least this basic function.

access controller (AC) The network entity in the centralized WLAN architecture that provides wireless termination points (WTPs) with access to the centralized hierarchical network infrastructure in the data plane, control plane, management plane, or a combination therein.

accounting Involves tracking the use of network resources by users. Accounting is an important aspect of network security, and is employed to keep a paper trail of who used what resource, when, and where.

active discovery The process used by 802.11 stations (STAs) to discover available access points and SSIDs by actively transmitting probe requests.

active survey A survey that is performed while maintaining a full 802.11-based association (bi-directional communication) to an AP.

adjacent channel interference Interference caused by power from a signal on an adjacent channel.

admission control A network requirement where admittance of new client or application sessions must be approved by an algorithm that measures the availability and usage of network resources.

AES-CCMP The default encryption method defined under the 802.11i amendment. This method uses the Advanced Encryption Standard (AES) cipher. It uses a 128-bit encryption key size and encrypts in 128-bit fixed-length blocks. An 8-byte message integrity check (MIC) is used that is considered much stronger than the one used with Temporal Key Integrity Protocol (TKIP). AES-CCMP is the default encryption method defined by Wi-Fi Protected Access 2 (WPA2).

aggregated MAC protocol data unit (A-MPDU) A Physical Layer Convergence Procedure (PLCP) structure containing multiple MPDUs that can reach a length of 64 kilobytes as compared to the legacy frame size limit of 2,304 bytes.

aggregated MAC service data unit (A-MSDU) An MPDU structure containing multiple MAC service data units that can reach a length of 7,935 bytes.

AIFS The interframe space used by QoS stations attempting to access the WLAN medium for data frame transmissions.

airtime fairness A proprietary frame queuing and scheduling feature designed to supplement standardized QoS by regulating and fairly distributing client device airtime usage.

airtime scheduling An algorithm that determines the order in which data frames are given access to system resources.

amplifier saturation An amplifier will provide linear gain up to a well-defined power limit. Above that limit, increasing the input power will not produce more output power. The input power at which the amplifier starts to decrease its gain is the point where the amplifier starts to go into saturation.

antenna diversity Antenna diversity incorporates the use of more than one antenna element for single-input, single-output (SISO) clients. Antenna diversity helps to mitigate the negative effects of multipath interference.

application-specific device (ASD) A hardware device designed for a single application; usually runs a proprietary operating system.

arbitration The process a transmitter uses to gain controller over the wireless medium.

association After a station has authenticated with the access point, the next step is for it to associate with the access point. When a client station associates, it becomes a member of the Basic Service Set (BSS). Association means that the client station can send data through the access point and exchange data with the distribution system medium.

asymmetric key encryption The encryption method that is used with public key infrastructure (PKI) systems and means that the encryption key that is used to encrypt a message (public key) is different from the one that must be used to decrypt the message (private key).

attribute-value pairs (AVPs) AVPs are data values that are often used in RADIUS communications. AVPs are used to dynamically assign WLAN users to roles, VLANs, and a variety of other attributes resulting from client authentications.

authentication The verification of user identity and credentials. Users must identify themselves and present credentials, such as usernames and passwords or digital certificates. More secure authentication systems exist that require multifactor authentication where at least two sets of different credentials must be presented.

authentication server (AS) When an 802.1X/EAP solution is deployed, an authentication server validates the credentials of the supplicant that is requesting access and notifies the authenticator that the supplicant has been authorized. The AS will maintain a user database or may proxy with an external user database to authenticate user credentials.

authenticator When an 802.1X/EAP solution is deployed, a device that blocks or allows traffic to pass through its port entity is known as the authenticator. Authentication traffic is normally allowed to pass through the authenticator whereas all other traffic is blocked until the identity of the supplicant has been verified. Typically, authenticators are switches, routers, access points, or controllers.

authorization The act involved in granting access to network resources and services.

autonomous WLAN architectures The WLAN access network architecture family in which all the logical functions, including both IEEE 802.11 and CAPWAP functions (wherever applicable), are implemented within each WTP in the network. The WTPs in such networks are also called stand-alone APs, or fat APs, because these devices implement the full set of functions that enable the devices to operate without any other support from the network.

availability A term used to represent uptime of systems.

B

backlobes The RF energy that is emanated from an antenna in nonprimary direction(s).

backoff timer The timer used during WLAN arbitration to count down time slots after a station has selected a contention value from the contention window.

balun A device on an antenna that is used as a transformer. It will transform a cable impedance so that it will match an antenna impedance.

band steering A proprietary feature designed to steer client devices to specific frequency bands.

bandpass filter A passive device that will pass signals within a band of frequencies and block all others.

Barker code A direct sequence chipping code with good autocorrelation characteristics. 802.11 uses a specific 11-chip Barker code.

basic rates Individual PHY rates that use specific modulation and coding mechanisms that all devices must support before being allowed onto the WLAN. Basic rates have strong implications for certain classes of wireless traffic transmissions such as management frames, broadcast and multicast traffic.

Basic Service Set (BSS) A network service group that is initiated by an AP and joined by a group of client stations.

bill of materials (BOM) A list of all hardware, software, and accessories needed to implement the network design.

Binary Phase Shift Keying (BPSK) A one-bit modulation scheme. Its constellation can be represented by two points, –1 and 1, on the I-axis.

biotelemetry Transmission of data (usually patient vital information) in healthcare environments.

black body radiation The radiation emitted by all objects. The amount of microwave noise power due to black body radiation is related to bandwidth and temperature.

blacklists A term that refers to a list of known and undesired entities or locations.

block acknowledgment (BA) policy A set of options that may be used to acknowledge received 802.11 frames to the transmitter.

bridges An AP that is used to bridge one network technology to another. For example, a wireless bridge can be used as a backbone segment to connect two wired LANs.

business requirements Requirements that map directly to business-related goals rather than to the technical details of how those goals will be realized. Here's an example: "Reduce operating expenses by 10%" can be a business requirement. Installing a voice over WLAN phone system to reduce long-distance charges could be a technical solution to that requirement.

C

calibration A term used in survey mapping software packages that allows a graphic file to be scaled to real-world dimensions and interpreted.

call signaling A control protocol for audio or video communications that establishes and tears down sessions.

Calling-Station-ID A RADIUS attribute that identifies the client requesting authentication. Typically this is tied to the MAC address of the client.

capacitance A measure of how much charge a capacitor can hold.

capacity-based network A network that is deployed to accommodate a high number of clients. To accomplish this, the goal is to use a greater number of APs through the use of lower transmit power levels and carefully chosen antennas to shape the RF coverage.

captive web portal A network redirection feature used for the HTTP and HTTPS protocols where all web traffic will be redirected to a network device typically requiring some form of authentication or acceptance of use policy before being allowed to send traffic through the device.

Carrier Sense The set of mechanisms used by 802.11 stations to determine the state (whether idle or busy) of the wireless medium.

Carrier Wave A microwave radio tone that has not been modulated with information.

cavity filter A type of low-loss filter. Generally a cavity filter is large and heavy.

CCA congestion CCA (clear channel assessment) is the process an 802.11-compliant radio uses to gain access to transmit on the wireless medium. When the medium is busy, it will cause delays in gaining access to the medium, which may affect applications.

centralized data forwarding Centralized data forwarding is where all APs in a WLAN architecture tunnel all data traffic back to a single device for it to then be decapsulated and dropped onto the distribution system.

centralized WLAN architectures The WLAN access network architecture family in which the logical functions, including both IEEE 802.11 and CAPWAP functions (wherever applicable), are implemented across a hierarchy of network entities. At the lower level are the WTPs, while at the higher level are the access controllers (ACs), which are responsible for controlling, configuring, and managing the entire WLAN access network.

certificate authority (CA) A role in a public key infrastructure that issues and vouches for authenticity of digital certificates.

certificate trust list (CTL) A list of certificate authorities (CAs) and other trusted third parties on a host computer. The CTL is referenced when a digital certificate is presented to it and is used to determine whether to trust the presenting party.

change order (CO) Issued when requests are made that are outside of the agreed-upon statement of work. Maps closely with the customer requirements document (CRD) as the CRD details what the project requirements are, and often the requirements expand over time, resulting in scope creep.

channel reuse plan An AP channel planning technique for MCA systems in order to space same-channel APs at the farthest RF distance from one another. This technique minimizes co-channel interference and therefore the contention domain.

characteristic impedance A characteristic of a transmission line. The characteristic impedance of a transmission line should be equal to its terminating load to avoid reflections.

chip rate The number of pulses per second at which a signal is transmitted and received. The chip rate for 802.11b is 11 Mchips/s. There are 11 chips for every bit transmitted. This spreads the spectrum to 11 times of what it would be if there was no chipping of the signal.

chipping A method of using several symbols to represent a single bit of actual data. Chipping allows for data recovery of the actual received transmission that may not have all been received exactly intact.

chipset The silicon chip that provides the MAC and PHY features for a WLAN radio.

Cisco Centralized Key Management (CCKM) A vendor-specific standard created by Cisco that allows for fast secure roaming on Cisco infrastructure environments. CCKM is part of the CCX standard and has been widely adopted by many client device vendors.

class of service (CoS) An OSI Layer 2 term used to reference 802.1p traffic classes, as determined by the user priority (UP) bits.

classification Identification of an incoming frame's QoS class and the handling behaviors that should be applied to that class.

clauses In IEEE standard documents, content is divided into clauses or sections. A clause is the highest order category usually notated using numerical values.

Clear Channel Assessment A physical carrier sense mechanism used in IEEE 802.11 to sense activity on the wireless medium before performing a transmission.

co-channel interference Commonly used to refer to interference from APs and client devices operating on the same RF channel. Sometimes it can also be used to refer to any other interfering RF signal source occupying the same channel as another system such as a Wi-Fi AP.

codec An abbreviation for coder-decoder, referring to computer algorithms that code a source signal (usually an audio or video source) into a form that can be transmitted over a network medium and then decoded back into a perceptible original form at the destination.

common access cards (CAC) A smart card issued by the United States Department of Defense that is used to prove identity.

Complementary Code Keying (CCK) A modulation scheme used by 802.11b and 802.11 radios.

computers on wheels (COWs) Mobile computers commonly used in healthcare environments; the same term is used in the mobile carrier industry to refer to cellular on wheels, where a wireless base station needs to be deployed quickly and often temporarily.

constellation A display of digital modulation showing its phase and amplitude. The points of a constellation show where the receiver will detect a symbol.

contention The condition when other devices are currently using the wireless medium and other devices wishing to transmit must wait.

contention domain A geographical coverage area for a single channel shared by multiple devices. Each device must arbitrate for transmit time on the wireless medium within a contention domain. Mobile devices communicating back to the AP at the edge of the AP's geographical coverage increases the contention domain for that channel from both the client and AP perspective; it is a single, dynamic system.

contention window The range of values from which a transmitting WLAN station randomly selects a backoff timer to contend for access to the wireless channel.

Control and Provisioning of Wireless Access Points (CAPWAP) The standards-based replacement protocol for LWAPP or other proprietary protocols. CAPWAP also supports Datagram Transport Layer Security (DTLS) encryption mechanisms.

control plane The conceptual communication zone where functions related to cooperation and interaction between wireless equipment in a network take place. Examples include radio resource management (RRM) coordination, mobility management, load balancing, and AP transition coordination.

cooperative autonomous AP A type of autonomous AP that performs all the functions of an independent autonomous AP, but one that has enhanced control plane coordination with other APs within the ESS.

core, distribution, and access layers The logical and physical areas of campus network design that many campus-based networks follow.

Counter Mode with Cipher Block Chaining Message Authentication Code Protocol (CCMP) See AES-CCMP.

coverage-based network A network that is deployed with fewer APs at higher power. The intent is to cover as much as possible with the least number of APs.

CTS-to-Self A protection mechanism whereby the transmitting station reserves the wireless medium by use of a clear-to-send (CTS) control frame prior to transmitting the intended data frame.

customer requirements document (CRD) A document that clearly and concisely details the customer requirements for the project. It is essential to make this document as detailed as possible as it is often used to help prevent scope creep.

cyclic shift diversity An adaptation of delay diversity to OFDM systems that can distinguish between symbols shifted in the time domain.

D

data plane The communication plane where all data frames between devices are sent. The actual workload of the wireless devices and applications are sent in the data plane.

dBc The ratio of a measured power to the unmodulated carrier.

dBd Antenna gain relative to a dipole antenna.

dB-Hz A measure of bandwidth in dB. It is the ratio of bandwidth (BW) to 1 Hz used in noise power calculations.

$$BWdB - Hz = 10 * Log10(BWHz)$$

dBi Antenna gain relative to an isotropic antenna.

dBm A measure of absolute power. dBm is a dB measure of power in milliwatts.

$$PdBm = 10 * Log10(PmW)$$

dBr dB relative (dBr) is the same as dB.

dBW A measure of absolute power. dBW is a dB measure of power in watts.

$$P_{dBW} = 10 * Log_{10}(PW)$$

decibelDecibel (dB) is a relative measure of power. A radio gain is an example of something measured in dB. Gain is measured as the ratio of the output power P2 to the input P1.

$$G_{dB} = 10 * Log_{10}(P2/P1)$$

delay spread The spread of delay values for the various multipath signals received.

Delivery Traffic Indication Message (DTIM) A DTIM Beacon requires that all power save stations wake up for subsequent delivery of all unicast and multicast traffic.

dielectric A material that resides between the plates of a capacitor that influences its charge storage capacity. It is the plastic material inside cables and has an effect on the cable's characteristic impedance.

Differential Binary Phase Shift Keying (DBPSK) A modulation scheme where bits are represented by a change in BPSK state. No change is a 0; change is a 1.

Differential Quadrature Phase Shift Keying (DQPSK) A modulation scheme where bits are represented by a change in QPSK state.

Differentiated Services Code Point (DSCP) An IP layer QoS mechanism used to classify IP packets and prescribe handling procedures in accordance with the desired priority.

Direct Sequence Spread Spectrum (DSSS) A method for spreading a modulated carrier with a chipping code.

distortion An error condition that typically exists when an RF amplifier overamplifies an input signal beyond which it can reliably reproduce the input signal at the new amplified power.

distributed antenna systems (DASs) A DAS can come in many varieties, but in the context of this book it is a multispectrum and multihost RF antenna system designed to host multiple types of radio technologies.

Distributed Coordination Function (DCF) DCF is a set of functions that define how WLAN radios coordinate among each other. DCF inherently has no mechanism to reserve airtime for transmissions for particular stations on predetermined intervals. DCF implies that each station must perform a set of actions in order to gain access to transmit on the wireless medium.

distributed data forwarding A method of forwarding data frames in a WLAN architecture without having to first tunnel it to a specific location. It is a data forwarding scheme more similar to the way switched Ethernet networks work today where the traffic is bridged locally.

distributed WLAN architectures The WLAN network architecture family in which some of the control functions (e.g., CAPWAP functions) are implemented across a distributed network consisting of peer entities. A wireless mesh network is an example of such an architecture.

distribution service The service that, by using association information, delivers MSDUs within the distribution system.

distribution system A system used to interconnect a set of Basic Service Sets (BSSs) and integrated local area networks (LANs) to create an extended service set (ESS).

distribution system services (DSS) The set of services provided by the distribution system (DS) that enable the MAC layer to transport MSDUs between stations that are not in direct communication with each other over a single instance of the wireless medium.

down-tilt A downward tilting of, usually, a directional antenna to provide coverage closer to the antenna mounting location. Using the appropriate amount of down-tilt can also minimize RF interference from distances greater than the area of required coverage.

duplex Refers to Ethernet duplex, which is a peer-to-peer configuration setting for an Ethernet link that specifies half for full-duplex communications. Half duplex means that only one device can transmit at a time, whereas with full duplex, each may transmit simultaneously without interference.

Dynamic Frequency Selection (DFS) DFS is a set of behavior that is defined in the 802.11h standard that helps to avoid interference from radar when operating in the 5 GHz UNII bands.

Dynamic Transport Layer Security (DTLS) A security protocol that is used with CAPWAP to encrypt network traffic even over a wired medium.

E

EAP-FAST Flexible Authentication via Secure Tunneling (FAST). EAP-FAST is defined in IETF RFC 4851 and is a type of EAP that uses a Protected Access Credential (PAC) to securely tunnel client authentication credentials to an authentication server.

EAP-GTC Generic Token Card (GTC). EAP-GTC is defined in IETF RFC 3748 and was developed to provide interoperability with existing security token device systems that use one-time passwords (OTPs). The EAP-GTC method is intended for use with security token devices, but the credentials can also be a username and password.

EAP-LEAP A legacy EAP type that uses a username and password-based authentication method for client devices.

EAP-MD5 A legacy EAP type that uses one-way authentication and is susceptible to offline dictionary attacks.

EAP-TLS Transport Layer Security (TLS). Defined in IETF RFC 5216, EAP-TLS is a widely adopted EAP type and is largely considered to be one of the most secure EAP methods available to WLANs today. It requires the use of client-side certificates in addition to a server certificate.

EAP-TTLS Tunneled Transport Layer Security (TTLS). An EAP type that uses a TLS tunnel to protect less secure inner authentication methods and supports more inner authentication methods than almost every other EAP type.

effective isotropic radiated power (EIRP) The product of transmitted power and transmit antenna gain (sum if the power is in dBm and gain in dBi). It is the transmit power required if the power measured at the highest gain point of the antenna was radiating isotropically (radiating everywhere equally).

endpoint agents A software agent that is installed on client devices that enforces security policies.

end-to-end QoS The principle of networking QoS that dictates that traffic must be prioritized at every hop from a data frame's source to its destination.

energy detect (ED) The portion of CCA carrier sense that assesses the state of the wireless medium by measuring raw RF power.

Enhanced Distributed Channel Access (EDCA) A set of contention-based 802.11 channel access mechanisms defined in 802.11e and adopted by the Wi-Fi Alliance in the WMM specification to enable 802.11-based QoS.

EtherChannel A technique used to virtually combine multiple independent Ethernet links into a single aggregated link shared between two peers.

exciter A device used by RTLS vendors such as AeroScout in order to provide granular position accuracy using non–Wi-Fi RF frequencies or ultrasound.

executive summary A section included in many documents that provides a high-level description, designed for the executive audience, of the document's purpose and contents.

Extensible Authentication Protocol (EAP) A protocol used to provide user authentication for an 802.1X port-based access control solution. EAP is a flexible Layer 2 authentication protocol that resides under Point-to-Point Protocol (PPP).

F

farads The unit of measure for capacitance.

Fast BSS Transitions (FT) Fast secure roaming mechanisms defined by the IEEE 802.11r-2008 amendment.

fast fading A rapid change in receive signal due to multipath constructive and destructive interference.

fast secure roaming (FSR) Mechanisms for faster handoffs when roaming occurs between cells in a wireless LAN using the strong security defined in a robust security network (RSN). Fast and secure 802.11 roaming is needed to meet latency requirements for time-sensitive applications in a WLAN.

fragmentation A feature that divides MAC frames larger than a specified threshold into multiple frames to improve transmission reliability.

free space path loss (FSPL) The reduction of RF signal amplitude over free space.

front-to-back ratio The ratio of antenna gain between the front and back of an antenna pattern. The front is considered the point of highest gain or the boresight of the antenna.

full LLD A variation of the low-level design document that includes extensive detail prior to the actual network deployment.

G

gas tube surge suppression A type of surge suppression device placed on an antenna transmission line that is used to protect radios from electrical storms.

Greenfield mode In the context of 802.11n, a mode of operation for an AP and client that allows for 802.11n communications without support for legacy modes.

guard interval (GI) The delay spread that an 802.11 receiver can tolerate before multipath signals cause intersymbol interference (ISI).

H

HCF controlled channel access (HCCA) HCCA is a set of QoS mechanisms that define medium reservation and contention-less transmission for QoS-capable stations. HCCA has not been adopted by the Wi-Fi Alliance for its standards.

hidden node A well-known condition in wireless communications where two wireless transmitters cannot detect each other's transmissions because of their relation to one another, which causes collisions at other receiver(s).

high-level design (HLD) A design document that specifies the network's design as a high-level, reusable framework from which other members of a design or implementation team can draw for extension or replication of the design.

hold harmless An indemnity clause or agreement. It is an agreement under which one or both parties agree not to hold the other party responsible for any loss, damage, or legal liability.

Hybrid Coordination Function (HCF) The 802.11 channel access function introduced by 802.11e for support of contention-based (EDCA) and contention-free (HCCA) QoS.

I

impedance A measure of a transmission line load's resistance, capacitance, and inductance. Matching a load's impedance to the characteristic impedance of a transmission line will minimize reflections.

independent autonomous AP The traditional interpretation of a stand-alone, autonomous access point that provides all of the MAC layer functions required by the IEEE Std 802.11. Little to no control functions exist between individual independent autonomous APs.

inductor An electrical device that stores current.

in-phase axis The in-phase (I) axis is the horizontal axis in a constellation plot.

integration service (IS) The service that enables delivery of MAC service data units (MSDUs) between the distribution system and an existing, non-IEEE 802.11 local area network (via a portal).

interframe space (IFS) The time interval immediately following the end of a frame transmission that must be observed before another frame may be transmitted or before contention can resume.

intersymbol interference (ISI) The interference that occurs when there is too much delay spread in a received set of multipath signals.

Inverse Square Law The mathematical relationship that occurs between amplitude and distance with free space path loss (FSPL).

isotropic antenna An antenna that radiates equally in all directions. This is only a theoretical concept. A true isotropic antenna cannot be constructed.

J

jitter A measure of deviation or variability over time of packet latency between endpoints. The standards-based term for jitter is packet delay variation (PDV).

Joint Commission (JHACO) A hospital accreditation organization in the United States that performs audits of healthcare facilities.

K

kick-off meeting The first meeting of a project that involves all the important project stakeholders.

L

latency The measurement of time delay experienced in the delivery of a frame.

Legacy mode A mode that an 802.11n AP and client operate in that allows for legacy communications only.

Lightweight Access Point Protocol (LWAPP) The first protocol designed to standardize interoperability of "lightweight" access point protocols within a centralized WLAN architecture. LWAPP was used as a basis for the development of CAPWAP.

Lightweight Directory Access Protocol (LDAP) An application protocol for querying and modifying directory services running over TCP/IP.

load balancing A vendor-specific feature that may be available to balance client load across one or more areas such as spectrum, different APs, and perhaps channels.

local MAC A subgroup of the Centralized WLAN Architecture, where the majority or entire set of 802.11 MAC functions (including most of the 802.11 management frame processing) are implemented at the WTP. Therefore, the 802.11 MAC stays intact and local in the WTP, along with PHY.

logical network design A part of a network design document that defines logical connectivity and data flow processes without specifying physical connectivity details.

loss The measurement of frames or packets lost in communication transit.

low-level design (LLD) A design document that specifies many of the detailed components and configurations of the network design.

low-noise amplifier (LNA) An amplifier used for a radio receiver. It is designed to have a low noise figure—that is, it adds little noise to the incoming signal.

M

MAC filtering Allowing or disallowing connectivity based on the MAC address of client's WLAN radios trying to authenticate.

MAC service data unit (MSDU) The data portion of a MAC frame. In IP networks, the MSDU would be the complete IP packet inclusive of all network layer overhead.

machine authentication An authentication approach that authenticates a host device to the network via 802.1X/EAP prior to user login.

management plane The communication plane within a WLAN architecture where network configuration, status reporting and monitoring, firmware management, and other common management-related tasks happen.

marking A QoS technique of indicating a specific classification for an outgoing frame to facilitate classification at the receiving station.

master services agreement (MSA) A legal contract that states the responsibilities and obligations of one party to another. It is often used as a master contractual document servicing a variety of professional services activities or engagements.

maximal ratio combining (MRC) A receive technique used with MIMO that receives the same signal from more than one antenna element and combines them in a constructive manner for additive receive gain.

media stream The voice and video communication traffic between devices.

mesh A type of wireless networking technology that forms a self-optimizing, wireless backhaul connection network.

micro-miniature coaxial (MMCX) A small RF connector used on some client devices.

Mixed mode A mode that an 802.11n AP and client operate in that allows both legacy and 802.11n communications to coexist. The term has also been used with 802.11b and 802.11g cohabitation.

mobile IP Mobile IP can have multiple definitions, depending on the industry and application. From the CWNP perspective, mobile IP is a means of keeping an IP address from the IP network the client originally associated with as it traverses network segments with different subnets.

mobility management The methodology and handing of mobile device transitions within an extended service set (ESS).

modulation The process of modifying a carrier signal to represent data.

multiband DAS See neutral-host DAS.

multi-channel architecture (MCA) A WLAN architecture where multiple channels are used by each AP using a channel reuse plan. MCA is the most common WLAN architecture.

multifactor authentication A method of authentication involving more than one type of credential in order to add strength of identity validation.

multipath A real-world phenomenon when RF signals reach a receiving antenna in more than one path.

multiple-input, multiple-output (MIMO) A radio design technique that incorporates multiple antennas and spatial streams at the transmitter and receiver to improve communication performance.

N

N connector A large RF connector used mostly on outdoor APs and antennas.

National Electrical Manufacturers Association (NEMA) enclosure A type of enclosure that is commonly used to house APs in outdoor environments.

network access control (NAC) Provides a technology framework to interrogate devices before they can gain normal access to the network. It will typically offer a remediation or quarantine network with no access to the normal network that allows devices to resolve issues such as antivirus definition updates or operating system service patches. Sometimes referred to network admission control.

Network Address Translation (NAT) overload A subset of NAT that may also be referred to as PAT (Port Address Translation). NAT overload is a method of translating TCP/UDP transmissions from a public network to a private network. It allows a single IP address on the public network to be shared by all the hosts on the private network.

network allocation vector (NAV) The virtual carrier sense mechanism used by stations to detect and defer to other RF transmissions on the medium. The NAV is a timer that is set by the Duration value in WLAN frames.

network operations center (NOC) A support operation that monitors all network operational events and provides a response to network performance issues.

network signal analysis A term used in analyzing the physical components of an RF signal, usually as it passes through transmission lines and antennas.

neutral-host DAS A DAS architecture where the system is designed to support a wide variety of RF technologies using a common RF fabric.

noise figure (NF) A measure in decibels of the output SNR to input SNR ratio when the input is at thermal noise levels. An amplifier's NF is a measure of how much noise it adds to an input signal.

non–light of sight (LOS) A term used in RF communications when two RF communication devices do not have a clear RF transmission path.

O

one-time password (OTP) A temporary password that is only valid for a single login session or transaction.

Open Systems Interconnection (OSI) model A model that describes subdividing communications systems into seven layers.

opportunistic key caching (OKC) A type of fast secure roaming that allows for preemptive pairwise master key (PMK) caching between multiple APs that are under shared administrative control.

Orthogonal Frequency Division Multiplexing (OFDM) A modulation scheme where multiple subcarriers are modulated on a main carrier. The subcarriers are digitally modulated and spaced so that nulls of each carrier fall on the peaks of the other subcarriers.

oversubscription ratio Oversubscription occurs when the maximum bandwidth capacity is less than the sum of the bandwidth available to connected devices if utilized to full capacity.

The oversubscription ratio is the comparison between the aggregate bandwidth of all input to the output capacity.

P

packet error rate (PER) The rate of errors of packets received or transmitted commonly expressed as a percentage.

pairwise master key (PMK) caching A fast secure roaming method used by APs and client stations to maintain Pair-wise Master Key Security Associations (PMKSAs) for a period of time while a client station roams to a target AP and establishes a new PMKSA. An authenticator and a client station can cache multiple PMKs.

passband The band of frequencies that can pass through a band pass filter.

passive discovery The process used by 802.11 stations (STAs) to discover available access points and SSIDs by passively listening to beacons of nearby APs.

passphrase A simple 8-63 ASCII character string that is converted to a 256-bit preshared key (PSK) in WPA/WPA2-Personal networks.

Payment Card Industry (PCI) documentation and support services (DSS) Refers to the PCI DSS regulatory standard for organizations that electronically process credit card transactions.

PEAPv0/EAP-MSCHAPv2 A type of EAP-PEAP that sends client credentials via the MS-CHAPv2 protocol inside an encrypted tunnel. It is the most common form of the Protected Extensible Authentication Protocol (PEAP).

PEAPv0/EAP-TLS A type of EAP-PEAP that sends client credentials using client-side certificates inside of an encrypted tunnel.

PEAPv1/EAP-GTC A type of EAP-PEAP that was introduced by Cisco that uses the EAP-GTC protocol inside an encrypted tunnel.

per-user preshared keys (PPSK) A proprietary feature for using unique, per-user PSKs for each client device.

PHY rates PHY (Physical layer) rates are the individual data rates for wireless transmissions. These include 1, 2, 5.5, 6, 9, 11, 12, and higher, measured in megabits per second.

physical network design A part of a network design document that defines all the physical connections and configurations of a network's design.

pigtail cable A cable that is used between an AP and a bulkhead connector usually mounted in a NEMA enclosure.

plenum An area usually above a ceiling or below a floor that is used for air circulation from inhabited areas.

Point Coordination Function (PCF) A legacy coordination method designed to provide coordinated communications by wireless stations.

point of sale (PoS) A term used for equipment involved in consumer purchase and payment activities.

point-to-multipoint (PTMP) A wireless bridging method that uses a single root bridge for multiple bridge links.

point-to-point (PtP) A term commonly used for an RF bridge link involving two devices.

polarization A term used for physical orientation and direction of oscillation of electromagnetic waves.

Port Address Translation (PAT) See Network Address Translation (NAS) overload.

Power over Ethernet (PoE) A means of providing DC power to a powered device (usually an AP or VoIP phone) by means of the Ethernet cable.

Power Save Multi-Poll (PSMP) A power save mechanism that provides a time schedule that is used by an AP and its stations to access the wireless medium.

prealignment A concept used when initially aligning directional wireless bridge antennas using GPS coordinates, compass readings, or other similar methods.

preauthentication A fast secure roaming method used by clients to establish a new Pairwise Master Key Security Association (PMKSA) with an AP prior to roaming to the AP. Preauthentication allows a client station to initiate a new 802.1X/EAP exchange with a RADIUS server while associated with the original AP.

predictive surveys Often referred to as predictive designs. Predictive surveys are RF network designs based on information supplied to a software program that attempts to predict signal coverage based on mathematical algorithms and user-specified input.

preshared key (PSK) A method of distributing encryption passphrases or keys by manually typing the matching passphrases or keys on both the access point and all client stations that will need to be able to associate to the wireless network. This information is shared ahead of time (preshared) by using a manual distribution and configuration method.

private key A decryption key that is kept secret and is commonly used with asymmetric encryption methods.

processing gain The gain that comes from DSSS spreading. For 802.11, the 11 bit Barker code achieves a processing gain of 10.4 dB.

project sponsor Typically the most senior leader of the project, who is responsible for advocating the project, implementing budgeting, and the overseeing the progression and direction of the project.

Protected Access Credential (PAC) A type of shared secret that is based on X.509 digital certificates; used by the EAP-FAST protocol.

Protected EAP (PEAP) A type of EAP that establishes an encrypted tunnel between the supplicant and the authentication server before the client transmits its identity information for authentication.

public key infrastructure (PKI) An arrangement that binds public keys with respective user identities by means of a certificate authority.

Q

Quadrature Amplitude Modulation (QAM) A modulation scheme where bits are represented as constellation points on a rectangular grid.

Quadrature Phase axis The Quadrature Phase (Q) axis is the vertical axis in a constellation plot.

Quadrature Phase Shift Key (QPSK) A modulation scheme where 2 bits form a square in a constellation.

quality of experience (QoE) A quantified measurement of end user satisfaction derived from application performance criteria.

quality of service (QoS) A generic term used to describe a networking procedure in which services are provided in a discriminating and prioritized fashion.

queuing The process of arranging frames into delivery or transmit queue.

R

radio resource management (RRM) A term used for channel and power settings for automated RF management within a WLAN architecture.

RADIUS shared secret A secret key that is shared between AAA clients (authenticators) and the RADIUS server (authentication server) for authentication and encryption of messages.

radome A plastic cover on an antenna that will not absorb microwave radiation.

RC4 algorithm A stream cipher used in technologies that are often used to protect Internet traffic, such as Secure Socket Layer (SSL). The RC4 algorithm is used to protect 802.11 wireless data and is incorporated into two encryption methods known as WEP and TKIP.

receive diversity A radio design where there are two or more receive paths that make up a receiver. The receiver can either combine the signals appropriately or decide which to use.

receive sensitivity The signal amplitude level a receiver can demodulate a transmitted signal usually at a specified PHY rate.

reflection coefficient A measure of microwave reflection energy from a transmission line termination.

Remote Authentication Dial-In User Service (RADIUS) A networking protocol that provides centralized authentication, authorization, and accounting (AAA) management.

Remote MAC A subgroup of the Centralized WLAN Architecture, where the entire set of 802.11 MAC functions (including delay-sensitive functions) is implemented at the AC. The WTP terminates the 802.11 PHY functions.

request to send/clear to send (RTS/CTS) The optional mechanism used by the 802.11 wireless networking protocol to reduce frame collisions by controlling station access to the medium. RTS/CTS is often implemented to minimize collisions among hidden stations.

return loss A logarithmic measure of microwave-reflected energy from a transmission line termination.

RF fingerprinting A technique used by RTLS products of calibrating an area of signal coverage by measuring signal propagation based on specific locations.

RFC 4118 An IETF document providing a taxonomy of the architectures employed in the existing IEEE 802.11 products in the market, by analyzing WLAN functions and services and describing the variants in distributing these functions and services among the architectural entities.

robust security network (RSN) A network that only allows for the creation of robust security network associations (RSNAs). An RSN utilizes AES-CCMP encryption as well as 802.1X/EAP authentication.

robust security network association (RSNA) A term that originated with WPA-based security associations that do not employ legacy authentication and encryption mechanisms.

role-based access control (RBAC) An approach to restricting system access to authorized users.

root bridge A bridge that is the primary coordinator for a bridge link. The root bridge determines information such as RF channel, security policy, and other similar information for nonroot bridges to connect to.

root mesh node A mesh node with a direct backhaul connection.

S

scope creep Refers to the uncontrolled expansion of a project's scope. In the event that an agreed-upon customer requirements document (CRD) and statement of work (SOW) are in place and the customer is requesting additional services not already covered, the services can either be done for free (scope creep) or they can be added via a change order.

sector antennas A type of antenna that provides coverage in a wide horizontal pattern with minimal backlobe energy.

self-signed certificates A type of digital certificate that has not been generated by a trusted third party. Self-signed certificates are usually not implicitly trusted by other devices.

service loops A term used with wired cabling that implies an excess amount of cabling looped up at the remote termination points that allows for extending or relocating at a later date if required.

Service Set Identifier (SSID) hiding A method of using a NULL value in the beacon SSID field; usually also implies that APs do not respond to broadcast probe requests.

shared key authentication A legacy form of 802.11 authentication that has been deprecated due to security vulnerabilities.

shield The outer conductor of a coaxial cable.

signal-to-noise ratio (SNR) A measure of signal quality. It is the ratio of signal-to-noise power within the receiver filter bandwidth usually expressed in decibels.

single-channel architecture (SCA) A vendor-proprietary channel architecture that uses a single channel for all APs in a WLAN deployment.

single-input, single-output (SISO) The technology used in 802.11a/b/g radio technology.

slot time A PHY-specific time interval that varies by 802.11 clause and is used as a basic time unit.

solar loading The heating caused by direct sunlight exposure.

space time block coding A type of transmit diversity that is used in 802.11n.

Spanning Tree Protocol (STP) A wired networking protocol designed to prevent loops while maintaining redundancy.

spatial multiplexing The method of sending multiple data streams from multiple transmit antennas and receiving on multiple receive antennas.

Spatial Multiplexing Power Save (SMPS) A power save method introduced with 802.11n that specifies behavior for disabling MIMO radio chains and spatial streams to conserve power.

spectral mask Regulations require that a modulated carrier contain energy within a given transmission profile. The profile is called a spectral or emission mask.

spectral regrowth A distortion condition caused by intermodulation when amplifier gain is set too high.

speed Referring to Ethernet speed, which is the PHY rate negotiated over an Ethernet link.

Split MAC A subgroup of the Centralized WLAN Architecture whereby WTPs in such WLAN access networks only implement the delay-sensitive MAC services (including all control frames and some management frames) for IEEE 802.11, while all the remaining management and data frames are tunneled to the AC for centralized processing. The IEEE 802.11 MAC, as defined by IEEE 802.11 Standards in [1], is effectively split between the WTP and AC.

statement of work (SOW) A formal document that details the work to be performed along with associated details such as timelines and pricing information. All customer-specific deliverables should be listed as well as acceptance criteria to mark the completion of the project.

station services (SS) The set of services that support transport of MAC service data units (MSDUs) between stations within a basic service set (BSS).

straw man low-level design (LLD) A variation of the LLD document that begins as a design framework and is expanded with detail in many stages along with the actual network deployment.

SubMiniature version A (SMA) connector A small RF connector. The RP version is commonly used on access points.

supplicant When an 802.1X/EAP solution is deployed, a supplicant is a host (typically a client device) software agent that performs the 802.1X transaction.

survey mapping software Software used to perform RF site surveys.

symbol An RF representation of data using waveform or signaling events.

symmetric encryption A method of encryption that uses identical cryptographic keys for both encryption and decryption.

system administrator A member of the IT team who is responsible for maintaining computer or network systems.

T

technical requirements Requirements that map directly to technical aspects of a design.

telemetry See biotelemetry.

Temporal Key Integrity Protocol (TKIP) An encryption protocol established with the 802.11i and WPA amendments that addresses all known weaknesses of WEP but still utilizes the RC4 algorithm.

threaded Neill-Concelman (TNC) connector A medium-sized RF connector. The RP version is commonly used on access points.

traffic specification (TSPEC) The QoS characteristics of a data flow to and from a QoS client station.

traffic stream A set of MSDUs to be delivered in accordance with the QoS parameters defined in a TSPEC.

Transition Security Network (TSN) An 802.11 wireless network that allows for the creation of pre-robust security network associations (pre-RSNAs) as well as RNSAs. A TSN supports 802.11i-defined security as well as legacy security, such as WEP, within the same BSS.

transmission line A medium to transfer microwave energy from one place to another using one or more conductors.

Transmit Power Control (TPC) An 802.11 protocol technique designed to facilitate client device transmit power settings to maximize link quality while maintaining battery life.

Transport Layer Security (TLS) A cryptographic protocol used to provide secure communications. The TLS protocol uses end-to-end encryption using asymmetric encryption techniques and is used in all tunneled-based EAP methods other than EAP-FAST.

triggers Configurable thresholds on a spectrum analyzer that can trigger actions to be performed.

U

U.FI A very small RF connector used on circuit boards.

Unscheduled Automatic Power Save Delivery (U-APSD) Introduced with 802.11e as an improvement over the legacy power save modes of operations. U-APSD uses a triggered method by a sleeping station to request the transmission of queued traffic.

unshielded twisted pair (UTP) A type of cabling commonly used in Ethernet networks.

user priority (UP) A value associated with an MSDU that indicates how the MSDU is to be prioritized.

V

Vector Network Analyzer or Analysis (VNA) Provides details of RF transmission lines, such as return loss, impedance measurements, and detailed information to quantify antenna tuning characteristics.

vendor-specific attributes (VSAs) Provides functionality that is not supported in standard RADIUS attribute-value pairs (AVPs).

virtual LANs (VLANs) Used to create separate broadcast domains in a Layer 2 network and often used to restrict access to network resources without regard to the physical topology of the network. In a WLAN environment, individual SSIDs can be mapped to individual VLANs, and users can be segmented by the SSID/VLAN pair, all while communicating through a single access point.

virtual private network (VPN) A private network that is created by the use of encryption, tunneling protocols, and security procedures. VPNs are typically used to provide secure communications when physically connected to a nonsecure network.

Voice Enterprise A Wi-Fi Alliance certification based on 802.11r set to be released in late 2010 that defines fast, secure roaming functions.

voltage standing wave ratio A measure of microwave reflection energy from a transmission line termination.

W

walkthrough An in-person event where you are able to physically see an environment involved with or important to the success of a project.

waveguide A single-conductor transmission line.

wavelength A measure of a radio signal's size. It is equal to the ratio of the speed of light and the radio signal's frequency.

whitelist Often used for guest networks; allows users access to specific websites or network destinations before they are authenticated. For example, this might be the company website or an enrollment page.

Wi-Fi Multimedia (WMM) A Wi-Fi Alliance interoperability certification based on the 802.11e amendment that provides QoS support to 802.11 networks.

Wi-Fi Protected Access (WPA) Prior to the ratification of the 802.11i amendment, the Wi-Fi Alliance introduced the WPA certification as a snapshot of the not-yet-released 802.11i amendment, supporting TKIP dynamic encryption key management.

Wired Equivalent Privacy (WEP) An 802.11 Layer 2 encryption method that uses the RC4 streaming cipher in a weak way and is considered a legacy protocol due to its security vulnerabilities.

wireless intrusion detection system (WIDS) A client/server solution that is used to constantly monitor for 802.11 wireless attacks such as rogue APs, MAC spoofing, Layer 2 denial of service, and so on.

wireless intrusion prevention system (WIPS) A system capable of mitigating wireless attacks using a variety of preventive techniques.

wireless medical telemetry service (WMTS) A dedicated wireless medical frequency band that the FCC set aside for healthcare biotelemetry operations.

wireless medium Refers to the RF medium used for 802.11 and other wireless transmissions.

wireless network management system (WNMS) A network management system used for wireless network architectures.

wireless switches A legacy term used for WLAN controllers.

wireless termination point (WTP) The physical or network entity that contains an RF antenna and 802.11 PHY to transmit and receive station traffic for the IEEE 802.11 WLAN access networks.

WLAN client utility The software on a host computer that allows a user to configure their WLAN radio for a specific network.

WMM Power Save (WMM-PS) A subset of the Wi-Fi Alliance WMM interoperability certification that defines power save functionality; also an interoperability certification.

workstation on wheels (WOWs) See computers on wheels (COWs).

WPA2 Based on the security mechanisms that were originally defined in the IEEE 802.11i amendment defining a robust security network (RSN).

Y

yagi antennas A type of high-gain antenna with a narrow horizontal and vertical beamwidth that is commonly used in PTP or long-range RF communication links.

Index

Note to the Reader: Throughout this index **boldfaced** page numbers indicate primary discussions of a topic. *Italicized* page numbers indicate illustrations.

D

Wiley Publishing, Inc.
End-User License Agreement

The Best CWDP Book/CD Package on the Market!

Get ready for your Certified Wireless Design Professional (CWDP) certification with the most comprehensive and challenging sample tests anywhere!

The Sybex Test Engine features:

- All the review questions, as covered in each chapter of the book

- Challenging questions representative of those you'll find on the real exam

- Two full-length bonus exams available only on the CD

Use the Electronic Flashcards to jog your memory and prep last-minute for the exam!

- Reinforce your understanding of key concepts with these hardcore flashcard-style questions.

- Now you can study for the CWNA anytime, anywhere.

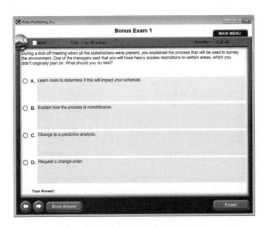

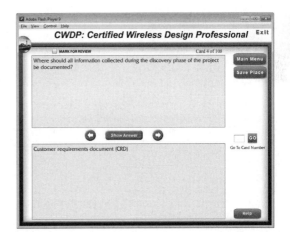

- An Assessment Test to narrow your focus to certain objective groups

Expert

Design

Secure

Troubleshoot

Earn all 3 Professional Level Certifications to earn CWNE

Comprehend

Network engineers and adminstrators, begin with CWNA to gain the foudational RF knowledge required to implement and manage enterprise Wi-Fi. CWNA is required for CWSP, CWAP, CWDP, and CWNE.

Begin

Newbies, non-techies, project managers, and technical sales professionals, start your wireless career with CWTS.